# THE
# WADING BIRDS
# OF NORTH AMERICA

Karl E. Karalus

# THE
# WADING BIRDS
# OF NORTH AMERICA
## (NORTH OF MEXICO)

TEXT BY

## *Allan W. Eckert*

PAINTINGS AND DRAWINGS BY

## *Karl E. Karalus*

WEATHERVANE BOOKS • NEW YORK

This 1987 edition is published by Weathervane Books, distributed by
Crown Publishers, Inc., 225 Park Avenue South, New York, New York
10003, by arrangement with Allan W. Eckert and Karl E. Karalus

Printed and Bound in Hong Kong

Design by M. Franklin-Plympton

LIBRARY OF CONGRESS CATALOGING-IN-PUBLICATION DATA

Eckert, Allan W.
The wading birds of North America.

Bibliography: p.
Includes index.
1. Ciconiiformes—United States.  2. Ciconiiformes—
Canada.  3. Gruiformes—United States.  4. Gruiformes—
Canada.  5. Birds—United States.  6. Birds—Canada.
I. Karalus, Karl E.  II. Title.
QL696.C5E25  1987      598′.34′097      87-10401
ISBN 0-517-63229-2
h g f e d c b a

# CONTENTS

*Color Plates and Species Sketches*     ix
*Acknowledgments*     xi
*Introduction*     xiii

Order *CICONIIFORMES* (Herons, Storks, Ibises, Flamingos, and Allies) Suborder *ARDEAE* (Herons, Bitterns, and Allies) Family *ARDEIDAE* (Herons and Bitterns) Subfamily *ARDEINAE* (Herons)

## Genus *BUTORIDES* Blyth
EASTERN GREEN HERON (*Butorides striatus virescens*)     3
FRAZAR'S GREEN HERON (*Butorides striatus frazari*)     12
ANTHONY'S GREEN HERON (*Butorides striatus anthonyi*)     14

## Genus *NYCTICORAX* Forster
BLACK-CROWNED NIGHT HERON (*Nycticorax nycticorax hoactli*)     19

## Genus *NYCTANASSA* Stejneger
YELLOW-CROWNED NIGHT HERON (*Nyctanassa violacea violacea*)     29

## Genus *ARDEA* Linnaeus
GREAT BLUE HERON (*Ardea herodias herodias*)     35
NORTHWESTERN COAST HERON (*Ardea herodias fannini*)     42
WARD'S HERON (*Ardea herodias wardi*)     44
TREGANZA'S HERON (*Ardea herodias treganzai*)     48
CALIFORNIA HERON (*Ardea herodias hyperonca*)     50
GREAT WHITE HERON (*Ardea herodias occidentalis*)     52

## Genus *FLORIDA* Baird
LITTLE BLUE HERON (*Florida caerulea caerulea*)     57

## Genus *HYDRANASSA* Baird
LOUISIANA HERON (*Hydranassa tricolor ruficollis*)     65

## Genus *BUBULCUS* Bonaparte
CATTLE EGRET (*Bubulcus ibis ibis*)     75

## Genus *DICHROMANASSA* Ridgway
REDDISH EGRET (*Dichromanassa rufescens rufescens*)     83
DICKEY'S EGRET (*Dichromanassa rufescens dickeyi*)     89

## Genus *CASMERODIUS* Gloger
GREAT EGRET (*Casmerodius albus egretta*)     93

## Genus *EGRETTA* Sharpe
SNOWY EGRET (*Egretta thula thula*)     101
BREWSTER'S EGRET (*Egretta thula brewsteri*)     106

_____

Subfamily *BOTAURINAE* (Bitterns)

## Genus *BOTAURUS* Stephens
AMERICAN BITTERN (*Botaurus lentiginosus*)     113

## Genus *IXOBRYCHUS* Billberg
EASTERN LEAST BITTERN (*Ixobrychus exilis exilis*)     121
WESTERN LEAST BITTERN (*Ixobrychus exilis hesperis*)     126

_____

Suborder *CICONIAE* (Storks, Ibises, and Spoonbills) Superfamily *CICONIOIDEA* (Storks) Family *CICONIIDAE* (Storks) Subfamily *MYCTERIINAE* (Wood Storks)

## Genus *MYCTERIA* Linnaeus
WOOD STORK (*Mycteria americana*)     129

_____

Superfamily *THRESKIORNITHOIDAE* (Ibises and Spoonbills) Family *THRESKIORNITHIDAE* (Ibises and Spoonbills) Subfamily *THRESKIORNITHINAE* (Ibises)

Genus *PLEGADIS* Kaup

GLOSSY IBIS *(Plegadis falcinellus falcinellus)* 137

WHITE-FACED IBIS *(Plegadis chihi)* 141

Genus *EUDOCIMUS* Wagler

WHITE IBIS *(Eudocimus albus)* 147

SCARLET IBIS *(Eudocimus ruber)* 153

Subfamily *PLATALEINAE* (Spoonbills)

Genus *AJAIA* Reichenbach

ROSEATE SPOONBILL *(Ajaia ajaja)* 157

Suborder *PHOENICOPTERI* (Flamingos)
Family *PHOENICOPTERIDAE* (Flamingos)

Genus *PHOENICOPTERUS* Linnaeus

AMERICAN FLAMINGO *(Phoenicopterus ruber)* 165

Order *GRUIFORMES* (Cranes, Rails, and Allies) Suborder *GRUES* (Cranes, Rails, and Limpkins) Superfamily *GRUOIDEA* (Cranes and Limpkins) Family *GRUIDAE* (Cranes) Subfamily *GRUINAE* (Cranes)

Genus *GRUS* Pallas

SANDHILL CRANE *(Grus canadensis canadensis)* 171

LITTLE BROWN CRANE *(Grus canadensis tabida)* 177

FLORIDA CRANE *(Grus canadensis pratensis)* 178

WHOOPING CRANE *(Grus americana)* 179

Family *ARAMIDAE* (Limpkins)

Genus *ARAMUS* Vieillot

LIMPKIN *(Aramus guarauna pictus)* 185

Superfamily *RALLOIDEA* (Rails, Gallinules, and Coots) Family *RALLIDAE* (Rails, Gallinules, and Coots) Subfamily *RALLINAE* (Rails)

Genus *RALLUS* Linnaeus

KING RAIL *(Rallus elegans elegans)* 191

NORTHERN CLAPPER RAIL *(Rallus longirostris crepitans)* 195

LOUISIANA CLAPPER RAIL *(Rallus longirostris saturatus)* 196

FLORIDA CLAPPER RAIL *(Rallus longirostris scottii)* 198

WAYNE'S CLAPPER RAIL *(Rallus longirostris waynei)* 200

MANGROVE CLAPPER RAIL *(Rallus longirostris insularum)* 202

CALIFORNIA CLAPPER RAIL *(Rallus longirostris obsoletus)* 204

YUMA CLAPPER RAIL *(Rallus longirostris yumanensis)* 206

LIGHT-FOOTED RAIL *(Rallus longirostris levipes)* 208

VIRGINIA RAIL *(Rallus limicola limicola)* 210

Genus *PORZANA* Vieillot

SORA *(Porzana carolina)* 213

Genus *COTURNICOPS* Gray

YELLOW RAIL *(Coturnicops noveboracensis noveboracensis)* 219

Genus *LATERALLUS* Gray

BLACK RAIL *(Laterallus jamaicensis jamaicensis)* 223

FARALLON RAIL *(Laterallus jamaicensis coturniculus)* 224

Genus *GALLINULA* Brisson

COMMON GALLINULE *(Gallinula chloropus cachinnans)* 227

Genus *PORPHYRULA* Blyth

PURPLE GALLINULE *(Porphyrula martinica)* 233

Subfamily *FULICINAE* (Coots)

Genus *Fulica* Linnaeus

AMERICAN COOT *(Fulica americana americana)* 237

Bibliography of Principal Sources 245
Index 249

# COLOR PLATES
# AND SPECIES SKETCHES

*(Plates appear after the given page number)*

PLATE I    EASTERN GREEN HERON *Butorides striatus virescens* (Linnaeus) (A.O.U. 201)   44

SKETCH 1    FRAZAR'S GREEN HERON *Butorides striatus frazari* (Brewster) (A.O.U. 201a)   13

SKETCH 2    ANTHONY'S GREEN HERON *Butorides striatus anthonyi* (Mearns) (A.O.U. 201c)   15

PLATE II    BLACK-CROWNED NIGHT HERON *Nycticorax nycticorax hoactli* (Gmelin) (A.O.U. 202)   44

PLATE III    YELLOW-CROWNED NIGHT HERON *Nyctanassa violacea violacea* (Linnaeus) (A.O.U. 203)   44

PLATE IV    GREAT BLUE HERON *Ardea herodias herodias* (Linnaeus) (A.O.U. 194)   44

SKETCH 3    NORTHWESTERN COAST HERON *Ardea herodias fannini* Chapman (A.O.U. 194a)   43

SKETCH 4    WARD'S HERON *Ardea herodias wardi* Ridgway (A.O.U. 194b)   47

SKETCH 5    TREGANZA'S HERON *Ardea herodias treganzai* Court (A.O.U. 194c)   49

SKETCH 6    CALIFORNIA HERON *Ardea herodias hyperonca* Oberholser (A.O.U. 194d)   51

PLATE V    GREAT WHITE HERON *Ardea herodias occidentalis* Audubon (A.O.U. 192)   60

PLATE VI    LITTLE BLUE HERON *Florida caerulea caerulea* (Linnaeus) (A.O.U. 200)   60

PLATE VII    LOUISIANA (or TRI-COLORED) HERON *Hydranassa tricolor ruficollis* (Gosse) (A.O.U. 199)   60

PLATE VIII    CATTLE EGRET *Bubulcus ibis ibis* Linnaeus (A.O.U. 201.1)   60

PLATE IX    REDDISH EGRET *Dichromanassa rufescens rufescens* (Gmelin) (A.O.U. 198)   76

SKETCH 7    DICKEY'S EGRET *Dichromanassa rufescens dickeyi* van Rossem (A.O.U. 198a)   90

PLATE X    GREAT EGRET *Casmerodius albus egretta* (Gmelin) (A.O.U. 196)   76

PLATE XI    SNOWY EGRET *Egretta thula thula* (Molina) (A.O.U. 197)   76

SKETCH 8    BREWSTER'S EGRET *Egretta thula brewsteri* (Thayer & Bangs) (A.O.U.) 197a)   107

PLATE XII    AMERICAN BITTERN *Botaurus lentiginosus* (Rackett) (A.O.U. 190)   76

PLATE XIII    EASTERN LEAST BITTERN *Ixobrychus exilis exilis* (Gmelin) (A.O.U. 191)   92

PLATE XIV    WESTERN LEAST BITTERN *Ixobrychus exilis hesperis* Dickey & van Rossem (A.O.U. 191a)   92

PLATE XV    WOOD STORK *Mycteria americana* Linnaeus (A.O.U. 188)   92

PLATE XVI    GLOSSY IBIS *Plegadis falcinellus falcinellus* (Linnaeus) (A.O.U. 186)   92

WHITE-FACED IBIS *Plegadis chihi* Vieillot (A.O.U. 187)   92

PLATE XVII    WHITE IBIS *Eudocimus albus* (Linnaeus) (A.O.U. 184)   108

PLATE XVIII    SCARLET IBIS *Eudocimus ruber* (Linnaeus) (A.O.U. 185)   108

PLATE XIX    ROSEATE SPOONBILL *Ajaia ajaja* (Linnaeus) (A.O.U. 183)   108

PLATE XX    AMERICAN FLAMINGO *Phoenicopterus ruber* Linnaeus (A.O.U. 182)    108

PLATE XXI    SANDHILL CRANE *Grus canadensis canadensis* (Linnaeus) (A.O.U. 205) 124
LITTLE BROWN CRANE *Grus canadensis tabida* (Peters) (A.O.U. 206)    124
FLORIDA CRANE *Grus canadensis pratensis* Meyer (A.O.U. 206a)    124

PLATE XXII    WHOOPING CRANE *Grus americana* (Linnaeus) (A.O.U. 204)    124

PLATE XXIII    LIMPKIN *Aramus guarauna pictus* (Meyer) (A.O.U. 207)    124

PLATE XXIV    KING RAIL *Rallus elegans elegans* Audubon (A.O.U. 208)    124

PLATE XXV    NORTHERN CLAPPER RAIL *Rallus longirostris crepitans* Gmelin (A.O.U. 211)    140

SKETCH 9    LOUISIANA CLAPPER RAIL *Rallus longirostris saturatus* Ridgway (A.O.U. 211a)    197

SKETCH 10    FLORIDA CLAPPER RAIL *Rallus longirostris scottii* Sennett (A.O.U. 211b)    199

SKETCH 11    WAYNE'S CLAPPER RAIL *Rallus longirostris waynei* Brewster (A.O.U. 211c)    201

SKETCH 12    MANGROVE CLAPPER RAIL *Rallus longirostris insularum* Brooks (A.O.U. 211d)    203

SKETCH 13    CALIFORNIA CLAPPER RAIL *Rallus longirostris obsoletus* Ridgway (A.O.U. 210)    205

SKETCH 14    YUMA CLAPPER RAIL *Rallus longirostris yumanensis* Dickey (A.O.U. 210a)    207

SKETCH 15    LIGHT-FOOTED RAIL *Rallus longirostris levipes* Bangs (A.O.U. 210.1)    209

PLATE XXVI    VIRGINIA RAIL *Rallus limicola limicola* Vieillot (A.O.U. 212)    140

PLATE XXVII    SORA *Porzana carolina* (Linnaeus) (A.O.U. 214)    140

PLATE XXVIII    YELLOW RAIL *Coturnicops noveboracensis noveboracensis* (Gmelin) (A.O.U. 215)    140

PLATE XXIX    BLACK RAIL *Laterallus jamaicensis jamaicensis* (Gmelin) (A.O.U. 216) 156
FARALLON RAIL *Laterallus jamaicensis coturniculus* (Ridgway) (A.O.U. 216.1)    156

PLATE XXX    COMMON GALLINULE *Gallinula chloropus cachinnans* Bangs (A.O.U. 219)    156

PLATE XXXI    PURPLE GALLINULE *Porphyrula martinica* (Linnaeus) (A.O.U. 218)    156

PLATE XXXII    AMERICAN COOT *Fulica americana americana* Gmelin (A.O.U. 221)    156

# ACKNOWLEDGMENTS

The illustrations for this book could hardly have been possible without the help of so many kind and patient people.

Melvin A. Traylor, Curator of Animals, Field Museum, Chicago, and a friend over the years, for criticism, encouragement, and the loan of many bird skins;

E. Joseph Koestner, Director of the Dayton Museum, Dayton, Ohio, for his encouragement;

Dr. Emmet Blake, Ornithologist, Field Museum, Chicago, Illinois, for criticism and patience;

Ms. Dianne Maurer, Curator of Birds, Field Museum, Chicago, Illinois, whose lunch hours were often spent aiding me in the selection of bird skins for this book, as well as *The Owls of North America;*

Tom O'Conor Sloane, III, Senior Editor, Doubleday & Company, Inc., for patience and understanding through difficult and trying times;

Diana Klemin, Art Director at Doubleday, for extreme patience;

Joseph Eckert, my field assistant, an unselfish young man whose willingness to tackle autopsies, skinning, and many other chores contributed enormously to this book;

The people at the Lemon Bay Conservancy, founded by Allan W. Echert at Englewood, Florida, for saving forever a series of beautiful islands where one may study the wading birds in comparative comfort: Mr. Jerry Chambers, Mr. James Cook, Mrs. Joan D. Eckert, Dr. Emil Swepston, Mr. Howard Mensel and Dr. Richard Campbell—sincere thanks to all;

Last but not least, my thanks to Russell Mason of Englewood, Florida, outdoor sports writer and an excellent field naturalist.

KARL E. KARALUS

Least
Bittern

Reddish
Egret

Green
Heron

Young
Night
Heron's

Green
Heron

Ibis

Black
Crowned

young
Bittern

Tricolored

Yellow
Crowned

Egret
chick
at nest

Snowy
Egret

# INTRODUCTION

In the preparation of this book, all known species and subspecies of wading birds of the North American continent north of Mexico have been studied closely. Mostly these are the typical waders—the long-legged and long-necked birds common to marsh and swamp. Yet, to aver that all the wading birds have long legs and long necks would certainly be incorrect, since in some cases the characteristics have become modified or are even absent.

In a book of this scope, it was important to include all known aspects of the life histories of each of the species and subspecies included under the orders Gruiformes and Ciconiiformes occurring on this continent north of Mexico. Since the Ciconiiformes and Gruiformes have many similar characteristics and these become progressively abundant as the classification is narrowed down through suborder, superfamily, family, subfamily, genus, species, and subspecies, tedious repetition in the text was likely to occur. It was necessary to avoid this possibility, yet without undermining the value of the descriptions for each of the subspecies. To do this, the most prominent, familiar, or representative wading bird of each genus and species has been selected for a major descrip-

tion. Other subspecies falling under each major species designation are described only as far as they *differ* from the representative species that is described in detail.

A word about subspecies is advisable here. The terms race, subspecies, and geographic variation are essentially synonymous. Subspecies are rarely constant in coloration, markings, and characteristics in the same sense that there is a constancy to species determination. The geographic variations—races or subspecies—are rarely separable into distinctly bounded geographic areas. Variation of a species on any continent is almost invariably continuous in smooth clines of intergrades and intermediates and therefore not neatly separable. Yet, to establish some sort of order, the subspecific scientific names become a necessity, however lacking they may be in the clarity one would hope to ascribe to them.

This, in itself, was a problem of considerable moment when it came to a determination of which geographical variations should be included in a book

---

Neck and head attitudes of resting herons, bitterns, ibises, etc. Field sketches made in the Everglades and elsewhere in south Florida.

(Overleaf) Field sketches of herons and egrets in flight, made on Manasota Key, Englewood, Florida, April 1974.

(Page xv) Sketches of dead birds washed ashore at Stump Pass, Englewood, Florida, April 20, 1974. (Thumbnail sketches not intended to show detail or scale.)

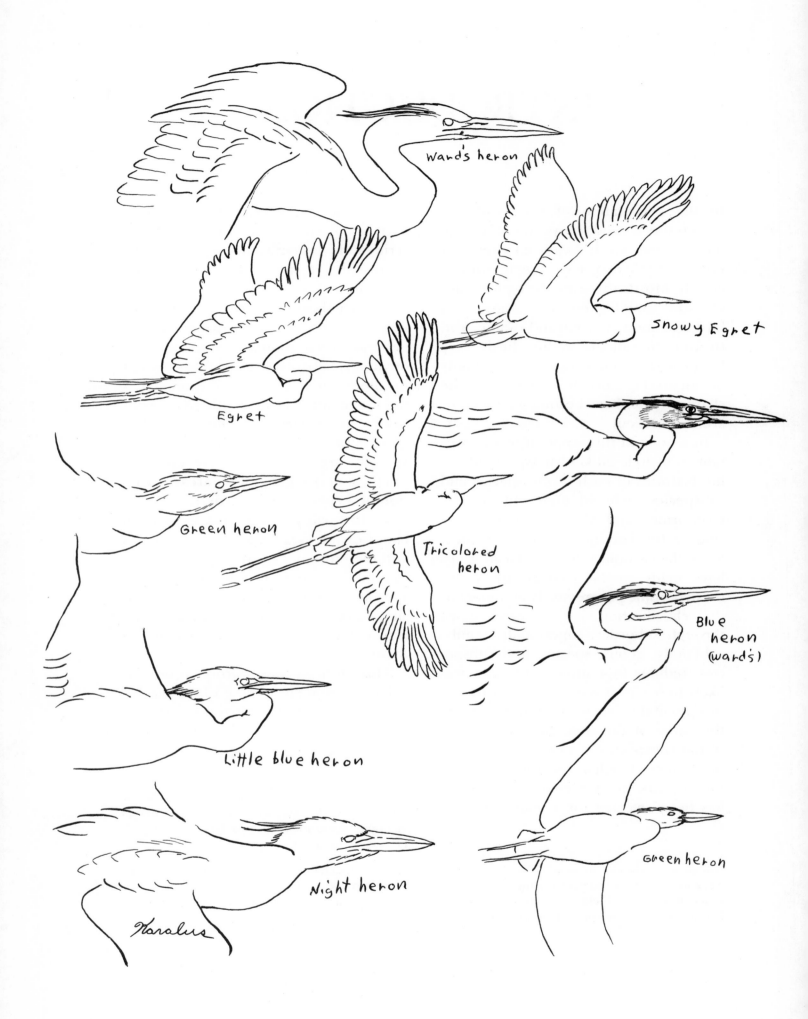

Ward's heron

snowy Egret

Egret

Green heron

Tricolored heron

Blue heron (ward's)

Little blue heron

Night heron

Green heron

Naralus

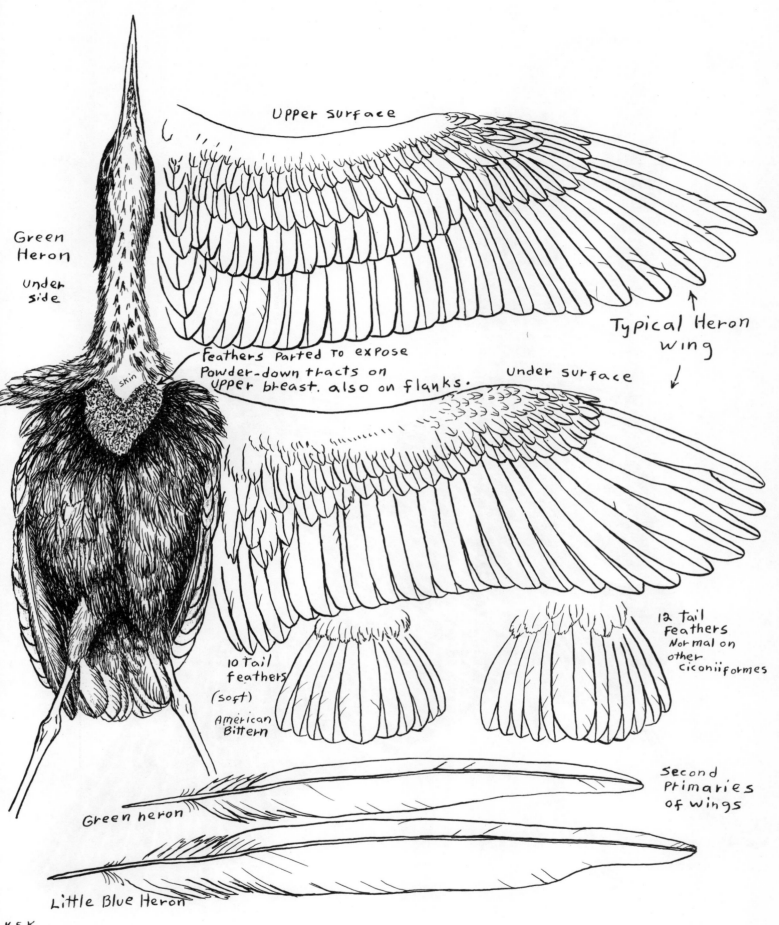

Upper Surface

Green Heron

under side

Feathers parted to expose
Powder-down tracts on
Upper breast. also on flanks.

skin

Typical Heron wing

Under surface

10 Tail Feathers

(soft)

American Bittern

12 Tail Feathers
Normal on other Ciconiiformes

Second Primaries of wings

Green heron

Little Blue Heron

K.E.K.

Karl E. Karalus

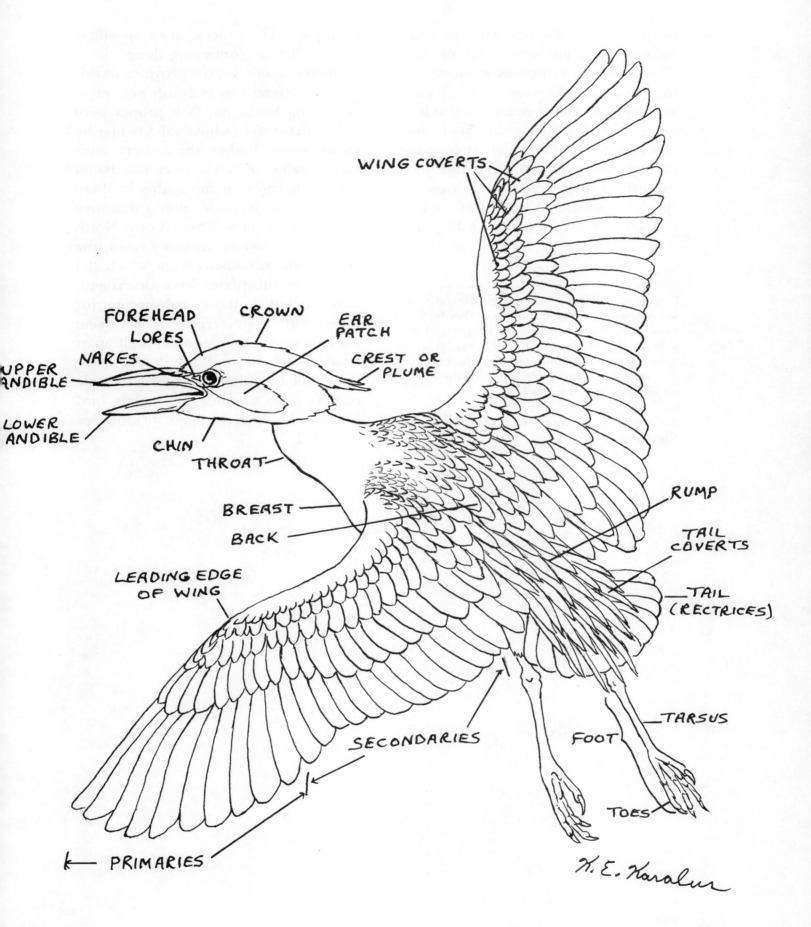

WING COVERTS

FOREHEAD
CROWN
LORES
EAR PATCH
NARES
CREST OR PLUME
UPPER ANDIBLE
LOWER ANDIBLE
CHIN
THROAT
BREAST
BACK
RUMP
TAIL COVERTS
TAIL (RECTRICES)
LEADING EDGE OF WING
TARSUS
FOOT
SECONDARIES
TOES
PRIMARIES

K. E. Karalus

1976

purporting to describe all continental subspecies of any one order of birds. The matter of taxonomy is more often than not a touchy issue. In some cases, wading birds that were accepted as legitimate species or subspecies some years ago may now be part of another species or themselves broken down into more extensive subspecies. Further, new subspecies continue to be named and described and often it becomes difficult to

keep pace. The process of subspecification is a living, continuing thing.

In no respect is it the province of this book to attempt to establish new races of wading birds, nor is it proper here to eliminate races whose validity may be questionable. Rather, the authors, after considerable research, after discussion with authorities far more able in these matters than we, and after exhaustive study of specimens from all over North America (including, in many cases, the actual type specimens from which the species or subspecies were described), have included those subspecies (or races) with characteristics which seem truly to set them reasonably well apart from others. Beyond any doubt, questions will be raised by knowledgeable readers as to whether this wading bird or that should have been included or excluded.

---

(Page xvi) Yellow-Crowned Night Heron, *Nyctanassa violacea violacea* (Linnaeus). This bird was studied for many hours on the property of Mrs. Joan D. Eckert, Lemon Bay, Florida. It would come in early afternoon to hunt wharf and soldier crabs until dusk. Normally shy, the bird allowed very close approach.

(Overleaf) Topography of a Yellow-Crowned Night Heron.

# *BUTORIDES* HERONS

---

ORDER:   *CICONIIFORMES*

SUBORDER:   *ARDEAE*

FAMILY:   *ARDEIDAE*

SUBFAMILY:   *ARDEINAE*

GENUS:   *BUTORIDES* Blyth

SPECIES:   *STRIATUS* (Linnaeus)

SUBSPECIES:   *virescens* (Linnaeus)
Eastern Green Heron

*frazari* (Brewster)
Frazar's Green Heron

*anthonyi* (Mearns)
Anthony's Green Heron

## COMMON NAME

Eastern Green Heron
(Color Plate I)

## SCIENTIFIC NAME

*Butorides striatus virescens* (Linnaeus). The generic name derives from the Latin *butio,* meaning "a heron," and the Greek *eidos,* signifying "resembling." The specific name is the Latin *striatus,* meaning "streaked." The subspecific name is the Latin *virescens,* meaning "growing green." In essence, then, the scientific name can be loosely translated to mean a bird "bearing a resemblance to a bittern, and streaked, but greener."

## OTHER COMMON OR COLLOQUIAL NAMES

CHALK-LINE After the white line of fecal matter often left behind when the bird is flushed.

CHRISTMAS HERON The origin of this name is unclear, but it is possibly based on the bird's predominantly green and reddish coloration, reminiscent of the Christmas colors.

CRAB-CATCHER From a particular item of prey it is fond of catching and eating in coastal waters, especially in southern Florida.

FLY-UP-THE-CREEK From its habit of doing just what the name suggests, when the bird is flushed along a stream.

GREEN BITTERN For its color and relationship to the bittern, especially the Least Bittern.

GREEN HERON For the lustrous coloration of its crest, shoulders, back, and wing coverts.

INDIAN PULLET Allegedly because formerly it was used as a food source, like chicken, by certain woodland tribes of American Indians.

KOP-KOP After the explosive call it makes.

LITTLE GREEN HERON For its size and coloration.

POKE Bag, as a diminutive of Shitepoke (see below), which is another common name.

REED HERON For its marked agility in moving about among the cattail reeds.

SHITEPOKE Literally, "bag of shit," after its habit of defecating voluminously when first flushed.

SKEER Apparently a dual-name form; first, after the fear it displays when flushed; second, after the piercing cry it utters at that time.

SKEO For much the same reason as Skeer, but with more consideration given to the articulation of the call.

SMALL BITTERN After the original description basis.

## SHAPE AT REST AND IN FLIGHT

The usual shape at rest is a hunched, drawn-in position on a branch, normally in protective cover, with the head couched on the body and showing little or no sign of the neck, or sometimes with the head drawn so far back that it seems to be growing out of the back. In this latter position it bears little resemblance to the characteristic at-rest pose of a heron. Relatively small and dark, it is not as large as a crow and often it is seen in its hunting posture along the margin of a stream or pond. That posture is with head, neck, and back nearly horizontal and the shanks of the legs so flat to the ground that the bird itself appears to be outstretched on the surface upon which it is standing. At such times it has been described as having a loglike appearance. Now and then, when startled unexpectedly, it will freeze in place to escape detection and its position then will be whatever position it happened to be in when it "froze." Occasionally it will stand with neck outstretched, head held high, beak slightly upward, and crest raised and spread. The tail is so short that it appears to be abnormally cut off. Sometimes the bird will "break" from its frozen position into an in-place nervous movement wherein it raises and lowers its crest and twitches its tail in irregular jerks. This is one of the smallest of the herons on the North American continent.

Although its initial takeoff when disturbed is not smooth it swiftly levels and can dart directly and with great skill through the overhanging branches of trees with relatively rapid wingbeats; strokes which are slightly faster than those of the closely related herons and equally faster and more coordinated than those of the Least Bittern, with which it is sometimes confused when it first rises. As well as the tail being short, the legs are relatively short and extend beyond the tail only a couple of inches. This, too, serves as a recognition factor since the legs and feet extend farther behind in flight than among other heron species. Ordinarily, in flight, the head is couched slightly on the shoulders, but it is not usually drawn in as much or with as great a neck curvature as is apparent with some of the other heron species.

## LENGTH AND WINGSPAN

The average length is 18 inches (457mm) and the average wingspan is just under 25 inches (629mm).

## BEAK

As in all the heron species, the beak is sharply pointed and, in the dorsal-ventral silhouette laterally, more or less symmetrical. In its coloration, the beak ranges from a pale clear greenish to a distinctly dusky greenish, with the lower mandible paler and more yellowish toward the base than the upper. In younger birds, the beak has a dusky ridge and is generally duller and a paler greenish than in adults.

## LEGS, FEET, AND CLAWS

In both adult and young birds, there is a slight webbing between the middle and outer toes. This aids young birds in swimming when they fall out of the nest, and aids adults when they deliberately plunge into the water after prey and return to shore or their hunting perch with it. The middle toe, including the claw, is about the same length as the tarsus, with legs and feet yellow in the adult and a pale and dull greenish gray in the young.

Green Heron, *Butorides striatus.*

serrate section
on inside of bill

franklin Park Illinois
may 20 1963

♂

studies near
Dayton Ohio

K. E. Karalus

chicks from nest
at myakka River
Charlotte co
florida

2 days old

12 days old

## CRESTS, PLUMAGE, ANNUAL MOLT

The long, soft, occipital crest is always raised when the bird is nervous and, at such times, is uneven and unruly, as if not properly combed. When the bird is hunting, the crest almost always lies flat against crown and nape. The crest feathers are a deep lustrous dark green. Although the crest is normally in its lowered position during flight, on very short flights not only is the neck extended and the head high but the crest is raised and spread. Very little seasonal difference occurs in adult plumage. A postnuptial partial molt occurs in late winter and early spring. Yearling birds tend to undergo their first postnuptial molt, at which time full adult plumage is acquired, occasionally as early as April, but more often in May or June.

## VOICE

*Butorides striatus virescens* makes a variety of sounds, some of them so distinctive to the bird that it has been dubbed with colloquial names which try to emulate the sound. Such names as Kop-Kop, Skeo, and Skeer, are derived from the sounds made by the bird, especially when startled from its perch. The most familiar of the cries is a loud, alarmed, raucous screech of *keow* or *skeow*, repeated as the bird wings away. Such a call is always explosively uttered and very distinctive. Once heard and identified, it is not mistaken for anything else when next encountered. In addition to that alarm call, however, there are a number of soft clucks, clicks, chuckles, squawks, cackles, and grunts made by the bird, especially during courtship and nesting. A particular courtship cry uttered by the male as he struts and displays before the female is a series of soft little sounds like *qua-qua-qua-qua-qua.* Sometimes this sound emerges as little more than a grunting repeated twice with a pause between of irregular duration before the call comes again. It may continue for an hour or more if the bird is undisturbed. A similar but slightly louder sound is sometimes made as the adult bird lands near the nest bearing young.

## SEXUAL DIFFERENCES: SIZE, COLORATION, VOICE

The male is slightly larger than the female, with a broader wingspan. There is no extensive difference in coloration between the sexes as adults and no real difference in tonal quality of the voice.

## COLORATION AND MARKINGS: ADULT

A deep, lustrous-but-not-quite-iridescent dark green is found on the crown and crest, and on the longer feathers of the shoulders and back. The latter plumage has a bluish-green, rather bronzish cast. The wing coverts are also green, but the edges of these feathers are buffy to tawny in color. The entire head (other than crown and crest) and neck are a deep, rich chestnut, sometimes tending toward a purplish cast. The upper throat is white with brownish-gray streakings. The gular area is dark brownish and the abdomen directly below is streaked with white. The primaries, secondaries, and rectrices are a dusky greenish, except that the leading edges of the wings are white. The beak is generally greenish above and paler greenish below, this color graduating to a chartreuse and then more distinctive yellowish near the base of the lower beak. The legs are yellow, but on occasion certain individuals will show more of a deep yellow ocher coloration on shanks and feet. The irides are a bright golden yellow and the bare skin surrounding the eyes is a pale bluish-green.

## COLORATION AND MARKINGS: JUVENILE

There is no crest and no green on the head of the juvenile bird. The head is generally brownish, with the neck and sides of the body a faintly lighter brown streaked with lighter tan. The throat and center of the gular area are dusky-streaked white. The back is a plain, non-lustrous greenish brown. The same occurs on the wing coverts and secondaries, but these feathers are white-tipped and white-edged. The undertail coverts are a dingy white, the legs are dusky green, and the beak is greenish with a grayish-green ridge. The irides are yellow.

## GENERAL HABITS AND CHARACTERISTICS

The Eastern Green Heron is commonly a very solitary bird, rarely associating with other birds, even of its own species. Except at times of courtship, nesting, or migration, it is almost always found by itself, generally along the margin of pond or stream.

## HABITAT AND ROOSTING

The Eastern Green Heron is rather selective about its habitat, preferring the edges of watercourses or ponds, especially where the water is sluggish and where there is dense growth of brush and trees to the water's edge and extending over the water. Areas of alders, willows, cottonwoods, and other such growth are particularly favored. This heron also shows a marked preference for areas where broken branches or logs extend from shore into the water, as these are favored as hunting perches. Even in coastal areas of salt water or brackish water, *Butorides striatus virescens* seeks out the tangled mangroves or areas of densest cover. In regard to roosting, it normally roosts alone in thick brush or close to the trunk of a dense tree growth near the water. Occasionally two will roost together and, even less often, three, but ordinarily the bird remains solitary.

## ENEMIES AND DEFENSES

The harsh alarm note it voices as it flushes may provide some sort of benefit in frightening or disconcerting would-be attackers. Also, the habit of waiting until the last possible moment to flush and then, in the very moment of flushing, defecating heavily may have considerable protective benefit. More than one would-be attacker has been struck full in the face with the bursting expulsion of the feces and been temporarily blinded and very thoroughly discouraged in the process. Becoming absolutely rigid at the sight of danger approaching is definitely another defense mechanism of considerable value. Even though the bird, moving, may be quite visible to an approacher, when it freezes in whatever position it may happen to be in, it is remarkable how difficult the bird is to detect, even though it is known where the bird was last moving. Even the very young Eastern Green Herons and subspecies utilize this process of freezing to avoid detection, doing so at a signal from the parent birds. Sometimes the "frozen" position will be held by young or adult birds alike until the intruder has approached to within a few short feet. Another trait which acts toward defense, though its utilization may be entirely accidental, is regurgitation of the stomach contents toward an intruder who is very close. Again, this is done by both young and adult birds, but whether it is an instinctive action brought about solely by fear or a deliberate attempt at defense against an enemy has not been ascertained positively. *Butorides striatus virescens* discriminates quite well in what constitutes danger and may be found perfectly content in an area where there is much adjacent auto traffic, human movement, and noise, as long as it is not molested. As an adult the bird has relatively few enemies and it is likely that more are killed by youngsters with air guns or small-caliber rifles who just wander along watercourses and "plink" at anything which catches their attention than by any other cause.

## FOOD AND FEEDING HABITS

What the Eastern Green Heron eats depends largely upon the environment in which it finds itself, whether marsh or swamp, saltwater or freshwater or brackish. The principal food, wherever it hunts, is fish—a variety of small species making up about 40 per cent of its diet. Insects are next in importance, making up close to 30 per cent of food intake, followed by crustaceans at 24 per cent and a variety of other material— spiders, snails, worms, small mammals— making up the remaining percentage. Surprisingly few reptilians are taken (snakes and lizards) and even more surprisingly, hardly any frogs. A partial listing of some of the prey most favored by the Eastern Green Heron would include a wide selection of minnows, especially including killifish, other fish up to about 6 inches in length, including carp, catfish, sunfish, eels, pickerel, goldfish, white perch, etc. Also favored are water insects and their larvae, dragonflies and damselflies, katydids and crickets, grasshoppers, crayfish and small crabs. Essentially a day-feeder, the Eastern Green Heron prefers to hunt in the morning hours, take a midday siesta, and then resume hunting again in late afternoon until twilight. It frequents the shallows when hunting, sometimes taking a perch on a branch or log just over the water and spearing whatever comes past which might represent food, but more often it stalks stealthily and with great skill and caution along the shorelines, head drawn back and couched between the hunched shoulders, as if on a spring and ready to snap forward and downward with unerring aim when prey appears. Infrequently the bird will actually plunge headlong into the water, usually successfully, after prey and then swim to shore or back to its perch with whatever it has caught, devouring it en route. It will frequently hunt in marshy meadows, especially for insects, but usually stay relatively close to good covering bushes along the edges.

## COURTSHIP AND MATING

*Butorides striatus virescens* will prance and dance in the most outlandish manner at times, sometimes on a gravel or sand bank, sometimes on a mud flat, sometimes in an inch or so of water. Most often it appears to be doing this for its own amusement, but such is not the case. Invariably the dancer is a male and he is performing a courtship ritual for a female who is close by, but probably well hidden from the eyes of an intruder. At such times the male will raise and twitch his crest, spreading it in a ragged fashion and tilting his head in a ludicrous manner as he dances, his tail bobbing up and down rapidly. He gets very caught up in the tempo of his display and sometimes will take several successive hops on one foot, then switch and do the same on the other; then spring forward four or five feet, then backward, then turn in small, dizzying circles. It is a fascinating display, but oddly graceless and appearing rather awkward and ridiculous, especially because he gives the illusion of doing it for his own amusement. Other courtship activities are not well documented, no doubt because of the solo habits of the bird. The actual copulation is reported to occur sporadically, several times daily over a period of from three to six or seven days.

## NEST AND NESTING HABITS

The Eastern Green Heron breeds anywhere within its range, but almost always only in pairs, rarely in small groups, and only in exceptional cases in any kind of breeding rookery. Its nest is by far the most frail constructed by any North American heron; a very poorly built platform of sloppily interwoven twigs which is almost flat on top. There is no cup shape to the nest, nor even a saucerlike depression to keep the eggs in the center, yet oddly enough there are virtually no accounts of the eggs having fallen out, even as the result of storms. Nevertheless, the nest is so flimsy that one can almost always see the eggs by standing right below the nest and looking up through the sticks of which the nest is constructed. The actual body of the nest is about 10 inches to a foot in diameter and, though ordinarily built anywhere from 10 to 20 feet high in living trees, it may sometimes be built in the very tops of trees or, contrarily, in low bushes or even on the ground in marsh grasses or thick meadow grasses. The nest is never lined with grasses, leaves, or any other sort of softening or buttressing material. Although the Eastern Green Heron prefers as a nesting site a tree in or very close to the water, such as dense willow or mangrove, it often nests quite far from the water in dry upland woods or even in orchards. Ornithologists of the past have written about relatively large rookeries of breeding Eastern Green Herons, but none of these writings are more recent than thirty or

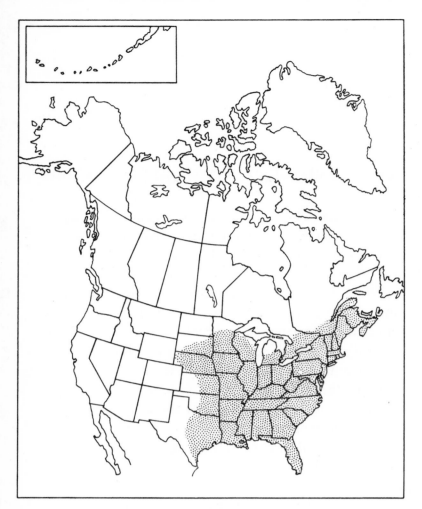

EASTERN GREEN HERON

*Butorides striatus virescens* (Linnaeus)

## YOUNG

All the eggs hatch at essentially the same time, almost without exception on the same day. They weigh approximately 21.25 grams on hatching (¾ ounce) and their weight increases by about 14 grams (½ ounce) daily until about the tenth day. They are fed by both parent birds, but the morning feeding (usually six or seven separate visits by the parents) generally occurs only between dawn and sunrise. A similar evening feeding begins in the later afternoon, perhaps no more than an hour before sunset, and continues until dusk, again with six or seven separate visitations by the parent birds. Feeding is by regurgitation, but the food material is not predigested by the parent birds. While still downy chicks, before beginning to assume juvenal plumage *(see Coloration and Markings: Juvenile)* the baby birds are clad in a nondescript down which ranges from a medium brown on the crestless crown to a light buff or buffy gray on the underparts. The young are quite ugly in the down period and until juvenile plumage is reasonably well developed.

forty years ago. No recent accounts speak of any sort of nesting rookery, although occasions are mentioned when, perhaps more or less accidentally, Eastern Green Herons nest near to or in conjunction with other heron species, or sometimes in the same areas with grackles or other birds.

## EGGS AND INCUBATION

Three to nine eggs are laid, though the usual number is four or five. They are smooth-shelled, pale greenish or bluish, and in size they average about 1.5 inches by 1.1 inches (38mm x 30mm). The twenty-day incubation is shared equally by the parent birds.

## MIGRATION

The southern movement begins, from the northern portion of its range, from as early as during the first few days of September to as late as mid-to-late October. Winters in north-central Florida (sometimes southern Georgia) southward through the West Indies and South America, with southward migration completed usually no later than November 25. The northern movement begins as early as mid-March and the birds have

*Eastern Green Heron*

settled into the northernmost portions of their range before the end of April.

# ECONOMIC INFLUENCE

*Butorides striatus virescens,* except in very isolated cases, has no significant economic impact. Its dietary habits are generally beneficial within the scheme of natural balance, except for occasions when it is of some economic detriment because of preying upon goldfish or minnows in areas where these are raised commercially. Probably is of considerable benefit in controlling injurious insects.

## COMMON NAME

Frazar's Green Heron
(Subspecies Sketch 1)

## SCIENTIFIC NAME

*Butorides striatus frazari* (Brewster). This subspecies was first discovered among the coastal mangroves at La Paz, Lower California, in 1887 by M. Abbott Frazar, who provided the type specimen for William Brewster.

## OTHER COMMON OR COLLOQUIAL NAMES

BAJA GREEN HERON For primary residence locality.

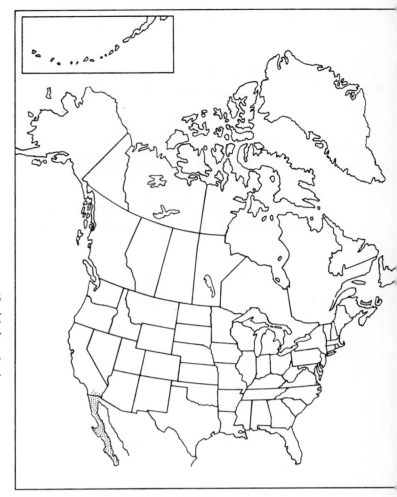

FRAZAR'S GREEN HERON

*Butorides striatus frazari* (Brewster)

## COLORATION AND MARKINGS: ADULT

It is generally darker and rather duller in coloration than *Butorides striatus virescens,* with the coloration more generally uniform. The neck is somewhat more purplish, the back and sides tend to be slightly more glaucous, and the light-colored throat line is more restricted.

## GENERAL HABITS AND CHARACTERISTICS

Since the habits of Frazar's Green Heron are virtually the same as those of the Eastern Green Heron, the principal differences are those of coloration and size, with Frazar's Green Heron averaging slightly larger and darker than the Eastern Green Heron.

## HABITAT

More frequently in mangrove areas and less often in upland areas or stream valleys.

---

1. FRAZAR'S GREEN HERON

*Butorides striatus frazari* (Brewster). Ensenada Baja, California. A.O.U. Number 201a

Karl E. Karalus

## COMMON NAME

Anthony's Green Heron
(Subspecies Sketch 2)

## SCIENTIFIC NAME

*Butorides striatus anthonyi* (Mearns). Dr. Edgar A. Mearns collected the first specimens of this subspecies just north of the Mexican border in the valley of the Colorado River in California during 1895. One of the birds he collected was the type specimen, and he named the bird in honor of his friend from San Diego, California, A. W. Anthony.

ANTHONY'S GREEN HERON

*Butorides striatus anthonyi* (Mearns)

## OTHER COMMON OR COLLOQUIAL NAMES

VALLEY GREEN HERON After the Colorado River valley which it inhabits.

DITCH HERON After the irrigation ditches it frequents throughout its range.

DESERT HERON Because it is the desert form of the Green Heron.

## COLORATION AND MARKINGS: ADULT

This is a much lighter subspecies; all the markings are paler, with those of the throat, neck, and wings being much less restricted and considerably paler than those of *Butorides striatus virescens*. Some of the markings fade out practically into whiteness in this desert form of the bird.

## NEST AND NESTING HABITS

On the average, the nest of Anthony's Green Heron is positioned slightly higher in the nesting trees than is the nest of the Eastern Green Heron, with the average nest height of the former approximately 30 feet high instead of 20.

---

2. ANTHONY'S GREEN HERON

*Butorides striatus anthonyi* (Mearns). San Diego, California. A.O.U. Number 201c

Karl E. Karalus

# BLACK-CROWNED NIGHT HERON

---

GENUS: *NYCTICORAX* Forster
SPECIES: NYCTICORAX (Linnaeus)
SUBSPECIES: *hoactli* (Gmelin)

## COMMON NAME

Black-Crowned Night Heron
(Color Plate II)

## SCIENTIFIC NAME

*Nycticorax nycticorax hoactli* (Gmelin).
*Nycticorax* means "Raven of the Night."

## OTHER COMMON OR COLLOQUIAL NAMES

QWOK From the call it utters.

NIGHT HERON Due to its almost exclusive tendency to hunt and fly nocturnally; and because the bird is rarely seen at any other time than during the night or the very deep twilight hours of morning and evening.

STRIPED NIGHT HERON Primarily due to the clear stripings on the plumage of birds less than four years of age, birds which have not yet acquired full adult plumage.

## SHAPE AT REST AND IN FLIGHT

Except when poised to strike prey, the Black-Crowned Night Heron almost always stands in a generally hunched posture with the head usually well couched on the shoulders. The bird is easily identifiable because of the stockiness of its body, stoutness of beak, and shortness of legs and neck in comparison with most other heron species.

The wings are long and broad, seeming almost abnormally so in flight for the size of the body, which appears to be blunt and short. In flight the head is tucked back in the shoulder plumage and the legs are drawn up tightly against the abdominal plumage, with the lower legs and feet trailing beyond the tail, as is the nature of all herons and egrets.

At takeoff, the wingbeat pattern is strong but fluttery, although very quickly the wingbeats settle to powerful, fairly slow regularity of approximately forty strokes per minute.

## LENGTH AND WINGSPAN

Average length of the Black-Crowned Night Heron is 26 inches (667mm) and the average wingspan is almost 46 inches (656mm).

## EYES

In adult birds, the irides are bright red. Young birds, however, go through a progression of iris coloration, from gray to yellow, to orange in the subadult, and red in the adult.

## CRESTS, PLUMAGE, ANNUAL MOLT

Generally, immature birds are streaky brown and white. Adult birds, from a distance, give the uniform impression of grayish coloration. There are no particular plumes except for the two or three

Common at dusk and at
night at Englewood Fla
Charlotte Co

Stump Pass channel
Englewood Florida
Dec 23 1976

A. E. Karalus

extremely long filamentous feathers which spring from the hind head. These few feathers are normally imbricated into one bundle. The average length of the longest plume in such a bundle is about 7 inches (183mm). There are eight complete plumage changes before full adult plumage is acquired. The annual molt, beginning about early June and completed by late October, is progressive and in no way hampers the bird's flight. The greasy, powdery substance exuded by the powder-down tracts on the breast is used to dress and oil the heron's contour feathers, as is the case with other heron species.

## VOICE

A brief and well-spaced series of deep-throated sounds similar to *quck* and *whuk* or *quock* are usually uttered immediately as the bird goes into flight, especially if it has been startled or forced to fly. A few of these same sounds may be uttered, in a somewhat lower and more placid tone, just prior to landing. When angered, especially during territorial squabbles or during incubation altercations *(see Eggs and Incubation)*, the bird may utter a harsh, grating screech.

## SEXUAL DIFFERENCES: SIZE, COLORATION, VOICE

The male bird is generally somewhat larger than the female, but coloration is identical. The voice of the male bird

---

Black-Crowned Night Heron, *Nycticorax nycticorax hoactli* (Gmelin).

tends to be a shade deeper and stronger and farther-carrying than the female's.

## MORTALITY

Hatchlings which are left unprotected in the nest can and quite often do fall prey to avian predators, especially crows and sometimes vultures and gulls. However, the highest death rate among young birds occurs when they are blown out of their flimsy nests during severe storms. It is believed that the Black-Crowned Night Heron in its wild state may live to around twenty years of age, and those in captivity may live to around age thirty.

## COLORATION AND MARKINGS: ADULT

The shoulders, back, and entire crown of this bird are jet black, while the remainder of the upper parts are a pale ash-gray, including wings and tail. The sides of the head, forehead, and throat are white, except that the throat generally blends into a pale lilac coloration. The remaining underparts are white. The beak is glossy black, the irides are scarlet, and the bare space around the eye is a light, delicate chartreuse. The legs are generally yellow.

## COLORATION AND MARKINGS: JUVENILE

In its natal plumage, the bird has head, neck, and dorsal tracts which are a dark mouse gray to a deep neutral gray. The outer three quarters of the crown filaments are white and these are especially conspicuous during the first few hours after hatching. The down of the ventral tract ranges from pallid neutral gray on the lower belly to a medium gray on the breast and then to a dark mouse gray on the neck. The down on the crown is always much longer than the body down and forms a distinct crest. The down, when dry, conceals the wings and aptera. When the hatchling is five days of age, the upper down fades to a neutral gray which can best be described as a mouse gray, as opposed to the lighter pale dull gray which the down becomes ventrally. Later, the entire plumage becomes grayish-white and is streaked on the head and breast as well as on the underbody with dark brown. There are also streaks and spottings of rusty-reddish and white on the back. The wing coverts are brown and these feathers have triangular white tips. The primaries are simply a dirty grayish-brown. The beak is a dull yellow and the feet are a pale chartreuse.

## GENERAL HABITS AND CHARACTERISTICS

This is a fairly large but decidedly stocky bird, with comparatively short legs for a heron. The neck, too, is much shorter than is commonly noted in other members of this family, and the beak is relatively short and stout. When seen perched from reasonably close up, the immature birds are generally brownish with much darker brown stripings, while the adults are a handsome gray with white underparts, and jet-black crown, back, and shoulders. Black-Crowned

Night Herons breed in colonies. They also occasionally gather in small groups of from three to seven individuals to feed or roost. Their migration is always in large flocks.

## HABITAT AND ROOSTING

This species particularly likes marshy areas with heavy reed growth and mangrove shorelines, especially those of small islands. It is uncommonly fond of alighting upon pilings, rocks, low docks, and other protuberances which project from the water. The Black-Crowned Night Heron is especially drawn to docks and other structures where artificial lighting at night tends to bring minnows and other small marine life to the surface. Roosting is usually low in dense, leafy trees—especially red mangroves in the coastal areas—fairly close to the water. In freshwater areas, roosting often occurs on floating matted bundles of dead cattails, especially within heavy standing growths of cattails.

## HUNTING METHODS, FOOD AND FEEDING HABITS

Unlike many of its longer-legged kin, the Black-Crowned Night Heron prefers *not* to stand in water when hunting. Rather, it likes to take a perch on a

---

Crustaceans most hunted by Black- and Yellow-Crowned Night Herons in the Lemon Bay, Florida, study area. These sketches were made from specimens collected by Joseph Eckert. They represent both live material and the stomach content of birds.

*Black-Crowned Night Heron*

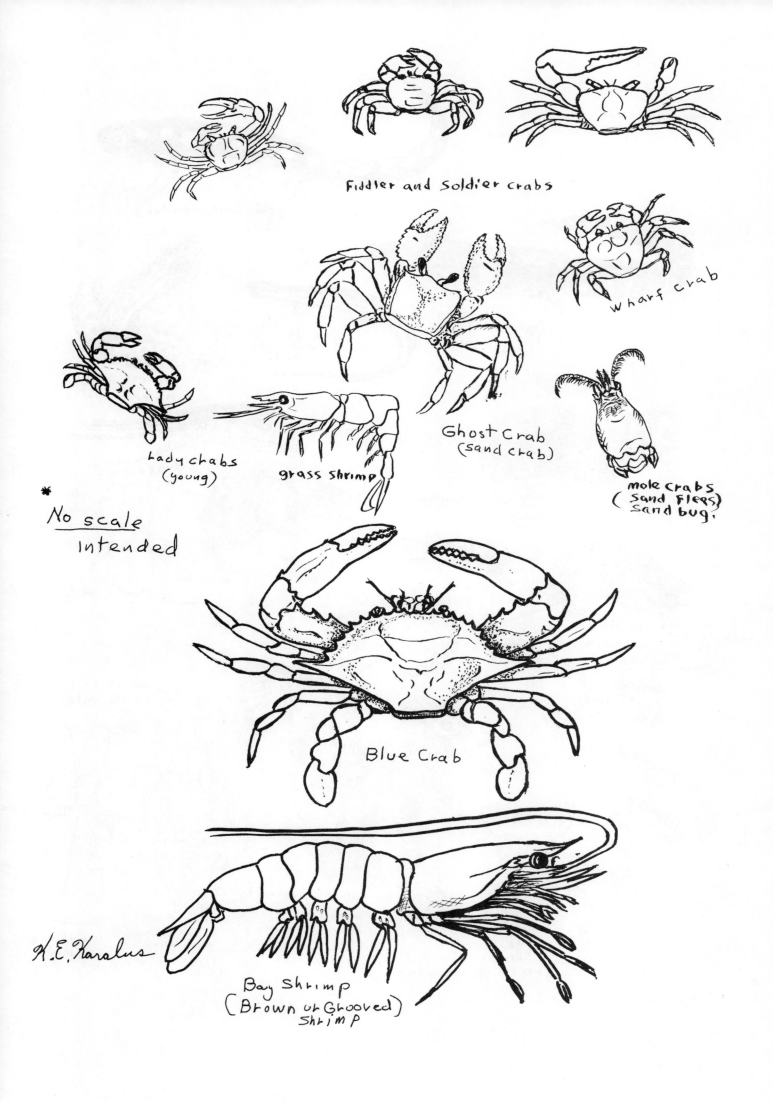

Fiddler and Soldier crabs

Wharf crab

Lady crabs
(young)

grass shrimp

Ghost Crab
(sand crab)

mole crabs
(Sand fleas)
Sand bug.

No scale
Intended

Blue Crab

H.E. Karalus

Bay Shrimp
(Brown or Grooved)
Shrimp

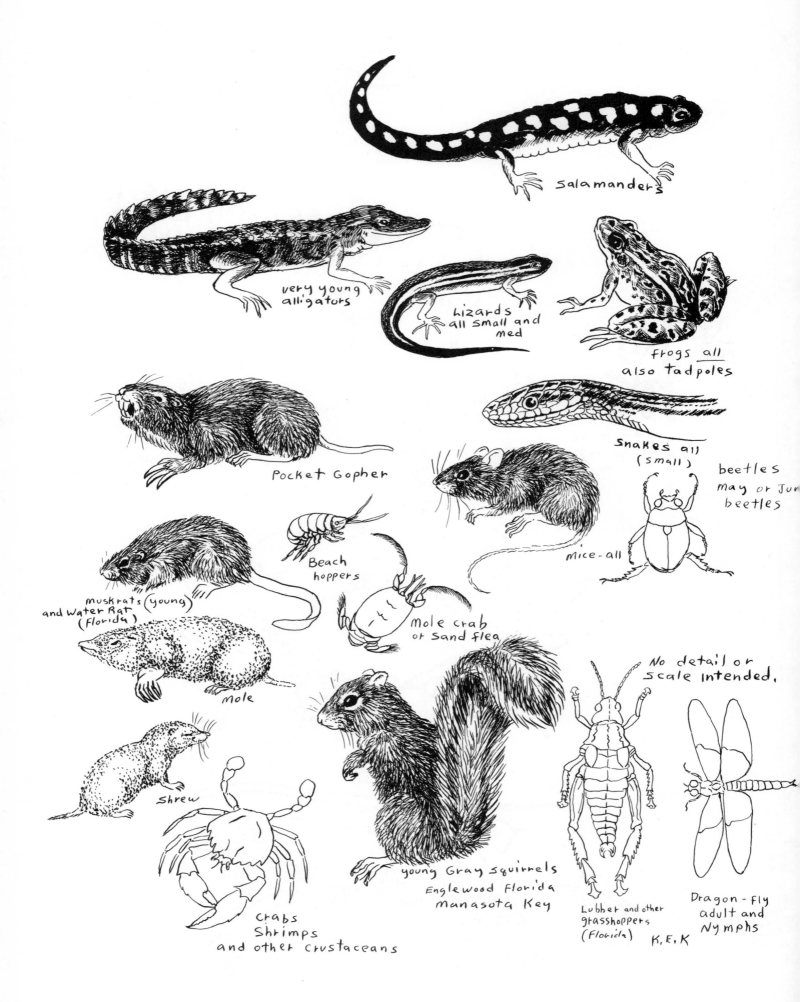

salamanders

very young
alligators

lizards
all small and
med

frogs all
also tadpoles

Pocket Gopher

Snakes all
(small)

beetles
may or Jun
beetles

mice-all

muskrats (young)
and Water Rat
(Florida)

Beach
hoppers

Mole crab
or Sand flea

Mole

No detail or
scale intended.

Shrew

young Gray squirrels
Englewood Florida
manasota Key

crabs
Shrimps
and other crustaceans

Lubber and other
grasshoppers
(Florida)

K.E.K

Dragon-fly
adult and
Nymphs

branch, mangrove root, piling, post, rock, or light fixture right at the water's edge and lean down to snatch up small unsuspecting prey swimming past on the water surface or just under the surface, or circling aimlessly in the halo of artificial light on the surface. Serrations of the beak aid in holding the often slippery prey.

Small fish of almost any variety up to four or five inches and occasionally even up to nine or ten inches are taken avidly by the Black-Crowned Night Heron. Occasionally it will also feed upon crayfish, shrimp, squid, insects, lizards, and amphibians. The captured prey is held very tightly crosswise in the beak and is usually shaken vigorously until thoroughly stunned and limp, or else dead. The prey is rarely dropped on the ground and speared, as is so often done by the larger herons with their prey. When the prey has been shaken to limpness, the bird then tosses it gently in its beak, juggling it about adroitly until it is positioned in a head-first manner toward the bird's throat. It is then swallowed.

The bird's digestive acids are so powerful that there is very little regurgitation of any ingested material. Almost all bone matter is dissolved in the digestive acids and this results in the feces taking on an unusually white, limy character due to the high content of dissolved bone calcium. More often than not, the nesting and perching areas used regularly by the bird become extremely unsightly because of the defecations which coat everything for yards.

---

Heron food-prey aside from fish. Lizards are grasped by the head and beaten repeatedly before being swallowed. The young of ground-nesting birds also make up part of the heron's diet.

## COURTSHIP AND MATING

Since much of this activity occurs during the nighttime hours, only the most spectacular efforts have been observed and described at any length. The males perform a sort of dance display and it is believed that at times the female will join in the prancing and leaping as the tempo seems to become infectious. On the whole, however, courtship displays are relatively simple and ordinarily rather brief. The male alights near the female and bends quite low, raising his crest and his back, breast, and neck feathers in display, to which the female responds similarly. Then begins a mutual caressing and preening with their beaks for a few minutes, after which they sit side by side, close together without movement. On occasion, it is the female who will fly in and perch close to the male and initiate the ceremony with an urgent squawking. In all cases, the male will grip the head of the female in his beak as he mounts her, at the same time raising his plumes and spreading his wings, as much for display as for maintaining balance as the copulation takes place.

## NEST AND NESTING HABITS

The nest is a crude, loosely constructed platform of coarse branches. It is usually quite low in the sturdier branches of low trees. Both male and female are active in the construction of the nest, a job which takes them from two to five days. This species will often nest in association with other species of herons and egrets.

BLACK-CROWNED NIGHT HERON

*Nycticorax nycticorax hoactli* (Gmelin)

be a full week ahead in their development beyond the last-hatched chick. Quite frequently the egg is pipped fully twenty-four hours before actual emergence occurs. The chick's eyes are open from the very beginning and by the end of twenty-four hours after hatching it can sit erect and be somewhat active. The hatchling utters a faint sound similar to a high-pitched "pip-pip-pip" when hungry or left alone. By the tenth day numerous pinfeathers appear, but vestiges of down remain on the young birds even after they have left the nest. The post-natal molt is not completed until the bird is from five to six weeks of age.

At the beginning of its fourth week, the bird has acquired the smooth, contoured appearance of the adult bird, but the complete growth of juvenile plumage does not occur until about the fiftieth day. There are eight distinct plumage changes before the full adult plumage is acquired.

## EGGS AND INCUBATION

The Black-Crowned Night Heron usually lays three or four bluish-green eggs, averaging 2.5 x 2 inches, between February and March and between June and July.

Incubation, beginning with the laying of the first egg, is undertaken by both parent birds. The incubation period of each egg is twenty-four to twenty-six days.

## YOUNG

Because of the interval of egg-laying, some of the chicks in the nest will often

## MIGRATION

*Nycticorax nycticorax hoactli* migrates in large flocks and almost without exception at night, resting in secluded areas during the daylight hours. The migration in spring to the north generally occurs from mid-February through mid-May. The autumn migration southward generally occurs from mid-July through October. Much of the population does not follow the pattern of a true migration, but merely moves about within the southern portions of its distributional range.

*Black-Crowned Night Heron*

# YELLOW-CROWNED
# NIGHT HERON

---

GENUS: *NYCTANASSA* Stejneger
SPECIES: *VIOLACEA* (Linnaeus)
SUBSPECIES: *violacea* (Linnaeus)

## COMMON NAME

Yellow-Crowned Night Heron
(Color Plate III)

## SCIENTIFIC NAME

*Nyctanassa violacea violacea* (Linnaeus). *Nyctanassa* derives from the Greek for "night fish trap." Species and subspecies name of *violacea,* from the Latin, "violet-colored."

## SHAPE AT REST

Although *Nyctanassa violacea violacea* is stocky in build, it is nonetheless more slender and graceful than *Nycticorax nycticorax hoactli* and its legs are slightly longer, its beak slightly stouter. A distinctive white check patch and yellow crown are good field marks.

## LENGTH AND WINGSPAN

The species averages, in length, about 24 inches (610mm) and the wingspan is just over 42 inches (1084mm).

## CRESTS, PLUMAGE, ANNUAL MOLT

The adult plumage includes a crest extending backward from the pate throughout the year. During the breeding season, however, both sexes produce from two to seven or eight long narrow white feathers, upward of 8 to 9 inches in length, that usually rest along the contour of the bird's back. Adult birds undergo a complete molt from August to October and a partial molt in late January and early February. Young birds get their first complete adult plumage at the age of thirty months when they undergo a complete postnuptial molt during July and August.

## COLORATION AND MARKINGS: ADULT

Generally the bird appears to be a medium grayish to violet-gray throughout its body at first look. The general blue-gray of the underparts is lighter than that of the back, where the feathers have dark centers and are strongly margined with lighter gray. The beak is black and the lores a pale greenish to greenish-gray. Crown and crest, including plumes, are creamy white to tawny yellow, with occasionally several jet-black plumes in the crest during the breeding season. The cheek patch extending backward from beneath the eye is whitish. The irides are bright orange-red in the adult, yellow in the juvenile. The upper body is dark violet-gray with long narrow streaks of black; lighter violet below. The wings also have black streakings and the primaries and rectrices are uniformly dark slate-gray. Legs and feet are yellow and black. Except for the cheek patch and crown-crest, the head and throat are black.

♀

Comb

fiddler
crab
Uca. sp

Yellow-Crowned Night
Herons show a
strong Preference for
crustacea in Florida
fiddler's a favorite food

Karl E. Karalius

## GENERAL HABITS AND CHARACTERISTICS

The Yellow-Crowned Night Heron, despite its name, is not essentially a nocturnal bird. Though it will often feed during the nighttime hours, it is as frequently found feeding during the daylight hours. The single exception, as adults, is when a pair is nesting in solitary manner, at which time they can sometimes be approached quite closely. When nesting in colonies, they take alarm easily and slip away from the nest before an intruder can come very close. While usually found only with its own kind, on rare occasions it will sometimes be found in mixed colonies made up of Ward's Herons, Little Blue Herons, Louisiana Herons, and Black-Crowned Night Herons.

## HABITAT AND ROOSTING

Most often *Nyctanassa violacea violacea* roosts alone or in company with only one or two others of its own species, usually in a dense tree close to the water. However, during nesting and migrational periods, colony roosting is not uncommon. The bird has a wide variety of habitat preference, ranging from rocky coasts or high cliffs or desert conditions to bayou swamp, cattail marsh, banks of rivers and creeks, and even forests in conjunction with slow-moving or

---

Yellow-Crowned Night Heron, *Nyctanassa violacea violacea* ♀ (Linnaeus). Field sketches made at Manasota Key, Englewood, Florida, April 1975.

stagnant water, such as with large cypress swamps and forests of Spanish moss-bedecked tupelos, water oaks, gum trees, and magnolias.

## FOOD AND FEEDING HABITS

The principal items of food for the Yellow-Crowned Night Heron are crawfish and crabs, although at times it will also eat such small coastal-area life as small fishes, small snakes and other reptiles, snails, baby birds that have tumbled from their nests, eels, young leeches, and aquatic insects. Oddly, very few frogs are eaten and there is no recorded instance of toads having been eaten. Although it is not unusual for this species to feed at night, it does so much less often than the Black-Crowned Night Heron. It is essentially diurnal, feeding most heavily during the early morning and late evening hours.

## NEST AND NESTING HABITS

Among the herons, *Nyctanassa violacea violacea* builds one of the most substantial of nests, constructed of relatively well-interwoven sticks. It is generally 18 to 22 inches in diameter and as much as 16 inches in depth, with a shallow depression in the center which is sometimes sparsely lined. The most common nesting site seems 'to be in a dense willow or black mangrove about 15 to 30 feet high. Most often the nesting occurs in conjunction with from ten to twenty pairs of its own species.

YELLOW-CROWNED NIGHT HERON

*Nyctanassa violacea violacea* (Linnaeus)

## EGGS AND INCUBATION

The four or five smooth-shelled eggs are a pale greenish-blue and, in size, average 2 inches x 1.4 inches (51mm x 37mm). Incubation appears to be identical to that of the Black-Crowned Night Heron and parental care is also the same. Eggs are laid from March through May. Incubation requires twenty-four to twenty-six days.

## YOUNG

Characteristics and development essentially the same as for the Black-Crowned Night Heron, the principal difference being that the young of the Yellow-Crowned Night Heron are a lighter slate color, with less brownish generally.

*Yellow-Crowned Night Heron*

# *ARDEA* HERONS

---

GENUS:     *ARDEA* Linnaeus

SPECIES:     *HERODIAS*

SUBSPECIES:     *herodias* (Linnaeus)
Great Blue Heron

*fannini* Chapman
Northwestern Coast Heron

*wardi* Ridgway
Ward's Heron

*treganzai* Court
Treganza's Heron

*hyperonca* Oberholser
California Heron

*occidentalis* Audubon
Great White Heron

## COMMON NAME

Great Blue Heron
(Color Plate IV)

## SCIENTIFIC NAME

*Ardea herodias herodias* (Linnaeus). From the Latin *ardea,* meaning heron, and the Greek *erodios,* also meaning heron.

## OTHER COMMON OR COLLOQUIAL NAMES

Practically all of its local names have to do with its size and color, sometimes coupled with (erroneously) the term "crane," which it is not. Often the bird is locally called simply a "crane," but this is in error. The other common or colloquial names include:

BIG BLUE HERON
BLUE CRANE
COMMON BLUE CRANE
CRANE

## SHAPE AT REST AND IN FLIGHT

When standing, the Great Blue Heron is about four feet high to the top of its raised head, a distinctive attitude of this bird. The legs are long, the neck thin and long, the tail relatively short, and the beak, which is thick at the base, symmetrically tapers to a very sharp point.

Occasionally the neck will be folded and the head couched on the shoulders. Often the bird will stand on one foot only, the other drawn up and all but hidden in the underside plumage. With the encroachment of another Great Blue Heron on its territory, the bird will stretch its neck upward fully, point its beak toward the sky, and advance slowly and menacingly toward the intruder, and chase it away.

In flight it is an uncommonly large bird, with long, broad, round-tipped wings. Except when first taking off and landing, the neck is folded back and the head is couched upon the folded neck. This, incidentally, quickly differentiates it from cranes and flamingos, which fly with heads and necks outstretched. The Great Blue Heron also trails its long legs far behind in flight.

The flight begins as the bird leans forward with neck outstretched. Then (sometimes with an assisting step or two) the great wings beat powerfully and it is launched. For a moment the neck remains outstretched and the legs dangle; but then the legs go back straight and stiff, trailing behind and acting as a rudder to assist the very short tail. At this point the head is couched on the folded neck. The early vigorous wingbeats settle down to slow, powerful strokes. Landing is slightly more graceful than the takeoff, as head and neck are again outstretched and long legs come forward, reaching for purchase as the broad wings brake the bird which drops lightly to the ground or onto its selected perch.

## LENGTH AND WINGSPAN

This species averages about 47 inches in length (1206mm) and has an impressive wingspan of around 70 inches (1789mm).

## BEAK

The sharp beak is about 5 inches long and yellowish, often turning considerably more orange during the breeding season.

## LEGS, FEET, AND CLAWS

Legs and feet are blackish in coloration, except that the soles of the feet are yellowish. The outer toe is longer than the inner. The hind toe is not elevated, but is on the same level with the others; all toes are long and slender, with small webbing connecting the base of the outer and middle toes. The long claw on the middle toe has comblike serrations on the underside (pectinations) which are used as an aid in preening.

## CRESTS, PLUMAGE, ANNUAL MOLT

The body plumage, generally, is loose and long. In the breeding season, the bird's back is without any lengthened and loosened plumes. The lower foreneck has considerably lengthened feathers and in the breeding season the crest, which is more or less present all year, becomes much more pronounced and develops two very long, slender, filamentous occipital plumes. The lores are bare.

## VOICE

The voice is a hoarse *gronnk* or *graack,* or occasionally a low, heavy, and coarse grunting *quuck.* It has been reported, though not verified, that when extremely angry, the Great Blue Heron will sometimes issue a very harsh shrieking sound not unlike the sound of a heavy desk being pulled across a wooden floor.

## SEXUAL DIFFERENCES: SIZE, COLORATION, VOICE

In coloration and voice, the sexes are virtually identical. The male is slightly larger than the female.

## COLORATION AND MARKINGS: ADULT

The sharply pointed beak is generally yellowish, especially on the lower mandible, with the upper mandible having a dusky greenish ridge. The lores are a faintly dusky bluish-green and the irides are a bright, clear chrome yellow. The brow and crown are pure white, but with the sides of the crown and the plume feathers black. The neck is a light gray with streaks of white, black, and rust on the sides of the neck toward the front. Cheeks and chin are white. The back and scapulars are a general slate-blue-gray. The tail is deeper slate-gray, as are the primaries, which shade into black. The longish plumes of the lower neck and breast are a light gray with, on the abdomen, streaks of rust interspersed on the white background. Undertail coverts are pure white and the legs and feet are a dusky gray, with the soles of the feet yellowish.

## COLORATION AND MARKINGS: JUVENILE

Much like the adults except for a generally browner coloration. Most of the crown is black and there are no lengthened feathers, either crest or plume, on the head. There is a strong rufous edging to the feathers of back and scapulars, while the lesser wing coverts are a rufous brown. The underside is an ashy gray-white, with the legs dingy grayish-black.

## GENERAL HABITS AND CHARACTERISTICS

The Great Blue Heron is the largest member of the heron family in the northern United States and Canada. It is also the most widely distributed, most commonly sighted, and therefore best-known of the North American herons. It is normally seen while flying with slow, graceful strokes of its great broad wings at relatively low (treetop) altitude, or while standing in dignified sentinel-like motionlessness in the shallows of stream, marsh, or bog. Yet, though it frequents watery areas, it is equally at home in meadows and highlands and is often seen in such areas walking about with stately grace, occasionally snatching some sort of prey—insects, young birds or small mammals, reptiles or amphibians. Most often solitary in its habits, *Ardea herodias herodias* shows a marked disdain for other wading bird species and even for other individuals of its own species, except during breeding and migratory seasons. Although it appears to be a tremendously large bird, equaling the turkey in general size, its weight is far less than that of the turkey, averaging only 6 to 8 pounds. Certainly it has to be considered as one of the most stately and recognizable of American birds.

## HABITAT AND ROOSTING

A wide variation of habitat is enjoyed by the Great Blue Heron but almost always on a solitary basis. It might be seen in newly plowed farm fields, in meadows, in marshes, swamps, bogs, and along the edges of lakes, streams, and ponds. Roosting is sometimes done on the ground and frequently the bird will sleep (often standing on one leg) while in knee-deep water. Most roosting is done, however, in relatively dense cover: heavy mangrove growth, deep willow margins, low swamp oak, and similar growth near watery areas. The roosting bird normally perches in a hunched position on a sturdy branch close to the trunk for long-period roosting. However, for short-term resting or observation, *Ardea herodias herodias* will very frequently land in the very uppermost branches of a tree and stand silhouetted against the sky.

## ENEMIES AND DEFENSES

Once it has acquired its full growth, the Great Blue Heron has few natural enemies. Its powerful beak is a formidable weapon. Unfortunately, because of its great size and distinctiveness, the Great Blue Heron is often destroyed by thoughtless or uncaring people with guns who are just looking about for something to shoot.

## FOOD AND FEEDING HABITS

*Ardea herodias herodias* is most often seen standing motionless waiting for prey in shallow waters. In the shallows it may move about in a very stealthy manner, walking slowly and carefully, so that no sound is heard and scarcely a ripple made. Very frequently in the marshes this is the principal means used by this species for capturing frogs and small turtles, which it devours greedily. In upland meadows and plowed fields it hunts field mice, shrews, moles, garter snakes, leopard frogs, and the young of ground-nesting birds. The principal prey, however, is fish of almost any variety. It captures fish by thrusting the powerful beak spearlike into the fish's side or back; then, partially opening the beak, it prevents the impaled fish from wriggling free until the fish can be carried to dry ground and stabbed again repeatedly until dead. The fish is then juggled until positioned headfirst and is swallowed with a series of convulsive gulpings. Often the size of the fish swallowed is remarkable. The authors have watched Great Blue (and Ward's) Herons in Florida coastal waters catch and quite successfully swallow ladyfish nearly two feet in length and just over two pounds, mullet upward of two pounds, and other such fish. Instinctive care seems to be taken, however, with species such as catfish which have spines that might prevent regurgitation. Smaller prey—whether fish, amphibian, or reptile—caught while the bird is wad-

ing, is not usually taken to shore. If not killed with the first thrust, the prey will be repeatedly tossed into the air, caught, and mouthed until dead (sometimes beaten against the water surface or against floating debris) and then juggled in the mouth until it is headfirst down the throat and swallowed. Practically without exception, immediately after swallowing the prey, whether in the water or out of it, the Great Blue Heron will dip its beak into the water and shake it back and forth several times, apparently to clean off any slime or other foreign matter which may be clinging to it, before resuming the hunt. Digestion is rapid and the digestive juices are of such acidity that bone matter swallowed is almost completely dissolved. Occasionally a compact pellet of undigested or partially digested feathers and fur is regurgitated.

## COURTSHIP AND MATING

Shortly after the spring migration north has been completed, the Great Blue Herons will sometimes assemble in large numbers to engage in mock fights. Soon the paired birds begin leaving for nesting areas.

Great Blue Herons usually copulate with the female standing on the ground. Even if she is on a low limb, invariably she will come to the ground itself before permitting the male to mount her for the brief copulatory activities.

---

Breeding displays of Great Blue Heron. Sketches made at Buttonwood Rookery, Lemon Bay, Englewood, Florida.

*Great Blue Heron*

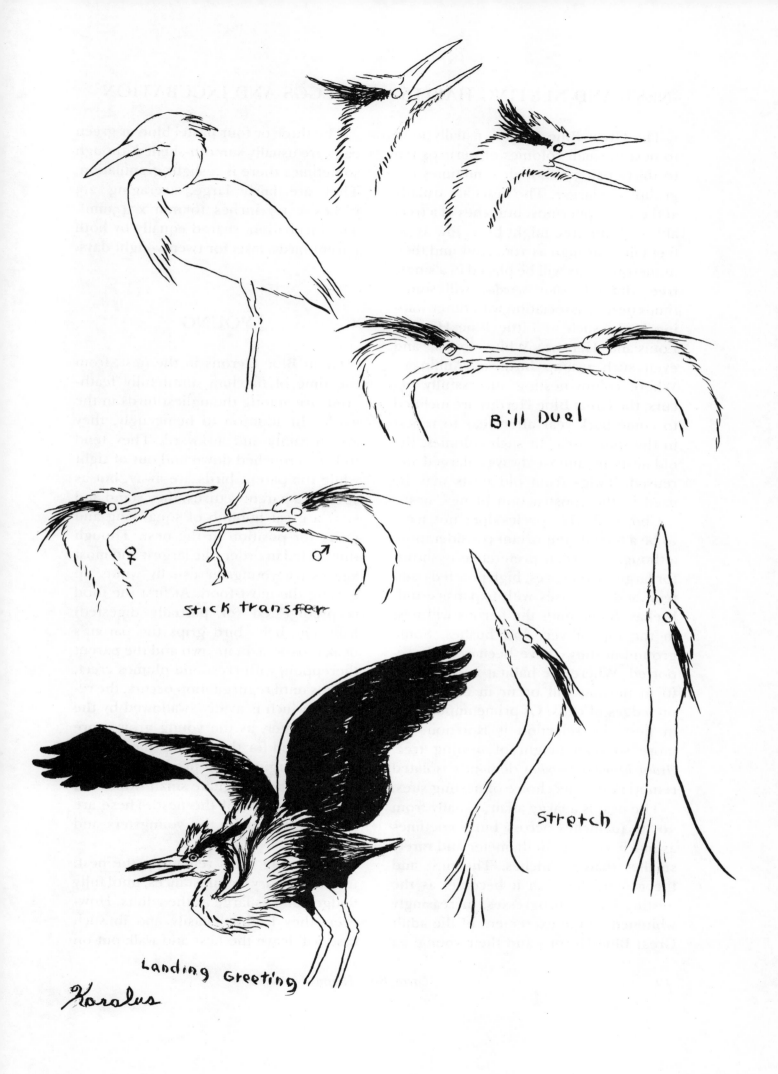

Bill Duel

Stick transfer

Stretch

Landing Greeting

Karalus

## NEST AND NESTING HABITS

The Great Blue Herons usually tend to nest in small colonies of perhaps ten to thirty pairs, although sometimes the groups are larger. The nests are usually at the very uppermost branches of a tree, although the tree might be as low as 10 feet tall or as high as 100. Now and then numerous nests will be placed in a single tree. *Ardea herodias herodias* will sometimes nest in association with other wading birds, such as Little Blue Herons, Louisiana Herons, White Ibises, and even such swamp birds as Anhingas. Where colony-nesting successfully occurs, the Great Blue Herons are inclined to come back year after year to renest in the same area. In such colonies, the old nests are almost always enlarged and reused. Twigs from old nests may be used in the construction of new nests.

Choice of tree species does not seem to be a terribly important consideration, although a certain preference is shown for larger mangroves, high pointed conifers, and cypresses with expansive umbrellas. Sometimes the herons will nest in the top of very low bushes. Some ground-nestings have been reliably reported. Where the habitat is conducive to it, nesting will occur in crevices or on ledges of cliffs. Of prime importance in nest site selection is isolation—far more so than height of nesting tree. *Ardea herodias herodias* demands isolated remoteness in its choice of nesting sites.

The nest is a large affair, usually from 30 to 40 inches across but sometimes as much as 4 feet in diameter and rarely smaller than 20 inches. The nest and the ground beneath it become, as the nesting season progresses, increasingly whitened by the excrement of the adult Great Blue Herons and their young.

## EGGS AND INCUBATION

The three or four pastel blue or green eggs are usually smooth-shelled, though sometimes there is a slight granulation. They are fairly large, averaging 2.5 inches x 1.7 inches (65mm x 45mm). The incubation, shared equally by both parent birds, lasts for twenty-eight days.

## YOUNG

Great Blue Herons in the nest, from the time of hatching until fully feathered, are among the ugliest birds in the world. In addition to being ugly, they are ungainly and awkward. They tend to keep crouched down and out of sight while the parent birds are away, but as soon as a parent returns, they stand and start a great hubbub of squawking and vying for position in the nest. Though they're fed in order, the largest and most aggressive youngster usually winds up getting the most food. At first the food is predigested (or partially digested) fish. The baby bird grips the parent's beak crosswise in its own and the parent thereupon, with crest and plumes erect, pumps until regurgitation occurs, the result of which is avidly swallowed by the young. Later, as the young grow more able to fend for themselves, the parents cease regurgitation of predigested food, and instead regurgitate small whole fish into the bottom of the nest. These are then picked up by the youngsters and swallowed.

The young birds remain in the nest, under ordinary circumstances, until fully fledged and as large as the adults. However, they frighten easily and in such case will leave the nest and walk out on the slender surrounding branches and remain perched there.

Full adult plumage is not assumed by the young bird until the first post-nuptial molt in its second year. After that there is little seasonal change except that the adult may be slightly more handsome in the spring breeding season than at other times of the year.

## MIGRATION

*Ardea herodias herodias* is definitely migratory in the northernmost portion of its range. Sometimes the bird migrates by itself or in flocks of from five to thirty birds. Many of the Great Blue Herons have winter ranges which overlap with the Ward's Heron or other subspecies to the south or west. The southward migration in autumn usually begins early in October. Northward migration in spring occurs in March or early April. Following the breeding and nesting season, young birds wander in all directions.

## ECONOMIC INFLUENCE

The Great Blue Heron has earned the enmity of man in some areas where gold-

GREAT BLUE HERON

*Ardea herodias herodias* (Linnaeus)

fish, turtles, frogs, or trout are raised commercially. Once one of these herons learns how simple it is to obtain food at a trout hatchery, for example, it may have to be trapped or shot. However, only individual troublesome birds justify this practice, which can only be done by permit.

# COMMON NAME

Northwestern Coast Heron
(Subspecies Sketch 3)

# SCIENTIFIC NAME

*Ardea herodias fannini* Chapman.

# BASIC SUBSPECIFIC DIFFERENCES

The Northwestern Coast Heron is the same size as, but considerably darker than, the Great Blue Heron. It is limited in distribution to the Pacific coastal area of the Northwest.

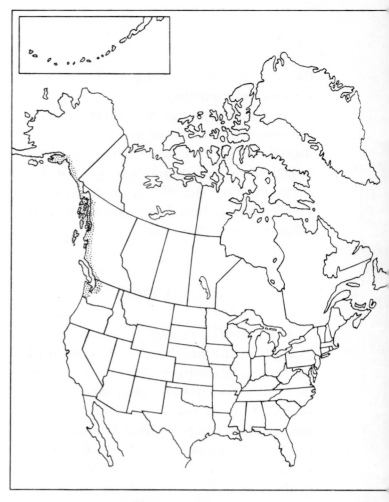

NORTHWESTERN COAST HERON

*Ardea herodias fannini* Chapman

---

3. NORTHWESTERN COAST HERON

*Ardea herodias fannini* Chapman. Campbell River, Vancouver Island, British Columbia, Canada. A.O.U. Number 194a

Karl E. Karalus

## COMMON NAME

Ward's Heron
(Subspecies Sketch 4)

## SCIENTIFIC NAME

*Ardea herodias wardi* Ridgway. At first suspected of being an intergraded hybrid of *Ardea herodias herodias* (Great Blue) and *Ardea herodias occidentalis* (Great White), but this distinction was ultimately given to a variety previously known as Wuerdemann's Heron.

## SHAPE AT REST AND IN FLIGHT

Generally larger than *Ardea herodias herodias,* but identical in basic contour.

## LENGTH AND WINGSPAN

Ward's Heron has an average length of about 51 inches (1315mm) and a wingspan over 6.5 feet (2033mm).

## COLORATION AND MARKINGS

The middle of the forehead is white, the sides of the crown and occiput are black, and the feathers are lengthened. The throat and sides of the head are white, while the neck is light drab streaked with black in front. The back,

wings, and tail are a dark smoky gray, with the primaries dark plum color. Underparts are mixed black and white and leg plumage is tawny. Unlike the Great Blue Heron, in which only the upper portion of the upper mandible is greenish, the entire beak of Ward's Heron is this color.

The variety formerly called *Ardea herodias wuerdemanni* (Wuerdemann's Heron), actually a hybrid of the Great White Heron and the Great Blue Heron (and found almost entirely in the Florida Keys), has white head and occipital crest feathers and a fuscous forehead. The underparts, also, are grayish-white.

## GENERAL HABITS AND CHARACTERISTICS

Ward's Herons will often construct their large nesting colonies in close proximity to (sometimes even surrounded by) such other species as the

---

I   EASTERN GREEN HERON

*Butorides striatus virescens* (Linnaeus). Franklin Park, Illinois, May 11, 1953. A.O.U. Number 201

II   BLACK-CROWNED NIGHT HERON

*Nycticorax nycticorax hoactli* (Gmelin). Near Dayton Museum of Natural History, Dayton, Ohio. A.O.U. Number 202

---

III   YELLOW-CROWNED NIGHT HERON

*Nyctanassa violacea violacea* (Linnaeus). Adult (left) and immature (right). Bay Oaks Circle, Manasota Key, Englewood, Florida. A.O.U. Number 203

IV   GREAT BLUE HERON

*Ardea herodias herodias* (Linnaeus). Lemon Bay, Sarasota County, Florida, January 19, 1974. A.O.U. Number 194

Karl E. Karalus
1973

Karl E. Karalus

Crown raised
in anger or display

K.E. Karalus

Little Blue Heron
Florida caerulea

Serrate section on bill of Green heron

Green Heron
Butorides striatus

Ward's Heron
Ardea herodias wardi
Southern variety of Great blue heron

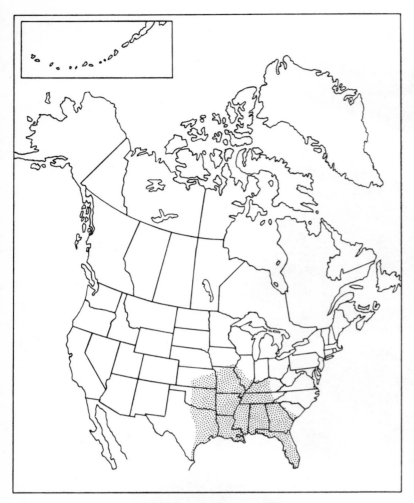

WARD'S HERON

*Ardea herodias wardi* Ridgway

Great White Heron, Great Egret, Snowy Egret, Reddish Egret, Louisiana Heron, and Black-Crowned Night Heron. Sometimes Boat-Tailed Grackles will be close by and even build their own nests in the bottom sticks of the Ward's Heron nests.

## HABITAT AND ROOSTING

The habitat most used, both for roosting and nesting, is densely tangled areas

of mangrove and other trees on floating islands or hammocks amid surrounding heavy marsh growth. Ward's Heron usually roosts and nests in an area of around 150 to 200 feet in diameter in the thickest portions.

## NEST AND NESTING HABITS

*Ardea herodias wardi* begins nesting activities as early as late November and continues right on through April. The nests themselves are usually quite large; built of interwoven sticks and measuring around 3 to 4 feet in diameter and 15 to 18 inches thick. Such nests are reused year after year if the nesting area remains undisturbed, with certain improvements made in the nest each new season. There may be as many as ten nests in a single tree, although occasionally the birds will nest on the ground amid clusters of prickly-pear cactus growth. If nesting among the oaks, water elms, or cypresses, Ward's Heron generally likes the nest to be about 40 to 50 feet from the ground.

## EGGS AND INCUBATION

The eggs are a bit larger than those of the Great Blue Heron, measuring on the average 2.5 inches x 1.8 inches (65mm x 46mm).

*(Overleaf)* Head and beak/bill studies from life; Stump Pass, Lemon Bay, Englewood, Florida; April 25, 1977. (Not to scale.)

4. WARD'S HERON

*Ardea herodias wardi* Ridgway. Englewood Beach, Florida. A.O.U. Number 194b

*Ward's Heron*

## COMMON NAME

Treganza's Heron
(Subspecies Sketch 5)

## SCIENTIFIC NAME

*Ardea herodias treganzai* Court.

## BASIC SUBSPECIFIC DIFFERENCES

While slightly larger than the Great Blue Heron *(Ardea herodias herodias)*, at an average height of 42 inches, it is somewhat smaller than Ward's Heron *(Ardea herodias wardi)*.

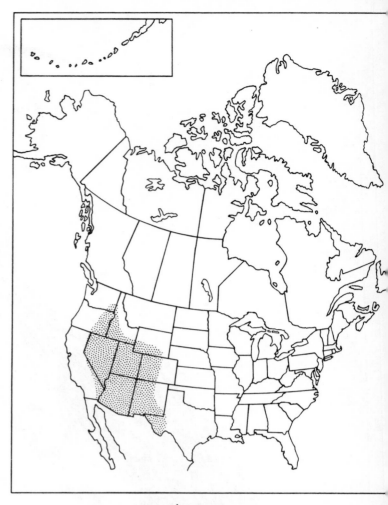

TREGANZA'S HERON

*Ardea herodias treganzai* Court

5. TREGANZA'S HERON

*Ardea herodias treganzai* Court. Green River, Wyoming. A.O.U. Number 194c

# COMMON NAME

California Heron
(Subspecies Sketch 6)

# SCIENTIFIC NAME

*Ardea herodias hyperonca* Oberholser.
*Hyperonca* means "of greatest bulk."

# BASIC SUBSPECIFIC DIFFERENCES

Identical in shape to the Great Blue Heron, but much larger than *Ardea herodias herodias,* and much darker than *Ardea herodias treganzai.*

**CALIFORNIA HERON**

*Ardea herodias hyperonca* Oberholser

# LENGTH AND WINGSPAN

The average length of the California Heron is about 50 inches (1287mm) and the average wingspan is almost 6 feet (1832mm).

# NESTING HABITS

The California Heron, which shows a somewhat more marked proclivity for colonial nesting than others of the subspecies, prefers a heavy tangle of brushy growth, from the midst of which rises one or more large trees. Here, at a height of about 40 to 80 feet, and sometimes with as many as twenty or more nests in the same tree, is where this subspecies is most inclined to nest. Having water close by is desirable, but evidently not a prerequisite.

---

6. CALIFORNIA HERON

*Ardea herodias hyperonca* Oberholser. Bakersfield, California. A.O.U. Number 194d

Karl E. Karalus

## COMMON NAME

Great White Heron
(Color Plate V)

## SCIENTIFIC NAME

*Ardea herodias occidentalis* Audubon.
The Latin name simply signifies that this
is a heron of the Western world.

## SHAPE AT REST AND
## IN FLIGHT

When at rest, this bird almost invariably sits on a mangrove branch outstretched over the water at a height of
6 to 20 feet, its head drawn down and
couched on the shoulders, and often
standing on one leg. As a matter of fact,
frequently one leg is a little larger than
the other as a result of its being used
more. When the bird is fishing it is usually standing erect in water nearly reaching its underside, patiently waiting for
a fish to swim close enough to impale.
At such times its head may be raised to
its greatest height for better visibility
downward into the water, or poised at
an angle on a neck bent into an S-curve
like a tight spring ready to be released,
as the bird observes prey coming close.
Its basic shape in flight is very similar
to that of the Great Blue Heron.

## LENGTH AND WINGSPAN

The average length of the Great White
Heron is 52.7 inches (1350mm) and
the wingspan averages 81.8 inches
(2097mm).

## BEAK

The beak is yellow on both mandibles,
usually becoming slightly greenish toward the tip. This is especially noticeable
on the lower mandible.

## LEGS AND FEET

The legs are yellowish, shading to
greenish on the front. The feet are also
yellowish with a faint greenish cast. The
general yellow coloration of the legs is
the best way to separate the Great White
Heron from the Great Egret, since the
legs of the latter are black.

## CRESTS, PLUMAGE,
## ANNUAL MOLT

The plumage of the Great White
Heron is much like that of Ward's
Heron, but white.

## EYES AND VISION

The irides of the Great White Heron
are a clear chrome yellow (with the lores
a pale bluish-green). The bird's vision
is excellent.

*Great White Heron*

## COLORATION AND MARKINGS: ADULT

The adults are always pure white in plumage, with the only coloration occurring in the irides (chrome yellow), the lores (bluish-green), the legs and feet (yellowish, tending toward greenish on the "shin" portions and on the upper surface of the toes), and the beak, which is yellow on both mandibles but usually slightly greenish toward the tip, especially on the lower mandible.

## COLORATION AND MARKINGS: JUVENILE

Like the adults, pure white, but often with the beak a little more greenish at the base than in the adult bird. The sequence of plumage and molts is the same as that in the Great Blue Heron, with fully adult plumage not being acquired until at least two years of age.

## HABITAT AND ROOSTING

This is the only heron species of the continent which is entirely coastal maritime in its choice of habitat. The rare occasions when the Great White Heron has been observed farther inland have almost without exception followed hurricanes or other severe storms. The preferred habitat is strictly of the low mangrove coastal area type, where extensive

**GREAT WHITE HERON**

*Ardea herodias occidentalis* Audubon

shallows afford good fishing and small but dense and tangled mangrove islands afford good nesting sites. Roosting almost always occurs in the denser areas of mangroves, relatively close to open water.

## COURTSHIP AND MATING

Courting activities which have been recorded are similar to those of *Ardea herodias wardi.*

# LITTLE BLUE HERON

GENUS: *FLORIDA* Baird
SPECIES: *CAERULEA* (Linnaeus)
SUBSPECIES: *caerulea* (Linnaeus)

## COMMON NAME

Little Blue Heron
(Color Plate VI)

## SCIENTIFIC NAME

*Florida caerulea caerulea* (Linnaeus). The Latin name signifies a sky-blue heron of Florida.

## OTHER COMMON OR COLLOQUIAL NAMES

BLUE EGRET For general coloration and for type of bird.

BLUE HERON For general coloration and type of bird, but might lead to confusion with Great Blue Heron, which is also often called simply "Blue Heron."

CALICO BIRD For the spotted coloration displayed by adult-sized immature birds.

CALICO HERON

LITTLE WHITE HERON Common for the adult-sized juvenile which may even be raising its own young, yet still wears the juvenile plumage of pure white with bluish primary tips. This name was used very commonly some years ago when it was incorrectly believed that the white bird was a color phase of the adult bird and that the Little Blue Heron was dichromatic.

PIED HERON After the coloration and mottled plumage of the young bird as it changes from white to the blue of the true adult.

SPOTTED CRANE For the same reason, but with erroneous designation of the type of bird.

SPOTTED HERON Again, for the type of bird and its mottled, intermediate plumage.

## SHAPE AT REST AND IN FLIGHT

This is a slender, streamlined heron which seems to be taller than it actually is because of its very slenderness and the fact that it rarely crouches and hunches when standing or perching, as other herons do. The neck is long and the head usually held high, with generally alert attitude and crest plumes not readily apparent. The beak is long and slender and very pointed and often the neck will be bent as if broken. At first glance from a little distance, the bird appears to be dark.

As do most herons, it flies with the head drawn in upon the shoulders and the long legs trailing behind, but with the body silhouette being somewhat less bulky than most other heron species.

Sometimes, when circling on a high wind, and almost always when coming in for a landing, *Florida caerulea caerulea* will set its wings and glide for a considerable distance. At times it will do this in unison with upward of a score of other birds of the same species, especially if it has been frightened from its perch. At such times it will frequently make a wide circle on relatively fast wingbeats and then come back, gliding the last dozen yards or more and landing lightly and gracefully with delicate strokes instead of with excessive wingbeating. Indeed, lightness and grace are characteristic of the flight of the Little Blue Heron.

## LENGTH AND WINGSPAN

The average length of the Little Blue Heron is just slightly over 2 feet (620mm) and its wingspan averages 40.25 inches (1032mm).

## BEAK

The beak is one of the features by which the white, immature but adult-sized Little Blue Heron can be told apart from the similar-sized and shaped Snowy Egret. The beak of the Little Blue Heron has a black tip and shades into a dark blue and then lighter bluish toward the base, while that of the Snowy Egret is essentially black or shading to grayish-black. Also the beak of the Snowy Egret is not quite as thick at the base as that of the Little Blue Heron, even though the latter's beak is relatively slender and very acute. On the upper mandible there is a gentle curve from base to tip (convex) and the lower mandible is straight or with only a very slight concave curvature.

## LEGS AND FEET

Again, as with the beak, legs and feet are a good means of distinguishing the immature Little Blue Heron from the Snowy Egret. The latter has black legs and bright yellow feet, while the immature Little Blue Heron has legs and feet which range from a medium greenish-yellow to a dark greenish.

## CRESTS, PLUMAGE, ANNUAL MOLT

Adult Little Blue Herons have a few short plume-like feathers in the back, but not really any outstanding aigrette feathers as do many of the related species. Beginning in February, the adult birds undergo a partial molt just prior to nuptials. Afterwards there is a complete molt beginning at the end of June and continuing until the wings themselves are finally molting in August. In its breeding plumage, *Florida caerulea caerulea* is a dark but extremely handsome bird with a beautiful plum-colored plumage frosted with a faint blush of powder from the powder-down tracts which imparts a delicate, temporal quality to the bird's general appearance.

## VOICE

The Little Blue Heron is usually a silent bird. However, there are times when it becomes downright garrulous, as during the nest-building period, when it seems to murmur constantly as it works, and during the early days of the hatching of its eggs, as it comes to the nest to feed its young through regurgitation. It often utters a loud, harsh, croaking cry when frightened.

## COLORATION AND MARKINGS: ADULT

Plumage of the head and neck range from a dark purplish-maroon to a purplish-red which is especially intense in the nuptial plumage (it is at this time that the slate-blue lengthened plumes on the back are more apparent). The lores and eyelids are blue and the rest of the bird's body and wings are dark plum color to slatey blue, but dusted with a delicate frosting of powder down of pale blue coloration. The Little Blue Heron is not dichromatic and does not have a white color phase, as was once believed. In winter plumage the head and neck are more evenly purple-colored with some white occurring on the throat and below the lower mandible. The irides are bright yellow.

## COLORATION AND MARKINGS: JUVENILE

The juvenile is snowy white with a tinge of blue tipping the primaries. The legs are green and the beak is bluish but tipped with black. Some of the young reach breeding age while still pure white, and this is what initially gave rise to the belief that dichromatism occurred in the species. However, it has now been proven that a white or pied bird is merely a young one changing color to the full adult plumage. When the change in plumage does occur (a change which takes place gradually over the entire year) the white birds get blotched, speckled, patched, and spotted with blue—a phenomenon unique among the herons.

## GENERAL HABITS AND CHARACTERISTICS

Probably the most immediately evident characteristic of *Florida caerulea caerulea* is its shy nature. It is not particularly reclusive, since it does take considerable pleasure in the company of its own kind as well as other heron species, but it tends to like isolated places to which it can retire and feed, roost, and nest undisturbed. When it travels to such areas, it generally travels in loose, rather disorganized flocks, with rarely more than fifteen or twenty birds in any one flying group, although these groups often converge at the final resting or feeding place. The Little Blue Heron shows a marked affinity for the company of the Louisiana Heron, and together they frequent isolated small ponds with densely tangled willow and myrtle banks, or else broad grassy open areas surrounding them. During daylight hours, when the birds are principally active, they like being in relatively small groups or even alone, but as evening comes on, they begin to collect in larger groups and then, in the twilight, take wing and fly to the roosting area, which may be several miles distant. As they reach it, they generally make an inspection pass first, then wheel about and glide in for their landing. These areas are shared not only with the Louisiana Heron, but sometimes with the Black-Crowned Night Heron and the Little Green Heron.

## HABITAT AND ROOSTING

Little Blue Herons generally roost among considerable numbers of birds, primarily of its own species, but sometimes, as noted above, with other herons. The roosting colonies are sometimes as small as twenty to fifty pairs of birds, but colonies as large as two thousand pairs have been recorded. The usual number seems to be anywhere from a hundred to three or four hundred birds. This roosting is done usually relatively low in clumps of bushes or dense trees on the margins of swamps and ponds, or on islands, generally well isolated and safe from molestation by man. Almost without exception these rookeries are far inland from the coast, even though the birds may have spent the day at the coastal flats feeding. In all cases, a freshwater habitat is preferred over a saltwater habitat, although now and then large colonies will frequent the dense mangrove swamps of the salt or brackish coastal areas. In the southern states the bird is especially fond of marshes and small pond habitats which are well grown with pickerelweed *(Pontederia cordata)* and dense barrier screens 8 to 20 feet high, closely stemmed bushes called ti-ti (or sometimes ty-ty). These *Cliftonia monophylla* borders become almost impenetrable to any enemy and certainly cannot be crossed without considerable disturbance being made. In addition to the swamps and marshes described above, Little Blue Herons like dense, tangled tree growths of willow, myrtle, black gum, sweet gum, pine, bay, water oak, and live oak, all growing from or on the margin of water that is mere inches to 2 or 3 feet in depth. These are the same sort of areas where nesting occurs and they are farther inland than the breeding areas of any of the other herons that breed in vast rookeries. After roosting for the night, the birds begin to fly away from the roost at the first light of early morning in small detached groups, heading for distant feeding grounds.

## FOOD AND FEEDING HABITS

Most often the Little Blue Heron feeds alone or in small groups during early morning and late evening, wading carefully about in the shallows and striking swiftly and usually unerringly with its sharp beak. Rarely if ever a night feeder, this heron usually feeds most determinedly in the early morning and early evening hours. If the small fish it is hunting in the shallows are specially abundant, it will often move about with great alacrity, stabbing here and there with its beak and rarely missing. Sometimes, like the Cattle Egret, it will alight near grazing cattle and follow them to pluck up the insects which are disturbed by the bovine movements. Most often, though, the food is small fish—ordinarily various species of minnows and killifish, along with occasional bluegills, sunfish, catfish, and other species, plus a fair amount of crawfish and a lesser number of grasshoppers, locusts, mole crickets, aquatic beetles, frogs, salamanders, small snakes and lizards, cutworms, and very young turtles.

## COURTSHIP AND MATING

The courtship of *Florida caerulea caerulea* is almost identical to that of *Hydranassa tricolor ruficollis* (the Louisiana Heron). The display begins with the male flying in to perch on the highest point of a low bush or small tree near

V   GREAT WHITE HERON

*Ardea herodias occidentalis* Audubon. Big Pine Key, Monroe County, Florida. A.O.U. Number 192

VI   LITTLE BLUE HERON

*Florida caerulea caerulea* (Linnaeus). Adult male (right) and immature (left). Stump Pass, Charlotte County, Florida. A.O.U. Number 200

*Little Blue Heron*

Karl E. Karalus

Karl E. Karalus

Karl E. Karalus

which a female bird is perched. There he begins his display by bowing low to her numerous times and moving farther and farther out on the branches until there is hardly a perch left for his feet. There he swings and sways precariously—yet with perfect balance—with every breeze which touches him. His neck moves in graceful serpentine curves and he rarely takes his eye from the female of his choice. Every now and then he will freeze in an especially attractive attitude and stay that way for five or ten seconds before once again beginning the dancing which moves him ever closer to the female. At last, when they are finally so close that their shoulders are actually rubbing, they lean against one another and rub heads and necks together and then copulation occurs. Following the mating, the paired birds fly off together and generally begin construction of their nest on the same day.

## NEST AND NESTING HABITS

The nest is usually in a bush or tree, sometimes as low as 2 feet above the water but more commonly at a height of 3 to 8 feet. On rare occasions it may be placed as high as 40 feet.

The extremely flimsy nests are actually no more than relatively flat unlined platforms of loosely interwoven twigs, perhaps 12 to 28 inches in diameter with a slight depression in the center. Sometimes some smaller, finer twigs are used for the top layer and for the depression. The nests have no lining other than that. Nest-building usually begins in mid-March and ends by mid-June, but on occasion it will take place much later—rarely as late as mid-August. Often numerous Little Blue Herons will nest in the same bush or tree.

## EGGS AND INCUBATION

There are usually four or five (sometimes six) smooth, delicate bluish-green eggs. The average egg size is 1.7 inches x 1.3 inches (44mm x 34mm).

Incubation, shared by both parents equally, begins with the first egg laid. It is not uncommon to find nests in which there is not only still a viable egg, but young ranging in age from one day to one week.

## YOUNG

Because of the staggered hatching, very often the smallest herons in the nest are eventually shoved out by the older nestlings. The baby birds appear in a first down that is pure white, and it is the body plumage which appears first, also pure white. The entire back is ordinarily well feathered before the baby bird is even half grown and considerably before the flight feathers break through their sheaths. The primaries and rectrices are not complete until the bird is

---

VII   LOUISIANA (OR TRI-COLORED) HERON

*Hydranassa tricolor ruficollis* (Gosse). South Manasota Key, Charlotte County, Florida (Nature Conservancy land), May 15, 1973. A.O.U. Number 199

VIII   CATTLE EGRET

*Bubulcus ibis ibis* Linnaeus. Cape Haze, Charlotte County, Florida, May 15, 1973. A.O.U. Number 201.1

LITTLE BLUE HERON

*Florida caerulea caerulea* (Linnaeus)

with the first post-nuptial molt when the young bird is just over a year old.

## MIGRATION

The movement northward which occurs from midsummer onward into autumn is not a true migration, but rather the wandering of the young adult birds out of the nest. Because these young are essentially in pure white plumage, they are very frequently mistaken for Snowy Egrets and reported as such. The northern population does undergo a true southward migration in late fall, withdrawing from the northern tier of its breeding range and not returning until late February to early May.

## ECONOMIC INFLUENCE

The Little Blue Heron is considered to be quite beneficial because of its habit of devouring large numbers of injurious insects (grasshoppers and locusts, along with cutworms of various kinds) and, in the areas where rice is grown (primarily Louisiana and southern Arkansas), eating great numbers of crayfish which dig holes into the embankments, weakening them and causing considerable damage. Because of these habits, *Florida caerulea caerulea* is probably the most beneficial of all the North American herons.

fully grown. The white plumage (with dark-tipped primaries) remains all during the first summer, fall, and winter. By the following February, some of the blue body plumage begins appearing. By this time the bird is old enough to breed itself and so some breeding takes place with young adults in interim plumage, ranging from pure white (pied) to almost all blue. Full adult plumage is apparent

# LOUISIANA (or TRI-COLORED) HERON

---

GENUS: *HYDRANASSA* Baird
SPECIES: *TRICOLOR* (Muller)
SUBSPECIES: *ruficollis* (Gosse)

## COMMON NAME

Louisiana Heron (or, almost as
frequently, Tricolor Heron,
or Tri-Colored Heron)
(Color Plate VII)

## SCIENTIFIC NAME

*Hydranassa tricolor ruficollis* (Gosse).
The name stems from the Greek and
Latin and means "rufous-necked, three-
colored water queen"—*hydr* meaning
water, *anassa*, a queen, *tricolor*, three-colored, *rufi*, rufous, and *collis*, neck.

## OTHER COMMON OR COLLOQUIAL NAMES

AMERICAN DEMIEGRET A misappelation
meaning that the bird is half egret and
half heron.

DEMOISELLE Because of its grace and
elegance.

LADY-OF-THE-WATERS Due to the delicate, dainty, and feminine mannerisms
of the bird when it is in and near the
water.

LOUISIANA EGRET Same as in Louisiana
Heron, but misapplied to egret.

## SHAPE AT REST AND IN FLIGHT

The Louisiana Heron is generally
alert, bright, and quick, moving with
dainty and delicate movements. It is a
medium-sized heron, as compared to the
Little Blue Heron and the Great Blue
Heron. The bird is slender, with a
smooth, clean silhouette.

Its shape in flight is similar to that
of other herons. The firm, regular wingstrokes are slightly faster than those of
the Great Blue Heron, but slower than
those of the Little Blue Heron. The
graceful flight usually terminates with
the wings gently cupping the air and the
outstretched feet neatly gripping the
perch without fumbling or stepping
about to retain balance. At times the
birds engage in some rather outstanding
aerial maneuverings. They approach the
feeding grounds, for example, with the
usual steady wingbeat, while flying at an
altitude of perhaps 200 feet or more.
Directly over the feeding ground they
will fold their wings and drop or tailspin
downward and then spread their wings
and swing from side to side as they come
in for the landing. This same action, often in much greater numbers, is performed over the roosting grounds in the
evening, once a preliminary pass has
been made over the area where the
roosting is to be done. The actual flights
to and from these areas in morning and
evening are usually made in non-forma-
tion flocks or sometimes in rather ragged, fluctuating long lines, often at considerable height. On the whole, this
heron is the most graceful of its entire
family.

## LENGTH AND WINGSPAN

The average length of the Louisiana
Heron is just over 25.5 inches (656mm)
and its wingspan averages 37.4 inches
(958mm).

## BEAK

The beak is very slender and, toward the middle, becomes contracted, so that the outline of both upper and lower beaks is slightly concave. It tapers on both mandibles to a very sharp point. During breeding season the beak is black at the end, shading into blue toward the base, then lilac at the base and to the lores. During non-breeding season, the beak is black and yellow.

## LEGS

The legs are a dingy yellowish-green behind and a dusky grayish in front, giving a general aspect of grayishness from a slight distance.

## EYES

The irides are a very bright and clear true red. During breeding season the lores are a pale lilac, but this becomes pale yellowish at other times.

## CRESTS, PLUMAGE, ANNUAL MOLT

The adult birds undergo a complete postnuptial molt beginning in late August, and lasting into early October. A partial molt, not including the flight feathers, occurs prenuptially in February and March. The nuptial plumage itself results in the growth of long white head plumes which are not evident at other times of the year. However, the other well-developed purplish head plumes are visible the year around, as are the purplish and dusky cinnamon back plumes. At all times except winter there is an exceptionally fine fringe-like train of feathers extending beyond the tail.

## VOICE

A variety of croaks and squawkings are issued at various times by the adults, sometimes low and chuckling in character, sometimes harsh. The young birds in the nests make an almost constant whining sound, low in tonal quality and inaudible very far from the nesting tree. However, they also make a very loud peeping cry, especially when hungry. This cry, which intensifies when an adult appears, can be heard for a considerable distance.

## SEXUAL DIFFERENCES: SIZE, COLORATION, VOICE

Males and females are essentially similar in coloration and voice.

## MORTALITY AND LONGEVITY

*Hydranassa tricolor ruficollis* is by far the most widespread and abundant heron species in the South, which may be due, in part, to the fact that the bird has been unmolested by plume or meat hunters.

---

Louisiana Heron, *Hydranassa tricolor ruficollis* (Gosse).

south Beach
manasota Key
Charlotte co
april 7.1975 Florida

N. E. Karolus

at nest
Peterson Island
Lemon Bay
Florida

Also, because it builds a more substantial nest than other heron species, there is less likelihood of storms destroying the nests and their contents.

## COLORATION AND MARKINGS: ADULT

On a very general basis, the bird is a dark grayish-blue in color with a white underside and white rump. This highly contrasting white underside (which is unique to the Louisiana Heron) is a key identification marking, and is apparent at all stages of the plumage and in all seasons. The adult's legs are a dingy yellowish-green in the rear and dusky grayish in front and on the tops of the toes.

## COLORATION AND MARKINGS: JUVENILE

Juveniles lack a crest and elongated plumes; the neck and back plumage is a dusky cinnamon in color, while the upper neck sides, nape, and head range from a deep chestnut to a bright reddish-bay in color. The center of the throat, the entire belly, and the underwings (exclusive of the primaries) are all white. The underwing primaries are purplish-blue, tipped with a deep chestnut. On the back, the primaries and rectrices are a pale mauve to lavender. The legs are one color—a dingy dust-green. Just after the nuptials, when the young bird is about sixteen months old, a molt occurs in which the last of the juvenile plumage is lost and the bird emerges with complete adult plumage for the first time.

## GENERAL HABITS AND CHARACTERISTICS

*Hydranassa tricolor ruficollis* is among the least shy of all the North American wading birds and sometimes can be approached and observed from very close range as it moves daintily about in its normal activities. As if conscious of its inherent elegance, this pretty heron may spend hours in the process of preening its plumage and thoroughly working the grease-powder from its powder-down tracts into the feathers, providing them with not only a degree of water repellency but also with an attractive dusty, almost silvery sheen.

## HABITAT AND ROOSTING

The rookeries—both breeding and roosting—are ordinarily located in wooded swamps or on densely treed and bushy islands or hammocks. The Louisiana Heron especially prefers as a habitat areas of tidal marsh, mangrove fringes in the coastal areas, small freshwater pond margins, the edges of lakes, creeks, and rivers, especially where these are well grown with brushy cover, marshy meadows, and along flooded ditches. Once in a while it will associate with the Cattle Egrets and Little Blue Herons as they follow meandering cattle through pasturage areas, in order to feed on the insects disturbed by the movements of the cattle.

## FOOD AND FEEDING HABITS

The Louisiana Heron prefers to move about slowly in the shallows, looking for prey, and, when it enters an area where prey is abundant, to dance about with rapid and agile steps, wings partially or fully outspread, spearing or snatching minnows or whatever other prey it has found. It is believed that this delicate prancing-about serves to muddy the water, causing the fish to get confused and to rise closer to the water surface, where the bird can more easily snap them up. When the Louisiana Heron strikes, it rarely misses. It has even been observed skillfully snatching flying insects out of the air. When feeding it prefers wading in water not over 6 inches in depth and preferably 3 or 4 inches deep. Like the Great Blue Heron, it will eat almost any fish, insect, crustacean, reptile, or amphibian it can catch, kill, and swallow.

## COURTSHIP AND MATING

Although the actual courtship dance is virtually identical to the dance of the Little Blue Heron, one part of it appears to be unique to *Hydranassa tricolor ruficollis*. This occurs when the male, toward the end of his display, allows his wings to droop until the tips of the primaries are dragging at which point he raises his head with the beak pointed skyward and the neck outstretched to its greatest limits, and gives voice to a peculiar low moaning sound. This sound is so muted that an observer only a dozen or so yards away would have to strain his ears to hear it, but it seems to excite the female.

## NEST AND NESTING HABITS

The Louisiana Herons usually nest in rookeries of considerable size. Accounts from years ago indicate that nesting colonies very often consisted of four to five thousand pairs of birds. Except that the nest is slightly more sturdily built, it is almost indistinguishable from that of the Snowy Egret. In Florida most of the nesting is done in mangrove tangles and dense willow clumps, and elsewhere the densest possible growth adjacent to water is what the Louisiana Heron likes most. Yet, in some areas where tree growth is scant and even bushes are few, it is not uncommon for this heron to nest on the ground or amid clusters of prickly-pear cactus. In the areas of willows and mangroves, the Louisiana Herons often nest in close proximity to other heron species, and in the ground nestings, they often share the area with nesting black skimmers, terns, and gulls. In the West, where tall cane borders marshy areas, strips of cane are often used for major braces in nest construction, while finer strips of the same material are used to line the nests. In their nest-building, the Louisiana Herons have a system that is seldom altered. The male seeks out the proper sticks and returns with them to the nesting site. There he gives them to the female, who does the actual nest construction. With each such stick presented to the female, the male raises his crest feathers, aigrettes, and neck plumage, struts with wings widespread, and utters a special long crooning cry. The female responds with a similar display and cry and then takes the stick from him. Almost at once he leaves to find another, while the female occupies herself with weaving the new stick into the nest, positioning and

bird runs forward
rapidly stopping
suddenly and
strikes

at times Heron's
head is held very
Low and Tightly
Withdrawn,
much Lower, tha
Illustration

Karalus

repositioning it until he returns with another.

## EGGS AND INCUBATION

The eggs are almost indistinguishable from those of the Snowy Egret. Both parents incubate in relatively equal segments during the daytime, usually changing position four times during the course of a day; but it is the female who does the incubating throughout the night, while the male roosts on a branch close by. Whenever one bird relieves another of the incubation duties, a ceremony of some importance is enacted. The approaching bird presents the sitting bird with a brief display of outstretched wings and a short crooning note as it hops from one branch to another while nearing the nest. The relieved bird relinquishes its position, but before leaving the area for any length of time, it presents the bird on the nest with anywhere from one to three twigs, which are then woven into the nest by the newly incubating bird. The incubation of an individual egg takes twenty-one days, but hatching is not simultaneous, due to staggered laying, and may occur over a period of four or five days, perhaps even a week.

## YOUNG

Young Louisiana Herons stay in the nest, under normal conditions, until they are fully two thirds the size of the

Feeding habits of the Louisiana Heron. Field sketches made at Manasota Key, Englewood, Florida, April 1974.

adult birds. Only then will they begin to climb about in the surrounding tangle of branches. They soon become quite adept at this, using feet, beak, and wings to do so. Falls often occur but rarely result in tragedy (such as a young bird hanging itself from a crotch or being gobbled up by an alligator). Most often when a fall occurs, the bird swims back to the tree and manages to climb back up, gradually working its way back to the nest, plaintively peeping all the while.

The downy baby birds have coloration unlike that of any other downy-young herons. The crown is covered with inch-long fawn-colored hairlike plumes, and the back is dense with a soft down of brown. Oddly, the white down of the underparts is rather more coarse. The beak, feet, and unfeathered skin all range from a dusky green to a dingy chartreuse in coloration.

The initial appearance of the juvenile plumage occurs on the back, then successively on head, neck, underparts, and tail. The last feathers to grow to full length are the flight feathers, and this doesn't occur until the bird has grown to full adult size.

## MIGRATION

Throughout its range, the Louisiana Heron is relatively permanent and abundant except for those populations in the coastal areas of Texas and Louisiana which abandon their usual habitat during the winter months. There are casual records from California, Arizona, southern Nevada, southern New Mexico, western Texas, southern Arkansas, southern Missouri, western Kentucky, southern Il-

LOUISIANA (OR TRI-COLORED) HERON

*Hydranassa tricolor ruficollis* (Gosse)

linois, southern Indiana, and even as far north as New Jersey and New York.

## ECONOMIC INFLUENCE

*Hydranassa tricolor ruficollis* is considered to be an ecologically valuable bird because of the large number of injurious insects and invertebrates it consumes, especially weevils and grasshoppers, which it devours in great quantities. It is also considered agriculturally valuable in rice-growing areas since it eats large numbers of crawfish, whose burrowing does considerable damage to rice dikes.

# CATTLE EGRET

---

GENUS: *BUBULCUS* Bonaparte
SPECIES: *IBIS* Linnaeus
SUBSPECIES: *ibis* Linnaeus

## COMMON NAME

Cattle Egret
(Color Plate VIII)

## SCIENTIFIC NAME

*Bubulcus ibis ibis* Linnaeus. *Bubulcus* is Latin for herdsman; *ibis* is Greek for wading bird.

## OTHER COMMON OR COLLOQUIAL NAMES

BUFF-BACKED HERON

## SHAPE AT REST AND IN FLIGHT

A short, stocky bird, easily identifiable because of the bright yellow beak, which distinguishes it from the black-beaked Snowy Egret. Even though stocky, it tends to stand very erect and its beak is much stouter than the beak of any other heron or egret with which it might be confused. Somewhat more erratic than that of other herons or egrets within its range, the flight pattern of the Cattle Egret tends to suggest a bouncing sort of movement through the air rather than the smooth level flight so characteristic of others of this family.

## LENGTH AND WINGSPAN

Average length for the Cattle Egret is 20 inches (514mm) and the average wingspan is 27.4 inches (702mm).

## BEAK

One of the most accurate and immediate means of identifying the Cattle Egret is its beak. In general physical appearance, only two other North American birds bear resemblance to the adult Cattle Egret; one is the mature Snowy Egret and the other is the immature Little Blue Heron. In the Snowy Egret and Little Blue Heron, however, the beak is very dark, whereas in the Cattle Egret it is yellow or greenish-yellow. Furthermore, the beaks of the other two birds are much more slender, longer, and more pointed than that of *Bubulcus ibis ibis*. During the breeding season the beak of the Cattle Egret may become a more vivid yellow, yellow-orange, or even reddish, but it is never dark (blackish or bluish) as in the case of the Snowy Egret or Little Blue Heron.

## LEGS

The legs may range in coloration from a dull, dingy yellowish or greenish-yellow to a darker orange. In winter, however, the legs are always a dark greenish-brown or blackish.

## EYES

The irides range from pure yellow to yellow-orange.

## CRESTS, PLUMAGE, ANNUAL MOLT

During the breeding season, elongated feathers appear on the back, lower nape, and crown; these range from distinctly pinkish in color to a rich cinnamon-buffy. The distinctive feathers are another excellent differentiating factor between this bird and the Snowy Egret and Little Blue Heron.

## VOICE

Although it is a gregarious bird in its normal daily activities, the Cattle Egret does not often vocalize beyond a few short *quck* sounds when alarmed. The hungry young in the nest will peep or make a faint squealing sound as the parent bird approaches, but otherwise are mostly silent.

## COLORATION AND MARKINGS: ADULT

Pure white plumage except in breeding season, when the feathers of the crown, lower rear of the neck, and upper back become buffy, cinnamon-buffy, or pinkish. Legs are greenish-yellow to dull reddish at this time, but dark olive-brown to blackish at other times.

## COLORATION AND MARKINGS: JUVENILE

Same as in the adult bird, except that there are no elongated buffy or pinkish feathers in crown, neck, or back. The beak is yellow and the legs are dark brown to greenish-brown or greenish-black.

## GENERAL HABITS AND CHARACTERISTICS

Probably the most characteristic trait of the Cattle Egret is that which gave it its name—its proclivity to associate with cattle. Often groups of three or four to twenty or more of the birds will follow close at the feet of grazing cattle, alert and ready to snatch up any grasshoppers or other insects, lizards, small snakes, and other such creatures which the casual movements of the cattle may disturb into motion. Sometimes the birds will land on the backs of the cattle, which are not bothered in the least by their presence. Not infrequently, the Cattle Egrets are joined in this activity by Snowy Egrets, Louisiana Herons, and Little Blue Herons, and occasionally even by Great Egrets. *Bubulcus ibis ibis* frequently engages in a very peculiar physical motion that is foreign to other birds of the family. During the midst of its feeding, it will pause and raise its head high, at which time a waving motion will begin in the head and neck and

---

IX  REDDISH EGRET

*Dichromanassa rufescens rufescens* (Gmelin). Light and dark phases. Tampa Bay, Florida. A.O.U. Number 198

X  GREAT EGRET

*Casmerodius albus egretta* (Gmelin). Bay Oaks Circle, Manasota Key, Charlotte County, Florida, April 20, 1975. A.O.U. Number 196

*Cattle Egret*

Karl E. Karalus

then, like a wave in a ribbon, move down the entire length of the bird's body. Usually two or three such waves will traverse down the bird's body before it lowers its head and resumes its normal feeding activities.

## HABITAT AND ROOSTING

The bird generally prefers to remain in pasture lands, associating with cattle in the manner mentioned above. Roosting is generally done in tangled areas of low trees or high bush growth and in groups of anywhere from twenty to one hundred birds. In recent years, as their numbers have increased and the range of the bird has become extended in North America, Cattle Egrets have become familiar sights in the ditches, on the shoulders, and on the median strips of modern highways and expressways. *Bubulcus ibis ibis* is also fond of foraging for food in marshy meadows, but it does not wade as much as other birds of its family.

## FOOD AND FEEDING HABITS

Insects make up by far the greater bulk of the Cattle Egret's diet. Snails,

slugs, worms, frogs, salamanders, small snakes, and lizards are also eaten, though in lesser volume. Feeding is done throughout the daylight hours, but most heavily in early morning and late afternoon.

## NEST AND NESTING HABITS

As nesting sites, low dense bushes are favored, well out of ordinary traffic areas which might bring danger. The basic foundation of the nest is a poorly built structure of twigs, to which is added a lining of smaller twigs (usually green) and both grasses and leaves which the bird plucks for the purpose. The nesting colonies ordinarily include around thirty or forty pairs of birds.

## EGGS AND INCUBATION

Usually five smooth-shelled, pale blue eggs are laid. Their average size is 1.4 inches x 1.1 inches (35mm x 29mm). Incubation is performed almost equally by both parent birds during the daylight hours, but more so by the female than by the male at night, at which time he roosts nearby.

## DISTRIBUTION

Each year the range of *Bubulcus ibis ibis* becomes more extended. This bird represents perhaps the classic example of a bird distributing itself throughout the world. Found on all major continents, the Cattle Egret is widely established throughout the Old World, Asia Minor, southern Asia, and Africa. It is

---

XI   SNOWY EGRET

*Egretta thula thula* (Molina). Palm Island, Stump Pass, Charlotte County, Florida. A.O.U. Number 197

XII   AMERICAN BITTERN

*Botaurus lentiginosus* (Rackett). Englewood, Florida, November 19, 1974. A.O.U. Number 190

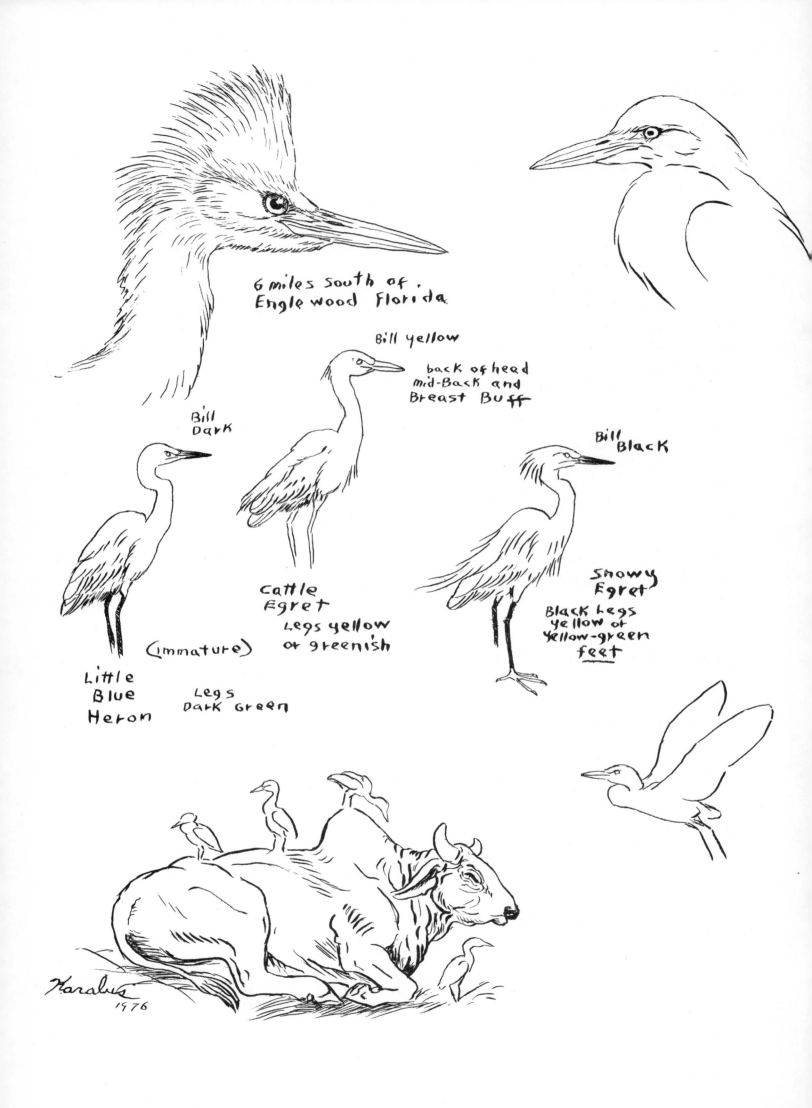

6 miles south of
Englewood Florida

Bill yellow

back of head
mid-Back and
Breast Buff

Bill
Dark

Bill
Black

Cattle
Egret

Legs yellow
or greenish

Snowy
Egret

Black Legs
yellow or
yellow-green
feet

(immature)

Little
Blue
Heron

Legs
Dark Green

Karalus
1976

believed to have come to the Western Hemisphere first in migration from Africa to Brazil sometime after 1850. By about 1877 it had spread to Surinam and by 1911 to Guyana. Movement through the Caribbean area via Central America and Mexico, and from island to island in the West Indies, was slow but relatively steady, with at least two major setbacks due to devastating hurricanes. However, by the late 1930s and early 1940s it had reached the Florida Keys and then the mainland of Florida. The extension of the bird's range was not particularly noted in ornithological literature until 1952, when, on April 23, a specimen was taken at Wayland, Massachusetts. By 1957 the species was breeding well throughout much of the southeast and spreading westward and northward quite rapidly. It has been nesting in southern Canada since 1962. Because it is continually in motion, it is difficult to state a definite range demarcation.

**CATTLE EGRET**

*Bubulcus ibis ibis* Linnaeus

## MIGRATION

There is a definite withdrawing of *Bubulcus ibis ibis* from the northern portions of its range in autumn, at which time the southern population seems almost to explode. With each spring's northward (and westward) migration, it seems that the bird extends its range.

It has now even been reported casually from southern Alaska.

## ECONOMIC INFLUENCE

Because of its propensity for devouring insects in large numbers, the Cattle Egret is considered to be a very beneficial bird agriculturally.

---

Field sketches of various egrets and one immature Little Blue Heron, made at North Port, Florida, September 1975.

# *DICHROMANASSA* EGRETS

---

GENUS: *DICHROMANASSA* Ridgway

SPECIES: *RUFESCENS* (Gmelin)

SUBSPECIES: *rufescens* (Gmelin)
Reddish Egret

*dickeyi* van Rossem
Dickey's Egret

## COMMON NAME

Reddish Egret
(Color Plate IX)

## SCIENTIFIC NAME

*Dichromanassa rufescens rufescens* (Gmelin). Scientific name from the Greek *dis* (twice) and *chroma* (color), referring to the two color phases (reddish and white), and from the Latin *rufus* (reddish).

## SHAPE AT REST AND IN FLIGHT

*Dichromanassa rufescens rufescens* in its colored phase bears a resemblance to the Little Blue Heron, except that it is larger and bulkier, has a slightly heavier beak, and its coloration is generally a bit lighter throughout. In its white phase it bears a resemblance to the Great Egret, except that it is shorter and not so trim and slender. A very distinctive characteristic of the bird is an unusually long tarsus for its size. Its movements on the ground have a peculiar grace.

The Reddish Egret looks most like the Little Blue Heron in shape while flying, except that its body is stouter and its wings broader. The flight pattern is more regular than that of other small or medium-sized herons, and the Reddish Egret generally flies a little higher. Occasionally, it will hesitate in its stroke and glide for two to five seconds before

stroking again. The wingstrokes are not as long and slow as those of the Great Egret or Great Blue Heron, and the flight is strong and fast as well as gracefully light.

## LENGTH AND WINGSPAN

Reddish Egrets average above 29 inches in length (751mm) and have an average wingspan of 47.3 inches (1213mm).

## BEAK

The terminal one third to one half of the beak is black, while the basal one half to two thirds is, in summer adults, a pale fleshy coloration. This particolored beak is a good field identification of the bird in its summer plumage. In winter, however, the beak is dusky.

## LEGS, FEET, AND CLAWS

The tibia is bare and, in the white phase, the toes are dark olivaceous instead of yellow, a factor that helps to distinguish the white-phase Reddish Egret from the Snowy Egret. In the colored phase, the legs and feet are blue with blackish scales on the tarsus. The middle toe and claw are lengthy.

## EYES

The irides of the Reddish Egret are milk-white, and both the lores and eyelids are a pale flesh coloration.

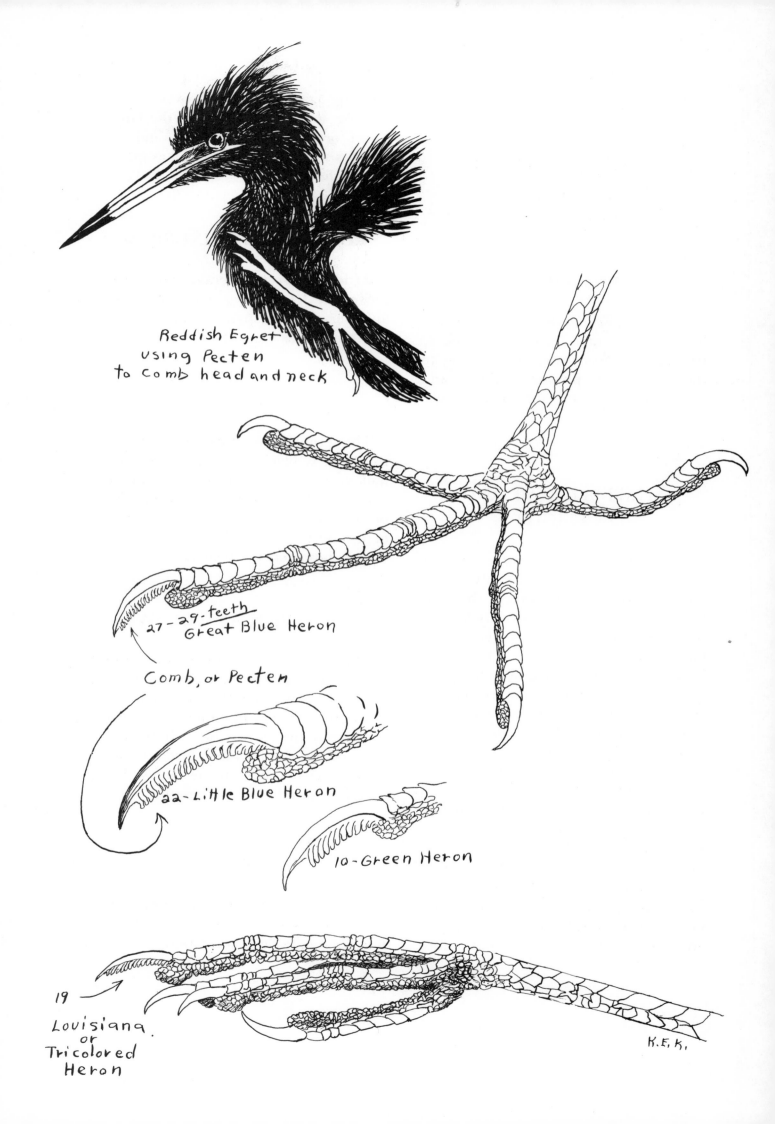

Reddish Egret
using Pecten
to comb head and neck

27-29-teeth
Great Blue Heron

Comb, or Pecten

22-Little Blue Heron

10-Green Heron

19
Louisiana
or
Tricolored
Heron

K.E.K.

## CRESTS, PLUMAGE, ANNUAL MOLT

Adult birds undergo a complete molt beginning in early to middle August, and lasting through mid-October. Also, in January and February, there is partial pre-nuptial molt which involves primarily the display plumes. These plumes of the head, neck, and breast are long and distinctive, with a peculiarly attractive pinkish brown to sometimes cinnamon coloration. These quills, when erected by the bird for display, stand out in a bristling array around the shoulders and on neck and back, appearing almost menacing, as if they are quills like a porcupine's. In wintertime, these quills and those of the back, which are a bluish-gray in coloration, are much shorter and less distinctive.

## VOICE

In at least one of its vocalizations, the Reddish Egret utters a far more musical note than do any of its heron or egret relations. This is a clear, bugling cry which is often given as it feeds on the tidal flats and, less often, as it settles into the rookery for the night. It also makes the more guttural croakings characteristic of most of the family. One other distinctive note, however, is a sort of booming, hollow sound with a rough, rasping quality which is uttered during the courtship displays.

## SEXUAL DIFFERENCES: SIZE, COLORATION, VOICE

There are no obvious differences between the sexes.

## COLORATION AND MARKINGS: ADULT

In its white phase, which is the less common, the Reddish Egret most closely resembles the Great Egret, but is shorter and stouter. The plumage is entirely white. The bird is dichromatic, with two well-defined color phases. In the more common colored phase, the bird resembles the Little Blue Heron but with the neck reddish-tan rather than dark purplish-blue. The rest of the body is, along with the wings, a neutral gray to a slight bluish-gray, but paler in this coloration on the underside. The ends of the train feathers are sometimes yellowish.

## COLORATION AND MARKINGS: JUVENILE

In the colored phase the young bird is a plain ashy gray, touched here and there with shades of reddish, from cinnamon-brown to rusty and fawn-colored. The beak is uniformly dusky. The white-phase bird is entirely white. The legs and the tops of the feet are a dark greenish-black and the soles of the feet are a dingy yellow.

---

The pecten, or comb, a peculiar structure found on the middle toenail of herons, bitterns, and egrets, is used to clean and dress plumage, sometimes in conjunction with the powder-down tracts on the upper breast.

## GENERAL HABITS AND CHARACTERISTICS

*Dichromanassa rufescens rufescens* is almost entirely diurnal in its habits, with its peak feeding activities in early morning and evening. At daybreak the birds fly from their rookeries or nesting colonies to the feeding areas, but they return before the sun is very high and spend much of the day dozing or playing at repelling intruders from their nests. Often they spend hours preening. When actively feeding, they are much more lively in their movements than any other heron, darting here and there with partially or fully outstretched wings—a distinctive trait which is called umbrella feeding—and sometimes punctuating these movements with peculiar little hopping flights of a dozen feet or less. Sometimes, however, they are content to stand in the tidal shallows and wait for food to come near enough to spear, or else move slowly about seeking their prey on the mud flats or sandbanks, remaining there until the incoming tide forces them to vacate.

## HABITAT AND ROOSTING

Sandy shoals, muddy banks, tidal flats, coastal marshes, narrow winding bays intermingled with mangrove islands—all these are indicative of the type of habitat most favorable for the Reddish Egret. Only on rare occasions does the bird stray very far from the immediate coastal areas, and it even prefers feeding in saltwater areas rather than brackish or freshwater locations. Most roosting is done in low trees on islands in rather isolated areas.

## FOOD AND FEEDING HABITS

With the approach of evening, the Reddish Egrets fly to their favorite feeding areas on the tidal flats and either snatch small crustaceans and fish from the shallows where the birds stand waiting, or else prowl about with steady stalking pace, hunting such prey. Often the prancing, darting, hopping sort of pursuit of prey is engaged in, with seemingly good results. The majority of the bird's diet consists of fish, but also a fair amount of crabs, grass shrimp, and snails are eaten. On those occasions when the bird does feed in less saline marshes and on the fringes of ponds or in moist meadows, frogs and tadpoles become important in the diet. Small snakes and lizards will be eaten as well.

## COURTSHIP AND MATING

As courtship begins, the males begin chasing one another with hoarse cries and considerable aerial acrobatics as the females watch, usually from the ground. The chasing flights involve swift turns, long curves, and harrowing zigzags low to the water and past obstructions. When the chasing male, whose crest has been raised in anger all during the chase, manages to oust the male he has been chasing, he then returns to where the female has been standing. Time and again, with all his display plumage as erect and bristling as he can force it to be, he parades back and forth in front of her in what seems to be a menacing manner, but in a way which evidently appeals to her greatly. Soon she stands close to him and for a while they rub necks together. Then, usually on the spot where this occurs, copulation takes place. Part of the male's display includes marching back and forth before her with his beak pointed skyward and his neck gracefully curved, all the while a deep, hollow coarse sound rumbling from his throat and his plumes trembling with the effort. No distinction is made among the birds regarding color phase; white and white, colored and colored, and white and colored pair up indiscriminately.

## NEST AND NESTING HABITS

Although the Reddish Egrets nest in colonies largely made up of their own species, they are not opposed to nesting in close proximity to or even among such other species as Great Blue Herons, Louisiana Herons, or Little Blue Herons; boat-tailed grackles also nest in conjunction with them. *Dichromanassa rufescens rufescens* is particularly adept at balancing on the thin and springy outermost branches of low bushes and trees, and it is here that the nests quite often are built. The nest is somewhat better made than the ordinary heron nest. The basic structure is still one of interwoven sticks, but the interweaving is a little better accomplished and the nest is not simply a flat platform, as is so often the case with other species in the family Ardeidae. Measuring from 20 to 26 inches in diameter, the nest is ordinarily about 10 inches high and has an inner hollow

**REDDISH EGRET**

*Dichromanassa rufescesn rufescens* (Gmelin)

about 1 foot in diameter and 3 or 4 inches deep. This hollow is well lined and smoothed with grasses, straws, and fine twigs. Not infrequently, the nest will be built on the ground.

## EGGS AND INCUBATION

Three or four pale bluish-green smooth-shelled eggs are laid which average 2 inches by 1.5 inches (52mm x 38mm). Both parent birds incubate on an essentially equal basis. Incubation lasts for twenty-four days.

## YOUNG

In their white phase, young Reddish Egrets are pure white, but in the colored phase the downy young have atop their heads inch-long hairlike plumes, a drab cinnamon in coloration, while the rest of the long and soft down is a mousy gray. The unfeathered throat, the beak, and the feet are all a dark olive-green. No fleshy coloration develops on the beak until the second year, when the bird reaches full adulthood.

## MIGRATION

There is no real migration among the Reddish Egrets and not as much general movement of young birds northward after they leave the nest as occurs with other heron and egret species.

# COMMON NAME

Dickey's Egret
(Subspecies Sketch 7)

# SCIENTIFIC NAME

*Dichromanassa rufescens dickeyi* van Rossem.

# PRINCIPAL SUBSPECIFIC DIFFERENCES

Dickey's Egret is included in this work because it moves casually into the United States from Mexico on a more or less annual basis, appearing with some regularity in southern California, especially in the coastal areas of San Diego County, and on occasion in the Colorado River valley as much as 50 miles north of the Mexican border. It has been known to wander as far as the Texas coast and north along the California coast to Los Angeles. Slightly larger than the Reddish Egret, it is also a bit lighter in general coloration. All the toes are markedly short for a member of the family Ardeidae.

The elongated plumes on the head and neck are quite well defined and form into tufts at the throat and occiput. Dickey's Egret, like the Reddish Egret, does

DICKEY'S EGRET

*Dichromanassa rufescens dickeyi* van Rossem

not have the white throat line of most herons.

More ground-nesting is done by Dickey's Egret than by the Reddish Egret, but the eggs are almost identical in size and coloration.

---

*(Overleaf)* 7. DICKEY'S EGRET

*Dichromanassa rufescens dickeyi* van Rossem. Isla Magdalena, Baja California, April 1963. A.O.U. Number 198a

head and neck of
This bird was much
darker compared
to Reddish Egret's
from Texas or florida

# GREAT EGRET

---

GENUS: *CASMERODIUS* Gloger
SPECIES: *ALBUS* Linnaeus
SUBSPECIES: *egretta* (Gmelin)

Karl E Karalus

Karl E. Karalus

# COMMON NAME

Great Egret (formerly American Egret)
(Color Plate X)

# SCIENTIFIC NAME

*Casmerodius albus egretta* (Gmelin). *Egretta,* from the French *aigrette,* a type of heron; also a plume. *Casmerodius* is Greek for gaping heron.

# OTHER COMMON OR COLLOQUIAL NAMES

This bird has quite a variety of local or regional names, although all are very similar. It is sometimes referred to as an egret, sometimes as a heron, and sometimes as a crane. For a great many years it was commonly called the American Egret.

BIG PLUME BIRD After its spectacular breeding plumage.

---

XV   WOOD STORK

*Mycteria americana* Linnaeus. Placida, Charlotte County, Florida. A.O.U. Number 188

XVI   GLOSSY IBIS (left)

*Plegadis falcinellus falcinellus* (Linnaeus). Naples, Florida. A.O.U. Number 186

WHITE-FACED IBIS (right)

*Plegadis chihi* Vieillot. Brownsville, Texas. A.O.U. Number 187

COMMON EGRET After the European egret to which it is so closely allied.

GREAT WHITE EGRET Because of its size.

GREAT WHITE HERON Erroneously, since this is the common name of *Ardea herodias occidentalis.*

LA GRANDE AIGRETTE French Canadian name.

LONG WHITE A very common name at one time, applied especially by the plume hunters in Florida.

WHITE CRANE Another case of misidentification, since the bird is not a crane at all.

WHITE EGRET Because of its pure white plumage.

WHITE HERON A misnomer for the species.

# SHAPE AT REST AND IN FLIGHT

A sleek, slender, well-shaped bird of grace and elegance and with uncommonly expressive posturings of the head and neck. Much larger than the Snowy Egret, it is very nearly the size of the Great Blue Heron, though not as bulky in body shape. During the breeding season a train of long graceful plumes extends far beyond the tail. The beak is relatively heavy for its size.

The basic shape in flight of the Great Egret is much like that of others of the heron family, with the neck folded back, the head between the shoulders, and the legs stretched far behind, acting as a rudder. When it takes to flight, the Great Egret springs very lightly into the air with legs and neck extended; even with neck drawn back and couched, this is still, in flight, the slenderest of the herons for its size. It also has an uncommonly buoyant flight silhouette, almost as if it were holding itself down with its wings in flight, instead of lifting itself up.

## LENGTH AND WINGSPAN

Excluding the plumes, which extend approximately a foot beyond the tail, the Great Egret has an average length of 37.3 inches (968mm) and a wingspan exceeding 4.5 feet (1489mm).

## BEAK

Most individuals have some degree of black on the very tip of the yellow-orange beak.

## LEGS AND FEET

The legs and feet are black, which is a key identification factor.

## CRESTS, PLUMAGE, ANNUAL MOLT

*Casmerodius albus egretta* has no crest, but its plumes are among the most beautiful to be found on any North American bird. These pure white plume feathers, as long as 680mm (approximately 26.5 inches), spring from the back and extend far beyond the tail almost in the manner of a bridal veil train. Though the shafts of these feathers are stiff and resilient, the barbs are soft and lack barbules. As many as fifty of the plumes have been found in the back of an individual bird, but the usual number is about thirty-five. These plumes are acquired during the pre-nuptial molt of adults, usually beginning in January, and are usually shed, in worn condition, toward the end of June. A complete post-nuptial molt begins in July or early August; this molt either produces no plumes at all or else back plumes which are relatively short and not as spectacular as those of the breeding plumage. While the plumes in the males generally extend about a foot beyond the tail feathers, those of the female birds average a couple of inches shorter.

## VOICE

The most familiar vocalization made by the Great Egret is a sort of coarse rattling croak, unpleasant squawkings, and raspy sounds, with the most raucous of all coming when the bird is alarmed. About the softest utterance is a soft gurgling sound made during courtship, ordinarily only by the male. Young birds demanding food issue a grating, almost constant *kak-kak-kak-kak-kak,* and adults approaching the nest often give utterance to a similar but deeper sound of *quck-quck-quck-quck,* which may go on for a quarter hour or more.

## MORTALITY AND LONGEVITY

As in most heron species, the infants suffer a relatively high mortality rate through tumbling from the nest into the water below and either drowning or being taken by predators before they are able to regain the security of the nest.

In former times, the greatest threat to the Great Egret came in the guise of the plume hunter, who destroyed great numbers of birds during the breeding season, with resultant destruction of whatever eggs or young were in the nests at the time.

## COLORATION AND MARKINGS: JUVENILE

Pure white, like adults, but without plumes. Legs and feet tend to have a more greenish cast.

## GENERAL HABITS AND CHARACTERISTICS

Great Egrets are primarily diurnal, rarely crepuscular, and almost never nocturnal in their habits. If harassed, they become very wary, but can become reasonably tame and easy to approach if left alone. When the breeding season is completed, young and old alike ordinarily scatter in all directions and become more solitary in their daytime habits, though still roosting at night in large groups.

## HABITAT AND ROOSTING

The most favored habitat is marshy or mangrove fringe. Sometimes the birds will be on open sand beaches, but far more often feeding occurs in the tidal flats among mangroves, or else in the midst of extensive marshes, usually along the fringes of more open water areas, such as channels or canals. Other areas holding an attraction for *Casmerodius albus egretta* are the margins of lakes, ponds, streams, ditches, rice fields, and bayous. Just prior to dark the birds gather in large numbers in the roosting areas—usually dense mangrove islands—and here they perch throughout the night in trees, only to scatter again after dawn.

## ENEMIES AND DEFENSES

The worst natural enemies of the Great Egret are crows, and boat-tailed grackles (the latter often playing havoc with the eggs when they are left unguarded, even briefly). By far, however, the greatest enemy of the Great Egret has been the plume hunter. At one point the species was teetering on the brink of extinction thanks to the vogue for plumed hats. Just before the turn of the century the plumes were worth, ounce for ounce, twice as much as gold. And it took the plumes of four birds to make one ounce. In 1886 New York dealers were paying 90 cents for the plumes of one bird, but the demand became so great and the prices went so high that in eleven years the feathers from one bird brought $10! At a single London auction in 1902, over a ton and a half of Great Egret plumes were sold. The actual weight was 48,240 ounces (3,015 pounds), which, with the feathers of four birds equaling 1 ounce, totals very nearly a fifth of a million birds. Add to this the fact that as a result of this slaughter of adults, probably around 600,000 eggs and young perished. And this was only one auction among a multitude of them! Fortunately, public outcry against such devastation resulted in the passage of tough legislation against plume-hunting. The Great Egret population, at an extremely low ebb by about 1905, has largely recovered and the species is no longer endangered. Due to man's own expansion, however, and the loss of great tracts of natural habitat, it is doubtful that *Casmerodius albus egretta* will ever again regain its former abundance.

## FOOD AND FEEDING HABITS

Sometimes in small groups, occasionally in large flocks, and most often in threesomes, pairs, or singly, the Great Egret feeds mainly in the shallows of marshes and coastal mangrove tidal flats. There it stands quietly in the shallows waiting for prey to come past or, nearly as frequently, wades slowly on the flats or in the marshy shallows, its neck drawn back like a coiled spring and its head poised, beak ready to thrust forward and impale or snatch whatever prey may be encountered. Food does not consist entirely of animal matter, although it does play a large part. A certain amount of vegetation, primarily in the form of seeds or small fruits and some green matter, is eaten. Mostly, though, food matter consists of fish, frogs, and crayfish, in about that order of importance. Also frequently eaten are large grasshoppers, dragonflies, moths, and other insects, especially of aquatic variety, along with lizards and small snakes, snails, small birds (rarely eggs), mice and moles, fiddler crabs, and such particularly favored fish as shad, suckers, and sunfish, along with minnows of any species.

## COURTSHIP AND MATING

All during the display period prior to actual pairing and copulation, the males show great antipathy for one another and battles of varying degrees of intensity are not uncommon. The male makes a great show of raising his plumes in a flashy manner, strutting, preening, and parading about before the female and crooning to her in a gurgling sort of way until she finally accepts him as mate. This display goes on for six days, each such display being followed by copulation. A lesser form of the display continues, by both sexes, at the nest throughout the remainder of the breeding season, and is especially noticeable at those times when the male and female are relieving one another of incubation or brooding duties.

## NEST AND NESTING HABITS

As with all of the herons, the nest is a simple structure of coarse sticks woven together to form a platform with a slightly depressed interior to help prevent the eggs from rolling off during bad weather. The nest is just slightly more substantial than that of the Snowy Egret or Louisiana or Little Blue Heron and it is sometimes lined with Spanish moss or a few mangrove leaves. Great Egrets are especially fond of building their nest in a tree, usually at a height of from 8 to 40 feet and most often about 20 feet high, where two substantial branches converge. Nesting is done in colonies of anywhere from a dozen pairs to fifty or more pairs, sometimes in company with brown pelicans and cormorants as well as other egret and heron species.

In the Gulf coastal areas, isolated mangrove islands are favored nesting sites. Away from the coastal areas, Great Egrets nest on densely overgrown hammocks of willow and bay, along with stands of cypress. Often they will build nests at the very tops of low bushes, but rarely in the tops of trees. The preference is for a nest site directly above water.

## EGGS AND INCUBATION

Ordinarily three or four pale bluish-green eggs are laid. The eggs are usually fusiform (somewhat pointed at both ends) and the shell is smooth. The average size is 2.2 inches by 1.6 inches (57mm x 41mm).

Incubation is undertaken by both sexes, but probably slightly more by the female than by the male. In most cases it is the female who incubates throughout the nighttime hours.

**GREAT EGRET**

*Casmerodius albus egretta* (Gmelin)

## YOUNG

If the nest is high in a tree, the young are inclined to remain within it until they can fly; if, however, it is low, they will generally leave earlier and crawl about with increasing skill through the low branches, sometimes falling but usually recovering. In most instances, two or three of the young are fed in a single feeding by the parent bird and in some manner not determined, the arriving second parent seems to know very well which of the birds was fed last and thus which should be fed next. Almost always the plumes of the parent bird, regardless of which parent, are raised as feeding is under way. The actual feeding, as with other heron species, is by regurgitation until the baby bird is old enough and capable enough to pick up food dropped into the bottom of the nest.

Juvenile plumage appears in succession on the back, wings, breast, crown, and tail, and finally the wings. The last down to disappear is that of the neck and underside. The growth of plumes in the juvenile plumage is extremely limited or absent. Full adult plumage is not acquired until the first postnuptial molt, occurring when the young bird is about fourteen months of age.

## NORTH AMERICAN DISTRIBUTION

Since the Great Egret was eliminated by plume hunters in much of the range it formerly occupied, it appears only casually in areas where once it was extremely abundant. The present breeding range has been expanding gradually, however, and is not quite so limited to the Gulf coastal areas as it was during the first half of this century.

## MIGRATION

The Great Egret withdraws from the more northerly portions of its range fairly early in autumn, with most of the birds vacating before mid-October and settling in for the winter in the Gulf coastal areas and southward into the Caribbean and Mexico, Central America, and South America.

## ECONOMIC INFLUENCE

Although, at one time, fortunes were made in the millinery trade with the plumes of the Great Egret, the bird is no longer considered economically important, as plume-hunting is now prohibited. Agriculturally the bird is of some benefit because of its habit of eating grasshoppers and other pests.

# *EGRETTA* EGRETS

---

GENUS:       *EGRETTA* Sharpe

SPECIES:       *THULA* (Molina)

SUBSPECIES:       *thula* (Molina)

Snowy Egret

*brewsteri* (Thayer & Bangs)

Brewster's Egret

## COMMON NAME

Snowy Egret
(Color Plate XI)

## SCIENTIFIC NAME

*Egretta thula thula* (Molina). *Thula,* Greek, means most northern.

## OTHER COMMON OR COLLOQUIAL NAMES

BONNET MARTYR This was a nickname affixed to the bird by ornithologists and bird-lovers at the time when plume hunters were making great inroads into the egret populations, and the name still is used in some localities.

COMMON EGRET An often used, though confusing terminology, since the Great Egret is also sometimes referred to by this name.

L'AIGRETTE NEIGEUSE French Canadian name meaning Snowy Egret.

LESSER EGRET As opposed to the "greater egret" (Great Egret).

LITTLE EGRET Descriptive of size and type.

LITTLE PLUME BIRD To differentiate it from the Great Egret, which was the big plume bird, though not referred to by that name.

LITTLE SNOWY Common term used by plume hunters.

LITTLE WHITE EGRET As opposed to "Great White Egret," meaning the Great Egret or, sometimes, the Great White Heron.

LITTLE WHITE HERON Same as the preceding.

SHORT WHITE The most common term for the bird used by the plume hunters, who thereby distinguished it from the "Long White," or the Great Egret. The term referred not only to the actual size of the bird, but to the relative sizes of the plumes.

SNOWY HERON A common appellation simply using the family term instead of the more specific term.

## SHAPE AT REST AND IN FLIGHT

A dainty and exquisite little egret, considered by many to be the most charming of all marsh birds and waders, *Egretta thula thula* is quite short and slender, though relatively not as slender as the Great Egret. Also, its beak is quite thin and dainty, as compared to the much heavier beak of *Casmerodius albus egretta.* When sitting hunched with head nestled between the shoulders and one leg drawn up, the Snowy Egret can look especially small.

Relatively speaking, the wings of the Snowy Egret are not as broad as those of the Great Egret and, while the Snowy Egret approximates the Cattle Egret in size, it is not as bulky a bird.

The wingstrokes of the Snowy Egret are somewhat faster than those of the Great Egret, but the flight is essentially as direct and purposeful, though perhaps not quite as light. It is much more inclined to fly close to the water surface—within 3 or 4 feet—than is the larger Great Egret. At times, though, the

Snowy Egret will travel rapidly at a height of about 200 feet until it reaches its destination and then it will abruptly pull its wings almost closed and fairly tumble groundward, braking itself only just in time to keep from crashing into ground or trees.

## LENGTH AND WINGSPAN

The average length of the Snowy Egret is just short of 2 feet (597mm) and the average wingspan is just about 38 inches (972mm).

## BEAK

The beak of the Snowy Egret is one of its most distinguishing characteristics. The all-black coloration of the beak immediately separates the Snowy Egret from the similarly sized and colored Cattle Egret (which has a yellow-orange beak) and the immature, all-white Little Blue Heron, which has a beak partially black and partially blue.

## LEGS, FEET, AND CLAWS

The legs and toes of *Egretta thula thula* clearly identify the species at a glance. The legs of the adult, as well as the tarsus, are black, but the toes are a brilliant yellow. The coloration change is so sharp and so apparent that at first glance it looks exactly as if a bird with black legs and feet had stepped into bright yellow paint which completely stained the toes. This color demarcation is not quite so distinct in the immature Snowy

Egrets, whose legs are more greenish than black. The claws are black.

## CRESTS, PLUMAGE, ANNUAL MOLT

The Snowy Egret, like the Great Egret, was destroyed in such vast numbers by plume hunters at the turn of the century that the species came very close to being made extinct. Although the plumes of the Great Egret are considerably longer than those of the Snowy Egret (but just as lacy and delicate in appearance), those of the smaller bird were in much greater demand because of the way they recurved toward their ends, with a lovely, graceful swirl. This made them especially appealing in the millinery trade and so literally millions of the birds were destroyed for the recurved plumes from about 1856 through 1905. About fifty of the long, filamentous scapular plumes appear on the bird's back when the Snowy Egret undergoes a partial pre-nuptial molt in mid-January through late February. These feathers, somewhat bedraggled after months of displaying, fighting, and preening, are finally shed with the complete molt which occurs from June to September. In the millinery trade, the recurved feathers of the back were known as "cross-aigrettes" and during the peak of the plume-hunting days, one bird's plumes might sell for as much as $20. Concurrent with the appearance of the recurved scapular plumes are similar but shorter and uncurved plumes on the lower neck. When these and the longer recurved plumes are shed in June, they are replaced by shorter, straighter winter plumes. Unlike the Great Egret, which has no crest feathers, the Snowy Egret has a well developed occipital crest extending over the crown and composed of long, loosely webbed feathers which it erects in a beautiful display during the breeding season as a compliment to the recurved scapular plumes. In its full courtship plumage of lacy white, filamentous, and recurved feathers, the Snowy Egret is indeed one of the most strikingly beautiful birds in the world.

## VOICE

The voice of the Snowy Egret is, like the voices of most of the birds of the heron family, ordinarily guttural and coarse. Although this species tends to be somewhat more silent than other species, it can become very vocal during the breeding season.

## COLORATION AND MARKINGS: ADULT AND JUVENILE

In both sexes and in both immature birds and adults, the plumage is always a pure, spotless, snowy white. Irides are chrome yellow in adults and slightly lighter yellow in immature birds. The lores are pale yellow.

## HABITAT AND ROOSTING

Open sandy beaches are a favorite feeding and resting place of the Snowy Egret, which shares such habitat on oc-

casion with Little Blue Herons. Often the delicate little Snowy Egrets will be seen running or stepping about in the upper portion of the surf, picking up minute fishes and tiny sand fleas. However, even more than on the Gulf beaches, the Snowy Egret is at home in tangled swamps, marshes, and bayous, and along the edges of more open ponds and streams. Probably the most favored roosting area is on the outer edges of a dense stand of mangroves which face the open water of some quiet and secluded bay. Here they roost from dusk to dawn (and sometimes in company with white ibises) in such numbers that the deep green foliage is practically white with them. The Snowy Egret seems to get along better with the white ibis than do any other of the herons, although why this should be so is not known.

## FOOD AND FEEDING HABITS

Though occasionally the Snowy Egret will stand silently waiting for food to swim past in the shallows, more often the bird darts about on the flats picking up minnows, shrimp, small crabs, and other food as it moves. In addition to the fry of fish, it also feeds heavily on tiny crustaceans and insects of a wide variety, including especially aquatic forms, such as dragonfly nymphs. In recent years the birds have taken to alighting on golf courses and feeding in early morning on the cutworms that have come to the surface during the night. Lizards and small snakes, along with frogs and tadpoles, make up a small portion of the diet, and some snails are also eaten.

## COURTSHIP AND MATING

Male Snowy Egrets tend to become very belligerent and quarrelsome during the breeding season and fights are not uncommon, although these are usually limited to a certain amount of sparring with the beak and batting at one another with their wings until one decides to give up before his beautiful plumage is spoiled. As for the plumage, it is fully displayed to its utmost beauty at every opportunity. Both males and females have plumes, but the males more than the females become highly active in showing off their finery. Passing back and forth before the chosen female, the male extends every plume feather to its utmost, so that he takes on the appearance of a gorgeous animated fan with recurved feather tips and a delicate laciness that is extremely attractive. The crest is raised to its highest vertical position, the breast feathers shoved forward and downward until they nearly touch the ground, the plumes of lower neck are spread wide, and the back plumes are fully extended and erectile. At the same time, the wings are partially opened with their tips sometimes nearly dragging on the ground. It is a lovely sight, evidently every bit as appealing to the female as it is to a human observer. Such displaying is at its peak during courtship, but goes on to a lesser degree all throughout nest-building, incubation, brooding, and later nesting activities.

## NEST AND NESTING HABITS

Almost without exception, both male and female birds, when approaching the nest, erect and display their showy plumage, caress one another, and croon softly. Both birds engage in the nest-building, the result of which is much like that made by any other heron. It is usually a flimsy and rather flat platform of intertwined sticks, coarser on the bottom and somewhat finer on the top, and occasionally lined with much finer twigs. Most often the nests are in dense bushes of trees near or directly over the water and from 8 to 20 feet in height. In western portions of their range, nesting is more often closer to the ground—usually under 6 feet high and sometimes on the ground itself. The nest is rarely over 1 foot in diameter and has a faint depression in the top which may be 3 or 4 inches in diameter. The bird almost always nests in colonies of from twenty to one hundred birds of its own species, and sometimes nests in company with such other species as Great Egrets, Louisiana Herons, and Little Blue Herons. Its nest and eggs are virtually indistinguishable from those of the Louisiana Heron and Little Blue Heron. Probably the favorite nesting trees are mangroves and willows, at a height of about 12 feet. Nesting generally begins in late March and continues through June.

## EGGS AND INCUBATION

Most often four eggs are laid, which may range in coloration from pale bluish to a pale bluish-green. Almost perfectly oval, these eggs are smooth-shelled but not glossy, and the average size is 1.7

*Snowy Egret*

inches x 1.3 inches (43mm x 32mm). Eggs are laid forty-eight hours apart. Incubation begins with the first egg laid and lasts for a term of eighteen days. The sexes share the incubation almost equally.

## YOUNG

Since incubation begins with the first egg laid in a nest with four eggs, the first bird hatched may be over a week old before the last egg hatches. The downy young, except for being smaller, are almost identical to the young of Great Egrets, with the naked portions of the skin a pale green and both beak and feet a pale yellow or yellowish-green. The legs shade to duskier greenish on the upper surface. Young birds are fairly helpless until they are about a week old. At twenty to twenty-five days, when they're half-grown, the young birds begin leaving the nest in the daytime to perch on nearby branches, returning to the nest at night. At about six weeks of age they leave the nest for good. Young birds finally become indistinguishable from adults when they are about eighteen months old.

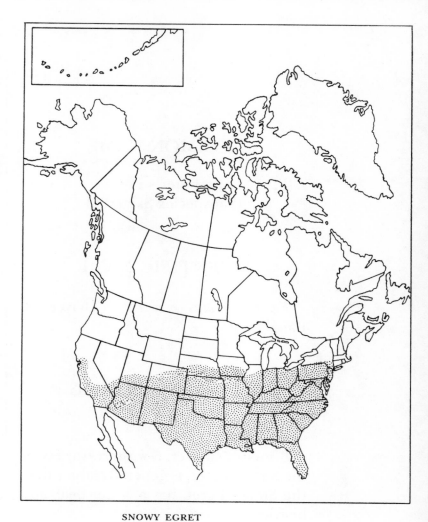

SNOWY EGRET

*Egretta thula thula* (Molina)

## ECONOMIC INFLUENCE

Because of its insect-eating habits and its propensity for seeking out injurious cutworms, the Snowy Egret is held to be a rather beneficial bird.

## COMMON NAME

Brewster's Egret
(Subspecies Sketch 8)

## SCIENTIFIC NAME

*Egretta thula brewsteri* (Thayer & Bangs).

## BASIC SUBSPECIFIC DIFFERENCES

Brewster's Egret, a western variety of the Snowy Egret, is generally larger than the Snowy Egret, has a larger beak and heavier legs.

BREWSTER'S EGRET

*Egretta thula brewsteri* (Thayer & Bangs)

---

8. BREWSTER'S EGRET

*Egretta thula brewsteri* (Thayer & Bangs). Saint George, Utah. A.O.U. Number 197a

# AMERICAN BITTERN

SUBFAMILY: *BOTAURINAE*
GENUS: *BOTAURUS* Stephens
SPECIES: *LENTIGINOSUS* (Rackett)

## COMMON NAME

American Bittern
(Color Plate XII)

## SCIENTIFIC NAME

*Botaurus lentiginosus* (Rackett). From *botaurus*, Latin, meaning a bittern, and *lentiginosus*, Latin, meaning spotted, in reference to the markings on the plumage.

## OTHER COMMON OR COLLOQUIAL NAMES

BOG BULL After the booming sound of its voice in the swamp or marsh.

BUTTER BUMP Because the sound of its voice, according to some, can be likened to the thump of a butter churn.

INDIAN HEN After the henlike appearance and size of the bird, and possibly after the fact that it is known to have been a common bill of fare for Seminole Indians in the Everglades as well as other Indian tribes elsewhere in the nation.

SHIT-QUICK Vulgar term extensively used, especially in the South, and descriptive of the habit of the bird to defecate voluminously immediately upon taking off.

STAKE DRIVER For the sound of the bird's voice which at a distance (though not up close) resembles the sound of a stake being driven with a mallet or an ax into the earth or mud.

SUN GAZER After the habit of the bird to assume a protective pose in which its beak is pointed directly skyward.

THUNDER PUMP After the sound of the bird's voice, which, at times, resembles the sound made by a wooden water pump.

## SHAPE AT REST AND IN FLIGHT

When alarmed, the American Bittern "freezes" into a posture which causes it to become well camouflaged in its surroundings, its beak pointed skyward and the pattern of its plumage blending almost perfectly with a cattail background. On either side of the neck there is a distinctive black stripe.

*Botaurus lentiginosus* has considerably smaller wings than similarly sized herons, and the tips of the wings are dark. As the bird first takes off, its legs dangle loosely below, the head is extended on the long, crooked neck, and the wings flap rather sloppily, the whole aspect being rather awkward. However, as it gets well under way, the legs are drawn up and back to extend beyond the short tail and act as a rudder, the neck is drawn in, the head couched snugly between the shoulders, and the wingbeats become more regular.

Ordinarily the flight is quite low, just over the reed tops, and of relatively short duration. The American Bittern alights again on the floor of the marsh or swamp, rarely if ever in a tree, as does the immature Black-Crowned Night Heron, which it most resembles. The American Bittern's takeoff is punctuated with harsh croaks but then, once the flight is well under way, the wingbeats become steady, firm, and powerful, as well as somewhat faster than those of herons of comparable size. The bird is then a strong and good flier.

## LENGTH AND WINGSPAN

The average length of the American Bittern is 30.7 inches (787mm) and the wingspan averages about 41.5 inches (1063mm).

## LEGS, FEET, AND CLAWS

The legs are a dull yellowish-green, darker and greener behind than in front. The claws are brown, with very little curvature.

## EYES

The irides are a brilliant clear yellow, made all the more startlingly bright by the dark brown loral striptin.

## CRESTS, PLUMAGE, ANNUAL MOLT

Adults undergo one complete post-nuptial molt annually, from about mid-July to September. They are somewhat hampered in their flight by this. There are, as with other heron species, two powder-down tracts on the breast. The neck feathers are quite long and loose. There are well-hidden nuptial plumes on the sides of the breast and neck which become conspicuous only when they are raised during courtship display, by both

sexes. At such times these white plumes are raised high above the shoulders.

## VOICE

Probably the most common vocalization by the American Bittern is a deep, hollow sound similar to *pump-er-lunk,* voiced mostly in early morning and late evening during spring and summer, and at almost any time of day or night during the breeding season.

## COLORATION AND MARKINGS: ADULT

The plumage is an interesting blend of spottings and streakings against a background buffy-brown coloration so like its surroundings that simply by compressing and extending its body, raising itself high, and standing still, the bird can become practically invisible at a distance of only a few feet from the observer. More than one observer has been amazed by the uncanny ability of the bird to blend with its background in an area where such blending seems well nigh impossible. The underparts of the wings of the adult bird are varying tones of yellowish-brown mingled with buffy and pale gray ashy coloration, and with numerous small-sized and irregular bars, spots, freckles, and streaks. The underside of the bird generally is a buffy yellowish-white to pinkish-buff with light brown streakings. There is a highly distinctive black stripe on each side of the

---

American Bittern, *Botaurus lentiginosus* (Rackett).

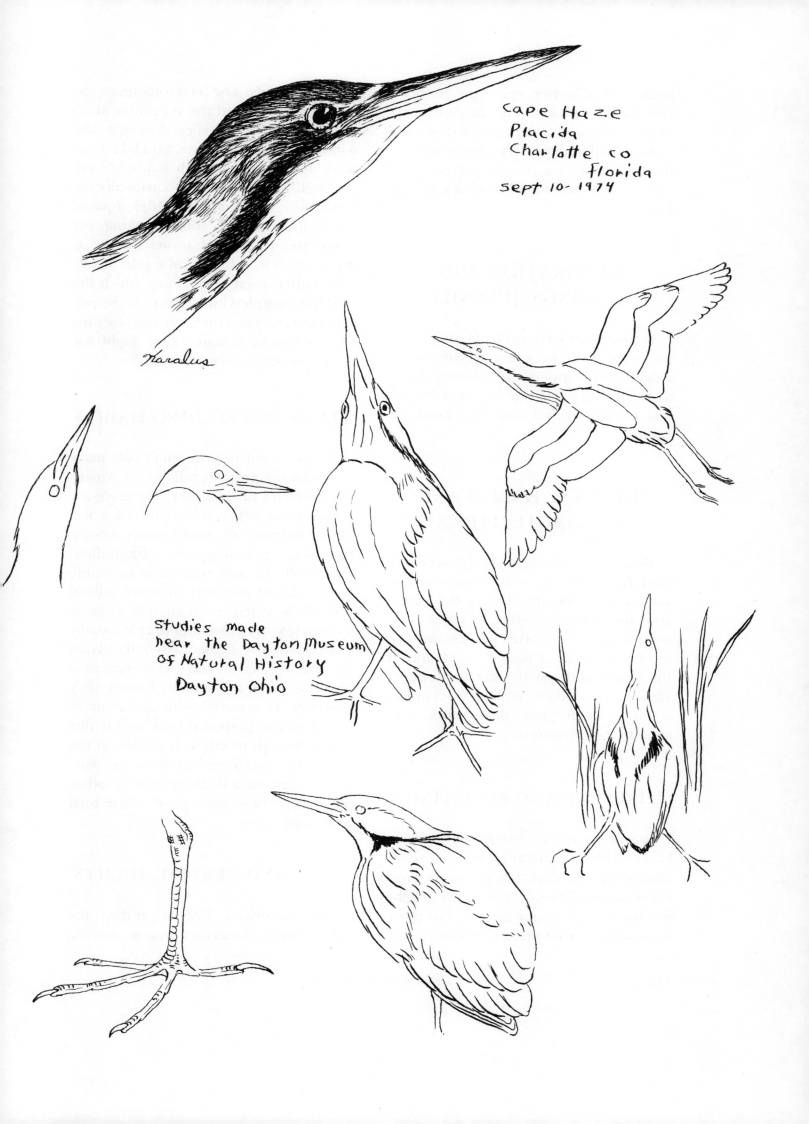

Cape Haze
Placida
Charlotte co
Florida
Sept 10-1974

Karalus

studies made
near the Dayton Museum
of Natural History
Dayton Ohio

neck and a rather yellowish to buffy streak over each eye. The throat is a sort of off-white with a dark stripe down the center. Dull brown covers the crown and the primaries are a greenish-black tipped with a warm brown. The tail is a similar brown.

## COLORATION AND MARKINGS: JUVENILE

Young birds have no black stripes on the sides of the neck and are somewhat more lightly striped and spotted. Aside from this, they are little different in general coloration and markings from the adults.

## GENERAL HABITS AND CHARACTERISTICS

*Botaurus lentiginosus* is a highly secretive bird, far preferring reclusiveness to gregariousness. Except during the courtship and nesting periods, it is almost always solitary. Very often it will stand well hidden beneath canopied vegetation of the marsh and quietly wait for food of some kind to pass it. When it does move, it moves with great deliberation and stealthy noiselessness.

## HABITAT AND ROOSTING

Grassy meadows, extensive marshes, brakes, bogs, canal banks, rush- or reed-choked margins of lakes, ponds, and waterways—all these form excellent habitat for the American Bittern, but most especially favored are the extensive cat-tail marshlands. The bird sometimes visits salt marshes and the vegetative areas bordering tidal marshes. Swamplands, willow and alder thickets, and lake shallows densely grown with bulrushes are also well-favored areas. Occasionally the birds will be found in drier upland meadows, stalking about looking for grasshoppers. Almost always the roosting is done in solitude on a pile of cattails, either dried or growing, which the bird has trampled into a heap. If the private roost remains undisturbed, the bird may return to it night after night for weeks, perhaps even for months.

## FOOD AND FEEDING HABITS

Frogs, crayfish, and small fish make up by far the greatest bulk of the American Bittern's normal diet, but there are a variety of other items this bird will eat, including snails, small snakes, lizards, tadpoles, grasshoppers, dragonflies, eels, mollusks, and even some vegetable food. Almost any sort of small animal life will be eaten, even animals as large as meadow mice. Smaller prey is usually grasped in the beak, tossed lightly in the air, recaught, and swallowed in a smooth, quick movement. Larger prey is generally speared with an accurate thrust of the powerful beak and if this is not enough to kill it, it is held in the beak and beaten against the water surface or against a floating stick or other piece of debris until dead, then torn apart and eaten.

## NEST AND NESTING HABITS

The American Bittern, unlike the other North American heron species, does not nest in colonies or even in small groups, but in separate pairs. The nesting is always on the ground level, or just above the water level in a nest constructed of reeds and either suspended just over the water or built up to be several inches above the surface. In the latter case it is built by the birds bending down dead dry reed stalks—or sometimes live ones—and forming them into a suspended platform in which some sticks may also be woven. The nests formed on the surface are also of reed material, usually either those that have been bent over or else material collected from close by where it has been floating in the water. At any rate, such a nest, loosely constructed, is built up to form an almost flat 7-inch platform a few inches above water level. At times the nest will be as much as a foot in diameter. There is practically no depression whatever in it for the eggs, but somehow the eggs manage to stay on the platform, even in severe weather. Rarely will the nest—either the suspended one or the one on the water surface—be constructed in an area where the water depth is over 18 inches. Now and then an American Bittern will nest in wet meadows or even in deeper grasses of dry fields.

Almost without exception, the American Bittern constructs out of trampled-down reeds or grasses two paths leading away from the nest. The bird lands at the end of one and walks to the nest through it, but exits from the nest using the other path, not going into flight until it has emerged from the opposite end. If the bird feels danger is close by, it may land at the end of the pathway it has built, but take anywhere from ten to twenty minutes just to walk the forty feet to the nest. In other areas of the marsh, where it is not following premade paths, the American Bittern will often walk a foot or so above the water by grasping clumps of reeds in the feet and moving along in a very agile manner and with surprising swiftness. Quite frequently a canopy of growing reeds will be bent over the nest by the American Bittern, hiding it from view. However well it hides its nest and endeavors to keep its location secret, by the time the nesting season is well under way, the whole nest area is pretty well befouled by fecal waste from the parent birds, and in time from the young ones as well.

## EGGS AND INCUBATION

Usually four or five eggs are laid. They are brownish-olive drab with a gray undertone, which matches exactly the coloration of dry cattail stalks, and which therefore helps in concealment of the eggs. The shell is smooth and has a slight gloss. The average egg size is 1.9 inches x 1.5 inches (49mm x 37mm).

Incubation begins with the second or third egg laid, and is primarily the responsibility of the female. Each egg requires twenty-four days of incubation. As the incubation (and later the brooding) proceeds, new cattail growth tends to cover the nest and make it even less visible than at the outset.

## YOUNG

Newly hatched nestlings are well covered with a long fluffy down of light buff coloration on back, rump, and head. On the underside the down is lighter in color and not as thick. The eyes are

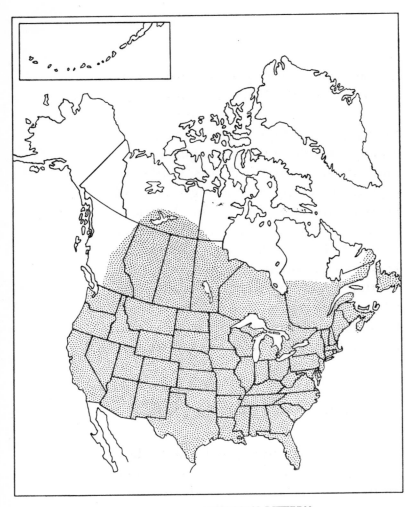

AMERICAN BITTERN

*Botaurus lentiginosus* (Rackett)

jerks her about. This causes the muscles of her throat to begin working in convulsive spasms. She drops her head and neck flat on the nest for a moment and then regurgitation occurs. All the young in the nest are fed at the same feeding and each, upon being fed, lies flat in the nest and rests.

## MIGRATION

The American Bittern is migratory, but the migrational flights are normally solitary, without the company of others of the same or other species. On the whole, it is more inclined to stay farther north in winter than any of the other herons of this continent. It has, for example, been found in winter as far north as Massachusetts in subzero weather. However, the population generally withdraws considerably farther south in winter, especially into the Gulf coastal regions, and most particularly to Florida. Florida's population of American Bitterns during summer, however, is very slight. The Everglades in Florida become heavily populated with American Bitterns during the winter months.

## ECONOMIC INFLUENCE

The American Bittern is, on the whole, considered to be a beneficial bird, largely because of the large numbers of injurious insects and crayfish which make up its diet.

yellow, the feet are flesh-colored with a greenish cast, and the entire beak is flesh-colored. By the time the nestlings are seven to ten days of age, they are already one half adult size and juvenile plumage has begun appearing. They begin leaving the nest at fourteen days.

Feeding of the nestlings is much the same as among the other heron species, through regurgitation by the adults. When the parent bird comes to the nest, the young become extremely excited and leap about until one grips her beak crosswise at the base and shakes and

# *IXOBRYCHUS* BITTERNS

---

GENUS: *IXOBRYCHUS* Billberg

SPECIES: *EXILIS* (Gmelin)

SUBSPECIES: *exilis* (Gmelin)

Eastern Least Bittern

*hesperis* Dickey & van Rossem

Western Least Bittern

## COMMON NAME

Eastern Least Bittern
(Color Plate XIII)

## SCIENTIFIC NAME

*Ixobrychus exilis exilis* (Gmelin). *Ixobrychus* is from the Greek, meaning deep bird lime; *exilis* is Latin for slender.

## OTHER COMMON OR COLLOQUIAL NAMES

CORY'S BITTERN After the form which was temporarily accepted as a subspecies and, later, a color phase.

LEAST HERON Former common name prior to separation of Eastern and Western forms of the Least Bittern.

## SHAPE AT REST AND IN FLIGHT

This is the smallest North American member of the heron family, and its small size immediately separates it from other heron species. In basic form it is very similar to the American Bittern, but in size it is no larger than the Wilson's snipe or the eastern meadowlark. When it is seen at rest, it is often in an uncommonly distorted pose, its body compressed into an extremely narrow form. *Ixobrychus exilis exilis* has short wings and a short tail. On brief flights, which are normally all it takes except during migrations, the long slender neck is extended, the feet are dangling, the wings are fluttering rapidly, and prominent buffy patches are visible on the wings. On long migrational flights the Least Bittern assumes more of the true heron flight posture, with neck drawn back, head tucked down between the shoulders, and legs drawn up and extended beyond the tail.

## LENGTH AND WINGSPAN

The Least Bittern has an average length of just under one foot (11.33 inches—291mm) and its wingspan averages less than a foot and a half (17.4 inches—446mm).

## BEAK

The slender beak is mostly pale yellow in coloration, with a dusky ridge ranging from brownish to blackish.

## LEGS AND FEET

The toes are yellow and the legs are a dull greenish.

## EYES

The irides are a very bright yellow and very distinct against the pale green coloration of the lores.

Rail-like in fligh[t]

Englewood florida
sept 20 - 1975

Kavalue

## CRESTS, PLUMAGE, ANNUAL MOLT

A complete annual molt takes place post-nuptially, beginning in late June or early July and extending into late August or early September. While there is a vague crest on the crown, there are no truly outstanding plumes, although the feathers of the lower neck are long and loose.

## VOICE

Far more silent than *Botaurus lentiginosus*, the Eastern Least Bittern is seldom heard or, if heard, the voice is seldom recognized by the listener. Yet, the bird has a fairly wide range of sounds. When intruded upon, it will sometimes hiss, and then utter a low *uk-uk-uk* sound. In the spring the male gives a soft cooing sound, of from five to eight notes, repeated for many minutes. This call will often draw a responsive clucking from the female, which the male evidently uses to locate her. When disturbed into flight, the bird utters a loud, harsh *qua* sound and, if really upset, flies off with a loud and rather startling *ca-ca-ca-ca*.

## SEXUAL DIFFERENCES: SIZE, COLORATION, VOICE

The sexes are dissimilar in size, coloration, and voice. The most apparent sexual difference is in coloration. The tail, back, and crown of the male bird

Least Bittern, *Ixobrychus exilis*.

are a glossy greenish-black, whereas these areas in the female are a dark chestnut in color; in addition, she has two white streaks along the shoulders. In young birds, the sexual difference in the plumage becomes apparent in the first spring, when the bird is approaching one year of age.

## COLORATION AND MARKINGS: JUVENILE

Juvenile coloration is similar to that of the adult female, but with the black feathers tipped with buff, and the crown and back plumage a lighter brown. Prominent dusky shaft streakings give a very distinct striped appearance to the upper breast and lower neck.

## GENERAL HABITS AND CHARACTERISTICS

Because it is so secretive and so retiring in its general habits, the Eastern Least Bittern is sometimes thought to be rare or even absent in areas where, in actuality, it is quite common. It is essentially a rather timid bird which endeavors to remain inconspicuous. It is rarely seen walking around on the ground or amid the reeds, but when it is seen in the shallows or walking on mud, matted vegetation in the water, or on dry land, its movements are quick and graceful, with the head characteristically shooting forward in a very distinctive manner at each step. This bird can compress its body laterally so much that it can pass through extremely narrow places.

## HABITAT AND ROOSTING

Cattail marshes, reedy swamps, along with margins of sluggish streams and ponds that are well grown with reeds, bulrushes, and heavy grasses, all these are habitat areas highly favored by the Eastern Least Bittern. Roosting is solitary. Freshwater marshy areas seem to be preferred, but the bird is no stranger to tidal flats and saltwater marshes, and it is sometimes seen moving about delicately through the most densely tangled coastal mangrove roots.

## ENEMIES AND DEFENSES

The principal natural enemies include birds of prey, crows, reptiles, and predatory mammals common to marshy habitat. Crows and snakes are especially detrimental to the eggs, and even the marsh wren has been observed deliberately destroying the unguarded eggs, though not eating them. Fledgling Least Bitterns evade danger or elude pursuit by climbing with great skill and speed among the reeds and hiding in the densest portions of reedy cover. The adult birds also escape danger by walking. Where the water is too deep for wading and the reeds grow closely together, the Eastern Least Bittern climbs swiftly through them about 2 or 3 feet above the water surface, as skillful in grasping the reeds with its feet and moving among them as a squirrel is in moving about in the trees. But, while able to slip away unnoticed in most cases, far more often the Eastern Least Bittern prefers to avoid danger by "freezing" in place and allowing its quite remarkable natural camouflage to hide it from any enemy.

## FOOD AND FEEDING HABITS

Insects, tiny fish, and small crustaceans make up the bulk of the Eastern Least Bittern's diet. Very young sunfish and perch, bluegills, topminnows, mud minnows, killifish, gambusias, and others are high on the preferential list, as are freshwater crayfish and such aquatic insects as dragonfly nymphs, giant water bugs, and marsh-dwelling caterpillars. Also eaten in fair amounts are frogs and tadpoles, shrews, mice, lizards, snails, very small snakes, leeches, and slugs. Almost the entire bulk of food is found by the bird within the marshy, reedy habitat in which it dwells. Only rarely will it leave this habitat to possibly catch grasshoppers in more open areas along the fringes of meadows and grassy fields.

## NEST AND NESTING HABITS

Most commonly the Eastern Least Bittern's nest is located in cattails and is itself made of cattails pushed and bent

---

XXI FLORIDA CRANE (left)

*Grus canadensis pratensis* Meyer. Englewood, Florida, July 10, 1974. A.O.U. Number 206a

SANDHILL CRANE

*Grus canadensis canadensis* (Linnaeus). Green Lake, Wisconsin, October 15, 1963. A.O.U. Number 205

LITTLE BROWN CRANE (right)

*Grus canadensis tabida* (Peters). Bassett, Nebraska, October 20, 1964. A.O.U. Number 206

XXII   WHOOPING CRANE

*Grus americana* (Linnaeus). Aransas National Wildlife Refuge, Texas. A.O.U. Number 204

Karl E. Karalus

Karl E. Karalus

Carl E. Karalus

Karl E. Karalus

down to form a loosely matted and yet fairly compact platform supported by the surrounding vegetation and from several inches to several feet above the water. The water itself is rarely over 2 feet deep where the nest is built. The same sort of nest construction is done in the Florida Everglades with saw grasses. The flat surface of the nest ordinarily measures about 5 inches x 7 inches. The Eastern Least Bittern is by no means gregarious and does not nest in colonies.

## EGGS AND INCUBATION

Normally there are four or five pale bluish-white smooth-shelled eggs which average 1.2 inches x .9 inch (31mm x 24mm). Though both sexes alternate in covering the nest, incubation, which takes sixteen to eighteen days, is primarily the responsibility of the female.

## YOUNG

The head and back of the young are fully covered with long, soft, buff-colored down. On the underside, this down is scantier and lighter in coloration. The young are fed by the typical heron family

---

XXIII   LIMPKIN

*Aramus guarauna pictus* (Meyer). Female. Moore County, Florida. July 10, 1956. A.O.U. Number 207

XXIV   KING RAIL

*Rallus elegans elegans* Audubon. Bensenville, Du Page County, Illinois, August 30, 1963. A.O.U. Number 208

EASTERN LEAST BITTERN

*Ixobrychus exilis exilis* (Gmelin)

method of regurgitation. If young birds are discovered, they will not hesitate to thrust their beaks with considerable viciousness at the intruder if he comes close enough.

## MIGRATION

The Eastern Least Bittern withdraws in winter from a very large portion of its northern summer range and tends to congregate in the Gulf coastal areas as well as the middle halves of the southern states and also into Mexico, Central America, and South America. In winter it has been found as far north as northern Georgia and central South Carolina, as well as central Arizona and southern California.

# COMMON NAME

Western Least Bittern
(Color Plate XIV)

# SCIENTIFIC NAME

*Ixobrychus exilis hesperis* Dickey & van Rossem. *Hesperis* is Greek for western.

# BASIC SUBSPECIFIC DIFFERENCES

The Western Least Bittern differs from the Eastern Least Bittern in that the former is considerably larger.

**WESTERN LEAST BITTERN**

*Ixobrychus exilis hesperis* Dickey & van Rossem

# WOOD STORK

---

| | |
|---:|:---|
| SUBORDER: | *CICONIAE* |
| SUPERFAMILY: | *CICONIOIDEA* |
| FAMILY: | *CICONIIDAE* |
| SUBFAMILY: | *MYCTERIINAE* |
| GENUS: | *MYCTERIA* Linnaeus |
| SPECIES: | *AMERICANA* Linnaeus |

## COMMON NAME

Wood Stork
(Color Plate XV)

## SCIENTIFIC NAME

*Mycteria americana* Linnaeus. From the Greek *mycteros*, meaning nose.

## OTHER COMMON OR COLLOQUIAL NAMES

FLINTHEAD The most commonly used colloquial name, especially favored in Florida and other southern states; after the dark, bare, flintlike head.

GOURDHEAD (Sometimes written as Goardhead.) After the naked gourdlike head of the bird.

IRONHEAD See derivation of Flinthead.

PREACHER For the solemn demeanor the bird often assumes as it stands motionless and contemplative, especially after a heavy meal.

WOOD IBIS Formerly the common name, though changed because the term ibis is inaccurate.

## SHAPE AT REST AND IN FLIGHT

The Wood Stork assumes, at rest, a very hunched posture, often perched on just one leg, head drawn in on shoulders, the huge beak resting on the breast feathers and pointing downward, the whole mien one of solemnity or dejection. It is a big white bird, 10 to 12 pounds, with a bare head and a huge beak. These traits, along with its distinctive combination of white and black plumage, unmistakably identify it in the field.

This is also an easily recognizable bird in flight, jet-black flight feathers contrasting with the prevailing whiteness of the bird, a long neck fully extended, long legs which trail far beyond the short black tail, and a very heavy beak. The black flight feathers make a fringe of black on the outer edge and rear of the outspread wing. The wingbeat is regular and strong, sometimes alternately flapping and gliding.

Now and then great flocks of the birds rise together and engage in spectacular aerial displays, seemingly for the sheer enjoyment of flying. The entire flock rises in an ever heightening spiral, the birds crossing and recrossing as they rise until they are mere specks in the sky and all but lost to human vision. For a while all will flap in unison and then, as if on signal, all will set their wings and sail along in great smooth circles. Abruptly the entire flock will dive down toward the earth, their plummeting bodies fairly whistling through the air and seeming sure to crash into the marsh or swamp below. Then, at the last moment, the great wings cup the air and thrust them into a long low glide which once more becomes a great spiraling climb upward to repeat the whole process. This is one of the really thrilling sights of nature.

## LENGTH AND WINGSPAN

The average length of the Wood Stork is just short of 44 inches (43.8 inches—

1123mm) and its average wingspan is
63.6 inches (1631mm).

## BEAK

The beak is not only long (8.7 inches
average), is is unusually thick, normally
measuring about 2 inches through at the
base. It is a dingy yellow on the sides
and the lower mandible, and dusky
along the upper ridge. It does not have
a nasal groove or membrane and the
nostrils directly perforate the beak high
up at the base of the upper mandible.
It is a long stout beak, gradually tapering
and ending in a downward curve at the
tip.

## LEGS, FEET, AND CLAWS

The toes are well lengthened and the
claws are compressed. The tibia, bare
for half its length, averages about
160mm in length (6.24 inches), and the
middle toe and claw average 123.70mm
(4.82 inches). The legs of the Wood
Stork range from a deep bluish-gray to
bluish-black, with the toes blackish. The
anterior toes are webbed at the base and
this webbing is tinged with yellow.

## EYES

The irides are a deep brown, so dark
as to appear almost black under certain
conditions of light.

## CRESTS, PLUMAGE, ANNUAL MOLT

The Wood Stork has no crests nor
even any peculiar plumage. A complete
molt of the adults occurs annually beginning in September, and this molt is normally completed by early November.

## VOICE

*Mycteria americana* is capable of producing quite a variety of sounds, although in most circumstances it is an
essentially silent species. The most commonly uttered note is a deep, grating
croak ordinarily uttered when the bird
has been disturbed or has become
frightened. The Wood Stork can also
voice very sharp and grating squalling
noises. The young birds make a sound
similar to the squeaking of a newly
hatched alligator. They also croak like
bullfrogs.

## SEXUAL DIFFERENCES: SIZE, COLORATION, VOICE

The male bird has a deeper voice and
is larger than the female, often by a considerable margin. There are no differences in coloration or markings.

## COLORATION AND MARKINGS: ADULT

Mostly, the plumage is all pure white,
the only exceptions being that the primaries, the primary coverts, and the rectrices are all rather blackish—the flight

*Wood Stork*

feathers a distinct bronzed greenish-black and the tail a similarly bronzed bluish-black, but sometimes shading to greenish. The head is bare of plumage and crowned with a horny plate. The naked, scaly skin of the head and down the neck is a dark blackish-gray.

## COLORATION AND MARKINGS: JUVENILE

In juvenile birds up until the time of the first molt, the head is well covered with a fuzzy brown down. This same down also covers the neck. All this fuzz, however, disappears with the first molt. The plumage is quite different in coloration from that of the adults, a dark grayish as opposed to the adult bird's white, and with the blackish feathering showing much less of the glaucous green.

## GENERAL HABITS AND CHARACTERISTICS

This is an uncommonly gregarious bird at almost all times and is rarely if ever seen alone. In eating, roosting, nesting, migration, and all other activities, it prefers the company of its own kind and often the company of other wading birds as well, such as Roseate Spoonbills, Great Egrets, Great Blue Herons, White Ibises, and others. However, gregarious though it is, occasionally small groups of birds, numbering from three or four to a half dozen or more, will break away from the main flock and wander off together. The Wood Stork is the only native stork in North America north of Mexico.

## HABITAT AND ROOSTING

Thickly wooded swamps and marshes with dense growths of reeds and bushes are especially favored areas, although now and again the Wood Stork will forsake the favored woodlands of cypress and mangrove for open pasturelands, sloughs, pond edges, and even roadside ditches. Though generally a freshwater bird, it is frequently observed in saltwater marshes as well. The hot, moist bottomlands of the southern states are greatly favored, especially in conjunction with stands of water oaks, large stands of cypress, willows, tupelo, and gums heavy with Spanish moss, and dense underbrush interlaced with tangled vines in areas of dark muddy pools of water. Such areas are favorite roosts of the Wood Stork, where hundreds, perhaps even thousands, of the birds gather.

## FOOD AND FEEDING HABITS

Wood Storks eat a wide variety of small life from the swamps and marshes they habitually visit. Fish of any kind, as long as they are small enough to be handled, frogs, baby alligators, water snakes, lizards, minnows, wood rats, fiddler crabs and other crustaceans, nestling grackles and rails, small turtles, tadpoles, water beetles, dragonfly nymphs, a variety of seeds, mosses and pond slime, catfish, carp, and crickets—all these and more make up the diet of the Wood Stork.

WOOD STORK

*Mycteria americana* Linnaeus

tion between two branches. On an especially favored branch there may be half a dozen nests in a row, the edges of each touching one another. As many as five thousand nests in one nesting rookery is not uncommon. On rare occasions, if tall trees are not available, they will nest in the very tops of shorter trees, such as red mangroves about 20 feet high.

For such a large bird, the nests are small and surprisingly flimsy. On the base of interwoven twigs, finer twigs are laced, mixed with finer stems and twigs of willows, oaks, maples, cypress, and other woody growth. The nest, when completed, is usually no more than 1.5 feet in diameter and about 5 inches thick, but with very little depression in the top for the eggs. Occasionally it is lined with Spanish moss or green leaves. Although these big birds are inclined to sharing their feeding areas with other wading birds, this is not the case with the nesting areas and they will normally drive away other birds which attempt to nest in their vicinity.

## NEST AND NESTING HABITS

Stands of huge cypress trees rising from water are the favorite nesting areas of the Wood Storks, although they will nest in other trees as well. They much prefer a high nest, from 50 to 100 feet up. Every major tree within the rookery is occupied by nests, with some of the larger trees containing as many as five to fifteen nests. At times the nests are so close together they are almost touching. A typical nest is constructed basically of large twigs, many of them torn from living trees and bushes by the birds, and interwoven together on a sturdy branch, especially at a good junc-

## EGGS AND INCUBATION

Two or three chalky white (but occasionally brown-stained) eggs are laid; the shells range from smooth-surfaced to rather rough and flaky. They are large eggs, averaging 2.7 inches x 1.8 inches (68mm x 46mm).

An interval of about forty to fifty hours (sometimes even longer) occurs between the laying of each egg. Both parent birds incubate, though the female somewhat more extensively than the male. Term of incubation is twenty-seven to thirty days and begins with the first egg laid.

*Wood Stork*

## YOUNG

When first hatched, the young are partially covered with a dense white down almost like wool, but the front half of the nestling's head and the spaces of skin between the feather tracts remain bare. The young tend to be noisy in the nest and this tendency increases for the first two thirds of their nest life, after which it decreases sharply.

As soon as they are large enough and strong enough, they begin leaving the nest and perching on the nearby branches, not infrequently losing their balance and hanging by necks and toes, flapping their wings desperately in an effort to regain their perch.

# *PLEGADIS* IBISES

---

SUPERFAMILY: *THRESKIORNITHOIDAE*
FAMILY: *THRESKIORNITHIDAE*
SUBFAMILY: *THRESKIORNITHINAE*
GENUS: *PLEGADIS* Kaup

---

SPECIES: *FALCINELLUS* (Linnaeus)
SUBSPECIES: *falcinellus* (Linnaeus)
Glossy Ibis

---

SPECIES: *CHIHI* Vieillot
White-Faced Ibis

## COMMON NAME

Glossy Ibis
(Color Plate XVI)

## SCIENTIFIC NAME

*Plegadis falcinellus falcinellus* (Linnaeus). From *plegadis*, Greek, meaning small sickle, after the shape of the bird's beak, and *falcinellus*, Latin, also meaning small sickle.

## OTHER COMMON OR COLLOQUIAL NAMES

BLACK CURLEW Because of its general coloration and, erroneously, because of its resemblance, due to the curved beak, to a curlew.

GREEN IBIS After the glaucous or somewhat metallic bronze-greenish cast to the feathers, especially under ideal conditions of sunlight.

SPANISH CURLEW "Spanish" origin uncertain, and "curlew" erroneously after the species it resembles to some degree.

## SHAPE AT REST AND IN FLIGHT

A slender, relatively long-necked bird with very distinctively downturned beak, which makes a graceful downward arc from base to tip. The shape of the head and beak is very reminiscent of that of the curlews, but this ibis is darker and larger than any curlew species.

In flight it presents a long, slender silhouette, with neck and head outstretched and held at a downward angle, and legs trailing behind. Flight is characterized by a generally rapid flapping and gliding at low altitudes, rarely over 500 feet.

## LENGTH AND WINGSPAN

The Glossy Ibis averages 2 feet in length (615mm) and has an average wingspan of 3 feet (922mm).

## LEGS AND FEET

The legs are grayish-black and the feet are equally dark.

## EYES

The irides are brown and the lores are a slaty bluish and broadly naked, with the bare space embracing the eye.

## CRESTS, PLUMAGE, ANNUAL MOLT

A complete molt occurs among the Glossy Ibises once a year beginning in mid-July and ending by late October. The plumages and molts of the Glossy Ibis are very similar to those of *Plegadis chihi.* (the White-Faced Ibis, see page 141).

## VOICE

Both adult sexes utter a very soft crooning sound in the midst of courtship and as they approach the nest throughout the nesting season. This sound is in marked contrast to their ordinary sound, a sort of bleating grunt, not unlike that made by the White Ibis, *Eudocimus albus*.

## SEXUAL DIFFERENCES: SIZE, COLORATION, VOICE

In coloration and voice the sexes are identical.

## COLORATION AND MARKINGS: ADULT

In general, the plumage is a rich purplish-chestnut with a greenish and purplish metallic iridescence on the crown, back, rump, wings, and tail. These are very distinct colorations, but the glaucous nature can only be seen well at close range. From a distance the bird looks entirely black.

## COLORATION AND MARKINGS: JUVENILE

The head and neck of the juvenile ranges from grayish-brown to grayish-black and is streaked with white. The upper parts are generally a dusky green with a metallic bronze-greenish gloss, while the underparts are an ordinary dull brownish-gray.

## GENERAL HABITS AND CHARACTERISTICS

The Glossy Ibis is a fairly quiet bird, content to perch, wade about, and fly in relative silence. It is gregarious within certain limitations with its own species, and occasionally with other ibises.

## HABITAT AND ROOSTING

The principal habitat is extensive marshland dotted well with low hammocks of tangled brush and low trees and with, here and there, well-hidden little lakes and ponds. Flooded meadows are also appealing, but the Glossy Ibis rarely lands along canals or ditches. Most roosting is done in densely overgrown willow islands or hammocks, such as those found centrally located in the Everglades. Especially favored for a roost are islands of this nature which have, in their centers, well-hidden little lakes. Although the Glossy Ibis will roost here with other species, it generally remains in little pockets of its own kind rather than intermingling.

## FOOD AND FEEDING HABITS

The Glossy Ibis is very definite about establishing feeding areas it particularly likes and then frequenting these areas to the exclusion of others, even though there may be no apparent difference in terrain or the sort of food available. It is not at all unusual for the Glossy Ibis, leaving its roosting area in the early morning, to fly fully 20 miles to a favorite feeding area, when just such an area may be within a mile or two of the roosting area. A wide range of food is eaten, though cutworms, grasshoppers, crayfish, and snakes make up the bulk of its intake. Water insects, frogs, and lizards, along with some snails and tadpoles, complete the Glossy Ibis' diet.

## NEST AND NESTING HABITS

In by far the majority of cases, nest-site selection is made by the female, but construction of the nest is undertaken by both birds. The nest is sloppily made of poorly interwoven twigs and is rarely completed before the female lays her eggs. Initial construction takes the pair two days, but after the young birds hatch, additional material is often added to the nest. If the first nest is destroyed, as often happens, a whole new nest will be constructed and more eggs laid.

Most nests are located about 10 to 20 feet high in dense tangles of brush and low trees, most often over shallow water. The Glossy Ibis is very jealous about its nesting area and will not permit any other species, regardless of size, to build its nest within 10 to 12 feet of its own. Sometimes it will tolerate such a nearby nest for a while, but when its own eggs are ready to hatch it will attack the other bird, even if it is the size of a Great Blue Heron, and eventually run it off. Then it will watch with disinterest as fish crows steal the eggs from the other nest, after which the Glossy Ibis will itself dismantle the other nest and sometimes use the twigs as additional material in its own nest. The nest is usually 1 to 1.5 feet in diameter and has a reasonably well-formed cup in the center.

**GLOSSY IBIS**

*Plegadis falcinellus falcinellus* (Linnaeus)

## EGGS AND INCUBATION

Normally four pastel greenish-blue smooth-shelled eggs are laid which have an average size of 2 inches x 1.4 inches (52mm x 37mm). The eggs are laid about twenty-four hours apart. Incubation does not begin until fully twenty-four hours after the last egg of the clutch has been laid. This incubation, which lasts for twenty-one days, is accomplished by both parents. The female incubates about eighteen hours out of each twenty-four.

## YOUNG

The beak of the downy young is yellowish and black, and the feet are yellow. During the first five days after hatching, the young are never left alone in the nest. One parent is always on hand. When the adult bird feeds the young, the food is regurgitated into the throat, not into the beak, as is the case with the herons. The young Glossy Ibis then shoves its own head and beak into its parent's mouth and feeds. One young bird is fed until it is entirely filled before another is fed. It takes only about two minutes to feed one of the nestlings and there is rarely a wait of over three minutes before the next nestling is fed. The young Glossy Ibises remain in the nest for six weeks, until they are able to fly. At this point they begin flying with their parents to the feeding ground and return with them at night to roost at the nest.

## MIGRATION

There is a casual, disbursement sort of migrational movement northward and westward following the nesting season, and a very strong autumn and spring migration. Winter range in the North American continent is seldom north of southernmost Florida.

---

XXV   NORTHERN CLAPPER RAIL

*Rallus longirostris crepitans* Gmelin. Yorktown, Virginia. A.O.U. Number 211

XXVI   VIRGINIA RAIL

*Rallus limicola limicola* Vieillot. Franklin Park, Illinois. A.O.U. Number 212

*Glossy Ibis*

Karl E. Karalus

Karl E. Karalus

Karl E. Karalus

Karl E Karalus

## COMMON NAME

White-Faced Ibis
(Color Plate XVI)

## SCIENTIFIC NAME

*Plegadis chihi* Vieillot.

## OTHER COMMON OR
## COLLOQUIAL NAMES

BLACK CURLEW Because of its coloration and its basic similarity in form to the curlew; term mainly used by hunters of this bird in California.

BRONZE IBIS After its general coloration; term used most commonly in Texas.

## SHAPE AT REST AND
## IN FLIGHT

Very similar in silhouette to the smaller curlew, with smooth slender

---

**XXVII SORA**

*Porzana carolina* (Linnaeus). Cape Haze, Placida, Charlotte County, Florida, September 14, 1956. A.O.U. Number 214 (Mrs. Joan D. Eckert, collector)

**XXVIII YELLOW RAIL**

*Coturnicops noveboracensis noveboracensis* (Gmelin). Cicero and 111 Street, Cook County, Illinois, April 17, 1937. A.O.U. Number 215

body, erect posture, longish neck, and smoothly arched, downcurved, slender beak. The White-Faced Ibis is difficult to distinguish in flight from the Glossy Ibis.

## LENGTH AND WINGSPAN

The White-Faced Ibis has an average length of 23.4 inches (599mm) and an average wingspan of 38.9 inches (996mm).

## CRESTS, PLUMAGE,
## ANNUAL MOLT

The feathers of the head sweep down the forehead, framing the bare skin of the face, and extend back beyond the eye in a posterior point. There are no particular plumes or crests at any season. Adults have a partial pre-nuptial molt beginning in March and a complete post-nuptial molt in July and August.

## COLORATION AND
## MARKINGS: ADULT

In outward appearances the White-Faced Ibis is identical to the Glossy Ibis except for the margin of white feathering that rims the bare flesh of the face and is fairly obvious even from short distances. Legs and feet are dusky reddish. The irides are bright red.

## COLORATION AND MARKINGS: JUVENILE

With traces of the down still remaining, the first plumage of the young birds is highly lustrous and iridescent. It is almost entirely bronze-greenish, without the violets, reds, and purples of the adults. When adult plumage finally appears, the greenish gives way to grayish-brown and then to the purplish-reds. In its first winter plumage, the young bird is lightly and irregularly streaked with light brownish and dull white on the body, while head and neck are already covered with adult plumage.

## HABITAT AND ROOSTING

*Plegadis chihi* shows a marked preference for tule swamps and marshes, marshy prairies, and lake margins well grown with reeds and rushes. It rarely roosts in trees, as does *Plegadis falcinellus falcinellus,* preferring to roost on low platforms of dead reed stems and rush piles amid heavy cover of marsh or swamp. Sometimes it roosts in plain sight on mud banks or projecting land spits in lakes or streams.

## ENEMIES AND DEFENSES

Man had been and to some extent still is the worst enemy of the White-Faced Ibis. Unfortunately for the species, it has a very fine-tasting flesh and was once a game species. Now it is protected, but still taken illegally in considerable numbers annually, as is the case with the White Ibis in Florida, *Eudocimus albus.*

## FOOD AND FEEDING HABITS

*Plegadis chihi* feeds primarily along riverbanks and the shallow shorelines of ponds, lakes, pools, marshes, and swamps, as well as along sluggish streams to a lesser degree. It also frequents marshy meadows, especially those where the ground tends to be torn up by cattle or other stock animals, because these are areas where it finds earthworms and other prey it favors. Almost any small vertebrate or invertebrate animals are eaten, along with a small amount of vegetative matter, but the principal diet items are, in addition to earthworms, crayfish, small mollusks, snails, insects and their larvae, small fish, frogs, leeches, newts, and slugs.

## NEST AND NESTING HABITS

Unlike the herons, the White-Faced Ibis makes a rather compact and well-constructed nest with a deep cup that is well and smoothly lined with fine tule reeds and grasses; the outer portion of the nest is 12 to 14 inches in diameter and formed of tightly interwoven dead tule reeds from the preceding year. It does not normally nest in trees or bushes, as does the Glossy Ibis, but instead builds its nest 10 or 12 inches above the water in thick stands of rushes or reeds and attached to these plants. Now and then the nests are actually partially afloat in the water. Almost invariably the water where the nests are built is less than 3 feet deep, but at least 2 feet in depth. The birds nest in very large rookeries numbering, at times, in the thousands of individual birds. They also nest in amiable conjunction with some of the herons.

## EGGS AND INCUBATION

Most often three or four eggs are laid which initially are a rather distinct pastel blue or green, but which soon fade to nearly white. Though usually smooth-shelled, sometimes the shells are finely pitted or granulated. The average egg size is 2 inches x 1.4 inches (52mm x 36mm).

The term of incubation is twenty-one days and is done by both parents, the female predominating.

## YOUNG

A very dull, unattractive blackish down covers the nestlings and there is a distinctive whitish patch at the back of the crown. The beak is a pale flesh color with a tip of black, a blackish base, and a black band in the middle. (This unusual beak coloration is also a characteristic of the juvenile plumage and does not disappear until the post-nuptial molt in September.) The young birds in the nest are uncommonly timid and, as soon as they are capable of it, they will flee the nest at any disturbance whatever, throwing themselves into the water and flapping across it to the nearest cover where they hide until the danger is past, at which time they return in less haste to the nest.

**WHITE-FACED IBIS**

*Plegadis chihi* Vieillot

## MIGRATION

The species withdraws from most of its northern range in the autumn and moves into semitropical or tropical climes, remaining in the United States primarily in Florida and to a lesser extent in Louisiana and Texas coastal areas, and in southernmost California. Ordinarily the birds have withdrawn from the northern range by mid-October, and begin returning in late March or early April.

# *EUDOCIMUS* IBISES

---

GENUS:   *EUDOCIMUS* Wagler
SPECIES:  *ALBUS* (Linnaeus)
             White Ibis
             *RUBER* (Linnaeus)
             Scarlet Ibis

# COMMON NAME

White Ibis
(Color Plate XVII)

## SCIENTIFIC NAME

*Eudocimus albus* (Linnaeus). *Eudocimus* from the Latin, meaning well known or familiar; *albus* also from the Latin, meaning white.

## OTHER COMMON OR COLLOQUIAL NAMES

CURLEW Because of its curved beak, resembling that of the curlews.

SPANISH CURLEW Allegedly because it was extensively hunted by the Spanish in Florida as food.

WHITE CURLEW For coloration and beak resemblance to curlews.

## SHAPE AT REST AND IN FLIGHT

This bird often stands dozing or looking about on bare tree branches, sometimes alone, frequently in groups of three to a dozen. If merely looking about, it generally stands erect with head held high. If dozing or resting, it often stands on one leg with the other drawn up and out of sight in the underside plumage, its head hunched down on the shoulders in heron fashion and the distinctly curved beak resting on its breast plumage.

In flight, the bird's head and neck, though outstretched, are angled slightly downward. The wings are fairly broad and the long curved beak is plainly visible in flight.

The flight of *Eudocimus albus* is characterized by rapid wingbeats interspersed by occasional to frequent periods of gliding. Usually such flight is in formation with others in long lines that are either straight abreast or diagonal. The flight is fairly swift and direct, and ordinarily quite low, seldom over 150 feet high. This is particularly true during the morning and evening flights to and from feeding and roosting areas. Sometimes the entire flock will perform spectacular acrobatics, including steep dives and recoveries, with such evolutions generally beginning at a very high altitude. The White Ibis is very partial to soaring high on thermals, as are Wood Storks.

## LENGTH AND WINGSPAN

The average length of the White Ibis is 26 inches (666mm) and its average wingspan is 39.3 inches (1008mm).

## BEAK

The 6-inch beak is curved downward for its entire length, from base to tip.

Myakka River
Charlotte co Florida

feet and Legs rather stout
compared to other Wading birds

wing tip
of white
Ibis

Button wood Rookery
Englewood Florida

white Ibis
Euclocimus albus

immature

Grass shrimp
Leptochela . SP.

* Grass shrimp and Larval
Stages of other Shrimps
and Some small crabs appear
to be the main food of
the Ibis and Spoon bills
at Buttonwood Rookery

* from stomach
contents.

K.E. Karalus

## EYES

The irides of the adults are a distinctive pearly blue, and those of the young birds are brownish.

## CRESTS, PLUMAGE, ANNUAL MOLT

There are no crests or unusually developed plumes at any time of the year. The adults undergo a complete postnuptial molt from early July usually into late September. There is also an incomplete prenuptial molt in late December and January. The face of the bird is bare of plumage and dull reddish at all times except after prenuptial molt, when this area becomes brilliant red.

## VOICE

The White Ibis is not a particularly vocal bird even during breeding season. If disturbed, it will rise and fly away with a peculiar soft grunting call similar to a muted honking. During the breeding season the females are normally silent, while the males make only a few soft cooing sounds and a gurgling sound sometimes repeated for several minutes and similar to a deep-throated *ulla-ulla-ulla.*

Studies of White Ibis and spoonbills made at Buttonwood Rookery and on the Myakka River, in Charlotte County, Florida.

## COLORATION AND MARKINGS: ADULT

The breeding plumage and non-breeding plumage are about the same, except that the latter has more dusky mottlings on the hind neck and crown rather than pure white. The beak, legs, and feet and the naked area of the face tend to range from flesh-colored to pinkish during the greater part of the year, but become bright red during the breeding season. There is also a throat sac—gular pouch—which becomes visibly extendable during breeding.

## COLORATION AND MARKINGS: JUVENILE

A very strong combination of contrasting dark brown and white, though the head is actually grayish. The browns are rich in tone but fade until by late winter they are dingy. The legs of young birds are bluish. The irides are brownish. In the first prenuptial molt the young are still mottled, but generally with more white than before. At the first complete postnuptial molt (when the young bird is about fifteen months old) an almost-adult plumage is assumed, but with a few immature traces remaining. Complete adult plumage is not assumed until the second postnuptial molt, when the bird is over two years of age.

## GENERAL HABITS AND CHARACTERISTICS

The White Ibis is generally rather active while on the ground, ordinarily feeding in the shallows and moving about in a sprightly manner, or even continuing the general activity as it groups with others in the low branches of mangroves or high in cypresses. It walks gracefully on the ground, swims well if the need arises, and flies smoothly. It can also climb quite well among the branches, beginning at an early age. Often it will perch for long periods of preening on an open branch. It enjoys the company of its fellows and other waders, such as the Wood Stork and Roseate Spoonbill, but is not garrulous.

## HABITAT AND ROOSTING

The White Ibis particularly likes small brushy islands, especially for roosting and nesting, but for feeding, it prefers more open shallow waters of pond margins, shallow swamp, and marsh waters and at times shows a keen fondness for flooded meadowlands. It prefers areas that are muddy to those which are sandy, but will frequent either. The birds especially like exposed tidal flats. Preferred roost tree include myrtle, mangrove, willow, cypress, elders, and bays. When approaching the roosts in the evening, they often travel in long wavering lines, sometimes numerous in the extreme and coming from all directions.

## ENEMIES AND DEFENSES

Man remains an enemy, for even though the bird is now fully protected by law, its flesh is so prized as meat that it is still illegally hunted in much of its range.

## FOOD AND FEEDING HABITS

Insects, crustaceans, and small snakes are the principal foods. Cutworms are a very big item in the diet, as are crayfish. Grasshoppers, too, are eaten in abundance, and, to a slightly lesser extent, fiddler crabs and soldier crabs. Snails and slugs are eaten, as are the larvae of many insects, especially aquatic varieties.

The White Ibis has developed an enterprising manner of hunting successfully for crayfish. In dry weather, when crayfish must burrow to reach water, they leave behind telltale mounds of mud at the hole entry. The White Ibis, seeing one of these, approaches quietly and, with the long curved beak, nudges some of the mud back into the hole. The bird then steps back a step or two and waits. In a short while the crayfish appears at the entry to dispose of the mud again on the pile already built up. As soon as it emerges from the hole as much as it is going to, the bird darts forward and snatches it.

## COURTSHIP AND MATING

Although the breeding coloration changes for both sexes, it is most vividly changed in the male, with the fleshy coloration of beak, face, gular pouch, and legs becoming brilliant red. Occasionally, though, the redness, which is common, gives way to a bright red-orange or true orange. The gular pouch extends about a half inch below the beak and is ordinarily a turkey red in coloration. When this pouch is distended, the male sometimes makes low cooing or clucking sounds to the female, which she may or may not echo.

## NEST AND NESTING HABITS

White Ibises nest in considerable colonies of their own species, but also frequently in close conjunction with herons, egrets, anhingas, grackles, and other birds. The nesting area is usually the outer fringe area of a hammock or island of dense brushy growth. If the island or hammock has a pond or lake in its center, then often the nesting will take place adjacent to or even overhanging this water. Often numerous nests will be in the same tree and from as low as 3 or 4 feet to as high as 20, but usually around 15 feet in height.

The nest is a poorly constructed one of coarse sticks, with a small depression in the center, that is occasionally lined with Spanish moss, leaves, or grasses. Sometimes, however, the eggs will be laid on the bare twigs. Surprisingly, for the size of the bird, the nests are quite small, often no more than 6 or 7 inches in diameter and seemingly hardly big enough to hold more than one or two eggs. In most cases, the nesting areas are inland, rather than in the immediate coastal areas.

## EGGS AND INCUBATION

Ordinarily four eggs are laid which are creamy-buff in color, often with some blotchings of brown at the larger end. The shell is smooth or very finely granulated and the average egg size is 2.25 inches x 1.5 inches (58mm x 40mm).

The incubation period is twenty-one

WHITE IBIS

*Eudocimus albus* (Linnaeus)

days and the incubation duties are shared by both parents on a relatively equal basis.

## YOUNG

The downy young, which peep much like chicks fresh from the egg, have glossy black heads, brownish-black throats and necks, and a mouse-gray body down, darker above than below. The beak is a pale flesh color with a dark tip and dark central band. Even when still unable to fly, the young birds are adept at climbing and usually move about in the trees around their nesting area with great agility. Falls are rare and when they do occur, the young bird swims to the first emergent branches and crawls out again quickly. In climbing, it uses not only its feet, but beak and wings as well. Within five weeks the young are able to fly and very quickly after this they are abandoned by the parents.

## MIGRATION

There is a general northerly movement of some degree from the breeding range in late summer and early autumn, but this does not last very long. During this period, however, individuals may appear with some regularity in southern California and, in the middle portion of its North American breeding range, as far north as Colorado, Illinois, Minnesota (rarely), Missouri, South Dakota, Ohio, New Jersey, New York, Pennsylvania, Virginia, North Carolina, and occasionally even Vermont.

## ECONOMIC INFLUENCE

The White Ibis, because of its propensity for devouring grasshoppers which cause crop damage, and crayfish which feed on the spawn of fish which are good mosquito controllers, is generally considered a very valuable and economically beneficial bird. In past years it was considered valuable for the quality of its flesh as table fare.

## COMMON NAME

Scarlet Ibis
(Color Plate XVIII)

## SCIENTIFIC NAME

*Eudocimus ruber* (Linnaeus). *Ruber* is Latin for red.

## OTHER COMMON OR COLLOQUIAL NAMES

BLOOD BIRD After its coloration.
RED IBIS After its coloration.

## PRINCIPAL DIFFERENCES FROM *EUDOCIMUS ALBUS*

The most immediate and striking difference between the two closely related birds is, of course, the coloration. The Scarlet Ibis is, as its name indicates, a brilliantly scarlet bird, especially so in its breeding plumage. The beak, bare skin of the face, gular pouch, plumage, and legs are all a deep blood-red, the only exception being the outermost tips of the primaries, which are a deep blue. Unlike the young of the White Ibis, which take two years to assume full adult plumage, that plumage does not occur completely in the Scarlet Ibis until the bird's fourth year. First-year birds are generally brown, but gradually begin assuming increasing areas of reddish coloration, mixed with some grayish and white. Incubation is slightly longer than

SCARLET IBIS

*Eudocimus ruber* (Linnaeus)

that for the White Ibis—twenty-four days instead of twenty-one.

Much more wary than the White Ibis, the Scarlet Ibis is rarely seen except at a distance. Although it has been known to interbreed with the White Ibis, this does not occur on a regular basis, and the pink offspring do not breed true color even with its own kind; resultant offspring are usually white.

At one time this bird was very rare anywhere in North America north of Mexico, but in recent years breeding colonies have become artificially established in southern Florida and possibly in south coastal Texas.

*(Overleaf)* Sketches of ibis and spoonbills made near Peterson Island in Lemon Bay, Englewood, Florida. (Sketches were made with the aid of 10 x 50mm glass.)

# ROSEATE SPOONBILL

SUBFAMILY: *PLATALEINEA*
GENUS: *AJAIA* Reichenbach
SPECIES: *AJAJA* (Linnaeus)

Karl E. Karalus

Karl E. Karalus

## COMMON NAME

Roseate Spoonbill
(Color Plate XIX)

## SCIENTIFIC NAME

*Ajaia ajaja* (Linnaeus). *Ajaia* is the Brazilian name for the bird.

## OTHER COMMON OR COLLOQUIAL NAMES

Most common or colloquial names other than Roseate Spoonbill have to do with the shape of the beak and the coloration of the bird. Some of the names used are:

BIGBILL
FLAME BIRD
FLATNOSE
PADDLEBEAK
RED SPOONBILL
SPOONBILL

---

**XXXI   PURPLE GALLINULE**

*Porphyrula martinica* (Linnaeus). Lake Wales, Florida. A.O.U. Number 218

**XXXII   AMERICAN COOT**

*Fulica americana americana* Gmelin. Charlotte Harbor, Charlotte County, Florida. A.O.U. Number 221

## SHAPE AT REST AND IN FLIGHT

The Roseate Spoonbill is a tall bird but most distinctive because of the large, spatulate character of the beak. Generally the bird stands quite erect, but with beak angled downward or hanging straight down.

In flight the head and neck are fully outstretched and, again, the spoonlike beak as it points straight forward is the most obvious distinguishing characteristic. Feet extend backward under the tail and beyond it during flight.

The flight pattern of the Roseate Spoonbill underlines its close relationship to the ibises, for the wingbeating and gliding are very nearly identical. In flock flight, which is customary, the Roseate Spoonbills generally assume long diagonal lines, but rarely fly abreast, as do the White and Scarlet Ibises. The Spoonbill, however, unlike those ibis species, frequently group together in wedge formation for flight, as in the manner of geese. The wingbeats are low and slow, interspersed with periods of gliding.

## LENGTH AND WINGSPAN

The Roseate Spoonbill has an average length of 33 inches (847mm) and a wingspan of 52.8 inches (1354mm).

## BEAK

The beak, as we have said, is extremely distinctive, a sure means of identifying the species at a glance. It is long and flat, narrow most of its length, and very much widened spoonlike at the outermost quadrant, (at that point it is about 2 inches wide). The nostrils are near the base and are long rather than round. The beak itself is a variety of colors, ranging from greenish and bluish to yellowish and black.

## EYES

The irides are carmine in coloration.

## CRESTS, PLUMAGE, ANNUAL MOLT

The finest plumage occurs with the completion of the prenuptial molt, which begins in November and is usually finished by late December. The postnuptial molt, which is complete in adults, begins about late May and finishes by mid-July. The highest perfection of adult plumage is not acquired until the bird has passed three years of age and sometimes not until four. There are no crests or plumes of a spectacular nature, although the species was once endangered by plume hunters who sought the wing feathers for hats. In some cases the entire opened wings were dried and sold as fans. Only a remnant population of the birds remained when legislation was enacted prohibiting the plume-hunting.

## VOICE

The young birds in the nest give voice to a number of different trilling and peeping sounds, which increase in speed and become more tremulous as the parent bird approaches the nest. The adults are largely quiet, even during courtship, although occasionally both sexes will exchange low-pitched grunts not unlike the clucking of a hen and not audible at any great distances. The author once heard a low murmuring, muted honklike sound from a flight of about a dozen Roseate Spoonbills passing overhead in the first light of dawn, but never encountered this sound from the birds again.

## COLORATION AND MARKINGS: ADULT

The head of the Roseate Spoonbill is bare, with yellowish-green to yellowish green-blue skin. The neck, breast, and back plumage is pure white, while the rest of the body and wings are a pale rose-pink, with the shoulders and tail coverts boldly splashed with a rich carmine. A tuft of small curly carmine feathers occurs in the center of the breast. In some birds, there is a suffusion of carmine or at least pinkish in the breast plumage. The tail is a rich ochraceous buff. The legs are red.

## COLORATION AND MARKINGS: JUVENILE

The juvenile plumage, acquired before the young birds leave the nest, is mainly white suffused with pinkish be-

Field sketches of spoonbills made at Buttonwood Rookery, Lemon Bay, Englewood, Florida, September 1976.

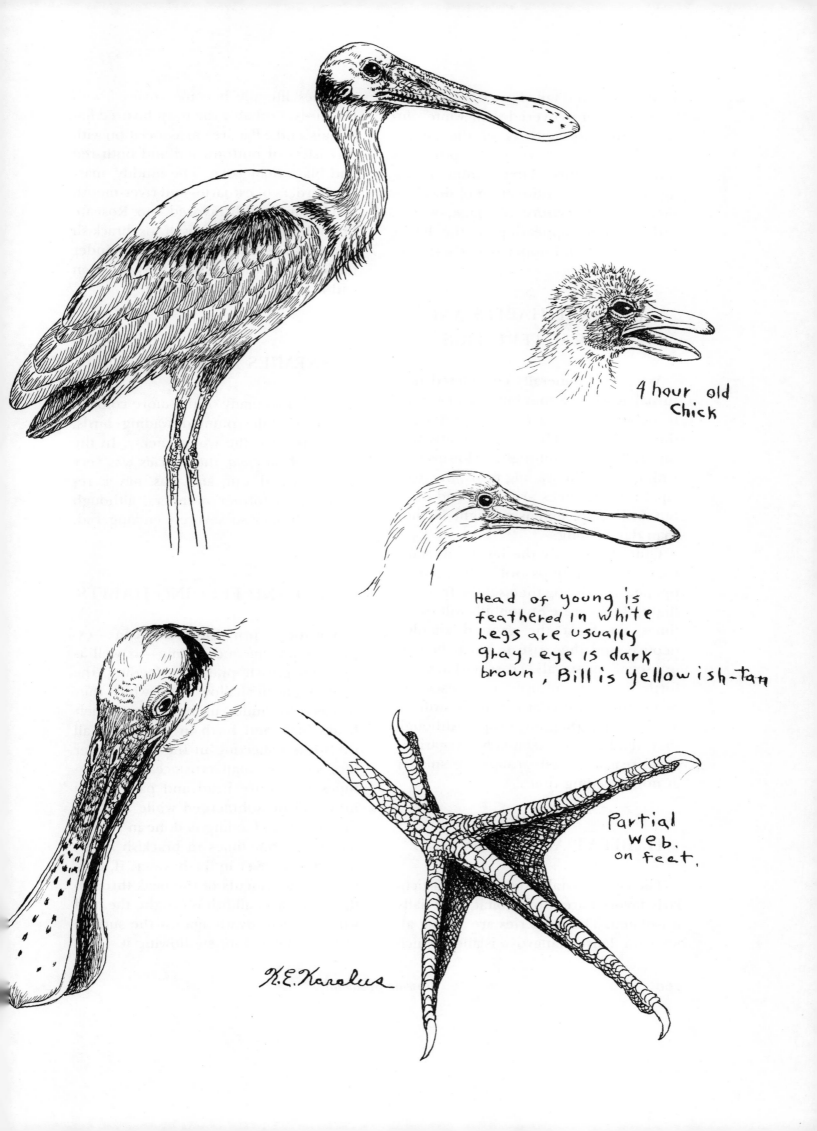

4 hour old
Chick

Head of young is
feathered in white
Legs are usually
gray, eye is dark
brown, Bill is yellowish-tan

Partial
web.
on feet.

K.E.Karalus

neath wings and tail. The crown, cheeks, and throat are covered with white plumage and are not, as in the adults, naked. The outer primaries have dusky tips. First winter plumage is simply a continuation of development toward mature plumage, with a little carmine appearing in the lesser wing coverts and upper tail coverts.

## GENERAL HABITS AND CHARACTERISTICS

While not generally considered nocturnal, Roseate Spoonbills are just as apt to be abroad and active at nighttime as during the day. This is particularly true on brightly moonlit nights. However, as with most of the wading birds, the principal feeding times are dawn and dusk, but with more extensive night feeding than day feeding.

Quite frequently the birds will stand together in groups with their wings opened as if drying themselves. In group flight, the Roseate Spoonbills will sometimes lift from the ground simultaneously and then rise to great heights in ascending spirals, crossing back and forth the way vultures and ibises are prone to do. Descent is usually swift, in a series of zigzagging drops. Although they tend to be essentially gregarious at all seasons, their groups are smaller at non-breeding times.

## HABITAT AND ROOSTING

The Gulf coastal estuaries are particularly favored areas of habitat, especially if isolated. The rookeries are almost always on dense mangrove islands, which at times literally become covered with the birds. Probably the most favored habitat is a tidal flat area in association with tiny islets of buttonwood and both red and black mangrove. The muddy, marshy borders of estuaries and river-mouth systems are highly favored, too. Roseate Spoonbills often visit salt or brackish ponds. Sometimes the birds will wander far inland, but most often they are seen within a mile of the coastline.

## ENEMIES AND DEFENSES

As with so many of the more colorful and beautifully plumed wading birds, man has been the worst enemy. In the case of *Ajaia ajaja*, the species was very nearly wiped out and has never recovered its former numbers, although it is no longer so severely endangered.

## FOOD AND FEEDING HABITS

The food is primarily crustaceans—especially prawns and shrimp—as well as fish and grasshoppers. In feeding, the birds alight in shallow water which they proceed to muddy up by swishing their beaks back and forth in the water, all the while collecting in the beaks water life, such as small crustaceans. Sometimes the entire head and part of the neck will be submerged while feeding. Practically all feeding is done in saltwater areas; sometimes in brackish areas, but almost never in fresh water. If, during the movements of the beak through the water, a small fish is caught, the bird will beat it to death against the surface of the water before swallowing it.

## COURTSHIP AND MATING

The courtship dance is engaged in by both sexes, though more strenuously by the male. Generally he approaches the female on the ground and as he walks toward her he opens his wings and vibrates them. He seems to make a point of approaching the female with the sun behind him so that the rays shining through the open plumage of his wings will bathe him in a rosy glow. Now and then he will execute little hops as he nears her and then she, too, will engage in small jumps. This may or may not be accompanied by more extensive wing opening (and some flapping) on the part of both. Head raising and lowering sometimes occurs with almost metronomic regularity. Actual copulation more often takes place on the ground than in a tree or bush.

## NEST AND NESTING HABITS

Prior to 1879, when plume-hunting began decimating the species, the Roseate Spoonbill nested all along the Gulf Coast of the United States. Huge nesting rookeries containing many thousands of birds could be found from southern Texas to southern Florida. Now most of the breeding is in the area south of a line across Florida which bisects Lake Okeechobee on an east-west direction. The Roseate Spoonbill's present breeding colonies are much smaller and are frequently found in conjunction with Louisiana Herons, Little Blue Herons, Great Egrets, anhingas, White Ibises, and Florida cormorants. Most often the nests are located in the outer fringe of small mangrove islands in saltwater areas or brackish estuarial systems, but always well hidden in the densest areas of the mangrove fringe.

The nests are almost always located in red mangroves at a height of about a dozen feet off the water or mud and are more often constructed on a horizontal branch than in the fork of branches. Though they nest in conjunction with White Ibises and medium-sized herons, nests of Roseate Spoonbills are easily recognizable because they are built of larger sticks and have a diameter of about 1.5 feet. The egg depression is shallow—only about 1 to 2 inches deep maximum—and about 6 inches in diameter. Occasionally the nest will be lined with smaller twigs, but not as a rule. Even more rarely, there will be a lining of moss or grasses or sometimes some leaves of the mangrove. On the whole, the nest is better constructed than are those of neighboring species.

## EGGS AND INCUBATION

There are usually four eggs to a clutch, of varied coloration. At times they are pinkish-creamy and speckled with dots and blotches of lavender, purple, brown, and gray-drab. Most often, though, the ground coloration is a dingy white, more or less regularly blotched and spotted with browns ranging from umber to russet. The eggs are thick-shelled, without gloss, and rather roughly granulated. The average egg size is 2.6 inches x 1.7 inches (65mm x 44mm). Incubation is shared by both parents.

ROSEATE SPOONBILL

*Ajaia ajaja* (Linnaeus)

## YOUNG

When first hatched, the young Roseate Spoonbills are very feeble and almost entirely helpless. For some hours they have difficulty even raising their heads. They are very strange-looking creatures, unable to stand, having enormous stomachs and a generally salmon-colored skin which is, at first, only very scantily covered by a soft down. The wing quills are well started at this time, but are still in sheaths and take a long time developing. The soft beak is turned downward slightly and rather ducklike at first. The down increases in quantity and length until, within a few days, the bird is entirely covered.

The young are fed through regurgitation, with a parent bird feeding one and then resting, then feeding another, until all the young are fed. Within a couple of weeks, the young birds begin to venture out onto nearby branches and quickly become skilled in climbing about, although they still fall quite frequently. When the parent birds are away from the nest, the young, after the first few days, rarely make any sounds.

## MIGRATION

There is not a general species-wide migration as such among the Roseate Spoonbills, although, as is the case with some others of the wading birds, there is a general northerly movement after the nesting seasons. The birds from southern Florida will sometimes go as far north as South Carolina and there have even been sightings recorded in Wisconsin, Illinois, Ohio, Pennsylvania, New York, and Indiana, as well as in Colorado, Utah, New Mexico, Arizona, and California, but these are isolated cases. The Roseate Spoonbill very rarely travels any great distances inland, and not too far northward from its normal range.

# AMERICAN FLAMINGO

SUBORDER: *PHOENICOPTERI*
FAMILY: *PHOENICOPTERIDAE*
GENUS: *PHOENICOPTERUS* Linnaeus
SPECIES: *RUBER* Linnaeus

## COMMON NAME

American Flamingo
(Color Plate XX)

## SCIENTIFIC NAME

*Phoenicopterus ruber* Linnaeus. From the Greek *phoenikopteros*, meaning a red wing.

## SHAPE AT REST AND IN FLIGHT

A very distinctive bird, immediately recognizable due to its long legs, relatively short, horizontal body, and very long neck. Also, the bent beak is unique among North American birds. Standing, the bird is about 5 feet tall.

In flight, as well as at rest, flamingos are very recognizable. The very long legs stretch far out behind, as with the herons. However, unlike the herons, the neck is well outstretched as in the manner of cranes and ibises. The tail is relatively short and the surprisingly narrow, pointed wings are just about exactly midway between beak and feet.

The strong, level, purposeful flight with medium-speed wingbeat is faster than the Great Blue Heron's, but slower than that of the White Ibis.

## HEIGHT AND WEIGHT

The American Flamingo has an average height of just over 5 feet (61.1 inches

—1567mm) and an average weight of 7.33 pounds (3.3 kg).

## LENGTH AND WINGSPAN

The average length is 47.75 inches (1225mm) and wingspan averages 61.3 inches (1571mm).

## BEAK

The beak of the flamingo is unique in shape; abruptly bent at midpoint, the beak's front upper surface faces straight forward and when the bird's head is upside down for feeding, the upper beak is on the bottom. The length of the beak actually exceeds the length of the head. Very large and thick, the beak is black at the tip, orange in the middle portion, and yellowish at the base.

## CRESTS, PLUMAGE, ANNUAL MOLT

The flamingo has no crests and no particularly elongated plumes at any season. The annual complete molt is postnuptial, but it begins while the adults are still nesting. The first feathers to be affected are those of the scapulars and crown. By the time this molt occurs, the breeding plumage is very worn and faded almost white. The least amount of fading has occurred on upper and under wing coverts. By mid-June the molt is full upon the bird, at which time it may be incapable of flight or at least greatly handicapped; if danger threatens at such time, the bird depends upon its running ability to escape. The molt is completed, at the latest, by early August. A partial prenuptial molt, which brings the spectacularly beautiful red breeding plumage, begins in about November and is completed by January.

## VOICE

The American Flamingo has a fairly extensive range of notes, most of which are guttural and croaky in character. Perhaps the most common is a sort of in-flight honking sound of three notes repeated regularly, the second note loudest. Another call, also usually uttered in flight, is more gooselike in character—a deep but not terribly melodious four-note or five-note honking. This is a call that may come from many of the birds simultaneously when they are in flight, and which becomes harsher and more strident if danger threatens. There is also a murmuring groanlike cry which is uttered upon approaching the nest, and a similar but slightly more grating cry uttered as a flight is terminated.

## COLORATION AND MARKINGS: ADULT

The perfect breeding plumage is practically all scarlet except for the primaries and most of the secondaries which are black on the terminal ends. In the words of the late Dr. Frank Chapman, "No other large bird is so brightly colored, and no other brightly colored bird is so large."

## COLORATION AND MARKINGS: JUVENILE

The first winter plumage of the immature flamingo begins to appear at five weeks of age, first on the scapulars and sides of the breast. The general coloration is a grayish-brown barely tinged with pinkish on the underside and wings. The back feathers have well-marked shaft streaks and the tail is pinkish in coloration with the feathers black-edged. The secondaries are black in the center and have white margins. The following July to August, when the bird is about eighteen months old, a postnuptial molt occurs in which the young bird assumes full adult plumage with the possible exception of some dusky discoloration on the wing coverts. Immature birds are always lighter in coloration than adults and they fly together, apart from the adults.

## HABITAT

The extremely rare American Flamingo favors the marl and mud flats of the coastal shallows. The author, who lived in southern Florida for many years and observed birds closely during all that time, saw American Flamingos only once—thirteen of them in flight just at dawn at the lower end of Lemon Bay in 1969.

## FOOD AND FEEDING HABITS

The flamingo's food consists almost entirely of shells of genus Ceritheum,

American Flamingo, *Phoenicopterus ruber* Linnaeus (no scale intended).

Feet Webbed

chick

nest
of mud
a few inches to
2 feet high

AMERICAN FLAMINGO
*Phoenicopterus ruber* Linnaeus

which are picked out by the beak as it probes and swishes and sifts through the muddy bottom, swallowed whole and then ground up in the stomach.

## EGGS AND INCUBATION

Most often only one egg is laid. Occasionally there will be two and very rarely three. They are dingy white, with an uncommonly thick shell that is often lumpy with flaky white calcium deposits on the surface. These are large eggs, averaging 3.6 inches x 2.2 inches (91mm x 56mm).

The incubation is about equally divided between both parents, with the parent not on the eggs ordinarily feeding during this period or standing guard near the incubating parent bird (guard duty usually falls to the male). The change of shift on the nest usually occurs in early morning and late afternoon. The incubation period is about thirty-one days.

## YOUNG

At the time it is first hatched, the American Flamingo chick is clad in a coat of thick white down which is a dingy blue on crown and back. The lores and areas surrounding the eyes are bare of down. At the age of one month, this coat of down is shed and another, ash-gray in color, replaces it. This second downy coat lasts for only seven to nine days. Before the hatchling begins feeding on its own, it is fed through regurgitation by the parent birds. The first material that the chick eats on its own is the trampled egg fragments still on the nesting platform. This is believed to be crucial to the bone-formation process. The young chick issues a series of sounds, including a puppylike yapping, a whistling sound, and then a slightly melodious crowing call.

## NORTH AMERICAN DISTRIBUTION

*Phoenicopterus ruber*, beyond any doubt one of the most spectacular birds of the Western Hemisphere, was once abundant in the southern portion of North America, but is largely extinct there now. Only rarely is it seen in southernmost Florida.

# THE CRANES

---

ORDER: *GRUIFORMES*
SUBORDER: *GRUES*
SUPERFAMILY: *GRUOIDEA*
FAMILY: *GRUIDAE*
SUBFAMILY: *GRUINEA*
GENUS: *GRUS* Pallas

---

SPECIES: *CANADENSIS* (Linnaeus)
SUBSPECIES: *canadensis* (Linnaeus)
Sandhill Crane

*tabida* (Peters)
Little Brown Crane

*pratensis* Meyer
Florida Crane

---

SPECIES: *AMERICANA* (Linnaeus)
Whooping Crane

## COMMON NAME

Sandhill Crane
(Color Plate XXI)

## SCIENTIFIC NAME

*Grus canadensis canadensis* (Linnaeus).
From the Latin *grus*, a crane.

## OTHER COMMON OR COLLOQUIAL NAMES

COMMON BROWN CRANE After basic coloration.
COMMON CRANE
RATTLING CRANE After peculiar vocal sounds.

## SHAPE AT REST AND IN FLIGHT

A very tall, upright, stately bird with a sharply pointed heron-like beak, long neck, no showy plumes, a heavy body, long legs, and long sturdy toes. Not as tall as the Whooping Crane, *Grus americana*.

During flight the birds gives the immediate impression of great wing force and direction with little real effort and without rapid wingbeating at any time. Occasionally long glides are enacted, especially in descent from high altitudes. This bird often soars and circles in a dizzying manner at great altitudes, evidently for the sheer enjoyment of flying.

## LENGTH AND WINGSPAN

The Sandhill Crane has an average length of 43.75 inches (1122mm) and an average wingspan of 80 inches (2053mm).

## LEGS AND FEET

The legs and feet are sturdily built, with considerably less of the long narrow delicacy characteristic of the legs of the egrets. Both legs and feet are black and heavily scaled and the toe span is very wide.

## EYES

The irides are brown, though sometimes with a faint touch of ruddy coloration, or paling down to yellowish.

## ANNUAL MOLT

A complete molt begins each year in August with the flight feathers, and lasts until replacement of the body plumage and wing coverts in December. There is said to be very little, if any, prenuptial molt.

## VOICE

The voice of the crane is very distinctive and has a powerful, far-carrying resonant quality caused by a peculiar series of tracheal convolutions which allow the windpipe to act as a sort of echo chamber. This capability seems to reach its peak of effectiveness in the Whooping Crane, which has upward of 30 inches of such convolutions. The Sandhill Crane has about 8 inches of convoluted windpipe, but enough to produce a rather thrilling and very far-carrying trumpeting, rattling cry, which, once heard and correctly identified, is never mistaken for the call of any other bird. In addition to the long, rattling, trumpeting cries, there are also numerous shorter, guttural rattles and croakings. Young birds are capable of uttering only a slight peeping sound and a rather plaintive whistling.

## COLORATION AND MARKINGS: ADULT

The primaries and coverts, as well as general body plumage, are slate-gray to brownish-gray. The coloration becomes somewhat lighter on head and neck, with the throat and chin sometimes almost whitish. Cheeks, too, are light. A bare space of bright red skin stretches from the base of the beak to mid-crown, the bottom line of this bareness passing through the median line of the eye on both sides. This is a very distinctive marking for the species. The rear portion of the crown, as well as the nape, is darker slaty gray. The underwings are lightish gray, almost white. Legs and beak are black.

## COLORATION AND MARKINGS: JUVENILE

For the most part like that of the adult except that the head is fully feathered

and thus lacks the bright red bare skin of the face, and the plumage is much more variegated with browns, chestnut, and rusty colorations. These are replaced by full adult plumage colorations with the second complete annual molt, when the bird is just over two years old.

## HABITAT AND ROOSTING

The Sandhill Crane particularly enjoys expansive prairie locations with relatively short grass, but is often found in sparse stands of cypress and pine. It prefers dry ground to wading, although is not disinclined to entering water which may be deep enough to reach almost to the abdomen. Wet meadows and slough edges are often frequented. Most often the roosting is done on low sturdy branches or the ground, usually in the company of a dozen or more of its own kind, but sometimes with only one or two others. It rarely roosts alone.

## FOOD AND FEEDING HABITS

Sandhill Cranes are probably most often observed as they walk slowly and sedately through the prairie grasses, here and there plucking things up with graceful movements of the head and neck and murmuring softly among themselves, in groups of from two or three to six or seven birds. The food matter they pick up at such times is considerably varied. A great deal of vegetation is eaten, espe-

Sandhill Crane, *Grus canadensis canadensis* (Linnaeus).

*Sandhill Crane*

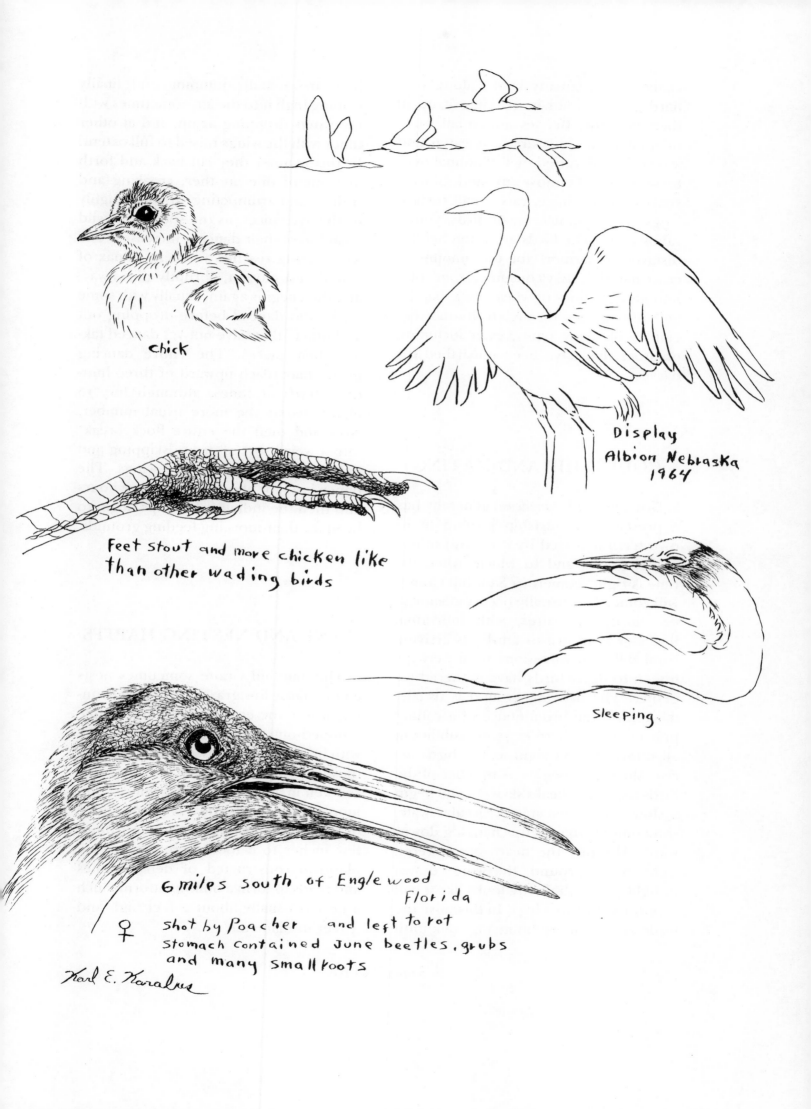

chick

Display
Albion Nebraska
1964

Feet stout and more chicken like
than other wading birds

Sleeping.

6 miles south of Englewood
Florida

♀ shot by Poacher and left to rot
stomach contained June beetles, grubs
and many small roots

Karl E. Karalus

cially seeds of many kinds, along with hard gravel to aid in grinding it up in their gizzards. Berries and small fruits of numerous kinds are also eaten and a surprisingly varied diet of animal matter—insects of almost any kind, lizards, snakes, moles, mice, rats, small turtles, frogs, fish, tadpoles, small birds, young rabbits, etc. The birds are often held in disfavor by farmers for the amount of crop materials they consume, from voluminous quantities of wheat, oats, barley, and other grains, through fruits and vegetables of many types, even including potatoes that have been unearthed for harvest.

## COURTSHIP AND MATING

*Grus canadensis canadensis* generally has a preselected courtship ground in its own territory, used by itself and others of its species and to which, when the time is right, numerous Sandhill Cranes will come. This usually occurs at sunrise or shortly thereafter, with individual flocks of from five to ten birds arriving from different directions until perhaps fifteen to thirty birds have gathered together. The dancing ground is usually located on the prominence of a rolling prairie, where there is good visibility in all directions. As soon as the birds arrive, the dance begins. A number of the birds raise their beaks skyward and begin a slow and rather stately circular walk, sometimes with wingtips hanging downward. Abruptly the heads are lowered right to the ground, the wings drawn in tightly, and the body looks like a ball supported by three legs. In this pose the birds begin a more bouncing walk until

they are actually jumping and finally leaping high into the air, sometimes with the wings dropping again, and at other times with the wings raised to full extent. In this manner they cut back and forth in front of one another, croaking and trilling and trumpeting in their highly distinctive voices, as the speed and wild abandon of their dancing increases. The whole thing reaches a violent climax of sound and motion, abruptly dies away, and then begins again, usually with some birds who danced before dropping out and others that have not yet danced taking their places. The entire dancing group may reach upward of three hundred birds at times, although fifty to eighty seems the more usual number. Now and then the entire flock breaks into a weird sort of group skipping and light leaping with upraised wings. The dance lasts for about two or three hours and then the individual groups begin to head for their morning feeding grounds.

## NEST AND NESTING HABITS

The Sandhill Crane sometimes nests among fairly low grasses in prairie country, where the eggs are laid in a simple scooped-out area of earth lightly lined with broad-leaved grasses. An advantage of such a locality is that the bird can see well in all directions. Far more commonly, though, the nest is in the fringe of a marsh or slough in water from a few inches to a foot deep, the nesting platform constructed of dense rushes and reeds to form a bulky platform. Such a nest is usually about 2 feet high and 4 feet in diameter.

*Sandhill Crane*

## EGGS AND INCUBATION

Almost always two eggs are laid which range from a pasty pale green to a pale brownish-green of pastel nature, overlaid by a series of brown, dark buffy-gray or purplish-gray spots and blotches. In general, the eggs are slightly lighter-colored than those of the other North American cranes. The shell is thick and usually smooth, though it is sometimes lightly pitted or granulated. The eggs are quite large, averaging about 3 inches x 2.4 inches (97mm x 63mm). Incubation is by both parent birds, but predominantly by the female.

## YOUNG

Sandhill Crane chicks emerge from the egg in about two to four hours, remain helpless for another hour or so beyond that, and within another hour are standing and demanding food from the parent birds. Although they tend to remain near the nest for the first couple of days, they can, if need be, leave the nest within three or four hours of hatching. In all cases the nest is abandoned fairly early and the chicks wander about under the protective care of the parent birds, being fed by them and learning to feed themselves. They remain with the parent birds until and even after they can fly very well themselves, with some families staying close-knit up until the time of the next nesting.

The downy young bird is clad in thick soft down which ranges from chestnut to a deep rich brown on crown, nape, back, and wings, to a rather lighter tawny-buff on the sides and throat, to a grayish-white on the underparts. These

**SANDHILL CRANE**

*Grus canadensis canadensis* (Linnaeus)

colors fade as the chick grows older and by the time the first juvenile plumage is appearing, the down has become dingy. Young cranes do not acquire their complete adult plumage until they are about thirty months of age.

## MIGRATION

Highly migrational, Sandhill Cranes, beginning usually in August and continuing into late September, gather in great migratory flocks which gradually grow larger and larger and which regularly take to wing and soar about at great altitudes and in thrilling performances prior to the actual directional movement of the migration. An almost constant din of their rattling, trumpeting cries fills the air as they whirl and circle and dip; this vocal demonstration tends to diminish somewhat during the actual migrational flights. The flights north and south are swift and strong and direct, occurring both day and night, with the birds stopping for brief hours here and there to feed and rest. A major migrational staging area is at Nebraska's Platte River. The Sandhill Crane is absent in winter from about the northern four fifths of its range north of Mexico. The northward migration sometimes extends across Alaska's Aleutian Islands and into Siberia.

## ECONOMIC INFLUENCE

Sandhill Cranes have gained the enmity of many farmers because of their depredations in grain fields, and in areas where fruit and vegetable crops are maturing. To some extent this adverse influence is offset by the considerable insect-eating and rodent-eating habits of the birds during practically any season.

## COMMON NAME

Little Brown Crane
(Color Plate XXI)

## SCIENTIFIC NAME

*Grus canadensis tabida* (Peters). *Tabida* from the Latin *tabidus,* meaning lesser.

## BASIC SUBSPECIFIC DIFFERENCES

The Little Brown Crane, also known as the Canadian Crane, Northern Brown Crane, and Big Brown Crane, is, despite its most common name, somewhat larger than the Sandhill Crane. Coloration is essentially the same, although with less grayish and more brownish-buff than in the Sandhill Crane.

The Little Brown Crane breeds in the far northern regions of the North American continent, across the northern portion of Alaska and Canada eastward to about the region of Hudson Bay. It is absent from all of that territory during winter, occurring in great abundance during the fall migration in the western states west of the Rockies. Lemmings make up a large portion of their summer diet.

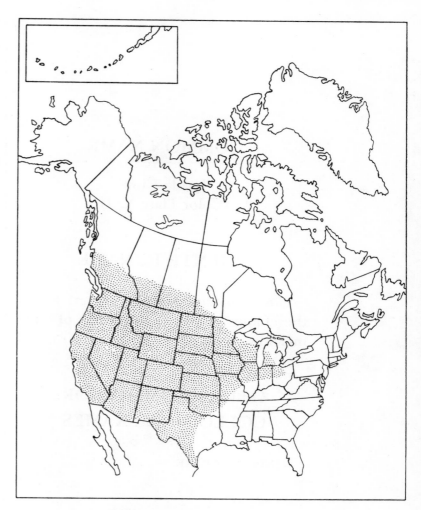

LITTLE BROWN CRANE
*Grus canadensis tabida* (Peters)

More often than the Sandhill or Florida Crane, the Little Brown Crane prefers a relatively dry nesting area on the ground. The nest is often no more than a cavity hollowed out of sandy soil, most often rather thickly lined with fine (rather than coarse, as with the other cranes) grasses and perhaps a few feathers. The eggs—usually two—are pale green with dark chocolate-colored blotches and spots. Average egg size is 3.5 inches x 2.2 inches (90mm x 55mm).

# COMMON NAME

Florida Crane
(Color Plate XXI)

# SCIENTIFIC NAME

*Grus canadensis pratensis* Meyer. From the Latin *pratensis,* meaning of the meadow.

# OTHER COMMON OR COLLOQUIAL NAMES

SANDHILL CRANE

# BASIC SUBSPECIFIC DIFFERENCES

The Florida Crane is on the average considerably smaller than the Little Brown Crane and slightly smaller than the Sandhill Crane.

There is a greater difference of coloration between the Florida Crane and the Sandhill than there is between the Sandhill and the Little Brown Crane. In the Florida Crane, the forehead and crown, as in the other subspecies, are bare and red, but the chin and throat are white, with the rest of the body mainly a rather darkish smoke-gray, with back and scapulars overlaid heavily with wood brown or fuscous. The primaries are a fuscous-black.

The Florida Crane depends to a greater extent on a diet of vegetation than the other subspecies, with animal

FLORIDA CRANE

*Grus canadensis pratensis* Meyer

matter (including insects, mammals, reptiles, amphibians, etc.) comprising only 2.5 per cent of the bird's diet. *Grus canadensis pratensis* most often frequents marshy meadows and wet prairies, but is also found in the pine flats and open pine forests in the vicinity of small ponds. It is in the area of such ponds that the Florida Crane ordinarily builds its nest, which is bulkier for the most part than that of the Little Brown Crane and usually more so than that of the Sandhill Crane.

The Florida Crane nest is 4 or 5 feet in diameter and constructed of sticks, grasses, reeds, and palmetto fronds, often to a height of more than a foot. There is no finer lining in the nest and usually not even very much of an egg depression.

## COMMON NAME

Whooping Crane
(Color Plate XXII)

## SCIENTIFIC NAME

*Grus americana* (Linnaeus).

## OTHER COMMON OR COLLOQUIAL NAMES

GREAT WHITE CRANE After general coloration and size.
WHITE CRANE For general coloration.
WHOOPER For vocal attributes.

## SHAPE AT REST AND IN FLIGHT

A very tall (over 5 feet), stately bird which, at a distance, looks pure white, with a distinctive red fleshy marking on the forecrown, extending from beak base to slightly below occipital area.

The Whooping Crane in flight is clearly recognizable by its well-extended neck and head, snow-white plumage with black primaries and secondaries, and black legs and feet extending far behind the tail. The beak is clearly yellow. This is one of America's most distinctive birds.

## LENGTH AND WINGSPAN

The average length of the Whooping Crane is 54.2 inches (1390mm) and the average wingspan is 7.5 feet (2308mm).

## CRESTS, PLUMAGE, ANNUAL MOLT

The Whooping Crane has no particularly elongated plumes at any season and no crest. However, the dull red fleshy area of the face and head becomes a much brighter carmine during the breeding season. There is a complete molt of the plumage once annually, beginning about early July and extending through November.

## VOICE

One of its most distinctive characteristics, the voice of the Whooping Crane is a far-carrying trumpeting call which is thrilling to hear and unforgettable. Its tremendous carrying power and clarion quality are the result of an extraordinarily long and amazingly convoluted windpipe that amplifies and trumpets the sounds made by the bird. This windpipe is often longer than the total length of the bird itself, averaging about 1428mm (55.69 inches). The cry is loud, clear and piercing and said to be audible for 2 or 3 miles under proper conditions. It has a greater clarity and less of a rattling quality than the calls of the Sandhill, Little Brown, or Florida Cranes.

## COLORATION AND MARKINGS: ADULT

The adult *Grus americana* is pure white throughout its plumage except for the primaries and secondaries, which are deep black and, in some lights, faintly iridescent with a bronze-green tone. Legs and feet are black and the beak is a dull greenish except during breeding season when it becomes more yellowish. The eye is a brilliant lemon-yellow and the fleshy area of the face and head, extending from the base of the beak to mid-crown and slightly beneath the eyes, is dull red except during breeding season, when it becomes more of a bright blood-red. There are scattered black hairlike feathers in this red fleshy area at all seasons.

## COLORATION AND MARKINGS: JUVENILE

The head of the juvenile bird is completely feathered and does not become bare until full adult plumage is acquired at the second annual molt. The plumage of the young bird is basically white, but with a rusty-brownish overcast at times.

## HABITAT AND ROOSTING

During its breeding season, the Whooping Crane (which now breeds almost solely in the area of Great Slave Lake) prefers slough country that is marshy and swampy, especially areas with extensive growths of aspen. During its migration, when it passes from the prairie wetlands of northwestern Canada southward through the Dakotas, Nebraska, Kansas, Oklahoma, and Texas, it lands to feed in grainfields and it is at this time that it becomes most vulnerable to waterfowl gunners.

## ENEMIES AND DEFENSES

Man is, of course, by far the worst enemy of the species. To his shame, man very nearly exterminated this bird, bringing its total wild population down to thirteen birds at one time. But, to his credit, man has, through extensive endeavors and great care, brought the total number into the hundreds again. The Whooping Crane is still an extremely endangered bird and conditions still remain all too precarious for it. One great natural blow in the form of a hurricane or other disaster striking the wintering birds at the National Wildlife Refuge at Port Aransas, Texas, near Corpus Christi, could well cause the ultimate extinction of the bird.

## FOOD AND FEEDING HABITS

Though generally omnivorous, the Whooping Crane eats somewhat more vegetative matter than animal matter. Nevertheless, it is known to eat large quantities of grasshoppers, beetles, dragonflies and other large insects and their larvae, as well as small rodents, shrews, lizards, snakes, frogs, and birds. Plant bulbs, tubers, succulent leaves and stems, small fruits, berries, grains, and other vegetable crops and foliage make up the bulk of the diet.

## NEST AND NESTING HABITS

Most often the nest is built in relatively shallow water, from a few inches to perhaps a foot or a little more in depth. The nest itself, made up of matted rushes, reeds, and grasses, extends anywhere from 6 to 14 inches above the water and is about 2 feet in diameter. Invariably it is extremely well hidden from casual view, yet almost always within mere feet of fairly open areas. The adult birds are very cautious about approaching the nest and if any sort of danger threatens, will walk casually past it as if it didn't exist and then try to make the intruder think the nest is elsewhere, some distance away. The nest itself is not just a floating platform of woven grasses and reeds, but a very dense structure built up from the bottom surface so that it can support considerable weight without sinking or even lowering appreciably.

**WHOOPING CRANE**

*Grus americana* (Linnaeus)

## EGGS AND INCUBATION

Most often two eggs are laid, although occasionally there will be only one, and on very rare occasions, three. The base color of the egg is a heavy buff to dull greenish-buff. In addition, the larger end of the egg is rather heavily blotched and spotted with brown. There is a slight granulation and glossiness to the shell, but it is nevertheless rather smooth and faintly glossy.

Arthur Cleveland Bent in *Life Histories of North American Marsh Birds* gives the average size of thirty-eight measured eggs as being 3.8 inches x 2.4 inches (98mm x 62mm).

Incubation is shared by both parent birds.

## YOUNG

The downy hatchling is generally pale beige in coloration, but darker on the back than elsewhere. The chicks are said to peep vigorously and plaintively while emerging from the egg, and are able to move about freely and well within a few hours of hatching. Within twenty-four hours of emerging from the egg, the chick will move off the nest platform and swim into hiding in the surrounding grasses and rushes if danger threatens.

Young birds are fed by regurgitation and this sort of feeding continues for several weeks, even after the chicks have begun eating food on their own.

In the first winter plumage the entire head, including even the lores, is feathered and there is no real indication of the reddish flesh of face and crown which the bird will have as an adult. The young are believed to remain with the parent birds up to and possibly through the fall migration, and it is even possible that the family groups again fly north together the following spring.

## NORTH AMERICAN DISTRIBUTION

While the Whooping Crane was once abundant all throughout America east of the Rocky Mountains, it is now extremely scarce and its distribution very limited—ranging from the breeding area in Canada down a narrow migrational corridor to the Texas coast. A few wild pairs are known to breed in Wood Buffalo Park, Mackenzie.

## MIGRATION

The Whooping Cranes leave the Great Slave Lake area of Mackenzie on their southward migration around October 1 and arrive at the Texas coast two or three weeks later. In spring, the northward migration generally begins about mid-April and ends by mid-May.

## ECONOMIC INFLUENCE

While no longer of any real economic influence, the Whooping Crane has a very great aesthetic value and its decline and gradual partial recovery provide an important lesson in conservation practices.

# LIMPKIN

---

FAMILY: *ARAMIDAE*
GENUS: *ARAMUS* Vieillot
SPECIES: *GUARAUNA* (Linnaeus)
SUBSPECIES: *pictus* (Meyer)

## COMMON NAME

Limpkin
(Color Plate XXIII)

## SCIENTIFIC NAME

*Aramus guarauna pictus* (Meyer). *Aramus,* derivation unknown; *guarauna,* a Brazilian name; *pictus,* painted.

## OTHER COMMON OR COLLOQUIAL NAMES

The Limpkin (a name derived from the bird's peculiar halting gait) has a wide range of common or colloquial names, including:

CARAU
CLUCKING HEN
COURLAN
COURLIRI
CRYING BIRD
FLORIDA COURLAN
GREATER COURLAN
HAMMOCK TURKEY
INDIAN PULLET
NIGGERBIRD
SCOLOPACEOUS COURLAN
SWAMP GROUSE
UP-N-DOWN

## SHAPE AT REST AND IN FLIGHT

The Limpkin is a large-bodied bird with relatively long legs and medium-long neck.

In flight, the down-angled neck and head, with distinctive oversized beak, are clearly evident. The long legs dangle at first but are drawn up to trail behind the tail, which is very short. Its flight, which seldom lasts long, always seems very heavy, effortful and quite slow. The Limpkin rarely flies more than a few feet above the reeds or grasses.

## LENGTH AND WINGSPAN

The average length of the Limpkin is 26.7 inches (684mm) and its wingspan is 3.5 feet (1077mm).

## BEAK

The beak is a dingy brownish shading to dark gray.

## CRESTS, PLUMAGE, ANNUAL MOLT

The Limpkin has no crests and grows no special plumes for the breeding season. Adults have a complete prenuptial molt which begins in February and concludes in April, and another complete molt, postnuptially, beginning in August and ending in November. The plumage is generally very dense, even though relatively short.

## VOICE

The voice of the Limpkin is a lonely, disconsolate, and yet altogether delightful sound of the marsh. Oddly, it is one of the few birds whose vocal qualities inspire almost completely different reactions in different people. For some it is chilling. For others it is a beautiful, gentle, and wholly pleasant auditory experience. Why this should be could make an interesting study. Whatever the case, the voice of the Limpkin is so completely distinctive that, like the voice of the Sandhill Crane, once heard it is never mistaken for that of any other bird. The call is a high-pitched rattling sound, followed by two equally high-pitched plaintive notes.

## COLORATION AND MARKINGS: ADULT

The basic coloration of *Aramus guarauna pictus* is a milk-chocolate brown, with sharp streakings and spottings of white throughout the plumage. The legs are a dingy green, the beak dark brownish-gray, and the eyes brown, sometimes with a faint orangish cast.

## COLORATION AND MARKINGS: JUVENILE

Young Limpkins are essentially the same color and pattern as the adults, except that the browns are paler and the whites duller.

## HABITAT AND ROOSTING

Although the Limpkin will frequently alight on low scrub-growth trees (especially those devoid of leaves) growing in marsh or swamp, and perch there for long sleepy minutes, most often it does not roost in trees at all but rather in the saw grass and reeds and rushes of the marsh habitat it favors. It is slow to take flight and quick to end its flight once airborne, dropping into the tall water grasses much in the manner of the rails. And, like the rails, it is an expert at slipping through the dense vegetation with the utmost facility. In addition to ordinary marsh-grass areas, the Limpkin favors areas of tree growth containing scattered cypresses, magnolias, maples, oaks, sabal palms, and pines, and also areas where the undergrowth of vines and brush are very thick. It also favors areas where there is little water current and extensive growths of water hyacinth and swamp lettuce, upon which it often walks as it searches for food.

## FOOD AND FEEDING HABITS

*Aramus guarauna pictus* eats very little vegetable matter, feeding almost exclusively on small animal life of the marshlands, especially snails, mollusks, crustaceans, insects, frogs, worms, and lizards, as well as occasional small snakes. Undoubtedly its favorite food is the apple snail so common to the Everglades and other Florida marsh areas. The Limpkin has a habit of bringing the snails and crustaceans it catches to a particular log or stump or clump of matted swamp grass and devouring them there, leaving behind the shells, which eventually grow into a telltale mound. The Limpkin is quite skilled at shaking the large snails free of their shells without breaking the shells themselves.

---

Limpkin, *Aramus guarauna pictus* (Meyer).

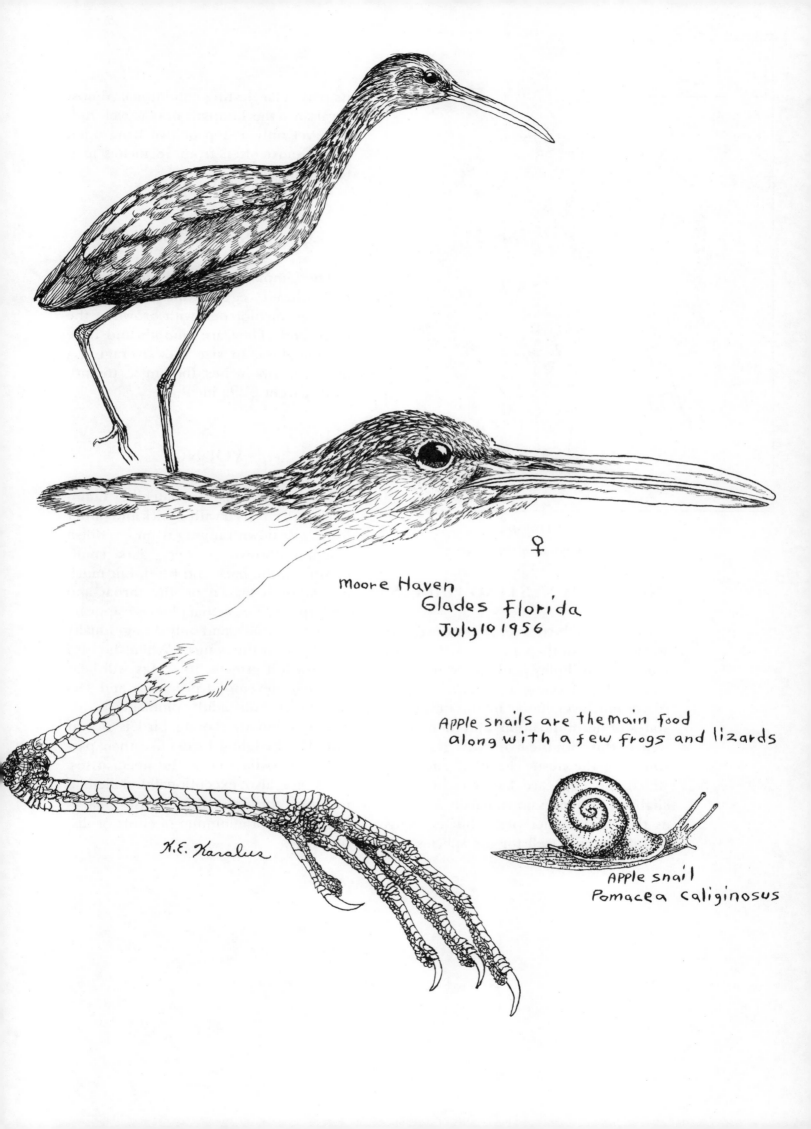

moore Haven
Glades Florida
July 10 1956

Apple snails are the main food
along with a few frogs and lizards

Apple snail
Pomacea caliginosus

K.E. Karalus

**LIMPKIN**

*Aramus guarauna pictus* (Meyer)

## NEST AND NESTING HABITS

Most often the nest of *Aramus guarauna pictus* is built in thick sawgrass. The bird constructs its bulky platform by bending over stalks of saw grass, upon which it places much vegetative matter in various states of decomposition, and then interweaves this with the living saw grass surrounding the nest. The platform upon which the eggs are laid has only the slightest of depressions, hardly as much as that of a dinner plate, but it seems to suffice quite well for the species and its particular nesting conditions. Almost invariably the Limpkin nest is well hidden, yet only a step or two from open water, most often from 18 inches to 2 feet in depth.

## EGGS AND INCUBATION

The Limpkin usually lays five to eight buff-colored eggs which are often streaked or blotched with brown at the large end. They are smooth and have a faint gloss. In size they average 2.3 inches x 1.8 inches (60mm x 46mm). Both parent birds incubate.

## YOUNG

Like young rails, the hatchling Limpkin is well covered with a thick and rather long, soft down ranging from a reddish cinnamon-brown to very dark snuff-brown on the back and head, but much lighter buffy-brown on the throat and underparts. The actual plumage appears first on the body, and only very gradually develops on the wings. (When the bird reaches full growth, its wings still bear only half-developed primaries and secondaries.) Full adult plumage is acquired when the young bird is a year old. The fledgling birds, like their parents, can swim well if the need arises. They are also exceptionally skilled at moving through the dense marsh grasses with a minimum of effort or disturbance.

# *RALLUS* RAILS

---

SUPERFAMILY: *RALLOIDEA*
FAMILY: *RALLIDAE*
SUBFAMILY: *RALLINAE*
GENUS: *RALLUS* Linnaeus

---

SPECIES: *ELEGANS* Audubon
SUBSPECIES: *elegans* Audubon
King Rail

---

SPECIES: *LONGIROSTRIS* Boddaert
SUBSPECIES: *crepitans* Gmelin
Northern Clapper Rail

*saturatus* Ridgway
Louisiana Clapper Rail

*scotti* Sennett
Florida Clapper Rail

*waynei* Brewster
Wayne's Clapper Rail

*insularum* Brooks
Mangrove Clapper Rail

*obsoletus* Ridgway
California Clapper Rail

*yumanensis* Dickey
Yuma Clapper Rail

*levipes* Bangs
Light-Footed Rail

---

SPECIES: *LIMICOLA* Vieillot
SUBSPECIES: *limicola* Vieillot
Virginia Rail

# COMMON NAME

King Rail
(Color Plate XXIV)

## SCIENTIFIC NAME

*Rallus elegans elegans* Audubon. From the Latin, *rallus* signifying a rail, and *elegans* meaning choice.

## OTHER COMMON OR COLLOQUIAL NAMES

FRESHWATER MARSH HEN This same name is applied to most of the rails without regard to species or subspecies.

MARSH HEN Probably the most common term, but too indefinite to be of value.

MUD HEN Also very common, though this name is also used in reference to the American Coot.

## SHAPE AT REST AND IN FLIGHT

The King Rail is not at all large in comparison to other Gruiformes, such as the cranes. It is well adapted to its life among close-growing reed stems, the body highly compressed and almost pointed in the front, then tapering back in a sort of wedge shape to a blunt, thick posterior with short up-tipped tail.

The wings are extremely short and rounded. When it first springs into the air, its legs dangle awkwardly beneath. They are not drawn up unless the flight is to be long, which is rare, since the bird ordinarily drops out of sight into the marsh grass after a very short flight just over the tops of the reeds. If, however, flight is to be protracted, the legs and the neck are fully extended.

Flight is slow and laborious in practically all circumstances. This is so pronounced that one wonders how the long migrational flights can be made. Even when in full flight with neck extended and legs fully back, the King Rail's movements appear difficult, slow, and weak. Yet, extensive migrations do take place. In most circumstances the flight is very short and vacillating, with rapid wing-beats which seem essentially ineffective. When pursued, they usually run for escape rather than take flight.

## LENGTH AND WINGSPAN

The King Rail has an average length of 1.5 feet (464mm) and an average wingspan of 2 feet (615mm).

## CRESTS, PLUMAGE, ANNUAL MOLT

There are no distinctive plumage changes throughout the seasons or from one molt to another. The flank feathers are barred, black and white. Adult birds undergo a complete molt which takes about two months, beginning in early August. There is also a partial molt of the contour plumage in spring prior to nesting.

## VOICE

The King Rail utters a three-note call, which sounds most like *kark-kark-kark*, and can be heard both day and night.

## COLORATION AND MARKINGS: ADULT

The King Rail has a general resemblance to the Northern Clapper Rail, *Rallus longirostris crepitans*, but is larger and slightly more brightly colored. The coloration and markings, in fact, are almost identical to those of the much smaller Virginia Rail, *Rallus limicola limicola*. On the upper portions, the adult King Rail is generally brownish and distinctly streaked. These markings enable the bird to camouflage itself very well among the reeds and rushes of the marsh. On the underside, the plumage is a cinnamon color, brightest on the breast. There is a light line from the base of the beak to over the eye, and a dark line through the eye. The irides are a rich chestnut. The lower eyelid is white. The flanks, as well as the lining of the wings, are quite blackish and very distinctly barred with white. Legs and feet are pale dusky green.

## HABITAT AND ROOSTING

Reedy marshes are the preferred habitat of the King Rail and the location where roosting occurs. It does not like tidal marshes and is rarely found along saltwater fringes, preferring a freshwater habitat for roosting, breeding, nesting, and feeding.

## FOOD AND FEEDING HABITS

The food of the King Rail consists of both animal and vegetable matter. Snails, slugs, leeches, insects, crayfish, tadpoles, small frogs, and lizards seem to make up the bulk of the animal matter, while seeds of various water and marsh plants, such as water cane, marsh oats, etc., make up the vegetable matter. Food matter is never probed for in the mud, as is the custom with woodcocks and shorebirds, but instead is plucked from the surface of the water or mud by the nimble bird.

## NEST AND NESTING HABITS

The nest is ordinarily a slightly raised platform—1 inch to 3 inches above the water surface—of matted reeds and other vegetation, often with surrounding vegetation bent over the top in a concealing manner.

## EGGS AND INCUBATION

Most often six to ten creamy beige (sometimes faintly olive) eggs are laid. Irregular spots and blotches appear toward either end of the eggs, which are smooth and faintly glossy. The eggs average about 1.6 inches by 1.2 inches (42mm x 30mm).

Incubation is divided equally between the parent birds and lasts for about 21 to 24 days.

---

Field sketches of various rails made at Cape Haze, Placida, Florida, March 22, 1964.

*King Rail*

Virginia Rail
Rallus limicola

King Rail
Rallus elegans

Clapper Rail
Rallus longirostris

Florida clapper Rail
Rallus longirostris scottii
Cape Haze florida
March 22, 1964

Virginia
Rail

K. E. Karalus

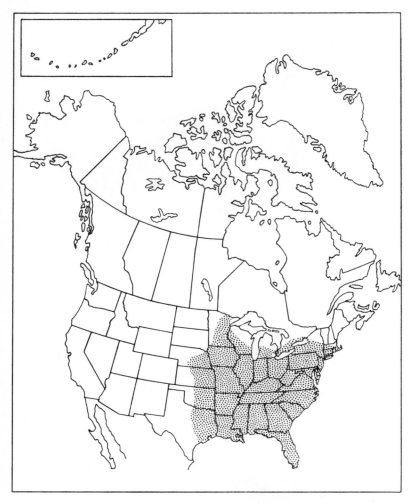

KING RAIL

*Rallus elegans elegans* Audubon

## YOUNG

A heavy coat of thick, short, black fluffy down covers the hatchling. By the November following its hatching, the fledgling bird has acquired virtually adult plumage, though the full richness of adult coloration is not acquired until the next August's molt. When all the young have hatched, they follow their parent birds dutifully about the marsh, quickly learning to snatch up and devour small insects and water life, along with the tender shoots of plants and some seeds. They become very quick in their movements quite soon and, if unexpectedly encountered, scatter in such a manner that one might well mistake them for a group of mice disappearing into the cover.

## MIGRATION

In the fall, the King Rail withdraws from most of its breeding range in North America north of Mexico except for southern Texas, southern Mississippi and Alabama, southernmost Georgia, and all of Florida, though with concentrations heavier in the south than in the north. The migrational flights, usually nocturnal, leave the north in about mid-September and return in April.

*King Rail*

## COMMON NAME

Northern Clapper Rail
(Color Plate XXV)

## SCIENTIFIC NAME

*Rallus longirostris crepitans* Gmelin. The Latin *crepitans* signifies clattering, and *longirostris*, long-billed.

## OTHER COMMON OR COLLOQUIAL NAMES

SALT-MARSH HEN For habitat and appearance.
SEDGE HEN Same.

## BASIC SUBSPECIFIC DIFFERENCES

This essentially grayish subspecies is more muted in coloration than the King Rail and lacks the reddishness which marks that species. As an adult the Northern Clapper Rail is variegated in color, with dark brownish to greenish-brown streaks. The same colors, but paler, appear underneath, becoming more grayish-white on throat and sides of breast, without chestnut shadings. The flanks, undertail, and underwings are deep gray with a brownish cast, sharply and narrowly barred with white. The primaries, secondaries, and tail are dull brown shading to gray and without ruddiness. The eyelids and the short line over the eye are grayish-white. Hatchlings are sooty black and juveniles are

NORTHERN CLAPPER RAIL

*Rallus longirostris crepitans* Gmelin

much like the adults but dusky white below.

The Northern Clapper Rail is particularly fond of salt marshes and is usually found in coastal areas.

## LENGTH AND WINGSPAN

The average length of the Northern Clapper Rail is about 15 inches (386mm) and average wingspan is 20 inches (513mm).

## EGGS

Six to fifteen buffy-white eggs are laid. These are randomly speckled and blotched with brown and faint lavender. In size they average 1.75 inches x 1.1 inches (45mm x 29mm).

## COMMON NAME

Louisiana Clapper Rail
(Subspecies Sketch 9)

## SCIENTIFIC NAME

*Rallus longirostris saturatus* Ridgway.
The Latin *saturatus* signifies dark-colored.

## BASIC SUBSPECIFIC DIFFERENCES

Generally, the Louisiana Clapper Rail is similar to the Northern Clapper Rail in shape and size, but with considerably darker coloration. On the back and upper areas it is a dark olive-gray and quite broadly striped in dark brown to black. The underside lacks the lightness of the Northern Clapper Rail and is a dull cinnamon-red.

LOUISIANA CLAPPER RAIL

*Rallus longirostris saturatus* Ridgway

9. LOUISIANA CLAPPER RAIL

*Rallus longirostris saturatus* Ridgway. Gulfport, Louisiana. A.O.U. Number 211a

# COMMON NAME

Florida Clapper Rail
(Subspecies Sketch 10)

# SCIENTIFIC NAME

*Rallus longirostris scottii* Sennett. Named after W. E. D. Scott, who discovered the bird.

# OTHER COMMON OR COLLOQUIAL NAMES

BLACK CLAPPER
SCOTT'S CLAPPER

# BASIC SUBSPECIFIC DIFFERENCES

This common Florida subspecies is just a bit smaller than either the Northern Clapper Rail or the King Rail, but the principal difference is in the coloration. On its upper portions, this bird is

FLORIDA CLAPPER RAIL

*Rallus longirostris scottii* Sennett

a deep sooty gray, shading into blackish and only a slight edging of olivaceous on the feather rims. On the underside the bird is very dark gray with just a faint touch of cinnamon. As in similar rails, the flanks, axillars, and undertail are well barred with white. The wing coverts are olive-brown to buffy-brown.

---

10. FLORIDA CLAPPER RAIL

*Rallus longirostris scottii* Sennett. Englewood, Florida. A.O.U. Number 211b

*Florida Clapper Rail*

from life

Buttonwood Rookery
Lemon Bay Conservancy Land
Englewood Florida
May 1-1975

## COMMON NAME

Wayne's Clapper Rail
(Subspecies Sketch 11)

## SCIENTIFIC NAME

*Rallus longirostris waynei* Brewster.

## BASIC SUBSPECIFIC DIFFERENCES

This subspecies is about the size of the Florida Clapper Rail and its range overlaps that of *Rallus longirostris scottii,* with some intergrading no doubt occurring. However, in general, Wayne's Clapper Rail does not have the overall conspicuous darkness of the Florida Clapper Rail. Its upper parts are generally much more grayish and the underparts, especially the breast, much lighter.

WAYNE'S CLAPPER RAIL

*Rallus longirostris waynei* Brewster

11. WAYNE'S CLAPPER RAIL

*Rallus longirostris waynei* Brewster. Cedar Key, Florida. A.O.U. Number 211c

A.E. Karalus.
Cedar Key florida
Nov 16-1976

## COMMON NAME

Mangrove Clapper Rail
(Subspecies Sketch 12)

## SCIENTIFIC NAME

*Rallus longirostris insularum* Brooks. *Insularum* is Latin for of islands.

## BASIC SUBSPECIFIC DIFFERENCES

The Mangrove Clapper Rail is very similar in size and markings to Wayne's Clapper Rail, except that the feathers of the upper parts of the Mangrove Clapper Rail are considerably more broadly edged with gray. The area beneath and behind the eyes on the sides of the head is a light neutral gray and the sides of the neck and the breast have a wash of the same coloration.

MANGROVE CLAPPER RAIL

*Rallus longirostris insularum* Brooks

12. MANGROVE CLAPPER RAIL

*Rallus longirostris insularum* Brooks. Big Pine Key, Florida. A.O.U. Number 211d

*Mangrove Clapper Rail*

K. E. Karalus
Big Pine Key
Florida
10 June 1973

## COMMON NAME

California Clapper Rail
(Subspecies Sketch 13)

## SCIENTIFIC NAME

*Rallus longirostris obsoletus* Ridgway. The Latin *obsoletus,* meaning obsolete, refers to the lack of those markings on the upper parts that characterize the King Rail, *Rallus elegans elegans.*

## BASIC SUBSPECIFIC DIFFERENCES

One of the better-marked subspecies, the California Clapper Rail is unique in that it has the characteristics of the Northern Clapper Rail, *Rallus longirostris crepitans,* on the upper parts, and the characteristics of the King Rail on the underparts.

CALIFORNIA CLAPPER RAIL

*Rallus longirostris obsoletus* Ridgway

13. CALIFORNIA CLAPPER RAIL

*Rallus longirostris obsoletus* Ridgway. Los Angeles, California. A.O.U. Number 210

*California Clapper Rail*

## COMMON NAME

Yuma Clapper Rail
(Subspecies Sketch 14)

## SCIENTIFIC NAME

*Rallus longirostris yumanensis* Dickey.

## BASIC SUBSPECIFIC DIFFERENCES

This rail, which is confined strictly to freshwater areas (as opposed to other California rails, which inhabit tidal estuarial salt-marsh systems), is similar in appearance to the Light-Footed Rail, *Rallus longirostris levipes,* but its general color is duller and with more of an olive tone on the upper wing and tail coverts; it also has paler underparts and more slender legs and beak.

## NORTH AMERICAN DISTRIBUTION

The Yuma Clapper Rail is non-migratory and has a very limited distribution. It occurs only in the fresh or (rarely) brackish marshes of the Colorado River in both California and Arizona, from Laguna Dam to Yuma and at the southeastern end of Salton Sea.

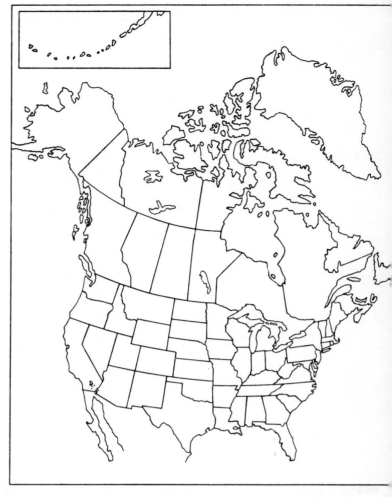

YUMA CLAPPER RAIL

*Rallus longirostris yumanensis* Dickey

14. YUMA CLAPPER RAIL

*Rallus longirostris yumanensis* Dickey. Grand Junction, Colorado. A.O.U. Number 210a

## COMMON NAME

Light-Footed Rail
(Subspecies Sketch 15)

## SCIENTIFIC NAME

*Rallus longirostris levipes* Bangs.

## BASIC SUBSPECIFIC DIFFERENCES

Despite its name, the Light-Footed Rail is not really any more light-footed than any other of the rails. It most resembles the California Clapper Rail—*Rallus longirostris obsoletus*—but its beak is more slender, and it is generally darker than *obsoletus*. The breast and the sides of the neck are rusty in coloration rather than grayish, with a tinge of rufous. The ground color of the flanks is darker and the superciliary streak is white instead of rusty.

## NORTH AMERICAN DISTRIBUTION

This is another of the non-migratory rails. It resides in the salt marshes and, occasionally, brackish or freshwater marshes of southern California from Hueneme in the north (formerly Santa Barbara) to San Diego and southward.

**LIGHT-FOOTED RAIL**

*Rallus longirostris levipes* Bangs

15. LIGHT-FOOTED RAIL

*Rallus longirostris levipes* Bangs. Rosario, Baja California. A.O.U. Number 210.1

K.E. Karalus

## COMMON NAME

Virginia Rail
(Color Plate XXVI)

## SCIENTIFIC NAME

*Rallus limicola limicola* Vieillot. *Limicola* is Latin for mud-dweller.

## LENGTH AND WINGSPAN

Average length of the Virginia.Rail is about 9.5 inches (245mm) and its average wingspan is 13.5 inches (348mm).

## VOICE

The very distinctive voice of the Virginia Rail is often heard, even though the bird itself is very infrequently seen. The sound has a strong metallic timbre and might well be compared to that of an anvil being struck by a light hammer. The Virginia Rail's call is best rendered as *ku-tic ku-tic ku-tic ku-tic.* This is sometimes repeated incessantly day and night.

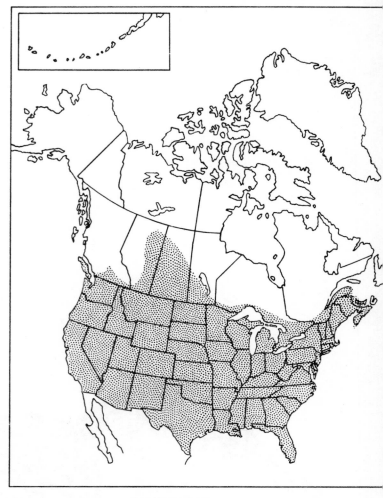

**VIRGINIA RAIL**

*Rallus limicola limicola* Vieillot

## EGGS

Normally there are six to ten eggs in a clutch, though sometimes as many as a dozen or as few as five. They are generally a pale buff, sometimes with a pinkish cast and liberally to sparingly sprinkled with blotches, spots, and streaks of dark brown to reddish-brown.

# SORA

---

**GENUS:** *PORZANA* Vieillot
**SPECIES:** *CAROLINA* (Linnaeus)

## COMMON NAME

Sora (or Sora Rail)
(Color Plate XXVII)

## SCIENTIFIC NAME

*Porzana carolina* (Linnaeus).

## OTHER COMMON OR COLLOQUIAL NAMES

CAROLINA CRAKE From its most common distributional area and from the sound of its voice.

CAROLINA RAIL Distributional nomenclature.

CHICKEN-BILLED RAIL For the character of its beak.

COMMON RAIL Because it is the most common and most widely distributed rail in North America.

LITTLE AMERICAN WATER HEN Descriptive.

MEADOW CHICKEN After its habitat and, to some extent, after its general appearance.

ORTOLAN After the Italian and French (and derived from the Latin *hortulanus*), relating to a garden; the true ortolan is *Emberiza hortulana*, a European bunting deemed a delicacy by gourmets, which is also true of the Sora.

## LENGTH AND WINGSPAN

The Sora's average length is about 8.5 inches (219mm) and its wingspan averages about 12.5 inches (322mm).

## CRESTS, PLUMAGE, ANNUAL MOLT

There are no particularly elongated or exceptional plumes and no crest. The adult birds undergo an incomplete molt, prenuptially, between January and March, but this molt involves only the contour plumage. Another molt, this one complete, occurs postnuptially beginning in July and ending in September.

## VOICE

The call of the Sora is a piglike *oink-oink*, and a loud, descending warbling whistle.

## COLORATION AND MARKINGS: ADULT

The upper parts are a light sepia well marked with black patches and narrow white streakings. The underparts are essentially a neutral gray; while the flanks are very distinctly marked with narrow, back-curved barrings of white. The undertail and underwing are dingy white. The crown is very dark, as are the face, chin, and lores. A dark, broad stripe (usually gray in the female and black in the male) runs down the throat. A light line originates at the base of the beak, runs over the eyes, and trails down the back sides of the head, fading out gradually. The beak is yellow and rather chick-enlike in form.

## COLORATION AND MARKINGS: JUVENILE

Much like the adults except that the underparts are mainly white and there is no black on the throat.

## FOOD AND FEEDING HABITS

The primary foods seem to be small mollusks or gastropods of the marsh, along with aquatic insects and their larvae and, to a lesser extent, seeds and the tender shoots of some young vegetation. Occasionally the bird will eat small tadpoles or earthworms and evidently at some times of the year caterpillars are important in the diet. In autumn, as seeds ripen, this sort of vegetation becomes important in the overall diet, too.

## NEST AND NESTING HABITS

The nest is very much like that of other rails. It is ordinarily constructed a few inches to a foot above the water level in densely reeded or rushed areas of the marsh. The fibers of the nest are interwoven with the surrounding grasses and the whole is rather haphazardly concealed by a canopy of grasses bent over the nest. The actual nest is about 6 inches in diameter, with an inner cavity about 3 inches across and a couple of

inches deep. Quite frequently a small runway of grasses leading the last yard or two to the nest will be constructed.

## EGGS AND INCUBATION

Ordinarily there are between eight and fourteen eggs to each nesting. These eggs range from a reddish to a yellowish beige, with this ground color overlaid with irregular streakings and spottings of brown, chestnut, and dark olive. They are smooth and quite glossy —much glossier, in fact, than those of the Virginia Rail. The average egg size is about 1.25 inches x .9 inch (32mm x 22mm).

Because there are so many eggs in the nest, the Sora, as a rule, puts the eggs in two layers, but even then the bird is hard put to cover and incubate well all that are in the clutch. Both parents incubate, evidently about equally, and incubation begins with the first, second, or third egg laid. Hatching is therefore staggered. The incubation period is fourteen days. As the first eggs hatch, one parent takes the young off, leaving the other parent to continue incubation.

## YOUNG

As with most other rail species, the downy chicks of the Sora are black and

---

Sora, *Porzana carolina* (Linnaeus). Field sketches made at Cape Haze, Placida, Florida, September 14, 1956. In the nest in which the female on the lower right was found were two normal eggs, plus a third that was one third larger than the others (the latter was in fact two eggs bound into one).

*Sora*

K. E. Karalus

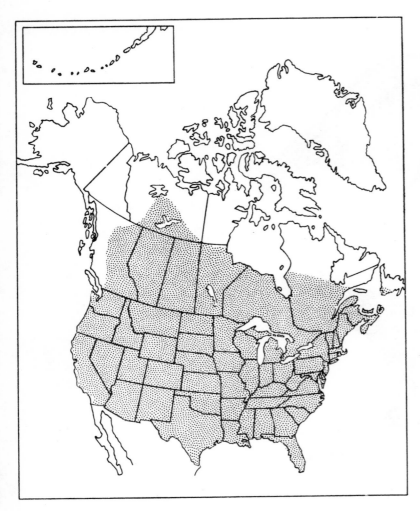

SORA

*Porzana carolina* (Linnaeus)

fluffy and very soon after hatching are able to move about and follow the parent birds. The only real difference between the down covering of the Sora and that of other rails is its glossiness and the fact that there are some stiff and usually curly bright yellow hairs on the chin. Full adult plumage is assumed by the first postnuptial complete molt, when the bird is about sixteen months old.

## NORTH AMERICAN DISTRIBUTION

The Sora is one of the most common and widely distributed rails in all of North America.

*Sora*

# YELLOW RAIL

---

GENUS: *COTURNICOPS* Gray
SPECIES: *NOVEBORACENSIS* (Gemlin)
SUBSPECIES: *noveboracensis* (Gemlin)

♀

white wingpatch
visible only when flushed
which is rare

H. E. Karalus

## COMMON NAME

Yellow Rail
(Color Plate XXVIII)

## SCIENTIFIC NAME

*Coturnicops noveboracensis noveboracensis* (Gmelin). From *coturnicops*, meaning quail-like, and *noveboracensis*, meaning New York.

## BASIC SPECIES DIFFERENCES

Slightly smaller than the Sora, the Yellow Rail, as its name suggests, is basically yellowish, especially on the underside and flank plumage, where the Sora is gray; it also lacks the blackness of face and lores that the Sora shows. Instead of red eyes, as the Sora has, its irides are yellowish.

There is a very basic quail-like appearance to the Yellow Rail when it is afoot, although this similarity vanishes as the bird takes wing, since its weak, fluttery flight pattern, like that of the other rails, has no quail-like quality. Basically in coloration it is streaked with blackish and brownish yellow on the upper parts, and thickly marked with narrow white semicircles and transverse barrings. The underparts are a pale brownish-yellow, deepest on the breast and fading on the belly. Many of the breast feathers are

Yellow Rail, *Coturnicops noveboracensis noveboracensis* (Gmelin).

**YELLOW RAIL**

*Coturnicops noveboracensis noveboracensis* (Gmelin)

tipped in black. The flanks are generally black with numerous barrings of white. The lining of the wings and the secondaries is white. A dark brownish stripe is under each eye. The average length of the Yellow Rail is 6.4 inches (164mm) and its average wingspan is 10 inches (254mm).

Although its distribution is quite wide on the continent, it is nowhere nearly as abundant as the Sora.

## EGGS

The usual clutch contains seven to ten eggs. These are a buffy warm brown with reddish-brown to dark brown spots and blotches, mostly at the larger end.

# *LATERALLUS* RAILS

---

GENUS: *LATERALLUS* Gray
SPECIES: *JAMAICENSIS* (Gmelin)
SUBSPECIES: *jamaicensis* (Gmelin)
Black Rail

*coturniculus* (Ridgway)
Farallon Rail

Laterallus of
jamaicensis
coturniculus
Point Reyes
California  Oct 29
1913

one specimen observed
near Dayton museum
of Natural History
Dayton Ohio
Oct 1974

Englewood florida
march 1973

Chick

Karl E. Karalus

## COMMON NAME

Black Rail
(Color Plate XXIX)

## SCIENTIFIC NAME

*Laterallus jamaicensis jamaicensis* (Gmelin). From *laterallus*, a rail.

## OTHER COMMON OR COLLOQUIAL NAMES

LITTLE BLACK CRAKE
LITTLE BLACK RAIL
JAMAICAN CRAKE
JAMAICAN RAIL

BLACK RAIL

*Laterallus jamaicensis jamaicensis* (Gmelin)

## BASIC SPECIES DIFFERENCES

A very small rail, no longer than a large sparrow. The crown is black, the nape and upper back are a deep red-brown, and the lower back a dark brown, flecked with white. The beak is black. Young birds are similar to the adults except that they are paler on the underside and white on the throat. The crown is brownish rather than black. Not terribly abundant, yet not as rare as it was once thought to be, an impression due to the extreme secretiveness of the bird in most circumstances.

Black and Farallon Rails (*Laterallus jamaicensis jamaicensis* [Gmelin] and *Laterallus jamaicensis coturniculus* [Ridgway]).

## EGGS

Quite different from those of either the Sora or the Yellow Rail. The usual clutch is from six to nine eggs which are 1.1 inches x .8 inch (27mm x 21mm) on the average. The basic coloration is cream-white with fine cinnamon to drab brown speckles on the large end of the egg.

# COMMON NAME

Farallon Rail
(Color Plate XXIX)

## SCIENTIFIC NAME

*Laterallus jamaicensis coturniculus* (Ridgway).

## OTHER COMMON OR COLLOQUIAL NAMES

CALIFORNIA BLACK RAIL (infrequent)
FARALLON BLACK CRAKE
FARALLON BLACK RAIL

FARALLON RAIL

*Laterallus jamaicensis coturniculus* (Ridgway)

## BASIC SUBSPECIFIC DIFFERENCES

Even smaller than the Black Rail, *Laterallus jamaicensis jamaicensis*, the Farallon Rail has an average wing length of only 2.5 inches (64mm). In almost all respects it is very similar to the Black Rail, except that it is much more uniform in its coloration and does not have the white specks which are so significant on the Black Rail. The bird is very rarely seen and very limited in its population north of Mexico.

## NORTH AMERICAN DISTRIBUTION

The subspecies is known to breed in a very limited scope in the southwesternmost point of California, specifically in the immediate area of San Diego. There was one record of a nesting near Chino, California. During the winter, it has been known to migrate coastally as far north as San Francisco. It is also found inland casually as far as Stockton, Riverside, and the Salton Sea in southern California.

*Farallon Rail*

# COMMON GALLINULE

---

GENUS: *GALLINULA* Brisson
SPECIES: *CHLOROPUS* (Linnaeus)
SUBSPECIES: *cachinnans* Bangs

## COMMON NAME

Common Gallinule
(Color Plate XXX)

## SCIENTIFIC NAME

*Gallinula chloropus cachinnans* Bangs. From the Latin, *gallinula,* meaning little hen; *chloropus,* meaning green-footed; and *cachinnans,* meaning laughing.

## OTHER COMMON OR COLLOQUIAL NAMES

MUD HEN A term descriptive of its habitat but one more commonly applied to the American Coot and certain of the rails, such as the King Rail and Northern Clapper Rail.

## SHAPE AT REST AND IN FLIGHT

This is a long-legged, short-bodied, and relatively short-necked marsh bird with a chickenlike beak and a rather sloping forehead marked by a scarlet unfeathered frontal plate. The toes are very long and with a considerable span. Generally, the tail is held upright.

In flight, the wings are rather short and rounded. The tail is short.

The flight of *Gallinula chloropus cachinnans* is not really very strong and has an excessively flapping, fluttery quality.

If the flight is short, which is ordinarily the case, the legs will dangle very awkwardly below. On longer flights the legs will extend back and be tight against the abdomen, extending far beyond the short tail. On long flights the head becomes more outstretched in front and the wingbeat somewhat smoother and stronger, with less visible effort.

## LENGTH AND WINGSPAN

The Common Gallinule has an average length of 13.1 inches (336mm) and a wingspan which averages 20.8 inches (533mm).

## LEGS, FEET, AND CLAWS

The feet, of a beautiful lime hue, are narrow-boned with long, slender toes. The legs are the same shade as the feet up to the first joint, above which they turn a shade of orange. The toes are marked by an evident (although only very slight) marginal membrane.

## EYES

The Common Gallinule's irides are generally red, sometimes shading into a chestnut-brownish.

## CRESTS, PLUMAGE, ANNUAL MOLT

There are no particular plumes of note, nor any crest. The adults have a complete molt, usually beginning in early August and lasting through most of September or into early October. There is also a partial prenuptial molt occurring in the spring, but neither molt brings much of a difference in coloration.

## COLORATION AND MARKINGS: ADULT

Most often the very tip of the beak will have a faint yellowish or even greenish-yellow cast, but the remainder is bright red, and this scarlet coloration is clearly offset by the slate-black coloration of the entire head and throat. This slate-black shades to a deep coot-like neutral gray on the foreback and belly. The mid and rear back is very dark brown and the wings fuscous. The middle undertail coverts are black and the outer ones are white (the latter appear as the bird moves as a couple of white patches). A ring of scarlet encircles the leg just above the heel and the rest of the tarsus (or shank) and foot is greenish.

## COLORATION AND MARKINGS: JUVENILE

Very similar to the adult, though less intense generally. The throat is white and the underparts are more or less mixed with white. The crown is a medium brown. Otherwise gray.

## HABITAT AND ROOSTING

The Common Gallinule is strictly confined to swampy areas, preferably where muddy conditions provide a good growth of lily pads and other surface vegetation upon which the bird can walk and search for food. It is less often seen in marsh areas that are strictly of a saw grass, rush, or reed character. The edges of slow rivers and bayous, especially where they are broadly muddy or overgrown with water hyacinth, are especially favored. Roosting is sometimes done in heavy marsh vegetation and at other times in dense brush which is contiguous to the water.

## FOOD AND FEEDING HABITS

Practically all the food eaten by the Common Gallinule is found amid floating or surface vegetation in water where there is little or no current. Popular belief had it that *Gallinula chloropus cachinnans* was essentially insectivorous, but recent studies have shown this is not the case; the bird is, in fact, about 85 to 90 per cent herbivorous, with the remainder comprised of aquatic insects and occasionally mollusks or gastropods. The vegetation eaten is primarily tender new shoots, rootlets, leaves, and seeds of various water plants.

## COURTSHIP AND MATING

When the male approaches the female he wishes to win, they are ordinarily in the water, either standing on floating vegetation or swimming. Usually it is the latter, at least for the male. As he nears her, he begins uttering his *tikka-tikka-tikka-tikka* mating call, at the same time holding his head so near the water surface that occasionally the beak touches the water and his neck is curved in a manner curiously like a swan's. His wings open partially and he raises and spreads his short tail to its utmost, exposing as much as possible the white undertail coverts, which seem to be the most important breeding feathers. He swims with his head bobbing back and forth, much in the manner of the American Coot. He paddles back and forth before her, drawing ever closer, occasionally raising his head high. At last, though no apparent visible or audible sign is given to signify her acceptance, he abruptly swims to her and they move off together into heavier cover to copulate. The copulation, and occasionally the male's display, are repeated daily for at least three or four days, at the end of which time the pair gets ready to build their nest.

COMMON GALLINULE

*Gallinula chloropus cachinnans* Bangs

## NEST AND NESTING HABITS

Ordinarily the nest is built amid dense stands of reeds or rushes, but with close access to reasonably open water. The nest is a dense interweaving of reeds to a height of about 8 inches above the water surface. The diameter of the nest is about 20 inches, but with an inner cavity diameter of only about 7 inches and a depth of less than 3 inches. Such a nest is usually anchored and often has an interwoven reedwork pathway leading to the nest from the water.

## EGGS AND INCUBATION

Most often there are from eight to twelve eggs, which vary from a pale buffy-olive to a distinct cinnamon-buff in their ground color. On this ground color are numerous irregular spots, dots, blotches and irregular streakings of dark brown, cinnamon-red, and olive-drab. The eggs are smooth, but with little or no gloss. In size they average about 1.5 inches x 1.2 inches (40mm x 31mm).

The incubation, by both parents, commences with the first egg, and lasts for twenty-one days.

## YOUNG

The downy young bird has only a few hairlike feathers on its head, but the remainder of the bird is covered with a thick and soft down of glossy greenish-black on the upper parts and dull black on the underparts. At this time the skin at the base of the beak is bright scarlet and there is a sharp spur protruding at the bend of the wing, which the young bird uses in climbing through dense cover. It is capable of leaving the nest and swimming shortly after being hatched. Curly white hairs occur frequently on the throats of the hatchlings. Full adult plumage is not acquired until the first postnupital molt the next year, when the bird is about fourteen or fifteen months old.

# PURPLE GALLINULE

---

GENUS: *PORPHYRULA* Blyth
SPECIES: *MARTINICA* (Linnaeus)

## COMMON NAME

Purple Gallinule
(Color Plate XXXI)

## SCIENTIFIC NAME

*Porphyrula martinica* (Linnaeus). From the Latin *porphyra,* meaning purple.

## BASIC SPECIES DIFFERENCES

In size, shape, and bearing, the Purple Gallinule is virtually identical to the Common Gallinule, but the immense difference is in the coloration. The Purple Gallinule is one of North America's most gorgeously colored birds. Sometimes called "Blue Pete," the Purple Gallinule has a beak much like a chicken's in shape, but bright yellow at the tip and bright red for the remaining two thirds of its length. The frontal shield, instead of continuing red, as in the case of the Common Gallinule, is a light pastel blue. The head and underparts are a very distinct, eye-catching purple with a certain amount of gloss if not true iridescence. The hind part of the bird from mid-back and the wings are a dark to very deep green, often shading into bluish-green. The legs and feet are greenish-yellow, but with more yellowish apparent than in the greenish-yellow legs of the Com-

PURPLE GALLINULE

*Porphyrula martinica* (Linnaeus)

mon Gallinule. The undertail coverts are white and, importantly, show as a very prominent white patch when the tail is raised.

The immature birds are less vividly colored, with the top of the head a warm sepia color, the throat white, and the breast a pale buff to tawny. The entire back is solidly greenish-brown except at the rump, which is a clove brown. Downy young are an unbroken greenish-black in coloration.

# AMERICAN COOT

SUBFAMILY: *FULICINAE*
GENUS: *FULICA* Linnaeus
SPECIES: *AMERICANA* Gmelin
SUBSPECIES: *americana* Gmelin

# COMMON NAME

American Coot
(Color Plate XXXII)

## SCIENTIFIC NAME

*Fulica americana americana* Gmelin. From the Latin *fuligo,* meaning soot, or a sooty color, referring to the general coloration of the bird.

## OTHER COMMON OR COLLOQUIAL NAMES

Because it is so common and so frequently seen, the American Coot is a very familiar American bird and, as a result, is known by a great number of common or colloquial names. Most are of obvious origin and some of the most frequently used names are

BLUE PETER
COOT
CROW-BILL
CROW-DUCK
FLUSTERER
HEN-BILL
IVORY-BILLED COOT
LA FOULQUE AMÉRICAINE
MARSH HEN
MEADOW HEN
MOOR HEN
MUD COOT
MUD HEN
PELICK
POND CROW
POND HEN
PULL-DOO (POULE D'EAU)
SEA CROW
SHUFFLER
SPLATTERER
WATER CHICKEN
WATER HEN
WHITE-BILL
WHITE-BILL COOT
WHITE-BELLIED MUD HEN

## SHAPE AT REST AND IN FLIGHT

The American Coot is rather ducklike when resting on the water surface as it ordinarily does, but easily distinguished from a duck by its white beak, very much like that of a chicken. When standing on the ground, its legs are slightly longer than those of a duck and the toes are lobed rather than webbed.

It is even more ducklike when in full strong flight, but differs from a duck when first taking off, at which time it begins flapping and running along the water surface until it is actually stepping on the water surface faster and faster until the rapidly beating wings can lift a body which seems too heavy. Often the American Coot will seem to give up before takeoff speed is reached and simply settle back onto the water surface, or dive if there is danger. The wings are are set well back in flight, like those of a duck. The neck is well extended, also in ducklike fashion, but the beak, instead of being pointed straight forward, is pointed slightly downward. The feet extend behind the tail a short way, with

---

*(Overleaf)* American Coot, *Fulica americana americana* Gmelin.

K.E. Karalus

April 1975

Near Dayton
Museum of
Natural History

Still water River
Dayton Ohio
Montgomery Co.

the toes pointing upward and helping to serve as a rudder to aid the tiny and ineffective tail. In local flight, the altitude is quite low, often just above the water surface. On longer flights, especially migrations, the flight is high and quite frequently in company with flocks of ducks.

## LENGTH AND WINGSPAN

The American Coot has an average length of just over 15 inches (386mm) and its wingspan averages about 25.5 inches (653mm).

## BEAK

The beak ranges from pure milk white to a sort of fleshy color, often with a clayish cast. It is marked with reddish-black near the tip and at the base of the frontal plate.

## LEGS, FEET, AND CLAWS

The legs and feet range from dull grayish-green to a rather bright yellowish-green, with black claws. All of the toes are lobed, facilitating better swimming than is possible for the gallinules, yet also permitting pad-walking, an ability shared with the gallinules. The hind-toe lobe is rudimentary.

## EYES

The irides are a bright carmine at all seasons.

## CRESTS, PLUMAGE, ANNUAL MOLT

Beginning in August, adults have a complete molt, which is usually finished before the end of September. A rather limited partial molt occurs prenuptially early each spring.

## VOICE

The American Coot is capable of a wide range of vocal utterances, most of them far from melodious. Some are simply guttural squawks and croakings. A few of the calls, however, have a somewhat pleasant sound. Foremost among these is a rather common early morning cooing sort of chatter that passes back and forth among them as they feed in the marsh fringe of open waters. There is also a less melodious clucking sound which is quite common and, less often, a heavy quack similar to that of a mallard duck.

## COLORATION AND MARKINGS: ADULT

The plumage is generally a dark slate-gray in color, slightly paler on the underside and noticeably darker, almost to black, on the head and neck. The dark gray gets a sort of olivaceous cast on the back. The crissum, the edge of the wing, and the tips of the secondaries are white, but these markings are generally hidden except when the bird is in flight. The primaries are dusky gray except for the outer edge of the first, which is white. The tail is gray-black.

*American Coot*

## COLORATION AND MARKINGS: JUVENILE

The young are colored very much like the adults except that the grays and blacks are not as crisp; there is a more general dullness of tone and the overall coloration is slightly paler than in the adult. There is considerably more white or dingy white on the underparts than in the adult. The frontal shield at the base of the beak is not developed and the beak is dingy in its coloration and lacks the distinctive reddish spots seen in adult birds. Full adult plumage is acquired after the first postnuptial molt when the young bird is over a year old.

## HABITAT AND ROOSTING

The marsh fringe is the American Coot's favored habitat, because of the plentiful food and security the marsh provides. Roosting is normally in small open pockets in the reed or rush banks and usually occurs in groups of from six to twenty birds, though the flocks grow much larger as migrational periods near. In migration and on wintering grounds, the bird often associates in large numbers with diving ducks.

## FOOD AND FEEDING HABITS

The great majority of the American Coot's food is vegetative—primarily seeds, tender grass sprouts, and some different sorts of greenery. Wild celery, milfoil, corn, millet, various cereal grains—all these are food for the American Coot, along with occasional animal matter such as grasshoppers and other insects. Another item of the diet is green algae, which the American Coot seems to have a special fondness for at certain times. Occasionally it will eat tadpoles, snails, and small fish.

## COURTSHIP AND MATING

Rivalry is very keen among the American Coots and reasonably serious fights between males during the courtship period are frequent. These fights are sometimes over territory and at other times to gain the acceptance of a female. In addition to fighting, the males will display before the females. Most often this amounts to the male swimming toward the female, his head and neck on the water surface, his wingtips raised high above the tail, and the ridiculous little tail itself spread and elevated so that the white markings on either side become very obvious. As he gets very near to her, the female, deciding in his favor, assumes the same position. When he gets to within a couple of feet of her, the male turns, shows his tail and starts slowly swimming away, encouraging her to follow. If she does not, he returns and repeats the act. When they are finally paired, the two birds will frequently swim directly toward one another, scatter droplets of water on each other, and then begin nuzzling and preening one another's neck and upper breast and back feathers.

## NEST AND NESTING HABITS

Although the male stays close at hand, most of the nest construction is under-

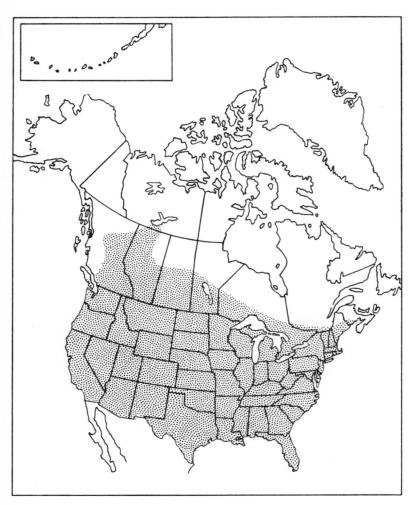

AMERICAN COOT

*Fulica americana americana* Gmelin

## EGGS AND INCUBATION

The usual number of eggs laid is from eight to sixteen, most commonly nine to eleven. They are a warm buffy color well covered with a multitude of tiny dots and blotches of dark brown and black over the entire surface. They are smooth with a slight gloss and in size they average about 1.9 inches x 1.3 inches (49mm x 34mm).

The incubation, shared by both parent birds, extends over a period of twenty-two days. Frequently the male will guard the female while she incubates, but rarely is the opposite true.

## YOUNG

The downy young are strikingly colored but not really very pretty. They appear shaggy, with a body down coloration of black and scattered orange hairs here and there. There are also scattered hairlike feathers, some curly and some short and stiff and straight of pure yellow or pure white. The bald crown is very reddish. The hatchlings are quite precocious; they leave the nesting platform and begin swimming within an hour or so of emergence. By the end of just a few hours they can dive with remarkable skill and stay under water for a surprising length of time—upward of three minutes. The feet grow much too fast for the body, resulting in chicks with enormously oversized legs and feet. Not until it is over a year old, at the first postnuptial molt, does the young bird assume full adult plumage. Swimming or walking, it bobs its head—as does the adult—with each movement of the feet.

taken by the female. She starts the nest by gradually building up a platform of living reed stems, which she bends over and fastens down by interlacing them together. In this manner a nesting platform is eventually built up. It is quite firmly fastened to the growing reeds of the area and well woven into a substantial basket. The outside diameter of the completed nest is about 15 inches. The inner diameter, well lined with soft plant materials, is about 7 inches, with the egg basin of the nest fully 8 inches above the water.

*American Coot*

## MIGRATION

American Coots are very hardy and, though they migrate long distances, they are among the last of the summer birds to leave the northernmost portions of their range in fall, and among the first to return in spring. Quite often they will not leave the northern lakes until forced to do so by the freezing of lake surfaces and the increasing scarcity of food. The birds come together into flocks numbering in the thousands and they literally darken the sky when they fly. In the dead of winter, they are rarely found north of the United States and, depending upon the severity of the winter, are often scarce in the northernmost tier of states.

## ECONOMIC INFLUENCE

While American Coots cannot be considered a top-notch game bird, they are nevertheless on the migratory waterfowl game lists and are hunted extensively each year. They travel with duck flocks quite often but, since they are not as maneuverable as ducks, nor as wary, nor as fast in flight, they are often killed when the ducks are not.

# BIBLIOGRAPHY

It is not possible to list here every source consulted in the preparation of *The Wading Birds of North America.* Oftentimes certain books, papers, theses, leaflets, and similar materials provided only a single minor datum which was incorporated into this volume; to list these, except in the most unusual of cases, would be virtually pointless. The following works, therefore, are those which we relied upon most heavily in the research of this book.

\* \* \*

Allen, Robert P. "Additional Data on the Food of the Whooping Crane," *The Auk,* No. 71, Vol. II, page 198, April 1954

———— "The Whooping Crane," *National Audubon Society Research Report,* No. 3, xxvi, July 1952

American Ornithologists' *Union Check-list of North American Birds,* Fifth Edition, Lord Baltimore Press, Baltimore, Maryland, 1957

Applegarth, John H. "The Ecology of the California Clapper Rail on the South Arm of San Francisco Bay," AM thesis, Stanford University, 1938

Bancroft, Griffing "Northern Breeding Record for Reddish Egret," *The Auk,* Vol. 88, No. 2, page 429, April 1971

Bent, Arthur Cleveland "Life Histories of North American Marsh Birds," *U.S. National Museum Bulletin,* No. 35, Washington, 1926

Billard, Ruth S. "An Ecological Study of the Virginia Rail *(Rallus limicola limicola)* and the Sora *(Porzana carolina)* in Some Connecticut Swamps," MS thesis, Iowa State College, 1947

Blaker, D. "Behaviour of the Cattle Egret *Ardeola ibis,*" *The Ostrich,* Vol. 40, No. 3, September 1969

Campbell, R. Wayne "The Green Heron in British Columbia," *Syesis,* Vol. 5, 1972, and *Biological Abstracts,* Vol. 55, No. 9, 1973

Caslick, James W. "Sandhill Cranes in Yellowstone Park," *The Auk,* Vol. 72, No. 1, January 1955

Chapman, Frank L. *Handbook of Birds of Eastern North America,* D. Appleton Co., New York, 1929

Cottam, Clarence "Food of the Limpkin," *Wilson Bulletin,* Vol. 48, No. 1, March 1936

———— "Supplementary Notes on the Food of the Limpkin," *The Nautilus,* Vol. 55, No. 4, April 1942

Coues, Elliott *Key to North American Birds,* Fifth Edition, Vol. II, The Page Co., Boston, Mass., 1927

Crosby, Gilbert T. "Spread of the Cattle Egret in the Western Hemisphere," *Bird Banding,* Vol. 43, No. 3, July 1972

Dennis, Clifford J. "Observations on the Feeding Behaviour of the Great Blue Heron," *The Passenger Pigeon,* Vol. 33, No. 4, Winter 1971

DeVore, Jon E. "The Sandhill Crane in Tennessee," *The Migrant,* Vol. 43, No. 2, June 1972

Dinsmore, James J. "Foraging Success of Cattle Egrets, *Bubulcus ibis,*" *The American Midland Naturalist,* Vol. 89, No. 1, January 1973

Drewien, Roderick C., and Elwood C. Bizeau "Status and Distribution of Greater Sandhill Cranes in the Rocky Mountains," *Journal of Wildlife Management,* Vol. 38, No: 4, October 1974

Dunmire, William W. *Birds of the National Parks in Hawaii,* Hawaii Natural History Association, Honolulu, Hawaii, 1961

Engeling, Gus A. "King and Clapper Rail," *Texas Game and Fish,* Vol. 8, No. 11, October 1950

Ferrigno, Frederick "Some Aspects of the Nesting Biology, Population Dynamics, and Habitat Associations of the Clapper Rail," MS thesis, Rutgers University, 1966

Friedmann, Herbert, Ludlow Griscom, and Robert T. Moore *Distributional Check-list of the Birds of Mexico*, Cooper Ornithological Club, Pacific Coast Avifauna, No. 29, Part I and Part II, Berkeley, California, 1950

Friley, Charles E., Jr., Logan J. Bennett, and George O. Hendrickson "The American Coot in Iowa," *The Wilson Bulletin*, Vol. 50, No. 2, June 1938

Glahn, James F. "Study of Breeding Rails with Recorded Calls in North-Central Colorado," *The Wilson Bulletin*, Vol. 86, No. 3, September 1974

Godfrey, W. Earl *The Birds of Canada*, Queen's Printer, Ottawa, 1968

Gullion, Gordon W. "The Displays and Calls of the American Coot," *The Wilson Bulletin*, Vol. 64, No. 2, June 1952

———— "Observations on Molting of the American Coot," *The Condor*, Vol. 55, No. 2, March–April 1953

———— "The Reproductive Cycle of American Coots in California," *The Auk*, Vol. 71, No. 4, October 1954

———— "Sex and Age Determination in the American Coot," *Journal of Wildlife Management*, Vol. 16, No. 2, April 1952

———— "Territorial Behaviour of the American Coot," *The Condor*, Vol. 55, No. 4, July–August 1953

Hall, Henry M. "Wakulla Limpkins," *Audubon Magazine*, Vol. 52, No. 5, September–October 1950

Hamerstrom, F. N., Jr. "Central Wisconsin Crane Study," *The Wilson Bulletin*, Vol. 50, No. 3, September 1958

Hamilton, Anne P. "Roseate Spoonbills in Georgia and Tennessee in 1972," *The Oriole*, Vol. 40, Nos. 1 & 2, March–June 1975

Harmon, William Z. "Notes on Cranes," *The Florida Naturalist*, Vol. 27, No. 1, January 1954

Henika, Franklin S. "Sandhill Cranes in Wisconsin and Other Lake States," *Proceedings of the North American Wildlife Conference*, 1936

Henny, Charles J., and Michael R. Bethers "Population Ecology of the Great Blue Heron with Special Reference to Western Ore-

gon," *The Canadian Field Naturalist*, Vol. 85, No. 3, July–September 1971

Hopkins, Milton N., Jr. "Does the Little Blue Heron Breed in the White Plumage?" *The Oriole*, Vol. 36, No. 4, December 1971

Hopkins, Milton N., Jr., and Philip G. Murton "Rookery Data from South Georgia," *The Oriole*, Vol. 34, No. 1, March 1969

Houston, C. Stuart "Longevity Record for Black-Crowned Night Heron: 16½ Years," *The Blue Jay*, Vol. 32, No. 3, September 1974

Howell, Arthur H. *Florida Bird Life*, Coward-McCann, Inc., New York, 1932

Jaeger, Edmund C. *A Source Book of Biological Names and Terms*, Charles C. Thomas, Publisher, Springfield, Illinois, 1955

Jenni, Donald A. "A Study of the Ecology of Four Species of Herons During the Breeding Season at Lake Alice, Alachua County, Florida," *Ecology Monographs*, Vol. 39, No. 3, Summer 1969

Johnson, Douglas H., and Robert E. Stewart "Racial Composition of Migrant Populations of Sandhill Cranes in the Northern Plains States," *The Wilson Bulletin*, Vol. 85, No. 2, June 1973

Jones, John C. "Food Habits of the American Coot, with Notes on Distribution," USDI, *Biological Survey Research Bulletin* 2, 1940

Kiel, William H., Jr. "Nesting Studies of the Coot in Southwestern Manitoba," *Journal of Wildlife Management*, Vol. 19, No. 2, April 1955

Kiel, William H., Jr., and Arthur S. Hawkins "Status of the Coot in the Mississippi Flyway," *Transactions of the 18th North American Wildlife Conference*, 1953

Kozicky, Edward L., and Francis V. Schmidt "Nesting Habits of the Clapper Rail in New Jersey," *The Auk*, Vol. 66, No. 4, October 1949

Kushlan, James A. "Aerial Feeding in the Snowy Egret," *The Wilson Bulletin*, Vol. 84, No. 2, June 1972

———— "Least Bittern Nesting Colonially," *The Auk*, Vol. 90, No. 3, July 1973

———— "Promiscuous Mating Behaviour in the White Ibis," *The Wilson Bulletin*, Vol. 85, No. 3, September 1973

———— "White Ibis Nesting in the Florida Everglades," *The Wilson Bulletin*, Vol. 85, No. 2, June 1973

Lemmon, Robert S. *Our Amazing Birds*, Doubleday & Company, Inc., Garden City, New
York, 1952

Lewis, James Chester "Ecology of the Sandhill
Crane in the Southeastern Central Flyway,"
Ph.D. thesis, Oklahoma State University,
December 1974

Littlefield, Carroll D. "Flightlessness in Sandhill
Cranes," *The Auk*, Vol. 87, No. 1, January
1970

Lowery, George H., Jr. *Louisiana Birds*, Louisiana
State University Press, Baton Rouge, Louisiana, 1955

Lumsden, Harry G. "The Status of the Sandhill
Crane in Northern Ontario," *The Canadian
Field Naturalist*, Vol. 85, No. 4, October–
December 1971

Mangold, Robert E. "Noisy Phantom of the Salt
Marsh: The Clapper Rail," *New Jersey Outdoors*, Vol. 23, No. 12, June 1973

McLeod, Edith R. "Sandhill Cranes at Meiss
Lake, Northern California," *The Condor*, Vol.
56, No. 4, July–August 1954

Meanley, Brooke "Natural History of the King
Rail," *North American Fauna*, No. 67, May
1969

———— "Nesting of the King Rail in the Arkansas
Rice Fields," *The Auk*, Vol. 70, No. 3, July
1953

Miller, Richard S. "The Brood Size of Cranes,"
*The Wilson Bulletin*, Vol. 85, No. 4, December
1973

———— "The Florida Gallinule: Breeding Birds
of the Philadelphia Region (Part III),"
*Cassinia*, Vol. 36, 1946

Miller, Richard S., Daniel S. Botkin, and Roy
Mendelssohn "The Whooping Crane *(Grus
americana)* Population of North America,"
*Biology and Conservation*, Volume 6, No. 2,
April 1974

Mock, Douglas W. "Aerial Hunting by Little
Blue Herons," *The Wilson Bulletin*, Vol. 86,
No. 3, September 1974

Munro, David A. "A Study of the Economic Status of Sandhill Cranes in Saskatchewan,"
*Journal of Wildlife Management*, Vol. 14, No.
3, July 1950

Naylor, A. E., A. W. Miller, and M. E. Foster
"Observations on the Sandhill Crane in
Northeastern California," *The Condor*, Vol.
56, No. 4, July–August 1954

Nesbitt, Stephen A. "Wood Stork Nesting in
North Florida," *The Florida Field Naturalist*,
Vol. 1, No. 2, Fall 1973

Oberholser, Harry C. "A Revision of the Clapper
Rails *(Rallus longirostris* Boddaert)," Smith-
sonian Institution, *Proceedings of the United
States National Museum*, Vol. 84 (3018), 1937

Oney, John "Fall Food Habits of the Clapper
Rail in Georgia," *Journal of Wildlife Management*, Vol. 15, No. 1, January 1951

———— "Final Report: Clapper Rail Survey and
Investigation Study," *Georgia Game and Fish
Commission Final Report Federal Aid Program
for Georgia*, W-9-R, 1954

Partch, Max "The 1972 Great Blue Heron Migration in Minnesota," *The Loon*, Vol. 44,
No. 3, Fall 1972

Pearson, T. Gilbert *Birds of America*, Garden City
Publishing Co., Garden City, New York,
1936

Peterson, Roger Tory *A Field Guide to the Birds*,
Second Edition, Houghton Mifflin Co., Boston, Massachusetts, 1947

Phillips, Allan, Joe Marshall, and Gale Monson
*The Birds of Arizona*, University of Arizona
Press, Tucson, 1964

Pospichal, Leo B., and William H. Marshall "A
Field Study of Sora Rail and Virginia Rail
in Central Minnesota," *The Flicker*, Vol. 26,
No. 1, March 1954

Pratt, Helen M. "Breeding Biology of Great Blue
Herons and Common Egrets in Central
California," *The Condor*, Vol. 72, No. 4, Oc-
tober 1970

———— "Nesting Success of Common Egrets and
Great Blue Herons in the San Francisco Bay
Region," *The Condor*, Vol. 74, No. 4, Winter
1972

Ramsey, J. J. "The Status of the Cattle Egret
in Texas," *Bulletin of the Texas Ornithological
Society*, Vol. 4, 1971 (from *The Auk*, Vol. 89,
No. 4, 1972)

Rapp, William F., Jr. "The Status of Cranes in
Nebraska," *The Wilson Bulletin*, Vol. 66, No.
3, September 1954

Reese, Jan G. "Unusual Feeding Behavior of
Great Blue Herons and Common Egrets,"
*The Condor*, Vol. 75, No. 3, Autumn 1973

Reynard, George B. "Some Vocalizations of the
Black, Yellow, and Virginia Rails," *The Auk*,
Vol. 91, No. 4, October 1974

Ridgway, Robert, and Herbert Friedmann "The Birds of North and Middle America, Part IX," *U.S. National Museum Bulletin*, No. 50, 1941

Roberts, Thomas S. *Bird Portraits in Color*, University of Minnesota Press, Minneapolis, 1934

Rudegeair, Thomas "The Gular Pouch of the Female White Ibis," *The Auk*, Vol. 92, No. 1, January 1975

Schmidt, F. V., and Paul McLain "The Clapper Rail in New Jersey," *New Jersey Division of Fish and Game*, 9-page mimeo, 1951

Shields, Robert H., and Earl L. Benham "Farm Crops as Food Supplements for Whooping Cranes," *Journal of Wildlife Management*, Vol. 33, No. 4, October 1969

Siegfried, W. R. "Communal Roosting of the Cattle Egret," *Transactions of the Royal Society of South Africa*, Vol. 39, No. 4, 1971

——— "The Nest of the Cattle Egret," *The Ostrich*, Vol. 42, No. 3, 1971

Sooter, Clarence A. "Ecology and Management of the American Coot (*Fulica americana americana* Gmelin)," *Iowa State College Journal of Science*, 1941

Stephenson, James Dale "Plumage Development and Growth of Young Whooping Cranes," MS thesis, Oregon State University, June 1971

Stevenson, James O., and Richard E. Griffith "Winter Life of the Whooping Crane," *The Condor*, Vol. 48, No. 4, July–August 1946

Stewart, Robert E. "Clapper Rail Populations of the Middle Atlantic States," *Transactions of the North American Wildlife Conference*, No. 16, 1951

——— "Migratory Movements of the Northern Clapper Rail," *Bird Banding*, Vol. 25, No. 1, January 1954

Sturgis, Bertha B. *Field Book of Birds of the Panama Canal Zone*, Putnam, Washington, D.C., 1928

Sutton, George Miksch *An Introduction to the Birds of Pennsylvania*, J. Horace McFarland Co., Harrisburg, Pennsylvania, 1928

——— *Mexican Birds: First Impressions*, University of Oklahoma Press, Norman, 1951

Tanner, Dean "Autumn Food Habits of the Sandhill Crane," *The Flicker*, Vol. 13, No. 2, May 1941

Thompson, Richard L. "Florida Sandhill Crane Nesting on the Loxahatchee National Wildlife Refuge," *The Auk*, Vol. 87, No. 3, July 1970

Turcotte, W. H. "The Sandhill Crane in Mississippi," *Mississippi Game and Fish*, Vol. 10, No. 12, June 1947

Vermeer, Kees, and Gary G. Anweiler "Great Blue Heron Colonies in Saskatchewan in 1970," *The Blue Jay*, Vol. 28, No. 4, December 1970

Vermeer, Kees, and David R. M. Hatch "Additional Information on Great Blue Heron Colonies in Manitoba," *The Blue Jay*, Vol. 30, No. 2, June 1972

Walkinshaw, Lawrence H. "The Sandhill Cranes," *Cranbrook Institute of Science Bulletin*, No. 29, 1949

Wilbur, Sanford R. "The Status of the Light-Footed Clapper Rail," *American Birds*, Vol. 28, No. 5, October 1974

Wilke, Ford, and Brooke Meanley "Fluctuation in the Fall Food of the Sora Rail," *Maryland Conservation*, Vol. 19, No. 4, Fall 1942

Williams, Lovett E., Jr., and Robert W. Phillips "North Florida Sandhill Crane Populations," *The Auk*, Vol. 89, No. 3, July 1972

Williams, Lovett E., Jr. "Spring Departure of Sandhill Cranes from Northern Florida," *The Auk*, Vol. 87, No. 1, January 1970

Wolford, James W., and David A. Boag "Distribution and Biology of Black-Crowned Night Herons in Alberta," *Canadian Field Naturalist*, Vol. 85, No. 1, January–March 1971

——— "Food Habits of the Black-Crowned Night Herons in Southern Alberta," *The Auk*, Vol. 88, No. 2, April 1971

Youngworth, William "Migration of the Sandhill Crane in Nebraska," *Iowa Bird Life*, Vol. 17, No. 4, December 1947

# INDEX

*Aigrette Neigeuse, L',* 101
*Ajaia ajaja* (Linnaeus), 157–62
American Bittern, 76, 77, 113–18, 121
American Coot, 156, 157, 191, 227, 229, 237–43
American Demiegret, 65
American Egret, 93
American Flamingo, 108, 109, 165–68
Anhingas, 40, 161
Anthony, A. W., 14
Anthony's Green Heron, 14, 15
*Aramus guarauna pictus* (Meyer), 185–88
*Ardea herodias fannini* Chapman, 42
*Ardea herodias herodias* (Linnaeus), 35–41, 48, 50
*Ardea herodias hyperonca* Oberholser, 50
*Ardea herodias occidentalis* Audubon, 44, 52–53, 93
*Ardea herodias treganzai* Court, 48, 50
*Ardea herodias wardi* Ridgway, 44–46, 48, 53
*Ardea herodias wuerdemanni,* 44

Baja Green Heron, 12
Beaks
    American Coot, 240
    American Flamingo, 165
    Cattle Egret, 75
    Eastern Green Heron, 4
    Eastern Least Bittern, 121
    Great Blue Heron, 36
    Great Egret, 94
    Great White Heron, 52
    Limpkin, 185
    Little Blue Heron, 58
    Louisiana Heron, 66
    Reddish Egret, 83
    Roseate Spoonbill, 157–58
    Snowy Egret, 102
    White Ibis, 147
    Wood Stork, 130
Bent, Arthur Cleveland, 181
Bigbill, 157
Big Blue Heron, 35
Big Brown Crane, 177
Big Plume Bird, 93
Black Clapper, 198
Black-Crowned Night Heron, 19–26, 31, 32, 44, 46, 59, 113
Black Curlew, 137, 141
Black Rail, 156, 223, 224
Blood Bird, 153
Blue Crane, 35
Blue Egret, 57
Blue Heron, 57
Blue Pete, 233
Blue Peter, 237
Boat-Tailed Grackles, 46
Bog Bull, 113
Bonnet Martyr, 101
*Botaurus lentiginosus* (Rackett), 113–18, 123
Brewster, William, 12
Brewster's Egret, 106, 107
Bronze Ibis, 141
*Bubulcus ibis ibis* Linnaeus, 75–79
Buff-Backed Heron, 75
*Butorides striatus anthonyi* (Mearns), 14
*Butorides striatus frazari* (Brewster), 12
*Butorides striatus virescens* (Linnaeus), 3–11, 12, 14
Butter Bump, 113

Calico Bird, 57
Calico Heron, 57
California Black Rail, 224
California Clapper Rail, 204, 205, 208

California Heron, 50, 51
Canadian Crane, 177
Carau, 185
Carolina Crake, 213
Carolina Rail, 213
*Casmerodius albus egretta* (Gmelin), 93–98, 101
Cattle Egret, 60, 61, 68, 75–79, 101, 102
Chalk-Line, 3
Chapman, Dr. Frank, 166
Chicken-Billed Rail, 213
Christmas Heron, 3
Ciconiiformes, general data on, xiii
Clucking Hen, 185
Coloration and markings
    American Bittern, 114–16
    American Coot, 240–41
    American Flamingo, 166
    Anthony's Green Heron, 14
    Black-Crowned Night Heron, 21–22
    Cattle Egret, 76
    Common Gallinule, 228
    Eastern Green Heron, 6–7
    Eastern Least Bittern, 123
    Frazar's Green Heron, 12
    Glossy Ibis, 138
    Great Blue Heron, 36–37
    Great Egret, 95
    Great White Heron, 53
    King Rail, 192
    Limpkin, 186
    Little Blue Heron, 58–59
    Louisiana Heron, 66, 68
    Reddish Egret, 85
    Roseate Spoonbill, 158–60
    Sandhill Crane, 172
    Snowy Egret, 103
    Sora, 213–14
    Ward's Heron, 44
    White-Faced Ibis, 141–42
    White Ibis, 149
    Whooping Crane, 180
    Wood Stork, 130–31
    Yellow-Crowned Night Heron, 29
Common Blue Crane, 35
Common Brown Crane, 171
Common Crane, 171
Common Egret, 93, 101
Common Gallinule, 156, 227–30, 233
Common Rail, 213
Coot, 237
Cory's Bittern, 121
*Coturnicops noveboracensis noveboracensis* (Gmelin), 219
Courlan, 185
Courliri, 185
Courtship and mating
    American Coot, 241
    Black-Crowned Night Heron, 25
    Common Gallinule, 228–29
    Eastern Green Heron, 9
    Great Blue Heron, 38
    Great Egret, 96
    Great White Heron, 53
    Little Blue Heron, 60–61
    Louisiana Heron, 69
    Reddish Egret, 86–87
    Roseate Spoonbill, 161
    Sandhill Crane, 174
    Snowy Egret, 104
    White Ibis, 150–51
Crab-Catcher, 3

Crane, 35
Crow-Bill, 237
Crow-Duck, 237
Crying Bird, 185
Curlew, 147

Demoiselle, 65
Desert Heron, 14
*Dichromanassa rufescens dickeyi* van Rossem, 89
*Dichromanassa rufescens rufescens* (Gmelin), 83–88
Dickey's Egret, 89, 90
Ditch Heron, 14

Eastern Green Heron, 3–11, 12, 14, 44
Eastern Least Bittern, 92, 121–25
Economic influence
    American Bittern, 118
    American Coot, 243
    Cattle Egret, 79
    Eastern Green Heron, 11
    Great Blue Heron, 41
    Great Egret, 98
    Little Blue Heron, 62
    Louisiana Heron, 72
    Sandhill Crane, 176
    Snowy Egret, 105
    White Ibis, 152
    Whooping Crane, 182
Eggs and incubation
    American Bittern, 117
    American Coot, 242
    American Flamingo, 168
    Black-Crowned Night Heron, 26
    Black Rail, 223
    Cattle Egret, 77
    Common Gallinule, 229
    Eastern Green Heron, 10
    Eastern Least Bittern, 125
    Glossy Ibis, 139
    Great Blue Heron, 40
    Great Egret, 97
    King Rail, 192
    Limpkin, 188
    Little Blue Heron, 61
    Louisiana Heron, 71
    Northern Clapper Rail, 195
    Reddish Egret, 87
    Roseate Spoonbill, 161
    Sandhill Crane, 175
    Snowy Egret, 104–5
    Sora, 214
    Virginia Rail, 210
    Ward's Heron, 46
    White-Faced Ibis, 143
    White Ibis, 151
    Whooping Crane, 181
    Wood Stork, 132
    Yellow-Crowned Night Heron, 32
    Yellow Rail, 219
*Egretta thula brewsteri* (Thayer & Bangs), 106
*Egretta thula thula* (Molina), 101–5
*Emberiza hortulana*, 213
*Eudocimus albus* (Linnaeus), 138, 142, 147–52, 153
*Eudocimus ruber* (Linnaeus), 153, 157

Farallon Black Crake, 224
Farallon Black Rail, 224
Farallon Rail, 156, 224
Flame Bird, 157
Flatnose, 157
Flinthead, 129
*Florida caerulea caerulea* (Linnaeus), 57–62
Florida Clapper Rail, 198, 199, 200
Florida cormorants, 161
Florida Courlan, 185
Florida Crane, 124, 177, 178, 179
Flusterer, 237
Fly-Up-The-Creek, 3
Food and feeding habits
    American Bittern, 116
    American Coot, 241
    American Flamingo, 166–68
    Black-Crowned Night Heron, 22–25
    Cattle Egret, 77

Food and feeding habits *(Continued)*
    Common Gallinule, 228
    Eastern Green Heron, 8–9
    Eastern Least Bittern, 124
    Glossy Ibis, 138–39
    Great Blue Heron, 38
    Great Egret, 96
    King Rail, 192
    Limpkin, 186
    Little Blue Heron, 60
    Louisiana Heron, 68–69
    Reddish Egret, 86
    Roseate Spoonbill, 160
    Sandhill Crane, 172–74
    Snowy Egret, 103–4
    Sora, 214
    White-Faced Ibis, 142
    White Ibis, 150
    Whooping Crane, 180
    Wood Stork, 131
    Yellow-Crowned Night Heron, 31
*Foulque Américaine, La*, 237
Frazar, M. Abbott, 12
Frazar's Green Heron, 12, 13
Freshwater Marsh Hen, 191
*Fulica americana americana* Gmelin, 237–43

*Gallinula chloropus cachinnans* Bangs, 227–30
Geographic variation, general data on, xiii–xviii
Glossy Ibis, 92, 93, 137–40, 141, 142
Gourdhead, 129
*Grande Aigrette, La*, 93
Great Blue Heron, 35–41, 42, 44, 46, 48, 50, 52, 53, 57, 65, 69, 83, 87, 93, 131, 139, 165
Great Egret, 46, 52, 76, 83, 85, 93–98, 101, 102–3, 104, 105, 131, 161
Greater Courlan, 185
Great White Crane, 179
Great White Egret, 93, 101
Great White Heron, 44, 46, 52–53, 60, 93, 101
Green Bittern, 3
Green Heron, 3
Green Ibis, 137
Gruiformes, general data on, xiii
*Grus americana* (Linnaeus), 171, 179–82
*Grus canadensis canadensis* (Linnaeus), 171–76
*Grus canadensis pratensis* Meyer, 178
*Grus canadensis tabida* (Peters), 177

Habitat and roosting
    American Bittern, 116
    American Coot, 241
    American Flamingo, 166
    Black-Crowned Night Heron, 22
    Cattle Egret, 77
    Common Gallinule, 228
    Eastern Green Heron, 7
    Eastern Least Bittern, 124
    Frazar's Green Heron, 12
    Glossy Ibis, 138
    Great Blue Heron, 37
    Great Egret, 95
    Great White Heron, 53
    King Rail, 192
    Limpkin, 186
    Little Blue Heron, 59–60
    Louisiana Heron, 68
    Reddish Egret, 86
    Roseate Spoonbill, 160
    Sandhill Crane, 172
    Snowy Egret, 103
    Ward's Heron, 46
    White-Faced Ibis, 142
    White Ibis, 150
    Whooping Crane, 180
    Wood Stork, 131
    Yellow-Crowned Night Heron, 31
Habits and characteristics
    American Bittern, 116
    Black-Crowned Night Heron, 22
    Cattle Egret, 76–77
    Eastern Green Heron, 7
    Eastern Least Bittern, 123
    Glossy Ibis, 138

Habits and characteristics *(Continued)*
 Great Blue Heron, 37
 Great Egret, 95
 Little Blue Heron, 59
 Louisiana Heron, 68
 Reddish Egret, 86
 Roseate Spoonbill, 160
 Ward's Heron, 44–46
 White Ibis, 149–50
 Wood Stork, 131
 Yellow-Crowned Night Heron, 31
Hammock Turkey, 185
Hen-Bill, 237
*Hydranassa tricolor ruficollis* (Gosse), 60, 65–72

Indian Hen, 113
Indian Pullet, 3, 185
Ironhead, 129
Ivory-Billed Coot, 237
*Ixobrychus exilis exilis* (Gmelin), 121–25
*Ixobrychus exilis hesperis* Dickey & van Rossem, 126

Jamaican Crake, 223
Jamaican Rail, 223

King Rail, 124, 125, 191–94, 195, 198, 204, 227
Kop-Kop, 3, 6

Lady-Of-The-Waters, 65
*Laterallus jamaicensis coturniculus* (Ridgway), 224
*Laterallus jamaicensis jamaicensis* (Gmelin), 223, 224
Least Bittern, 4
Least Heron, 121
Lesser Egret, 101
*Life Histories of North American Marsh Birds* (Bent), 181
Light-Footed Rail, 206, 208, 209
Limpkin, 124, 125, 185–88
Little American Water Hen, 213
Little Black Crake, 223
Little Black Rail, 223
Little Blue Heron, 31, 40, 57–62, 65, 68, 69, 75, 76, 83, 85, 87, 96, 102, 103, 104, 161
Little Brown Crane, 124, 177, 178, 179
Little Egret, 101
Little Green Heron, 3, 59
Little Plume Bird, 101
Little Snowy, 101
Little White Egret, 101
Little White Heron, 57, 101
Long White, 93, 101
Louisiana Clapper Rail, 196, 197
Louisiana Egret, 65
Louisiana Heron, 31, 40, 46, 59, 60, 61, 65–72, 76, 87, 96, 104, 161

Mangrove Clapper Rail, 202, 203
Marsh Hen, 191, 237
Meadow Chicken, 213
Meadow Hen, 237
Mearns, Dr. Edgar A., 14
Migration
 American Bittern, 118
 American Coot, 243
 Black-Crowned Night Heron, 26
 Cattle Egret, 76
 Eastern Green Heron, 10–11
 Eastern Least Bittern, 125
 Glossy Ibis, 140
 Great Blue Heron, 41
 Great Egret, 98
 King Rail, 194
 Little Blue Heron, 62
 Louisiana Heron, 71–72
 Reddish Egret, 88
 Roseate Spoonbill, 162
 Sandhill Crane, 175–76
 White-Faced Ibis, 143
 White Ibis, 152
 Whooping Crane, 182
Moor Hen, 237
Mud Coot, 237
Mud Hen, 191, 227, 237
*Mycteria americana* Linnaeus, 129–33

Nest and nesting habits
 American Bittern, 116–17
 American Coot, 241–42
 Anthony's Green Heron, 14
 Black-Crowned Night Heron, 25
 California Heron, 50
 Cattle Egret, 77
 Common Gallinule, 229
 Eastern Green Heron, 9–10
 Eastern Least Bittern, 124–25
 Glossy Ibis, 139
 Great Blue Heron, 40
 Great Egret, 96–97
 King Rail, 192
 Limpkin, 188
 Little Blue Heron, 61
 Louisiana Heron, 69–71
 Reddish Egret, 87
 Roseate Spoonbill, 161
 Sandhill Crane, 174
 Snowy Egret, 104
 Sora, 214
 Ward's Heron, 46
 White-Faced Ibis, 142–43
 White Ibis, 151
 Whooping Crane, 181
 Wood Stork, 132
 Yellow-Crowned Night Heron, 31
Niggerbird, 185
Night Heron, 19
Northern Brown Crane, 177
Northern Clapper Rail, 140, 192, 195, 196, 198, 204, 227
Northwestern Coast Heron, 42, 43
*Nyctanassa violacea violacea* (Linnaeus), 29–32
*Nycticorax nycticorax hoactli* (Gmelin), 19–26, 29

Ortolan, 213

Paddlebeak, 157
Pelick, 237
*Phoenicopterus ruber* Linnaeus, 165–68
Pied Heron, 57
*Plegadis chihi* Vieillot, 137, 141–43
*Plegadis falcinellus falcinellus* (Linnaeus), 137–40, 142
Poke, 3
Pond Crow, 237
Pond Hen, 237
*Porphyrula martinica* (Linnaeus), 233
*Porzana carolina* (Linnaeus), 213–16
*Poule d'Eau*, 237
Preacher, 129
Pull-Doo, 237
Purple Gallinule, 156, 157, 233

Qwok, 19

Race, general data on, xiii–xviii
*Rallus elegans elegans* Audubon, 191–94, 204
*Rallus limicola limicola* Vieillot, 192, 210
*Rallus longirostris crepitans* Gmelin, 192, 195, 204
*Rallus longirostris insularum* Brooks, 202
*Rallus longirostris levipes* Bangs, 206, 208
*Rallus longirostris obsoletus* Ridgway, 204, 208
*Rallus longirostris saturatus* Ridgway, 196
*Rallus longirostris scottii* Sennett, 198, 200
*Rallus longirostris waynei* Brewster, 200
*Rallus longirostris yumanensis* Dickey, 206
Rattling Crane, 171
Reddish Egret, 46, 76, 83–88, 89
Red Ibis, 153
Red Spoonbill, 157
Reed Heron, 3
Roseate Spoonbill, 108, 109, 131, 150, 157–62

Salt-Marsh Hen, 195
Sandhill Crane, 124, 171–76, 177, 178, 179, 186
Scarlet Ibis, 108, 153, 157
Scolopaceous Courlan, 185
Scott, W. E. D., 198
Scott's Clapper, 198
Sea Crow, 237
Sedge Hen, 195

Shitepoke, 3
Shit-Quick, 113
Short White, 101
Shuffler, 237
Skeer, 3, 6
Skeo, 3, 6
Small Bittern, 3
Snowy Egret, 46, 58, 69, 71, 75, 76, 77, 83, 93, 96, 101–
    5, 106
Snowy Heron, 101
Sora (Sora Rail), 140, 141, 213–16, 219, 223
Spanish Curlew, 137, 147
Species, general data on, xiii–xviii
Splatterer, 237
Spoonbill, 157
Spotted Crane, 57
Spotted Heron, 57
Stake Driver, 113
Striped Night Heron, 19
Subspecies, general data on, xiii–xviii
Sun Gazer, 113
Swamp Grouse, 185

Thunder Pump, 113
Treganza's Heron, 48, 49
Tri-Colored (Tricolor) Heron, 65–72

Up-N-Down, 185

Valley Green Heron, 14
Virginia Rail, 140, 192, 210, 214
Voice
    American Bittern, 114
    American Coot, 240
    American Flamingo, 166
    Black-Crowned Night Heron, 21
    Cattle Egret, 76
    Eastern Green Heron, 6
    Eastern Least Bittern, 123
    Glossy Ibis, 138
    Great Egret, 94
    King Rail, 192
    Limpkin, 185–86
    Little Blue Heron, 58
    Louisiana Heron, 66
    Reddish Egret, 85
    Roseate Spoonbill, 158
    Sandhill Crane, 171–72
    Snowy Egret, 103
    Sora, 213
    Virginia Rail, 210
    White Ibis, 149

Voice (Continued)
    Whooping Crane, 179
    Wood Stork, 130

Ward's Heron, 31, 38, 41, 44–47, 48, 52
Water Chicken, 237
Water Hen, 237
Wayne's Clapper Rail, 200, 201, 202
Western Least Bittern, 92, 126
White-Bellied Mud Hen, 237
White-Bill, 237
White-Bill Coot, 237
White Crane, 93, 179
White Curlew, 147
White Egret, 93
White-Faced Ibis, 92, 93, 137, 141–43
White Heron, 93
White Ibis, 40, 108, 131, 138, 142, 147–52, 153, 157, 161,
    165
Whooper, 179
Whooping Crane, 171, 172, 179–82
Wood Ibis, 129
Wood Stork, 92, 93, 129–33, 147, 150
Wuerdemann's Heron, 44

Yellow-Crowned Night Heron, 29–32, 44
Yellow Rail, 140, 141, 219, 223
Young, the
    American Bittern, 117–18
    American Coot, 242
    American Flamingo, 168
    Black-Crowned Night Heron, 26
    Common Gallinule, 230
    Eastern Green Heron, 10
    Eastern Least Bittern, 125
    Glossy Ibis, 140
    Great Blue Heron, 40–41
    Great Egret, 97
    King Rail, 194
    Limpkin, 188
    Little Blue Heron, 61–62
    Louisiana Heron, 71
    Reddish Egret, 88
    Roseate Spoonbill, 162
    Sandhill Crane, 175
    Snowy Egret, 105
    Sora, 214–16
    White-Faced Ibis, 143
    White Ibis, 151–52
    Whooping Crane, 124, 181–82
    Wood Stork, 133
    Yellow-Crowned Night Heron, 32
Yuma Clapper Rail, 206, 207

# THE TETRA
# ENCYCLOPEDIA OF FRESHWATER
# TROPICAL
# AQUARIUM
# FISHES

Cichlasoma biocellatum (C. octofasciatum)

Symphysodon aequifasciata aequifasciata

# THE TETRA
# ENCYCLOPEDIA OF FRESHWATER
# TROPICAL
# AQUARIUM
# FISHES

Dick Mills
Dr. Gwynne Vevers

Consultant
Douglas G. Campbell

16060

Published by Tetra Press,
3001 Commerce Street,
Blacksburg,
VA 24060.

© Salamander Books Ltd.,
129-137 York Way,
London,
N7 9LG,
United Kingdom

Revised and updated Edition 1989.

ISBN 1-56465-131-2

## Credits

Editor: Geoff Rogers
Designer: Roger Hyde

Color separations: Bantam Litho Ltd.,
    England. Rodney Howe Ltd.. England.

Filmset: Modern Text Typesetting.
    England. Em Photosetting. England.

Printed in Belgium by
    Proost International Book Production

# THE AUTHORS

## PART ONE

*Dick Mills is an experienced fishkeeper and author with a very clear understanding of the needs and aspirations of beginners to the aquarium hobby. His ability to explain unfamiliar and often quite complex concepts in a clear way is put to good use in the first part of this book. Dick has an excellent 'pedigree' in the fishkeeping world, having kept a wide range of fishes over a period of more than 20 years and pursuing an active involvement in the Federation of British Aquatic Societies, for which he regularly lectures and produces a quarterly News Bulletin. He is the author of several books on a range of fishkeeping subjects.*

## PART TWO

*Gwynne Vevers, M.B.E., M.A., D.Phil., F.L.S., F.I.Biol., followed a distinguished academic career in the zoological sciences, culminating in his appointment as Curator of the Aquarium at the London Zoo, a post he held until 1981. In addition to undertaking biological expeditions to places as far afield as Iceland and the Solomon Islands, Dr. Vevers found the time to write, translate and edit many books on the subject of aquarium fishes. His broad experience is reflected on the pages of Part Two of this book.*

# THE CONSULTANT

*Douglas G. Campbell, currently an aquarist at the Houston Zoological Gardens, has practical as well as academic knowledge of fishkeeping. He has spent six years in the retail fish trade, and written over 50 articles on fish subjects. He was formerly a Contributing Editor of Freshwater and Marine Aquarium magazine.*

# CONTENTS

## PART ONE **PRACTICAL SECTION**

A complete practical guide to setting up and maintaining a tropical freshwater aquarium, from selecting a tank to exhibiting fishes at a competitive show.

*Selecting a Tank 10*
*Heating, Lighting, Filtration, Aeration 12*
*Aquatic Plants 16*
*Furnishing the Aquarium 22*
*Water: The Vital Ingredient 24*
*Setting Up the Aquarium 26*
*Basic Fish Anatomy 34*
*Fishes: Making the Right Choice 36*
*Feeding and Maintenance 38*
*Diseases: Prevention and Treatment 40*
*Breeding Fishes in the Aquarium 44*
*Expanding the Interest 48*

## PART TWO **SPECIES GUIDE**

A detailed survey of 200 tropical freshwater fishes. These are presented in family groupings that are arranged in order of evolutionary development, from the more primitive to the more specialized. Within each family the fishes are presented in alphabetical order of scientific name. The principal families featured are listed below.

*The Characins 54*
*The Carps and Barbs 92*
*The Catfishes 120*
*The Egg-laying Toothcarps 132*
*The Live-bearing Toothcarps 144*
*The Cichlids 160*
*The Labyrinth Fishes 184*

*Further Reading 198*
*Glossary 198*
*Index 201*
*Picture Credits 208*

## Publisher's note

Fishkeeping is a hobby full of technical terms and scientific names. This book tries to avoid becoming too complicated, but understanding a technical language is a necessary part of this hobby, as it is with many others. When technical terms are introduced they are explained in the text. However, if questions should arise, the glossary contains clear descriptions of all the terms used in this book. The scientific names of fishes, plants, disease organisms, etc. may seem awesome at first, but anyone seriously interested in fishkeeping as a hobby will soon realize that understanding these standardized terms makes life easier. Measurements in the book are quoted in the units in everyday use in the United States, i.e. feet, inches, pounds, ounces, US-gallons, degrees Fahrenheit, etc. The metric equivalents, which are used in scientific circles, are given in parentheses where necessary. British Imperial equivalents are also given where appropriate. To show the sex of fishes, the standard scientific symbols have been used — ♂ male, ♀ female. In the end, however, as the authors are quick to point out, the rewards of fishkeeping will not come from a preoccupation with the technical details and scientific names, but from the pleasure of nuturing and displaying some of the world's most beautiful living things.

# PART ONE

# PRACTICAL SECTION

*Fishkeeping, although not a new hobby, now bears little resemblance to its form of 100 years ago. Technical advances, especially fast air transportation, have resulted in a modern, satisfying hobby that appeals to people everywhere.*

*Concentrating on the history of fishkeeping would not necessarily introduce the newcomer to the hobby. Naturally, he wants to 'get on with it' as soon as possible. Therefore, the first section of this book will concentrate on preparing a modern-day aquarium for its living occupants, whether they are fishes or plants. However, respectful recognition is given to those pioneering aquarists whose efforts have made the hobby as popular as it is today.*

*Compared with other hobbies and pastimes, fishkeeping requires relatively little time from the hobbyist. Even when increasing costs are considered, the rewards, when compared with the capital outlay, seem to be proportionately higher than with other hobbies.*

*Fishkeeping is a quiet, self-contained interest and has little nuisance value either to the neighbors or to the hobbyist's vacation plans. If the aquarium is prepared correctly and the guidance on aquarium management is followed, this should be a very fulfilling pastime. The only real problem will be finding room for those extra tanks!*

*Left: Many specimen plants are grown in plastic baskets filled with growing medium. To plant them, simply bury the basket in the gravel as shown here.*

# SELECTING A TANK

An aquarium makes good use of a corner.

*S*electing a tank is very similar to choosing a house. It should be big enough for the number of occupants (including room for any possible increases); it must be in the right location and of sound construction; you must be able to live with it; and it must be within your price range. The style and design are personal choices. The main aim should be something that fishes can live in comfortably, and that will remain functioning with a minimum of maintenance. Carry out a survey of existing aquariums in your neighborhood. Make friends with their owners and ask all the questions you want. Find out from them which types have stood the test of time. Your local aquatic store will have all the information about modern tanks and which ones are the best buys. Be guided by people with practical experience, not seduced by a gimmick-laden creation. You owe it to your fishes.

Think reasonably big. There are several good reasons for this: Conditions in a large aquarium remain more stable (and therefore more controllable) than in a small one; more fishes can be kept; and the overall appearance of the aquarium when fully furnished will be more pleasing. Any tank longer than 24in (60cm) with a width of 12in (30cm) and a water depth of 12 to 15in (30 to 38cm) is suitable.

The overall water capacity of the tank is not the most important contributing factor to the tank's fish-carrying capacity. Fishes do have more room to swim and set up their territories in a larger tank, but much more important than size is the shape or proportions of the tank. A tall, slim tank may well hold the same amount of water as a shallow, wide tank, but the latter will house more fishes. The reason for this is that the oxygen content of the water depends upon how easily it can be supplied: The only place that this can occur is at the water surface, so the larger the water surface offered to the atmosphere, the better. The shallow, wide tank outscores the narrow tank in this respect.

Similarly, the opportunity for carbon dioxide (exhaled by the fishes) to be expelled from the water also occurs primarily at the water surface, and again a large water surface area is preferable.

In terms of numbers of fishes that may be stocked in any particular size tank, the following guide may be usefully considered:

Freshwater tropical species
10in² per inch body length
(25cm² per cm body length)
Freshwater coldwater species
30in² per inch body length
(75cm² per cm body length)
Marine tropical species
48in² per inch body length
(120cm² per cm body length)

Note: In all fish measurements used in these calculations the tail (caudal fin) is excluded.

An example: A tank 24x12x12in (60x 30x30cm) has a water surface area of

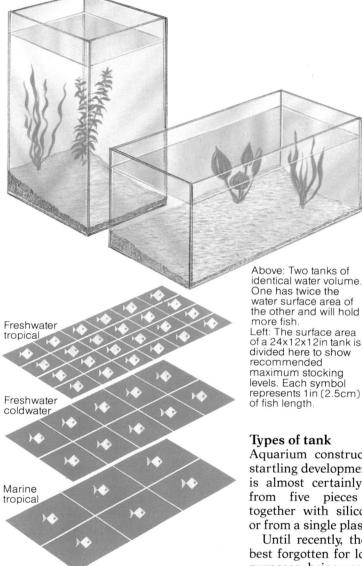

Freshwater tropical

Freshwater coldwater

Marine tropical

Above: Two tanks of identical water volume. One has twice the water surface area of the other and will hold more fish.
Left: The surface area of a 24x12x12in tank is divided here to show recommended maximum stocking levels. Each symbol represents 1in (2.5cm) of fish length.

Below: All-glass aquariums are made from five pieces of glass bonded with silicone-rubber adhesive. Plastic tanks are also available.

All-glass bonded tank

Plastic molded tank

288in² (1800cm²) and will comfortably hold:
24in (60cm) of freshwater tropical fishes
10in (25cm) of freshwater coldwater fishes
15cm (6in) of marine tropical fishes.

Consideration must be given to the final sizes that the fishes will reach in the aquarium; fishes bought from dealers are usually juveniles and can be expected to double in size at least.

## Types of tank

Aquarium construction has undergone startling developments, and today's tank is almost certainly to be made either from five pieces of glass bonded together with silicone-rubber adhesive, or from a single plastic moulding.

Until recently, the plastic types were best forgotten for long-term fishkeeping purposes, being used mainly for nursery, breeding tank, hospital, or quarantine quarters. The main drawback was that they were generally of small dimensions, and the plastic soon became scratched and discolored. Modern plastic tanks are gaining popularity, particularly in the U.S., where such tanks may be found in all sizes, and reports indicate that discoloration is no longer a problem.

Angle-iron framed tanks, glazed with putty, have been superseded by all-glass types. Some all-glass models are framed with anodized aluminum or plastic strips, but these are simply to improve

the appearance of the tank rather than to provide basic structural support.

Tanks are commercially available in standard sizes (quoted either by dimensions or by water capacity), but the hobbyist can make his own tank to suit his exact requirements. Any glass used should be optically clear, free from distortion and of sufficient thickness to withstand the considerable water pressure exerted on it.

Secondhand tanks are occasionally available and, if of sound construction, are a good buy.

## Siting the tank
Given a free choice of possible locations for the tank, there are several places that are definitely not suitable. A window location, especially one that faces the sun, is probably the worst place of all, because in hot weather the amount of light reaching the tank would be excessive and would not only result in the rapid growth of unwanted and unsightly algae, but also cause the water temperature to rise too high. In cold weather, a tropical aquarium thus situated will be fighting to conserve heat.

An aquarium should not be placed directly opposite a constantly opening door, since an accidentally slammed door will frighten the fishes and may even crack a glass panel. Again, a heated

Above: This splendidly furnished aquarium not only provides a focal point in the apartment but also acts as a very decorative room divider. Filtration equipment is hidden beneath the aquarium and is easily accessible.

aquarium may be subject to cold drafts.

Another important factor to keep in mind is that a fully furnished aquarium is heavy. A conveniently placed bureau or sideboard may seem an ideal site, but at best any drawers or doors in it will become unopenable under the weight of the aquarium, and at worst the legs may collapse. A strong stand or plinth is recommended, and the site should be located over the floor joists in such a way that the load is spread. Specially made aquarium stands are available commercially; these are designed to accommodate 'standard' sized tanks, and are usually made of wrought-iron. Provision should be made to protect decorative floor coverings from damage by the metal legs.

The ideal location for an aquarium is in a dark alcove. Here, the lighting conditions can be carefully controlled, there are unlikely to be cold drafts or physical disturbances, and as a bonus the illuminated aquarium will liven up that dark corner!

An aquarium can be placed in an unused fireplace, used as a free-standing room-divider or built in alongside book

shelves. Wherever the tank is finally sited, it must be accessible for regular maintenance and for feeding.

Additionally, whatever type of aquarium is planned, coldwater or tropical, there should be an electrical socket nearby to power the tank lights, air pump, filtration equipment, and heating (if required).

## Installing the tank
Having chosen the tank's permanent position, make sure that, in addition to being firm, it is also level. An uneven supporting surface will produce stresses in the glass base of the tank, which could crack when the aquarium is filled. Place a thick slab of polystyrene (cut to the tank's base dimensions) beneath the tank to cushion it and even out any irregularities in the supporting surface. It will also conserve heat in a tropical aquarium.

A frequent fear, if not of the aquarist then certainly of other members of the family, is that of a leaking tank—a reasonable concern when considering the mess that 15 gallons of water might make!

It is wise to check any tank (even a new one) for leaks before final installation. This is especially important if the tank has not held water for some time; a slight weeping at the joints may occur when it is refilled. New all-glass tanks are not likely to leak, but if a leak is found, empty the tank and dry it out before repairing the seams with silicone-rubber adhesive. You can apply this straight from a tube or, for larger quantities, from a cartridge using a sealing gun. The sealant gives off strong fumes smelling of vinegar, and so be sure to carry out this repair work in a well-ventilated area. This is particularly important because this is the sort of job you can only do properly by bending over the tank.

It is important to use only sealants specifically approved for aquarium use; the sealants used in bathrooms and for window-fixing contain mildew retardants that are toxic to fish.

If you want the aquarium to have a decorative background, it must be fixed in place before the tank is put in its final position. Or you may paint the outside of the rear and side panels a dark color.

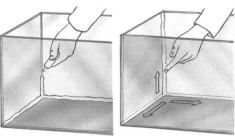

Above: Aquarium sealant should be applied in a continuous bead to all interior seams, and then smoothed over with a finger. It is vital to allow the sealant to cure for 24 hours before using.

# HEATING, LIGHTING, FILTRATION, AERATION

Fluorescent tube fitted in an aquarium hood.

*B*efore furnishing a tank, the newcomer should have a clear understanding of how the environment for fishes in captivity is maintained. For many decades it was believed that an aquarium should be self-cleaning and—apart from the addition of food by the hobbyist—self-perpetuating. Modern understanding has revised that thinking and it is now agreed that technology may be allowed to lend a hand. There are four areas in which the hobbyist has the controlling influence: Heating, lighting, filtration, and aeration. Today's aquarium equipment is completely reliable and almost foolproof. Very little technical knowledge, beyond the ability to wire up an electrical plug, is needed to install and operate the equipment safely. But never place your hands in the aquarium without first disconnecting the electrical power supply.

The majority of fishes kept are tropical species. Since many fishkeepers live outside the tropical areas from which their fishes come, it is necessary for them to heat the aquarium water to the temperature of the fishes' natural waters, approximately 75°F (24°C).

Aquarists with several tanks in one room may find it to their financial advantage to heat the room rather than each individual tank, but for the purposes of this book it is assumed that only one tank is planned at the outset and therefore only individual tank heating will be examined.

Aquarium heaters are heat-resistant, submersible glass tubes containing a wire heating element wound on a ceramic former. Electricity is supplied via a cable, which enters the tube through a watertight cap. It would be impossible to choose a heater of any particular size that would exactly counterbalance heat losses for any tank, bearing in mind the diversity of likely ambient temperatures around the world, and so the aquarium heater needs to be thermostatically controlled.

Today, both heater and thermostat are housed in the same watertight container, the electro-mechanical (or more often, electronic) thermostatic unit being mounted above the heating coil with its temperature adjustment control emerging through the waterproof cap for ease of use. Some models show the temperature setting very clearly indeed. External heating pads, sited under the tank, can also be used and these are controlled by an external electronic thermostat with a sensing probe that hangs in the water.

Thermostats effectively stabilize the water temperature by switching off the supply to the heater when the required temperature is reached and switching it on again when the water has cooled by a degree or two. These temperature fluctuations occur quite slowly, particularly in a tank of the recommended size.

Heating similar-sized tanks with multiple heaters controlled by one master thermostat is possible, but this method can be unreliable as a heater failure in the master tank will lead to the others becoming dangerously overheated.

The size of heater (measured in watts) should be selected with care. An overlarge heater will cause a rapid rise in water temperature (which could be fatal to the fishes), should the thermostat fail while in an 'on' position. On the other hand, a small heater may have to work overtime to keep up, with the result that the thermostat's contacts will become burned and pitted, with eventual failure.

Allow 10 watts per gallon (3.8 liters) as a rough estimate when choosing a heater. For large tanks, 36in (90cm) and over, two heaters may share the total required wattage, each being controlled by its own built-in thermostat.

Do not worry about severe temperature loss in the event of electrical power failure. This will not occur for hours following the cut in electrical supply. You can take immediate steps by wrapping the tank in a blanket or with thick layers of newspaper. Bottles of hot water (heated by alternative means) can be placed in the aquarium if the power remains off for too long and the temperature appears to be falling to a critical level. Some aquarists insulate the outside of the sides and rear

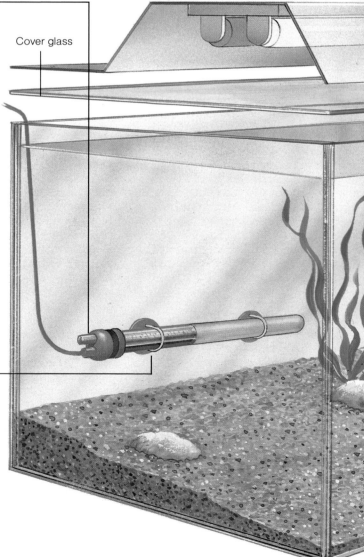

Right: Combined heater/thermostats are usually mounted on the rear wall of the aquarium, either at an angle or near vertical in a corner. Check whether the unit is suitable for total immersion before use. Temperature adjustment is made by means of the protruding knob. It is important that the heater does not rest directly on the gravel, as this will prevent adequate circulation of water around the heater and cause localized overheating of the unit, possibly resulting in the glass tube fracturing. Use two heater/thermostats in large tanks in order to spread the heat more quickly and evenly.

Cover glass

Heater mounting clips should be made from non-toxic materials. Avoid placing a clip over the hottest part of the heater tube — the nearer the thermostat end the better.

of a tank with polystyrene sheeting to conserve heat.

The temperature is easily measured with an aquarium thermometer. This may be one of several types: Floating or stick-on internal models, or a liquid-crystal display external type. Although water temperatures will vary by a degree or so over a period of hours, this is nothing to worry about; this fluctuation is far less than the fishes experience in nature, where the day-night-day differences can be quite considerable.

## Lighting

Light is not provided just to enable the hobbyist to see his collection of fishes. It acts as a stimulus to the fishes, and is needed by aquatic plants for photosynthesis. This latter function is most important, for while the plants photosynthesize they absorb carbon dioxide from the water, thus lowering the level of this unwanted gas.

The amount of light is fairly critical, and the final balance between the brightness and the illumination time is best found by trial and error. Naturally the hobbyist will want the aquarium lit to suit his viewing habits (usually in the evenings), and the plants will also require a certain minimum amount of light to flourish properly. Fortunately, these two requirements are quite compatible and the aquarium is normally lit for 10 to 15 hours each day.

Two methods of lighting can be used: lamps either enclosed collectively in a hood/reflector or individually in separate reflectors suspended above an open-top tank. Lamps used may be fluorescent tubes or high-intensity metal-halide or mercury vapour lamps.

**Fluorescent lighting:** Tube lighting.
*Advantages:* Long lamp life, inexpensive to run, cool running, even light distribution, various colors available to enhance fish or promote plant growth.
*Disadvantages:* Slightly complicated to install due to the need for starting units. Lamp length may not correspond exactly to hood size chosen.

**High-intensity lamps:** Bulb-shaped lamps mounted in separate reflectors.
*Advantages:* Very good for deep tanks; can be used to highlight individual features or create variable light levels.
*Disadvantages:* Expensive; produce more heat; not quite so unobtrusive as built-in lighting; require ceiling or wall fixing.

Both systems can be combined to suit aquarium plant requirements and both may be operated by means of a time-switch for accurate and regular light control (convenient during vacations.)

It is normal practice to use a cover glass between the tank top and the hood to prevent excessive water evaporation, fish escape attempts, and damage to the light fittings by condensation.

Plants do best in light with certain wavelengths predominating—blue-green and orange-red. Fluorescent lamps that provide this spectrum are available but aquarists usually supplement these lamps with the more normal 'warm-white' tubes to give better colored light for viewing.

Although bright light may well suit the viewing fishkeeper, too much light results in excessive growth of algae (remember the warning against window locations). The amount of light may be reduced by installing lower wattage lamps, reducing the illumination time, or providing a cover of floating plants. Alternatively, an increase in the number of aquatic plants may well do the trick by out-competing the algae for the available light.

Light should be used as efficiently as possible. The reflector can be painted white inside or lined with reflecting metal foil. Direct the light downwards and slightly backwards into the tank to avoid casting shadows on the undersides and viewer-facing sides of the fishes. Keep cover glasses meticulously clean so as not to reduce the brightness of the light.

Another factor affecting efficiency is the clarity of the water—water containing particles of dirt in suspension will cut down the amount of light reaching the plants. It is to the aquarium's advantage if the water can be maintained in a clear condition at all times.

## Filtration

The efficiency of any filter is often gauged by its ability to maintain crystal clear water, but modern filters can also be used to alter the water's pH or hardness to some degree in addition to just removing suspended matter. Filters, depending on design and mode of operation, can provide three methods of filtration—mechanical, chemical, and biological. Filters may be fitted either inside or outside the tank and be operated by either compressed air or electrically powered water pumps. Most filters that provide mechanical and chemical processes are box- or cylindrical-shaped containers holding the necessary filter media through which the water is passed.

Left: A combination of different color tubes can be fitted in the hood. Here, a tube designed to promote plant growth is paired with a daylight tube. For lush plant growth, it may be necessary to install several tubes in the hood.

Back            Front

Above: Place a thermometer in or on the tank at a convenient position for easy reading.

Left: Liquid crystal thermometers are sturdy and reliable for aquarium use. They stick on the outside of the tank glass.

Above: The position of the light in the hood affects the aquarist's view of the fish. With a center position (top) any fish near the front glass will cast a shadow towards the viewer. A front-located lamp (below) will cast all shadows behind the fishes being viewed, thus showing all the fishes' colors and beautiful iridescences.

The slotted undergravel filter plate is a popular form of biological filtration; water drawn through the gravel encourages bacteria to act on toxic wastes.

## Mechanical and chemical filters

Pumped air is used either to draw water through internal types or to return filtered water from an external type back into the aquarium.

Internal filters are best used in sparsely furnished tanks, such as those used for raising young fishes, because the necessary regular maintenance would otherwise disturb a heavily planted tank. Internal filters can be of a very simple or very complicated design.

The widely used outside filter has few maintenance problems, although when it is initially installed some cutting of the tank hood may be necessary. Outside filters cannot overflow—as soon as the water in them rises to the same level as that in the main aquarium the inlet siphon action stops. When sufficient clean water has been returned to the tank the level in the filter falls and the siphon starts again.

## Electrically powered filters

Usually referred to as 'power filters', these filters have a far greater water flow and may be of an 'open' or 'closed' type. The 'open' type is merely an upgraded version (by the addition of an electric pump) of the outside box filter. The 'closed' type—the canister models favored by European aquarists—can be fully submersible, semi-submersible, or situated outside the tank, even some distance from it. To prevent accidental emptying of the tank when using an external power filter, make sure that all water hose connections are firmly made and that the return tube and spray bar are securely fixed.

## Filter media

In filters used as trapping devices, matter suspended in the aquarium water is removed by filter 'wool', usually a man-made fiber. Glass-wool must *not* be used because tiny particles of it can find their way back into the tank and irritate and damage the fishes' delicate gills. Filter wool can be re-used (after washing) to some degree. This poses the question how often should the filter medium be changed. There is no definite answer to this because it depends on how dirty the water was in the first place and how fast the filter does its job. But regular filter maintenance should be the rule rather than the exception.

Modern filters often come ready equipped with their own custom-made, preformed foam media inserts; these are graded to suit the designed flow rate of the filter and are easy to maintain. While

equally efficient alternative media may be used, make sure they are non-toxic and avoid packing them too tightly; they may impede water flow.

Although the water in an aquarium may appear to be quite clear of suspended matter, it will contain dissolved waste products excreted by the fishes and organic materials from decaying matter such as dead leaves. Some of these unwanted substances can be removed by the use of activated carbon in the filter. One drawback of this material is that it will also adsorb any medication added to the water when treating the aquarium for sickness. Filters that contain activated carbon should be turned off during the period of treatment. Alternatively the carbon can be removed and the filter left running to provide water circulation and aeration since many medications reduce the oxygen content of the water.

Peat and ion-exchange resins may also be used within the filter body; these are useful when keeping species that require special water conditions.

Some aquarists argue that they have never seen a stream or pond fitted with a

filtration system and they scorn such devices. Unfortunately the static aquarium does not benefit from the cleansing actions of wind, rain, and water movements enjoyed by natural bodies of water, so the modern aquarist has to employ artificial aids (including partial water changes) to keep the aquarium in top condition.

## Biological filtration

Working with no moving parts and no filter media and needing no maintenance except a periodic stir of the gravel to help remove detritus, the undergravel filter is probably the most misunderstood piece of aquarium equipment and is often blamed for poor plant growth. If a sufficient depth of gravel (of correct particle size) is used above the filter plate, there should be no problems.

The newcomer to the hobby ought to be warned that the biological filtration *versus* plant growth debate is a controversial subject among aquarists everywhere, although a few minutes' examination of the function of this type of filter will reveal just what a naturally

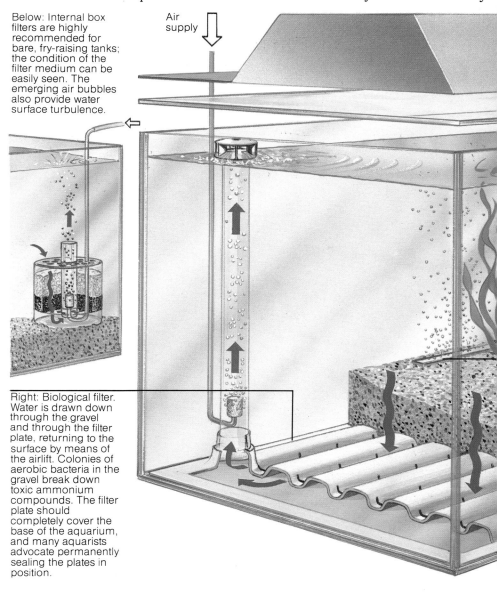

Below: Internal box filters are highly recommended for bare, fry-raising tanks; the condition of the filter medium can be easily seen. The emerging air bubbles also provide water surface turbulence.

Air supply

Right: Biological filter. Water is drawn down through the gravel and through the filter plate, returning to the surface by means of the airlift. Colonies of aerobic bacteria in the gravel break down toxic ammonium compounds. The filter plate should completely cover the base of the aquarium, and many aquarists advocate permanently sealing the plates in position.

efficient job it can usefully perform.

Water is drawn through the aquarium gravel in either a downward or an upward direction depending on the filter's design. This oxygenated water flow encourages aerobic bacterial growth, which continues to thrive only as long as the water flow continues. For this reason, the air supply to a biological (or undergravel) filter system should never be disconnected.

The bacterial colony in the aquarium gravel breaks down toxic substances such as ammonium compounds into less harmful forms by a three stage process. Ammonia is produced by the fish either directly from the gills during respiration, or indirectly because their fecal material is further metabolized by bacteria that produce ammonia as a waste product. *Nitrosomonas* bacteria metabolize ammonia and in doing so produce a waste product called nitrite. Next, *Nitrobacter* bacteria turn the nitrite into a waste product, nitrate. Ammonia and nitrite, both toxic to fish, have now been changed into nitrate, which (although not proven to be harmful to fish) may inhibit growth.

Plants can use nitrate as a food source and nitrate levels can be further reduced (by dilution) as a result of partial water changes.

Biological filtration has several advantages over other filtration systems, the main ones being that it is unobtrusive, does not take up excessive room in the tank, and does not require any physical allowances (such as cutting the tank hood) made for it. The majority of U.S. aquarists have proved that it is not the demon it is often thought to be.

## Choice of filtration systems

The use of any filtration system will greatly alleviate any deteriorating conditions in the aquarium, but the fishes' requirements and their everyday activity must be considered when choosing a filtration system.

Many cichlid fishes — particularly those of African origin—will nullify the use of biological filtration once the filter plates are uncovered by the fishes' digging actions, unless the gravel above the filter has a protective mesh fitted about an inch above the filter plates.

A filter's actions should also be considered during any fish's breeding period. A powerful, high water-flow rate filter causing much surface turbulence will be very frustrating for a Dwarf Gourami (*Colisa lalia*) trying to build a bubble-nest only to find it constantly disintegrating. Internal box filters need regular medium changes and it can almost be guaranteed that a pair of cichlid fishes will choose to spawn on the very day such maintenance has been planned by the aquarist. Any intrusion into their tank at this stage will cause them to panic and eat their eggs or newly hatched fry. Filtration systems used in breeding tanks should be either external or of a type that is unlikely to disturb the fishes during maintenance operations.

## Aeration

The use of air has already been discussed as a motive power for filtration systems, which incidentally fulfill an 'aeration' purpose while they operate. If filters are not used, what does straightforward aeration do? Aeration has the effect of enlarging the tank's fish-holding capacity. By agitating the water surface it exposes oxygen-depleted water to the air-water interface, thus allowing oxygen from the oxygen-concentrated atmosphere to enter into solution. Similarly, air bubbles from a submerged airstone contain more oxygen than the water surrounding them and lose oxygen by diffusion into the water as they rise to the surface. Aeration also drives free carbon dioxide from the water more rapidly by bringing greater amounts of respired water (containing carbon dioxide) to the water surface.

'More oxygen, less carbon dioxide = more fishes' is an equation that holds good only if the aeration system is kept running. Should the air supply fail, there will be a rapid build-up of carbon dioxide and the fishes may asphyxiate. Sheer numbers of fishes is not generally a problem.

Air pressure is provided by the air pump, whose usual form is of a small electric vibrator operating a diaphragm that pumps air through a one-way valve to the aquarium equipment.

Once the compressed air reaches the aquarium (by way of neoprene tubing) it passes through an airstone, which breaks up the air flow into tiny bubbles. The amount of air may be controlled either by a clamp on the air-carrying tube or by a control on the air pump itself. Although a vibrator air pump can have its output controlled by a clamp, excessive air from a piston pump should not be restricted in this way but bled away to the atmosphere.

Compressed air can also be used to operate an aquarium 'vacuum cleaner' — a device that sucks up detritus.

Above: This sponge filter not only strains out dirt mechanically but, in time, will also act biologically.

Below: An internal power filter of the fully submersible type. An electric impeller in the top housing draws water in at the base and through the filter medium contained in the body of the filter. The small tube allows controllable amounts of air to be added to the outgoing water flow.

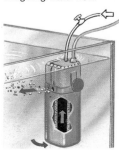

Above left: The stream of bubbles from an airstone helps to aerate the water in the tank directly as well as by constantly agitating the water surface.

# AQUATIC PLANTS

A highly contrasting planting arrangement.

*In addition to their obvious visual impact, aquarium plants provide the following services: (1) They reduce the carbon dioxide in the water (during the aquarium's illuminated period only). (2) They provide shelter, shade, and sanctuary for the fishes. (3) They give a natural look to the aquarium. (4) They provide spawning sites or food for certain fishes. Many plants are anchored in the gravel by roots but not all draw nourishment through them. Salts are also absorbed from the water through their leaves. Plants suitable for the aquarium can be classified for convenience into three groups: Rooted plants, floating plants, and cuttings. Of course, plants may be classified in other ways, but the categories above coincide with how the plants are grouped when shown competitively at fish shows, and the newcomer may find this easier than trying to remember the scientific names.*

Rooted plants form the major proportion of aquarium plants, and there are many diverse leaf forms from which to choose. Rates of growth vary from genus to genus. Some plants require less light than others. There are many shades of green to blend or provide contrast.

The various genera of aquarium plants are generally recognizable by their leaf shapes and colors, but some species readily hybridize to produce confusing varieties. In one genus, the only positive way to identify the species accurately is to allow the plant to grow in shallow water and then to study the flower structure above the surface.

It is not necessary to pre-cultivate the gravel to any great extent in order for the plants to flourish. After the introduction of the fishes, the aquarium plants will be provided with food by the action of bac-

**Microsorium pteropus**
*Java Fern*
India to Far East. Leaves up to 12in (30cm) long. Rootstock clings to logs and rocks. Young plants form on leaves. Does well in any light conditions.

**Riccia fluitans**
*Crystalwort*
Worldwide. Multibranched floating plant forms dense mats. Ideal refuge for fry and for shading the aquarium. Light requirement not critical.

**Acorus gramineus** var **pusillus**
*Dwarf Japanese Rush*
Eastern Asia. A 4in (10cm) foreground plant. A slow grower in the aquarium. Best suited for the cooler aquarium.

**Vallisneria natans**
*Eelgrass*
Throughout tropics. Up to 36in (90cm). Favorite background plant. Several varieties (one with tightly spiraled leaves). Propagation by runners.

**Najas guadelupensis**
Central America. Brittle, multistemmed plant with 1in (2.5cm) leaves. Forms dense clumps. Ideal spawning medium. Propagation by stem division. Synonym—*N. microdon*.

teria on the fecal material excreted by the fishes. Some aquarists provide a layer of peat or loam beneath the gravel when setting up the aquarium, placing the additional 'soil' in nylon bags to prevent it being stirred up by fishes digging in the gravel. However, you may wish to use only aquarium gravel for a first tank and use the special liquid or tablet fertilizers and foods for aquarium plants that can be purchased from an aquatic dealer, should the urge towards underwater gardening become overwhelming. Alternatively, if you are convinced that certain plants require extra nourishment, they can be planted in shallow pots (which contain clay or loam-enriched gravel) sunk in the aquarium gravel. Looking on

Right: An imaginative plant layout that gives not only color contrasts but also, by using plants of different heights, a sense of spaciousness.

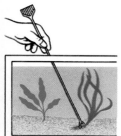

Below: A planting stick may be useful in rooting plants in inaccessible locations or for stirring the gravel. The reverse end of many planting sticks has provision for mounting razor-blades; they can then be used as algae-scrapers to clean the aquarium glass.

**Aponogeton crispus**
Sri Lanka. Has a rhizome rather than roots. Leaves up to 12in (30cm); variable in color, may be reddish. Suited to bright light. Requires cool rest period in winter.

**Hygrophila polysperma**
Far East. The 1 to 2in (2.5 to 5cm) leaves are alternate on stem. Fast growing; forms bush when cuttings taken. Propagation easy; cuttings root quickly. Ideal aquarium filler.

**Nomaphila stricta**
Thailand. Larger, woodier version of *H. polysperma*. Its 4in (10cm) leaves may be eaten by snails. Propagation by cuttings. Prefers hard water. Purple flowers above water.

**Salvinia natans**
Asia. Floating leaves up to 1in (2.5cm) long. Roots provide shelter for fry. Often grows abundantly, covering the entire surface. Use cover glass to avoid lamp-scorching.

**Aponogeton madagascariensis**
*Madagascar Laceplant* Malagasy. The 8 to 12in (20 to 30cm) leaves are skeletal. Needs bright light, water changes, enriched gravel, and a rest period.

the pessimistic side, if things then do not turn out right, only the pots will need removing and a total aquarium stripping and rebuilding is avoided. On the optimistic side, specimen plants that do flourish in their pots will continue to do so undisturbed by any other aquarium rearrangement and the plants can even be transferred, still undisturbed, to new aquatic locations.

The gravel supplied by an aquatic dealer is usually adequate, the only stipulation being that it should be neither too coarse nor too fine—a particle size of about 0.125in (3mm) is suitable. This particle size is also suitable when using biological filtration.

Fast-growing, tall, grasslike plants such as *Vallisneria* and *Sagittaria* are ideal for masking the rear and sides of the aquarium. Bushy plants should be used to fill the corners (in front of the taller plants); Water Wisteria (*Synnema*, now also known as *Hygrophila difformis*) is an excellent choice along with other species of *Hygrophila, Ludwigia,* and *Ceratopteris.*

Foreground plants, visually very effective when placed in front of a rocky outcrop, may be of shorter stature and slower growing. Hairgrass (*Eleocharis*) and Dwarf Japanese Rush (*Acorus*) are often used in this position.

No aquarium scene would be complete without one or two featured 'specimen' plants. The Amazon Swordplant (*Echinodorus*) fills this role admirably, while dense, low clumps of members of the *Cryptocoryne* genus carpet the open swimming area. The sturdy broad leaves of these two genera provide excellent spawning sites for fishes that deposit their eggs on vertical surfaces. The Amazon Swordplant is a natural choice for its piscean companion, the Angelfish (*Pterophyllum* sp.); the Asian *Cryptocoryne* plays an unconscious host to the eggs of the Harlequin Fish (*Rasbora heteromorpha*), which deposits its eggs on the undersides of the leaves.

It will not matter if *Cryptocoryne* plants are shaded from the light by larger plants, because they are quite happy with low light levels.

Mention must be made of the splendid genus *Aponogeton* from Africa and Malagasy, carrying wide, ruffle-edged leaves; the famous Lace Plant (*A.madagascariensis*) has skeletal leaves, completely devoid of tissue between the veins. *Aponogeton* species do not have roots in the literal sense but have a rhizome. It is normal aquarium practice to rest these

**Sagittaria subulata**
*Arrowhead*
North America. Leaves 12in (30cm) long. Aquarium favorite similar to *Vallisneria*. Tolerates hard water. Propagation by runners.

**Pistia stratiotes**
*Water Lettuce*
Tropical areas. Wedge-shaped leaves are 4in (10cm) long and velvety. Long trailing roots. Grows very large in nature, smaller in the aquarium.

**Hygrophila difformis**
*Water Wisteria*
Far East. Light green leaves, up to 4in (10cm) spread, may vary in shape depending on the lighting. Roots easily. Synonym—*Synnema triflorum.*

**Echinodorus bleheri**
Brazil. Up to 20in (50cm). A popular Amazon Swordplant. Often featured as a specimen plant in the aquarium. Plantlets form on long runners sent out from the main plant.

**Cabomba caroliniana**
North America. Up to 1.5in (3.75cm) across whorls. A popular plant and spawning medium. Needs clean water, otherwise sediment will clog leaves. Roots easily.

Left: The fishes and plants in this aquarium have been very carefully chosen to contrast and complement each other. Note how the red of the fishes (center) keys in with the color of the plants (left). The silvery shapes of the other fishes add brilliance and movement. The aquarium lights may be adjusted, in both direction and intensity, to favor specific groups of plants, creating patches of light and shade to further the illusion of space and depth. In order to maintain such luxuriant plant growth, as in this Dutch aquarium, a great amount of light is needed—at least 40 watts (fluorescent) per sq. foot (900cm²) of water surface area.

flowering, seed-setting species during the winter months by transplanting them into a shallower, cooler aquarium until the following spring, when they regain their former glory once more.

It is a little difficult to classify *Microsorium;* it does have hairlike roots emerging from a creeping rhizome, but it is not anchored in the gravel, preferring to cling to rocks and tree roots, which it soon overgrows. Another plant that adopts a surface to cling to is Java Moss (*Vesicularia*); along with the coldwater Willow Moss (*Fontinalis*), its tangled mass of tiny leaves provides an excellent spawning medium for egg-scattering fishes, whose eggs are soon caught in these plants and well-protected from the hungry adult fishes.

Being totally submerged, plants in the aquarium tend to reproduce vegetatively

**Echinodorus magdalenensis**
*Dwarf Amazon Swordplant*
Tropical America. Up to 8in (20cm). Used as a foreground plant. Sends out many runners with young plants.

**Azolla caroliniana**
*Fairy Moss*
America. Velvety leaves up to 0.5in (1.25cm) may also be reddish in color. Provides shade and a haven for young fishes. Shown raised for detail.

**Ceratophyllum demersum**
*Hornwort*
Worldwide. Up to 1in (2.5cm) across whorls. Shown rooted, but mostly floats freely. Propagation by cuttings. Temperate species die in warm water.

**Ludwigia repens**
North America. Leaves up to 1.5in (3.75cm) long have reddish undersides. Needs good light. Propagation by cuttings. Popular plant used in terrariums. A bog plant in the wild.

**Eleocharis acicularis**
*Hairgrass, Needlegrass*
Worldwide. Up to 8in (20cm) tall. Common name most apt, different in form from any other plant. Needs good light. Propagates by root runner.

by sending out runners from which new plants develop, or new daughter plants may emerge on the leaves of certain species. One group of plants, the Aponogetons, actually flowers above the water surface and can be pollinated by the aquarist to produce seed pods. The seeds can then be sown in shallow water and will grow into new plants.

## Floating plants

Although regarded as pests by some aquarists, these floating species do serve a useful purpose in the aquarium. They offer shade for the fishes from the almost perpetual glare of the lights, and provide a sanctuary for newly born young fish, which find safe refuge in the trailing roots hanging down into the water. Members of the Gourami family, notably *Colisa* species, utilize fragments of these plants in the construction of their bubble-nests, the plant's texture helping to prevent the nest from disintegrating.

The size of floating plants ranges from the diminutive *Lemna, Salvinia,* and brightly colored red and green *Azolla,* through the brittle strands of *Riccia* and *Najas,* to the massive velvety bulk of *Pistia*—which can almost push the aquarium hood off!

Referring back to lighting, another need for cover glasses becomes apparent here; they prevent the leaves of floating plants from being scorched by the heat from the lamps hanging low over the water surface.

## Cuttings

This is an artificially created group, because plants within this category do root in gravel, but they are more usually propagated by means of cuttings. The top section of a plant is cut off and planted in the gravel, where it soon roots and forms a new plant. One effect of this pruning is to encourage the donor plant to take on a more bushy shape, as side replacement shoots develop.

Plants in this group (also known as 'bunch' plants in the U.S.) include the fine-leaved species such as the tropical *Cabomba, Limnophila,* and coldwater *Ceratophyllum* and *Myriophyllum.* Members of the *Hygrophila* genus may also be propagated by cuttings, and a severed leaf left floating in the aquarium will usually develop roots of its own accord.

Replicas of aquarium plants, modeled in some form of plastic, are also commercially available, and these will be discussed in the section dealing with decorative materials. (See page 22.)

**Egeria densa**
South America. One inch (2.5cm) opposite leaves on long stem. Receives nourishment through leaves, roots serving merely as an anchorage. Prefers hard water.

**Cryptocoryne balansae**
Far East. Up to 24in (60cm) tall. Long, narrow leaves make this plant ideal for a deep tank. Propagation by runners. Flowers above surface when grown in shallow water.

**Cryptocoryne willisii**
Sri Lanka. Variable in size, up to 8in (20cm) tall. Useful foreground plant shown pot-planted. This avoids any disturbance when transplanting to another aquarium.

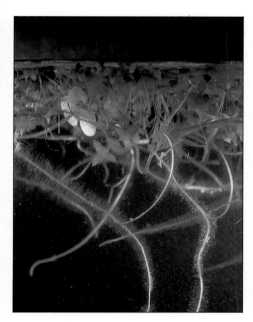

Left: Floating plants (here including *Lemna* sp.) offer shade from the aquarium lights and also provide safe hiding-places for newly born fishes.

Right: Increased plant stocks can be achieved by severing young plants from the parent and re-rooting. Some plants will develop roots from cuttings readily; the top portion is cut off and left to float until roots emerge. Alternatively, the cut portion can be rooted in the gravel immediately and it is usual practice to remove existing leaves from the bottom inch or so of the cutting's stem before planting so that roots are encouraged to form.

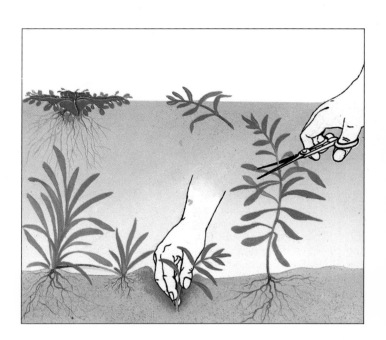

**Ceratopteris thalictroides**
*Indian Fern*
Southeast Asia. Up to 20in (50cm) tall. Grown rooted or floating. Roots from floating example very long. Leaves flat on water surface. Growth vigorous, propagation by daughter plants appearing on leaves. Often attacked by snails. Requires good light and warmth. Floating plants provide shade but must be kept in check.

**Cryptocoryne wendtii**
Sri Lanka. 4 to 12in (10 to 30cm). Leaf color variable from specimen to specimen. Identification of *Cryptocoryne* species only positive through study of flower above shallow water.

**Vesicularia dubyana**
*Java Moss*
Southeast Asia. Leaves 0.1in (2.5mm) long on branched stems. A clinging moss needing a good light and protection from sediment and algae.

# FURNISHING THE AQUARIUM

Correct gravel particle size is 0.125in (3mm).

*Clumps of plants and avenues of tall grasses may be very artistic but for dramatic effect an outcrop of rocks cannot be topped. Rocks also provide shelter, territorial areas, and breeding sites. It is true that some fishes—such as those from the African Rift Valley Lakes—are more at home among rocks than among plants, and a tank especially created for these species (Pseudotropheus, Julidochromis, Labeotropheus etc.) should be furnished with plenty of terraced rocks, giving ample opportunity for each fish to find a cave of its own. Gravel is not only a medium in which the plants can root; it can also serve as a filtration bed and as a spawning site. In order to make the aquarium look even more natural, aquarists usually include roots and sunken branches in the aquarium's decor. There are many artificial decorations available, too.*

The choice of rock should be made keeping in mind the shape, texture, stratum detail, color (matched to the gravel, ideally), and chemical composition. Although most rocks will be chosen mainly for their appearance, it must be appreciated that the fishes will live in close proximity to the rocks. There should be no sharp edges, nor should the rocks be erected in precarious, overhanging piles.

By far the most important consideration is the effect the rocks will have on the water's chemical composition. Rocks that are at all soluble, particularly those of a calcareous nature, should not be used in the freshwater aquarium where a soft water condition is required. However, water-hardening rocks may be valuable in aquariums containing fishes that tolerate hard water, such as the Rift Valley Lake species. Calcareous rocks are beneficial in saltwater aquariums, where they help to maintain the required high pH reading. (See section on water, page 24.)

Many newcomers to the hobby are tempted to add branches of dead coral as decoration, assuming that this normally submerged material is relevant to the aquarium. Although some fishes may enjoy amusing themselves among the coral, it should be barred from use in a freshwater aquarium since coral's high calcium content may adversely affect the water chemistry. Coral is also extremely sharp and will cut and scratch freshwater fishes. Of course, there are no such restrictions about its use in a marine aquarium.

Examples of suitable rocks for aquarium use are granite, basalt, quartz, and slate. Crumbly sandstone, limestone, and rocks carrying any metal ore should not be used.

## Gravel

Much of what has been said about the selection of rocks also applies when choosing gravel for the aquarium. Very often, gravel dredged up off-shore will contain many fragments of calcium-rich seashells, which will again harden the water over a period of time. Some aquatic dealers stock lime-free gravel, and although it will invariably be more expen-

sive, it will be a worthwhile investment if softwater fishes are to be kept.

The particle size of the gravel is important. Coarse gravel is unsuitable for two reasons: Food will quickly fall beyond the reach of the fishes and will decay, beginning a pollution risk; and if biological filtration is used, coarse gravel will not provide enough surface area for the bacteria to colonize, and the water flow through the gravel will be too fast.

If the gravel is too fine, it will pack down too tightly. Under these conditions, the plant roots will have difficulty penetrating the gravel, and the water flow rate through a biological filter will be severely impeded.

A medium-size gravel must be found and, as mentioned earlier, a particle size of 0.125 (3mm) is ideal. So much for size; what about the color and the amount needed to furnish your aquarium?

A dark gravel is best from several standpoints. In the wild, a fish swimming over a light-colored river bed would be easily seen by any predator—fish, bird, or even man. Freshwater fishes normally have a dark-colored back or top (dorsal) surface, which camouflages them as they swim over a dark river bed. In the aquarium, light from above will be reflected back up from any light-colored gravel, washing out the colors of the fish, which will then appear faded to the viewing aquarist. (The exception to this might seem to be in marine aquariums, where the bright colors of the fishes are apparently not affected as they swim above brilliant white coral sand. As we shall learn later, only coloration due to reflective material is affected, and the marine fishes' pigmented colors are not diluted.) For this reason, exhibition tanks at fish shows usually have the bottom glass painted black (on the outside!).

Some aquatic dealers stock colored gravel, but there is something slightly unnerving about a bed of yellow, green, or even mottled red and white gravel. There is also a danger that the colors used to dye the gravel may leach out into the water and release toxic substances.

If the color of the rockwork does not blend with the color of the gravel, there is an easy trick to match the two colors—some of the rock can be smashed up into small pieces that are then scattered on the surface of the gravel. Wrap the rock in a piece of cloth before smashing it, to stop flying splinters and to collect the pieces all in one operation.

The amount of gravel needed for any one tank may surprise you. The plants must have an adequate depth in which to root, and if biological filtration is to be used, at least 2 to 3in (5 to 7.5cm) of gravel must be placed over the filter plate to avoid any adverse effects on plant growth. (Incidentally, plants grown in pots will not suffer from biological filtration, being isolated from water flow.)

In practical terms this means approximately a 2 gallon (7.6 liter) bucketful for every 1ft² (900cm²) of tank floor area; if the gravel is to be landscaped, considerably more will be needed.

## Other tank decorations

Wood is a favorite material for furnishing the aquarium naturally. Sunken logs and twisted roots are notable features in a well-appointed aquarium. Such material can be collected from rivers, marshes, and forests, the only reservation being that any wood obtained this way must be long dead, with no traces of rotting.

Wood intended for aquarium use must be boiled in several changes of water and immersed in water for several weeks until completely waterlogged, then it may be considered fit for use. There should be no sign of discoloration of the water from the tannins in the wood. Alternatively, dead wood can be sealed with several coats of polyurethane varnish. Florists sometimes sell pieces of petrified wood for flower arrangements and this can also be used, after sealing, in an aquarium. Aquatic dealers will also stock this wood occasionally.

Another suitable natural material is cork bark, often used as a backdrop or to form terracing. The color is most pleasing, and it is easily cut to shape.

Modern technology has provided a synthetic substitute for natural wood decoration, and very realistic molded-resin 'logs' and 'tree roots' are commercially available. Modeled on real-life branches, after a few weeks in the aquarium they soon become coated with algae and it is difficult to tell them from the real thing.

Imitation plants are also a result of modern technology and, thanks to patient development in design tools and processing methods, it is now possible to purchase extremely lifelike replicas of the more popular aquarium plants—even down to the wet, floppy feel when taken out of water.

Of course, these artificial substitutes will not perform the same chemical and biological processes as their living counterparts, but they can provide shelter and spawning sites. Soon disguised by a covering of natural algae, artificial plants bring a touch of greenery to any aquarium in which boisterous fishes or those with vegetarian dietary habits are to be kept.

Several other objects of an artificial nature sometimes find their way into aquariums under the guise of being 'decorative'; these range from miniature, precast brick walls to sunken galleons, divers, treasure chests, and even mermaids. Usually out of scale, such ornaments are really quite out of place in the aquarium, and often the materials will emit color or poisonous substances into the water and endanger the fishes.

Quartz
Slate
Granite
Basalt
Cork bark
Twisted roots

Above: It is important to use only those rocks that will not adversely affect the water chemistry. Wood and cork bark should be sealed.
Left: A tank furnished to suit these rock-dwelling Malawi Blue Cichlids (*Pseudotropheus zebra*).

Below: Plastic plants will provide decorative 'greenery' and shelter in tanks with herbivorous fishes. Algae will soon cover them and make them look more natural. The gray 'rock' and 'log' in this tank are also artificial.

# WATER: THE VITAL INGREDIENT

The Discus Fishes need soft water.

*We now come to the main ingredient of the aquarium, without which it would be unable to function — water. Water is the fishes' atmosphere and serious consideration must be given to its supply and condition. The fishes we keep in our freshwater aquarium can come from several different types of water depending upon location. It says much for our fishes' tolerance that, generally, it is not too difficult to maintain quite successfully a truly cosmopolitan collection of fishes (from all manner of natural waters) in one common type of water, usually tap water. This may be called 'fishkeeping', whereas 'fish-breeding' may well require a deeper knowledge of the water qualities needed to bring about the successful reproduction of a particular species of fish. There are still many fishes that have not been bred in an aquarium and water management is probably the key to success.*

The water of all streams, rivers, and lakes begins ultimately as rain. The water then collects and drains across the land until it eventually reaches the sea, from which the evaporation and condensation cycle starts again. As rain falls through the atmosphere, it collects dust and minerals and absorbs gases, so that the water in rainfall is no longer pure. According to where the rain falls, the run-off is also affected by rocks and vegetation. Water falling on granite and flowing across moorland will be different from water that seeps through chalk hills. Lakes formed in rocky basins are again different in mineral composition from jungle streams. Yet we blithely expect to keep fishes from all these locations in water that probably resembles none of their natural habitats.

## Water quality

Tap water is supplied for one purpose — human consumption. It is carefully screened, cleaned, treated with prophylactic chemicals, and pumped into our homes for our use. It does not however carry a guarantee that it is suitable for fishkeeping!

Before you put it in an aquarium, tap water should be left standing for a day or two and, if possible, subjected to strong aeration to remove the chlorine in the water. Alternatively, a dechlorinating agent can be used. This can be obtained in liquid form from your aquatic dealer and is just mixed into the water. The amount to be used will be stated in the accompanying instructions.

Water drawn through copper piping can be toxic to fish (especially if the pipework or storage tank is new). So the first batch of water that flows through the tap, which may have been standing in the system for some time, should not be used.

Normally there is not too much to worry about, for any fish that is purchased locally will have been kept by the dealer in water similar to your supply while awaiting sale. If you are likely to buy the more exotic species (perhaps requiring special water conditions) or to bring fishes back from other areas, it might be wise to inquire about the water

conditions they are used to, in case these are different from yours.

Many aquatic publications deal in great depth with water chemistry, and the newcomer to fishkeeping is likely to be confused about the mystery surrounding such a normally taken-for-granted commodity.

There are two yardsticks used when describing water quality, and although they do bear some relationship to each

Above: The waters of the vast Amazon rain forest — whether they are rivers, streams, or lakes — are very soft and have an acidic reaction (pH value below 7) due to the large amounts of decaying vegetation present in the water.

other, it is suggested that the hobbyist treat them as separate entities right from the start to avoid any confusion. The properties of water are classified under two main headings: pH (acidity or alkalinity), and hardness.

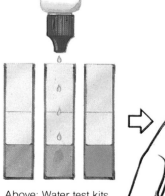

Above: Water test kits are simple to use. A measure of aquarium water is taken (left), the liquid indicator added (center), and the mixture's color compared with the standard color wheel. The pH value of the sample can be read off against the scale.

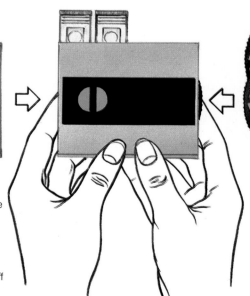

Above: Color wheels calibrated for different pH values are inserted into the water sample holder. The right-hand vial contains only aquarium water (to pre-color the viewing window) thus allowing for any discoloration in the aquarium water when comparing colors.

Above: The Rift Valley Lakes in Africa are gigantic clefts in the rocky basin, filled with water. Some fishes are endemic to their own lake, not being found elsewhere. The high mineral content of the water makes it hard and alkaline.

Right: *Labeotropheus trewavasae*, a cichlid found in Lake Malawi.

## The pH scale

The pH scale measures the strength of acidity or alkalinity on a range from 0 (very acid) to 14 (very alkaline) and is logarithmic; that is, pH 8 is ten times and pH 9 a hundred times more alkaline than pH 7 (the neutral point). The scale concerns the aquarist over only a narrow band; water used in freshwater tanks generally lies between pH 6.5 and 8.2.

```
pH values    0 1 2 3 4 5 6 7 8 9 10 11 12 13 14
             ←—Acid——  |  ——Alkaline——→
                       Neutral
```

The pH of any sample of water can be tested with inexpensive test-kits. These may employ sensitized papers or test liquids, and are quite accurate enough for the beginner. Much more accurate (and therefore expensive) electronic test apparatus exists, but this is usually well beyond the financial means and actual requirements of the average hobbyist.

To give an example of the practical use of pH: Freshwater fishes from jungle streams and rivers are usually found in waters with a pH below 7, whereas fishes from African rocky basins with waters of a high mineral content will require a pH above 7.

Much of the theory of pH and the fishes' needs is nullified by the fact that many fishes are bred commercially in water not always corresponding to that of their original natural habitat. Following their export to the aquarium markets of the world, they are then restocked into whatever water is convenient to the dealer, before finally ending up in a domestic aquarium.

Should it be necessary to stabilize the aquarium water around a definite pH value (for instance when trying to breed a species that requires very precise water conditions) a great deal of thought has to be given to everything that will be put into the tank (in the way of decoration and gravel), to avoid altering the pH. This is not generally necessary in the running of a cosmopolitan community collection of fishes, and it is only when the hobbyist decides to specialize with the more delicate species that water chemistry technology becomes important.

For those readers who are naturally curious, the pH of tap water in the U.S. is around 7.8-8.2. In most European domestic supplies it is around 7.2, but may be higher in some places. All are a convenient average for the aquarium.

## Water hardness

Probably a better-known property of water, hardness is also an important factor in the fishes' comfort and general well-being. Hardness is due to dissolved salts, usually of calcium and magnesium, and is one of two types — general (GH) or temporary/carbonate (KH). Temporary hardness can be removed by boiling but general hardness can be removed or reduced only by chemical means or by distillation. A quick method of reducing hardness (if necessary) is by dilution with *unpolluted* rainwater or by using special aquarium water softeners.

Most egg-laying fishes prefer soft water since any excessive hardness may prevent the development of the fertilized eggs. Live-bearing fishes and some African cichlids require hard water. Similarly, plants also have their preferences: *Echinodorus* will tolerate soft to medium-hard water, but *Cabomba* prefers soft and *Vallisneria* hard. (Many aquarists feel that certain plants are incompatible in each other's company; this may be so, but it also follows that the water composition could be wrong for some of the plants and not for others.)

Most methods of describing hardness refer to amounts of calcium carbonate ($CaCO_3$) present, either as mg/liter or as the equivalent ppm (parts per million), but the units used may vary from country to country. Taking the American °hardness 1mg/liter $CaCO_3$ as the standard, the British °Clark represents 14.3mg/liter, the German °dH 17.9mg/liter and the French °fH 20mg/liter. Soft, moderately hard and very hard water rate as up to 3°dH (0-50 mg/liter), 12-18°dH (200-300mg/liter), and over 25°dH (over 450mg/liter).

Usually, soft waters have an acidic reaction (lower than pH7) and hard water is usually alkaline (above pH7).

The hardness of the domestic water supply varies from region to region, depending upon the original source of water catchment. Water pumped from reservoirs in mountainous areas will generally be soft, whereas water collected from chalk soils will be very hard.

The newcomer should not feel intimidated by these brief notes on the technicalities of water management since, it should be stressed, thousands of hobbyists pursue a successful interest in fishkeeping without knowing the slightest thing about water chemistry. A simple way to ensure good healthy aquarium water is to undertake regular partial water changes, say 20 to 25% every three to four weeks, ensuring that the replacement water is of the same temperature and quality as that removed. In the marine aquarium, evaporation losses should be replaced not with salt but with fresh water, since none of the dissolved salts will have been lost during evaporation.

In every instance, fishes should not be subjected to drastic changes in water temperature or quality, and methods of ensuring this will be discussed in a later section. (See page 37.)

# SETTING UP THE AQUARIUM

Keep the final design in mind during setting up.

*Now that you understand the equipment and furnishings for the aquarium, you are ready to begin. There are three points to remember. First, the aquarium must be set up well in advance of the purchase of the livestock, for reasons that will become clear in the following chapter. Second, although the emphasis throughout this book has been concentrated upon tropical aquarium fishkeeping, much of the foregoing information (with the obvious exception of the section on heating) will also be applicable to the setting up of a coldwater aquarium. Finally, the photographs and diagrams in this section are from a studio performance carefully prepared to show the greatest detail. You may not be blessed with as much elbow room and things may be a little more cramped. But any variations, particularly in tank layout and design, are your prerogative.*

Setting up an aquarium can be an inconvenient, and sometimes messy, operation. Usually the source of water (and the place to dispose of it) is nowhere near the proposed site for the aquarium. If this is the case, as much preparatory work as possible should be done before moving to the actual aquarium site. Repeated journeys with dripping buckets, to and from the kitchen sink by way of the carpeted hall, are not guaranteed to endear the fishkeeper to the rest of the family. A certain amount of setting up can be done, if necessary, at the sink—

gravel and rocks can be installed in tanks up to 24in (60cm) in length and then carried into position. But for demonstration purposes in this book everything will be put into the tank in one location.

A small table next to the tank's position is very useful; on it you can keep all the

Fit the biological filter plate first (1). The correct size is one that fits snugly over the entire aquarium base. The vertical airlift tube may be fitted at either end (or both). For non-standard tanks, consider modular filter plates (1A) that you can fit together to match the shape of the base exactly.

Make sure that the plate is sitting flat on the glass base of the tank, then add gravel (2). At least 2in (5cm) depth will be needed for rooting plants, and this may be increased to 3 or 4in (7.5-10cm) at the rear to give a contoured effect; push pieces of rock into the gravel (3) to stop subsidence.

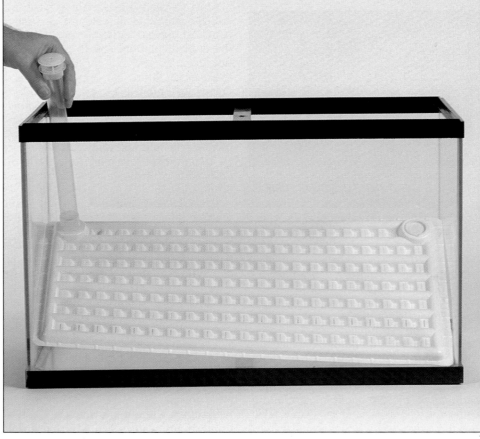
1

1A

2

3

necessary equipment close at hand. Tools required will be a small screwdriver, pliers, scissors, a pair of metal shears, a glasscutter, a small hammer, and a tube of aquarium sealant. Although this sounds a formidable line-up, every tool may not be needed in every setting-up situation, but without all of these, you can almost guarantee that the very thing you want will not be there when it is required.

## Advance preparation

Certain tasks, such as washing the gravel and selecting the rocks and plants, can be carried out in advance. The gravel is best washed out of doors, half a bucketful at a time, under a running hose until the water runs clear from the bucket. Rocks can be worked to the correct proportions with a few well-directed blows from a

hammer (protect your eyes!) and pieces can be glued together with sealant into preformed grottoes and caves ready for placing in the tank. At this stage a rocky backdrop can be constructed and glued directly onto the rear wall of the tank, or a decorative background can be fixed to the outside of the tank. The plants should be laid out in groups of species between sheets of very wet newspaper to prevent them from drying out as they await their turn to be placed in the tank.

It will be assumed that the site chosen for the tank fulfills all the requirements stated earlier, and that the empty tank is in position on its polystyrene base awaiting our attention.

## Setting up

Before beginning to furnish an aquarium, make a plan of the desired layout. In this

way, you will have a clear picture and you will not waste time in trying (and rejecting) many ideas. While following this plan it is also wise to keep looking through the front panel of the aquarium to see how things are progressing!

The decision to use a biological filter or not has to be made at the outset because, if such a filter is to be used, it goes into the tank before anything else.

Gravel is then added to a depth of 2 to 3in (5 to 7.5cm) and contoured to suit; vertical slabs of rocks (resting on the tank base) are used to form terracing, and other rocks and items such as wood branches are firmly fixed in position. Note that the gravel should slope from back to front to give a more pleasing appearance. When 'rock-scaping' remember to allow room for the plants and for the extra visual effect they will give.

4

The heater/thermostat unit is held in position by clips and suction pads. Simply slide the clips onto the heater tube (4) and space them a suitable distance apart. Do not position one clip over the hottest part of the heater. Mount the unit diagonally on the back glass (5), ensuring that it is clear of the gravel bed so that water can circulate freely around it to transfer warmth.

Below, left to right. A powerhead pump (A) will increase the flow rate through an undergravel filter. An outside box filter (B) with custom-made filter media blocks. An efficient inside power filter (C); these may feature variable flow rates and a facility for aeration. External power filters (D) can be sited remotely from the tank with a spraybar to return the filtered water across the aquarium surface.

5

A

B

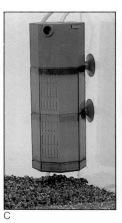

C

D

While the aquarium is dry, and so far reasonably uncluttered, is the best time to fit the filtration system (unless a biological system is already in position), heating system, air supply tubing, and airstones.

Combined heater/thermostat units generally have mounting clips provided but, if not, always fix the heater unit using non-metallic clips. Use two units for large tanks and always make the wiring connections outside the tank, installing drip loops where necessary.

Filter boxes are fitted to one end of the tank or to the rear wall, ensuring that the water flow is reasonably unimpeded to the inlet siphon tube. Do not obstruct the water flow with a huge rock. If possible, the returned cleaned water from the filter should be directed away from the inlet siphon by fitting an extension tube to the

filter's outlet pipe or, in the case of filters with provision of a separate return pipe, by fitting the return pipe at the opposite end of the tank. The return and inlet tubes to external power filters must be securely fastened to the side or rear walls of the tank and special care must be taken to ensure that the holes in the return tube spray bar face across the tank, preferably downwards!

Airstones can be located behind rocks for good visual effect and the connecting air tubing may be buried under the gravel and held down by a piece of rock. Provision must be made for an anti-siphon loop in the air tubing, or the air pump itself should be situated above the eventual water level. The air supply to the filters can be connected at this stage.

For the moment, all wires from filters, air pumps and heater/thermostats are

left unconnected to avoid the risk of accidental switching on at this time.

## Planting the aquarium

The aquarium may be planted dry or wet. The wet method is generally preferable, as the plants instantly take up their natural positions in the water and the hobbyist can see at a glance if the planting plan is working out to his liking. So the tank must now be filled with water.

To avoid overflowing when the planter's arms and hands are in the tank, it should be filled only three-quarters full at the planting stage. Water must be added in such a manner as not to disturb the carefully contoured gravel and terracing. It is best done by means of a hose pipe running first into a saucer or other container sitting on the aquarium floor. The overflow from this container will then

Use a ganged valve (6) to split the main air supply from the pump into separate outlets for each piece of air-operated equipment. Note the airstone in the airlift tube. Ideally, site the air pump above the tank to guard against water siphoning back into it when the power is switched off. Or use an anti-siphon valve in the airline (to the left of the pump) or loop the airline a few inches above the level of the tank to gain the same effect.

Below: A cable tidy (7) makes connecting electricity both safe and convenient. The central neon lamp shows that the supply to the unit is on. Removing the cover (8), shows the wiring. Two switched circuits control air pump and lighting, while the circuits for heating and a spare circuit (for power filters, etc.) are continuous. Be sure to position the cable tidy where it will not be splashed with water; avoid fixing it to the tank glass.

6

7

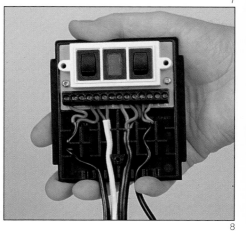

8

gently fill the aquarium without any undue disturbance. Cold water can be brought to approximately the correct temperature by adding some hot water.

Planting is done working from the edges of the tank towards the center. The tall plants go around the sides and back, with the bushy plants behind and between the rocks. Shorter plants look effective immediately in front of rocks, and 'specimen' plants are best planted away from groups of other plants. Remember that the crown (base) of a plant should be level with, or just above, the surface of the gravel. In cold-water aquariums, it is recommended that plant crowns are protected by a few small pebbles to prevent uprooting by fishes.

Most of the plants will take up their final positions almost immediately, but others may take some time to respond to the aquarium light, delaying your evaluation of the full effect of the planting.

### Final preparations

Once planting has been completed, the aquarium can be filled with water and it is time to get the whole thing operating. The filter box should be filled with filter medium and activated carbon, and the filter siphon started. The filter will then fill with water and stop, until air is supplied. External, cannister-type power filters are filled by temporarily removing the return tube (at the filter end) and sucking air through the filter, thus drawing water from the aquarium into the filter container (previously filled with the filter medium). As soon as water emerges from the filter outlet, the return tube should be securely replaced. The filter will not work until power is supplied to the motor, ideally via a switched circuit.

The wires from the heater/thermostat, power filter (if fitted), air pump, and lamps can now be connected to their respective supplies; the lamps' supply needs to be switchable. Use can be made of a 'cable tidy', a proprietary piece of aquarium equipment that serves as an electrical connection box and switching center and is fixed to the outside of the aquarium by adhesive pads. An aquarium thermometer should be fixed in place, depending on the type used, so it can easily be seen by the hobbyist. Similarly, a row of airline valves may usefully be stuck to the aquarium outside, and the airline connections from the pump to the filter and airstone made secure.

The cover glass should now be fitted, and the aquarium hood put into place. Finally, a suitable plug is fitted to the

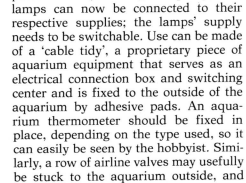

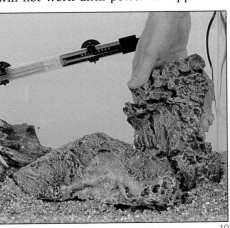

Build up interesting formations (9, 10, 11) from pieces of rock and decorative materials, taking care to place large rocks deep into the gravel to prevent toppling. Terraces filled with gravel will allow plants to grow at various levels. Use taller rocks to hide aquarium hardware, although the plants will do the same once established. Aim to create an illusion of front to back depth and hide the corners of the aquarium.

Fill the tank with care (12, 13), so as not to flatten out any contoured gravel. Pour the water onto any suitable object (saucer, jar or even a rock) to disperse the water flow gently. Stop when the tank is just over three-quarters full. This is the best stage to put in the plants; they will take up their natural positions, supported by the water, and the effect of planting can be seen and adjusted easily. See page 30 for adding plants.

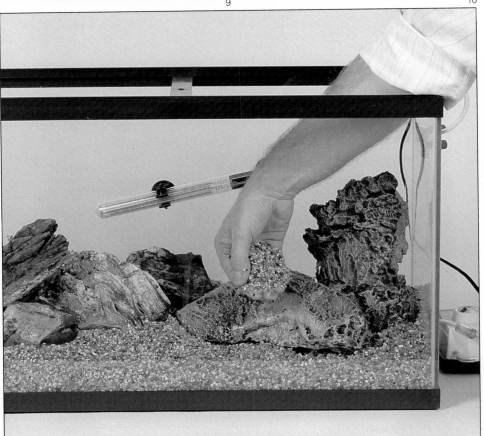

| Water capacities, weights and recommended heater sizes | | | | | | |
|---|---|---|---|---|---|---|
| Tank size | Volume | | | Weight of water | | Heater size |
| | US Gallons | Imp Gallons | Liters | Lbs | Kg | |
| 12 x 8 x 8in (30 x 20 x 20cm) | 3.0 | 2.5 | 11.4 | 25 | 11.3 | 75W |
| 18 x 10 x 10in (45 x 25 x 25cm) | 6.0 | 5.0 | 22.7 | 50 | 22.7 | 100W |
| 24 x 12 x 12in (60 x 30 x 30cm) | 14.4 | 12.0 | 54.5 | 120 | 54.3 | 150W |
| 24 x 15 x 12in (60 x 38 x 30cm) | 18.0 | 15.0 | 68.2 | 150 | 67.9 | 150W |
| 36 x 15 x 12in (90 x 38 x 30cm) | 27.6 | 23.0 | 104.5 | 230 | 104.1 | 2 x 100W |
| 48 x 15 x 12in (120 x 38 x 30cm) | 36.0 | 30.0 | 136.4 | 300 | 135.7 | 2 x 150W |

Above: Thermometers with liquid displays make temperature checking easy. Mount them on the tank in an easily visible position, as here.

14

With the hardware fitted (but not connected to any electrical supply), and with the gravel and rocks in place, the partially filled tank (14) is ready for planting. Not filling the tank completely leaves space for any displacement of the water as you reach in to position the plants. Start in the rear corners (15) with clumps (not single plants) of tall species such as *Vallisneria* or *Sagittaria*. Spread out and bury the roots in the gravel but leave the crown (where roots and stem join) just exposed. Use space-filling species of plants such as *Cabomba* or *Hygrophila* to hide the heater (16). Many specimen plants are cultured commercially in small individual plastic baskets filled with a growing medium. Simply bury each basket in the gravel; (17) in time, the growing medium inside will rot away as the roots spread out into the gravel.

15

17

16

supply cable to the cable tidy and the connection can be made to the electrical supply. The switches can now be operated and the aquarium is in action.

At this stage, several things will happen, and just as likely, several other things will not. Expected occurrences, such as the lights coming on and the air-pump and filter motors starting, usually function the first time. A glow from the neon indicator on the thermostat indicates that electrical power is reaching the heating system, but until the thermometer indicates a change in temperature there will be no visible reassuring evidence of heat emerging from the heater—don't be tempted to take the heater out of the water to feel it.

One possible annoyance may be that air-operated filters and airstones seem to refuse to work in harmony with each

other. This problem is easily overcome by adjusting the air flow to each, by means of the air flow valve, until the water pours from the filter return tube together with a satisfactory column of bubbles from the airstone and/or the biological filter system.

### Running in
It is understandable that now that the aquarium is to all intents and purposes ready for livestock, the hobbyist will want to lose no time in acquiring the fishes. Ideally, the aquarium should be functioning as a wholly complete unit (biologically speaking) when the fishes are introduced.

Modern thinking and aquarium practices have done away with the necessity of letting the aquarium 'mature' itself for a few weeks before adding the livestock.

Water conditioners are available that neutralize the chlorine from tap water and that will precipitate heavy metals almost immediately.

The biological filter will not function unless the bacteria in the gravel have something to work upon and, as we have seen previously, this means a source of ammonia. It is often suggested that some gravel from an established aquarium is used to 'seed' the new gravel bed, or that a piece of food (meat, for example) is allowed to rot away in the new, uninhabited aquarium. It is now normal practice to let the fishes themselves provide the ammonia, although the newcomer is advised not to risk very expensive fishes at this initial stage—a few hardy species will do just as good a job.

During this initial period, some plants may shed their leaves or become uprooted

The starting gear for fluorescent lighting can be accommodated in the rear of some hoods (18), if not already built-in. The unit is fitted with a switch but it may be more convenient to leave this switch in the on position and operate the lights by means of the cable tidy switch. Although the tank will have a plastic condensation tray, or cover glass, the pins on each end of the fluorescent tube are further protected by waterproof caps on the cable connectors. Most hoods have fittings for only one lighting tube; there is usually enough room for at least one more tube but remember you will need an extra set of starting gear. This need not be fitted in the hood if no space is available. Hoods usually have cut-outs or press-out panels for the passage of cables and airlines, but may need further alteration to cater for tall powerheads or the tubes of outside filters. The hood (19) has a white interior to reflect as much light as possible down into the water. To help this further, keep cover glasses and condensation trays spotlessly clean. The front part of the hood is hinged for easy maintenance and feeding purposes. Where tanks have a strengthening bar midway across the top, ease access by arranging the cover glass in two sliding halves. Cut off corners of the cover glasses or trays to facilitate entry of cables and airlines.

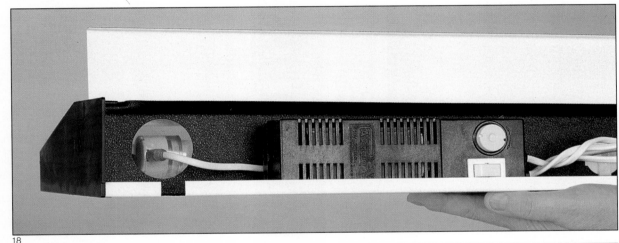

18

19

Above: Float the bag for several minutes to equalize temperatures, then add water to gradually acclimatize the fish before gently releasing them into their new home (right).

until enough roots develop to anchor the plants more firmly. Additionally, the presence of fishes in the tank from the beginning will mean that food will be available for the plants too, as they will utilize nitrates as a food source. This period is also a convenient time to assess the lighting requirements of the aquarium. The duration and/or brightness of the illumination can be adjusted accordingly, although the final evaluation cannot be made until the plants are at their full growth rate.

Another task that is best accomplished during the running in of the aquarium is getting to know as much as you can about the fishes before you purchase them. As you become acquainted with your developing aquarium you can mentally picture fishes inhabiting the aquatic landscape of your creation. Using the following pages to learn of the fishes' widely varied characteristics and how to look after them and the aquarium in the future will provide you with a basic knowledge. Then, armed with Dr. Vevers' information on the selection of the colorful fishes themselves, you can go ahead and complete the living picture that is the aquarium with all its fascinations. We wish you well.

# BASIC FISH ANATOMY

The Swordtail's 'sword' is purely decorative.

*S*ince fishes play the major role in an aquarium, it is recommended that the hobbyist becomes familiar with the animal and its general physiological characteristics as early as possible. In every book about fishes, the author invariably describes the fishes' appearance and habits using words that are unfamiliar to the novice fishkeeper. To avoid this common problem, this section of our book explains the structure of the fish's body, and its more general characteristics are noted. But it is a hypothetical fish that is described; there may well be several slight variations between this fundamental 'blueprint' and the widely varied living specimens in your own aquarium, because each of the many worldwide fish species has evolved different physical characteristics to suit its natural environmental conditions, in order to give that species the best chance of surviving and flourishing.

Not every fish conforms to the traditional torpedo shape since body shape reflects individual living and feeding habits. Ultra-streamlined bodies indicate fast-swimming, open-water predators whose large tail fins are often complemented at the other end by a large tooth-filled mouth. Laterally compressed fishes such as the Angelfish (*Pterophyllum* sp.) inhabit slower flowing, reed-filled waters and vertically compressed specimens live on the river-bed itself.

The position of the mouth often indicates in what level of the water the fish generally lives. An upturned mouth indicates a swimmer just below the surface, whose mouth is structured ideally for capturing insects floating on top of the water. These fishes usually have a straight, uncurved dorsal surface. Fishes whose mouths are located at the very tip of the head, on a horizontal line through the middle of the body, are mid-water feeders taking food as it falls through the water, although they can feed equally well from the surface or from the river-bed, should the mood take them. Many other fishes have underslung mouths. This, coupled with a flat ventral surface, clearly shows a bottom-dwelling species. A slight variation on this development is those fishes whose underslung mouths are used for rasping algae from rock surfaces (and the sides of the aquarium), in which case the fishes may not be entirely bottom-dwelling. Some bottom-dwellers have whiskerlike barbels around the mouth, which are often equipped with taste buds, so the fish can more easily locate its food as it forages.

## The scales
A fish's scales provide not only protection for the body but also aerodynamic streamlining. A variation from a scale covering is found in the Armored Catfish group (Callichthyidae), whose bodies are covered with two or three rows of overlapping bony scutes. Some catfishes, particularly those of the Mochokidae and the Pimelodidae, are covered in neither scales nor scutes.

## The fins
The fish uses its fins for locomotion and stability, and in some cases as spawning aids either during courtship or in the hatching period of the eggs. Fins may be either single or paired. The caudal fin provides the final impetus to thrust the fish through the water—fast swimmers have a deeply forked caudal fin. The Swordtail (*Xiphophorus* sp.) has an elongated lower edge to the caudal fin.

The dorsal fin may be erectile (as in the Sailfin Mollies—*Poecilia velifera, P. latipinna*) and will often consist of hard and soft rays. In some species two dorsal fins may be present, but these should not be confused with the adipose fin, a small fin (usually of a fatty tissue) that is found in some species, notably the Characoid group, between the main dorsal fin and the caudal fin.

The anal fin is another single fin mounted under the body just forward of the caudal fin. Mostly used as a stabilizer, in the male live-bearing fishes it has become adapted to serve as a reproductive organ. In some Characoid fishes the anal fin of the male carries tiny hooks that help to hold the two fishes together during spawning.

The pelvic, or ventral, fins are paired and are carried forward of the anal fin. In many of the Anabantid fishes (Gouramies) these fins are filamentous and are often used to explore the fish's surroundings. The Angelfish also has narrow, elongated pelvic fins, but these are not so maneuverable, nor are they equipped with tasting cells. The Armored Catfishes in the *Corydoras* genus use their pelvic fins to transport their eggs to the spawning site.

Pelvic fins in some species of Gobies are often fused together to form a suction cup that anchors the fish to the river-bed and prevents it from being swept away by the water currents.

Pectoral fins emerge from just behind the gill cover or operculum. Primarily used for maneuvering, pectoral fins have also been adapted for other uses. The Hatchetfishes emulate the marine Flying Fishes as they skim across the water surface by means of their well-developed pectoral fins. The marine Gurnard literally walks across the seabed on 'legs' formed by rays of its pectoral fins.

Many aquarium fishes have overlong, decorative fins. Fish breeders developed these exaggerated fins through deliberate breeding programs and such fin developments are not found in fishes in the wild.

## The fish's senses
The fish has the same five senses that a person enjoys—sight, touch, taste, smell, and hearing. Of these, the last two are more highly developed than those of humans. Many fishes detect food through

**Basic fish anatomy**
Knowledge of the fish's anatomy will help the aquarist to understand how a fish works and to use information found in aquatic books.

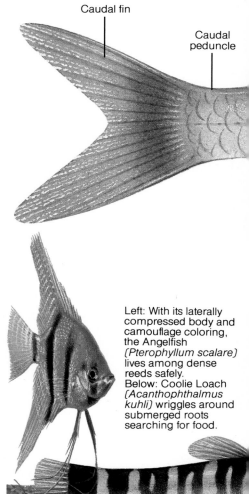

Caudal fin

Caudal peduncle

Left: With its laterally compressed body and camouflage coloring, the Angelfish (*Pterophyllum scalare*) lives among dense reeds safely.
Below: Coolie Loach (*Acanthophthalmus kuhli*) wriggles around submerged roots searching for food.

smell, often over great distances. A fish's nostrils are not used for breathing, only for smelling. It is debatable where the sense of actual hearing ceases and the detection of low frequency vibrations begins in the fish world. This is because fishes are equipped with a sixth sense—the lateral line system. Through perforations in a row of scales, the fish's nervous system can detect minute vibrations in the surrounding water. This warns of other fishes or obstacles nearby. The Blind Cave Characin (*Astyanax mexicanus*) copes quite easily with life in an aquarium, navigating by means of its lateral line system.

Some fishes have developed sophisticated aids to help them cope in darkness or in murky waters, and these include the ability to generate a weak electromagnetic field. The Electric Catfish (*Malapterurus electricus* sp.), although scaleless, needs little protection against predators, because it packs a hefty electric shock. It is thought that it uses this shock to stun smaller fishes.

## The swim-bladder

A feature exclusive to fishes is a hydrostatic buoyancy organ known as a swimbladder. This enables the fish to position itself at any level in the water, automatically giving the fish neutral density. Some fishes, notably the marine sharks, lack this organ.

## Color

Apart from attracting fishkeepers color plays an important role in the fish world. It serves to identify the species in general

Above: The Three-banded Pencilfish (*Nannostomus trifasciatus*) is seen here displaying its daytime colors; like related species, it has a different color pattern at night.

and the sexes in particular. It camouflages a fish from predators or gives clear visual warning that a species may be poisonous. Color presents false targets to an attacker and gives some clue to a fish's disposition, for instance frightened or angry.

Color is determined by two methods—by reflection of light and by pigmentation. Those silvery, iridescent hues seen on the flanks of many freshwater species are due to reflective layers of guanin. Guanin is a waste product that is not excreted from the kidneys and body, but stored just beneath the skin. The color seen depends upon the angle at which light hits and is reflected from these crystals. Many fishes, when lit by light coming through the front glass of the aquarium, seem to be colored differently than when lit by light coming from directly overhead. This also explains why a light-colored gravel appears to wash out the fishes' coloring.

Fishes with deeper colors have pigment cells in their bodies, and some species are able to control the amount of color they display. This can be seen quite easily in those species that tend to rest on the gravel surface or on rocks, where their colors are adapted to suit the background. Other fishes take on nocturnal colorations. The popular Pencilfishes (*Nannostomus* sp.) are notable examples and the hobbyist may be initially surprised at finding these fishes a different color pattern each morning. Fishes effect such color changes by contracting or expanding the pigmented cells (chromatophores) to intensify or dilute the color.

Color intensity is likely to be heightened in the male fish during the breeding period in order to attract a mate, and some female fishes within the Cichlid group may also have their colors exaggerated in order to be recognized by their subsequent offspring. A good example of this is seen in the *Pelvicachromis* genus, where the females are often more colorful during breeding than the males.

It is possible to intensify fishes' colors by feeding them so-called 'color foods'. These contain additives, such as carotin, that will accentuate colors. The Tiger Barb (*Barbus tetrazona*) is a favourite fish that responds quite startlingly to color feeding, each scale becoming edged with black, giving a netted appearance. Unfortunately, in fish competitions the judges are quick to notice such artificial practices, and color-fed fishes are likely to be down-graded for not complying with the natural colors of their species. The use of color-enhancing lamps will also give the impression of more brightly colored fishes, but naturally the fishes will regain their normal colors when removed to more normally lit environments using standard lamps.

Dorsal fin

Swim-bladder

Adipose fin

Scales

Lateral line system

Liver

Kidney

Gills (Gill cover, or Operculum, cut away to show detail.)

Eye

Nostril

Mouth

Barbels

Heart

Vent (Anus and Urinogenital opening)

Anal fin

Ovary

Intestine

Esophagus, leading to Stomach (hidden behind Ovary)

Pectoral fin (paired)

Pelvic, or Ventral, fin (paired)

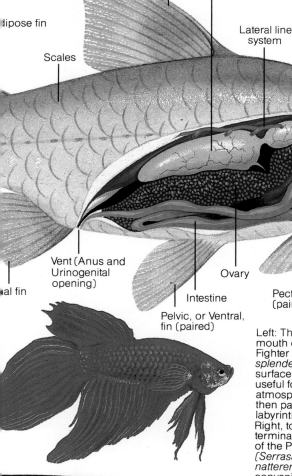

Left: The upturned mouth of the Siamese Fighter (*Betta splendens*) indicates a surface feeder. It is also useful for breathing atmospheric air, which then passes into the labyrinth organ.
Right, top: The terminally located teeth of the Piranha (*Serrasalmus nattereri*) are conveniently placed for biting anything!
Right: Barbels around the mouth of the *Corydoras* catfish are equipped with taste cells to assist in the search for food.

# FISHES: MAKING THE RIGHT CHOICE

The voracious Piranha is its own best company.

*The choosing of the fishes for your collection should not be rushed. The success of keeping fishes in captivity depends upon the selection of healthy, suitable stock, followed by proper handling and a careful introduction into the aquarium. The treatment your fishes receive at this stage of their progression from the dealer's tanks to your aquarium is yet another traumatic experience for them to survive. Remember, they may already have traveled halfway around the world, perhaps under extremely trying conditions, and a stress-free introduction into your aquarium will be appreciated and rewarded. A fish that is under considerable stress is likely to contract disease much more readily than a contented one, so get your fishes off to a good start by caring right from the beginning. Any failure to apply a few commonsense rules at this stage is certain to mean disappointment.*

In order to make full use of the available aquarium space a selection of fishes that will occupy all levels in the water should be chosen, by studying their physical forms as described earlier.

Another factor to be considered is the size that any fish will eventually attain. Most of the fishes offered for sale are juveniles and it is likely that in the aquarium their size will at least double. In practical terms, it would be foolish to buy a number of 1in (2.5cm) fishes of different species, if some of them grow to 5in (13cm) and the remainder mature at 1.5in (3.75cm), since the law of the wild is often 'eat, or be eaten'. The hobbyist will not want this law demonstrated in his fish tank. Your aquatic dealer should be able to advise you on the likely adult sizes of his fishes.

Some fishes, although seen quite clearly in the shop's brightly lit but barely furnished tanks, may well be nocturnal by nature, so don't be surprised if they display this habit, hiding in the plants by day and swimming at night, when settled into your comfortable aquarium. Herbivorous fishes have been known to strip a lushly planted aquarium bare of vegetation—obviously a case for rocks and artificial plants!

Slow-moving fishes with exaggerated fins are often discomforted by the presence of faster-moving species, but this can be alleviated by providing retreats and refuges for the slower species. Gregarious fishes should not be purchased in ones or twos: A shoal of six or more will not only look more attractive, but the fishes will feel happier too. In addition, some male fishes are ardent suitors and it is then better to buy trios of a species (two females to one male) to ensure that one female is not harassed.

We now come to the situation where we have mentally chosen our fish and are faced with the actual moment of selection in the aquatic shop. Look for a healthy fish. The majority of freshwater fishes will swim with the dorsal fin erect. A folded-down dorsal fin usually indicates an ailing fish. The fish's body should be well-filled, with no 'knife-edge' dorsal or ventral surfaces. Colors should be dense and any color patterns clearly defined

with no smudging between different color areas. The act of swimming should be effortless, with no undue wobbling, and the fish should be able to remain at any depth in the water without bobbing to the surface or sinking to the floor.

Do not purchase fishes with obvious defects such as deformed bodies or missing fins; similarly, fishes with spots or open wounds should also be passed over.

Determining the sex of the fishes is not difficult. The live-bearing species are

easily distinguished by the obvious difference between the shapes of the anal fins. The general rule for egg-laying species is that the male fish is usually slimmer and more brightly colored, and often has more developed and pronounced finnage. Purchasing a number of specimens is more likely to provide both males and females than if you purchased only two or three.

Although the more exotic specimens are certainly appealing, they should be

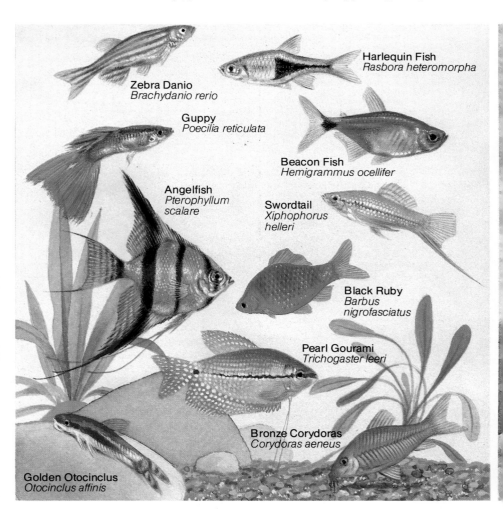

Zebra Danio
*Brachydanio rerio*

Harlequin Fish
*Rasbora heteromorpha*

Guppy
*Poecilia reticulata*

Beacon Fish
*Hemigrammus ocellifer*

Angelfish
*Pterophyllum scalare*

Swordtail
*Xiphophorus helleri*

Black Ruby
*Barbus nigrofasciatus*

Pearl Gourami
*Trichogaster leeri*

Bronze Corydoras
*Corydoras aeneus*

Golden Otocinclus
*Otocinclus affinis*

## Fishes for a community aquarium

Fishes for the community tank should be chosen to make full use of all swimming space and water levels in the aquarium; additionally, the many various shapes, colors, and swimming habits of the fishes are automatically included in such a cosmopolitan collection. Similarly, it is quite usual to find aquatic plants from worldwide locations sharing the same aquarium. Avoid mixing boisterous species with the more timid fishes, and those of a vegetarian nature should not be included in a well-planted tank. Live-bearing fishes will interbreed within the same species regardless of color pattern; do not mix colors if you want pure strains.

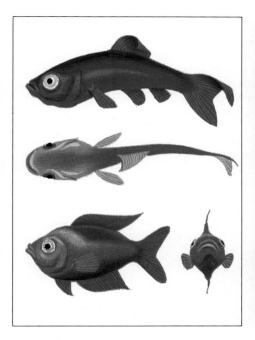

Above: Fishes exhibiting severe wasting symptoms such as hollow bellies and emaciated bodies are not necessarily in need of a good meal. They may be suffering from fish diseases.

Above: When buying live-bearers, such as these Sailfin Mollies *(Poecilia velifera),* it is easy to select pairs since sex differences are obvious; the male has a taller dorsal fin and a modified anal fin.

ignored (even if they are within your financial grasp) when you choose the original stock, and left until practical experience has been gained.

## Transport and introduction into the aquarium

Fishes are usually transported in a plastic bag. Should the homeward journey be lengthy, however, there is a risk that tropical species may become chilled. It is advisable to wrap the plastic bag in a layer or two of newspaper or, better still, place the bag in an insulated box.

Despite such precautions, there will still be a temperature difference between the water in the transportation bag and in the prepared aquarium. To avoid any thermal shock to the fishes, the water temperatures must be equalized before the fishes are released into the aquarium. This is easily achieved by floating the plastic bag in the aquarium for several minutes. To accustom the fishes to the water quality of the aquarium, some hobbyists introduce increasing amounts of the aquarium water into the plastic bag during this temperature equalization. It may also be advisable to carry out the introduction of the fishes with the aquarium lighting off, so that they can accustom themselves to their new home under subdued lighting, and thus be protected from any shock brought on by environmental changes.

The introduction of fishes into an aquarium should always be made as calm an operation as possible. When adding new fishes to an already stocked aquarium, it can be a useful ploy to give the existing fishes some food to divert their attention away from the newcomers; in any case, make sure that there are always adequate retreats and refuges available for the more timid ones to take advantage of during their settling-in.

**Trewava's Cichlid**
*Labeotropheus trewavasae*

**Malawi Golden Cichlid**
*Melanochromis auratus*

**Malawi Blue Cichlid**
*Pseudotropheus zebra*

**Golden Julie**
*Julidochromis ornatus*

**Blue Discus**
*Symphysodon aequifasciata haraldi*

**Lyretail**
*Aphyosemion australe*

**Oscar**
*Astronotus ocellatus*

**Clown Loach**
*Botia macracantha*

## Fishes for a rocky aquarium
These very territorial fishes are all originally from the hard waters of the African Rift Valley Lakes, and the rocky background should provide at least one retreat per fish. Many browse upon algae and plants, so the aquarist may wish to use artificial plants to decorate the otherwise barren tank, since natural plants may suffer.

## Fishes for a species aquarium
These fishes may adapt to community life but their individual requirements (or anti-social behavior) are better provided for (or guarded against) in separate aquariums. Some may need special care or be of nocturnal habits; others may be your favorite shoaling fishes that you may prefer to keep on their own.

# FEEDING AND MAINTENANCE

A cube of safe freeze-dried *Tubifex* worms.

*We have seen how fishes have become adapted to suit their varying environments by evolving different body shapes, mouth positions, finnage, and so on. Similarly, we have learned that the aquarium water needs to be kept in good condition by means of filtration systems and aquatic plants. But things in the aquarium are not the same as in nature and many of the fishes' needs must be supplied, or carried out, by the hobbyist. The attention of the hobbyist is particularly drawn to the provision of a varied and nourishing diet for the fishes, together with a good service record in maintaining the aquarium's hygiene. Whenever it is impossible to recreate exact conditions any substitute must be as near the fishes' natural norm as possible. Again, in order to protect the fishes from any undue stress, changes to new conditions must be made gradually.*

Having read about the fishes' natural diet (insects, smaller fishes, amphibians, water crustacea, etc.) the newcomer may be concerned as to how to keep his fishes from starving. Fortunately, fish nutrition has been the subject of research and production for many years and now vast industries keep the market well stocked with fish foods.

Modern fish food is far removed from the old-fashioned 'ants' eggs' approach. It is now possible to buy food to suit any fish's particular requirement, whether carnivorous or herbivorous. Nor is the choice limited to food content, for foods can be of various forms — flake, liquid, tablet, paste, powder, or freeze-dried lumps. These have been developed not only to suit the different feeding habits of fishes, but also to suit a fish throughout its whole life — from tiny, newborn fry (when microscopic-sized food is necessary) right up to adulthood (when a large chunk is taken without effort).

Despite the undoubted excellence of manufactured foods, which can provide a complete and varied diet, feeding exclusively with one type of food can have its drawbacks. The fishes can become bored with an unchanging diet and go off their food, but the main danger when feeding 'artificial' foods is that of overfeeding. No, the fishes will not develop a weight problem — unlike humans, they do not over-indulge. The problem arises from the food that is not eaten. These leftovers will decay in the aquarium and pollute it sooner or later, requiring a complete dismantling and refurnishing.

The rule is to feed 'little but often'. The fishes should be able to clear up all the food you give them in a matter of a few minutes. If you share the responsibility of looking after the aquarium with other members of the family, do tell them when you have fed the fishes. This will prevent someone else doing it again a few minutes later, with the result that overfeeding becomes a risk. A feed for the fishes morning, noon and night is quite acceptable, provided that only small amounts are given at any one time. The feed just before 'lights out' at night is important, as those fishes with nocturnal habits are then not neglected.

In addition to the modern, protein-filled dried foods that are available, fishes can be given live foods. Such foods can be captured from ponds, or cultured.

Water fleas (*Daphnia pulex*), *Tubifex* worms, mosquito larvae, bloodworms, etc. are all excellent foods. Fishes benefit from the chase after the wriggling foods almost as much as from eating them.

There is a real risk of introducing disease (or predators) when using some wild-caught live foods, especially those collected from fish-inhabited waters. *Tubifex* worms, found in river mud usually near to sewage outfalls, may be particularly suspect. If you wish to feed *Tubifex*, clean it well before use under running water. Some fishkeepers decline to use it altogether.

Small earthworms may also be given (do not use worms from ground that has been treated with weedkillers), and many fishes relish household scraps. Lean raw beef, ox heart, peas, lettuce, spinach, and wheat germ are quite common extras to the fishes' menu. However they may need to be trained to accept the new foods over a period of time.

Above left: A selection of dried foods. (1) Multiflavored flake, (2) floating pellets, (3) freeze-dried *Tubifex* cubes, (4) flour-fine fry food, (5) stick-on tablet food, (6) granulated high protein food, (7) freeze-dried shrimp, and (8) green (vegetable formula) flake food. Tubed liquid fry food is also available.

Above right: Live foods. Water fleas and mosquito larvae can be caught in ponds. Eggs of brine shrimps hatch in warm salt water.

Water crustacea should not be collected from fish-carrying waters (they are unlikely to be there in worthwhile numbers anyway), so as not to introduce any fish diseases into the aquarium. An even greater danger is that the catch will also contain predators that will attack small fishes. Such predators include the larval forms of the great diving beetle (*Dytiscus marginalis*), water boatman (*Notonecta*), whirligig beetle (*Gyrinus*) and dragonflies (*Aeshna, Libellula, Sympetrum*). It is also possible to introduce *Hydra*, leeches, and snails together with other waterborne creatures when netting foods from natural waters, so all collected foods should be carefully screened.

Mosquito and gnat larvae may be collected in any garden rain-barrel, and

The removal of algae from the front glass of the tank is made easy by abrasive pads, either mounted on a long handle (above left) or on self-parking magnetic blocks (left). Detritus from the floor of the aquarium can be sucked up by a useful air-operated 'vacuum cleaner', the detritus automatically collecting inside the cloth bag (above) and the water returning to the tank.

these wriggling foods are much relished by aquarium fishes.

Live foods that can be cultured by the hobbyist include micro-worms, grindal worms and white worms; these are listed in ascending order of size. Micro-worms are very tiny and white worms not much thicker than a heavy thread. Such worms are fed on cereal foods and need to be grown in progressive cultures—as one culture becomes exhausted (or turns sour), a portion of it is used to start a new one.

A live food that plays a most important role in feeding aquarium fishes (particularly young newborn specimens) is the brine shrimp (*Artemia salina*). The eggs of this marine crustacean may be stored indefinitely, and hatched when required by immersing them in salt water. The resulting newly hatched shrimps, or nauplii, are an ideal first food for fry. They are highly nutritious and completely disease-free, unlike pond-caught food, which may carry fish diseases. Again, it is recommended that cultures of brine shrimp are started in rotation to ensure a continuing supply of the food. Brine

shrimp eggs are available in two forms—with and without shells—the latter form being produced commercially; the shells are already dissolved away and a higher hatch yield is expected.

### Routine maintenance

Commonsense checks and chores need take no more than a few minutes a day, or perhaps an hour or two each month. Many of the checks will be made automatically while the hobbyist is watching his fishes, and it really is true that fishkeeping offers rewards far in excess of the necessary effort put into it.

A daily check easily carried out at feeding time is to see if all the fishes are well and present. Any missing fish should be located at the earliest opportunity, since a decomposing body (if it is dead) will pollute the tank or spread disease. A quick look at the thermometer will indicate if all is well with the heating system, and the filtration and aeration systems have readily visible proof of working. Faulty lamps should be replaced.

Depending upon the dirtiness of the tank (or the habits of the fishes) the filter

medium can be changed as needed, probably about every two to four weeks. When maintaining power filters, remember to check the tightness of all pipe unions and connections. Dead leaves should be removed from the aquarium; any rampant plants can be pruned, and the cuttings planted elsewhere. Algae should be scraped from the front glass, but may be left undisturbed on side and rear walls of the aquarium for the benefit of vegetarian species.

Each month or so, 20 to 25% of the aquarium water should be removed and replaced with fresh water of the correct temperature. During this process any detritus should be siphoned from the floor of the aquarium. Cover glasses should be cleaned at this time, too. Over a period of time, airstones become clogged; this may not be due to algae forming on the airstone's surface, nor due to the hardness of the water. Most airstones clog up from the inside through drawing poorly filtered air into the aquarium via the air pump. The better models of air pump are fitted with filter pads (usually in the base, where they are conveniently forgotten). Regular cleaning or replacement of air pump filters is recommended. Where biological filtration is used, there may be a tendency for the gravel to bed down; it is good practice to rake over the gravel periodically to ensure a continued water flow through the system.

### Vacation worries

Unlike other pets, fishes do not present many problems when the annual vacation looms. Although fishes cannot be left at a neighbor's house, they can easily be looked after by a friend, provided that exact feeding instructions are given. The danger is that people without fishkeeping experience disbelieve the amount of food stated in any instructions and nearly always over-feed, with dire results. It is not unusual for a whole tin of fish food to be used by well-meaning 'fish-sitters' over a two-week vacation.

If the fishes have been well fed during the weeks running up to the holiday, they are quite able to endure a week or two without food or light. Of necessity, a hungry fish will search for food, and the aquarium will be well scoured by the time the owner returns. The plants, too, may have lost their covering of algae during the period of darkness, and another noticeable effect will be that the plants will have tilted themselves towards the front glass in their efforts to receive any available light.

Automatic feeders and time switches will keep an aquarium in full operation during absence. It may be a bit extravagant (or just impossible) to go to these lengths for the sake of a few weeks in the year when they will be needed.

# DISEASES: PREVENTION AND TREATMENT

Typical signs of 'hole-in-the-head' disease.

*Most of the illnesses to which fishes succumb may be regarded as nothing more serious than the occasional colds and influenza attacks that affect human beings. Without doubt, fish diseases will strike at your fishes at one time or another. "It won't happen to my fish," is a cry all too frequently heard from aquarists who, in truth, do not really care. Although the following information is broadly based, due to the diversities of proprietary brands of treatments available worldwide, the hobbyist must be prepared to face the occasional setback in his fishes' health. Nearly all ailments are curable, and more often than not the hobbyist puts his fishes at more risk from poor aquarium management than they are facing from disease. In addition, disease may be introduced into the aquarium through ignorance or laziness, when simple quarantine measures would avoid such occurrences.*

With the exception of the initial furnishing and stocking of an aquarium (the settling down period may be regarded as a quarantine process), any further addition—be it fish or plant—should be well screened for potential disease before its introduction into the aquarium.

A separate small tank should be set up for quarantine purposes. It need not be fully furnished, but one or two rocks can be provided to give the new fish a sense of security. A period of two to three weeks should be enought time for latent diseases (if any are present) to manifest themselves. During this time, a careful watch should be kept on the fish for any spots, pimples etc. Should an ailment become noticed, the quarantine tank can immediately be converted into a hospital tank in which the fish can be treated.

Although plants may not develop such visible signs of disease as do fishes, they should be carefully prepared for use in an aquarium. The plant should be searched for unwanted 'passengers', particularly snails' eggs, which could result in an infestation of snails in a very short time. To make more sure of safety, some aquarists advocate that new plants be given a rinse in a weak solution of potassium permanganate to destroy any minute animal life that might otherwise be introduced with the plants.

Very often an outbreak of disease follows the addition of new stock, which is consequently blamed, as is the dealer from whom the new fish was purchased. The reason for this coincidence is that the new fish is often placed under stress due to the change in its environment, and it is thus more prone to those diseases to which the existing fishes of the aquarium may have built up some degree of immunity. It may therefore be unfair to blame the dealer for unhealthy stock. A good dealer will quarantine his stock before offering it for sale. If you want to buy a new fish from a dealer, inquire whether it can be quarantined and reserved for purchase at a later date.

Should the aquarist progress to multiple tanks, a risk of infection can occur by using a single net between all the tanks. Each tank should have its own net, disinfected after every use. It should be unnecessary to warn against the transfer of water from an infected tank to a healthy one.

Aquarium water can become contaminated by such things as cigarette smoke, aerosols, fumes from paint or furniture polish, industrial smells, etc, all of which are pumped into the aquarium by the air pump. Metals and cement are also liable to contaminate the water, and nitrogenous compounds (ammonia, nitrite and—less harmful—nitrate) should be kept to a minimum by biological filtration and regular partial water changes.

Despite the excellent quality of prepared foods, a full varied diet should be given to avoid any vitamin deficiencies, and live food will greatly improve a fish's health and breeding potential.

## Treatments

In order for any disease or disorder to be treated successfully, an accurate diagnosis must first be made. Fortunately, the most common (but curable) ailments are all easily recognizable and, thanks to modern research, the necessary treat-

**Basic treatment or quarantine tank**
To quarantine new arrivals and/or to treat ailing fishes, set up a small tank along the lines shown below. The accent should be on simplicity and ease of maintenance. Do not share any equipment, such as nets, with the display aquarium. Locate this tank away from the main one where it will be undisturbed.

Dim lighting will help to reduce stress on the fish and provide a calm environment. It may help to shade the tank to prevent strong daylight affecting certain medications.

Use an internal power filter (without any activated carbon) or an air-driven foam filter. Maintain these filters regularly and make frequent partial water changes.

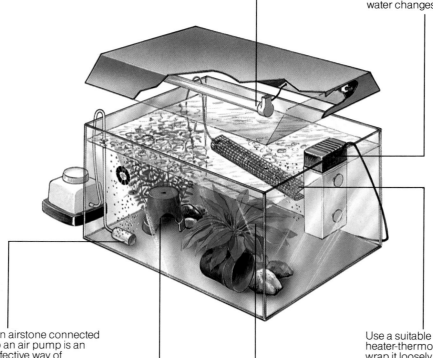

An airstone connected to an air pump is an effective way of keeping the oxygen level high and also helps to circulate warmth from the heater around the tank.

Smooth stones and plant pots (plastic ones are best) form excellent refuges for nervous fish. But keep the groupings fairly open so that you can keep an eye on things.

Plastic plants are ideal for the tank; they are durable and will not be affected by any medications. They also provide interest in an otherwise bare tank.

Use a suitable heater-thermostat and wrap it loosely in a plastic mesh. This will prevent fishes from resting on the heating element and injuring themselves.

## GUIDELINES FOR GOOD HEALTH

ENVIRONMENT: Don't overcrowd —stresses are set up, and any outbreak of disease spreads quickly. Don't keep large fishes with small ones, and provide plenty of retreats. Don't overfeed—uneaten food will cause pollution.
Don't underfeed—a starving fish has less resistance to disease.
Feed a varied diet—a fixed diet may not provide a correct balance of vitamins and may cause digestive disorders.
Avoid possible toxins entering the aquarium—tobacco smoke, paint fumes, aerosols, etc.
Keep filters clean, and make regular partial water changes.
Avoid stressing the fishes—don't change water conditions suddenly.

LIVESTOCK: Always buy healthy stock. Quarantine all new additions before introducing them to the main collection. Check plants for snail eggs and other unwanted aquatic animals; disinfect with a rinse in potassium permanganate. Remove any sick fishes as soon as possible.

TREATMENTS: Follow medication instructions as closely as possible in order to avoid overdosing.
Some medications adversely affect plants, or are affected by light—treat sick fishes away from the main aquarium if possible.
Some medications reduce oxygen levels, so increase aeration during treatment.
Remove activated carbon from filters during any course of medication.
Some chemicals (such as snail-killers) may adversely affect biological filtration, and may cause pollution problems if used to destroy snails that burrow in the gravel, whose dead bodies then decompose.

## A TROUBLE-SHOOTING QUESTIONNAIRE

The following questionnaire is a basic template that you can adapt to your own special situation. The answers to the questions should enable a person with some fishkeeping experience either to identify the most likely cause of a problem or at least to eliminate the most obvious causes. Of course, the questionnaire is not foolproof, and it is vital to view each problem in the light of your particular situation.

1 How many years experience in fishkeeping?

2 Types of fishkeeping experience, such as coldwater, tropical, marine, etc.

3 Number of tanks at the present time.

4 Special interests within the hobby.

5 Local tapwater conditions:
   pH value
   Hardness
   — Total (GH)
   — Carbonate (KH)
   Nitrate ($NO_3^-$)

6 When did the problem begin?

7 Describe the symptoms seen on the affected fish.

8 Which are the worst affected species?

9 List any unaffected species in the same tank.

10 Are other tanks affected?

11 Conditions in the affected tank:
   pH value                    Ammonia ($NH_3$)
   Hardness                   Nitrite ($NO_2^-$)
   — Total (GH)             Nitrate ($NO_3^-$)
   — Carbonate (KH)     Copper
   Temperature
   Stocking level (species and sizes)
   Tank volume and surface area
   Method of filtration
   Time since setting-up

12 Extent and nature of routine maintenance, such as:
   Partial water changes
   Filter maintenance

13 How long is the aeration and filtration left running each day?

14 Any recent
   Fish or plant introductions?
   Use of live food; which type?
   New tank decorations?

15 Could any of the following have gained access to the aquarium?
   Aerosols          Tobacco fumes
   Sprays            Other fumes
   Paint fumes      or chemicals

16 Type of food and frequency of use.

17 Any new plumbing in the house or mains work by the water supply company?

18 Any new equipment used in the tank?

19 Any recent use of disease remedies or water treatments? Were doses correct?

20 Has *anything* been done to the tank recently which is out of the ordinary?

ment is usually easily available and administered. It is natural that a newcomer to the hobby will hope that any such ailments will not occur in his aquarium, but nevertheless he should be able to recognize the symptoms early.

Over-production of mucus by the fish is an indication that something is wrong. Mucus is a protective slime produced by the fish. It can immediately coat a wound, but it can be deceiving because it can also hide parasites from view.

A brief outline of the more common ailments and disorders follows on the next two pages. Suspected problems that are beyond the scope of this chapter should be referred to the nearest knowledgeable source, such as an experienced aquarist, your local aquatic dealer, or even a veterinarian. With respect to veterinarians, it is reassuring to find that many more are becoming both qualified and interested in fishkeeping.

Treatments vary in method of application from individual baths to the dosing of the complete aquarium. Individual baths are generally only for short periods of time (a matter of minutes) while the treating of a complete aquarium is classified as a 'long-term' bath (until the medication ceases to be effective or the treatment is complete) and is carried out at a much lower concentration level of medication. Occasionally, a fish may need to be treated 'out of water', when dealing with a wound, for instance, or a parasitic infection that is large enough to be treated in this way.

It is important that doses of medication are calculated as accurately as possible because overdosing can be dangerous. Medications should always be dissolved into liquid form and prepared in basic stock solution strengths before being used. In some cases, medication can be administered internally to a fish by the simple method of soaking the fish's food in the medication before feeding. This method is a little uncertain, as no definite dosage can be proved to have been taken.

**During the treatment of the whole aquarium, carbon should be removed from any filters to prevent it adsorbing the medication** (thus reducing its effect), but the filter should be left running to assist water movement. Medications often reduce the level of oxygen in the water and extra aeration can usefully be employed during the period of treatment. Some aquarium plants may be adversely affected by the addition of medication to the aquarium; usually the fine-leaved specimens are the worst affected. At the end of any long-term bath of medicated treatments, the fish should be gradually acclimatized to fresh, clean water again by the replacement with clean water over a period of days.

**White spot disease** (*Ichthyophthiriasis*) This is the most common parasitic ailment and probably the easiest to diagnose. The fish's body is covered with tiny white spots, which extend to cover the fins. The disease is of a cyclic nature. The parasite leaves the fish's body to form cysts on the aquarium floor and upon hatching the parasite is then free-swimming, seeking a new host. It can be attacked by treatment at this stage. As the disease is likely to affect all the fishes in an aquarium, the whole tank should be treated. Proprietary cures are readily available, simple to administer, and extremely effective.

**Fungus** (*Saprolegnia*) In this disease, white tufts appear on the body or it may be covered with a fine layer of cobwebby or dusty fungus. Proprietary remedies, such as those containing phenoxyethanol and nirfurpirinol, and also dip treatments are all recommended. Although salt baths (about 4oz/gallon or 3gm/liter) can be used as a supportive measure, with perhaps three times this strength where exposed skin is evident, as a fungus cure in itself it is not reliable and can cause rapid pollution unless frequent water changes are made.

Similar in appearance, and often confused with body fungus, is 'mouth fungus'; this is caused by a quite different agent, a slime bacterium, *Flexibacter columnaris*, and will not necessarily respond to the same treatments used against body fungus. Phenoxyethanol has proved effective, as has treatment with antibiotics.

**'Shimmying'** The symptoms are aptly described, since the fish just makes rapid undulating movements without any forward movement occurring. One cause of this ailment is a drop in water temperature, so that the fish becomes chilled. The obvious remedy is to check the aquarium's heating system for any malfunction and to raise the temperature to the correct level. One species in particular seems prone to 'shimmying', the very popular Black Molly (*Poecilia* hybrid).

**'Dropsy'** Occasionally a fish's body becomes bloated to such a degree that the scales protrude outwards. This is due to the body cavities filling with liquid. There is some confusion as to what exactly causes this to happen, but the majority of hobbyists refer to the condition as 'dropsy'. It is difficult to cure, although it is possible for a veterinarian to draw off excess fluid using a fine syringe. Since dropsy can be contagious, it is best to isolate the affected fish until it recovers or has to be painlessly destroyed.

**'Finrot'** The degeneration of the tissue between individual rays of the fins is caused by a bacterial infection that is often encouraged by poor water conditions. The fins may have become damaged by bad handling techniques, or by a bullying fish. This allows the bacterial infection to gain a hold on the injured fins. A general clean-up of the aquarium water will be required, together with better aquarium management in the future. Proprietary cures will assist rapid recovery to full fin health, but these medicines cannot overcome neglect by the hobbyist.

**Gill flukes** Fishes are sometimes seen scratching themselves on rocks or plants, accompanied by an increased respiration rate with the gills gaping and obviously inflamed. Such fishes are infected with *Gyrodactylus* and *Dactylogyrus* parasites, which burrow into the skin or collect on the delicate gill membranes. The para-

**White spot infection cycle**

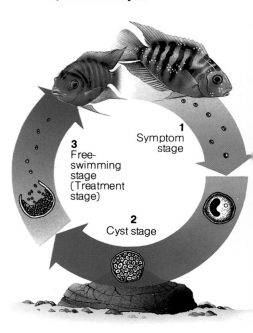

1 Symptom stage

2 Cyst stage

3 Free-swimming stage (Treatment stage)

---

### Fish diseases

Illustrated below are some of the more common ailments that befall fishes in the aquarium. Some are due to parasites introduced into the aquarium with live food or plants from other waters; others are bacterial infections brought about by poor aquarium hygiene and lack of proper maintenance.

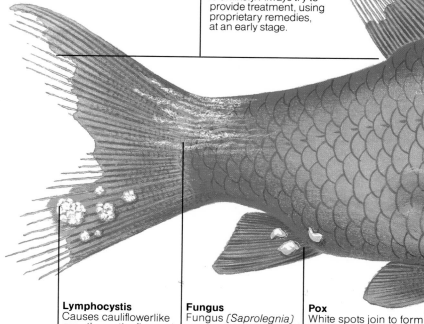

**Tailrot/Finrot**
The very obvious symptoms appear on fishes of poor health. Low temperatures, physical damage, and unhygienic conditions all encourage the harmful bacterial action. Should tailrot reach the body of the fish, a satisfactory cure is unlikely. Always try to provide treatment, using proprietary remedies, at an early stage.

**Lymphocystis**
Causes cauliflowerlike growths on the fins and skin, together with a decrease in weight. Individual cell growth rapid. Rare in freshwater fish.

**Fungus**
Fungus (*Saprolegnia*) attacks fishes already weakened by physical damage, parasitic attacks, or poor conditions. Also liable to affect fishes if they are transferred to differing aquarium waters. As healthy fish will not be infected, it is only necessary to remove the infected fish for treatment.

**Pox**
White spots join to form large patches. Fish is emaciated and often left twisted. Faulty diet, lack of vitamins likely causes. May heal itself under good conditions.

Left: Infection cycle for white spot disease. (**1**) The symptoms appear. (**2**) Parasites leave fish and form cysts. (**3**) The cysts produce new free-swimming parasites to re-infect fish. Treatment is effective during this stage only.

Right: This fine dusting of gold spots, here on an Indian glassfish, is typical of velvet disease, caused by the single-celled parasite *Oodinium*. At first glance, it can be confused with white spot, but in the latter the spots are larger and more clearly white in color. Proprietary treatments are effective against both of these conditions.

**White spot disease**
*Ichthyophthiriasis* is a common ailment and well described. Many aquarists believe it lies dormant in every tank waiting to strike any weakened fish. Responds to treatment.

**Velvet disease**
Infected fishes have a dusty look. Caused by *Oodinium*, which undergoes an encystment stage. Treatment similar to white spot disease.

**Skin flukes**
*Gyrodactylus* make fish feeble and cause colors to fade; they rest frequently near surface. Gills may be attacked, too. Responds to treatment.

**Eye infections**
Cloudy or protruding eyes (pop-eye) may be due to several causes, including fungus, bacterial infections, eye flukes, and even fish tuberculosis.

**Mouth 'fungus'**
Unrelated to body fungus and unaffected by some similar treatments. Usually due to slime bacterium *Flexibacter columnaris*.

**Slimy skin**
Thin gray film covers the body. Parasites *Chilodonella* and *Ichthyobodo (Costia)* cause the fish to produce excess slime.

**Dropsy**
Protrusion of scales due to accumulated liquid in body. Fluid from infected fish may infect others. Remove sick fish at once.

**Gill flukes**
Caused by *Dacty-logyrus*, a flatworm that hooks onto the fish's gills.

sites may be removed by immersing the fishes in relatively low-dosage, long-term baths of suitable remedies. The easiest way to do this is to treat the whole aquarium, although it is important to check the manufacturer's instructions carefully to see whether plant life (or invertebrate life in marine tanks) will be harmed at the recommended dosages. The alternative method of giving affected fishes short-term baths in much stronger dosages should only be used in emergencies; while this method may eradicate the problem, it may be more stressful to the fish in the process.

Well-established remedies, such as formalin, methylene blue and acriflavine, have been superseded by more modern proprietary treatments; for example, metriphonate (an organophosphorus insecticide) has also been found to be effective against gill and skin flukes. Although many modern substances have replaced more outmoded treatments, they are not always to be found universally throughout the hobby, as supplies may be strictly limited according to prevailing drug laws in different countries.

If fishes are removed for treatment in a separate 'hospital tank' (using the same long-term remedial bath technique described above), any parasites remaining in the original aquarium will die off after a few days in the absence of the necessary fish host on which they depend for survival and reproduction. Gill flukes, for example, produce eggs that hatch into larvae that must find a suitable fish host within 6-8 hours to survive.

It is often easy to jump to wrong conclusions. Fishes panting at the surface may not be afflicted by parasites at all—they may be gasping for oxygen because of an excess of carbon dioxide in the water. Immediate relief can be provided by extra aeration, but better aquarium management is the real answer.

### Serious diseases

More serious ailments result from internal causes such as tuberculosis, threadworms and tapeworms, which are unseen by the fishkeeper. Usually when the symptoms become apparent it is too late to effect a cure. Diagnosis of these conditions can be done only by examination of the organs of the diseased fish (which in practical terms means a post-mortem) and this aspect of disease is beyond the capability of the beginning aquarist.

There are several diagnostic services available by mail order, but as these will only reveal the cause of death (from examination of the corpse), this course of action, which can be rather expensive, may be regarded as a little too retrospective, to say the least!

# BREEDING FISHES IN THE AQUARIUM

Spraying Characins spawning out of the water.

*O*ne of the attractions of fishkeeping is that the fishes may multiply in captivity. But, because of the confined space within an aquarium, it is often impossible for fishes to find enough seclusion or safe territory in which to raise a family, and any fry that are born soon get eaten by larger fishes. These difficulties are easily solved by providing a separate aquarium in which prospective breeders can be kept. That second tank kept for quarantine can be used. Fish-breeding can be divided into two phases: Events leading up to spawning, and the care of the young fry. In both phases the aquarist can have a fair measure of control: Selecting and conditioning the adult fishes; preparing the breeding aquarium; supervising spawning; and raising the fry. Add to these the challenge of producing a new variety and you will understand why this aspect of the hobby is so popular.

The egg-laying fishes spawn in a variety of ways: Egg-scattering, egg-burying, egg-depositing, nest-building, or mouth-brooding. Faced with these, the aquarist needs to prepare the breeding aquarium accordingly. Egg-scattering fishes are not protective towards their eggs and will eat them, given the chance. Various methods are used by aquarists to ensure that the eggs survive. The main principle is to separate the eggs and adult fishes as soon as possible after the eggs are released and fertilized. A layer of marbles on the aquarium floor provides fish-proof crevices into which the fertilized eggs fall. Thick bunches of plants also trap the adhesive eggs and effectively hide them from the adults or, alternatively, the fishes may be spawned above a net or grid submerged in the water through which the eggs fall.

Egg-burying species require the floor of the aquarium to have a deep layer of peat placed on top of the gravel into which the fish can dive and bury the eggs. The egg-depositors are very protective towards their eggs and young fry, but the aquarium needs to be furnished with suitable rocks or caves to provide a choice of spawning sites for these fishes. Nest-builders won't need extra material to help construct their nests; the fishes will collect fragments of plants. Their aquarium should be well planted to provide shelter for the female after spawning.

The incubation of the mouth-brooders takes place within the mouth and buccal cavity of the female fish, and all that she will appreciate is peace and quiet while this occurs—she won't even take food!

At birth, the young fry born to live-bearing fishes are free-swimming miniatures of their parents, but a well-planted nursery tank with a layer of floating plants will allow them to escape any cannibalistic tendencies on the part of their parents.

The breeding aquarium will have a low stocking level, and so a powerful filter will not be needed; even an under-gravel filter may draw young fry into the gravel if driven by a too powerful air pump. A simple sponge filter is best in breeding aquariums, as this presents no danger at all to the young fishes.

The breeding aquarium should have the same water temperature and quality as the main aquarium. Should the breeding fishes require different water conditions (to induce spawning, for instance) they should be acclimatized to these over a conditioning period. This must be lengthened if necessary to allow the alterations to the water quality without shocking or stressing the fishes.

The breeding aquarium for live-bearing fishes will act as nursery accommodation for the gravid (pregnant) female fish only and she should be placed into it early in her 30-day gestation period. Breeding traps can have a quite traumatic effort on the female fish, who is very likely to give birth prematurely (to non-fully-developed fry) as a result of this confinement.

## Selection and conditioning

Whether your choice of fishes to breed belongs to the egg-laying or the live-bearing group of fishes, the first task is to find a true pair—one male and one female. Referring to the notes on the fish's fins (page 34) indicates that determining the sex of live-bearing fishes does not raise too much of a problem, since males have a modified anal fin. Such obvious differences do not occur between the sexes of egg-laying species, but there are some rough guidelines that may help. Usually the male fish is slimmer and more colorful, and may have more pronounced finnage than the female. Fishes

**Egg-scatterers**
Above: The problem of Zebra Danios *(Brachydanio rerio)* eating their own eggs can be solved by placing a layer or two of pebbles or glass marbles on the aquarium floor. The eggs quickly fall between the crevices beyond the reach of the fishes, which should be removed after spawning is completed.

**Egg-buriers**
Above: The egg-burying Argentine Pearlfish *(Cynolebias bellotti)* needs a deep layer of peat on the aquarium floor. After spawning, the peat (complete with fertilized eggs) can be removed and stored almost dry for a few months. The hatching process is activated by immersing the peat in the aquarium water again.

from the Cichlid group select partners themselves, and any two fishes that keep together (often excluding others from their area of the aquarium) are likely to be a true pair.

Fishes selected for breeding should be healthy and free from disease and deformities. They should be chosen for good points like strong coloration, fin development, and so on. This is particularly the case when attempting to breed a definite color strain or more exaggerated finnage into the young. Live-bearing fishes are so ready to interbreed with any of their own species, regardless of color variety, that a very controlled breeding program has to be maintained in order to keep the strain pure.

'Absence makes the heart grow fonder' is one ploy to ensure more success when putting egg-laying fishes together to breed. It is usual to separate the sexes for a few weeks before introducing the fishes to each other in the breeding aquarium. During this period the isolated fishes are fed intensively with high quality foods, with live food predominating. This ensures that the female will be full of roe when spawning time approaches. If she is considered unready by the male fish, he will often attack her. For this reason the female is best introduced into the breeding aquarium first; it then becomes her territory and the male has to court

Left: The female live-bearer's anal fin is fan-shaped; the male's is modified (fully or partly, depending on genus) into a reproductive organ.
Right: Jewel Cichlids *(Hemichromis bimaculatus)* spawning on a piece of wood. Both parents guard the eggs.

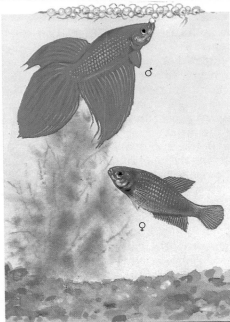

### Egg-depositors
Above: 'Kribs' *(Pelvicachromis pulcher)* are secretive spawners and prefer the privacy of a flowerpot or rocky cave in which to spawn. Unfortunately, this often means that the hobbyist is not aware of spawning taking place until the proud parents bring their free-swimming youngsters out into the open.

### Bubble-nest builders
Above: Siamese Fighters *(Betta splendens)* use fragments of plants in the construction of their bubble-nest. The female is often attacked by the male if he considers her not ready for spawning. For this reason the female should be put into the breeding aquarium before the male, so that he has to court her in her own territory.

### Mouth-brooders
Above: Egyptian Mouth-brooders *(Pseudocrenilabrus multicolor)* need no special breeding quarters. During incubation, the female (who undertakes this task solely) takes no nourishment and becomes very thin. The free-swimming fry seek shelter in their mother's mouth whenever danger threatens.

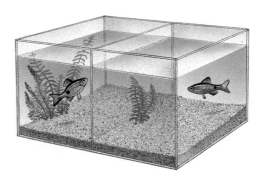

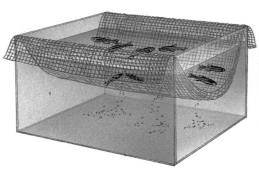

Left: Separating the male and female for two or three weeks and feeding them with high-quality and live foods ensures that both fishes are at peak condition for spawning and are keen to do so. They may be reunited by simply removing the partition.

Left, below: A layer or two of marbles on the bottom of the tank provides a fish-proof egg trap and prevents the adult fishes—in this case Tiger Barbs (*Barbus tetrazona*)—from eating the eggs. The shallow water level reduces the time that the falling eggs are at risk.

Right: The four photographs show a spawning of Rosy Barbs (*Barbus conchonius*). The more highly colored male nudges and butts the female (1-3) until they take up a side-by-side attitude (4); eggs are then released and fertilized.

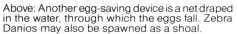

Above: Another egg-saving device is a net draped in the water, through which the eggs fall. Zebra Danios may also be spawned as a shoal.

Above: Tetras lay adhesive eggs that may be trapped in a dense clump of plants where the female has been driven by the male to spawn.

Above: Live-bearers can give birth in breeding traps, the fry escaping to safety. A heavily planted separate nursery tank is preferable for them.

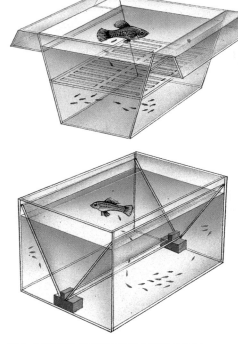

her. To conserve space, a breeding pair can be conditioned in the breeding aquarium by the use of a tank-divider; this may be made of glass or of sheet plastic, and some aquarists believe that the sight of each other, although physically separated, stimulates the two fishes towards successful spawning. It is then simplicity itself at the desired spawning time to introduce the fishes to each other by withdrawing the partition.

The prolific live-bearing fishes hardly need any encouragement to breed, but in order to maintain a certain quality, their spawning activities should be controlled. A collection of the many colored varieties of one species will not prove to be a stable strain for long. It may be more rewarding to specialize in one color variety only.

### Spawning and after

The spawning should be supervised. Some male fishes are very active drivers of the female and will continue to harass her even after spawning; other males may not always accept the female as a partner at the outset and will attack her.

In both cases, the aquarist, if on hand, can rescue the ladies in distress. Egg-scattering fishes of both sexes are best removed from the breeding tank after spawning to eliminate the risk of them eating their own eggs. In any case, the aquarist usually wants to see what is going on and may even wish to photograph the events, particularly when observing the more ritualistic spawnings of the cichlid fishes.

Despite their reputation for being good parents, occasionally the cichlids do not fulfill their responsibilities and may well ignore, or even eat, their carefully laid eggs. In these instances the aquarist must either remove one of the parents (letting the remaining fish do its parental duty), or remove both fishes and artificially hatch the eggs by placing an airstone near the eggs and allowing the water currents to act as a substitute for the parents' fin-fanning actions.

The eggs of the egg-laying Toothcarps (Cyprinodontidae) may be deposited in bunches of natural plants, mops of nylon wool, or the peat layer on the aquarium floor. Depending on the species, the eggs

Top: A floating breeding trap that can be conveniently placed within the main aquarium. Above: Two pieces of glass quickly convert a spare tank into a live-bearer's nursery.

Left: A male American Flagfish *(Jordanella floridae)* is here guarding its eggs, which can be seen in the plants. This species is said to spawn and guard its eggs in a depression dug in the aquarium gravel but, unusually, this fish has spawned in among plants! Fishes obviously do not read the same books as aquarists. The female fish is best removed immediately after the spawning is completed, for her own safety.

Right: The Paradisefish *(Macropodus opercularis)*, despite having a reputation for pugnacity, was probably the first tropical fish imported into Europe and has remained a firm favorite ever since. Here, the male inspects the bubble-nest as the female turns away after the spawning embrace. Again, the female should be removed after spawning.

Above: Some killifishes bury their eggs. There should be a deep layer of peat to accommodate such species as *Cynolebias,* shown here.

Above: Other killifishes *(Aphyosemion)* lay their eggs on artificial mops, from which they are collected and hatched in shallow dishes.

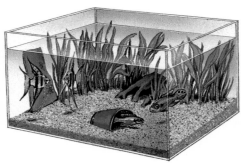

Above: Depending on the species, cichlids will require rocks, pieces of slate, flowerpots, or broad-leaved plants as spawning sites.

should be collected and either left in shallow water to hatch or kept in almost-dry peat for two or three months before re-immersing in water to activate hatching. Due to the vigor of the male fishes it is usual practice to spawn these fishes as trios, one male to two females. Female fishes of the bubble-nest building species are best removed after spawning: The male guards the nest and the fry quite fanatically.

After giving birth, female live-bearing fishes should, if possible, be allowed a further few days' rest before being returned to the main aquarium, otherwise they may be unable to cope with the renewed attentions of ardent males so soon after their confinement.

## Care of the fry

As soon as any young fish begins swimming, it will require food, but until it actually swims it receives enough nourishment from its yolk-sac. It is pointless to give food before this time as the young fish cannot eat it and the added food will pollute the tank.

The first food for a fish depends upon the size of the fish. Not all fishes are the same size at birth. Generally fry from egg-scattering and nest-building species require smaller food than Cichlid and live-bearer fry.

Proprietary foods are available in liquid, paste, and fine powder forms, formulated to suit egg-laying or live-bearing species' requirements. Green water — cultures of infusorians — are very suitable for the smallest of fry. Micro-worms, screened *Daphnia,* and grindal worms are suitable for most young fishes, but the best food (as soon as the fry can cope with it) is brine shrimp. Soon the growing fry can be given white worms, crushed flake foods, and any other foods suitably reduced in size.

With the Anabantid fishes, such as the Siamese Fighting Fish *(Betta splendens)* and the Gourami families, the fry are susceptible to cold drafts, which may enter the aquarium hood; many aquarists drape the hood with a towel to minimize this risk.

Young fishes should feed continually and a low-power light should be left burning over the aquarium to encourage this. As the fish mature, partial water changes should be made, the aeration rate increased, and the filtration system upgraded. This increase in water movement and the effect of the water changes will stimulate healthy growth. As the fishes grow and take on the familiar shapes and colors of their parents, the slow developers or stunted ones should be culled. At this time, a careful watch should be kept on live-bearer fry and the sexes separated as early as possible; again, fry not conforming to the required color or finnage pattern should be discarded. Although it may appear a callous act, unwanted fish fry make excellent food for other adult fishes. It is not good practice to raise large numbers of mediocre fishes out of soft-heartedness; if such specimens are introduced either back into your main collection or into the hobby (via friends or a retailer) the outcome will be a general lowering of fish quality.

A final note: Do keep written records of spawning attempts, particularly with the more difficult species. You may be the first hobbyist to get it right!

# EXPANDING THE INTEREST

"Will it win?" thinks this young competitor.

*It has been estimated that about one household in every ten either keeps an aquarium or has a garden pond. It is also probable that the majority of these fishkeepers are perfectly content with their decorative pets and have no desire to expand the number of their aquariums or to become involved with the organized side of the hobby. However, there are a number of advantages in joining an aquarist society, particularly if you want more from your hobby than just a pleasant 'living picture' in your home. Even the single aquarium has a good deal to offer within itself by way of information and education. Geography, biology, chemistry, physics, and mathematics are all skills that need to be exercised by the aquarist in the pursuit of fishkeeping. As a teaching aid, the aquarium may be far larger on the inside than we outsiders think! But was there ever a more enjoyable way of learning?*

Aquarist societies—usually meeting monthly—offer regular lectures by visiting speakers, competitive Bowl Shows, inter-society quizzes and shows, trips to public aquariums, conventions, etc. Within these societies aquarium hobbyists can find all the latest information on recently imported species, plus all the practical hints to be had by the newcomer —from initial problems to how to cope with the more exotic species. In addition to local societies there are aquatic groups specializing in certain species of fishes including Catfishes, Cichlids, Goldfish, Koi, Live-bearers, and Marine Fishes.

Most local societies are affiliated with larger national bodies. In the U.S. the largest is the Federation of American Aquarium Societies (F.A.A.S.). Canada has the Canadian Association of Aquarium Clubs (C.A.A.C.), and Britain has the Federation of British Aquatic Societies (F.B.A.S.). European aquarists can affiliate as individuals (rather than by societies) with their respective countries' aquatic governing bodies: Germany — Verband Deutscher ver Aquarien (V.D.A.); France—Fédération Français des Associations Aquaphile et Terrariophile (F.F.A.A.T.); Belgium—Belgique Bond Aquaria et Terraria (B.B.A.T.); Netherlands—Nederlands Bond Aquaria et Terraria (N.B.A.T.); Denmark—Dansk Akvarie (D.K.A.); Norway—Norsk Akvarieforbund (N.A.F.); Poland—Polski Zwiazeke Akwarystow (P.Z.A.); Luxemburg—Federation Luxembourg Aquariophile et Terrariophile (F.L.A.T.); and Sweden—Sveriges Akvarietföreningars Riksförbund (S.A.R.F.). All these organizations are in turn members of the Aquarium Terrarium International (A.T.I.).

The aquarium hobby may not appear to be quite so tightly knit in Australia, where the large distances between societies is a contributory factor, but New Zealand aquarists enjoy the services of the Federation of New Zealand Aquatic Societies.

These national bodies lay down rules that are used by the local societies which organize open competitive shows and also publish much valuable information on nomenclature and the sizes attained by aquarium fishes.

During the show season there is a fish show somewhere every weekend. Even if the newcomer is not particularly competitive, a visit to an open show will reveal a whole selection of fishes suited to aquariums, together with superbly set-up, furnished tanks and aquatic plants. It is an excellent showcase for products and a meeting place for anyone interested in keeping fishes.

It is natural for a newcomer to look for assistance with issues that seem important to him. Aquarist magazines, with their advisory columns, are a good source of information; and most fish food and aquatic equipment manufacturers operate an advisory service or issue information packs that can be helpful.

Above: The fishkeeper often has a well-developed eye for beauty and an artistic appreciation. The way that the aquarium has been incorporated into this room amply illustrates this design sense to stunning effect.

## Showing

As with other organized competitive pet shows, aquarium shows in the U.S., Canada, and Britain revolve around the animals on display. They are generally divided into classes based roughly on broad family groups—Cyprinids, Characins, Cichlids, Catfishes, Anabantids, Live-bearers, etc. Fishes are shown singly (except for pairs and breeders, classes) in bare tanks. Each fish may earn up to a maximum of 100 points (under one system), divided into five groups of 20 points each. Points are awarded for size, body, fins, color, and condition and deportment. Speciality clubs may differ in their allocation of points. Each entry is judged individually (about five judges evaluating approximately 500 entries in two hours) and the results are displayed for the benefit of exhibiting owners and for visitors to the show. In addition to single fish classes, there may be opportunities to see furnished aquariums, aquatic plants, pairs and breeders' teams —a group of four or six fishes of the same species bred by the owner. The main interests of the day's show are to see which fish is going to be 'Best in Show' and whether the host society can win the trophy for gaining the most winning places.

The show scene on the continent of Europe is slightly different; there, the show may not be so competition-orientated and the accent is more likely to be upon informative (and extremely decorative) furnished aquariums for display purposes only, coupled with lectures and seminars during the exhibition. Another type of competition (shared by many aquarist societies the world over) is where the hobbyists' home-furnished

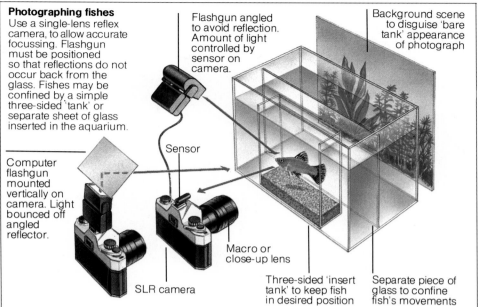

**Photographing fishes**
Use a single-lens reflex camera, to allow accurate focussing. Flashgun must be positioned so that reflections do not occur back from the glass. Fishes may be confined by a simple three-sided 'tank' or separate sheet of glass inserted in the aquarium.

Flashgun angled to avoid reflection. Amount of light controlled by sensor on camera.

Background scene to disguise 'bare tank' appearance of photograph

Computer flashgun mounted vertically on camera. Light bounced off angled reflector.

Sensor

Macro or close-up lens

SLR camera

Three-sided 'insert tank' to keep fish in desired position

Separate piece of glass to confine fish's movements

aquariums compete against each other and are evaluated by a visiting panel of judges.

Often, the competitive aspect of the hobby is frowned upon by non-competitors but aquarium shows do provide the main impetus for further interest

in serious fishkeeping and breeding, bringing more and more new species to the attention of the aquarist, together with vital information as to how they may be successfully kept in the aquarium.

### International connections
Many aquarists subscribe to specialist societies that have evolved into international groups. The fact that Killifishes' eggs can be directly mailed to aquarist acquaintances around the world certainly strengthens the ties between hobbyists who are interested in these fishes. With air travel becoming more convenient and vacations taking people further from home than ever, contacting fishkeepers and societies wherever you travel can be a fun and friendly way to meet people in foreign places.

### Photography
If an aquarist also is a competent photographer, here is an ideal parallel interest. With modern high-speed color-correct films allied to electronic flash photography, it is not too difficult to capture some of your favorite fishes and aquascapes on permanent film.

With the advent of macro-lenses and the now ubiquitous single lens reflex (SLR) camera, even spawning sequences can be recorded. Should you see an unfamiliar fish at a fish show, a photograph of it, together with its scientific name from the show's judging sheets on display, will provide you with perhaps another new aquatic interest.

The video-recorder provides the aquarist with yet another means of capturing live aquatic action in pictorial form, with the extra benefit of 'action-replays' whenever desired. From here you can add commentary on a synchronized soundtrack and thus provide a fully documented visual record of your living hobby.

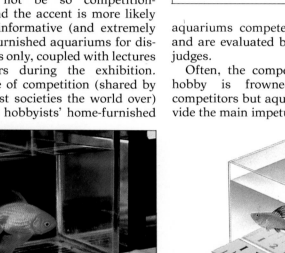

Above: Judging fishes is a skilled job. Each fish (in this case a coldwater goldfish) is accurately measured for size.
Below: A magnifying glass reveals any scale damage or split fins. An essential show check.

Above: Rulers with mirror-image markings help to measure fishes easily; watch the reflection of the ruler in the glass. Move the ruler *away* from the tank to measure a fish at rear of tank—the image follows the fish.

# PART TWO

# SPECIES GUIDE

Two hundred tropical freshwater fishes
are featured here, with details on their shape
and coloration, their diet and breeding habits,
and—most important—the conditions under
which each species can be kept.

The vast majority of the world's
freshwater fishes live in warm-water lakes
and rivers, particularly in tropical America,
Africa, and Asia. It is these fishes that
provide the aquarist with such a galaxy of
different shapes, sizes, and colors.

Most aquarium fishes belong to a small
number of large groups, each with quite
distinctive characteristics. These are the
Characins, the Carps and Barbs, the
Catfishes, the Toothcarps, the Cichlids, and
the Labyrinth Fishes. The remainder are
members of a large number of small families.

Every kind of fish—indeed, every kind of
animal—is given a scientific name consisting
of two words, the genus or generic name and
the species or specific name. These scientific
names are used internationally, whereas the
common names are mostly confined to a
limited area or language. There are a few
fishes that have been given more than one
scientific name and these have been
indicated in the text. However, do not get
too involved in the intricacies of fish
nomenclature; it is better to spend time and
energy on getting to know the habits and
biological requirements of your fishes.

Left: The contrasting shapes of
Angelfishes (Pterophyllum scalare)
and Neon Tetras (Paracheirodon innesi).

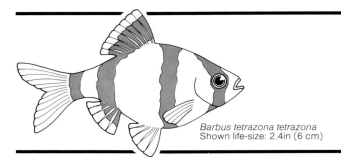

*Barbus tetrazona tetrazona*
Shown life-size: 2.4in (6 cm)

## Family POLYPTERIDAE

This is a small group of fishes found only in tropical Africa. Characterized by the ability to swallow air at the surface and use it as an aid to respiration, these fishes are also distinguished by the dorsal fin, which is divided into a number of finlets.

Family POLYPTERIDAE
### Calamoichthys calabaricus
*Reedfish*

● **Distribution:** Africa: Cameroon and Niger Delta at Calabar
● **Length:** Up to 14.6in (37cm), possibly more
● **Tank length:** 36in (90cm)
● **Diet:** Worms, crustaceans, insects
● **Water temperature:** 73 to 83°F (23 to 28°C)
● **Community tank:** Will eat small fish in the aquarium

Also known as *Erpetoichthys calabaricus,* this is a very elongated, cylindrical, eellike fish with seven to 13 small, well-separated dorsal fins. These fins are usually kept folded down. There are no ventral fins. The two nostrils are developed into tubular

processes. The fan-shaped pectoral fins serve as paddles when swimming, and also as struts to support the body when the fish is resting on the bottom. The swim-bladder has an open connection with the esophagus, and functions as a lung; air swallowed at the surface passes into the swim-bladder where its oxygen content is absorbed into the blood system. The anal fin has 12 to 14 rays in the male and nine to 12 in the female. The back is a delicate olive-green; the flanks are a pale green and the underparts are yellow. There is a large black marking at the base of each pectoral fin.

This hardy fish should be kept in a tank with a good lid, and with rocks and roots arranged to provide hiding-places. This species must have access to air. The tank should not be too full so that there is a space between the water surface and the tank lid. It is mainly active at night, preferring to remain hidden during the day. The water can be soft or medium-hard. The species has not yet been bred in captivity.

This is the only species in its genus, but the family Polypteridae contains several species in the genus *Polypterus,* all from tropical waters of Africa. They are known colloquially as bichirs, and most are quarrelsome among themselves. Like the Reedfish, they are nocturnal, rather secretive fishes. Little is known about their reproductive habits. The young are known to have treelike external gills and are similar in appearance to newt larvae.

Left: **Calamoichthys calabaricus**
*This is a rather shy fish that lurks among vegetation on the bottom, moving about like a snake.*

## Family NOTOPTERIDAE

This is a small family with representatives in tropical Africa and Southeast Asia. These active, nocturnal fishes have a swim-bladder that serves as an accessory respiratory organ.

Family NOTOPTERIDAE
### Xenomystus nigri
*African Knifefish*

● **Distribution:** Africa: Nile westwards to Liberia
● **Length:** Up to 8in (20cm)
● **Tank length:** 36in (90cm)
● **Diet:** Worms, crustaceans, insects, snails, meat
● **Water temperature:** 75 to 83°F (24 to 28°C)
● **Species tank:** Or in a community of medium-sized, peaceful fishes such as Angelfish and Gouramis.

The African Knifefish is elongated and very laterally compressed. Its large mouth has two nasal tentacles. The anus is situated very far forward on the body. The dorsal fin is lacking, but the anal fin is very long, starting immediately behind the anus and extending to the rear tip of the body where it fuses with the caudal fin. This fringelike anal fin is the fish's main organ of propulsion, and its undulatory

movements enable the fish to swim forward or backward. The general coloration is dark brown or dark gray with paler underparts. The flanks sometimes have one or more rather indistinct longitudinal stripes.

This is a shy, retiring fish, which comes to the surface from time to time to swallow air. The brief sounds emitted at intervals are due to the expulsion of air from the swim-bladder into the alimentary tract. A shoal of young individuals can be kept in a tank with subdued lighting, areas of dense vegetation, and a tangle of rocks and roots that will provide shelter. The fishes rest in a slightly oblique position with the head down. They come out at dusk and during the night to hunt for prey. The species has not yet been bred in captivity.

The related *Notopterus afer,* from Congo to the Gambia in Africa, reaches a length of about 24in (60cm), but is suitable for the home aquarium only when young.

Above: **Xenomystus nigri**
*This is an interesting fish to watch as it moves to and fro using the long anal fin for propulsion.*

**A practical reminder**
You will get maximum enjoyment from fishkeeping only if your fishes are provided with the very best conditions. Only then will they be able to repay you by looking their best and living the longest.

## Family PANTODONTIDAE
This family, containing only one genus and one species, is found in tropical West Africa. The large pectoral fins allow the fish to glide over the surface of the water. It does not, however, beat its fins as do the the hatchetfishes. It is active mainly at night.

Family PANTODONTIDAE
# Pantodon buchholzi
*Butterflyfish*
- **Distribution:** Africa: Niger Cameroon, Zaire
- **Length:** Up to 4in (10cm)
- **Tank length:** 24in (60cm)
- **Diet:** Crustaceans, insects, fish
- **Water temperature:** 75 to 84°F (24 to 29°C)
- **Community tank:** May swallow smaller specimens

This fish is boat-shaped with a flat dorsal surface and rounded underparts. The large, winglike pectoral fins are held out from the body. The dorsal fin is quite small, rounded, and positioned far back on the body. The anal fin and the central rays of the caudal fin are elongated. The large mouth faces upward, and the nostrils are elongated and tubular. The upperparts and flanks are silvery or greenish and are marked with an irregular pattern of brown spots and streaks. The rays of all the fins show alternating dark and pale rings. A dark band runs from the forehead, across the eye, to the lower jaw.
   This is a surface-living fish of standing waters. It is capable of

Right: **Pantodon buchholzi** ♀
*Although it takes most of its food from the surface, this fish can also leap out to catch flying insects.*

leaping out of the water and gliding for short distances with the help of the outstretched pectoral fins, though the pectorals are not beaten or flapped. The Butterflyfish can be kept in a tank with floating plants to cover only a part of the surface and a few rooted plants with leaves that grow up to the water surface. There should, of course, be a well-fitting lid to prevent 'flying'. The water must be soft, slightly acid, and filtered through peat. The sexes are not difficult to distinguish since the rear edge of the anal fin is straight in the

female, but concave in the male. Spawning is preceded by vigorous driving. Afterward the fishes coil around one another and the eggs and sperm are shed in batches. The eggs, which are brown or almost black, hatch in

36 to 48 hours. Spawning has been observed on many occasions, but successful rearing of the fry is very rare. Tiny nauplii can be offered, but the fry do not chase them, taking only those that drift past in the surface waters.

## Family MORMYRIDAE
This is an exclusively African family. Some long-nosed species probe the substrate for food, while others hunt in midwater. Muscles at the rear of the body have developed to form an electric organ that serves mainly for orientation, for species recognition, and for delimiting territories. Most species in the family have poor eyesight.

Family MORMYRIDAE
# Gnathonemus petersi
*Elephant Nose*
- **Distribution:** Africa: Congo, Cameroon to Niger
- **Length:** Up to 9in (23cm), possibly more
- **Tank length:** 24in (60cm)
- **Diet:** Worms, insects, dried food
- **Water temperature:** 75 to 83°F (24 to 28°C)
- **Community tank**

This is an elongated and laterally compressed fish with a small round mouth. The lower jaw has a mobile, trunklike extension, hence the popular name. The caudal fin is deeply cleft, and the dorsal and anal fins are almost opposite one another. The brain is very large and—relative to body weight—is comparable to the brain of a human being. The slender caudal peduncle contains an electric organ that is not used for stunning

Right: **Gnathonemus petersi**
*A peaceful fish that prefers to hide during the day, this species has a large brain in relation to body size.*

prey as in the Electric Eel, but is used for finding its way about in turbid water. The organ emits about 20 electric pulses per minute, thus producing an electrical field. Objects in the vicinity will disturb this field and this is detected by sense organs in the head of the fish. The general coloration is blackish brown with violet iridescence when seen in reflected light. There are two irregular, yellowish-white

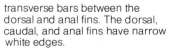

transverse bars between the dorsal and anal fins. The dorsal, caudal, and anal fins have narrow white edges.
   This is an active fish that lives close to the bottom where it probes (mostly at night) for food with the long snout. It is territorial and is usually rather aggressive towards members of its own species. However, it is quite peaceful with other fishes. It can be kept in a tank with dense

vegetation, a soft substrate, and a number of rocks and roots arranged to form hiding-places. The lighting should be subdued or it can be installed so that some parts of the tank are dark. The composition of the water is not very critical, but it should preferably be mature, and about a quarter of it must be changed once a month or so. The Elephant Nose has not yet been bred in the aquarium.

# THE CHARACINS

Above: *Poptella orbicularis*, a South American member of the family Characidae.
Right: A peaceful stretch of water in tropical Amazonia, a typical habitat for characins.

*T*his large group of fishes consists of several closely related families with some 200 species in Africa and about 1,000 species in South America, Central America, and southern North America. The body is typically scaled, but the head has no scales and no barbels. There is usually, but not always, an adipose fin. Many of the species live in shoals and are active during the day. Brood protection occurs only rarely. The parent fishes show no interest in their brood except that, at least in captivity, many species chase and eat their own eggs. The suborder contains carnivores, omnivores, and herbivores.

The group contains the following families.

The Characidae or true characins occur in Africa and more numerously in Central and South America. Many are small or very small fishes with a short dorsal fin, usually an adipose fin, and a deeply cleft caudal fin. Most species spawn at random and the eggs are adhesive.

The Serrasalmidae or piranhas of central and northern South America are aggressive predators with powerful jaws and numerous very sharp teeth. Only small individuals are suitable.

The Gasteropelecidae or hatchetfishes, restricted to tropical America, are very compressed fishes with the pectoral fins forming 'wings' that can be beaten to propel the body out of the water.

The Lebiasinidae of South America are slender, elongated fishes with a short dorsal fin; some species have an adipose fin.

The Anostomidae of tropical America are elongated, spindle-shaped fishes with a wedge-shaped head and a small mouth. Only a few species have been bred in the aquarium.

The Curimatidae of South America are very similar to the Anostomidae. They have an elongated body, and an adipose fin is usually present.

The Citharinidae are restricted to tropical Africa. Many are medium-sized to large fishes that are suitable only when young.

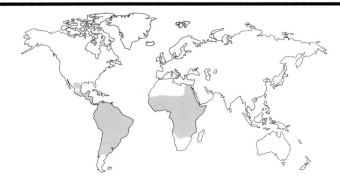

Left: Most species in this large group are typically shoaling fishes living in fresh waters. The numerous species in South America inhabit different types of water. In the Amazon region there are clear greenish waters and white water rivers, so-called because of their content of clay particles. Finally, there are 'black' waters, which are perfectly clear but colored dark brown by their content of organic compounds.

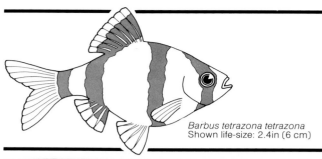

*Barbus tetrazona tetrazona*
Shown life-size: 2.4in (6 cm)

Family CHARACIDAE
## Alestes longipinnis
*Long-finned Characin*
● **Distribution:** Tropical West Africa, from Sierra Leone to the Congo
● **Length:** Up to 5in (13cm)
● **Tank length:** 24in (60cm)
● **Diet:** Flies, beetles, small cockroaches
● **Water temperature:** 73 to 77°F (23 to 25°C)
● **Community tank**

The Long-finned Characin is a laterally compressed, olive-green to yellow-green fish with marked silvery iridescence and a broad black band on the caudal peduncle. In males the dorsal fin is much elongated and the anal fin has a white border. The eyes are bright golden-red.

This is an attractive fish for a large community tank, where it can be kept in a shoal. Take care to have a close-fitting lid, because this fish jumps very well. They mostly swim in the middle water layers and the tank should have groups of fine-leaved plants to provide shelter.

Above:
**Alestes longipinnis** ♂(t), ♀(b)
*This is sometimes a shy, nervous fish and any disturbance in the aquarium should be avoided.*

For breeding it is essential that the water should be soft and slightly acid. Spawning is preceded by vigorous driving among the plants. The female lays 300 or more eggs, which hatch after about six days. The fry can be fed at first on rotifers and very small nauplii.

The related Chaper's Characin (*A. chaperi*) from West Africa (Ghana to Nigeria) is a smaller fish (up to 2.8in/7cm) with grass-green flanks and red dorsal and anal fins with broad yellow borders. It requires similar conditions to *A. longipinnis*, but has probably not yet been bred successfully in captivity.

Family CHARACIDAE
## Aphyocharax anisitsi
*Bloodfin*
● **Distribution:** South America: Rio Paraná, Argentina
● **Length:** Up to 2.2in (5.5cm)
● **Tank length:** 12in (30cm)
● **Diet:** Worms, small insects and crustaceans, dried food
● **Water temperature:** 72 to 83°F (22 to 28°C)
● **Community tank**

Bloodfins are shoaling fishes which swim mainly in the upper and middle water layers. The elongated body is yellow to grayish green with a bluish sheen. The basal parts of the dorsal, caudal, anal, and ventral fins are blood-red, hence the popular name. Tiny hooklets on the anal fin of the male often become entangled with the meshes of the net when the fish is being caught. If this happens, the fish should not be pulled away from the net, because this may tear off the hooklets. The fish will survive this loss, but will not be able to mate since during mating, the hooklets

of a male are briefly engaged with the anal fin of the female.

Spawning takes place usually in early morning, after a period of very active driving by the male. The water must be soft and slightly acid. The female lays a large number of glass-clear eggs, sometimes 700 to 800, which sink to the bottom of the tank. These must be protected from the parents, which will eat them if given the chance. The eggs hatch in about 20 to 25 hours, and after a day or two the fry can be fed on rotifers and small nauplii. Under favorable conditions they grow very rapidly.

Right: **Aphyocharax anisitsi**
*This attractive shoaling fish is easy to breed in the aquarium. A fine mesh netting just above the bottom will safeguard the eggs.*

**A practical reminder**
Select as large a tank as you can accommodate, with the largest water surface area, regardless of its total capacity. This makes for a stable environment and lessens changes in water temperature and conditions.

Family CHARACIDAE

# Arnoldichthys spilopterus
*Red-eyed Characin*
● **Distribution:** Tropical West Africa: Niger estuary to Lagos
● **Length:** Up to 4in (10cm)
● **Tank length:** 24in (60cm)
● **Diet:** Worms, small insects, crustaceans, dried food
● **Water temperature:** 75 to 81°F (24 to 27°C)
● **Community tank**

These are rather shy, shoaling fishes that require sufficient space for swimming and not too many plants. The body is elongated, with green or bluish green flanks and a yellowish belly. The dorsal fin has a prominent black marking. The scales on the upper half of the body are much enlarged, a characteristic that helps to distinguish this particular species—the only one in the genus *Arnoldichthys*—from related African characins, such as *Alestes.* The eye is bright red. Females show less green coloration.

This species requires soft,

Above: **Arnoldichthys spilopterus**
*The color and pattern of this fish are variable; in some males the anal fin has a blood-red spot at the base. In hard water the species is susceptible to infection with fish turberculosis.*

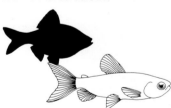

slightly acid water and preferably a diet of live insects, but will also take dried food. It is not an easy species to breed in the aquarium: In fact, this was not accomplished until 1967. After vigorous driving the female lays up to 1000 eggs, which hatch in 30 to 34 hours, depending upon the temperature. The fry are free swimming after six or seven days, and can then be fed on tiny nauplii and rotifers. When conditions are just right the young grow rapidly, but they are often difficult to rear.

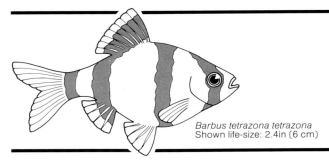

*Barbus tetrazona tetrazona*
Shown life-size: 2.4in (6 cm)

Family CHARACIDAE
## Chalceus macrolepidotus
*Pink-tailed Characin*
- **Distribution:** South America, in Guyana
- **Length:** Up to about 9.5in (24cm)
- **Tank length:** 24in (60cm)
- **Diet:** Worms, insect larvae, and small fishes
- **Water temperature:** 75 to 81°F (24 to 27°C)
- **Community tank**

Sometimes classified in a separate family, the Chalceidae, these elegant shoaling fishes are predatory and require plenty of space for swimming. They mostly live near the surface and at times they jump out of the water. The body is elongated and laterally compressed, but the most striking and characteristic feature is the arrangement of the scales. The upper half of the body has three

rows of very large scales, but the lower half has considerably smaller ones. There is a medium-sized adipose fin; the dorsal fin is set slightly behind the middle of the back; and in the caudal fin the lower lobe is larger than the upper lobe. The flanks are silvery with violet or greenish iridescence while the belly is shiny white and the back relatively dark. The anal fin is red or yellowish red. The dorsal, caudal, and ventral fins are usually wine-red, but may be more yellowish. There is a prominent dark brown marking just behind the gill cover.

In addition to live food, this fish can also be fed on chopped lean beef. The species is not often available to aquarists, and it has not yet been bred in captivity.

Right: **Chalceus macrolepidotus** ♂
*An elegant fish best kept in a shoal in a tank with a good lid.*

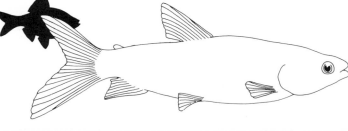

Family CHARACIDAE
## Astyanax mexicanus
- **Distribution:** North and Central America, from Texas south to Panama
- **Length:** Up to 3.5in (9cm)
- **Tank length:** 24in (60cm)
- **Diet:** Insects, crustaceans, worms, dried food
- **Water temperature:** 66 to 77°F (19 to 25°C)
- **Species tank**

There are two forms of this species, the normal one and a blind form found in subterranean streams in the Mexican province of San Luis Potosi. The normal form is brassy or silvery in

Left: **Astyanax mexicanus** ♂
*This blind form comes from underground waters and shows an uncanny ability to navigate without functional eyes.*

**A practical reminder**
Make sure the tank is standing on a
firm and level foundation away from
windows. It should be situated near an
electrical power outlet, and in a place where
regular maintenance is easy.

# Cheirodon/
# Paracheirodon axelrodi
*Cardinal Tetra*
- **Distribution:** South America,
  in tributaries of the Orinoco and
  Rio Negro
- **Length:** 1.6 to 1.8in (4 to
  4.5cm)
- **Tank length:** 12in (30cm)
- **Diet:** Worms, small crus-
  taceans, dried food
- **Water temperature:** 73 to
  79°F (23 to 26°C)
- **Community tank**

This is one of the most attractive
and popular of the tropical
American characins. It mostly lives
in a shoal in the middle water
layers. Females are usually a little
larger than males. The body is
elongated and laterally
compressed, and there is an
adipose fin. The most striking
feature, however, is the coloration.
A broad, iridescent blue-green
longitudinal band extends from
the tip of the snout, through the
eye, to the caudal peduncle.
Below this there is a bright red
band also extending to the base of
the tail. The fins are colorless, and
the back is brownish-red.
   Cardinal Tetras do best, and also
look most attractive, when kept in
subdued light in a tank with a dark
substrate. The water should be soft
and slightly acid. Under such
conditions spawning may take
place, often at night or at any rate in
subdued light. The eggs hatch in
24 to 30 hours and the fry are
free-swimming after three or four
days. Feed them on very small
nauplii and rotifers.
   The related *P. meinkeni* from
coastal areas of Brazil (Bahia to Rio
de Janeiro) is a little larger, up to
2in (5cm) long, but less brilliantly
colored. The flanks are silvery with
an olive tinge and an iridescent
longitudinal band.

coloration with an olive upper
side. The caudal peduncle has a
roundish dark marking with pale
yellow borders in front and
behind.
   The blind form of *A. mexicanus*,
known as the Blind Cave
Characin, is an altogether more
interesting fish. For many years it
was called *Anoptichthys jordani.*
The body is flesh-colored with
silvery iridescence, the fins being
colorless or reddish. The two
forms can mate with one another,
and the offspring may be
intermediate.
   Juveniles of the blind form often
have normal vision in their early
stages, but as they get older the
eyes become covered with skin
and are then non-functional. The
fishes find their way about by their
sense of smell and by the lateral
line organs; they have no difficulty
in finding food or avoiding
obstacles.
   Both forms of *A. mexicanus*
breed quite readily in an
aquarium. The eggs, which are
laid at random, hatch in about 25
hours, and the fry are free-
swimming after four or five days.
They can then be fed on fine live
and dried food, and they grow
rapidly into healthy young fish.

Below: **Paracheirodon axelrodi**
*The Cardinal Tetra looks like a larger
and more brilliantly colored version
of* Paracheirodon innesi, *the Neon
Tetra. With its full-length area of
carmine red topped by electric blue,
this species is seen to best
advantage as a contented shoal in a
tank furnished with a dark substrate,
bogwood decorations, fine-leaved
plants and under subdued lighting.
Breeding is possible, but the young
may be difficult to rear.*

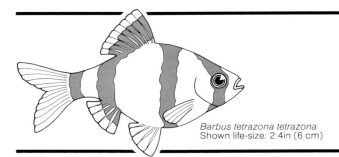

*Barbus tetrazona tetrazona*
Shown life-size: 2.4in (6 cm)

Family CHARACIDAE

## Ctenobrycon spilurus
*Silver Tetra*

- **Distribution:** South America: coastal districts of Venezuela, Guyana and Surinam
- **Length:** Up to 3.5in (9cm)
- **Tank length:** 24in (60cm)
- **Diet:** Worms, crustaceans, insects, plant matter, dried food
- **Water temperature:** 68 to 81°F (20 to 27°C)
- **Community tank:** Sometimes aggressive

The Silver Tetra is a hardy characin with a very laterally compressed body that is almost lozenge-shaped when seen from the side. As in the related Disk Tetra *(Poptella orbicularis)* the anal fin is very long, an adipose fin is present, the dorsal fin is short and pointed, and the caudal fin is forked. The sexes are similarly colored. A large blue-black marking, just behind the iridescent green gill cover, is united to a similar marking on the caudal peduncle by a thin, greenish longitudinal band.

This is an active fish that should be kept as a shoal in a tank with other characins of similar size. There should be a few tough plants, bearing in mind that the species tends to nibble the leaves of soft-leaved plants. The composition of the water is not

critical for the adults.

For breeding a well-fed and compatible pair should be placed in a separate tank, preferably with soft or medium-hard water. There is usually a vigorous courtship among the plants and the female lays about 1000 eggs, sometimes more, which must be protected from the parent fishes. At a temperature of 77°F (25°C) the eggs hatch in 24 hours. The fry should then be fed on *Paramecium,* rotifers and a plentiful supply of brine shrimp nauplii. Large broods should be divided up if they are growing rapidly.

This species has a reputation of nibbling the fins of Angelfishes.

Right: **Ctenobrycon spilurus**
*A good shoaling fish for the community tank, although it may be aggressive to smaller species.*

Family CHARACIDAE

## Gymnocorymbus ternetzi
*Black Tetra*

- **Distribution:** South America: Mato Grosso area of Rio Paraguay and Rio Negro
- **Length:** Up to 2.4in (6cm)
- **Tank length:** 18in (45cm)
- **Diet:** Worms, small crustaceans, insects, dried food
- **Water temperature:** 73 to 79°F (23 to 26°C)
- **Community tank**

This is an excellent aquarium fish that is particularly attractive when young. In juveniles the flanks are black, but they become smoky-gray with increasing age. The

Left: **Gymnocorymbus ternetzi**
*A good all-round fish, tolerant of others and generally easy to breed.*

60

**A practical reminder**
Tanks can be insulated with polystyrene sheets to conserve heat; you can paint these in dark colors or decorate them with underwater scenes. Do not forget to put a thick slab underneath the tank to cushion it.

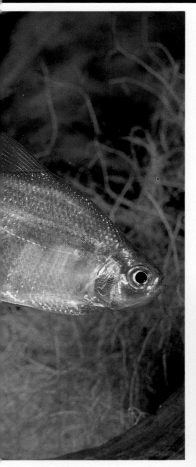

Family CHARACIDAE

# Hemigrammus caudovittatus
*Buenos Aires Tetra*
● **Distribution:** South America, in the Rio de la Plata Basin
● **Length:** Up to 2.8in (7cm)
● **Tank length:** 18in (45cm)
● **Diet:** Worms, crustaceans, insects, plant matter, dried food
● **Water temperature:** 64 to 83°F (18 to 28°C)
● **Community tank**

This is a very undemanding fish, and particularly suitable for the beginner. The female is somewhat stouter than the male. The back is blackish brown or olive brown, the flanks are iridescent silvery, and the upper part of the iris is red. In males the dorsal, adipose,

and anal fins and the lobes of the caudal fin are red or yellowish red. The ventral fins are reddish. Just behind the gill cover there is a comma-shaped dark marking, which is best seen in reflected light. However, the most characteristic marking is a black streak on the caudal peduncle, which extends back onto the center of the caudal fin with a yellowish white area above and below. There is a color variant in which the caudal fin lobes are lemon-yellow. The females are less colorful, with delicate pink or almost colorless fins and a more rounded body.

This is an easy fish to breed at a water temperature of about 75°F (24°C). Spawning takes place among plants, the eggs being laid at random. They hatch very

quickly, usually in 20 to 24 hours, and after a few days the fry can be fed on tiny live food such as rotifers and nauplii.

This is one of the hardiest tropical fishes for the home aquarium, and it has been popular for almost 60 years. It has a tendency to eat delicate plants.

Below:
**Hemigrammus caudovittatus**
*A hardy fish ideal for beginners.*

back is olive-green and the belly whitish with a silvery sheen. Behind the gill cover there are two prominent black bands. The dorsal, anal, and adipose fins are black or blackish. The ventral and pectoral fins are more or less colorless. A selected form with longer fins is sometimes available. The female is a little larger at the rear than the male, with the body cavity rounded; this can be seen when the fish is observed against the light. In the male, the rear part of the body cavity is pointed, and the caudal fin has white spots, which do not occur in the female. This is a fish of the middle and upper water layers, which should preferably be kept as one of a small shoal.

Before mating the male swims around the female with fins spread out, sometimes in circles, or sometimes following a zigzag track. The tiny, transparent eggs are laid at random among plants, preferably those with feathery leaves; at this point the parent fishes should be removed to prevent them eating the spawn. The eggs usually hatch in 24 to 26 hours, and the fry are free-swimming three to five days later. They should then be fed on rotifers and tiny nauplii.

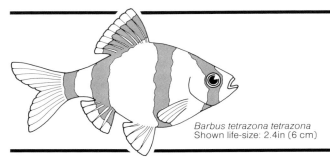

*Barbus tetrazona tetrazona*
Shown life-size: 2.4in (6 cm)

Family CHARACIDAE

## Hemigrammus erythrozonus
*Glowlight Tetra*

- **Distribution:** Northeastern parts of South America
- **Length:** Up to 1.6in (4cm)
- **Tank length:** 18in (45cm)
- **Diet:** Worms, small crustaceans, plant matter, dried food
- **Water temperature:** 75 to 83°F (24 to 28°C)
- **Community tank**

This species is one of the most beautiful of the South American characins, and similar in shape to the Neon Tetra. It lives mostly in the lower water layers of the tank, which should have patches of dense vegetation and plenty of open water for swimming.

The background coloration of the body is gray-green, the back brownish olive, and the belly silvery. A broad ruby-red band extends back from the upper lip, through the upper part of the eye, and along each flank to the base of the caudal fin. At its rear this band widens into a gleaming spot, hence the popular name. The front of the dorsal fin is bright red, but all the other fins are a delicate pink or colorless, and more or less transparent. The tips of the dorsal, anal, and ventral fins are ivory-white.

This species thrives best in soft, slightly acid water, and this is essential for breeding; filtration through peat is also strongly recommended. At the moment of spawning the parent fishes swim in among the plants, which should preferably be those with feathery leaves. The eggs usually fall to the bottom of the tank, and must then be protected from the parents; the safest method is to remove the pair from the tank. The eggs hatch in 20 to 25 hours, and when free-swimming the fry can be fed on rotifers and very tiny nauplii.

Right: **Hemigrammus erythrozonus**
*Popular in the aquarium world since the 1940s, this fish's common name refers to the bright spot of red at the base of the tail, which shines in a well-lit tank.*

Family CHARACIDAE

## Hemigrammus ocellifer
*Beacon Fish*

- **Distribution:** Northern South America
- **Length:** Up to 1.8in (4.5cm)
- **Tank length:** 12in (30cm)
- **Diet:** Worms, small insects, crustaceans, plant matter, dried food
- **Water temperature:** 72 to 81°F (22 to 27°C)
- **Community tank**

There are two subspecies of Beacon Fish and this has caused some confusion. The one usually seen is *H. ocellifer falsus,* which was introduced into the aquarium world around 1910. The other, *H. ocellifer ocellifer,* was not widely known until 1960.

In *H. ocellifer falsus* the flanks are brownish to greenish yellow with silvery iridescence. Behind the gill cover there is a rather indistinct dark marking within an area of iridescent green. At about the level of the dorsal fin there is the start of a narrow dark band, which extends back to the base of the tail. There, it is crossed by a dark transverse bar flanked by brilliant golden-yellow spots, which give this fish its popular name. The other subspecies is perhaps even more attractive. The marking behind the gill cover is black, with a golden area in front and behind, and there is red at the base of each caudal fin lobe.

Both subspecies have been

Right: **Hemigrammus ocellifer ocellifer**
*This colorful fish is highly suitable for a community tank.*

bred in the same way as the Buenos Aires Tetra. The swim-bladder of the slimmer male can be clearly seen when the fish is viewed against the light, but it is usually masked in the more robust female.

**A practical reminder**
Choose the correct size heater. Allow 10 watts per gallon (3.8 liters). Large tanks need two heaters to spread heat evenly and quickly. Do not test heaters out of water. Always switch off the power before adjusting

Family CHARACIDAE
# Hemigrammus pulcher
*Pretty Tetra*
- **Distribution:** South America: the Peruvian part of the Amazon, above Iquitos
- **Length:** Up to 1.8in (4.5cm)
- **Tank length:** 12in (30cm)
- **Diet:** Worms, small crustaceans, plant matter, dried food
- **Water temperature:** 73 to 81°F (23 to 27°C)
- **Community tank**

This is a deep-bodied, rather high-backed characin living in the middle water layers. Depending upon the angle of light the flanks are pale grayish green to coppery. The back is brownish green and the belly whitish. The head is dark green, becoming darker towards the black snout. The iris is bright purple above, blue-green below. Just behind the gill cover there is a shiny copper-red marking and the upper part of the caudal peduncle has a brilliant golden area. Below this there is an area of black, which extends forwards to below the dorsal fin. The dorsal, caudal, and anal fins are violet or reddish. In the male, which is more slender than the female, the swim-bladder is clearly visible when the fish is viewed against the light, but it is only partly visible in the female. The first four rays of the male's anal fin each end in a tiny hook.

This is not always an easy fish to breed. Some pairs do not succeed in spawning; if this happens, the male should be replaced. Once a pair have spawned successfully they will usually continue to do so. It is probably advisable to attempt breeding in a tank at least 18in (45cm) long, with a water temperature two to four degrees Fahrenheit (one or two degrees Centigrade) above the normal. The water should be soft, slightly acid and preferably filtered through peat. Spawning takes place in the same manner as *Hemigrammus caudovittatus.*

Left: **Hemigrammus pulcher**
*Successful breeding of this fish depends upon finding a compatible pair. Once established such a pair is usually very prolific.*

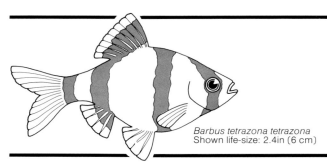

*Barbus tetrazona tetrazona*
Shown life-size: 2.4in (6 cm)

Family CHARACIDAE

# Hyphessobrycon callistus

*Blood Characin*

- **Distribution:** South America, in the Basin of Rio Paraguay
- **Length:** Up to 1.6in (4cm)
- **Tank length:** 12in (30cm)
- **Diet:** Worms, crustaceans, insects, plant matter, dried food
- **Water temperature:** 73 to 79°F (23 to 26°C)
- **Community tank**

This deep-bodied characin is much compressed laterally, and is very suitable for the beginner. The ground coloration of the body is brownish red with silvery iridescence, the belly yellowish brown, becoming much rounded and blood-red in females that are ready to spawn. Just behind the gill cover there is a vertical black marking, which becomes less prominent with increasing age. The dorsal fin is black but its base is a transparent yellow or yellowish brown. An adipose fin is present but colorless. The anal fin is red, the rear part with a black border. The caudal, ventral, and pectoral fins are also red.

This is not a difficult fish to breed. Spawning is preceded by vigorous driving by the male during the early hours of the day. The brownish eggs mostly fall to the bottom, and must be protected, because the parents are notorious spawn-eaters. This can be done either by removing the parents or by installing a fine-mesh grating 1in (2.5cm) above the bottom—the eggs fall through this and are then beyond the reach of the parent fishes. The fry are darkly pigmented.

There is a blood-red fish, known as *Hyphessobrycon 'minor'*, which is now regarded as a variant of *H. callistus;* its fry are pale reddish. There are also several other very closely related species of *Hyphessobrycon*, including the well-known *H. serpae,* which has often been confused with *H. callistus* but is now regarded as a distinct species. Its eggs and newly hatched fry are almost colorless.

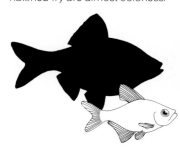

Right: **Hyphessobrycon callistus**
*Striking in appearance and easy to breed, this species has several variants differing in coloration.*

# Hyphessobrycon erythrostigma
*Bleeding Heart Tetra*
- **Distribution:** Northern South America: Colombia
- **Length:** Up to 2.8in (7cm)
- **Tank length:** 36in (90cm)
- **Diet:** Worms, crustaceans, plant matter, dried food
- **Water temperature:** 73 to 77°F (23 to 25°C)
- **Community tank**

Also known as *H. rubrostigma,* this is a hardy shoaling characin.

Left: **Hyphessobrycon erythrostigma** ♀(t), ♂(b)
*Living up to four years, this fish is hardy but not easy to breed.*

The body is very deep and almost lozenge-shaped, and an adipose fin is present. The back is brownish to grayish green, often with a reddish tinge, particularly when the fish is excited. The flanks are silvery and iridescent, and the underparts are orange. Just behind the gill cover there is a large red marking, which accounts for the popular name, and a red longitudinal band extends back from the middle of the body to the base of the tail. The dorsal fin is red, somewhat prolonged in the male, with a white border and with black rays at the front. In the female this fin is shorter with a black marking. The caudal fin is red with bluish white streaks in the male; the ventral fins are reddish; and the adipose fin is bluish white. In the male the anal fin is elongated, with a black edge and a bluish white base, but in the female it is reddish with a whitish area in the front.

Attempts at breeding this species have rarely been successful. The males often drive by swimming around the plants, but the females seldom react, even though they appear to be full of spawn. This is a pity, as the species is very handsome and lives often for two to four years.

# Hyphessobrycon flammeus
*Flame Tetra*
- **Distribution:** South America: Rio de Janeiro, Brazil
- **Length:** Up to 1.8in (4.5cm)
- **Tank length:** 18in (45cm)
- **Diet:** Worms, small crustaceans, plant matter, dried food
- **Water temperature:** 68 to 77°F (20 to 25°C)
- **Community tank**

This colorful old favorite was introduced into the aquarium world around 1920, and is a very good fish for a beginner. It is sometimes known as the Red Tetra from Rio. The shape of the body, but not the color pattern, is very similar to that of Griem's Tetra; an adipose fin is present. The back is grayish olive, and the belly silvery; the flanks are a brilliant brassy color. However, the characteristic feature is the rear part of the body, which is a particularly brilliant red, as are all the fins except the pectoral fins, which are colorless. In the male the tips of the ventral fins and the edge of the anal fin are black. These fins are not so brightly colored in the female and they lack the black edge.

Above:
**Hyphessobrycon flammeus** ♂
*Ideal for a beginner, this peaceful charadin will brighten a community tank with its red markings. It is easy to breed.*

This is a peaceful shoaling fish, swimming mainly in the middle and lower water layers. The tank can have areas of dense vegetation, leaving sufficient open water for swimming. Although it probably does best in soft water, it will tolerate and even breed in medium-hard water. The female lays 200 to 300 eggs, which hatch in two to three days. The fry hang from fine-leaved plants for three more days and can then be fed on rotifers and small nauplii.

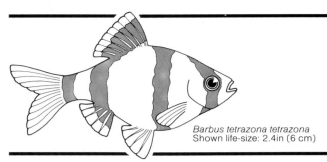

*Barbus tetrazona tetrazona*
Shown life-size: 2.4in (6 cm)

Family CHARACIDAE

# Hyphessobrycon griemi

*Griem's Tetra*

- **Distribution:** South America: the Goyaz area of Brazil
- **Length:** Up to 1.2in (3cm)
- **Tank length:** 18in (45cm)
- **Diet:** Worms, crustaceans, plant matter, dried food
- **Water temperature:** 72 to 81°F (22 to 27°C)
- **Community tank**

Griem's Tetra is a very small, dainty characin, and a relative newcomer to the aquarium, being first introduced in 1956. The body is similar in form to that of the Flame Tetra, but significantly smaller. The background color is a delicate chestnut-brown or olive-brown, flushing to a shade of cinnabar-red when the fish becomes excited. There are two dark vertical markings behind the gill cover, surrounded by a zone of yellow; the first marking is often rather indistinct. The dorsal and anal fins have white tips; an adipose fin is present.

Griem's Tetra does well when kept in a small shoal in a tank with soft or even medium-hard water, where it swims about in the middle layers. It is not difficult to breed. The female is stouter than the male and usually a little longer. As in other related characins the eggs are laid at random, often among clumps of dense vegetation such as Milfoil *(Myriophyllum)*.

An even smaller relative is *Hyphessobrycon georgettae,* sometimes known as the Strawberry Tetra. The average length is 0.8in (2cm), the female a little longer, the male slightly shorter. In males the body and fins are blood-red or strawberry-red, in females yellowish red, and there is no dark marking behind the gill cover. Although quite easy to breed it is not very prolific.

Right: **Hyphessobrycon griemi**
*Although small, this fish may be aggressive to others in the tank.*

Family CHARACIDAE
# Hyphessobrycon herbertaxelrodi
*Black Neon*
- **Distribution:** South America: Rio Taquari, Mato Grosso area of Brazil
- **Length:** Up to 1.4in (3.5cm)
- **Tank length:** 12in (30cm)
- **Diet:** Worms, small crustaceans, plant matter, dried food
- **Water temperature:** 75 to 81°F (24 to 27°C)
- **Community tank**

Named after the well-known American ichthyologist and aquarist Dr. Herbert Axelrod, this is a relatively recent arrival in the aquarium world. The general shape of the body is very similar to that of the Flag Tetra (*Hyphessobrycon heterorhabdus*). The back is a delicate brownish color, and the scales have dark edges that give a reticulated appearance. The belly is silvery and an adipose fin is present. The characteristic feature, however, is the flank pattern: A broad, black longitudinal band extends back from the gill cover to the root of the tail. Parallel to and above this, there is a narrower brilliant iridescent green to yellowish green stripe. The iris is bright blood-red above, iridescent green below.

This is a typical shoaling fish of the upper and middle water layers. It is peaceful, and best kept in a tank with soft, slightly acid water, some patches of vegetation, and space for swimming. Spawning takes place in the open water, sometimes while the sexes are swimming along the side panes of the tank. The parent fishes should be removed immediately after egg-laying has ceased, or the eggs can be protected by a fine-mesh grating. The eggs hatch in 24 to 30 hours and the fry can be reared initially on very fine live food.

Family CHARACIDAE
# Hyphessobrycon heterorhabdus
*Flag Tetra*
- **Distribution:** South America: Rio Tocantins, lower Amazon
- **Length:** Up to 1.8in (4.5cm)
- **Tank length:** 12in (30cm)
- **Diet:** Worms, crustaceans, plant matter, dried food
- **Water temperature:** 73 to 77°F (23 to 25°C)
- **Community tank**

This species, introduced to the aquarium about 1910, is not as hardy as many of the other tetras described. The general shape of the body is similar to that of the Black Neon. The females appear bulkier, with the rear end of the body cavity rounded, whereas the males are more slender and the body cavity has a pointed rear end. There is an adipose fin.

The back is reddish brown and the belly silvery, sometimes with an olive-green tinge. The flanks are yellowish brown marked with a three-colored band extending from the gill cover back to the base of the tail. The central broad band is whitish or golden, the upper narrow band bright red, and the lowermost band black, with a rather indistinct lower border. The fins are colorless or a delicate yellowish color.

This is an active shoaling fish best kept in a tank with soft, slightly acid water, preferably filtered through peat. Clumps of plants should be arranged so as to leave sufficient open water for swimming. Spawning takes place in the same way as Black Neon, but the broods are sometimes relatively small and may fall prey to disease.

Below:
**Hyphessobrycon heterorhabdus**
*This is a delicate characin and not easy to breed successfully.*

Left:
**Hyphessobrycon herbertaxelrodi**
*Distinctively striped, this species will swim peacefully in the middle and upper water layers of the tank. It is not a prolific breeder.*

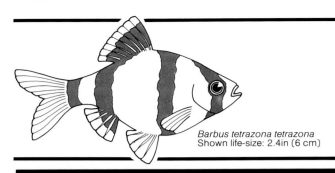

*Barbus tetrazona tetrazona*
Shown life-size: 2.4in (6 cm)

Family CHARACIDAE

## Hyphessobrycon pulchripinnis
*Lemon Tetra*
- **Distribution:** South America, the precise area is unknown
- **Length:** Up to 1.6in (4cm)
- **Tank length:** 12in (30cm)
- **Diet:** Worms, crustaceans, plant matter, dried food
- **Water temperature:** 73 to 77°F (23 to 25°C)
- **Community tank**

Although this small tetra was introduced to the aquarium as long ago as about 1932, the exact place where the original stock was caught is still a mystery. It has sometimes been incorrectly known as *Hemigrammus erythrophthalmus.* The body is fairly deep and translucent with a tinge of yellow; an adipose fin is present. Behind the gill cover there is a rather indistinct marking. The eyes are large and the upper part of the iris is bright red, a point noted in the erroneous specific name *(erythrophthalmus* means 'red eye').

The flanks are silvery, with a scarcely visible longitudinal band

Above:
**Hyphessobrycon pulchripinnis ♂♂**
*A small characin of beautiful color.*

extending back from the rear edge of the gill cover to the root of the tail. In general, the fins are yellowish. The front rays of the anal fin are somewhat elongated and lemon-yellow, and the same color occurs at the tip of the dorsal fin. In the male the anal fin has a broad black edge, but in the female this is narrower and only blackish.

This is a quiet shoaling fish of the middle and lower water layers, and it thrives best in soft water. For successful breeding the females must be given a varied diet of live food. Even so, spawning may not take place as readily as in most other tetras. Sometimes, however, a female may be very productive.

Family CHARACIDAE

## Hyphessobrycon scholzei
*Black-line Tetra*
- **Distribution:** South America, in the Pará region of Brazil
- **Length:** Up to 1.8in (4.5cm)
- **Tank length:** 24in (60cm)
- **Diet:** Worms, small crustaceans, plant matter, dried food
- **Water temperature:** 72 to 77°F 22-25°C
- **Community tank**

This is a hardy, shoaling species with the typical tetra body form. The back is greenish to brownish, the belly silvery; the flanks are iridescent bluish. The characteristic feature, however, is a narrow black longitudinal stripe extending back from the rear of the gill cover to the basal part of the caudal fin, where it widens out into a blackish area on the central caudal fin rays. The pectoral fins are colorless, but all the other fins have a reddish tinge, the tip of the anal fin being white. The iris is yellow.

This is a peaceful fish that is perfectly hardy and very suitable for a beginner. It is not difficult to

breed in a tank with soft to medium-hard water. Before spawning the male carries out a courtship display in front of the female. The female lays her eggs at random and these hatch in about 30 hours. The tiny fry are free-swimming a few days later and can then be fed on live food such as rotifers and very small nauplii. As they grow the young fishes can be gradually accustomed to taking some dried food.

There are several related groups in the large genus *Hyphessobrycon,* and the Black-Line Tetra is considered to be most closely related to *H. heterorhabdus, H. herbertaxelrodi* and *H. metae* (from the Rio Meta).

Right: **Hyphessobrycon scholzei**
*Introduced into the aquarium in the 1930s, this fish is easy to breed.*

**A practical reminder**
Heavily planted tanks require a lot of light—
40 watts (fluorescent) per square foot
(900cm²) of water surface area.
Illumination time should be 12 hours daily,
with reduced lighting for a pleasant
evening's viewing.

Left: **Megalamphodus megalopterus**
*Their large blackish fins identify
these fishes clearly as males of the
species. Females have reddish fins.*

Family CHARACIDAE
# Megalamphodus megalopterus
*Black Phantom Tetra*
● **Distribution:** South America:
Rio Guapore on the border
between Bolivia and Brazil
● **Length:** Up to 1.8in (4.5cm)
● **Tank length:** 18in (45cm)
● **Diet:** Worms, small insects,
crustaceans, dried food
● **Water temperature:** 73 to 79°F
(23 to 26°C)
● **Community tank**

This peaceful shoaling fish has the
typical body outline of the tetras. In
general, the male is grayish with a
blackish back and a paler belly.
The flanks have a prominent black
vertical marking situated behind
the gill cover and surrounded by
an iridescent turquoise-green
area. The pectoral fins are
colorless, but all the other fins are
blackish; the dorsal fin is quite
elongated. In the female the back
is gray; the flanks are brownish-
red and the vertical marking is
similar to that of the male. The
dorsal and caudal fins are grayish
or blackish, the pectoral fins
reddish, and the adipose and
ventral fins bright red.
This is a species that should
always be kept in a tank with soft,
slightly acid water, whether for
breeding or at other times. The
lighting should be subdued and
the planting generous, but leave
plenty of space for swimming.
This species is very susceptible to
fish tuberculosis. Breeding is not
always easy and it seems that
older fishes cease to breed.
Spawning behavior is similar to
that in members of the genus
*Hyphessobrycon.* Newly hatched
fry can be fed on rotifers and very
small nauplii.
Fishes belonging to the genus
*Megalamphodus* are very similar
to many other characin genera,
but they are separated from these
by differences in the dentition and
in the structure of the skull.

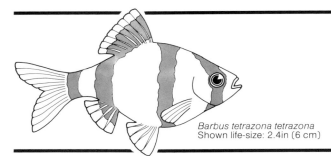

Barbus tetrazona tetrazona
Shown life-size: 2.4in (6 cm)

Family CHARACIDAE
## Megalamphodus sweglesi
*Red Phantom Tetra*
- **Distribution:** South America: Orinoco region, Rio Muco and the upper reaches of the Rio Meta
- **Length:** Up to 1.6in (4cm)
- **Tank length:** 18in (45cm)
- **Diet:** Worms, small insects, crustaceans, dried food
- **Water temperature:** 73 to 79°F (23 to 26°C)
- **Community tank**

This relatively recent introduction to the aquarium has a body outline very similar to that of *M. megalopterus*. Both species are shoaling fishes, swimming mostly in the lower water layers. The

general body coloration is yellowish red. There is a more or less rounded marking on the flanks just behind the gill cover. The belly has a faint shiny golden tinge. In the male the dorsal fin is considerably longer than in the female, with a tapering point. In the female the dorsal fin has a rounded tip and is marked with a conspicuous dark blotch. The dorsal, caudal, anal, and ventral fins are bright yellowish red.

On the whole this is a peaceful species; at times a couple of males may indulge in a sparring match with their fins, but they do not damage one another. Spawning behavior takes place as in members of the genus *Hyphessobrycon*. Some authorities recommend that peat should not be added to the tank,

maintaining that although the embryos may develop normally the peat has a tanning action on the egg coverings that prevents the fry from breaking out, and they then die within the egg coverings.

This species is not as susceptible to disease as *M. megalopterus*.

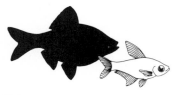

Below:
**Megalamphodus sweglesi** ♀
*This colorful shoaling fish will thrive in a community tank.*

Family CHARACIDAE
## Micralestes interruptus
*Congo Tetra*
- **Distribution:** Central Africa: Zaire region
- **Length:** Males up to 3.2in (8cm), females to 2.4in (6cm)
- **Tank length:** 24in (60cm)
- **Diet:** Worms, small insects and crustaceans, plant matter, dried food
- **Water temperature:** 75 to 79°F (24 to 26°C)
- **Community tank**

Formerly known as *Phenacogrammus interruptus*, this is one of the most elegant of the medium-sized characins, with large eyes, a laterally compressed body, and large scales. In the male the dorsal fin is much elongated and so are the central rays of the caudal fin. In the rather smaller female these parts are scarcely elongated. In reflected light the flanks of the male are iridescent greenish blue with a tinge of reddish brown, yellow, or sometimes violet. The back is brownish, and the dorsal and caudal fins are gray; the anal and caudal fins have a white border.

This is not a difficult species to keep, but for the male's fins to develop fully the tank must have soft, slightly acid water filtered through peat, not too many plants, plenty of space for swimming, and preferably a dark substrate. Under these conditions spawning may occur during the hours of morning sunshine. After vigorous driving by the male, the female lays up to 300 eggs, sometimes more, which sink to the bottom. The eggs hatch after about six days, and the fry can be fed immediately on rotifers and very small nauplii.

Right: **Micralestes interruptus** ♂♂
*Although it appears rather delicate, this species has proved perfectly hardy when kept in the soft, slightly acid water that it needs, and it breeds quite successfully. For the male fins to develop properly as shown here the fish should have a spacious tank.*

**A practical reminder**
Use inside filters for unfurnished fry-raising
tanks. Outside filters are much better for
fully planted tanks, however, since you will
not have to disturb the planting layout to
carry out the necessary regular maintenance.

Left: **Moenkhausia pittieri** ♂
*The beautifully developed dorsal
and anal fins identify this as a male
specimen of this hardy species.*

Family CHARACIDAE
# Moenkhausia pittieri
*Diamond Tetra*
● **Distribution:** Northern South
   America: Lake Valencia in
   Venezuela
● **Length:** Up to 2.4in (6cm)
● **Tank length:** 18in (45cm)
● **Diet:** Worms, crustaceans,
   insects, dried food
● **Water temperature:** 72 to 81°F
   (22 to 27°C)
● **Community tank**

This is a particularly active
shoaling fish of the middle and
upper water layers; it was
introduced to the aquarium in the
early 1930s. In the male the dorsal
fin is quite elongated and the anal
fin is also better developed than in
the female. In males the body and
fins are a delicate violet color with
golden iridescence when seen in
reflected light, and small iridescent
greenish dots. Apart from the
colorless pectoral fins all the other
fins have white borders. The
females are paler in coloration
and usually yellowish with slight
iridescence.

   This is a hardy fish, best kept in
soft, slightly acid water filtered
through peat. Plant patches of
vegetation, but leave sufficient
water for swimming. In most
cases spawning takes place quite
readily and the female is usually
very prolific. In fact, the species
has been known to breed in quite
small tanks (about 5 gallons/20
liters) and the parents do not
normally eat the eggs. The young
hatch after about 25 to 30 hours
(possibly longer) and then hang
for a few days from plants or
sometimes the glass panes of the
tank. They will then be free-
swimming and can be fed at first
on rotifers and tiny nauplii. When
the water conditions are right the
young feed voraciously and grow
rapidly.

   The related Glass Tetra
(*Moenkhausia oligolepis*), up to
4.7in (12cm) in length, comes
from the Amazon and Guyana
regions, and can be kept in the
same way as *M. pittieri*.

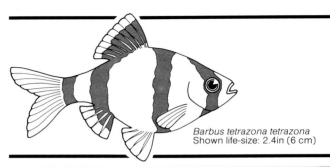

*Barbus tetrazona tetrazona*
Shown life-size: 2.4in (6 cm)

Family CHARACIDAE

## Moenkhausia
## sanctaefilomenae
*Red-eye Tetra*

- **Distribution:** South America: Rio Paraguay and Rio Parnaiba
- **Length:** Up to 2.4in (6cm)
- **Tank length:** 24in (60cm)
- **Diet:** Worms, insects, crustaceans, plant matter, dried food
- **Water temperature:** 70 to 79°F (21 to 26°C)
- **Community tank**

This relatively deep-bodied characin, lives in small shoals, mainly in the middle water layers.

It was introduced to the aquarium in the middle 1950s. The females have a markedly rounded belly profile when ready to spawn.

In general the body is silvery, with the back pale greenish or brownish and iridescent. The scales, particularly those on the upper side, have dark edges. The caudal peduncle has a wide iridescent yellow area and the base of the tail carries a broad black transverse bar. The fins are colorless or more or less smoky-gray, except that the dorsal and anal fins have white tips. The upper half of the eye is a brilliant blood-red. The Red-eye Tetra resembles a smaller, more

colorful version of *M. oligolepis*.

Red-eye Tetras should be kept in a spacious tank with tough plants arranged to leave sufficient open water for swimming; members of this species have a tendency to nibble soft plants. They need some plant matter in their diet, and this can be conveniently supplied by having a small piece of lettuce in the tank. This must be removed, however, as soon as it shows signs of rotting in the warm water.

The tank water should be soft to medium-hard and there will be no difficulty in getting this species to spawn. The fry should be treated like those of the Diamond Tetra

Above:

**Moenkhausia sanctaefilomenae**
*This is one of the best shoaling charactins. It behaves peacefully in a community tank and breeds easily. Ideal for a beginner.*

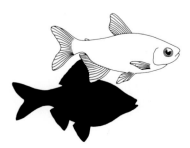

**A practical reminder**
Biological filtration relies on bacterial activity
and must have a constant water flow
through the gravel. Do not disconnect the
air supply to such filters or the water flow
will stop and all the bacteria will die.

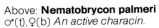

Above: **Nematobrycon palmeri**
♂(t), ♀(b) *An active characin.*

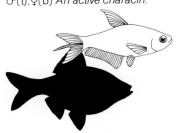

Family CHARACIDAE

# Paracheirodon innesi
*Neon Tetra*
- **Distribution:** Northern South
  America: Upper Amazon
- **Length:** Up to 1.6in (4cm)
- **Tank length:** 12in (30cm)
- **Diet:** Worms, small insects and
  crustaceans, plant matter, dried
  food
- **Water temperature:** 70 to 79°F
  (21 to 26°C)
- **Community tank**

Originally described in 1936 as
*Hyphessobrycon innesi,* after the
American aquarist W.T. Innes, this
brilliantly colored small characin is
one of the most popular fishes for
the home aquarium.

The body is slender, spindle
shaped and only slightly laterally
compressed, and has an adipose
fin. The back is dark olive-green,
the belly yellowish white. The
flanks show a brilliant iridescent
greenish blue stripe extending
from the front of the eye back to
the level of the adipose fin. Below
this, but beginning only in the
middle of the body, there is a
broad, very bright red band that
extends back to the root of the tail.
(In the closely related Cardinal
Tetra, the red band extends from
the mouth to the tail base.)

Neon Tetras are active
characins, swimming mostly in
the lower and middle water layers,
and thrive best in a tank with a
dark substrate and subdued
lighting. The adults can be
acclimatized to medium-hard
water, but for breeding it is
essential that the water be soft and
slightly acid. The breeding tank
can be quite small (length 8in/
20cm) with just one clump of
vegetation. A pair introduced to
such a tank may spawn the
following morning. The female
lays a relatively small number of
eggs, which hatch in about 24
hours. The parent fishes should
be removed after spawning. The
fry are free-swimming four days
after hatching and can then be fed
on very small live food.

Left: **Paracheirodon innesi**
*Widespread and universally popular
in the aquarium world, this species
is active, colorful, and hardy, and
breeds readily in soft water.*

Family CHARACIDAE

# Nematobrycon palmeri
*Emperor Tetra*
- **Distribution:** Northern South
  America: Colombia
- **Length:** Up to 2.2in (5.5cm)
- **Tank length:** 12in (30cm)
- **Diet:** Worms, crustaceans,
  finely chopped meat, dried food
- **Water temperature:** 73 to 79°F
  (23 to 26°C)
- **Community tank**

An active and very colorful fish,
the Emperor Tetra swims mostly
in the lower water layers. The
body is relatively tall and there is
no adipose fin. The male has an
elongated dorsal fin and a
conspicuously developed caudal
fin, the central rays being very
elongated. The anal fin is very
long, with a narrow dark band
along its outer edge. The female
lacks the elongations of the dorsal
and anal fins. In both sexes the
back is olive-brown and the flanks
have a broad, iridescent grass-
green or sometimes blue-green
longitudinal band that extends
from the gill cover to the caudal
peduncle. Below this runs a broad
blackish band that extends onto
the caudal fin. The iris is an
iridescent blue-green.

This very attractive characin
should be kept in a tank with a
dark substrate, patches of dense
vegetation, and sufficient space for
swimming. The lighting should be
subdued, and this can be best
achieved by having some floating

plants at the surface. These
conditions help to enhance the
Emperor Tetra's brilliant
coloration. The water should be
soft and slightly acid.

This is not always an easy fish to
breed. Provided a compatible pair
can be found, the male drives the
female very actively. The eggs are
laid among fine-leaved plants.
Once they are free-swimming the
fry can be fed on very small live
food. They grow quickly.

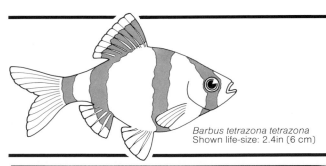

*Barbus tetrazona tetrazona*
Shown life-size: 2.4in (6 cm)

Family CHARACIDAE
## Petitella georgiae
*False Rummy-nose*

- **Distribution:** South America: the upper Amazon
- **Length:** Up to 2in (5cm)
- **Tank length:** 12in (30cm)
- **Diet:** Worms, small crustaceans, plant matter, dried food
- **Water temperature:** 75 to 79°F (24 to 26°C)
- **Community tank**

The False Rummy-nose is a peaceful shoaling fish. The body is silvery with blue-green iridescence and a dark longitudinal stripe that extends from the caudal fin forwards onto the caudal peduncle. This characin has been much confused with the very similar Red-nosed Tetra *(Hemigrammus rhodostomus)*, in which the flanks are silvery and iridescent, with a

Left: **Petitella georgiae**
*This colorful fish is best kept in a small shoal, which will swim in the middle and lower water layers.*

Family CHARACIDAE
## Poptella orbicularis
*Disk Tetra*

- **Distribution:** South America: Amazon Basin, Guyana and Paraguay
- **Length:** Up to 4.7in (12cm)
- **Tank length:** 36in (90cm)
- **Diet:** Worms, insects, crustaceans, plant matter, dried food
- **Water temperature:** 77 to 81°F (25 to 27°C)
- **Community tank**

This species was formerly known as *Ephippicharax orbicularis*. It is a disk-shaped, laterally compressed, omnivorous fish that is perfectly hardy in an aquarium. The flanks are silvery with a greenish, yellowish, or bluish sheen, depending upon the lighting. The upper side is dark green and there are two curved dark markings just behind the gill cover. The scales are relatively large and the fins almost colorless except that the dorsal, anal, and caudal fins are marked with small dark dots. There is also an adipose fin. Although this species is not as colorful as many other characins, its more unusual shape adds variety to the tank.

This is a shoaling fish living mostly in the middle and lower water layers, which does best in a tank with plenty of space for swimming and a dark substrate. The light should be fairly subdued. For breeding the tank should have soft, slightly acid water. The eggs are laid at random and the females are normally very productive. The fry should be fed at first on tiny live food, such as rotifers and small nauplii.

Right: **Poptella orbicularis**
*A handsome fish, first introduced into the aquarium in the 1930s.*

**A practical reminder**
The biological filter plate should cover the entire base of the tank. If it is sealed in place permanently, there is no possibility of water finding a path around it and the whole gravel bed becomes a colony of bacteria.

dark longitudinal stripe extending back from the center of the body to the caudal peduncle and onto the end of the caudal fin, where it becomes appreciably wider.

When the fish is in good condition the iris and the snout are blood-red, hence the popular name. The lobes of the caudal fin are whitish, sometimes yellowish white, each with a prominent black blotch. The other fins are colorless.

The False Rummy-nose does not produce a large number of eggs and the fry are evidently rather delicate. This species should be kept in soft, slightly acid water, but it is not an easy fish to breed. The fry grow slowly at first.

Family CHARACIDAE
## Pristella maxillaris
*X-ray Fish, Water Goldfinch*
● **Distribution:** Northern South America and Lower Amazon
● **Length:** Up to 1.8in (4.5cm)
● **Tank length:** 18in (45cm)
● **Diet:** Worms, small crustaceans, insects, dried food
● **Water temperature:** 70 to 79°F (21 to 26°C)
● **Community tank**

This is an old favorite introduced into the aquarium world in the middle 1920s. The body is laterally compressed and fairly elongated, particularly in the males and juveniles, but females have a more rounded belly profile; the popular name refers to the remarkably translucent body. An adipose fin is present. The caudal fin is deeply cleft. In general, the translucent body has a pale yellowish or greenish tinge, and appears silvery in reflected light. The dorsal and anal fins have an area of lemon-yellow at the base, a black marking in the middle, and white tips. The caudal fin is red. Just behind the gill cover there is a distinct black blotch.

This is a hardy, shoaling characin that should be kept in a tank with a dark substrate and subdued light. The water can be soft to medium-hard, although the former is preferable.

Breeding is not all that easy. It seems that some pairs are not compatible. If two fishes have spawned successfully, they should be kept together and may then go

Above: **Pristella maxillaris**
*This lively fish should be kept in a shoal in subdued light. Breeding success needs a compatible pair.*

on breeding for four years or so; the female will usually produce about 300 eggs at each spawning. These hatch in 24 hours, and the very tiny fry should be fed on fine live food as soon as they become free-swimming.

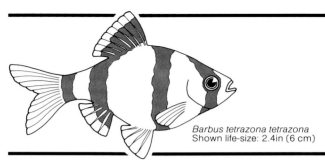

*Barbus tetrazona tetrazona*
Shown life-size: 2.4in (6 cm)

## Family CHARACIDAE

### Thayeria boehlkei
*Boehlke's Penguin Fish*
- **Distribution:** South America: Amazon Basin
- **Length:** Up to 2.4in (6cm)
- **Tank length:** 24in (60cm)
- **Diet:** Worms, small insects and crustaceans, dried food
- **Water temperature:** 73 to 79°F (23 to 26°C)
- **Community tank**

Boehlke's Penguin Fish is a hardy shoaling fish found mostly in the upper water layers. It swims in a characteristic oblique position with the head upward. The body is laterally compressed; an adipose fin is present. The back is brownish or olive. The main distinguishing feature is the prominent black longitudinal band on the flanks. This starts immediately behind the gill cover and extends back to the tail, where it bends downwards and ends at the tip of the caudal fin's lower lobe. Beneath and parallel to this band there is a greenish golden stripe. The fins are more or less colorless, except that the anal fin and the lower lobe of the caudal fin are yellowish white. As in most related characins the females are stouter when sexually mature, with a more rounded belly profile than the males.

These striking fishes do best in soft water, but will tolerate medium-hard water. For breeding the tank should have clumps of fine-leaved plants such as Milfoil *(Myriophyllum),* and the water must be soft and slightly acid. Before spawning takes place (usually at twilight) the pair indulge in vigorous driving and the female then lays a large number of eggs. These hatch in about 20 to 24 hours and the fry are free-swimming four or five days later.

There has been some confusion between this species and the very similar *Thayeria obliqua.* However, in the latter the dark longitudinal band starts just behind the dorsal fin (rather than behind the gill cover) and runs back to the lower lobe of the caudal fin.

Below: **Thayeria boehlkei**
*An elegant, hardy fish that swims typically in an oblique position.*

## Family GASTEROPELECIDAE

### Gasteropelecus sternicla
*Common Hatchetfish*
- **Distribution:** South America: middle Amazon, Guyana
- **Length:** Up to 2.6in (6.5cm)
- **Tank length:** 24in (60cm)
- **Diet:** Worms, crustaceans, insects, dried food
- **Water temperature:** 73 to 86°F (23 to 30°C)
- **Community tank**

This very tall, strongly compressed fish has an almost straight dorsal profile as far back as the dorsal fin, behind which it dips down to the caudal peduncle. But the throat and belly are very convex. This peculiar development of the underparts is due to the enlargement of the shoulder girdle and the powerful muscles attached to it. These give power to the pectoral fins, which the fish is able to beat rapidly. Thus it can fly over the water for distances of up to 16.5ft (5m).

There is a small adipose fin. In reflected light the fish shows silvery iridescence. The scales are actually gray and those on the upperparts have dark edges. The flanks are marked by a dark longitudinal band that extends from the edge of the gill cover to the root of the caudal fin. This band is bordered above and below by a paler line. In some individuals the front edge of the dorsal fin has dark markings, but otherwise the fins are almost colorless. Adult males appear thinner than adult females when viewed from above.

This is an active, peaceful fish that lives at the surface of the water. It is quite a hardy species when kept under suitable conditions. The tank must have a well-fitting cover to prevent the fish from 'flying' out and landing on the floor. The nature of the substrate is not important for the hatchetfishes and can be made suitable for any other occupants of the tank. A few floating plants and some roots will supply the

**A practical reminder**
Most air pumps have filter pads to clean the
air. You should clean these regularly to
keep the pump performing in peak
condition. Air valves should also be kept
clean and mechanical pumps well oiled.

Family SERRASALMIDAE
## Serrasalmus nattereri
*Red Piranha*
- **Distribution:** South America:
  Amazon, Orinoco, Paraná
- **Length:** 12in (30cm)
- **Tank length:** 48in (120cm)
- **Diet:** Insects, worms, fish, meat
- **Water temperature:** 75 to 81°F
  (24 to 27°C)
- **Species tank**

Sometimes known as
*Rooseveltiella nattereri,* the Red
Piranha is an aggressive,
predatory fish. The body is tall and
very compressed laterally and an
adipose fin is present. The back is
bluish-gray and the belly strikingly
red. The flanks are pale brown to
olive with numerous shiny spots,
but the coloration varies
somewhat, depending to a certain
extent on the age of the fish. The
dorsal and caudal fins are dark
and the anal fin usually has a
broad black border. The keel of

Left: **Serrasalmus nattereri**
*Only young specimens are really
suitable for a home aquarium.*

the belly has a number of
serrations.
Only young specimens are
really suitable for the home
aquarium. They need a tank with
a few tough plants, and possibly
some rocks and roots for
decoration. The water should be
soft, slightly acid, and filtered
through peat.
The Red Piranha and related
species have been bred in large
public aquarium tanks. A single
spawning may produce 4000 to
5000 large eggs, which adhere to
the plants and are not attacked by
the parent fishes. These hatch in
nine or 10 days.
In general, the ferocity of the
Red Piranha and its relatives has
been overstated. They are
aggressive but will usually attack
only when they smell blood in the
water. Their extremely sharp
dentition and powerful jaws
enable them to reduce even a
large animal such as a tapir to a
skeleton in a matter of minutes.
The genus *Serrasalmus* and
related fishes were formerly
classified in the family Characidae.

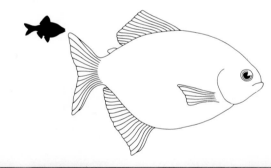

decoration. The water must be
soft, slightly acid, and filtered
through peat. This species has
been bred on a few occasions,
but the details are sketchy.
Spawning has not been observed,
but probably takes place at dusk.
The eggs have been seen
hanging from fine-leaved plants or
lying on the substrate. The fry
have been reared on rotifers and
small nauplii.

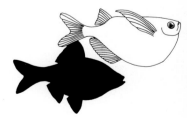

Right: **Gasteropelecus sternicla**
*This surface-dwelling fish is quite
capable of leaping out of an
uncovered tank. The species will
thrive in soft water but has not
been bred with great success.*

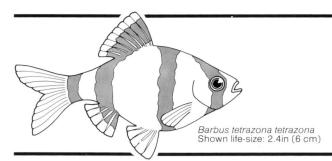

*Barbus tetrazona tetrazona*
Shown life-size: 2.4in (6 cm)

Family GASTEROPELECIDAE

## Gasteropelecus levis
*Silver Hatchetfish*

- **Distribution:** South America: lower Amazon
- **Length:** Up to 2.4in (6cm)
- **Tank length:** 24in (60cm)
- **Diet:** Worms, crustaceans, insects, dried food
- **Water temperature:** 75 to 86°F (24 to 30°C)
- **Community tank**

The shape of this species is exactly the same as that of the Common Hatchetfish and the coloration is also similar. The dorsal profile is straight back to the dorsal fin with a short concave part in the region of the small adipose fin. The underparts are very convex. The body is more silvery, particularly on the lower half, than that of the Common Hatchetfish and there is a dark marking at the base of the dorsal fin. The longitudinal band is more pronounced and there is sometimes a thin black line along the base of the anal fin.

This is an active fish that lives at the surface of the water, where it also takes much of its food. In general, it is not as hardy as the Common Hatchetfish. The tank must have a well-fitting lid and a few floating plants, with sufficient open water available for

swimming. Occasionally these fishes chase after food that is sinking to the bottom. The water must be soft, slightly acid, and filtered through peat. This species is not known to have been bred in captivity.

The related Spotted Hatchetfish, *Gasteropelecus maculatus,* comes from the area between western Colombia and Panama, and is up to 3.5in (9cm) in length. The flanks are gray-green with strong silvery iridescence and brownish spots arranged in transverse rows. A black longitudinal band extends from the gill cover to the base of the tail and it is bordered above by a shiny silver line. The fins are almost colorless, except for the dorsal fin, which has a dark edge. This species has not been bred successfully in an aquarium.

Right: **Gasteropelecus levis**
*Sometimes rather delicate in an aquarium, this is a lively 'jumper'.*

Family GASTEROPELECIDAE

## Carnegiella marthae
*Black-winged Hatchetfish*

- **Distribution:** Venezuela, Peru, Amazon, Rio Negro, Rio Orinoco
- **Length:** Up to 1.4in (3.5cm)
- **Tank length:** 18in (45cm)
- **Diet:** Crustaceans, insects, dried food
- **Water temperature:** 73 to 84°F (23 to 29°C)
- **Community tank**

This is the dwarf among the hatchetfishes. The body is the same shape as in the other species except that there is no adipose fin. The flanks are silvery with a dark longitudinal line running from the gill cover to the base of the tail. This is bordered above by a delicate golden or silver line. The central part of the pectoral fins has a black marking, and the keel of the belly and

breast has a black border. There are two black cheek markings.

This is a peaceful, surface-living fish that has usually been found to be rather delicate for an aquarium. It should be kept in a tank with a well-fitting cover to prevent jumping. A few roots and plants with fine leaves, as well as floating plants, will help to subdue the light. The other inmates of the tank should be peaceful fishes that live on or near the bottom. The Black-winged Hatchetfish feeds entirely at the surface and does not chase prey or other food that is sinking in the water. Hence, insects that are trapped at the surface of the water form a large portion of its diet in the wild. This habit can certainly be encouraged in the aquarium.

Spawning has been seen on a few occasions. It takes place among roots of floating plants, the male performing a fluttering dance and then swimming just below the female as spawning begins. The eggs adhere to plants and hatch in 24 to 36 hours. The fry remain hanging from the plants while they consume the contents of the yolk-sac and are free-swimming about five days after hatching. They are not difficult to rear and take infusorians as a first live food.

Left: **Carnegiella marthae**
*This small species needs careful attention from the aquarist.*

**A practical reminder**
Vibrator type pumps run quieter with back pressure applied; piston pumps must have any excess air bled away since back pressure due to clamping causes wear. Air from these pumps must be filtered to remove oil.

Family GASTEROPELECIDAE
## Carnegiella strigata
*Marbled Hatchetfish*
- **Distribution:** South America: Amazon, Guyana
- **Length:** Up to 1.8in (4.5cm)
- **Tank length:** 18in (45cm)
- **Diet:** Crustaceans, insects, dried food
- **Water temperature:** 75 to 84°F (24 to 29°C)
- **Community tank**

This is an attractive fish with a belly profile that is almost semi-circular. The ventral fins are very small. Between these fins and the caudal fin the profile is almost straight. The dorsal fin is fairly short and positioned far back on the body. The winglike pectoral fins are almost half the length of the body. There is no adipose fin. The general coloration is silvery-green to silvery-violet. A longitudinal band that is pale above and dark below runs from the gill cover to the root of the tail. The marbled pattern is formed by three dark brown oblique bands on the belly which are irregularly toothed and partly broken up into separate spots. The back is dark brown, and the keel in the breast region is yellowish. The fins are all colorless. There are no external sex differences.

This is a peaceful fish that is mainly active at dusk. It can be kept in a tank with a good lid to prevent unwanted flights, and with some feathery-leaved plants. A few floating plants will provide shade; the colors of this species tend to fade if the light is too strong. The water must be soft, slightly acid, and filtered through peat. The species has been bred on a few occasions. After a preliminary period of courtship, during which the male flutters around the female, spawning takes place among the fine-leaved plants. The eggs adhere to these plants and will hatch in about 30 hours. The fry are swimming five days later. They feed at first on infusorians, and, at this period, they are not confined to the surface waters. They start to develop the typical adult form when they are about 20 days old.

Left: **Carnegiella strigata**
*A peaceful, surface-dwelling fish that thrives in shady conditions.*

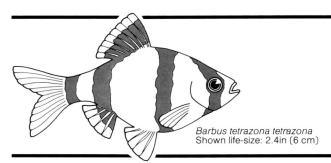

*Barbus tetrazona tetrazona*
Shown life-size: 2.4in (6 cm)

Family LEBIASINIDAE

# Copeina guttata
*Red-spotted Copeina*

- **Distribution:** South America, in tributaries of the middle Amazon
- **Length:** Up to 3.2in (8cm)
- **Tank length:** 24in (60cm)
- **Diet:** Worms, insects, small crustaceans, dried food
- **Water temperature:** 75 to 81°F (24 to 27°C)
- **Community tank**

Nowadays this species and the following one, *Copella arnoldi,* are classified in the family Lebiasinidae, but they were formerly placed in the Characidae.

This is a hardy aquarium fish that shows some interesting biological features. The body is slender with small short fins, but lacks an adipose fin. The caudal fin is forked, and in males the upper lobe is rather larger than the lower one. In males the flanks are pale blue to greenish blue, the belly is white, and the back is brownish green. There are reddish dots at the base of each scale, giving the impression of longitudinal rows. The smaller females show paler coloration, with yellowish gray fins. The dorsal fin has a fairly prominent black marking.

For successful breeding the water should be soft and slightly acid. At spawning time the male, after some vigorous driving and prodding of the female, comes alongside and slightly below her. The male then pushes an open pocket (formed by his anal fin) below the genital opening of the female. She releases her eggs into this and the male fertilizes them and allows them to drop into a small pit in the sand that he has previously prepared. The male fans the eggs with his fins until they hatch, in about 25 hours, and he continues to protect the fry until they are free-swimming. The fry can be fed at first on tiny nauplii.

Below: **Copeina guttata** ♂♂
*This attractively marked fish tends to jump, so the tank must have a close-fitting lid. Not difficult to breed, this species has an unusual spawning behavior. The male fans the eggs and protects the brood.*

**A practical reminder**
The aeration rate should always be increased when you use the tank for sick fishes, because some medications reduce the level of oxygen in the water. Aeration also helps to drive carbon dioxide from the water.

Family LEBIASINIDAE
## Copella arnoldi
*Spraying Characin*
- **Distribution:** South America: lower Amazon and Rio Paru.
- **Length:** Male up to 3.2in (8cm), female up to 2.4in (6cm)
- **Tank length:** 18in (45cm)
- **Diet:** Worms, insects, crustaceans, dried food
- **Water temperature:** 73 to 81°F (23 to 27°C)
- **Community tank**

This fish, formerly known as *Copeina arnoldi,* has now been assigned to the genus *Copella* on the basis of certain rather small differences in jaw structure. However, there is still some doubt about its new classification, and the subject requires further detailed analysis by professional ichthyologists. The fish's real

Left: **Copella arnoldi** ♀
*Of particular interest because it spawns above the water surface.*

interest to aquarists lies in the unusual method of breeding.
In the male the flanks are yellowish, the scales have dark edges, and the gill cover has a greenish gold marking. When excited during courtship or fights, the male becomes black with silvery dots. The dorsal fin of the male is elongated and roughly triangular, red at the tip and marked with a black blotch that has a white base. The other fins of the male are yellowish red and elongated. The coloration of the female is more subdued, and the fins are not so well developed.
Spraying Characins spawn on the undersides of leaves growing above the surface of the water. The male and female swim vertically to the surface, flick their tails and leap up to a leaf, which may be 1.6 to 2.4in (4 to 6cm) above the surface. The female lays from five to eight eggs on the leaf and these are immediately fertilized by the male. This highly original spawning procedure is repeated many times, until some hundreds of eggs have been laid. The male then keeps the eggs damp by flicking his tail to spray them with water. As they hatch, the fry fall into the water. In an aquarium, the eggs are often laid on the underside of the tank lid.

Family LEBIASINIDAE
## Nannostomus beckfordi
*Golden Pencilfish*
- **Distribution:** South America: Guyana to Rio Negro
- **Length:** Up to 2.6in (6.5cm)
- **Tank length:** 12in (30cm)
- **Diet:** Worms, crustaceans, insects, dried food
- **Water temperature:** 75 to 81°F (24 to 27°C)
- **Community tank**

The Golden Pencilfish is elongated and torpedo-shaped with slight lateral compression. It has a symmetrical caudal fin but no adipose fin. The dorsal and ventral fins are immediately opposite one another. With such an extensive geographical distribution it is not surprising that the coloration varies and several color variants or subspecies have been discovered. The subspecies *N. beckfordi anomalus* is probably no longer on the aquarium market. On the other hand, *N. beckfordi aripirangensis,* from Aripiranga Island in the lower Amazon, is often available. In the male of this subspecies, the flanks and the bases of the dorsal, caudal, anal, and ventral fins are blood red — particularly when the fish is excited. There is a broad, blue-black longitudinal band running from the snout to the root of the tail, and this is accompanied above by a golden-yellow band. The female is not as brightly colored and only the fin bases are red.
The Golden Pencilfish should be kept in a tank well stocked with areas of dense vegetation, including plants with feathery leaves, and sufficient open water for swimming. The water must be soft, slightly acid, and filtered through peat. The lighting should be subdued. At spawning time the male and female swim alongside one another. Several batches of one to five eggs are laid among the fine-leaved plants, with a total of up to 200 eggs in some cases. The eggs hatch in 30 to 40 hours and the fry are free-swimming about six days later. They can then be fed on brine shrimp nauplii or other live food of the same size.

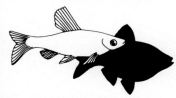

Left: **Nannostomus beckfordi**
*Variable in color, this species should be kept in a shoal.*

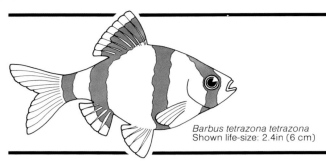

*Barbus tetrazona tetrazona*
Shown life-size: 2.4in (6 cm)

Family LEBIASINIDAE
## Nannostomus eques
*Tube-mouthed Pencilfish*
- **Distribution:** South America: central Amazon
- **Length:** Up to 2in (5cm)
- **Tank length:** 12in (30cm)
- **Diet:** Worms, crustaceans, insects, dried food
- **Water temperature:** 72 to 79°F (22 to 26°C)
- **Community tank:** Best kept with other small, non-aggressive species

Also known as *Poecilobrycon eques,* this is a slender, spindle-shaped pencilfish with a pointed head. The lower lobe of the caudal fin is larger than the upper lobe. The adipose fin is very small or non-existent. The male is slender with an almost straight belly profile; the female is stouter with convex underparts. This species swims in an oblique position with the head up, becoming almost vertical when at rest. The back is pale brown to silvery-gray with five rows of dark dots. Below these dots there is a broad dark brown longitudinal band that extends from the tip of the snout to the lower lobe of the caudal fin. The upper lobe is colorless. The anal fin is black and red with a white border, but the dorsal fin is colorless. In the males the ventral fins have bluish-white

tips. In general, the females are less colorful than the males. During the night, two broad dark and somewhat oblique transverse bars appear on each flank.

This peaceful fish swims mostly near the surface and should be kept in a shoal in a tank with other small, non-aggressive species. There should be areas of dense vegetation interspersed with space for swimming. The water should be soft, slightly acid, and preferably filtered through peat. Spawning is preceded by active driving, during which the male may swim obliquely above the female. The actual spawning takes place on the underside of leaves; the eggs are laid in batches of about four. Most of them sink to the bottom and they may have to be protected from the parent fishes. They hatch in 25 to 30 hours and the fry are usually free-swimming about five days later. They can be fed on brine shrimp nauplii.

Below: **Nannostomus eques**♂♂
*A surface-dwelling, peaceful fish that swims in an oblique position.*

Family LEBIASINIDAE
## Nannostomus espei
*Comma Pencilfish*
- **Distribution:** South America: Rio Mazaruni, Guyana
- **Length:** Up to 1.4in (3.5cm)
- **Tank length:** 12in (30cm)
- **Diet:** Worms, crustaceans, insects, dried food
- **Water temperature:** 75 to 79°F (24 to 26°C)
- **Community tank**

This elongated, spindle-shaped fish has a pointed snout, a very small mouth, and an adipose fin. The caudal fin is deeply forked with both lobes pointed. The male is more slender than the female. It is characteristic of the species to swim in a slightly oblique position with the head up. The general coloration is pale gray-brown; the back is a delicate olive and the underparts are silvery. The flanks are marked by a golden longitudinal band that runs from the snout across the eye to the root of the caudal fin. In the head region this golden band is accompanied below by a shorter dark marking that runs over the gill cover to the pectoral fin area. However, the most striking features of the pattern are the four short, dark oblique bars on the

**A practical reminder**
Plants not only look nice, but also provide shelter and breeding sites for fishes. Many water plants can be easily propagated by cuttings, which root quickly when they are planted in the aquarium gravel.

Family LEBIASINIDAE

# Nannostomus trifasciatus
*Three-banded Pencilfish*

- **Distribution:** South America: Guyana, central Amazon, Rio Negro
- **Length:** Up to 2.4in (6cm)
- **Tank length:** 12in (30cm)
- **Diet:** Worms, crustaceans, insects, dried food
- **Water temperature:** 72 to 79°F (22 to 26°C)
- **Community tank**

The Three-banded Pencilfish is an elongated, spindle-shaped fish with slight lateral compression. It has a pointed snout and a protruding upper jaw. The adipose fin is either very small or lacking. The male is slender with a rounded edge to the anal fin; the female has a more convex belly profile and a truncated or slightly concave edge to the anal fin. The back is olive and the flanks and

Left: **Nannostomus trifasciatus**
*The three longitudinal stripes are replaced at night by broad bars.*

underparts are silvery-white. There are three dark longitudinal markings. The first and uppermost mark is a narrow band from the upper edge of the eye to the caudal peduncle; the second and most prominent is a broad band running from the snout across the eye to the root of the caudal fin; and the third is a short band from the ventral fins to the anal fin. The dorsal, caudal, anal, and ventral fins are red at the base but otherwise colorless. At night these bands fade into scarcely visible blotches.

This rather delicate pencilfish swims in a horizontal position in the upper and middle water layers. It can be kept in a tank with a certain amount of dense vegetation, including fine-leaved plants, and sufficient space for swimming. The water should preferably be soft and slightly acid, possibly with peat filtration or with a little peat in the substrate. Spawning takes place among the plants. In some instances the eggs have been laid on fine-leaved plants such as Java Moss. However, this is not an easy species to breed and it is doubtful if there have been many successful rearings. The newly hatched fry should at first be fed on *Paramecium* and rotifers as they may not be able to take brine shrimp nauplii in the first few days.

lower half of the body and a similar bar on the caudal peduncle. The fins are translucent or very pale red-brown.

This peaceful fish of the upper and middle water layers should be kept in a small shoal with plenty of dense vegetation, leaving an adequate area of open water for swimming. The water must be soft, slightly acid, and possibly filtered through peat. The species has the reputation of being slightly delicate. A sexually mature pair introduced into a breeding tank will usually start to spawn among the plants within a few hours, often producing a total of 50 to 70 eggs. These hatch in 30 to 40 hours and the fry are free-swimming five or six days later. They can be fed initially on brine shrimp nauplii. Growth is rapid and it is not unusual for the fish to reach sexual maturity in six or seven months.

Right: **Nannostomus espei**
*Possibly delicate in an aquarium.*

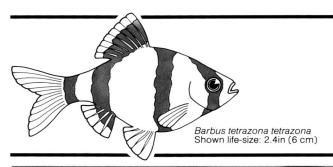

*Barbus tetrazona tetrazona*
Shown life-size: 2.4in (6 cm)

Right: **Pyrrhulina laeta**
*The photograph shows a spawning pair. This species swims and takes most food in the upper layers.*

Family LEBIASINIDAE
## Pyrrhulina laeta
*Half-banded Pyrrhulina*
● **Distribution:** South America: Guyana and Middle Amazon
● **Length:** Up to 3.2in (8cm)
● **Tank length:** 24in (60cm)
● **Diet:** Worms, crustaceans, insects, dried food
● **Water temperature:** 70 to 83°F 21 to 28°C)
● **Community tank**

The body of the Half-banded Pyrrhulina is elongated and very slender, with only slight lateral compression. The back is dark gray or dark brown and the belly whitish or yellowish. The flanks are delicate gray-brown with pale bluish or violet iridescence. Some of the scales have dark edges. A blackish or dark brown band runs from the tip of the snout, across the eye, and obliquely back to end just above the anal fin; this is a characteristic feature of the species. The fins are delicate yellowish or reddish, the dorsal fin having a large dark marking in the middle. The upper lobe of the caudal fin is elongated in the male.

This very attractive fish should be kept in a tank with a dark substrate and a few broad-leaved plants, such as the Amazon Sword Plant (*Echinodorus sp.*). The water should be soft, slightly acid, and filtered through peat. Specimens kept in water that is too hard and lacking in peat may survive but they do not thrive. This species has evidently not yet been bred in an aquarium.

The related Striped Vittata (*Pyrrhulina vittata*) has obliquely positioned blackish markings on the flanks. This is not a particularly difficult fish to breed. The female spawns on the upper surface of a leaf and the eggs hatch in 26 to 30 hours. After a few days the very tiny fry will be free-swimming and can then be fed on rotifers. The female is not very prolific and usually lays about 90 to 100 eggs at a spawning.

Family LEBIASINIDAE
## Nannostomus unifasciatus
*One-lined Pencilfish*
● **Distribution:** South America: middle and lower Amazon, Guyana
● **Length:** Up to 2.8in (7cm)
● **Tank length:** 18in (45cm)
● **Diet:** Worms, crustaceans, insects, dried food
● **Water temperature:** 73 to 81°F (23 to 27°C)
● **Community tank**

Also known as *Poecilobrycon unifasciatus,* this is a very elongated pencilfish with an adipose fin and symmetrical caudal fin lobes. There are two subspecies distinguished by a slightly different color pattern. The edge of the anal fin is rounded in the male but straight-cut in the female. The swimming position is slightly oblique, with the head upward. In *N. unifasciatus unifasciatus* the upperparts are a delicate beige color and the underparts are silvery-white. The yellow-brown or golden-brown flanks are prominently marked with a broad, black longitudinal band that extends from the tip of the snout across the eye to the caudal peduncle and ends in the lower lobe of the caudal fin. It is sometimes accompanied above by a narrow golden streak. The upper lobe of the caudal fin is transparent, and the other fins are all colorless. The front edge of the anal fin appears soft-white in both sexes, and the ventral fins have white tips in the male. The other subspecies, *N. unifasciatus ocellatus,* has the same general coloration and pattern but is distinguished by the lower lobe of the caudal fin. This lobe has a black eye-spot, bordered above with white and below with red. During the night the whole body becomes very dark and two broad transverse bars appear on the flanks.

This is a peaceful pencilfish, which should be kept in a small

Above: **Nannostomus unifasciatus**
*This is the most slender pencilfish. When the fish is healthy the scales on the back have dark edges.*

shoal in a tank with dense vegetation and sufficient space for swimming. The water should be soft, slightly acid, and preferably filtered through peat. There is still some confusion about the breeding of this species in captivity. Some authorities say that spawning takes place among plants, preferably *Hygrophila* and *Ludwigia.* Others suggest that the species has not yet been bred in the aquarium. It may well be that it has been bred, but only rarely.

84

**A practical reminder**
Fast-growing plants are best used for
background decoration and for corner-
fillers; more slow-growing plants are used
as foreground or feature plants. Fine-leaved
plants are often nibbled by herbivorous fishes.

Family LEBIASINIDAE
# Pyrrhulina metae
*Rio Meta Pyrrhulina*
- **Distribution:** South America,
  Peruvian Amazon, Rio Meta
- **Length:** 2.4in (6cm)
- **Tank length:** 24in (60cm)
- **Diet:** Worms, crustaceans,
  insects, dried food
- **Water temperature:** 70 to 83°F
  (21 to 28°C)
- **Community tank**

Also known as *Copella metae,* this
is a very slender species with only
slight lateral compression. The
mouth faces slightly upward. In
the males the back is chestnut-
brown and the underparts are
whitish. The brownish flanks are
marked with a broad, longitudinal
dark band that extends from the
tip of the snout to the caudal
peduncle; it is bordered above by
a cream-colored stripe. At times
the dark band becomes much
paler. Each scale on this part of
the body is marked with a blood-
red spot. The fins are reddish to
brownish, and somewhat
elongated. The females are
generally paler, with shorter fins.
   This very elegant species
should be kept in a tank with a
dark substrate (preferably of peat)
and a number of plants with
broad leaves that grow up to the
water surface; these help to
subdue the light. If it is too bright
the fishes become scared and
their colors do not develop fully.
The water should be soft, slightly
acid, and filtered through peat.
The eggs are laid on the upper
surface of a large leaf, which has
been previously cleaned by the
male. Up to 300 eggs may be laid
and they are fanned by the male
until they hatch after 26 to 30
hours. The very tiny fry lie near the
water surface for a few days.
Once they are free-swimming they
can be fed on rotifers and very
small nauplii. Although spawning
may take place quite readily, the
fry grow rather slowly and they are
not easy to rear.
   The genera *Pyrrhulina, Copeina,
Copella,* and *Nannostomus,*
now placed in the family
Lebiasinidae, were formerly
classified in the family Characidae.

Left: **Pyrrhulina metae**
*The photograph shows a
spawning pair. Some eggs have
already been laid on a leaf.*

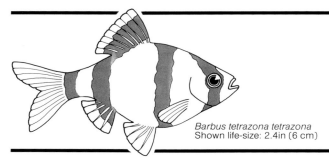

*Barbus tetrazona tetrazona*
Shown life-size: 2.4in (6 cm)

## Family ANOSTOMIDAE
### Anostomus anostomus
*Striped Anostomus*
● **Distribution:** South America:
Amazon, Orinoco, Guyana
● **Length:** Up to 6.3in (16cm)
● **Tank length:** 36in (90cm)
● **Diet:** Worms, crustaceans,
insects, plant matter, dried food
● **Water temperature:** 75 to 81°F
(24 to 27°C)
● **Community tank:** Occasionally
aggressive

Because of its interesting shape
and striking markings, the Striped
Anostomus is a favorite of
aquarists. It is very elongated and
spindle-shaped with a pointed
head, a small mouth that faces
upward, and an adipose fin. The
body is mostly held obliquely with
the head down. The general
coloration is yellow with three dark
longitudinal bands that have finely
toothed edges. The upper band
starts on the head and runs along
the back; the middle band starts at
the mouth, crosses the eye, and
extends back along the flanks to
the root of the tail; the bottom
band runs from the throat, over
the insertion of the pectoral fin, to
the lower part of the caudal
peduncle. The fins are reddish at
the bases, and yellow or colorless
towards the edges.
    The tank for this handsome fish
should have roots to give hiding-
places and a few plants with long

leaves, such as *Echinodorus*.
There should be plenty of open
water for swimming. The water
must be soft, slightly acid, and
filtered through peat—or the
substrate can contain peat. The
fishes are very adept at removing
algae from leaves and the
aquarium glass. The species is not
known to have bred in an
aquarium, but has probably
been bred in a few commercial
hatcheries.
    The related Three-spot
Anostomus, *Anostomus
trimaculatus,* is not as slender as
the Striped Anostomus. The body
is olive-gray marked with three
black blotches—one on the gill
cover, the second in the middle of
the flanks, and the third on the
caudal peduncle.

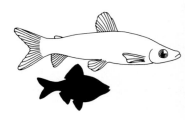

Below: **Anostomus anostomus**
*This handsome fish feeds with the
head pointing downward, often
with the body held vertically. It has
not been bred in an aquarium.*

## Family ANOSTOMIDAE
### Abramites hypselonotus
*Headstander*
● **Distribution:** South America:
lower Amazon, Guyana
● **Length:** Up to 5.5in (14cm)
● **Tank length:** 24in (60cm)
● **Diet:** Worms, crustaceans,
insects, plant food, dried food
● **Water temperature:** 77 to 81°F
(25 to 27°C)
● **Community tank:** Old
individuals are often very
quarrelsome

Sometimes known as *Abramites
microcephalus,* the Headstander
is an elongated, quite tall fish with
strong lateral compression, a very
small head, and a pointed snout.
The height of the body increases
with age and is greatest in old
females. The body is held
obliquely with head downward—
a striking characteristic of the
family. Coloration varies but it is
usually pale to dark brown and
marked with seven to nine broad
dark transverse bars that are
irregular in shape. There is a
bright yellow area in the forehead
region. The adipose fin is bright
yellow in the middle and has a

**A practical reminder**
The plant's crown—the junction between stem and root system—should not be buried when planting. It should be level with, or just above, the surface of the gravel; otherwise the plant will rot away.

Family ANOSTOMIDAE
# Leporinus fasciatus
*Banded Leporinus*
- **Distribution:** Northern and central South America
- **Length:** Up to 12in (30cm)
- **Tank length:** 36in (90cm)
- **Diet:** Worms, crustaceans, insects, plant matter, dried food
- **Water temperature:** 75 to 79°F (24 to 26°C)
- **Community tank:** Sometimes aggressive, particularly in small tanks

The Banded Leporinus is an elegant, elongated and laterally compressed fish. It has large eyes, a cleft upper lip, a small mouth, and an adipose fin. The caudal fin is deeply cleft, the upper lobe

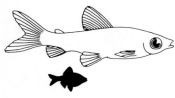

Left: **Leporinus fasciatus**
*The pattern is sometimes variable in this species, but the dark vertical bars are characteristic. The related species* Leporinus striatus *has longitudinal stripes.*

being slightly larger than the lower lobe. The general coloration is yellow, lemon-yellow, or almost golden. It is marked with nine or 10 broad dark transverse bars that gradually fade away towards the underparts. The first bar runs over the forehead and ends at each eye, the second crosses the edge of the gill cover, and the last is immediately in front of the caudal fin. The fins are colorless or delicate gray. Adult males are more slender than females and often have an orange-red or blood-red throat. There are, however, several color varieties, which is not surprising in view of the very wide geographical distribution (Rio Orinoco to Rio de la Plata).

This peaceful fish lives mainly in the lower water layers and has a taste for soft vegetation. In an aquarium the vegetarian part of its diet can include lettuce, boiled spinach, and soaked oat flakes. Like other members of the family Anostomidae, it swims in an oblique, head down position. This fish is a keen jumper so it should be kept in a tank with a good lid. Some rocks and roots and a few plants with tough leaves should also be included. The water must be soft, slightly acid, and filtered through peat. This species, like many other members of the genus *Leporinus*, has not yet been bred in captivity.

broad black border. The fins are generally yellow, the bases of the dorsal and anal fins being dark. The iris of the eye is blood-red above, golden-yellow below.

This rather timid fish dwells in the middle and lower water layers. It comes from shallow water along the banks of rivers, where it moves about in shoals among the vegetation. It should be kept in a tank with a good lid (it is a jumper) with some rocks and roots to provide shelter, a few scattered plants, and a dark substrate. The water must be soft, slightly acid, and preferably filtered through peat. The Headstander relishes plant matter, and in an aquarium this can be provided by lettuce and boiled spinach.

This species has not yet been bred in captivity.

Right: **Abramites hypselonotus**
*A shy species that swims with the head held obliquely downward.*

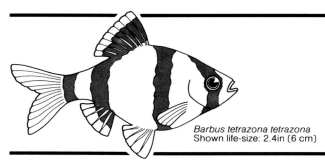
*Barbus tetrazona tetrazona*
Shown life-size: 2.4in (6 cm)

Family ANOSTOMIDAE
## Leporinus striatus
*Striped Leporinus*
● **Distribution:** South America: Upper Amazon, Mato Grosso in Brazil
● **Length:** Up to 10in (25cm)
● **Tank length:** 36in (90cm)
● **Diet:** Worms, crustaceans, insects, plant matter, dried food
● **Water temperature:** 75 to 79°F (24 to 26°C)
● **Community tank**

The Striped Leporinus is an elongated, spindle-shaped fish with little lateral compression, a tapering pointed head and a small mouth. The genus *Leporinus* is characterized by the cleft upper lip or hare-lip (*Leporinus* means 'of a hare'). The eyes are relatively large. The upperparts and flanks are brown and the underparts are yellow. There are four longitudinal stripes. The central dark brown one is always the most prominent and the other stripes are pale brown. The fins are almost colorless and translucent. The anal fin, however, may have a brownish base and the adipose fin is also brown. The sexes show no external differences.

This is an active but peaceful fish that swims mainly in the lower water layers. It should be kept in a tank with a well-fitting lid to discourage jumping. Arrange rocks and roots to provide hiding-places, and scatter some tough-leaved plants since any plants with soft leaves will soon be consumed. The water must be soft, slightly acid, and filtered through peat, or the substrate can be peat. In addition to helping condition the water, a dark substrate of peat enhances both the color and pattern of the fish.

The related *Leporinus frederici* from Guyana to the Amazon is yellowish gray with slight silvery iridescence, and the flanks are marked with three dark blotches: One below the dorsal fin, one in front of the adipose fin, and the third at the rear end of the caudal peduncle.

Neither of these species has been bred in captivity.

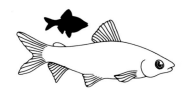

Right: **Leporinus striatus**
*The two middle teeth of the upper jaw protrude, which accentuates the harelike expression of this fish.*

Family CURIMATIDAE
## Chilodus punctatus
*Spotted Headstander*
● **Distribution:** South America: Amazon, Guyana
● **Length:** Up to 4in (10cm)
● **Tank length:** 24in (60cm)
● **Diet:** Worms, crustaceans, insects, plant matter, dried food
● **Water temperature:** 70 to 83°F (21 to 28°C)
● **Community tank**

Formerly placed in the family Anostomidae, this is an elongated, spatulate fish with moderate lateral compression, a small head, and a small mouth with a thick upper lip. When swimming the body is held obliquely, head down. The female is larger than the male. The general coloration is gray or brown with a slightly darker back and silvery-white underparts. Each scale on the flanks has a dark base, giving it a spotted appearance. From the upper lip the spots fuse to form a short horizontal line that crosses the eye and ends just behind it. A narrow longitudinal line may run from below the dorsal fin, along the flanks, to the root of the tail. The fins are all colorless and translucent except for the dorsal fin, which is spotted with a dark brown front edge and tip.

This active fish inhabits the middle and lower water layers. It is peaceful towards other species but may quarrel with members of its own species. It should be kept in a tank with rocks and roots, a few plants (including some that float), and a dark substrate. The water must be soft, slightly acid, and peat-filtered. Spawning takes place on the bottom. The male curls his caudal peduncle under the female as the eggs and sperm are shed. The parent fishes should then be removed from the tank. The fertilized eggs swell to reach a diameter of 0.08in (2mm) and hatch in three or four days. The fry can be fed almost immediately on rotifers and brine shrimp nauplii, but they are not easy to rear.

Right: **Chilodus punctatus**
*The characteristic oblique swimming position adopted by the headstanders may help them to hide among vegetation.*

**A practical reminder**
Rocks form caves and territories for fishes
in addition to providing dramatic decoration.
Be careful to use only rocks that will not
affect the aquarium water chemistry.
Stand large rocks directly on the tank floor

Family CITHARINIDAE

# Distichodus sexfasciatus
*Six-banded Distichodus*
● **Distribution:** Central Africa: middle and lower Congo (Zaire)
● **Length:** Up to 10in (25cm)
● **Tank length:** 36in (90cm)
● **Diet:** Worms, crustaceans, insects, plant matter, dried food
● **Water temperature:** 75 to 81°F (24 to 27°C)
● **Community tank:** May be aggressive. Their large size may intimidate smaller species

This moderately elongated fish with strong lateral compression has large eyes, a relatively small pointed head, an adipose fin, and a forked tail. The fins are all well-developed. The head is blackish but the rest of the body is bright orange with golden or silvery iridescence. The underparts are paler. The flanks are noticeably marked with six or seven dark transverse bars, which may become less prominent in older individuals. The adipose fin is whitish with a dark edge, and the other fins are blood-red. In young individuals the dorsal fin often features dark dots.

In the wild this peaceful fish lives in shoals that swim in the lower water layers of rivers. It can grow quite large and is, of course, suitable for a home aquarium only when relatively young and small. The tank can have rocks and roots both to decorate and to provide hiding-places, but it should contain no plants because this species likes to eat the young shoots. The plant requirements of the diet can be supplied by soaked oat flakes, and boiled lettuce and spinach leaves. The water must be soft and slightly acid. This species has not yet been bred in captivity.

The genus *Distichodus* contains several species, varying in length from 3.2 to 24in (8 to 60cm), and some of them are caught for food in certain parts of Africa.

Below: **Distichodus sexfasciatus**
*Only young specimens of this fish are suitable for the aquarium. Breeding behaviour is not known.*

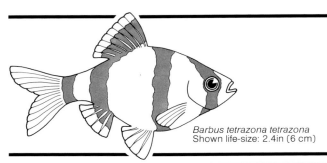

*Barbus tetrazona tetrazona*
Shown life-size: 2.4in (6 cm)

Family CITHARINIDAE

## Nannaethiops unitaeniatus

*One-striped African Characin*

- **Distribution:** Tropical West Africa to the White Nile
- **Length:** Up to 2.6in (6.5cm)
- **Tank length:** 24in (60cm)
- **Diet:** Worms, crustaceans, insects, dried food
- **Water temperature:** 73 to 79°F (23 to 26°C)
- **Community tank**

The One-striped African Characin is elongated with moderate lateral compression, a small mouth, a deeply forked caudal fin, and a rather large adipose fin. The upperparts are brownish and the underparts yellowish white; they all show silvery iridescence. A narrow dark longitudinal band runs from the mouth across the eye to the root of the caudal fin. This band is bordered above by an iridescent golden line. The fins are yellowish to pale green, and the first rays of the dorsal fin are black. The larger females have duller coloration than the males. At spawning time the front part of the dorsal fin and the upper lobe of the caudal fin become blood-red in the male.

This is a peace-loving but quite active fish that lives mostly in the upper and middle water layers. It can be kept in a tank with a sandy substrate and a few areas of vegetation, leaving sufficient space for swimming. The water should be soft, slightly acid, and filtered through peat. If possible, the tank should be positioned so that it receives a certain amount of sunshine, preferably in the morning, as this stimulates spawning. This is a very productive species. The eggs are laid at random among the plants or in the open water. They will be attacked by the parent fishes, which should therefore be removed from the tank as soon as spawning has ceased. At temperatures of 77 to 79°F (25 to 26°C) the eggs hatch in 26 to 32 hours. The fry live on the contents of the yolk-sac for about five days and are then free-swimming and ready for rotifers and small nauplii.

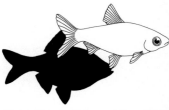

Right: **Nannaethiops unitaeniatus** ♀
*The only species of its genus, this fish is ideal for a community tank.*

**A practical reminder**
Gravel size should not be too fine or too coarse; 0.125in (3mm) is about right. A gravel depth of at least 2 to 3in (5 to 7.5cm) is needed for good plant growth. Fragments of smashed rock can be used to 'color match' the gravel.

# Phago maculatus
*Pike Characin*
- **Distribution:** Tropical West Africa
- **Length:** Up to 6in (15cm)
- **Tank length:** 24in (60cm)
- **Diet:** Large insects, fish
- **Water temperature:** 79 to 83°F (26 to 28°C)
- **Species tank**

This elongated, pikelike fish has a flat forehead and little lateral compression. The mouth is deeply cleft with beaklike jaws. Each jaw has two rows of teeth; the upper jaw moves upwards. The fins are relatively small. The caudal fin is deeply forked and the adipose fin is very small. The upperparts are chestnut-brown to dark brown, and the belly is very

Left: **Phago maculatus**
*Although not suitable for a beginner, this fish provides a rewarding challenge for the serious aquarist.*

pale yellow. The flanks are yellow-brown or reddish brown with several thin brown transverse bars. The fins are yellowish. The dorsal and caudal fins have black longitudinal bands, usually two on the dorsal and three or four on the caudal.

This predatory fish must be kept away from smaller fishes, it is said to swim with lightning speed out of its hiding-place to bite off the fins of larger fishes. It should be kept in a tank with subdued lighting and plenty of vegetation to provide cover as it lies in wait for prey. The composition of the water is not critical. The species has not yet been bred in captivity.

The closely related species *Phago loricatus* is an even more slender fish that comes mainly from the Niger Basin. It has a dark brown back and yellowish white underparts. The flanks are reddish brown with two or three dark longitudinal bands, of which the central one is the broadest. These bands are separated by narrow golden-yellow lines. The fins are similar to those of *P. maculatus* but the central rays of the caudal fin have a black wedge-shaped marking. And like *P. maculatus*, *P. loricatus* has not yet been bred in captivity.

# Neolebias ansorgei
*African Redfin*
- **Distribution:** Central Africa
- **Length:** Up to 1.4in (3.5cm)
- **Tank length:** 24in (60cm)
- **Diet:** Worms, crustaceans, insects, dried food
- **Water temperature:** 73 to 83°F (23 to 28°C)
- **Species tank**

The African Redfin, a relatively short fish with little lateral compression, has no adipose fin. The caudal fin is slightly forked, and the dorsal and anal fins are relatively short. The back is brownish green and the underparts are yellowish with iridescent grayish green or blue-brassy iridescence. The flanks are green and are marked with a broad grass-green to moss-green longitudinal band. There is a narrow black longitudinal bar on the caudal peduncle. The dorsal, caudal, and ventral fins are reddish. At spawning time the fins of the male, except the pectoral fins, become blood-red. The females have a more rounded belly, and just before spawning the eggs can be seen in the body cavity when the fish is viewed in transmitted light.

This is a peaceful fish that swims in the lower water layers and can be kept in a small shoal.

The tank should have some large rocks, areas of dense vegetation around the edges, and a sandy substrate. If kept in a community tank, this species will retreat into the vegetation and its colors will become much paler. The water should be soft. Spawning is preceded by a period of driving, during which the male tries to coax the female into the vegetation. The male and female come together side by side very briefly and the sperm and eggs are shed. The female may lay 50 to 60 eggs per day, in batches of five to 10. This may go on for two to four days, giving a total of about 200 eggs. The eggs hatch in about 40 hours and the fry usually lie on the bottom for four or five days. They can then be fed on infusorians and very small sieved nauplii. After eight days they can be given brine shrimp nauplii. However, they are not easy to rear.

Right: **Neolebias ansorgei**
*After spawning, the male has been seen to use his tail to flick the fertilized eggs in among the plants.*

# THE CARPS AND BARBS

Above: *Barbus nigrofasciatus,* a prolific fish
from the fresh waters of Sri Lanka.
Right: A quiet backwater in Sri Lanka, the type
of habitat in which many barbs live.

*This very large family of fishes includes about 1,250 species distributed throughout Europe, Africa, Asia, North America, and northern Central America, almost exclusively in fresh waters. The body is typically elongated and torpedo-shaped with the dorsal and ventral profiles equally convex. The jaws have no teeth, but there are rows of teeth in the pharynx, which are used to grind up the food. The number, shape, and position of these teeth are used by ichthyologists to distinguish species that are otherwise very similar. In many cyprinids, often known colloquially as carps and barbs, there are one or two pairs of barbels at the corners of the mouth; but there is never an adipose fin. There are usually scales on the body but not on the head.*

*Most cyprinid species live in standing or slow-flowing warm waters, although a few have become adapted to living in colder, fast-flowing waters. Almost all species live in shoals, particularly when young. Many feed on small invertebrates or solely on plants, but the majority are omnivorous, a fact that helps the aquarist in his task of supplying a suitable diet.*

*Most cyprinids spawn at random above or among plants, and the small eggs sink and adhere to the leaves. They usually hatch in a few days and the fry then hang vertically from plants or other objects, while consuming the contents of the yolk-sac. Other species lay their eggs on the bottom. Only a few species practice any kind of brood protection. Spawnings of several thousand eggs are not uncommon.*

*Many of the small, attractive barbs from tropical and subtropical waters are kept in the aquarium, where they are undemanding and not at all difficult to breed. In temperate regions some members of the family, such as the Common Carp (Cyprinus carpio), are used as human food, and are also kept and bred in outside ponds or, more rarely, in cold-water aquarium tanks.*

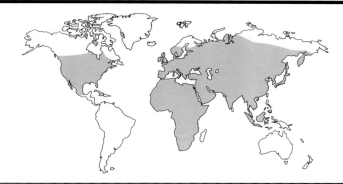

Left: Like the catfishes, the members of the family Cyprinidae are found in all continents except Australia. They do not occur in South America, which is the home of so many characins and catfishes. Unlike many of the characins, which require special types of water, the carps and barbs are most undemanding in this respect. Perhaps this accounts for their wide geographical distribution. Many are ideal for beginners.

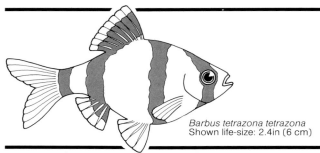

*Barbus tetrazona tetrazona*
Shown life-size: 2.4in (6 cm)

Family CYPRINIDAE

# Barbus arulius
*Arulius Barb*

- **Distribution:** Southern and southeastern India
- **Length:** Up to 4.7in (12cm)
- **Tank length:** 36in (90cm)
- **Diet:** Worms, crustaceans, insects, plant matter, dried food
- **Water temperature:** 73 to 79°F (23 to 26°C)
- **Community tank:** May be too active for smaller varieties, such as characins.

Arulius is a hardy barb that swims mostly in the middle and lower water layers. Its body is elongated and moderately compressed

laterally, and a pair of fairly long barbels appears on the upper jaw. The general coloration is greenish to reddish with silvery or violet iridescence, the scales being marked with several very small shiny dots. The gill cover has an iridescent green spot. The main pattern on the flanks consists of dark blue vertical markings, the most distinct being below the front of the dorsal fin, just above the anal fin, and on the caudal peduncle. The iris of the eye is dark and marked with iridescent green dots. In mature males the rays of the dorsal fin are elongated, but in females they are quite short. The anal and caudal

fins are yellowish or reddish yellow with a red border.

The tank for this species should have clumps of plants with tough leaves—this may prevent the fishes from nibbling them. The substrate should be soft to allow them to dig. Adult fishes will usually tolerate medium-hard water, but for breeding the water should be soft.

For spawning, a tank containing 8 gallons (30 liters) of water should be quite sufficient. The females are usually put in the breeding tank a day or two before the males are introduced, in the evening. After intense driving, spawning takes place. The eggs must then be

Above: **Barbus arulius**
*This barb is not very prolific in the aquarium; a brood of 100 young would be a good result.*

protected from the voracious parent fishes. The eggs hatch in about 25 hours; the fry are free-swimming about two days later and ready to feed on tiny live food.

94

## A practical reminder

Coarse gravel may trap uneaten food where it will rot and cause pollution; and the water flow through the biological filter will be too fast. But very fine gravel will impede filter water flow and plant root growth.

Family CYPRINIDAE

# Barbus chola

*Swamp Barb*

- **Distribution:** Eastern India and Burma
- **Length:** Up to 6in (15cm)
- **Tank length:** 36in (90cm)
- **Diet:** Worms, crustaceans, insects, plant matter, dried food
- **Water temperature:** 72 to 77°F (22 to 25°C)
- **Community tank:** May be too large for smaller tankmates

Another hardy shoaling barb, Swamp Barb has a rather stocky body and a single pair of relatively short barbels on the upper jaw. Its back is olive-green, its flanks are yellowish with silvery iridescence, and the belly is whitish. On the gill cover there is an ill-defined golden-yellow marking; and the caudal peduncle has a black spot, which may be surrounded by a golden area. The eye is a brilliant orange or red. The dorsal fin is yellowish or orange, sometimes with brown dots in older specimens. The other fins are pale yellowish, possibly slightly reddish in the smaller males.

This is a peaceful fish that mostly swims in the middle and lower water layers. The tank should have a soft substrate, some vegetation around the edges, and a few separate clumps of plants with tough leaves to curb the barb's nibbling tendency. Adults are not fussy about the water and will do well in medium-hard water. For breeding, however, the water should be soft. Spawning takes place after a period of courtship, the female laying eggs at random, usually among the plants. The Swamp Barb is a remarkably hardy fish and has been known to spend the winter in water as low as 62 to 68°F (17 to 20°C).

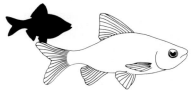

Below: **Barbus chola**
*In the wild this barb is quite common in rice fields. In an aquarium it is hardy and prolific.*

Family CYPRINIDAE

# Barbus bariloides

*Orange Barb*

- **Distribution:** Southern Africa: Angola, Zimbabwe
- **Length:** Up to 2in (5cm)
- **Tank length:** 18in (45cm)
- **Diet:** Worms, crustaceans, insects, plant matter, dried food
- **Water temperature:** 73 to 79°F (23 to 26°C)
- **Community tank**

An attractive shoaling barb, Orange Barb lives mainly in the middle and lower water layers. Its body is elongated, with a distinctly arched back and a relatively long caudal peduncle. There is a pair of quite long barbels at the front of the upper jaw. The general coloration is orange to reddish, becoming more brownish on the back and silvery on the belly. The flanks are conspicuously marked with 12 to 16 transverse dark bars. The iris is bright red. In general, the fins are reddish or yellowish; the front part of the dorsal fin has a large carmine-red marking, which is sometimes not very clearly defined.

A peaceful barb, this fish is not difficult to keep in a tank with clumps of robust vegetation placed around the edges to leave sufficient room for swimming. The substrate should be dark and the lighting subdued. If the lighting is too bright, the fishes become timid and scared. Although the composition of the water is not critical, it is always better to use 'old' or 'mature' water. This means water that has stood in a tank with plants for a few weeks. A portion of the water—about 20 per cent—should be renewed about every month. The species has been bred in the aquarium, although probably not very often.

Left: **Barbus bariloides** ♂(t), ♀(b)
*This is a shy barb that is easily upset by bright lighting levels.*

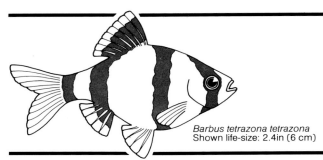

*Barbus tetrazona tetrazona*
Shown life-size: 2.4in (6 cm)

Family CYPRINIDAE

# Barbus conchonius
*Rosy Barb*

- **Distribution:** Northeastern India, particularly Bengal and Assam
- **Length:** Up to 5.5in (14cm)
- **Tank length:** 24in (60cm)
- **Diet:** Worms, crustaceans, insects, plant matter, dried food
- **Water temperature:** 72 to 77°F (22 to 25°C)
- **Community tank:** May be too active for some small characins.

Rosy Barb has been an extremely popular aquarium fish for about 80 years. It is ideal for a beginner. The body is stocky and the female is somewhat stouter than the male. These fishes have no barbels. The back is iridescent olive-green and the belly is silvery, sometimes with a reddish tinge. The flanks are reddish with silvery iridescence, becoming brilliant red around spawning time. The female is not as brightly colored as the male. At the front end of the caudal peduncle there is a black marking usually with a yellow border. In the male the fins are pink and the tip of the dorsal fin is black. In the female the fins are almost colorless, the dorsal fin showing only a darkish tinge.

This is a most undemanding fish, and can be kept in a tank with rather subdued lighting, conveniently achieved by having a few floating plants at the surface. The substrate should be soft sand because the fishes like to burrow. Adult Rosy Barbs do well in medium-hard water, but for breeding the water should be soft, neutral, and preferably mature. After a very vigorous driving the pair spawn among the plants. The eggs must be protected by the aquarist immediately to prevent them from being eaten by the parents. Some aquarists do this by removing the parents from the tank. The eggs hatch in about 24 hours and the fry live for a few days on the contents of the yolk-sac before becoming free-swimming. They should then be fed on rotifers and small nauplii.

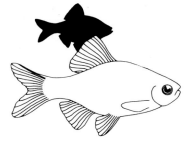

Below: **Barbus conchonius**
*This is one of the best species for a beginner, but if spawning takes place you must try to prevent it from eating the eggs.*

**A practical reminder**
Wood is a favorite aquarium decoration. Any wood used must be long dead and should be boiled and sealed before being put into the tank. A plate bolted to the wood and buried in the gravel will prevent floating.

## Barbus cumingi
*Cuming's Barb*

- **Distribution:** Sri Lanka
- **Length:** Up to 2in (5cm)
- **Tank length:** 18in (45cm)
- **Diet:** Worms, insects, crustaceans, plant matter, dried food
- **Water temperature:** 77 to 81°F (25 to 27°C)
- **Community tank**

Cuming's Barb is a relatively tall-bodied barb with no barbels. The back is grayish brown, but the general coloration of the flanks is grayish white with some silvery or golden iridescence, each scale having a dark edge. The eye is an iridescent golden color. Just behind the gill cover there is a dark (sometimes black) vertical bar, which extends down to the rear end of the pectoral fins. There is a similar dark marking on the caudal peduncle. The dorsal and ventral fins are orange, the anal and caudal fins pale yellow, and the pectoral fins colorless. The fins of the slightly larger female are not as brightly colored.

This is an active barb from the forest streams in the mountains of Sri Lanka. In an aquarium it usually swims in the middle and lower water layers. The tank should have a soft substrate and some tough-leaved plants arranged to leave sufficient open water for swimming. The composition of the water is not critical for adults, but breeding should be attempted only in a tank with soft, neutral water. The parents perform an active courtship drive before spawning. The eggs, usually laid among vegetation, hatch in about 25 hours. The fry should be free-swimming in a few days and can be fed at first on rotifers.

Below: **Barbus cumingi**
*An active fish best kept in a shoal.*

## Barbus everetti
*Clown Barb, Everett's Barb*

- **Distribution:** Singapore and Borneo
- **Length:** Up to 6in (15cm)
- **Tank length:** 36in (90cm)
- **Diet:** Worms, crustaceans, insects, plant matter, dried food
- **Water temperature:** 77 to 81°F (25 to 27°C)
- **Community tank:** Very active. May be quarrelsome with smaller species

This is a hardy Asiatic barb that has two pairs of barbels. Clown Barb's back is brownish or red-brown, sometimes with an orange tinge, and the belly is almost white. The flanks are reddish with golden or silvery iridescence and marked with somewhat irregular black or blue-gray vertical markings. Unlike certain related species, this barb has no dark stripe running through the eye. The fins are mostly a pale reddish color and may occasionally have dark tips. The slightly larger and stouter females are not as colorful as the males.

This is a lively barb living in the lower water layers and best kept in a small shoal. The tank should have marginal vegetation and a soft substrate, but the plants should have tough leaves, as this fish is another plant nibbler. The water should be soft.

The Clown Barb is not always easy to breed. Experience has shown that it is best to keep the prospective breeding fishes apart for about three weeks. During this time give them a varied and plentiful diet of white worms, insect larvae, and greens such as lettuce. They spawn in the sunshine of early morning, preferably among fine-leaved plants, such as Milfoil (*Myriophyllum*).

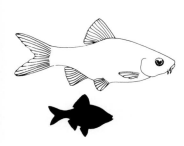

Left: **Barbus everetti**
*A relatively large fish for an aquarium, this species has two pairs of barbels and thrives best when kept in a small shoal. It will nibble any soft-leaved tank plants.*

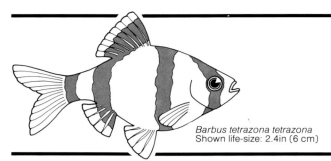
*Barbus tetrazona tetrazona*
Shown life-size: 2.4in (6 cm)

## Family CYPRINIDAE
## Barbus fasciatus
*Striped Barb*
- **Distribution:** Malaya, Sumatra, Borneo
- **Length:** Up to 2.4in (6cm)
- **Tank length:** 24in (60cm)
- **Diet:** Worms, crustaceans, insects, plant matter, dried food
- **Water temperature:** 72 to 79°F (22 to 26°C)
- **Community tank**

A species with the typical barb shape and a laterally compressed body, Striped Barb has two pairs of barbels. Its back is greenish with a few irregular black markings; the flanks are red, with a violet sheen that becomes paler ventrally so that the belly is almost white. The flanks are marked with four or five dark blue longitudinal stripes that extend back from the rear end of the gill cover to the base of the caudal fin. The dorsal and anal fins are red or sometimes pale yellow, but the other fins are nearly colorless. The female is slightly larger than the male, and has paler coloration and a more rounded belly profile.

This is a very active barb and is not difficult to keep in a domestic aquarium. The tank should have a soft substrate to allow for burrowing, and the plants should be mostly installed along the back and sides to leave plenty of open water for swimming. For breeding the temperature should be 81 to 83°F (27 to 28°C) and the water preferably soft. After the usual driving the female lays eggs at random among the vegetation. These hatch and can be reared in the same way as fry of the Rosy Barb.

There is a very similar species known as the Lined Barb *(Barbus lineatus),* which comes from southern Malaya. It has almost the same pattern on the flanks, but it has no barbels.

Right: **Barbus fasciatus**
*This is an active barb that thrives in an aquarium. It needs plenty of open water for swimming.*

## Family CYPRINIDAE
## Barbus gelius
*Golden Dwarf Barb*
- **Distribution:** India, Bengal, and Assam
- **Length:** Up to 1.6in (4cm)
- **Tank length:** 18in (45cm)
- **Diet:** Small crustaceans and insects, dried food
- **Water temperature:** 68 to 72°F (20 to 22°C)
- **Community tank**

A somewhat transparent small barb, the female Golden Dwarf Barb is stouter than the male and has no barbels. Backs of both sexes are olive-green to brownish; the underparts are white with a silvery sheen. The flanks are iridescent gold with irregular dark blotches. In addition there is a reddish gold longitudinal stripe that extends back to the caudal peduncle, where it widens into a shiny coppery marking. The eye is pale green. The caudal fin is pale red; the pectoral fins are colorless and the other fins yellowish.

In the wild this tiny but hardy barb lives in standing and slow-flowing waters. It is one of the most undemanding aquarium fishes and can even be kept at temperatures as low as 61 to 64°F (16 to 18°C). For breeding, the water temperature should not exceed 70 to 72°F (21 to 22°C). The eggs are laid among the plants, to which they adhere, and hatch in about 24 hours. For a few days the tiny fry live on the contents of the yolk-sac and then swim free. At this point they can be fed on rotifers and nauplii, and possibly a little finely powdered dried food. The parents do not eat their own eggs, but it is probably best to remove them from the tank anyway as soon as they have finished spawning.

Below: **Barbus gelius**
*This is an excellent barb for a beginner or for anyone without sufficient space for a large tank. The markings on the flanks are rather variable between individuals.*

**A practical reminder**
Of the artificial aquarium decorations available, molded logs are the most natural looking. Sunken galleons, mermaids, and opening shells are quite out of place. Other pre-cast 'rocks' may be toxic.

Family CYPRINIDAE
# Barbus lateristriga
*Spanner Barb*
- **Distribution:** Thailand, Malaysia, Indonesia
- **Length:** Up to 7in (18cm)
- **Tank length:** 36in (90cm)
- **Diet:** Worms, crustaceans, insects, plant matter, dried food
- **Water temperature:** 66 to 77°F (19 to 25°C)
- **Community tank:** May be too active for smaller species

This handsome barb would be too large for a home aquarium if it were to reach the maximum size of Spanner Barbs grown in the wild. In practice, however, this does not happen, and a good aquarium specimen would be 2.4 to 4in (6 to 10cm) long. The body of a young fish is slender, but with increasing age it becomes deeper and dorsally more arched; there are two pairs of barbels.

The back is greenish orange, the belly orange, and the flanks are yellowish brown with golden iridescence. On the front of the body there are two prominent blue-black markings, which straddle the back and extend down each flank to end in a tapered point. A black longitudinal bar extends from below the dorsal fin to the caudal peduncle and onto the caudal fin. The fins are red, more noticeably so in the male. In general, however, the colors and patterns of this species vary greatly, but this is not surprising in view of its wide geographical distribution.

Breeding is not difficult. After a period of vigorous driving,

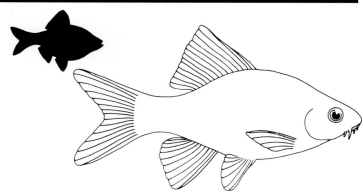

spawning takes place among the plants. As soon as this has finished, the parent fishes should be removed from the tank because they sometimes eat their own eggs. Although the composition of the water is not critical for the parents, it is probably best to use soft water for successful breeding.

Below: **Barbus lateristriga**
*Half-grown specimens are more suitable; the pattern fades with age.*

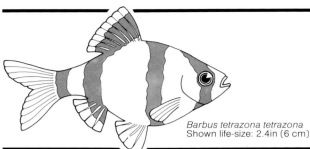

*Barbus tetrazona tetrazona*
Shown life-size: 2.4in (6 cm)

Family CYPRINIDAE
# Barbus nigrofasciatus
*Black Ruby, Purple-headed Barb*

- **Distribution:** Sri Lanka
- **Length:** Up to 2.4in (6cm), possibly more
- **Tank length:** 36in (90cm)
- **Diet:** Worms, insects, crustaceans, plant matter, dried food
- **Water temperature:** 72 to 75°F (22 to 24°C)
- **Community tank:** Tank size often affects behavior; a larger tank usually results in less aggression

This is a hardy, deep-bodied fish without barbels, and it is very suitable for a beginner. In both sexes the head of Black Ruby is a beautiful crimson color. The flanks are mainly yellowish gray marked with three or four dark transverse bars. The edges of the scales are silvery, so that together they form rows of glistening dots. In males the dorsal fin is black, the anal fin is dark red, and the ventral fins are reddish. In females the colors are much paler, and the fins are yellowish without dark edges.

This is one of the most accommodating barbs for an aquarist. The tank should have a soft substrate and marginal vegetation arranged to leave sufficient open water for swimming. A few floating plants will help to subdue the light and this will benefit the fishes. For decorative purposes there can be a few isolated plants with tough leaves.

At spawning time the males assume a dramatic color change. The whole of the front part of the body becomes deep purplish red, the back velvety green, the caudal peduncle and the caudal fin almost black, and the rows of dots on the flanks green. For spawning the temperature of the water should be raised to 77 to 83°F (25 to 28°C). The female lays a large number of eggs, usually in the morning sunshine, and these hatch in about 25 hours.

Right: **Barbus nigrofasciatus**
*For spawning, many aquarists recommend that the tank should have plants with feathery leaves, to which the eggs will adhere. It is important to remember, however, that the parents are spawn-eaters.*

**A practical reminder**
Tap water is quite suitable for the majority of fishes providing the chlorine in it is neutralized by dechlorinators before use. Aeration will also help to drive out chlorine.

Family CYPRINIDAE
## Barbus oligolepis
*Island Barb, Checker Barb*
- **Distribution:** Sumatra
- **Length:** Up to 2in (5cm)
- **Tank length:** 18in (45cm)
- **Diet:** Worms, small crustaceans, insects, plant matter, dried food
- **Water temperature:** 72 to 77°F (22 to 25°C)
- **Community tank**

The name Island Barb refers to the fact that this species was originally found only on the island of Sumatra. It was introduced into the aquarium world about 1925. The body has the typical barb shape, and there is a single pair of small barbels at the corners of the mouth. There may also be a pair of very small barbels on the snout.

The general coloration is a delicate ocher to red-brown, the back somewhat darker with bluish iridescence, the belly yellow; the flanks have a mother-of-pearl sheen. The scales on the flanks each have a broad black edge and a bluish spot at the base. In males the dorsal and anal fins are reddish, with dark edges. In females these fins are yellowish, without dark edges. It is sometimes known as the Checker Barb because the pattern formed by the scales on the flanks resembles a checkerboard. This barb should be kept in a tank with a soft substrate and a reasonable amount of vegetation, mainly around the edges. The water composition is not critical for adults, but it should be mature and not straight from the tap. For

Above: **Barbus oligolepis** ♀
*This attractive barb is best kept in a shoal. It is easy to breed.*

breeding, which presents no special problems, the water should preferably be on the soft side. Spawning takes place in the same way as the Black Ruby.

Family CYPRINIDAE
## Barbus phutunio
*Dwarf Barb, Pygmy Barb*
- **Distribution:** Eastern India and Sri Lanka
- **Length:** Up to 3.2in (8cm)
- **Tank length:** 12in (30cm)
- **Diet:** Worms, crustaceans, insects, plant matter, dried food
- **Water temperature:** 70 to 77°F (21 to 25°C)
- **Community tank**

This is another of the very small barbs. The body, which has the typical barb shape, becomes deeper with increasing age. There are no barbels. The back is brownish green or grayish green, and the belly white with a silvery sheen. The flanks are also silvery, but with bluish or violet iridescence. The scales are relatively large and each has a dark base and a pale glistening edge. When the fish is excited, five blue transverse bars can be seen on the flanks, but these later fade leaving usually three dark blotches. The coloration is less pronounced in the stouter female. The pectoral fins are colorless but the other fins are yellowish to red. In the male an oblique dark bar often runs across the dorsal fin.

This is a peaceable, hardy barb that lives mostly in the middle water layers. It should be kept in a small shoal, in a tank with marginal vegetation and a good

Above: **Barbus phutunio** ♂
*For best results a breeding pair of this species needs a separate tank.*

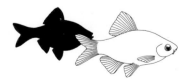

space in the center for swimming. The water should be soft. This is not a very prolific species, and a spawning of 60 to 80 eggs at a time can be regarded as successful. The fry can be reared in the usual way in a planted breeding tank, but they often turn out to be rather delicate.

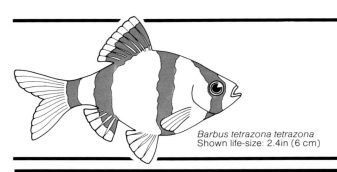

*Barbus tetrazona tetrazona*
Shown life-size: 2.4in (6 cm)

Family CYPRINIDAE

## Barbus schwanenfeldi
*Schwanenfeld's Barb, Tinfoil Barb*

- **Distribution:** Thailand, Malaysia, Indonesia
- **Length:** Up to 14in (35cm), may grow larger
- **Tank length:** 36in (90cm)
- **Diet:** Worms, crustaceans, insects, plant matter, dried food
- **Water temperature:** 68 to 77°F (20 to 25°C)
- **Community tank:** Keep with larger species only

This elegant barb has a compressed body with a profile that looks like an elongated lozenge. It has two pairs of barbels on the upper jaw. The back, flanks and underside are all silvery, sometimes with yellow or bluish iridescence. This brilliant coloration has earned the fish its other common name, Tinfoil Barb. The iris of the eye is golden. The dorsal fin is bright red with a dark marking near the tip. A thin dark stripe running along the edge of each lobe marks the red caudal fin. The other fins are paler and usually yellowish or orange. The sexes cannot be distinguished on the basis of coloration.

This is a very active barb, which should be kept in a small shoal. The fishes are only suitable for a home aquarium when they are relatively small, 2.4 to 3.2in (6 to 8cm) in length. Large specimens become somewhat aggressive and may attack and eat smaller species. The tank should be spacious enough to allow for swimming and the substrate should be soft. Like so many other barbs this species is partial to vegetation and will eat aquarium plants. This annoying habit can be prevented, to some extent, by giving Tinfoil Barb plenty of lettuce leaves.

Tinfoil Barb has not yet been bred in captivity.

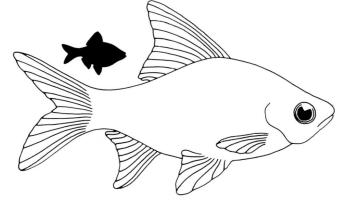

Above: **Barbus schwanenfeldi**
*Small specimens of this barb are suitable for the home aquarium. It needs a good supply of plant food to prevent it from eating the tank vegetation. It grows very rapidly.*

**A practical reminder**
Some fishes require special water conditions whose quality may be checked by the use of inexpensive test kits. Any necessary changes to the water must be introduced gradually to avoid stressing the fishes.

Family CYPRINIDAE

# Barbus semifasciolatus

*Green Barb, China Barb, Half-banded Barb*
- **Distribution:** Southeastern China
- **Length:** Up to 4in (10cm)
- **Tank length:** 24in (60cm)
- **Diet:** Worms, crustaceans, insects, plant matter, dried food
- **Water temperature:** 72 to 77°F (22 to 25°C)
- **Community tank**

The Green Barb is a fairly elongated barb with a slightly arched back, which is more pronounced in old specimens. On the upper jaw at the corners of the mouth is a single pair of very short barbels. The back is brown to reddish brown and the belly is whitish. The flanks, which are greenish to yellow with some iridescence, are usually marked with from five to seven narrow black transverse bars. The scales all have dark edges and the upper part of the iris is blood-red. The dorsal, caudal, and anal fins are brownish red or sometimes brick-red, the pectoral fins are colorless, and the ventral fins are brownish to yellowish.

This is a hardy barb, which should be kept in a small shoal. It swims mainly in the middle and lower water layers. The tank should have a soft substrate and a reasonable amount of vegetation, and should be set up with bright lighting. Although the optimum water temperature is 72 to 77°F (22 to 25°C), an occasional drop to 64 to 68°F (18 to 20°C) will not be harmful. The water should be soft and slightly acid.

For breeding, the tank needs to be at least 24in (60cm) long to allow for the very vigorous courtship behavior. During this time the male circles around the female, pushing her with open mouth and striking her with his tail to drive her in among the plants, where they will spawn. The yellowish eggs hatch in about 25 hours and the fry should be reared in the same way as those of the Rosy Barb.

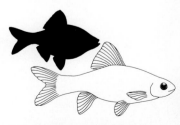

Right: **Barbus semifasciolatus**
*This is a peaceful shoaling fish that will thrive in conditions of relatively low oxygen concentration.*

Family CYPRINIDAE

# Barbus 'Schuberti'

*Golden Barb, Schubert's Barb*
- **Distribution:** Unknown
- **Length:** Up to 2.8in (7cm)
- **Tank length:** 18in (45cm)
- **Diet:** Worms, crustaceans, insects, plant matter, dried food
- **Water temperature:** 68 to 77°F (20 to 25°C)
- **Community tank**

This barb first appeared in the aquarium world several years ago in North America. Apparently nobody knew where the fish came from. It was named 'Schuberti' without giving it a proper description in a recognized scientific journal. The name 'Schuberti' is therefore invalid and can only be regarded as a nickname. This fish is now thought to be a yellow form of *Barbus semifasciolatus*.

Notwithstanding such an illegitimate origin, Golden Barb is quite attractive, and perfectly hardy in the aquarium. The ground coloration is golden-yellow, the underparts being more silvery. Just below the dorsal fin there is a single black blotch, and the base of the tail also has distinct very dark markings. Old specimens sometimes have small black spots on the flanks. The fins are reddish. The females are less colorful but more robust than the males.

This barb should be kept in a small shoal, which will swim in the middle and lower water layers. The tank can be furnished in exactly the same way as for the Green Barb, described on this page. The fish spawns very freely; some aquarists, in fact, find that it spawns even more readily than the Green Barb.

Below: **Barbus 'Schuberti'**
*Although of unclear origin, this fish is a perfect aquarium subject. It is hardy and breeds very easily.*

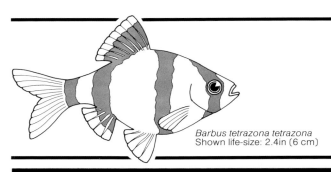

*Barbus tetrazona tetrazona*
Shown life-size: 2.4in (6 cm)

Family CYPRINIDAE
# Barbus ticto stoliczkae
*Stoliczka's Barb*
- **Distribution:** Southern Burma, in the lower Irrawaddy River
- **Length:** Up to 2.4in (6cm)
- **Tank length:** 24in (60cm)
- **Diet:** Worms, crustaceans, insects, plant matter, dried food
- **Water temperature:** 68 to 77°F (20 to 25°C)
- **Community tank**

This small deep-bodied barb with no barbels is often known as *Barbus stoliczkanus,* but here it is treated as a subspecies of *B. ticto.*

The back is dark olive-green, sometimes moss-green, and the belly whitish. The flanks are silvery with yellowish to bluish iridescence, depending upon the angle of the light, and the scales have dark edges. There are two large dark markings, one just behind the gill cover, the other at the start of the caudal peduncle. In the male the dorsal fin is reddish at the base and black above, the base of the caudal fin is yellowish, the anal and ventral fins are reddish, and the pectoral fins are colorless. The female has

Above: **Barbus ticto stoliczkae**
*In this popular aquarium fish the mouth faces slightly upward. It differs from* Barbus ticto ticto *in the arrangement of the scales on the flanks. It is easy to breed.*

colorless fins except for the dorsal fin, which is a delicate red.

This is a popular shoaling fish, mostly swimming in the middle and lower water layers. It requires a tank with a soft bottom but the composition of the water is not critical. For breeding the temperature range should be 75 to 79°F (24 to 26°C). The eggs hatch in 25 to 30 hours.

The related and very similar Two-spot Barb *(Barbus ticto ticto)* comes from India and Sri Lanka. It can be kept in water as cool as 61°F (16°C).

**A practical reminder**
Fishes from rivers in tropical rain forests are used to soft water. Cichlids from African Lakes like very hard water. But both can be gradually acclimatized to live happily in normal tap water.

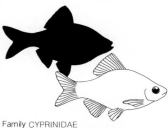

Left: **Barbus tetrazona tetrazona**
*This is the most widespread of the barbs with dark vertical bars. When spawning, the male's normal bright colors turn noticeably paler.*

## Barbus tetrazona tetrazona
*Sumatran Barb, Tiger Barb*
● **Distribution:** Sumatra and Borneo
● **Length:** Up to 2.4in (6cm)
● **Tank length:** 24in (60cm)
● **Diet:** Worms, small crustaceans, plant matter, dried food
● **Water temperature:** 68 to 77°F (20 to 25°C)
● **Community tank:** May be quarrelsome with other community species; a larger tank often reduces aggression

One of the more colorful barbs and one particularly suitable for a beginner is the Sumatran or Tiger Barb. The body is relatively high-backed and the mouth area has no barbels. The back is brown or brownish red and the belly is whitish. The flanks are silvery with reddish or yellowish iridescence and the scales, particularly those on the upper part of the body, have dark edges. The characteristic pattern on the flanks consists of four broad, black, transverse bars, from which the common name Tiger Barb is derived. The first bar runs through the eye and the second is just in front of the dorsal fin. The third bar is at the back of the dorsal fin and extends onto the base of this fin and the anal fin. The fourth bar is at the base of the tail. The outer parts of the dorsal and anal fins are blood-red.

This species should be kept in a small shoal, which will swim about in the middle layers of the water. The tank should have a soft substrate and some vegetation around the edges, with plenty of space left for swimming since this is a very active fish. Medium-hard water can be used but it is preferable to have soft water, especially for the breeding tank. Spawning habits are the same as those of the Green Barb described on page 103.

The Sumatran Barb has a reputation for nibbling the fins of Angelfishes, so it is best to keep the two species apart.

Family CYPRINIDAE
## Barbus tetrazona partipentazona
*Banded Barb*
● **Distribution:** Thailand and Malaysia
● **Length:** Up to 2.4in (6cm)
● **Tank length:** 18in (45cm)
● **Diet:** Worms, insects, small crustaceans, plant matter, dried food
● **Water temperature:** 68 to 79°F (20 to 26°C)
● **Community tank:** May harass smaller species

The body of this subspecies is slightly more slender than that of the Sumatran Barb. The Banded Barb's back is brownish red and the underparts are white. The flanks are silvery with a brilliant yellowish or red sheen, and the scales on the upperparts have dark edges. However, the distinguishing feature of the Banded Barb is the short bar that runs down from the dorsal fin to the middle of the body, giving the flanks a rather incomplete appearance. The fins are more or less the same as those of the Sumatran Barb. Tank conditions should also be similar, but Angelfishes should be excluded to prevent their fins from being nipped.

For breeding it is best to use fishes that are one to two years old. The tank should have soft water and a soft susbtrate. After a short period of driving, during which the female becomes paler, the male coils the rear part of his body (from above) around the rear part of the female. The eggs are then shed with the pair in this position. A female in good condition may produce 600 to 1000 eggs at each spawning and these hatch in 26 to 30 hours. The fry become free-swimming a few days later and can be fed at first on rotifers and brine shrimp nauplii.

Left:
**Barbus tetrazona partipentazona**
*This is a very prolific breeder.*

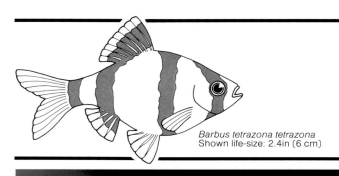

*Barbus tetrazona tetrazona*
Shown life-size: 2.4in (6 cm)

Family CYPRINIDAE

# Brachydanio albolineatus

*Pearl Danio*

- ● **Distribution:** Southeast Asia
- ● **Length:** Up to 2.4in (6cm)
- ● **Tank length:** 18in (45cm)
- ● **Diet:** Worms, small crustaceans, dried food
- ● **Water temperature:** 70 to 77°F (21 to 25°C)
- ● **Community tank:** Very active

Slender and rather elongated, the Pearl Danio is slightly compressed laterally and has two pairs of barbels. The caudal fin is somewhat forked and the anal fin is relatively long. When seen in reflected light the body is iridescent violet or blue, but in

Left: **Brachydanio albolineatus**
*In the wild this is a very active fish and the same liveliness is seen in good aquarium specimens. The flanks are beautifully iridescent.*

transmitted light it appears green. The belly is pale bluish and the back is darker blue or blue-gray. There is a longitudinal red streak, edged in blue-green, starting in the center of the body and ending on the caudal peduncle. The basal part of the anal fin is red or orange-red, its outer part transparent greenish. The other fins are also translucent green, with a tinge of red. The female is slightly larger, stouter, and less brightly colored than the male.

This peaceable fish was introduced to the aquarium in about 1911. It swims mostly in the upper and middle water layers. Unlike some of the other members of the family Cyprinidae, such as the rather shy Cherry Barb, this species loves sunshine; in fact, it develops the full delicate colors only when kept in sunlight.

The tank should have some vegetation, and a good lid to prevent jumping. The water can be soft or medium-hard, even for breeding. Spawning typically takes place in the morning sunshine and may last some hours. A fully mature female may lay up to 600 eggs and these must be protected from the parents; they hatch in about 24 hours. The fry take several days, usually six or seven, before they are free-swimming and ready to be fed on tiny live food such as rotifers.

**A practical reminder**
Do not worry unduly about the water quality. The chances are that if the fishes survive in your local store's water then they will be at home in yours.

Family CYPRINIDAE

## Barbus titteya
*Cherry Barb*
- **Distribution:** Sri Lanka
- **Length:** Up to 2in (5cm)
- **Tank length:** 18in (45cm)
- **Diet:** Worms, small crustaceans, plant matter, dried food
- **Water temperature:** 73 to 81°F (23 to 27°C)
- **Community tank**

An elegant small barb, the Cherry Barb has a relatively elongated body and one pair of barbels on the upper jaw at the corners of the mouth. The back is chestnut-brown with greenish iridescence. Flanks are silvery with red tones. A dark brown or blue-black stripe

**Left: Barbus titteya**
*This is a beautiful but shy barb. During spawning the parent fishes can be fed on white worms.*

extends from the mouth to the center of the tail base, being broadest in the middle of the body. Above this dark stripe there is a broad iridescent yellow band, which becomes greenish towards the rear. When the fish is excited a double row of dark dots may be discerned below the dark stripe. The iris of the eye is golden-red, and the gill cover is red. The whole body of the male, especially the underparts, becomes an intense red as spawning approaches. The fins are red in the male, yellowish in the female. In general, the coloration of the female is considerably paler than that of the male.

In the wild, Cherry Barbs live in shady streams, so in captivity the tank should be given subdued lighting and marginal vegetation. A few isolated plants with tough leaves will provide shelter. The water should be soft, and for spawning the water temperature should be 79 to 81°F (26 to 27°C). This is not a very prolific fish, the female usually laying 150 to 250 eggs at each spawning. These hatch in about 24 hours, and the fry should be free-swimming a few days later, and ready to feed on rotifers and nauplii. They are timid at first.

Family CYPRINIDAE

## Brachydanio rerio
*Zebra Danio*
- **Distribution:** Eastern India and Bangladesh
- **Length:** Up to 2in (5cm)
- **Tank length:** 12in (30cm)
- **Diet:** Worms, small crustaceans, dried food
- **Water temperature:** 64 to 77°F (18 to 25°C)
- **Community tank**

Zebra Danio is a slender fish with a slightly compressed body and two pairs of barbels. The female, with a more rounded belly profile, is a little larger than the male. The back is brownish olive, the belly whitish. The coloration and pattern of the flanks are quite characteristic.

In males the background color is golden, strikingly marked by four deep blue longitudinal streaks, which extend the whole length of the body from the gill cover to the end of the tail. This pattern is repeated on the anal fin. The dorsal fin is olive with a bluish white border, and the pectoral and ventral fins are colorless. The gill cover has rather indistinct blue markings.

This is a remarkably hardy tropical fish, highly suitable for a

beginner because it has no special requirements. The tank can have a reasonable amount of vegetation, leaving plenty of space in the upper water layers for swimming, and it must have a good lid to prevent the fishes from leaping out. For breeding the tank should have soft or medium-hard water and a few clumps of plants with feathery leaves, such as Milfoil *(Myriophyllum)*. After vigorous driving the male chases the female in among the plants, where spawning takes place. The eggs must be protected from the parents, which are notorious spawn-eaters.

**Below: Brachydanio rerio**
*This is an old favorite, introduced into the aquarium in 1905. For breeding, many aquarists recommend using dark males with shiny gold stripes and white-tipped fins.*

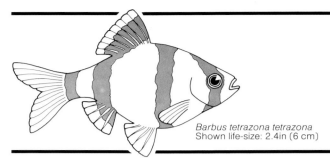

Barbus tetrazona tetrazona
Shown life-size: 2.4in (6 cm)

Family CYPRINIDAE
## Danio aequipinnatus
*Giant Danio*
- **Distribution:** Sri Lanka and west coast of India
- **Length:** Up to 4.7in (12cm), but mature at 2.8in (7cm)
- **Tank length:** 36in (90cm)
- **Diet:** Worms, crustaceans, insects, dried food
- **Water temperature:** 68 to 75°F (20 to 24°C)
- **Community tank:** Very active. May disturb other species

A giant only in relation to the other danios, *Danio aequipinnatus* is a more slender fish than *Danio devario*, and it has one pair of barbels. The body is markedly compressed laterally. The back is grey-green to bluish and the underparts are pale pink. Flanks

have three or four pale blue or indigo bands separated by thin golden-yellow longitudinal stripes. In the male the central blue band runs straight, but in the female it turns upwards at the base of the caudal fin. The gill cover has a bright yellowish green or golden .marking and the iris is iridescent golden. Apart from the pectoral fins, which are colorless, all the other fins are pink or a delicate blue, sometimes with a reddish tinge at their bases. The stouter female is not as brightly colored as the male.

Giant Danio is a very handsome fish and should be kept in a shoal swimming in the upper water layers. The tank should have plants around the edges, leaving sufficient space in the center for swimming. For breeding the

substrate can be fine gravel, which will provide some shelter for the eggs after spawning. This is a prolific species and it is not unusual for the female to lay over 1000 eggs.

The related *Danio regina* from southern Thailand is similar in coloration, but has a blue-back marking behind the gill cover.

Right: **Danio aequipinnatus**
*This striking and undemanding fish is suitable for a community tank with other robust fishes.*

Family CYPRINIDAE
## Danio devario
*Bengal Danio*
- **Distribution:** Pakistan, northern India, Assam, Bangladesh
- **Length:** Up to 4in (10cm)
- **Tank length:** 24in (60cm)
- **Diet:** Worms, small crustaceans, insects, dried food
- **Water temperature:** 68 to 75°F (20 to 24°C)
- **Community tank:** Very active. May distrub smaller species.

This is a stockier fish than the Zebra Danio with a markedly convex belly profile and no barbels. The basic coloration of Bengal Danio varies somewhat, but is usually a pale silvery-green, the back a little darker and the belly silvery-white. Behind the

iridescent green gill cover, the flanks show vertical blue and yellow streaks. The rear part of the body has three longitudinal blue stripes, bordered by thin yellow lines. The dorsal fin is grayish brown with a whitish border, and the ventral and anal fins are brownish or red. The upper lobe of the caudal fin is a delicate pink, the lower lobe usually more or less colorless. The iris of the eye is an attractive golden-green.

This active fish, introduced to the aquarium world in about 1939, is best kept in a small shoal, which will swim mainly in the upper water layers. The composition of the water is not critical and even during breeding it can be kept medium-hard. The tank should have clumps of fine-

Above: **Danio devario** ♀(t), ♂(b)
*Like the Giant Danio, this is an active fish that may jump out of the tank unless a lid is fitted.*

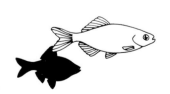

leaved plants, such as Milfoil *(Myriophyllum)*. If the tips of the shoots are held together by a rubber band, the fish will drive through the middle part of the plant when spawning. The plants will also help to give the sinking eggs some degree of protection from the greedy parents.

Family CYPRINIDAE
## Epalzeorhynchus kallopterus
*Flying Fox*
- **Distribution:** Sumatra and Borneo
- **Length:** Up to 5.5in (14cm)
- **Tank length:** 24in (60cm)
- **Diet:** Worms, crustaceans, insects, plant matter, dried food
- **Water temperature:** 72 to 81°F (22 to 27°C)
- **Community tank**

This barb has an elongated but only slightly compressed body, a mouth facing downward, and two pairs of barbels. The back is brown to olive-green and the underparts are white. Below the back there is a broad golden-

**A practical reminder**
The level of unwanted substances in the aquarium water can be kept to a safe minimum by efficient filtration (mechanical, chemical, and biological) and by regular partial water changes (20 to 25% per month).

yellow longitudinal band, which reaches from the tip of the snout to the caudal peduncle. Immediately below this band there is a blackish band running from the snout to the central rays of the caudal fin. The fins are mainly pink or reddish brown; the dorsal, anal, and ventral fins have a black bar and a white border. The iris of the eye is bright red.

This is a hardy fish that should be kept in a tank with dense vegetation and scattered rocks and roots. The substrate should be soft. The species is perfectly peaceful in a community tank. However, the Flying Fox will fight with other members of its own kind because each individual likes to have its own territory near the bottom, usually among dead branches and tree roots. When at rest they like to balance on their pectoral fins in the same way as marine bottom-living gurnards.

The ventral position of the mouth is adapted for rasping algae from rocks and roots, and also from the aquarium glass. It is unlikely that this species has been bred in captivity.

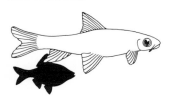

Right: **Epalzeorhynchus kallopterus**
*In addition to algae, this fish also browses on flatworms.*

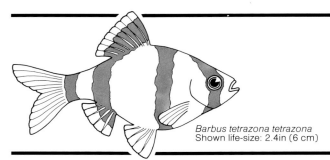

*Barbus tetrazona tetrazona*
Shown life-size: 2.4in (6 cm)

Family CYPRINIDAE

# Rasbora borapetensis
*Red-tailed Rasbora*
- **Distribution:** Thailand
- **Length:** Up to 2in (5cm)
- **Tank length:** 18in (45cm)
- **Diet:** Worms, insects, crustaceans, dried food
- **Water temperature:** 68 to 79°F (20 to 26°C)
- **Community tank**

Red-tailed Rasbora is an elegant, elongated fish, with a typically forked tail and a mouth turned slightly upward. The back is olive-green. The front of the dorsal fin is just behind the insertion of the ventral fins. The flanks are greenish yellow with silvery iridescence. A wide black longitudinal stripe extends from the rear of the gill cover to the rear of the caudal peduncle, and is bordered by a thin golden line that has a tinge of green. There is also a thin black line running along the midline of the back, and a similar line along the base of the anal fin. The dorsal and caudal fins are delicate red, but the other fins are more or less colorless. The sexes are similar in coloration, but the female is slightly more robust.

This is an active small fish, which should be kept in a shoal. The tank should have a certain amount of vegetation, but there should be plenty of open water so that the fishes can swim freely. The water must be soft and slightly acid with some added peat, or it can be filtered through peat. For breeding, the same type of water should be used. The tank should have no substrate, but should be provided with scattered groups of anchored feathery plants such as *Cabomba*. During spawning the male curls his body around the female, who lays eggs at random. Those eggs that fall among the plants have some protection from the parent fishes.

Below: **Rasbora borapetensis**
*Shallow water and subdued light will help this species to breed.*

Family CYPRINIDAE

# Labeo bicolor
*Red-tailed Labeo*
- **Distribution:** Thailand
- **Length:** Up to 4.7in (12cm)
- **Tank length:** 24in (60cm)
- **Diet:** Worms, crustaceans, insects, plant matter, dried food
- **Water temperature:** 72 to 79°F (22 to 26°C)
- **Community tank**

This elongated fish has slight lateral compression and a dorsal profile more convex than the ventral. The mouth faces slightly downward and has swollen lips and two pairs of barbels. The fins, particularly the dorsal fin, are well developed and usually held spread out. The females grow larger than the males. When in good condition the whole body—including the dorsal, anal, and ventral fins—is velvety-black, while the caudal fin is orange or red. The pectoral fins are also orange, but are sometimes very dark. There are local races that lack the velvety-black coloration; in this case, the body is pale gray or very dark brown and the caudal fin is yellowish red. Specimens kept in unsuitable conditions are also paler.

Right: **Labeo bicolor**
*Many aquarists use coconut shells or flowerpots to provide hiding-places for this species.*

This is a hardy fish that has been known to live for several years in the home aquarium. It can be kept in a tank furnished with rocks and roots; these provide hiding-places and enable the fishes to establish territories. Although aggressive towards other members of its own species, the Red-tailed Labeo normally does not molest other species. The tank can also have patches of dense vegetation. The water must be soft, slightly acid, and filtered through peat. It is also advisable to have subdued lighting. The species has been bred on only very few occasions. The eggs hatch in 30 to 50 hours and at first the fry are gray.

This species is sometimes known as the Red-tailed 'Shark', but this is very misleading as it is in no way related to true sharks.

**A practical reminder**
Before setting up your tank, plan everything ahead and have all the necessary tools at hand. Gravel can be washed beforehand and rocks can be contoured and glued together to make cliffs and caves.

Family CYPRINIDAE
## Rasbora einthoveni
*Brilliant Rasbora*
- **Distribution:** Southeast Asia: Thailand to Indonesia
- **Length:** Up to 3.5in (9cm)
- **Tank length:** 36in (90cm)
- **Diet:** Worms, crustaceans, insects, dried food
- **Water temperature:** 75 to 79°F (24 to 26°C)
- **Community tank**

Sometimes known as Einthoven's Rasbora, this is an elegant elongated shoaling species that swims mainly in the upper water layers. The back is yellow-brown to greenish brown and the belly is yellowish or silvery. The flanks are grayish blue with silvery iridescence and they are marked with a longitudinal black band, showing greenish iridescence, which extends from the tip of the snout to the caudal peduncle. Just above this band there is a reddish golden iridescent stripe. In some individuals the front rays of the dorsal fin are dark, but otherwise the fins are colorless. The female has a more convex ventral profile than the male.

This is a hardy species that can be kept in a tank with some

Above: **Rasbora einthoveni**
*For breeding, this species needs a spacious, infusorian-free tank.*

vegetation around the edges, leaving the shoal a good length of water for swimming. Although this species will live in medium-hard water it is much better—and essential for breeding—to use soft water that has been filtered through peat. For breeding, some aquarists use a tank without substrate, but with a few plants anchored at the bottom by glass rods. Spawning takes place at random in the water and when it has finished the parents must be removed, as they are spawn-eaters. The eggs will normally hatch in 26 to 30 hours and the fry will be free-swimming in three or four days. They can then be fed initially on rotifers and later on brine shrimp nauplii. About 25% of the water should be changed every month.

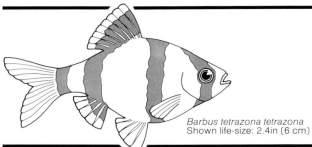

*Barbus tetrazona tetrazona*
Shown life-size: 2.4in (6 cm)

Family CYPRINIDAE

# Rasbora dorsiocellata

*Eye-spot Rasbora*

- **Distribution:** Malayan Peninsula and Sumatra
- **Length:** Up to 2.4in (6cm)
- **Tank length:** 18in (45cm)
- **Diet:** Worms, crustaceans, insects, dried food
- **Water temperature:** 75 to 79°F (24 to 26°C)
- **Community tank**

This is a relatively slender species of *Rasbora*. However, the females are slightly larger than the males, with more rounded bellies. The back of the Eye-spot Rasbora is brown or brownish olive, and the underparts are silvery-white. The flanks are also silvery but with bluish or violet iridescence, depending upon the angle of the light. There are two narrow black longitudinal lines that may be somewhat indistinct, running from the back of the head to the base of the tail. However, the distinguishing feature of this fish is the very prominent eye-spot in the middle of the dorsal fin. The caudal fin is yellow or pale red and the iris of the eye is yellowish.

This is one of the smaller *Rasbora* species and it should be kept in a tank with marginal vegetation and a sufficient length of open water for swimming. The water should be soft, slightly acid, and filtered through peat. For breeding, the tank can have a few isolated clumps of plants. The female will lay eggs among the plants and both parents should then be removed from the tank. The eggs hatch in about 30 hours and the fry at first hang more or less motionless from the plants. After three to five days they should be free-swimming and can then be fed on rotifers and small nauplii.

The subspecies *R. dorsiocellata macrophthalma,* which grows to 1.4in (3.5cm) long, has relatively larger eyes, with the lower half of the body iridescent blue-green.

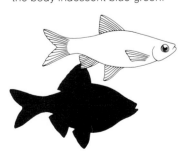

Right: **Rasbora dorsiocellata**
*This is an elegant and normally very prolific member of the genus. The eggs may be observed adhering to the uppersides of leaves.*

**A practical reminder**
Decide on the type of filtration system first.
If you have already put the gravel into the
tank, you will have to take it out again when
you come to fit a biological filter! Keep
thinking ahead at all times.

## Rasbora maculata
*Spotted Rasbora*
● **Distribution:** Malay
Archipelago, Sumatra
● **Length:** Up to 1in (2.5cm)
● **Tank length:** 12in (30cm)
● **Diet:** Worms, small crusta-
ceans, dried food
● **Water temperature:** 70 to 77°F
(21 to 25°C)
● **Community tank**

This is the pygmy of the *Rasbora*
genus, and indeed one of the
smallest aquarium fishes. The
body is fairly squat, the female
having distinctly rounded
underparts. The general
coloration of the Spotted Rasbora
is brick-red with a tinge of
greenish brown on the back. The
belly is usually yellowish. There
are blue-black markings of
varying sizes above the pectoral
fins, at the base of the anal fin, and

Right: **Rasbora maculata** ♀
*The colors of this fish appear
vivid against a dark substrate.*

on the caudal peduncle. The front
rays of the dorsal and anal fins are
dark, the other parts being
yellowish or red. The caudal and
ventral fins are reddish at the
base.

This diminutive fish should be
kept in a small shoal, in a tank
with a dark substrate and areas of
dense vegetation. The water
should be soft, slightly acid, and
filtered through peat. As in some
of the other *Rasbora* species,
breeding is not always easy. The
breeding tank should not contain

other species. It is best to keep the
breeding pair in separate tanks for
a week or two, and to supply them
with a rich and varied diet. After
they have been put together there
is often a delay of some days
before spawning takes place. After
spawning has finished, the
parents must be removed from
the tank to prevent them from
eating their own brood. The eggs
hatch in 24 to 30 hours and the
fry are free-swimming three or
four days later, and ready to feed
on the smallest live food.

## Rasbora heteromorpha
*Harlequin Fish*
● **Distribution:** Thailand, Malay
Archipelago, Indonesia
● **Length:** Up to 1.8in (4.5cm)
● **Tank length:** 12in (30cm)
● **Diet:** Worms, crustaceans,
insects, dried food
● **Water temperature:** 72 to 77°F
(22 to 25°C)
● **Community tank**

This is an old favorite, introduced
into the aquarium as long ago as
1906. The body is stockier than
the other species of *Rasbora,* but
the male is more slender than the
female. The general coloration of
the Harlequin Fish is silvery. The
back is bright pink to violet and
the flanks are a more delicate
pink. The underparts are pale
silvery-white. The characteristic
feature is the wedge-shaped blue-
black marking on the rear half of
the body. In the male this marking
is sharply defined and its lower,
front edge reaches down to the
center point of the belly. In the
female, this marking has a much
hazier outline and does not extend
as far down the belly. The dorsal
fin is red, becoming yellowish
towards the tip. The outer rays of
the caudal fin are red, the inner
rays pale yellow.

Harlequin fishes should be kept
in a small shoal, in a tank with
areas of dense vegetation
arranged to leave sufficient space
for swimming. This will mostly
take place in the upper water
layers. In this species it is
important that the water be soft,
slightly acid, and filtered through
peat. After vigorous driving, the
breeding pair arrive beneath a
leaf. The male curls his tail around
the female and spawning takes
place. The eggs hatch in 26 to 30
hours and the fry are free-
swimming three to five days later.
Feed them on rotifers and small
nauplii. The fry grow quickly.

Left: **Rasbora heteromorpha** ♂♂
*Many aquarists breed this species
successfully, but sometimes only
with difficulty. Spawning is often
delayed for a few days after the
breeding pair is put together.*

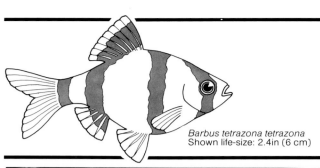

*Barbus tetrazona tetrazona*
Shown life-size: 2.4in (6 cm)

Family CYPRINIDAE

# Rasbora trilineata
*Scissor-tail*

- **Distribution:** Malay Archipelago, Sumatra, Borneo
- **Length:** Up to 6in (15cm)
- **Tank length:** 24in (60cm)
- **Diet:** Worms, crustaceans, insects, dried food
- **Water temperature:** 66 to 77°F (19 to 25°C)
- **Community tank**

This is an elongated, laterally compressed *Rasbora* species with a deeply forked and well-developed tail. Females can be distinguished by their more rounded underparts. In general, the body of the Scissor-tail is very translucent, particularly in young fish. The back is green to olive-yellow, and the belly is silvery-white. The flanks are grayish yellow, becoming more silvery when seen in reflected light. A narrow dark longitudinal line starts above the ventral fins and extends back along the middle of the flanks to the tail. A thinner dark line runs from the base of the anal fin along the underside of the caudal peduncle to the tail. The pattern of the caudal fin lobes is particularly striking. Each lobe has a broad black transverse marking, but the main characteristic of this species is the continuous scissoring action of the two lobes, hence the popular name.

This is an active shoaling fish, unlikely to exceed a length of 2.8in (7cm) in an aquarium. The tank should have a dark substrate and marginal vegetation to leave a good length of open water for swimming. After an active courtship with driving, spawning takes place in the open water. The eggs sink to the bottom, and hatch in 26 to 30 hours. The

Above: **Rasbora trilineata**
*This is an active fish that needs soft water for breeding. Water should be low on infusorians.*

parents must be removed as soon as spawning has finished. The fry should be free-swimming in three to five days and can then be fed on rotifers and the smallest brine shrimp nauplii.

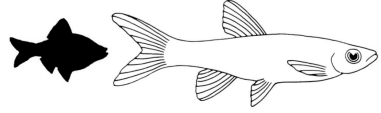

**A practical reminder**
Large rocks should be stood on the tank floor (or filter plate) before any gravel is added. This gives them extra stability. Otherwise, digging fishes may easily cause them to topple and crack the tank glass.

Left: **Tanichthys albonubes**
*This is one of the most undemanding of all fishes, partly because of its temperature range.*

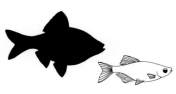

Family CYPRINIDAE
## Tanichthys albonubes
*White Cloud Mountain Minnow*
● **Distribution:** China, near Canton
● **Length:** Up to 1.6in (4cm)
● **Tank length:** 12in (30cm)
● **Diet:** Worms, small crustaceans, dried food
● **Water temperature:** 68 to 72°F (20 to 22°C) in summer; 61 to 64°F (16 to 18°C) in winter
● **Community tank**

A Chinese boy named Tan is said to have discovered this fish on the White Cloud Mountain near Canton around 1930. The genus name, *Tanichthys,* comes from the boy's name; the species name, *albonubes,* means 'white cloud'.

The body is elongated and moderately compressed. The small mouth faces slightly upward and there are no barbels. The back is dark brown or olive-brown with greenish iridescence, and the belly is white. The flanks are paler than the back and strikingly marked with a narrow iridescent golden band, bordered below by a thin dark blue line. Under this line is a broader red to chestnut-brown longitudinal band. The base of the dorsal fin is red, and the edge is silvery-blue.

This is a particularly hardy species and ideal for a beginner. In the wild it is found in mountain streams, so a regular replacement of a portion of the water is beneficial. The tank can have short plants around the edges and isolated clumps of Milfoil (*Myriophyllum*). The composition of the water is not important.

For breeding, the water temperature should be allowed to rise to 68 to 72°F (20 to 22°C). Spawning takes place among the plant clumps. The male curls the rear part of his body around the female, and the eggs adhere to the plants. Provided they are well fed, the parents do not usually attack their eggs, which hatch in about 48 hours. The fry feed at the surface on pulverized dried food or tiny live food such as rotifers.

Family CYPRINIDAE
## Rasbora vaterifloris
*Pearly Rasbora, Fire Rasbora*
● **Distribution:** Sri Lanka
● **Length:** Up to 1.6in (4cm)
● **Tank length:** 18in (45cm)
● **Diet:** Worms, small crustaceans, dried food
● **Water temperature:** 75 to 77°F (24 to 25°C)
● **Community tank**

This is a relatively short, tall-bodied, and laterally compressed *Rasbora* species, with a deeply forked tail and pointed fins. The back is green and the belly pale orange to almost white. Flanks are grayish green with a delicate pearly iridescence that varies

according to the angle of the light. The iris of the eye is golden-red. The dorsal and anal fins are orange or red and the base of the caudal fin is similarly colored. The fins of the female are more yellowish, but the pectoral fins of both sexes are colorless.

For this very beautiful species of *Rasbora,* the tank should have a certain amount of vegetation and subdued lighting. For breeding, it is strongly recommended that there be no substrate, but the tank should have groups of plants with feathery leaves, such as Milfoil (*Myriophyllum*). These plants can be anchored to the bottom with glass rods. The water must be soft, slightly acid, and filtered

Above: **Rasbora vaterifloris**
*Opinions differ, but this fish is not usually difficult to breed.*

through peat. After a period of driving, spawning takes place among the plants and the parents should then be removed. The eggs hatch in about 30 hours, and once the fry are free-swimming they should be fed at first on rotifers. After about a week they can be offered very small brine shrimp nauplii.

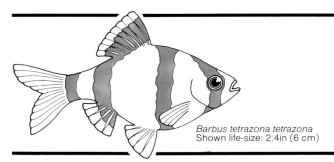

*Barbus tetrazona tetrazona*
Shown life-size: 2.4in (6 cm)

## Family COBITIDAE

Small to medium-sized, these are mainly bottom-living fishes with species in North Africa, Europe, and particularly Southeast Asia. They have a characteristic spine in front of the eye. Air swallowed at the surface passes along the alimentary tract to the hind-gut where its oxygen is absorbed by blood capillaries.

Family COBITIDAE

### Botia hymenophysa
*Banded Loach*
- **Distribution:** Thailand, Malaya, Borneo, Sumatra, Java
- **Length:** Up to 8.3in (21cm), possibly more
- **Tank length:** 24in (60cm)
- **Diet:** Worms, crustaceans, insects, dried food
- **Water temperature:** 77 to 86°F (25 to 30°C)
- **Species tank**

This is an elongated and slender loach with a conical pointed head. Its mouth faces downward and it has three pairs of barbels. Below the eye there is a forked, erectile spine; its length is the same as the diameter of the eye. The upperparts are brownish or yellowish brown and the underparts are pale yellow. The flanks are grayish yellow or gray-green; 11 or more dark transverse

Below: **Botia hymenophysa**
*The pattern is variable; there may be up to 15 dark transverse bars.*

bars, which are positioned slightly obliquely, mark the flanks. These bars are separated by narrow pale areas, but they do not reach the belly. The fins are yellowish or greenish; the dorsal and caudal fins have thin dark bands.

This rather shy loach can be aggressive. It lives on the bottom, remaining hidden by day but coming out at night to burrow for insect larvae and worms. It can be kept in a tank with a soft substrate and sufficient rocks and roots to provide plenty of hiding-places. The water should be soft, and at least a quarter of it should be renewed every month. As with Hora's Loach, there are no external sex differences and the species has not yet been bred in captivity.

The related *Botia berdmorei*, up to 10in (25cm) long, comes from Thailand and Burma. It is an elongated loach, similar in shape to *B. hymenophysa*, and it also has three pairs of barbels. The general coloration is cream or pale yellow. The flanks have 10 or 11 rather indistinct transverse bars—much fainter than in *B. hymenophysa*—and numerous dark dots and streaks arranged in longitudinal rows. The fins are yellowish. This species, too, has not yet been bred in captivity.

Family COBITIDAE

### Botia macracantha
*Clown Loach*
- **Distribution:** Sumatra, Borneo
- **Length:** Up to 12in (30cm)
- **Tank length:** 24in (60cm)
- **Diet:** Worms, crustaceans, plant matter, dried food
- **Water temperature:** 75 to 86°F (24 to 30°C)
- **Community tank**

The most colorful and most popular of the loaches, the Clown Loach is moderately elongated and laterally compressed. It has an arched back, an almost straight belly profile, and four pairs of barbels. The barbels located on the lower jaw are very small. The head is large and the mouth faces downward, with thick fleshy lips. The spine in front of the eye is quite short. The general coloration is bright orange and the flanks are crossed by three wide, wedge-shaped black bands. The first band runs from the top of the skull across the eye and then obliquely down to the region of the mouth; the second starts in front of the dorsal fin and extends down to the

belly; and the third covers a large part of the caudal peduncle and runs down onto the anal fin. The pectoral, ventral, and caudal fins are red; the dorsal and anal fins are yellowish with black markings.

This is a very attractive loach that is not as shy as the other species. Often active by day, it can be kept quite successfully in a community tank with other fishes. In fact, Clown Loaches have even been seen to form a small shoal with armored catfishes. The tank should have a soft substrate that will allow the fishes to burrow for live food. Rocks and roots suitably placed will provide shelter. The water should be soft.

Once they are established, Clown Loaches live for several years in an aquarium, where they grow slowly but never reach the size recorded for wild specimens. They have not been bred in captivity—perhaps because they do not reach full sexual maturity.

Right: **Botia macracantha**
*Also known as the Tiger Botia, this is the most colorful loach. There are no external sex differences.*

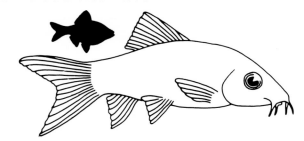

**A practical reminder**
Most aquarists contour the gravel to add the interest of varying levels in the tank. If it slopes down from the back to front, accumulated detritus is easily seen and siphoned off before it becomes a menace.

Left: **Botia morleti**
*This very active loach can be kept successfully with larger tankmates.*

Family COBITIDAE
# Botia morleti

- **Distribution:** Thailand
- **Length:** Up to 4in (10cm)
- **Tank length:** 12in (30cm)
- **Diet:** Worms, crustaceans, insects, plant matter, dried food
- **Water temperature:** 79 to 86°F (26 to 30°C)
- **Species tank:** Possible for community tank, but should be carefully watched

This is a squat, laterally compressed loach with a straight belly profile and prominently arched back. The dorsal fin lies directly above the ventral fins and therefore well forward of the anal fin. There are only eight soft rays in the dorsal fin. The head is pointed and relatively long, and the mouth faces downward and has three pairs of quite short barbels. Below the eye there is a two-pointed spine that can be

erected and locked into position. The general coloration is yellowish green with a paler belly and grayish upperparts. The flanks have four quite short narrow transverse bars but these are sometimes not very distinct. A black stripe starts at the tip of the snout and runs along the ridge of the back. It ends just in front of the caudal fin where it joins an intense black transverse bar on the caudal peduncle. The caudal fin is

yellowish, and sometimes has dark spots. The other fins are either almost colorless or gray-green.
This is a hardy and quite peaceful loach that lives near the bottom. It remains hidden by day but comes out at night (unless the aquarium is brightly lit) to search for food. It can be kept in a tank with a soft substrate and a number of rocks and roots arranged to give plenty of hiding-places. The water should be soft, and about a quarter of it should be changed once a month or so. There are no external sex differences and the species has not yet been bred in captivity.

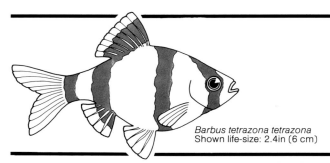

*Barbus tetrazona tetrazona*
Shown life-size: 2.4in (6 cm)

## Family COBITIDAE
# Botia modesta
*Orange-finned Loach*

- **Distribution:** Thailand, Vietnam, Malaysia
- **Length:** Up to 4in (10cm)
- **Tank length:** 12in (30cm)
- **Diet:** Worms, crustaceans, insects, dried food
- **Water temperature:** 77 to 86°F (25 to 30°C)
- **Species tank**

Though rather stocky and lacking the typical snakelike body of most loaches, the Orange-finned Loach has a laterally compressed shape and other features that easily identify it as a cobitid. It has three pairs of barbels. The back is moderately arched and the belly profile very slightly convex. The front rays of the dorsal fin lie directly above the ventral fins and well in front of the anal fin—again, this is a characteristic of most tropical loaches. The caudal peduncle is short but quite high. The general coloration is gray-green to grayish blue and slightly darker on the head. There is a dark marking at the root of the tail but it is usually indistinct. Otherwise, there are no transverse bars or other markings that are usually found in so many of the related species. The caudal fin is bright yellow, and the other fins are grayish yellow.

This is a hardy but rather shy loach that usually hides away during the day and comes out at night when it burrows for small

crustaceans and insect larvae. It can be kept in a tank with a soft substrate and scattered rocks and roots. Since this fish is a vigorous digger, rooted plants are not suitable for this aquarium. However, a few floating plants would provide decoration in the upper parts of the tank. This species has not yet been bred in captivity.

Loaches utilize their intestines

as an accessory respiratory organ. This enables them to live in oxygen-depleted waters. They rise to the surface and gulp a mouthful of air, which passes along the alimentary canal to the hind gut. There the oxygen is extracted by the dense accumulation of capillaries that line this part of the gut; the residue of air is passed out at the anus. However, clean water and aeration are important.

Above: **Botia modesta**
*Active at night, this species, like other loaches, uses its barbels to detect food in the substrate.*

**A practical reminder**
Terraces can be formed by using pieces of rock embedded in the gravel to hold back higher areas. Try to achieve an illusion of space and avoid perfectly flat 'aquascapes' and symmetrically grouped plants.

Family COBITIDAE

# Botia sidthimunki
*Dwarf Loach, Chained Loach*
- **Distribution:** Thailand
- **Length:** Up to 1.4in (3.5cm)
- **Tank length:** 12in (30cm)
- **Diet:** Worms, crustaceans, insects, plant matter, dried food
- **Water temperature:** 77 to 86°F (25 to 30°C)
- **Species tank**

The dorsal and ventral profiles of this elongated small loach are only slightly convex. The scales are very small but are not present on the head. The mouth has three pairs of barbels. The back is brownish and the belly is silvery-white. The flanks are golden-brown with a very variable pattern of dark brown markings arranged in four longitudinal bands. Two of these bands are close to the ridge of the back; the others appear at about the level of the vertebral column. These longitudinal bands are connected to one another by similarly colored transverse bars giving an almost netlike appearance. In young individuals the dark markings are black. The fins are almost colorless.

In the wild this loach lives in shoals that, unlike most other species of *Botia*, swim above the bottom—mostly in the middle water layers. It is active by day and night. In an aquarium, Dwarf Loaches can be kept in a small shoal in a tank with a soft substrate and a number of rocks and roots arranged to form suitable hiding-places. The water should be soft and approximately one quarter of it should be replaced every month.

The spines in front of the eyes, which occur in all loaches, are raised when the fish is excited or threatened. The spines may get caught in the meshes of a net when the fish is being moved from one tank to another. It is important to disentangle the fish very gently. Also, great care should be taken to avoid the sharp spines, which can cause painful wounds to the hands.

Below: **Botia sidthimunki**
*An active loach best kept in a shoal.*

## Family GYMNOTIDAE
This is a small family with species in Central and South America. These fishes have no dorsal, caudal, or ventral fins. The very long anal fin is the main organ of propulsion. Air swallowed at the surface is used for respiration. The scales are small and very numerous.

Family GYMNOTIDAE

# Gymnotus carapo
*Banded Knifefish*
- **Distribution:** Central and South America, Guatemala to Rio de la Plata
- **Length:** Up to 24in (60cm)
- **Tank length:** 48in (120cm)
- **Diet:** Worms, insects, meat, fish, plant matter, dried food
- **Water temperature:** 73 to 83°F (23 to 28°C)
- **Species tank**

The front part of the body of this eellike fish is almost cylindrical; the rear part is compressed and ends in a point. There are no dorsal, caudal, or ventral fins. However, the anal fin has a very long base that starts below the head. This fin is the main organ of propulsion—its undulations enable the fish to move backward or forward. The numerous scales are very small. The mouth is very broad and armed with conical teeth. Coloration varies. Young individuals are flesh-colored to pale yellow and marked with several broad transverse bars. Old specimens, on the other hand, have dark background coloration marked with oblique pale bars.

The Banded Knifefish has a weak electric organ which emits pulses that help the fish orientate in murky waters. It also has accessory respiration, so that it can rise to the surface and swallow air from which the oxygen is absorbed. This enables the fish to live in waters that are poor in oxygen. It is aggressive towards other members of its own species, so that the tank must be spacious and furnished with numerous roots to provide hiding-places. It is mainly active at night when it comes out to hunt for food. If the tank is kept fairly dark it may come out by day to feed.

The Banded Knifefish has not yet been bred in captivity.

Left: **Gymnotus carapo**
*Active mainly at night, this fish uses its long anal fin to move.*

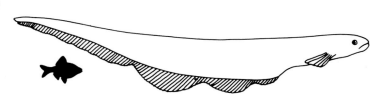

# THE CATFISHES

Above: *Corydoras aeneus,* one of the best-known
of the South American armored catfishes.
Right: A swampy area in Trinidad. Such places
are home to many types of catfishes.

*The order Siluriformes contains some 30 families with about 2,000 species, which have an almost worldwide distribution in fresh waters, particularly in Africa and South America. A few marine species occur in tropical and subtropical coastal waters.*

*The skin of catfishes is naked or covered with bony plates, but it never has true scales. Most species live on or near the bottom. They are solitary fishes, mainly active at dusk or during the night. Only a few form shoals. Their nocturnal habits are related to their poorly developed eyes, and the possession of highly sensitive barbels around the mouth. These structures help the fish to orientate in darkness and to find food.*

*Several of the families contain species that make excellent aquarium fishes. These include:*

*The Siluridae of Europe, Africa, and Asia, which lack scales or bony plates and an adipose fin, but have a long anal fin, a very small dorsal fin, and one to six pairs of long barbels.*

*The Schilbeidae of Africa and southern Asia, with two to four pairs of barbels and a small adipose fin. Some are active by day.*

*The Clariidae of Africa and southern Asia, usually with a long dorsal and anal fin, no adipose fin, and four pairs of long barbels. Most species in this family are too large for domestic aquariums.*

*The Mochocidae (or Mochokidae) of Africa south of the Sahara, which have three pairs of barbels and a very large adipose fin.*

*The Pimelodidae of tropical America with three pairs of long barbels and an adipose fin.*

*The Callichthyidae of South America and Trinidad, with a well-developed armor of overlapping bony plates, an adipose fin, and a varying number of barbels.*

*Finally, the Loricariidae, restricted to northern and central South America, with a few rows of bony plates along each flank, and an adipose fin in some species, not in others.*

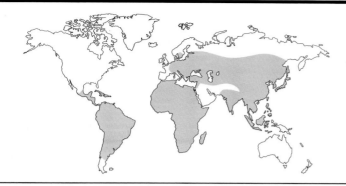

Left: The many catfish families
have an extremely wide distribution,
occurring in all continents except
Australia. Most catfishes live in
tropical fresh waters but a few
occur in marine habitats, particularly
off the coasts of southern Asia.
Within the group there are vegetarians
that suck algae from rocks,
carnivores that pursue other fishes,
and also true scavengers that burrow
in the substrate for scraps of food.

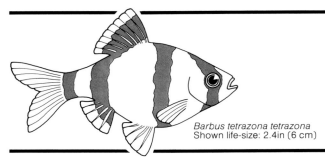

*Barbus tetrazona tetrazona*
Shown life-size: 2.4in (6 cm)

Family SILURIDAE
# Kryptopterus bicirrhis
*Glass Catfish*
● **Distribution:** Thailand, Java, Sumatra, Borneo
● **Length:** Up to 4in (10cm)
● **Tank length:** 18in (45cm)
● **Diet:** Worms, crustaceans, insects, dried food
● **Water temperature:** 70 to 79°F (21 to 26°C)
● **Community tank**

The body of the Glass Catfish is scaleless and very strongly compressed. The backbone and other internal organs are clearly visible; in fact, this is one of the most transparent of all tropical fishes. There is one pair of long

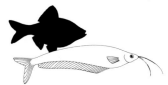

Below: **Kryptopterus bicirrhis**
*Many aquarists have tried to breed this attractive and unusual fish, but so far without success.*

barbels on the upper jaw and these can be extended forwards. The dorsal fin consists of only a single ray and there is no adipose fin. The caudal fin is deeply forked and its lower lobe may be slightly longer than the upper lobe. The anal fin is very long, but its rear end does not connect with the caudal fin. In general, the body is highly iridescent and the actual colors seen depend upon the angle of the light.

*Kryptopterus bicirrhis* is a delicate species. It swims mostly in the upper and middle water layers with the body positioned obliquely and head turned upward. The tail constantly moves from side to side. These diurnal catfishes can be kept in a tank with patches of vegetation where they can hide. They do swim about in the open water, but not as actively as the African Glass Catfish, *Eutropiellus debauwi*. They should be kept in a small shoal, possibly with other species of about the same size. Under no circumstances should a single specimen be kept on its own because it will soon languish.

This species is not known to have been bred in captivity.

Family SCHILBEIDAE
# Eutropiellus debauwi
*African Glass Catfish*
● **Distribution:** Central Africa: Congo Basin
● **Length:** Up to 3.2in (8cm)
● **Tank length:** 24in (60cm)
● **Diet:** Worms, crustaceans, insects, dried food
● **Water temperature:** 73 to 79°F (23 to 26°C)
● **Community tank**

African Glass Catfish is elongated and small with the caudal peduncle much laterally compressed. Its short dorsal fin—positioned above the pectoral fins—has a spiny first ray. There is a relatively well-developed adipose fin. The anal fin is very long and the caudal fin deeply forked. There are three pairs of short barbels on the upper jaw. The body is translucent with silvery underparts. The flanks are marked with three prominent longitudinal bands, which become more pronounced with increasing age. The head is quite short with a small terminal mouth. The eyes are large.

This is a very peaceful but active

Right: **Eutropiellus debauwi**
*This species is not as delicate as the Glass Catfish, but it has the same characteristic tail-wagging. A shoal of six is ideal.*

catfish. It does well in a tank with other species of a similar size. Because single specimens do not thrive, it should always be kept in a shoal. The tank should have a few areas of vegetation. However, there must be plenty of open space for swimming—this species seems to be always on the move. The water should be soft and slightly acid. When swimming, the body is positioned rather obliquely in the water with the tail downward. The caudal fin appears to beat from side to side constantly—an activity that is not completely understood.

This species has not yet been bred in captivity.

**A practical reminder**
Heaters should be mounted clear of the gravel to ensure adequate water circulation around them. Nonmetallic heater/thermostat clips are preferable as they are nontoxic to fishes and rust-proof.

Family MOCHOCIDAE
# Synodontis nigriventris
*Upside-down Catfish*
- **Distribution:** Central Africa: Congo Basin
- **Length:** Up to 3.2in (8cm)
- **Tank length:** 24in (60cm)
- **Diet:** Insects, crustaceans, plant matter, dried food
- **Water temperature:** 73 to 81°F (23 to 27°C)
- **Community tank**

Upside-down Catfish is squat, scaleless, and only slightly compressed laterally. It has three pairs of barbels—one smooth pair on the upper jaw, and two feathered pairs on the lower jaw. The adipose fin is particularly long, and the caudal fin is deeply forked with pointed lobes. The general coloration is cream to pale gray with dark brown or black markings. These patterns sometimes fuse to form transverse bars. Though the fins are colorless, they have dark markings. The belly is black. The light-colored back and black belly, in accordance with its usual upside-down position, give the fish its popular name.

This is a peaceful catfish that is generally active at night and swims in shoals. By swimming upside-down the fish is able to browse algae from the under-surfaces of leaves. It can be kept in a tank furnished with rocks and roots and a number of plants with large leaves. The composition of the water is not critical.

This unusual fish has been bred on only a few occasions. Shortly before spawning, the brownish coloration changes to yellowish white and this makes the markings of the fish even more conspicuous. The pale yellowish eggs, with a diameter of about 0.1in (2.5mm), hatch in seven or eight days, and the fry live for four days on the contents of the yolk-sac. They can then be fed on tiny brine shrimp nauplii. At first they swim belly downward, but after about eight weeks they start to swim upside-down.

Left: **Synodontis nigriventris**
*The mottled pattern of the upturned belly probably helps this catfish to remain undetected by predatory birds. Difficult to breed.*

123

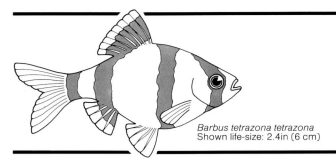

Barbus tetrazona tetrazona
Shown life-size: 2.4in (6 cm)

## Family PIMELODIDAE
## Pimelodella gracilis
*Graceful Pimelodella*
- **Distribution:** South America: in Orinoco, Amazon, La Plata
- **Length:** Up to 6.7in (17cm), possibly more
- **Tank length:** 24in (60cm)
- **Diet:** Worms, insects
- **Water temperature:** 66 to 75°F (19 to 24°C)
- **Community tank:** Keep with larger species only

Young specimens of *Pimelodella gracilis* have dark gray upperparts and silvery-white or silvery-green flanks. A black longitudinal band extends from the gill cover to the base of the caudal fin. Adult females are similarly colored, but adult males are a uniform blue-black with strong iridescence. The fins in both sexes are colorless. There is a pair of very long barbels on the upper jaw, and two pairs of shorter barbels on the lower jaw.

The Graceful Pimelodella is a fish suitable for a tank with other fishes of its own size, but it should not be kept with smaller species.

The tank should have rocks and roots to provide hiding-places and some plants around the edges. However, sufficient space should be allowed for swimming. The water should be soft. This species is mainly active at dusk, when it swims about in the middle and lower water layers. It is not known to have been bred in captivity.

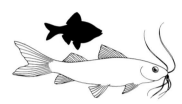

Below: **Pimelodella gracilis**
*This is a useful fish to have in a community tank as it spends much of its time scavenging for waste food. Keep in subdued light.*

## Family CALLICHTHYIDAE
## Corydoras aeneus
*Bronze Corydoras*
- **Distribution:** South America: Trinidad, Venezuela, southwards to La Plata
- **Length:** Up to 2.8in (7cm)
- **Tank length:** 18in (45cm)
- **Diet:** Worms, crustaceans, insects, plant matter, dried food
- **Water temperature:** 66 to 79°F (19 to 26°C)
- **Community tank**

This is perhaps the most commonly kept species of *Corydoras.* The body is stocky and deep, with a very arched back. The female is more robust than the male, and is usually a little longer. Each side of the body has two rows of bony plates, the upper row having 21 to 23 plates, the lower 19 to 21. The upper jaw has two pairs of barbels, which, if folded back, would reach almost as far as the gill opening. The background coloration is yellow-brown or a delicate reddish brown. The head and flanks have strong iridescence that appears greenish, coppery, or golden,

depending upon the angle of the light. The middle part of the flanks is usually darker. The fins are grayish and without markings.

The tank should have a sandy substrate. Decorative plants, such as *Cryptocoryne,* can be used sparingly. The composition of the water is not critical although it should not be too acid.

Spawning is preceded by very vigorous driving, and it has been observed that the female often takes the more active part. The actual spawning may go on for one to three hours, with the female laying from five to 12 eggs at a time, with a final total of up to 200 eggs. The eggs are usually laid on the plants and they hatch in five or six days. The fry fall to the bottom, where they feed at first on infusorians and rotifers.

Right: **Corydoras aeneus**
*This is another fish that scavenges for waste food in the aquarium.*

## Family CALLICHTHYIDAE
## Callichthys callichthys
*Armored Catfish*
- **Distribution:** South America: eastern Brazil to La Plata
- **Length:** Up to 4in (10cm), possibly more
- **Tank length:** 24in (60cm)
- **Diet:** Fish, insects, plant matter, dried food
- **Water temperature:** 68 to 79°F (20 to 26°C)
- **Community tank**

This elongated catfish has an arched back and an almost straight belly profile. The caudal peduncle is tall and laterally

compressed. The head of the Armored Catfish is broad and flattened, and it has relatively small eyes. The upper jaws carry two pairs of barbels. The body is enclosed in two series of bony plates—a characteristic of the whole family. The upper row has 26 to 29 plates, the lower row 25 to 28. In addition, between the dorsal and adipose fins there are some small bony plates separated by naked skin from the upper row of lateral plates. The adipose fin has a powerful spine in front and the caudal fin is rounded. In the males the first pectoral finray is thickened. The coloration is not particularly attractive. The upperparts are dark olive-green or dark

green with a slight bluish or violet sheen; the underparts are grayish blue. Both areas have a variable number of dark spots. The fins are translucent and grayish with dark spots, the edges red or yellowish orange. In general, the colors are more intense in the males than in the females.

This catfish remains more or less hidden by day and comes out at night to hunt for fish and insects. For this reason the aquarium should have rocks and roots to provide hiding-places, and some areas of dense vegetation. For breeding, a nest of air bubbles coated with saliva is built on the underside of a large leaf. The eggs are attached to the

nest and guarded by the male. They hatch in four to six days. The parents should then be removed. The fry live for about two days on the contents of the large yolk-sac and will then eat small live food.

Right: **Callichthys callichthys**
*It is quite normal for this species to swallow air at the surface for intestinal respiration The male grunts while guarding the eggs.*

**A practical reminder**
Make all electrical connections *outside* the
aquarium. Do not switch on heaters unless
they are covered by water. Always switch
off the power before putting your hands
into the aquarium for any reason.

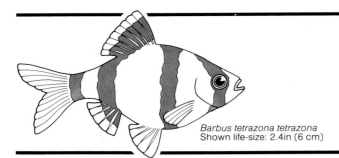

*Barbus tetrazona tetrazona*
Shown life-size: 2.4in (6 cm)

Right: **Corydoras julii**
*This is one of the most striking species in the genus* Corydoras.
*The barbels are relatively short.*

Family CALLICHTHYIDAE

## Corydoras julii
*Leopard Corydoras*

- **Distribution:** South America: Brazil, in lower Amazon tributaries
- **Length:** Up to 2.4in (6cm)
- **Tank length:** 18in (45cm)
- **Diet:** Worms, crustaceans, insects, plant matter, dried food
- **Water temperature:** 66 to 79°F (19 to 26°C)
- **Community tank**

Leopard Corydoras is a fairly squat armored catfish with an arched forehead and two pairs of relatively short barbels on the upper jaws. The armor on the flanks consists of 21 or 22 bony plates in the upper row and 20 or 21 in the lower row. There is a spine towards the front of the adipose fin. The general coloration is silvery-gray with delicate green iridescence. A characteristic pattern of black spots covers the back and flanks but not the underparts. On the gill cover and the upper side of the head, the spots are replaced by a pattern of wormlike squiggles. Near the midline of the body, between the two rows of bony plates, there is a wavy or almost jagged dark longitudinal band that extends from the end of the gill cover to the end of the caudal peduncle. A silvery-gray line borders each side of this prominent band. The outer part of the dorsal fin has a large black marking, and the caudal and anal fins have a few rows of dark spots.

*Corydoras julii* is an active fish best kept in a small shoal. The tank should have a soft sandy substrate because—like other species of *Corydoras*—Leopard Corydoras lives on or near the bottom, where it likes to burrow. It has been bred though not easily or often. Spawning may take place over a period of several days.

This catfish has also been known as *Corydoras leopardus*.

Family CALLICHTHYIDAE

## Corydoras melanistius
*Black-spotted Corydoras*

- **Distribution:** South America: Guyana, in the Essequibo River
- **Length:** Up to 2.4in (6cm)
- **Tank length:** 18in (45cm)
- **Diet:** Worms, crustaceans, insects, plant matter, dried food
- **Water temperature:** 66 to 79°F (19 to 26°C)
- **Community tank**

A small squat catfish with an arched back, the Black-spotted Corydoras has two pairs of barbels on the upper jaw. The armor on the flanks consists of 21 to 23 bony plates in the upper row and 19 or 20 in the lower row. The rear edge of the dorsal fin is concave. A scattered, irregular pattern of brown dots marks the flanks, which can be grayish white or yellowish white with a slight reddish tinge. Starting at the top of the head, an almost triangular marking runs down across the eye to the lower part of the head. Also a wedge-shaped black bar extends from the front of the dorsal fin to a position just above the insertion of the pectoral fins. Small dark dots, which may be arranged in rows, mark the caudal and anal fins. The other fins are usually colorless and without markings.

*Corydoras melanistius* is a hardy, active catfish best kept in a shoal. The fishes swim near the bottom, where they scavenge for scraps of food. In fact, all the species of *Corydoras* are marvelous scavengers that help to keep the tank clean. The tank should have a soft, sandy substrate, in which the fishes will burrow with their snouts. However, this activity will usually discourage plant growth. After a period of driving, spawning may take place at intervals over several days. The eggs hatch in five or six days. The fry fall to the bottom, where they feed at first on various kinds of very tiny live food.

Right: **Corydoras melanistius**
*This rather soberly colored armored catfish with short barbels is an efficient scavenger.*

**A practical reminder**
The air pump should be situated above the water level if possible. Failing this, an anti-siphon loop in the air tubing will prevent water siphoning into the pump if it stops due to an electrical failure.

Left: **Corydoras myersi**
*This particularly attractive species has been bred in the aquarium, but probably not very frequently. It is a hardy, inquisitive fish that is well worth keeping.*

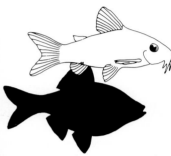

Family CALLICHTHYIDAE
## Corydoras myersi
*Myers' Corydoras*
- **Distribution:** South America: upper Amazon River in small tributaries
- **Length:** Up to 2.4in (6cm)
- **Tank length:** 18in (45cm)
- **Diet:** Worms, crustaceans, insects, plant matter, dried food
- **Water temperature:** 66 to 79°F (19 to 26°C)
- **Community tank**

A fairly deep-bodied armored catfish with a slightly arched back and three pairs of barbels, *Corydoras myersi* was first given a scientific description in 1942. The lateral armor has 22 or 23 bony plates in the upper row and 20 or 21 plates in the lower row. This is one of the more brightly colored of the *Corydoras* species. The general coloration is orange, but the top of the head and the throat are yellowish. Starting behind the head there is a broad, almost black band that extends back to the upper part of the tail base. The area around the gill cover may be iridescent green, and the eye and its immediate surroundings are very dark. The fins, which have no markings, are pale gray.

The many species of *Corydoras,* and also *Callichthys callichthys,* supplement the oxygen-gathering activity of their gills with an accessory respiratory organ. When living in waters that are low in oxygen or polluted, they rise to the surface and take in air through the mouth. The air is then passed through the alimentary tract to the hind-gut, where blood vessels extract the oxygen. Residual air passes out through the anus. If the atmosphere is sufficiently humid, it is not unusual for this and other species of *Corydoras* to come out on land and move about, using the spines of the pectorals as stilts to raise the body above the ground.

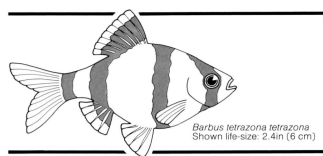

*Barbus tetrazona tetrazona*
Shown life-size: 2.4in (6 cm)

Family CALLICHTHYIDAE

## Corydoras paleatus
*Peppered Corydoras*

● **Distribution:** South America, in southeastern Brazil and La Plata Basin
● **Length:** Up to 2.8in (7cm)
● **Tank length:** 18in (45cm)
● **Diet:** Worms, crustaceans, insects, plant matter, dried food
● **Water temperature:** 66 to 79°F (19 to 26°C)
● **Community tank**

Peppered Corydoras is a tall-bodied catfish with two pairs of rather short barbels. The lateral armor has 22 to 24 bony plates in the upper row and 20 to 22 in the lower row. In the caudal fin the upper lobe is somewhat larger than the lower lobe. The dorsal fin is tall and pointed, and in the male the outer edge is ragged. The upperparts are dark olive-green or olive-brown and the underparts are pale yellow. The flanks are greenish with some iridescence, marked with large black spots that sometimes fuse to form transverse bands. This happens to some extent in the upperparts, and the body is more or less covered with small black dots. The dorsal and anal fins are gray, with a few dark dots. Dark spots also mark the caudal fin. These spots increase in number towards the tip of the fin.

*Corydoras paleatus* is probably the best-known and most widely kept species of *Corydoras*. This is not surprising, since the fish is very undemanding. The tank should have a soft bottom—preferably of sand—so that the fish can burrow. The composition of the water is not critical.

This is undoubtedly the beginner's catfish. It came into the aquarium world in the early 1890s, but it had already been bred in Paris in 1878 by M. Charbonnier. The breeding behavior is the same as in other species of *Corydoras*. This species may sometimes continue to spawn over several days.

Below: **Corydoras paleatus** ♂
*This is the easiest to breed of all the* Corydoras *catfishes. It is ideal for a beginner, being hardy and long-lived in the aquarium.*

Left: **Corydoras reticulatus**
*Often rests on smooth rocks.*

Family CALLICHTHYIDAE

## Corydoras reticulatus
*Reticulated Corydoras*

● **Distribution:** South America, in the Amazon River near Monte Alegre
● **Length:** Up to 2.8in (7cm)
● **Tank length:** 18in (45cm)
● **Diet:** Worms, crustaceans, insects, plant matter, dried food
● **Water temperature:** 66 to 79°F (19 to 26°C)
● **Community tank**

First described in 1938, Reticulated Corydoras is one of the most attractive of the armored catfishes. The body is high-backed and rather short and it has two pairs of barbels. The head, flanks, and back are iridescent

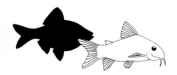

greenish or dark brown, marked with a bold netted pattern in black. The much paler belly shows little trace of this pattern. The young are gray to reddish with rather inconspicuous markings, and the full netted pattern is attained only when the fishes are sexually mature. There is a thin yellowish stripe running along the back from the base of the dorsal fin to the caudal fin. The dorsal fin itself is dark at the base with black dots in its outer part. The anal and caudal fins also have dark markings, but those on the caudal fin are arranged in rows. In general, the female is not as brightly colored as the male.

Spawning behavior follows the customary pattern for species of *Corydoras*. As usual the parents must be removed from the tank as soon as the female stops laying eggs. Some aquarists prefer to rear the brood in a carefully cleaned tank without substrate. This cuts down the risk of infection, and also enables any food remains to be removed.

**A practical reminder**
Plant the aquarium when it is three-quarters full. Use plants of the same species for best effect. Remember, not all plants tolerate the same water conditions and some will not grow happily together.

Family LORICARIIDAE

# Loricaria filamentosa
*Whiptail*

- **Distribution:** South America, in Rio Magdalena
- **Length:** Up to 10in (25cm)
- **Tank length:** 24in (60cm)
- **Diet:** Worms, insects, plant matter, dried food
- **Water temperature:** 72 to 79°F (22 to 26°C)
- **Community tank**

This elongated catfish has a dorso-ventrally flattened body that is covered by several rows of bony plates. Whiptail's mouth is ventral with lobed lips. The caudal peduncle is very long, and the upper lobe of the caudal fin ends in a whiplike prolongation. There is no adipose fin. The upperparts are gray-brown to yellowish brown and are marked with numerous irregular dark brown streaks and dots. On the caudal peduncle the markings coalesce to form transverse bars. The fins have dark tips and, with the exception of the caudal fin, they all start with a powerful spine. The sexes can be distinguished by the bristly outgrowths, which occur only in the adult male.

Whiptail is not difficult to keep in a tank with patches of dense vegetation and an arrangement of rocks and roots. This is all kept clean by the suction feeding of the fish. The water should be soft to medium-hard.

Before spawning the fishes clean a flat rock. The male and female lie over this spawning site as the eggs and sperm are shed. The eggs are guarded by the male, who fans fresh water over

them with his fins. As many as 100 to 200 amber-colored eggs may be laid. They are about 0.08in (2mm) in diameter. Hatching occurs in about nine days, and the fry should be kept in shallow water and fed on fine food.

Below: **Loricaria filamentosa** ♀♂
*This fish will keep the aquarium clean as it scavenges for food.*

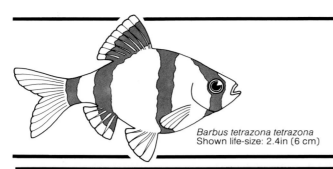

*Barbus tetrazona tetrazona*
Shown life-size: 2.4in (6 cm)

### Family LORICARIIDAE
# Otocinclus affinis
*Golden Otocinclus*
● **Distribution:** South America, in Brazil around Rio de Janeiro
● **Length:** Up to 1.6in (4cm)
● **Tank length:** 12in (30cm)
● **Diet:** Worms, plant matter, dried food
● **Water temperature:** 66 to 77°F (19 to 25°C)
● **Community tank**

This is a small catfish with a moderately elongated body covered with bony plates. The mouth is ventral and acts as a sucker, and there is no adipose fin. The flanks of the Golden Otocinclus are silvery-white with a broad black longitudinal band that extends from the gill cover to the base of the tail. The belly is whitish and the fins are colorless, without any pattern.

*Otocinclus affinis* is a bottom-living fish that does well in a tank with areas of vegetation and some rocks and roots, preferably covered with algae. This fish is mainly active at night. During this time it browses algae, which helps to keep the tank clean.

After a period of courtship the eggs are laid—more or less at random—on rocks, leaves, or the glass panes of the tank. They hatch in about two days and the fry can be reared on tiny nauplii, micro-worms, and sieved hard-boiled egg yolk.

The very similar *Otocinclus flexilis* can be distinguished by its pattern of spots on the dorsal, anal, and ventral fins.

Right: **Otocinclus affinis**
*This small, mainly nocturnal catfish is not very easy to breed.*

130

**A practical reminder**
Avoid disturbing the contoured gravel
when filling your tank. Direct the water into
a jug or shallow dish standing on the
gravel. Bring the water up to the
appropriate temperature by adding hot water.

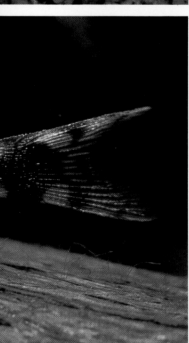

Family LORICARIIDAE
# Hypostomus punctatus
*Suckermouth Catfish*
● **Distribution:** South America, in southern Brazil
● **Length:** Up to 12in (30cm)
● **Tank length:** 24in (60cm)
● **Diet:** Worms, plant matter, dried food
● **Water temperature:** 66 to 79°F (19 to 26°C)
● **Community tank**

Formerly known as *Plecostomus punctatus*, this catfish can grow to a length of 6 to 8in (15 to 20cm) in a public aquarium but is unlikely to reach this size in a home aquarium. The body is elongated and slightly compressed laterally.

Suckermouth Catfish is covered in bony plates everywhere except on the belly. The head is very broad and flattened with a ventral sucking mouth and two barbels. The back and flanks are brown or brownish gray with dark dots and five oblique transverse bars. The belly is whitish to pale brown and the fins are brownish with fairly large rounded spots arranged in rows. The dorsal fin is particularly tall and flaglike, and the first ray is spiny. An adipose fin is present.

The Suckermouth is a very hardy and peaceful catfish. It is best kept in a tank with rocks and roots to provide hiding-places and with a few floating plants at the surface. It is mainly nocturnal and can scarcely be described as colorful. This is an excellent consumer of algae, browsing

Above and above left:
**Hypostomus punctatus**
*This is an excellent fish when small. It cleans the tank as it browses algae with its large sucking mouth.*

from rocks and aquarium glass. The tank should have medium-hard water. Approximately one teaspoonful of sea salt should be added to every 2.5 gallons (10 liters) of fresh water.

*Plecostomus punctatus* and the related *P. commersoni* are not known to have bred in captivity.

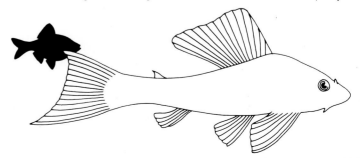

# THE EGG-LAYING TOOTHCARPS

Above: *Aphyosemion australe*, a toothcarp from
the acid waters of western Africa.
Right: A lake in Senegal, West Africa, the
typical home of many egg-laying toothcarps.

*These egg-laying toothcarps form a family of mostly small
fishes with representatives in Africa, America, Asia, and
Europe. The majority live only in fresh waters, a few in
brackish waters, and very few in the sea. The body is always
elongated and the top of the head is flattened. The mouth is
usually protrusible and faces upward; thus it is well adapted for
feeding at the surface. Many species vary in color and pattern
and there are numerous subspecies or local forms. Sex differences
are almost always quite distinct, the males being larger with
longer fins and having more intense coloration.*

*There are two main breeding patterns. Some species lay their
eggs among the vegetation, and the eggs adhere to the leaves; others
spawn within the substrate. Almost all the substrate spawners
are annual fishes. This means that they live in relatively small
bodies of water that dry up at certain times of the year.
Spawning takes place before this occurs and the parents leave the
eggs in the substrate. Then the parent fishes die when the water
recedes. The eggs, which have remarkably hard shells, remain in
the damp substrate for a resting period of several weeks or
months, and hatch only when the rains return. The fry grow
rapidly and become sexually mature during a single season in
much the same way as annual plants. This unusual method of
reproduction means that, during the dry season, each species
survives only as a varying number of fertilized eggs—without any
adult individuals.*

*Skilled home aquarists have contributed much to our knowledge
of the biology of fish reproduction from observing fishes of the
Cyprinodontidae.*

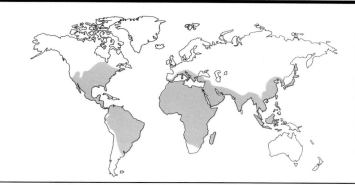

Left: The family Cyprinodontidae contains about 450 species, classified into eight subfamilies. The majority live in tropical America, Asia, or Africa. There are very few species in Europe or North America. Some live only in acid waters; others prefer alkaline waters, sometimes with a certain amount of salt. A few egg-laying toothcarps in South America and Africa live in temporary ponds.

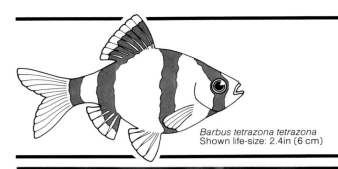

*Barbus tetrazona tetrazona*
Shown life-size: 2.4in (6 cm)

Family CYRINODONTIDAE

## Aphyosemion australe
*Lyretail*

- **Distribution:** West Africa: Gabon, Cameroon, Congo
- **Length:** Up to 2.2in (5.5cm)
- **Tank length:** 12in (30cm)
- **Diet:** Worms, crustaceans, insects, dried food
- **Water temperature:** 73 to 83°F (23 to 28°C)
- **Species tank**

Lyretail is an elongated species. The dorsal and anal fins are set far back on the body and their tips are more prolonged in the male. The upper and lower rays of the caudal fin are also elongated and pointed in the male. The whole body is markedly lyre-shaped. The fins of the female are more rounded.

The coloration of the sexes differs considerably. The background coloration of the male is yellowish brown to brownish orange. Bright red dots appear on the flanks and on the dorsal and caudal fins. The area of the gill cover is bluish or pale green. The caudal fin has a blue center, surrounded by a red

Above: **Aphyosemion australe** ♂
*Sometimes known as the Cape Lopez Lyretail, this toothcarp is fairly hardy when kept in soft water.*

border. The elongated tips of the lobes are white. A white border encloses the dorsal fin. Comparatively plain, the female is pale brown with scattered red dots.

This species is best kept as a pair in a tank without other fishes. The substrate should be dark and the vegetation fairly dense. The water must be soft, slightly acid, and filtered through peat. The eggs are laid on leaves and they adhere to them. It is best to remove the eggs to a separate small tank with shallow water. The eggs hatch in 12 to 20 days and the young can be fed immediately on rotifers and tiny nauplii.

A very attractive orange variety— Hjerresen's Aphyosemion has been bred in the aquarium.

Family CYPRINODONTIDAE

## Aplocheilus blocki
*Green Panchax, Dwarf Panchax*

- **Distribution:** Southern India and Sri Lanka
- **Length:** Up to 2in (5cm)
- **Tank length:** 12in (30cm)
- **Diet:** Worms, crustaceans, insects, dried food
- **Water temperature:** 72 to 83°F (22 to 28°C)
- **Species tank**

*Aplocheilus blocki* is a moderately elongated toothcarp. The front part of its body is roundish in the cross section and the rear part is laterally compressed. When viewed from the side its head appears flat and rounded. The dorsal fin is positioned far back over the rear end of the anal fin. The general coloration of the male is yellow-green or olive-green with longitudinal rows of bright yellow or reddish dots. The underparts are more blue-green. The dorsal, anal, and caudal fins are slightly yellowish with brown or red dots. Though far less colorful—usually yellowish gray—the female has a characteristic black marking at the base of the dorsal fin.

This is the smallest of the *Aplocheilus* species from

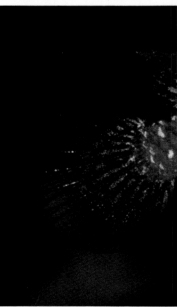

southern Asia. It lives and feeds mainly just below the surface of the water. The tank should have some vegetation but, more important, the water should be soft and preferably filtered through peat. The male swims around the female in a kind of aquatic

**A practical reminder**
Specimen plants may be grown in shallow pots buried in the gravel. This will enable you to give them special feeding if necessary and the plant will not be unduly disturbed if it is transplanted to another tank.

Family CYPRINODONTIDAE

# Aphyosemion filamentosum
*Plumed Lyretail*
● **Distribution:** West Africa, in Nigeria.
● **Length:** Up to 2.2in (5.5cm)
● **Tank length:** 12in (30cm)
● **Diet:** Worms, crustaceans, insects, dried food
● **Water temperature:** 68 to 75°F (20 to 24°C)
● **Species tank**

The dorsal and anal fins of this relatively short-bodied toothcarp lie opposite one another and are positioned far back on the body. In the male these fins are well developed and have toothed edges, but in the female they are somewhat smaller and the edges are not toothed. The upper and lower rays of the male's caudal fin are elongated, but not as much as in the Lyretail *(Aphyosemion australe)*.

The general coloration of the male is sky-blue to greenish marked with bright red dots. The belly is violet. The red markings on the flanks may appear to be arranged in diagonal rows. This is particularly so on the gill cover.

Above: **Aphyosemion filamentosum** ♂(t), ♀(b)
*Some aquarists carefully transfer the newly laid eggs of this species to a separate unlit tank.*

The dorsal and caudal fins have smaller red dots. The anal fin is blue and marked with a red horizontal band. The female is similarly colored but not nearly as brightly.

This species swims mainly in the middle water layers. It should be kept as a pair in a tank with some vegetation and a dark substrate. However, some aquarists dispense with the substrate and place a sheet of black paper below the bottom glass of the tank. The water must be soft, slightly acid, and filtered through peat. The eggs are laid on plants or sometimes on the bottom of the tank. They hatch in 20 to 40 days and the fry can be fed immediately on rotifers and very small brine shrimp nauplii.

courtship dance. Spawning takes place among the plants. The eggs are laid on the leaves and hatch in 12 to 15 days. It is best to remove the parent fishes before this happens. The fry should be fed on very tiny live food, such as rotifers and small nauplii.

Above: **Aplocheilus blocki**
*A tiny fish best kept as a pair.*

135

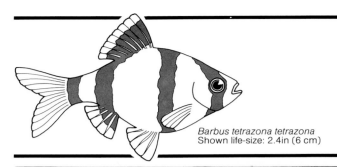

Barbus tetrazona tetrazona
Shown life-size: 2.4in (6 cm)

Family CYPRINODONTIDAE

## Aplocheilus dayi
*Ceylon Killifish*

- **Distribution:** Sri Lanka
- **Length:** Up to 2.8in (7cm)
- **Tank length:** 12in (30cm)
- **Diet:** Worms, crustaceans, insects, fish, dried food
- **Water temperature:** 70 to 77°F (21 to 25°C)
- **Community tank:** Keep with larger species only

This elongated, laterally compressed toothcarp has a flat head and a pointed snout. The short dorsal fin of the Ceylon Killifish is positioned over the last few rays of the much longer anal fin, which is pointed in the male and rounded in the female. The back of the male is golden-brown and the belly is pale bluish. The flanks are an iridescent yellow-green and each scale is marked with a shiny yellow dot. The fins are mainly yellow-green with small red markings. The iris of the eye is greenish or pale yellow. Although the female has the same type of coloration, she is much duller. Also a few dark transverse bars appear on the rear part of the body. These markings are evident

Above: **Aplocheilus dayi** ♀(t),♂(b)
*The growing fry should be sorted into sizes to prevent cannibalism.*

in young males, but are lost in adult males.

*Aplocheilus dayi* is a hardy toothcarp that should be kept only with larger fishes. The tank must have a good lid to prevent jumping. Some areas of dense vegetation, a few floating plants, and some well-washed roots should be included. Soft water, filtered through peat if possible, is best. During courtship the male swims in circles around the female. They spawn together near the bottom, often on the plants or roots. Spawning may go on for one or two weeks. The female lays eight to 10 eggs a day. Plants with attached eggs can be transferred to a separate tank. Hatching should take place in 12 to 14 days, and the fry can be reared on very tiny live food.

Family CYPRINODONTIDAE

## Aplocheilus panchax
*Blue Panchax*

- **Distribution:** India to Malaysia
- **Length:** Up to 3.2in (8cm)
- **Tank length:** 12in (30cm)
- **Diet:** Worms, crustaceans, insects, fish, dried food
- **Water temperature:** 70 to 77°F (21 to 25°C)
- **Community tank:** Keep with larger species only

This old favorite, introduced into the aquarium around 1899, is usually considered to be the most suitable toothcarp for a beginner. The body of the Blue Panchax is similar in shape to the other two species of *Aplocheilus* described in this book, but the coloration is quite different. In general, the male is a grayish yellow that becomes darker on the back and paler with blue iridescence on the underparts. The popular name refers to the scales on the flanks, which are iridescent blue in the middle with a thin dark edge. The dorsal fin is pale blue in the center and blackish at the base and edge. The anal fin is orange at the base and becomes reddish towards the edge. The caudal fin

is also orange at the base but white towards the rear edge. The female shows paler colors and more rounded fins.

Like many other toothcarps, *Aplocheilus panchax* is somewhat predatory so it can only be kept in a community tank with larger fishes. In addition to a good lid, the tank should have roots on the bottom, dense vegetation, and a few floating plants. If possible, the water should be soft. After vigorous driving by the male, the pair spawn among the plants. This goes on for some days. During this period plants with eggs should be moved to a separate tank with exactly the same type of water. The eggs hatch in 12 to 14 days and the fry are then fed on rotifers and small nauplii.

Right: **Aplocheilus panchax** ♂
*With a rich and varied diet the young usually grow very rapidly.*

**A practical reminder**
Sandwich activated carbon between filter wool when placing it in the filter body. Fill box filters with water by siphon tubes before switching on the air supply to start a water flow through the filter.

Family CYPRINODONTIDAE

# Aplocheilichthys macrophthalmus
*Lamp-eye Panchax*

- **Distribution:** Tropical West Africa
- **Length:** Up to 1.6in (4cm)
- **Tank length:** 24in (60cm)
- **Diet:** Worms, crustaceans, insects, dried food
- **Water temperature:** 72 to 79°F (22 to 26°C)
- **Species tank**

Lamp-eye Panchax is a handsome toothcarp with a slender, elongated body and strikingly large eyes that reflect golden-green iridescence. The dorsal fin is positioned far back on the body. It is pointed in the male and rounded in the female. The rear edge of the caudal fin is truncated or slightly convex. The body, as a whole, is more or less translucent. The upperparts are pale olive or yellowish gray and the underparts are yellowish with a bright sheen. There is a reddish stripe along the midline of the back. The pale yellow flanks have two iridescent blue-green stripes running back from behind the gill cover. The upper stripe is bordered by a thin black streak. The dorsal and anal fins are translucent with pale gray or blue edges. The caudal fin is blue with orange dots.

This very small toothcarp lives in the upper water layers, often right below the surface. It should be kept in a small shoal and in a tank with some vegetation planted to leave sufficient space for swimming. The water flowing out of a filter can be allowed to produce a surface current. For juveniles and adults the water should be hard or neutral because this reduces the risk of tuberculosis. On the other hand, breeding is more successful in soft or medium-hard water. Spawning goes on over a period of about two weeks. The female lays 15 to 20 eggs a day. These hatch in 11 to 14 days, and the fry can be reared on *Paramecium*, rotifers, and pulverized dried food.

Above:
**Aplocheilichthys macrophthalmus**
*Well-aerated water is recommended.*

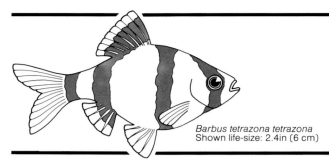

*Barbus tetrazona tetrazona*
Shown life-size: 2.4in (6 cm)

Family CYPRINODONTIDAE
## Cynolebias bellotti
*Argentine Pearlfish*
- **Distribution:** South America, in Rio de la Plata
- **Length:** Male up to 2.8in (7cm), female slightly less
- **Tank length:** 18in (45cm)
- **Diet:** Worm, crustaceans, insects, dried food
- **Water temperature:** 66 to 86°F (19 to 30°C)
- **Species tank**

The body of the Argentine Pearlfish is tall and laterally compressed. It has rounded fins. The dorsal fin is directly above the anal fin. These fins have about four more rays in the male than they do in the female. The dark blue male is covered with whitish or pale blue iridescent dots, which extend onto the head and the bases of the dorsal, caudal, and anal fins. During spawning the background coloration becomes almost black. A dark diagonal band runs from the nape across the eye. The pale yellow female has irregular dark markings and a large round dark spot in the middle of the flanks.

*Cynolebias bellotti* is an annual or seasonal toothcarp. In the wild it lives in waters that dry up during the dry season. The adult fishes then die, but they have spawned, leaving fertilized eggs in the mud.

These habits are so deeply ingrained that the fishes live only a short period in an aquarium, and their eggs require a resting period in a semi-dry state. A mature pair placed in an all-glass tank with peat and soft water will start to spawn almost immediately— usually after some courtship display. The eggs may be pushed into the soft substrate by the anal fin of the female, or both fishes may burrow into the substrate to spawn. This procedure sometimes goes on for two or three weeks. The eggs should be kept for six weeks or longer in damp peat at 64 to 68° (18 to 20°C). They hatch when the tank is flooded, and the fry should be fed immediately on pulverized dried food.

Below: **Cynolebias bellotti** ♂♀♀
*The males quarrel, so this species is best kept as a single pair.*

Family CYPRINODONTIDAE
## Cynolebias nigripinnis
*Dwarf Argentine Pearlfish*
- **Distribution:** South America, in Rio de la Plata and Rio Paraná
- **Length:** Male up to 2in (5cm), female slightly less
- **Tank length:** 12in (30cm)
- **Diet:** Worms, crustaceans, insects, dried food
- **Water temperature:** 64 to 77°F (18 to 25°C)
- **Species tank**

*Cynolebias nigripinnis* is a smaller, but somewhat more slender, version of *Cynolebias bellotti*. The rear edges of the dorsal and anal fins of the male are more pointed than those of the female. In mature males, body and fins are a brilliant blue-black with numerous iridescent blue or green dots. Just below the edge of the dorsal fin, the dots fuse to form an iridescent longitudinal band. On the caudal fin and the edge of the anal fin, the dots are arranged in rows. The female is yellow with irregular dark markings, but lacks the flank spot seen in *Cynolebias bellotti*.

Although the Dwarf Argentine Pearlfish is a rather delicate fish, it often behaves quite aggressively. So at no time should the tank contain two males. A mature pair should be placed in a small tank with a soft peat substrate, some marginal vegetation, and open water for swimming. The water should be soft and slightly acid. The pair should have been well fed in separate tanks for at least a week before being put together. After a period of driving they spawn on the bottom and the eggs are laid in the peat substrate. This usually continues for eight to 10 days. Afterwards the pair should be removed from the tank, and the water should be drained. The eggs must be left in the damp peat— in the dark— for 90 days at 68 to 72°F (20 to 22°C). The eggs start to hatch as water is added to the tank. The fry should be fed immediately on pulverized dried food.

Right: **Cynolebias nigripinnis** ♂(t)♀
*More strikingly patterned than C. bellotti, this species is not always easy to keep and is certainly not suitable for a beginner.*

**A practical reminder**
Reduce pressure of water returning from power filters by the use of a spray bar, which distributes the water across the whole aquarium. Ensure that all the hose connections and fixtures are secure.

Family CYPRINODONTIDAE

# Epiplatys sexfasciatus
*Six-barred Epiplatys*

● **Distribution:** West Africa: Ghana to Gabon
● **Length:** Up to 4in (10cm)
● **Tank length:** 18in (45cm)
● **Diet:** Worms, crustaceans, insects, fish, dried food
● **Water temperature:** 72 to 83°F (22 to 28°C)
● **Species tank**

Six-barred Epiplatys is an elongated, predatory toothcarp that was introduced to the aquarium around 1910. Both the dorsal and anal fins are positioned far back on the body, giving the fish a pikelike appearance. The dorsal fin, however, is considerably shorter than the anal fin. The back of the male is pale brown to olive-brown and the belly is whitish. The flanks are iridescent bronze, green, or blue, and the scales have red dots that are sometimes edged with black. There are six transverse bars on the lower part of the body. The dorsal, caudal, and anal fins are blue, orange, red, or green. The dorsal and anal ones have pointed tips. The eye is dark green enclosed within a narrow golden circle. The lips are black. The female is much paler and has rounded anal and dorsal fins. The great variation in coloration of this species is related to the very extensive geographical range.

This is a surface-living fish that can be kept in a tank with some areas of dense vegetation around the edges and a few floating plants. The water should be soft, slightly acid, and filtered through peat. The substrate should consist of fine sand. Spawning takes place among the plants and the

Above: **Epiplatys sexfasciatus** ♂
*The eggs of this rather timid fish hatch over a long period and the fry must be sorted according to size to prevent cannibalism.*

female usually lays one egg at a time. This may continue for 12 to 15 days with a final yield of 120 to 300 eggs. These usually hatch in 10 to 12 days, but the period varies. Soon after hatching, the fry start to swim at the surface and to feed on nauplii.

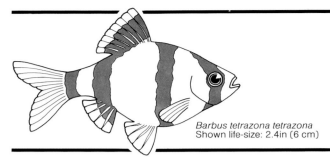

*Barbus tetrazona tetrazona*
Shown life-size: 2.4in (6 cm)

Family CYPRINODONTIDAE
## Jordanella floridae
*American Flagfish*
- **Distribution:** North America. Florida and Mexico
- **Length:** Up to 2.4in (6cm)
- **Tank length:** 24in (60cm)
- **Diet:** Worms, crustaceans, insects, plant matter, dried food
- **Water temperature:** 66 to 72°F (19 to 22°C)
- **Community tank**

*Jordanella floridae* is a short, rather squat species with a tall caudal peduncle and a dorsal fin that starts in the middle of the back and forwards of the anal fin. The caudal fin has a rounded rear edge. The back is brownish olive and the belly is yellowish to silvery-white. The flanks are olive-green and each scale has an iridescent blue or yellow-green spot. This combination of colors produces rows of glistening dots, which are particularly striking when seen in reflected light. The anal and dorsal fins are greenish or yellowish with rows of red-brown dots or bands. The general coloration of the female is yellow with a checkerboard pattern of dark markings on the sides of the body and a dark spot at the rear of the dorsal fin.

This species can be kept at a relatively low temperature in a tank with a dark substrate, dense

Right: **Jordanella floridae** ♂
*This hardy fish has interesting breeding habits that resemble those of the brood-protecting cichlids.*

marginal vegetation, and a few isolated plants with tough leaves. If the aquarium glass has a growth of algae, it will not matter because the American Flagfish is largely a vegetarian and will soon clear up any soft plant matter. The males establish territories, and when placed in an aquarium they become quite aggressive towards one another. For breeding, it is best to have only a single male in the tank. The composition of the water is not important. After vigorous driving, the pair spawn in a small pit that was previously prepared by the male. About 100 eggs are laid. The male will carefully guard them until they hatch in six to nine days. The fry will feed at first on tiny live food and can later be moved to a tank with a good growth of algae, which are their favorite food.

Family CYPRINODONTIDAE
## Oryzias melastigma
- **Distribution:** India and Sri Lanka
- **Length:** Up to 2in (5cm)
- **Tank length:** 18in (45cm)
- **Diet:** Worms, crustaceans, insects, dried food
- **Water temperature:** 73 to 79°F (23 to 26°C)
- **Community tank**

*Oryzias melastigma* is a moderately elongated, laterally compressed toothcarp with a very convex belly profile. The head and nape region are noticeably flat. The dorsal fin is small and positioned close to the rear of the body. The anal fin has a long base and is rounded in the

Left: **Oryzias melastigma** ♂ ♀
*This photograph shows the female (below the male) just after spawning, with the eggs still attached.*

male, but truncated or slightly concave in the female. The caudal fin is fanlike. When viewed in reflected light the body appears rather translucent with pale blue iridescence. There are several dark markings on the flanks and a narrow longitudinal streak. The dorsal, caudal and anal fins are colorless or pale orange. In the slightly larger female the dorsal and anal fins are smaller than in the male.

This is an active small fish that should be kept in a shoal in a tank with a substrate of fine sand and a few floating plants. For adults the water should be hard, but for spawning it should be soft and slightly acid. This is the same paradoxical situation seen in the Lamp-eye Panchax. At spawning time the male and female nudge each other with the rear part of the body, and the male wraps his anal fin around the female. The eggs are laid, then fertilized by the male. For a few hours the female swims around with the eggs still attached to her, but eventually she rubs them onto the plants. They hatch in 12 to 16 days and the fry are then fed on infusorians, rotifers, and tiny nauplii.

**A practical reminder**
Learn to recognize a fish's likely living and feeding habits by its appearance. Torpedo shape—fast swimmer. Upturned mouth—surface feeder. Underslung mouth and flat belly—bottom-dweller.

Family CYPRINODONTIDAE
# Pachypanchax playfairi
*Playfair's Panchax*

● **Distribution:** Seychelles, Zanzibar, probably also East Africa
● **Length:** Up to 4in (10cm)
● **Tank length:** 18in (45cm)
● **Diet:** Worms, crustaceans, insects, fish, dried food
● **Water temperature:** 72 to 77°F (22 to 25°C)
● **Community tank**

Playfair's Panchax is an elongated toothcarp with a flattened forehead and nape region. The body is round in front and laterally compressed at the back. The dorsal fin is positioned above the rear half of the anal fin. The back of the male is brown, and the underparts are yellowish. The flanks are bright emerald-green with longitudinal rows of red dots. The dorsal, caudal, and anal fins are yellow-green with rows of tiny red dots; the caudal and anal ones have a narrow black border. The female is more uniformly colored, with colorless fins, except that the dorsal fin has a prominent black spot at the base.

This is an active—often aggressive—toothcarp that can be kept in a tank with clumps of dense vegetation. Any other occupants of the tank should be equal in size or larger. The substrate should be fine sand; the water should be soft or medium-hard. A few floating plants would also be suitable. For breeding, it is usually best to put one male and two females together. After a short period of courtship, with the male and one female pressing against each other, spawning takes place among the plants. The female may lay 100 to 150 eggs over a period of 12 to 14 days, and these hatch in 10 to 12 days. The fry start to feed shortly after hatching. By that time most of them will already be swimming at the surface. Some aquarists remove the eggs from the breeding tank and put them into a separate tank for hatching and rearing.

Below: **Pachypanchax playfairi** ♂
*At certain times, and particularly during spawning, the scales of the male stick out. This is wrongly interpreted as a sign of disease.*

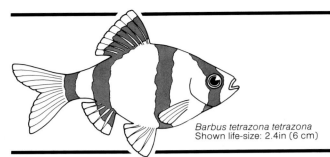

*Barbus tetrazona tetrazona*
Shown life-size: 2.4in (6 cm)

Family CYPRINODONTIDAE

## Pterolebias longipinnis

*Featherfin Panchax*

● **Distribution:** South America, in Brazil.
● **Length:** Up to 4in (10cm)
● **Tank length:** 18in (45cm)
● **Diet:** Worms, crustaceans, insects, dried food
● **Water temperature:** 72 to 79°F (22 to 26°C)
● **Species tank**

An elongated, short-lived toothcarp, Featherfin Panchax has some lateral compression in the region of the caudal peduncle. In the male the dorsal and anal fins are particularly well developed and their pointed tips extend back far beyond the base of the caudal fin. In the slightly smaller female the fins are rounded and not as large. The male is mainly dark brown with paler brown on the underparts. The flanks show

grayish blue iridescence and oblique rows of green or yellow dots. The smaller female is paler brown and lacks the rows of dots. Just above the base of the pectoral fins the male has an irregular cinnabar-red shoulder marking. The fins are brown with dark spots and streaks.

*Pterolebias longipinnis* is one of the annual species and it is best kept in a separate tank with a substrate of peat, marginal

vegetation, and sufficient space for swimming. The water should be soft and slightly acid. For breeding, the tank can have a pair or, if the male drives too vigorously, one male and two females. Before this the fishes should be kept apart and fed for at least a week on a rich diet, such as white worms and insect larvae. They usually spawn very soon after being put into the breeding tank. The eggs are laid in the substrate. Spawning may continue for eight to 10 days. When spawning is over, the parents must be moved to another tank. The breeding tank water should then be drained off carefully, leaving the eggs in the damp peat. They should remain there for 55 to 70 days. They will hatch when water is subsequently added to the tank.

Left: **Pterolebias longipinnis** ♂
*Some eggs of this species may remain dormant for several months.*

Family CYPRINODONTIDAE

## Roloffia occidentalis

*Red Aphyosemion*

● **Distribution:** Africa, in Sierra Leone
● **Length:** Up to 3.5in (9cm)
● **Tank length:** 12in (30cm)
● **Diet:** Worms, crustaceans, insects, dried food
● **Water temperature:** 70 to 75°F (21 to 24°C)
● **Species tank**

Red Aphyosemion is a moderately elongated, short-lived toothcarp. The dorsal fin sits roughly above the anal fin in the rear part of the body. The caudal fin is fan-shaped in the male, but ovate in the female. The coloration of the male—though always brilliant—varies. The back is orange-yellow with a yellow border. The usually bright blue throat becomes even darker at spawning time. The flanks are orange-red to golden with irregular dark red dots and streaks. The dorsal fin has areas of blue and red. The anal fin is similarly colored, but may have a white tip. There are two red bands on the caudal peduncle, one above and one below, and these extend back to the rear edge of the caudal fin. The female is red-

brown with indistinct brown markings.

This rather aggressive fish swims mostly in the middle and lower water layers. The tank should have a few areas of dense vegetation and a substrate of peat. The water must be soft and slightly acid. After a period of courtship the pair spawn in the substrate. In the wild the waters dry up, and the parents die. The

eggs, which were left in the mud, hatch only when the waters return at the start of the next rainy season. In an aquarium the water should be drained off and the eggs should remain in the damp peat for at least six weeks. They hatch when the tank is refilled with water. The fry start to feed almost immediately on rotifers and small nauplii. The eggs should be checked for mold during storage.

Above: **Roloffia occidentalis** ♂
*The eggs of this African toothcarp may hatch after several weeks rather than a rest of several months.*

**A practical reminder**
Disk-shaped fishes inhabit slow-moving or still waters. Fishes with large eyes live in deep or muddy waters. Fishes with no eyes navigate with lateral line systems, sensing obstructions by reflected vibrations.

### Family ANABLEPIDAE
This is a very small family (only two species) distributed from southern Mexico to northern South America. The horizontal partitioning of each eye allows the fish to see above and below water at the same time.

Family ANABLEPIDAE
## Anableps anableps
*Four-eyes*
- **Distribution:** Southern Mexico to northern South America
- **Length:** Up to 8in (20cm), possibly more
- **Tank length:** 36in (90cm)
- **Diet:** Insects
- **Water temperature:** 73 to 77°F (23 to 25°C)
- **Community tank:** May eat smaller fishes

Four-eyes has a flat head and very protruding eyes. The dorsal fin of this elongated fish is very small and set far back on the body; the caudal fin is oval. The male is easily distinguishable by the prominent gonopodium. The back is bluish gray, and the flanks and underparts are yellowish with no distinct markings. The fins are blue-gray.

The cornea, pupil, and retina of the eyes are separated into two parts by a horizontal bridge of tissue. The fish swims at the surface of the water with the upper half of the eye above the surface. Distant objects out of the water are perceived by the upper eye and registered on the lower half of the retina, while closer objects under water are seen by the lower half-eye and registered in the upper half of the retina. The upper eye, therefore, allows the fish to see enemies approaching.

This unusual-looking fish requires a shallow tank with a well-fitting lid, as it is a good jumper. The water must have added sea salt (about 5 teaspoonsful to every 2.5 gallons/ 10 liters of fresh water).

The genital opening of about half of all female Four-eyes faces to the left, and in the other half it faces right. Some of the males have the gonopodium turning to the right, others to the left. Males with a gonopodium turning to the right mate with females that have the genital opening facing left, and vice versa. The females produce a small number of live young (about six) twice a year, but these are already 1.2 to 2in (3 to 5cm) long.

Above: **Anableps anableps**
*Bifocal eyes enable this fish to see both above and below the water.*

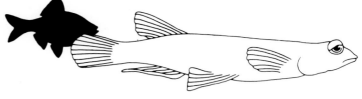

# THE LIVE-BEARING TOOTHCARPS

Above: *Xiphophorus variatus*, a live-bearer
from Mexico that breeds very freely.
Right: A river in Mexico, the natural habitat
of many of the popular live-bearers.

*These live-bearing toothcarps are mostly small fishes distributed from the southern United States, throughout Central America including the West Indies, and south to northern Argentina. However, some species have now been taken by man to many other tropical areas, where they are bred in large numbers for the aquarium trade. A few species have been introduced into malarial areas to control mosquito larvae.*

*Female live-bearers are usually larger than the males, but the latter have more striking colors and patterns, and often longer fins. The males also have a special organ, known as the gonopodium, which develops from the anal fin and is used to transfer packets of sperm to the female. The gonopodium consists of the third, fourth, and fifth rays of the anal fin; the other rays of this fin are much smaller. During mating the gonopodium is turned forward and its fin rays form a trough that is closed by the ventral fin to form a tube. The packets of sperm pass down this tube into the oviduct of the female. There the packets break up to release the sperm, some of which fertilize the ripe eggs, while the remainder are stored in the folds of the oviduct wall. A single mating is sufficient for several pregnancies. The yolky eggs develop within the oviduct and the young are born alive. In most species the female's tissues do not nourish the embryo, but in a few species the female may pass nutrients to the embryos.*

*The live-bearing toothcarps are among the most popular aquarium fishes. This is due to their small size and handsome coloration, and the ease with which they can be bred. Over a period of several years, aquarists have bred and selected a large number of new color variants and also new fin shapes.*

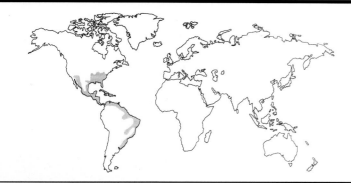

Left: The map shows the natural range of the family Poeciliidae, of which about 130 species are known, in addition to the numerous varieties produced in the aquarium. Most of the species occur in areas north of the equator. The Amazon River evidently forms a barrier, and few species occur further south. Most live-bearing toothcarps live in lakes or close to river banks, and some extend into brackish waters.

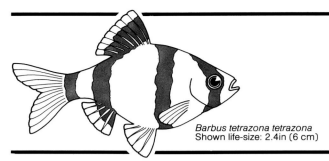

*Barbus tetrazona tetrazona*
Shown life-size: 2.4in (6 cm)

Family POECILIIDAE
## Gambusia affinis
*Mosquito Fish*
- **Distribution:** Southeastern United States, Texas and northern Mexico
- **Length:** Male up to 1.6in (4cm), female to 2.6in (6.5cm)
- **Tank length:** 24in (60cm)
- **Diet:** Worms, crustaceans, insects, plant matter, dried food
- **Water temperature:** 64 to 68°F (18 to 20°C)
- **Species tank**

There are two subspecies of *Gambusia affinis.* The typical one is *Gambusia affinis affinis* from Texas, and the very similar *G. affinis holbrooki* comes from the southeastern United States and northern Mexico. The following description is based on the typical subspecies. *Gambusia affinis affinis* is a spindle-shaped fish with a dorsal fin that starts behind the middle of the body, and with a fan-shaped caudal fin. As in other members of the Poeciliidae, part of the anal fin is modified to form a gonopodium. The back of the male is brown or olive-brown, and the underparts are silvery. In general, the flanks are gray with a delicate bluish iridescence and are sometimes marked with a few black dots. These markings also occur on the dorsal and caudal fins. The fins are otherwise colorless or very pale yellow. The female usually has the same coloration as the male but a larger anal fin. The Mexican subspecies differs only in that it has irregular black markings on the flanks.

Although quite small in size, Mosquito Fish is an aggressive live-bearer that nips the fins of other fishes. Therefore, it is best kept in a species tank. The composition of the water is not at all critical. In an aquarium the fishes breed at all times of the year. The females produce up to 60 live young after a gestation period of six to eight weeks. The parents are apt to eat their young.

*G. affinis* has been introduced in many areas for the control of mosquito larvae. It is very hardy and can be kept in winter at temperatures as low as 50 to 54°F (10 to 12°C).

Below:
**Gambusia affinis holbrooki** ♂
*The gonopodium is clearly seen on this male of the Mexican subspecies.*

Family POECILIIDAE
## Heterandria formosa
*Least Killifish*
- **Distribution:** North America, from North Carolina to Florida
- **Length:** Male up to 0.8 (2cm), female to 1.4in (3.5cm)
- **Tank length:** 12in (30cm)
- **Diet:** Worms, crustaceans, plant matter, dried food
- **Water temperature:** 68 to 75°F (20 to 24°C)
- **Community tank:** Keep with small, peaceful species

Least Killifish is an elongated live-bearer with moderate lateral compression and rather poorly developed fins. The male is much more slender than the female. The background coloration is yellowish brown or red-brown with striking pearly iridescence when seen in reflected light. An irregular dark brown band extends from the tip of the snout to the base of the caudal fin and it is crossed by six to 12 similarly colored short transverse bars. These bars become paler with increasing age. The fins are yellowish to brownish. The base of the anal fin has a black spot; the base of the dorsal fin has a similar spot with an orange border.

This very active fish swims mainly in the middle and lower water layers. The tank can have some vegetation but filamentous algae should be removed. Any other occupants of the tank should be small and peaceful. The water should be hard and slightly alkaline.

The males are often aggressive towards one another. After a period of courtship, the male—using his copulatory organ (gonopodium)—introduces sperm into the female's genital opening. In this particular species, but not in the other live-bearers described in this book, the eggs derive some nourishment from the female. Over a period of six to 10 days a single female may produce two or three young per day. These fry should be fed on very fine live food and pulverized dried food, and protected from their parents.

Right: **Heterandria formosa** ♀
*This fish is one of the smallest of all known vertebrates.*

**A practical reminder**
Some bottom-dwelling species, such as Gobies, have their ventral fins joined together to form a suction disk. This anchors them to rocks and keeps them from being swept away by water currents.

Family POECILIIDAE

## Poecilia hybrid
*Black Molly*

● **Distribution:** Venezuela, Colombia, Mexico
● **Length:** Up to 4in (10cm)
● **Tank length:** 18in (45cm)
● **Diet:** Worms, crustaceans, insects, plant matter, dried food
● **Water temperature:** 77 to 83°F (25 to 28°C)
● **Community tank**

The common name Molly comes from the genus *Mollienisia,* which is no longer used. The various species are now included in the genus *Poecilia.* The exact origin of some of the black hybrid Mollies is somewhat vague, but it is probable that the original male parent was *Poecilia sphenops.*

The dorsal fin of the male Black Molly is enormous—up to 0.6in

(1.5cm) or even 0.8in (2cm) tall—with a rather angular, only slightly rounded shape. The male is an intense black color, but females vary in coloration. Some are entirely black, but others have only black spots and black edges to the scales.

Another hybrid, known as the Crescenty Black Molly, was produced by crossing the original Black Molly with the Sailfin Molly (*Poecilia latipinna*). In the male of this hybrid the dorsal fin is 1.6 to 2in (4 to 5cm) tall and sail-shaped like *P. latipinna.* There is yet another black hybrid that has a lyre-shaped tail.

Black Mollies do well in a tank with plenty of vegetation, and water that is medium-hard and slightly alkaline. The addition of approximately one teaspoonful of sea salt to every 2.5 gallons (10

Above: **Poecilia hybrid** ♂
*This is one of many hybrid forms developed by aquarists. The large dorsal fin will develop only if the fish has plenty of space.*

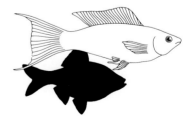

liters) of the tank water is the concentration recommended. The period of gestation is 40 to 70 days, and the female produces a brood of 20 to 60 live young—sometimes more. They can be fed at first on brine shrimp nauplii and sieved nauplii.

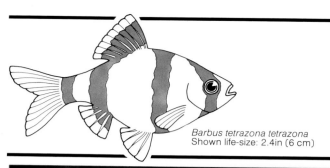

*Barbus tetrazona tetrazona*
Shown life-size: 2.4in (6 cm)

Family POECILIIDAE

# Poecilia latipinna
*Sailfin Molly*

- **Distribution:** Mexico, Texas, Florida, the Carolinas to Virginia
- **Length:** Male up to 4in (10cm), female to 4.7in (12cm)
- **Tank length:** 24in (60cm)
- **Diet:** Worms, crustaceans, insects, plant matter, dried food
- **Water temperature:** 68 to 75°F (20 to 24°C)
- **Community tank**

Formerly known as *Mollienisia latipinna*, Sailfin Molly is an elongated, laterally compressed fish with a very large dorsal fin. The dark olive-green coloration is sometimes tinged with yellow, becoming slightly darker on the back and paler on the underparts. The scales on the back and flanks are pearly and iridescent and each is marked with a dark spot. These prominent markings unite to form a number of longitudinal stripes. There are six or seven dark, almost black transverse bars at the rear end of the body. The dorsal fin of the male is bluish with very dark vertical stripes and an orange-red border. The center of the caudal fin is orange surrounded by metallic green. This fin is edged in black.

This very handsome species requires a spacious tank without too much vegetation. The water should be medium-hard and slightly alkaline with an addition of approximately one teaspoonful of sea salt to every 2.5 gallons (10 liters) of fresh water. It is best to keep only a single pair in a tank because the males may fight one another. The female gives birth to 20 to 80 young after a gestation period of eight to 10 weeks; she should then be removed from the tank. The young can be reared on

Above: **Poecilia latipinna** ♂(t)♀(b)
*The large dorsal fin of the male does not develop fully until the fish is two years old.*

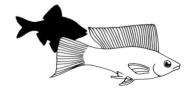

nauplii and finely sieved matter, but the water temperature should not exceed 75°F (24°C).

**A practical reminder**
Color is produced in the fish either by reflective guanin deposited beneath the scales or by pigmentation. Some fish genera, such as the pencilfishes *(Nannostomus),* change their color pattern at night.

Family POECILIIDAE
**Poecilia melanogaster**
*Black-bellied Limia*
● **Distribution:** Jamaica and Haiti
● **Length:** Male up to 1.6in (4cm); female to 2.4in (6cm)
● **Tank length:** 24in (60cm)
● **Diet:** Worms, crustaceans, insects, plant matter, dried food
● **Water temperature:** 72 to 83°F (22 to 28°C)
● **Community tank**

Black-bellied Limia, a rather squat fish, is more brightly colored than the Cuban Limia. It has a deep caudal peduncle and a relatively short dorsal fin that starts in the middle of its back. In the male, the back is olive-green and the underparts are dark orange. The iridescent steel-blue flanks have a number of ill-defined, almost black transverse bars on the caudal peduncle. The eye is a pale golden color. The fins are usually yellowish. The dorsal fin has a very dark edge and a black bar running parallel to the outer border. Sometimes the caudal fin has a black border. The female lacks the black edge to the dorsal fin but the transverse bars on her caudal peduncle are much more clearly defined than they are in the male, and their rear edges are silvery. However, the striking characteristic of this species is the very large black mark of

pregnancy on the female's belly, hence the popular name. The species name, *melanogaster,* means "black belly'.

This fairly active live-bearer needs a higher water temperature than the Cuban Limia, and, more important, a definite amount of sunshine. The tank should have clumps of plants. The water should be medium-hard and slightly alkaline with a supplement of approximately one teaspoonful of sea salt to every 2.5 gallons (10 liters) of fresh water. The female produces a brood of 20 to 40 live young (on occasion they have been known tó produce up to 80) every six or seven weeks. The offspring must be protected from the female.

Right **Poecilia melanogaster** ♀(b)
*This active, highly prolific live-bearer needs a spacious tank with plenty of open water for swimming.*

Family POECILIIDAE
## Poecilia reticulata
*Guppy*
● **Distribution:** Northern Brazil, Venezuela, Guyana, Barbados, Trinidad
● **Length:** Males up to 1.2in (3cm); females to 2.4in (6cm)
● **Tank length:** 12in (30cm)
● **Diet:** Worms, crustaceans, insects, plant matter, dried food
● **Water temperature:** 72 to 83°F (22 to 28°C)
● **Community tank:** Fancy varieties may be harassed

The Guppy is probably the best-known of all tropical aquarium fishes. In the 1860s a few living pairs were sent to the British

Left: **Poecilia reticulata** ♂♂
*This is a prolific and immensely popular fish. The females may produce young every four weeks.*

Museum in London by Robert John Lechmere Guppy, hence the popular name that is now used in all parts of the world. Until 1963 this fish was mostly known as *Lebistes reticulatus.*

Even specimens caught in the wild — particularly the males — show considerable variation in color and pattern. The females have duller coloration. Since its introduction into the aquarium world, this small live-bearer has been admired for its wide range of forms. This applies not only to the numerous color variants, but also to a whole series of caudal fin variants, such as round tail, spadetail, speartail, pintail, fantail, and many others. These various possibilities are now the preoccupation of enthusiasts who have established Guppy societies in many parts of the world.

Guppies are not difficult to keep, with a certain amount of vegetation. The water should be medium-hard and slightly alkaline, but added salt is not necessary and is not always tolerated. After a gestation period of four to six weeks the female produces 20 to 100 live young. The fry should be kept in a separate tank and fed like young Mollies.

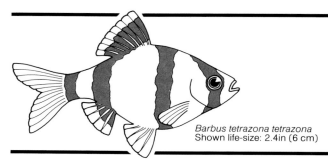

Family POECILIIDAE

# Poecilia sphenops
*Pointed-mouth Molly*

- **Distribution:** Venezuela, Colombia, Mexico, Texas, Leeward Islands
- **Length:** Males up to 2.8in (7cm); females to 4in (10cm)
- **Tank length:** 18in (45cm)
- **Diet:** Worms, crustaceans, insects, plant matter, dried food
- **Water temperature:** 73 to 83°F (23 to 28°C)
- **Community tank**

*Poecilia sphenops* (formerly known as *Mollienisia sphenops*) varies greatly in color. In general, the coloration is bluish with four to six longitudinal rows of orange-red dots. Between these rows there are numerous iridescent bluish or greenish spots. The dorsal fin is rather angular with black dots at the base. The dots are arranged between the fin's eight to 11 rays, and the border is red or orange with an outer edging of black. The pectoral and ventral fins are colorless and the gonopodium is orange. The much paler female has colorless fins.

Pointed-mouth Molly, an active live-bearer, lives mainly in the upper water layers. It should be kept in a tank furnished with rocks and roots, and some robust plants arranged to leave sufficient space for swimming. The water should be medium-hard and slightly alkaline with added sea salt (as recommended for *Poecilia vittata*). After a gestation period of about two months ,the female gives birth to a brood of 100 to 120 live young, each about 0.4in (1cm) long. The female should then be removed from the tank. The young are best kept in shallow water and fed on small nauplii and finely sieved plant food.

Below: **Poecilia sphenops** ♂
*This species probably provided the male parent for the Black Molly.*

Family POECILIIDAE

# Poecilia vittata
*Cuban Limia*

- **Distribution:** Cuba
- **Length:** Male to 2.4in (6cm), female to 4in (10cm)
- **Tank length:** 24in (60cm)
- **Diet:** Worms, crustaceans, insects, plant matter, dried food
- **Water temperature:** 72 to 79°F (22 to 26°C)
- **Community tank**

This species, formerly known as *Limia vittata,* is a stocky live-bearer with a fanlike caudal fin and a dorsal fin that starts in the middle of the back (behind the level of the gonopodium). The pectoral fins are positioned relatively high up on the sides of the body and are set just behind the gill cover. The back is yellow and the underparts are pink or pale yellow. The background coloration of the flanks is a darker yellow, showing some blue iridescence when seen in reflected light. The pattern of markings on the flanks varies, but there is usually a poorly defined dark longitudinal streak and a number of narrow dark cross bars that become more distinct on the caudal peduncle. These bars are fairly short and are normally apparent only in the middle of the body. The dorsal and caudal fins are yellow to orange-red and usually have dark edges and irregular dark markings.

Cuban Limia is a very hardy and peaceful live-bearer, which can be kept in a tank with areas of dense vegetation. The water should be medium-hard and slightly alkaline; the addition of approximately one teaspoonful of sea salt to every 2.5 gallons (10 liters) of fresh water is also to be recommended. After a gestation period of three to five weeks, the female produces a brood of between 20 and 60 live young. However, larger broods of young sometimes occur.

Right: **Poecilia vittata** ♂(t)
*This is an undemanding live-bearer that is ideal for a community tank.*

Family POECILIIDAE

# Poecilia velifera
*Mexican Sailfin Molly*

- **Distribution:** Southeastern Mexico
- **Length:** Male up to 6in (15cm), female to 7in (18cm)
- **Tank length:** 24in (60cm)
- **Diet:** Worms, crustaceans, insects, plant matter, dried food
- **Water temperature:** 77 to 83°F (25 to 28°C)
- **Community tank**

This is one of the larger Mollies, formerly known as *Mollienisia velifera*. It is very similar in appearance to *P. latipinna* but differs in several details. The dorsal fin of the Mexican Sailfin Molly starts further forward and has 18 or 19 rays, compared with Sailfin Molly's 14 rays. In *P. velifera* the pale spots at the base of the dorsal fin are roundish, rather than elongated as in *P. latipinna*. In males of *P. velifera* the flanks have large numbers of shining blue-green spots. The females are not as brightly colored but they still have varying numbers of dots. Some individuals of this species are almost completely black.

This species should be kept in a well-lit tank with growths of algae on at least some of the glass panes. An overcrowded tank will lead to stunted growth. The water must be medium-hard and slightly alkaline with added salt—a concentration of approximately one teaspoonful of sea salt to every 2.5 gallons (10 liters) of fresh water—and good filtration is essential. A virgin female should be mated with a well-developed male that is about 18 months old. The period of gestation is about two months, and the female should be removed as soon as she has produced her young. The broods usually contain 30 to 50 young, but births of up to 200

Above: **Poecilia velifera** ♀(t),♂(b)
*The large dorsal fin will develop only in a scrupulously clean tank.*

have been recorded. The young should at first be kept in shallow water (about 3.5in/9cm deep) and fed on brine shrimp nauplii with some fine plant food.

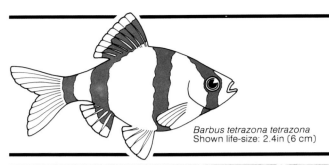

*Barbus tetrazona tetrazona*
Shown life-size: 2.4in (6 cm)

## Family POECILIIDAE
# Xiphophorus helleri
*Swordtail*

- **Distribution:** Southern Mexico, Guatemala
- **Length:** Males up to 4in (10cm) excluding sword; females to 4.7in (12cm)
- **Tank length:** 24in (60cm)
- **Diet:** Worms, crustaceans, insects, plant matter, dried food
- **Water temperature:** 70 to 79°F (21 to 26°C)
- **Community tank:** May be aggressive to smaller species, particularly in a small tank

*Xiphophorus helleri,* a slender, laterally compressed live-bearer, has a long 'sword' formed by the lowermost rays of the lower lobe of the caudal fin. The female is more squat and has no sword. The back of the original wild form is olive-green. The flanks are yellowish green and the edges of the scales are brown. A dark violet or red band extends from the snout, across the eye, and to the base of the tail. In the male it continues on towards the sword. This dark band is bordered on each side by a pale green zone. The sword may be green, orange red, or yellow. All are edged with black along the top. The dorsal fin is yellowish with one or more

Above: **Xiphophorus helleri** ♀(t),♂(b)
*This is a fine pair of the very popular red variety of Swordtail.*

rows of red dots. The female is similarly colored but somewhat duller.

This peaceful, lively species is very suitable for a beginner. The Swordtail can be kept in a tank with dense vegetation and areas of open water for swimming. The water should be medium-hard and slightly alkaline, and salt should not be added. For breeding, a pregnant female should be moved to a separate tank with dense vegetation. The gestation period is from four to six weeks and the female gives birth to 20 to 100 or more living young. The number of fry depends upon the size of the mother.

The Swordtail has been crossed with other members of the genus *Xiphophorus,* particularly *X. maculatus.* Some forms have lyre-shaped tails or even tails with an upper and lower sword.

## Family POECILIIDAE
# Xiphophorus maculatus
*Platy*

- **Distribution:** Southern Mexico, Guatemala, Honduras.
- **Length:** Males up to 1.6in (4cm), females to 2.4in (6cm)
- **Tank length:** 12in (30cm)
- **Diet:** Worms, crustaceans, insects, plant matter, dried food
- **Water temperature:** 68 to 77°F (20 to 25°C)
- **Community tank**

*Xiphophorus maculatus* was known as *Platypoecilus maculatus,* hence its popular name. It is a relatively elongated live-bearer, but squat, high-backed forms also occur. The dorsal fin has nine or 10 rays and is usually quite small. In the original Platy the upperparts are dark olive and the underparts are white. The flanks are an iridescent bluish color marked in the males with from two to five dark, though sometimes indistinct, transverse bars. The caudal peduncle has a pattern of black markings. The coloration is, however, extremely variable both in the wild and as a result of hybridization and selection in the aquarium. Hybrids include: the Red Platy with red

Above right:
**Xiphophorus maculatus**
*This is a very variable fish; one authority lists over 40 different hybrids and selected forms.*

body and fins; the Tuxedo Platy with the underparts black and the rest of the body red or greenish; and the Gold Platy with yellow upperparts, a red dorsal fin, and a pale belly.

The tank can have some areas of dense vegetation. The water must be medium-hard and slightly alkaline, but with no added salt. A pregnant female, transferred to a separate tank, will give birth to 10 to 80 or more live young after a gestation period of four to six weeks. The young, which are 0.28 to 0.32in (7 to 8mm) long at birth, grow rapidly.

**A practical reminder**
Male fishes are generally brighter in color
and slimmer, and have longer pointed fins
than the females of the same species. Male
live-bearers have their anal fins adapted
into a reproductive organ (gonopodium).

Family POECILIIDAE
# Xiphophorus variatus
*Variatus Platy*
- **Distribution:** Mexico
- **Length:** Males up to 2.2in
  (5.5cm), females to 2.8in
  (7cm)
- **Tank length:** 12in (30cm)
- **Diet:** Worms, crustaceans, in-
  sects, plant matter, dried food
- **Water temperature:** 68 to 75°F
  (20 to 24°C)
- **Community tank**

This member of the Poeciliidae
family is a moderately squat live-
bearer with the belly profile of both
sexes more convex than the back.
The dorsal fin is large and has 11
or 12 rays. The typical body is
yellowish to orange, greenish, or
bluish and marked with an
irregular pattern of black dots. The
caudal fin is usually orange or
reddish. All the other fins are
yellowish green. Underparts may
be silvery or golden. The females
show similar coloration but are
much paler—some simply
yellowish or grayish brown with
colorless fins.
    There are several aquarium
hybrids and color varieties. One
such variety is the Red Variatus,
showing orange or yellow flanks
with a greenish golden
iridescence when seen in reflected

Above and below left:
**Xiphophorus variatus**
*This is an excellent live-bearer for a
beginner, even though it may be
difficult for an aquarist to discover
which of the many different
varieties he is keeping.*

light. The dorsal fin is orange and
sometimes exhibits red dots.
    Variatus Platies can be kept in a
well-lit tank with a few areas of
dense vegetation. The water
should be medium-hard and
slightly alkaline, but salt should not
be added. For breeding, a
pregnant female can be
transferred to a separate tank with
the water at 73 to 81°F (23 to
27°C). Depending upon her age
and size, she will produce, over a
period of some days, from 20 to
150 (or even more) live young.
They may reach sexual maturity in
six or eight months and be fully
grown in a year.

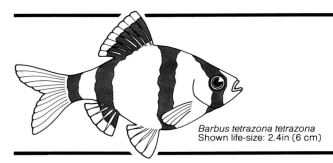

*Barbus tetrazona tetrazona*
Shown life-size: 2.4in (6 cm)

## Family EXOCOETIDAE

This is a family of fishes from tropical seas as well as fresh and brackish waters. It includes flying fishes that are not suitable for the aquarium, but the freshwater halfbeaks are kept and bred successfully. These fishes are live-bearers that feed near the water surface.

Family EXOCOETIDAE

### Dermogenys pusillus
*Halfbeak, Wrestling Halfbeak*
● **Distribution:** Thailand, Malaya, Sumatra, Java
● **Length:** Up to 2.8in (7cm)
● **Tank length:** 12in (30cm)
● **Diet:** Worms, crustaceans, insects, dried food
● **Water temperature:** 68 to 79°F (20 to 26°C)
● **Community tank:** Should be kept singly; two or more males may fight

This live-bearer is elongated with only moderate lateral compression. The dorsal fin is set very far back, close to the caudal fin. This gives the fish a pikelike appearance. However, the characteristic feature is the long thin lower jaw, which is not movable. The upper jaw, on the other hand, is much shorter and can move up and down with the skull. The caudal fin is ovate. In the male the front part of the anal fin is modified to form a gonopodium. Coloration varies considerably according to the locality, which is not surprising in view of the very extensive geographical distribution. The upperparts may be brownish or green, and the belly may be pale yellow or silvery-white. The flanks are silvery and, when seen in reflected light, may show blue iridescence. The iris is bright green. On each side of the long lower jaw is a red and a green line. A dark marking is usually quite distinct in the shoulder area, and there is another dark spot near the base of each pectoral fin. The fins are usually lemon-yellow. The anal fin has a black edge, and the dorsal fin of the male has a red spot.

These are lively fishes that live at the surface in both fresh and brackish waters. They can be kept in a large shallow tank with a few floating plants. The water should be medium-hard and slightly alkaline with 3 teaspoonfuls of sea salt per 2.5 gallons (10 liters) of water. During courtship the male swims up under the female and touches her belly with his snout, and at the subsequent spawning the two come alongside one another. The female has a long gestation period of up to eight weeks. Each brood consists of 12 to 20 live young, which are about 0.4in (1cm) long at birth. The female should then be removed and the young will start to feed on very tiny live food. At birth the upper and lower jaws are almost the same length, but the lower jaw starts to grow longer after about five weeks.

Below: **Dermogenys pusillus** ♂
*When alarmed, this fish may dash against the tank glass and damage its lower jaw.*

## Family CENTRARCHIDAE

These are small to medium-sized freshwater fishes of central and eastern North Ameria. In many species the male guards the eggs in a pit on the bottom. Some species have become naturalized in Europe.

Family CENTRARCHIDAE

### Elassoma evergladei
*Everglades Pygmy Sunfish*
● **Distribution:** North America, Carolina to Florida
● **Length:** Up to 1.4in (3.5cm)
● **Tank length:** 12in (30cm)
● **Diet:** Crustaceans, plant matter, dried food
● **Water temperature:** 50 to 77°F (10 to 25°C)
● **Species tank**

This is a moderately elongated fish with slight lateral compression. The caudal fin is fan-shaped and the anal fin lies below the rear part of the dorsal fin. The mouth is small. The body of an older female is taller than that of a comparably aged male. The general coloration is yellowish with scattered silvery and blackish dots, and it sometimes shows irregular, rather indistinct dark transverse bars. At spawning time the male becomes more intensely colored with a velvety-black body marked with numerous iridescent green dots; the fins also become black. The females are less brightly colored and at spawning time the reddish eggs can be seen through the body wall.

This is a particularly hardy fish that should definitely be kept at a temperature of 46 to 50°F (8 to 10°C) during the winter. In summer the species is usually kept at 61 to 77°F (16 to 25°C) or even higher, but at high temperatures the water must be sufficiently aerated. The tank should have dense vegetation and a number of rocks arranged so that each male can establish a territory. The water must be medium-hard or hard, and alkaline. Spawning takes place among the vegetation. The eggs are usually laid on feathery leaves. They hatch in two or three days and the fry become free-swimming about three or four days later. They can then be fed on brine shrimp nauplii. At this time they swim mostly just below the water surface.

In some areas this species will breed very successfully in an outdoor tank during summer.

Left: **Elassoma evergladei**
*In this species there is no need to remove the parent fishes after spawning has finished.*

Family CENTRARCHIDAE

### Lepomis gibbosus
*Pumpkinseed*
● **Distribution:** North America: Great Lakes to Texas and Florida
● **Length:** Up to 8.7in (22cm)
● **Tank length:** 36in (90cm)
● **Diet:** Worms, crustaceans, insects, dried food
● **Water temperature:** 50 to 72°F (10 to 22°C)
● **Species tank**

This is a thick-set fish with strong lateral compression. The dorsal fin has a large number (usually 10 to 12) of spiny rays, unlike species in the genus *Elassoma*, which have only four or five such rays. This fish is at its most attractive when 1.6 to 4in (4 to 10cm) long. At this time the general coloration is brownish yellow with pearly iridescent greenish-blue transverse bars and numerous red dots. The gill cover is iridescent green and the characteristic rear flap (sometimes called the 'ear') is deep black with an orange-red marking at the back. The throat and underparts are bright orange, and the fins are greenish or yellowish. In older individuals the general coloration is more brownish and the transverse bars on the flanks are iridescent greenish blue. The head is marked with numerous dark red spots.

**A practical reminder**
Always buy healthy stock from a quarantined source. Fishes with spots, pimples, split fins, or wounds and those that have difficulty in swimming or maintaining a stable position should be avoided.

## Family CENTROPOMIDAE
This group of mainly marine fishes is native to the tropical Atlantic, Indian and western Pacific Oceans. A few species inhabit fresh waters in Asia; these include the very translucent glassfishes that are kept in the aquarium. Some fishes in the group have two dorsal fins.

Family CENTROPOMIDAE
### Chanda ranga
*Indian Glassfish*
- **Distribution:** India, Burma, Thailand
- **Length:** Up to 2.8in (7cm)
- **Tank length:** 18in (45cm)
- **Diet:** Worms, crustaceans, dried food
- **Water temperature:** 64 to 77°F (18 to 25°C)
- **Community tank**

Tall and diamond-shaped, this fish has strong lateral compression. In old individuals the forehead is conspicuously indented. There are two separate dorsal fins: The first has only spiny rays, the second has one spiny ray and a number of soft ones. The caudal fin is deeply cleft with pointed lobes. In transmitted light the very translucent body has a greenish yellow tinge; in reflected light it shows golden and greenish iridescence. The flanks have a violet longitudinal line at the level of the backbone and a number of thin lines composed of tiny dark dots. The fins are yellow at the base and rust-red towards the edge. The second dorsal and the anal fin have a pale blue border in the male. In reflected light the caudal fin shows iridescent gold.

This timid fish is best kept only with others that are also peaceful. The tank can have patches of vegetation and a dark substrate. The water should be hard and slightly alkaline with added sea salt (approximately 3 to 6 teaspoonfuls per 2.5 gallons/10 liters of water). For breeding, about a third of the water should be renewed and the temperature raised a few degrees. There is active driving during spawning — the female lays four to six eggs at a time, with a total of 200 or more. The eggs adhere firmly to fine-leaved plants and are not bothered by the parents. They hatch in 20 to 24 hours and the fry hang vertically from plants for three or four days

Above: **Chanda ranga**
*Spawning in this timid species is stimulated by morning sunshine.*

and can then be fed on very tiny nauplii. They do not chase after the food, however, but take only what is close to their mouths. They are not easy to rear.

This is a peaceful fish that in the wild lives in clear standing waters with a good growth of aquatic plants. It is best kept in a tank with patches of dense vegetation and a fine sandy substrate. The water must be clean and rich in oxygen, but the actual chemical composition is not critical. Before spawning the male digs a pit in the sand in which he and the female come together, belly to belly, as spawning takes place. The female may lay up to 1,000 eggs; the male guards the eggs, beating his fins to fan fresh water over them. He usually drives the female away as soon as spawning has finished. The eggs hatch in four to six days and the male usually fans the fry into a clump of plants. They hang onto the plants until free-swimming. At first they feed on brine shrimp nauplii and later on micro-worms.

Right: **Lepomis gibbosus**
*Where the climate allows, this fish can be kept in a garden pool during the summer, and it will even survive outdoors in a mild winter.*

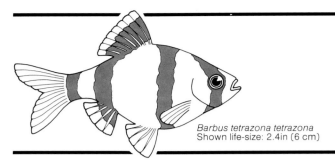

*Barbus tetrazona tetrazona*
Shown life-size: 2.4in (6 cm)

## Family MONODACTYLIDAE

A very small family with species living in the sea and brackish coastal waters of West Africa and the Indian and western Pacific Oceans. Most species live in shoals.

Family MONODACTYLIDAE
### Monodactylus argenteus
*Fingerfish*

- **Distribution:** Coastal areas, Red Sea to Australia
- **Length:** Up to 9in (23cm)
- **Tank length:** 36in (90cm)
- **Diet:** Worms, crustaceans, insects, plant matter, dried food
- **Water temperature:** 75 to 81°F (24 to 27°C)
- **Community tank:** A very fast-moving fish that is easily frightened. It may not be compatible with all other community varieties and will eat small specimens as it grows

The Fingerfish is a tall, disk-shaped fish with strong lateral compression. The head is relatively small, as is the mouth, which has fine teeth. The eyes are large. The dorsal and anal fins are almost opposite one another, and their front parts are much elongated. The very small scales extend onto the bases of the dorsal, caudal, and anal fins. The ventral fins are very small and positioned below the pectoral fins, and the edge of the caudal fin is almost straight. The body is very silvery, becoming yellowish green on the upperparts. The principal markings are two narrow dark transverse bars. The front bar, which starts on the nape, runs across the eye and ends on the cheek. The second one runs from the front edge of the dorsal fin in a curve across the gill cover and on to form the dark front edge of the anal fin. The dorsal, caudal, and anal fins are mostly yellowish to orange. The sexes are almost impossible to distinguish.

In the wild this attractive shoaling fish is found in fresh, brackish, and sea water. Young individuals can be kept quite successfully in hard fresh water, but they do better if the water has a small amount of salt (about 3 teaspoonfuls to 2.5 gallons/10 liters of water). As they grow the amount of salt should be gradually increased since old Fingerfishes thrive best in pure sea water. The species has not yet been bred in the aquarium. On the other hand, the related Striped Fingerfish, *Monodactylus sebae,* from coastal areas of tropical West Africa, has been bred successfully. After a stormy courtship the female lays up to 15,000 or more eggs, which hatch in about 24 hours.

Below: **Monodactylus argenteus**
*This fish should be kept in a shoal.*

## Family SCATOPHAGIDAE

This small family of fishes lives in coastal areas and reefs of the tropical Indo-Pacific. The juveniles are often found in fresh and brackish waters.

Family SCATOPHAGIDAE
### Scatophagus argus
*Argusfish*

- **Distribution:** Tropical Indo-Pacific, in coastal areas
- **Length:** Up to 12in (30cm)
- **Tank length:** 36in (90cm)
- **Diet:** Worms, crustaceans, insects, plant matter, dried food
- **Water temperature:** 70 to 83°F (21 to 28°C)
- **Community tank:** Often aggressive

This is a very tall, much laterally compressed fish with a small head. The spiny front section of the dorsal fin is relatively low, except for the third and fourth rays; but the soft-rayed part of this and the anal fin are well developed and separated from the caudal fin by only a narrow gap. The mouth is small with rows of fine teeth. The body and head have small scales and these extend onto the bases of the dorsal and anal fins. The coloration varies considerably with age. For the home aquarium only small specimens are suitable, and these are more attractively colored than old fishes. In individuals about 2 to 2.4in (5 to 6cm) long the flanks are silvery-brown or green and marked with either large round blackish blotches or irregular transverse bars. The soft-rayed parts of the dorsal and anal fins are translucent. Older individuals are greenish with black spots and the bases of the fins often have a yellowish brown or blackish pattern. Specimens with red markings on the back have often been called *S. rubrifrons* but they are really only color variants of *S. argus.*

The young are often seen in both fresh and brackish waters

**A practical reminder**
Choose compatible fishes. Your dealer should know what size your chosen fishes will reach. Large fishes will eat smaller ones. Slow-swimming timid fishes will not be happy with more boisterous tankmates.

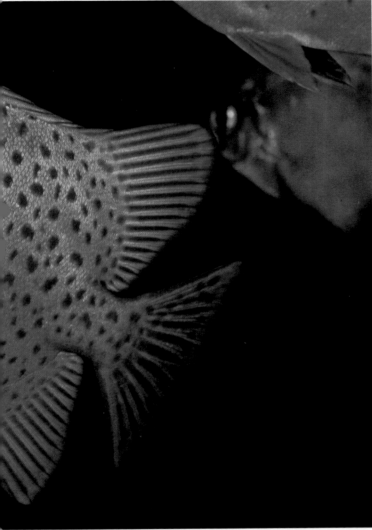

## Family TOXOTIDAE
This very small family (one genus with six species) is found in the coastal waters of Southeast Asia and the western Pacific. The fishes catch some of their food by shooting down insects with drops of water.

Family TOXOTIDAE
# Toxotes jaculator
*Archerfish*
● **Distribution:** Southeast Asia to Polynesia and northeastern Australia, mostly in brackish waters
● **Length:** Up to 10in (25cm)
● **Tank length:** 36in (90cm)
● **Diet:** Worms, insects
● **Water temperature:** 77 to 83°F (25 to 28°C)
● **Species tank**.

Also known as *T. jaculatrix,* the Archerfish is a moderately elongated, laterally compressed fish with a pointed head. The dorsal profile, between the forehead and the start of the dorsal fin, is almost straight. The eyes are strikingly large and the deeply cleft mouth faces slightly upward. The dorsal and anal fins are situated far back on the body, and the caudal fin has a slightly concave edge. The back is yellow-green or brownish; the flanks are pale gray to silvery and marked with four to six broad black transverse bars. The first bar runs across the eye and the last one is on the caudal peduncle. This last bar extends to the rear end of the dorsal fin on the top and to the border of the anal fin on the bottom. There are no reliable external sex differences.

Archerfishes are well known for their ability to shoot drops of water to dislodge insects above the water surface. The tongue and the roof of the mouth form a tube. When the mouth is filled with water, the sudden closure of the gill covers forces this water along the tube and out of the mouth. Young individuals start to learn how to shoot when only about 1in (2.5cm) long. The range of the shot varies with the size of the fish. Large, old individuals can bring a fly down at a range of 5ft (1.5m). These interesting fishes are best kept in a tank with rocks and shallow water, and with plants that grow up above the surface. The water should have added sea salt at the rate of one teaspoonful per gallon (4 liters); a quarter of the water must be renewed at regular intervals. The species has not yet been bred in captivity.

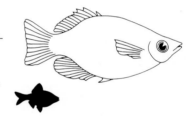

Below: **Toxotes jaculator**
*In an aquarium, prey such as crickets, flies, or mealworms placed on leaves above the surface will soon be shot down.*

Above: **Scatophagus argus**
*This greedy fish will eat almost anything, including boiled lettuce or spinach, and soaked oat flakes.*

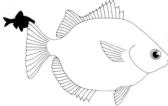

but adults mostly live in the sea, close to the coasts, where they often feed on sewage. They can be kept in a tank with rocks. The water should contain some added salt or sea water. However, because of the large amount of food these fishes consume, the tank will soon accumulate excessive amounts of detritus. This must be removed and a portion of the water replaced. There are no external sex differences. The species has probably not been bred or, if so, only very rarely.

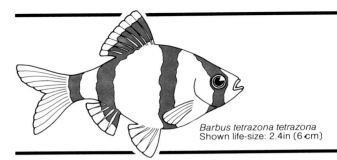
*Barbus tetrazona tetrazona*
Shown life-size: 2.4in (6 cm)

## Family NANDIDAE
The species of this small family of voracious predators are native to South America, Africa, and southern Asia. Most species are relatively small, robust fishes with large heads and deeply cleft, usually protrusible mouths. The dorsal fin has spiny and soft rays.

Family NANDIDAE
# Monocirrhus polyacanthus
*South American Leaf-fish*
- **Distribution:** South America: Amazon, Rio Negro, Guyana
- **Length:** Up to 3.2in (8cm)
- **Tank length:** 12in (30cm)
- **Diet:** Fish
- **Water temperature:** 75 to 83°F (24 to 28°C)
- **Species tank**

When seen from the side, this fish appears ovate with very marked lateral compression. It has a large pointed head with a slightly concave forehead. The mouth is large and protrusible, and the lower lip has a wormlike growth. The dorsal and anal fins have long bases; the front part of each is supported by numerous short spines. In general the fins are very poorly developed. The coloration, which is always inconspicuous and can change according to the surroundings, often gives the flanks the appearance of a dead leaf. When lurking among plants, the body, iris, and spiny parts of the fins are greenish yellow, but in open water they are pale yellow or brownish with irregular dark markings. There are three thin dark lines radiating from near the eye; the first runs obliquely up to the nape and on to the origin of the dorsal fin, the second obliquely down to the edge of the belly, and the third from above the gill cover to the root of the tail.

This is an extremely predatory, voracious fish, which remains mostly in an oblique position, with head down, lying in wait for prey. The prey is literally sucked into the protrusible mouth. The South American Leaf-fish should be kept in a well-established tank with dense vegetation and subdued lighting. The water must be soft, slightly acid, and filtered through peat. The pair cleans a spawning site (a rock, a leaf, or an area of the aquarium glass) and starts to spawn without a period of courtship. The male guards and fans the small eggs, which hatch after three to four days. The fry live on the yolk-sac contents until six or seven days after hatching and then feed on tiny crustaceans.

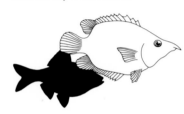

Below: **Monocirrhus polyacanthus**
*The female should be removed from the tank after spawning, leaving the male to tend the brood.*

Family NANDIDAE
# Badis badis
*Badis*
- **Distribution:** India
- **Length:** Up to 3.2in (8cm)
- **Tank length:** 12in (30cm)
- **Diet:** Worms, crustaceans, insects, dried food
- **Water temperature:** 79 to 83°F (26 to 28°C)
- **Community tank**

Badis is a somewhat elongated fish with only slight lateral compression. The dorsal fin starts above the pectoral fin and it has a very long base. The caudal fin has a rounded rear edge. The females are smaller and have a more convex belly profile, while the males usually have slightly concave underparts. In the adults the general coloration of the flanks is yellowish, brownish, or greenish; healthy males exhibit a mosaiclike pattern of yellow, red, or black scales. A black streak runs from the mouth, across the eye, to the insertion of the dorsal fin. The back is olive to dark blue and the underparts are greenish or bluish. The fin colors vary and may be bluish, dark blue, or green. The dorsal fin may be marked with red or green longitudinal stripes. Females are similar, but not as brightly colored. Young individuals often have six to 10 dark transverse bars, but these usually disappear with age.

This is a very peaceful fish of the middle and lower water layers, which does not quarrel with other members of its species even in a community tank. Keep it in a tank with areas of dense vegetation and be sure to furnish the tank with rocks and roots to provide hiding-places, since this is a shy fish. The composition of the water is not critical. Spawning takes place in one of the hiding-places (a flowerpot is very suitable), and the male guards the eggs. These hatch in three days and the fry are kept together until they have consumed the contents of the yolk-sac. At this point the parent fish should be removed from the tank. The fry will only feed on live food, such as brine shrimp nauplii.

Right **Badis badis**
*This is the most peaceful member of an otherwise aggressive family.*

**A practical reminder**
Avoid wide temperature changes when
introducing fishes into the tank. Float their
transporting bag in the aquarium for a few
minutes to equalize water temperatures
before you release the new fishes.

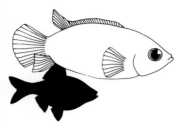

**Left: Polycentrus schomburgki**
*This interesting predatory fish is
reasonably sized for an aquarium,
but not suitable for beginners.*

Family NANDIDAE
# Polycentrus schomburgki
*Schomburgk's Leaf-fish*
- **Distribution:** Northern South
  America and Trinidad
- **Length:** Up to 4in (10cm)
- **Tank length:** 12in (30cm)
- **Diet:** Worms, insects, fish
- **Water temperature:** 73 to 79°F
  (23 to 26°C)
- **Species tank**

Another stocky, ovate and laterally
compressed leaf-fish, the stocky
*Polycentrus schomburgki* has a
large pointed head and a deeply
cleft, protrusible mouth. The rear
edge of the gill cover is armed
with a spine. The dorsal and anal
fins are similar to one another.
The rear parts of the fins—with
soft rays—are quite small, but the
front parts—with spiny rays—have
relatively long bases and are quite
low. The coloration changes
according to the surroundings, the
temperature of the water, and the
mood of the fish; but it is usually gray
to brownish with irregular dark and
pale markings. Three dark stripes
radiate from the eye—one to the
nape, one to the snout, and the
third to the edge of the gill cover.
At spawning time the male
becomes velvety-black marked
with silvery and blue-green dots,
while the female is very pale.
 This is a highly predatory fish,
which can be kept in a tank with
dense vegetation and some rocks
and roots where the fish can lie in
wait for prey. The water must be
soft, slightly acid, and filtered
through peat. The lighting should
be subdued. Spawning takes
place in a small cave or under an
overhang of rock. The eggs,
which are guarded by the male,
hatch in 60 to 70 hours and the
fry are free-swimming about six or
seven days later. They can be fed
on small nauplii. However, the fry
do not chase their prey but, like
their parents, wait until it appears
before their mouths.

# THE CICHLIDS

Above: *Pseudotropheus zebra*, one of the cichlids
found only in Lake Malawi, East Africa.
Right: A Rift Valley lake in East Africa with
hard, alkaline water that suits cichlids.

*T*his is a large family of fishes, mostly heavy-bodied and
distinguished more for their interesting breeding habits than
for their intrinsic beauty. They are widely distributed in South and
Central America and tropical Africa, with a few in southern Asia,
and one species is found in southern North America. Most cichlids
live in lakes or slow-flowing waters, often in shallow areas close
to the shore where rocks and vegetation provide good hiding-places.

Breeding is in most cases based on a territory, which may not
be very large but is always vigorously defended by the male. In
most home aquariums, therefore, a single pair is usually
sufficient for the average tank. The eggs are laid on rocks, timber,
or leaves, or in a pit dug in the sand by the male. Because of this
digging behavior the tank should not contain any rooted plants,
although a few floating plants will look attractive and provide some
degree of shelter.

There are two main spawning patterns. Some species lay
their eggs out in the open; both sexes take part in clearing the
spawning site, guarding the territory, and tending the eggs and
young. In these the sexes are similar in form and coloration and
difficult to distinguish.

In other cichlids, known in general as shelter-breeders, the sexes
are clearly distinguished, the males being larger and more
brightly colored than the females. Their eggs are either laid and
guarded in small caves or laid on the substrate and then taken
immediately into the mouth, usually of the female, where they are
incubated. Such eggs hatch in six to 10 days and the fry are
then tended for a while longer by the female.

For most cichlids the composition of the tank water is not
critical. The exceptions include the rather delicate discus fishes
from South America, which require soft, acid, peat-filtered
water, and certain species from Africa. The well-known
Mozambique Mouth-brooder normally lives and breeds in fresh
water, but it has been known to spawn successfully in sea water.

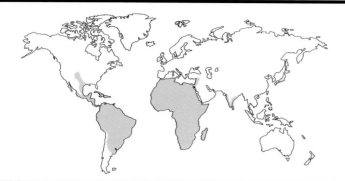

Left: The family Cichlidae has about 650 species, most of which live in the fresh waters of Africa or Central and South America. A few cichlids occur in brackish waters, but the vast majority live in rivers or standing inland waters. Most species are omnivorous, taking a wide range of foods, but some are active predators and others live mainly on a vegeterian diet, usually by scraping algae.

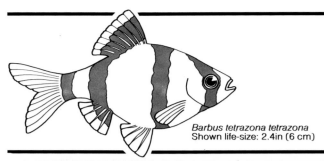
*Barbus tetrazona tetrazona*
Shown life-size: 2.4in (6 cm)

## Family CICHLIDAE
## Aequidens/Cichlasoma portalegrensis
*Port Acara*
- **Distribution:** Southern Brazil, Porto Alegre, Paraguay, Bolivia
- **Length:** Up to 8.7in (22cm)
- **Tank length:** 36in (90cm)
- **Diet:** Worms, crustaceans, insects, dried food
- **Water temperature:** 61 to 73°F (16 to 23°C)
- **Species tank**

Port Acara is a moderately squat cichlid with a deep, laterally compressed body and a massive head. The general coloration is greenish in the male but more brownish or red in the female. The flanks have reddish or bluish iridescence when seen in reflected light. A broad dark longitudinal band starts at the back of the eye and extends along the body. It ends in a dark greenish or brown marking on the dorsal side of the caudal peduncle. During periods of excitement, such as spawning time, the whole body in both sexes becomes almost black. The caudal and anal fins are green or brownish green, and the dorsal

Above:
**Cichlasoma portalegrensis** ♂(t)♀(b)
*This is a spawning pair. Some eggs have already been laid and these can be seen on the substrate beneath the belly of the female.*

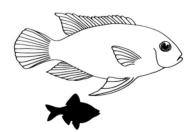

fin is bluish gray with small dark markings on its rear half.

This is a hardy cichlid that can be kept at temperatures as low as 61°F (16°C) during the winter. The tank can have rocks and roots to provide hiding-places, but should contain no rooted plants since the Port Acara is a great digger—particularly before spawning. The eggs are laid out in the open, and the newly hatched fry are assiduously guarded by both parents. Water changes are essential for healthy fishes.

## Family CICHLIDAE
## Aequidens maronii
*Keyhole Cichlid*
- **Distribution:** Guyana, Surinam
- **Length:** Up to 4in (10cm)
- **Tank length:** 36in (90cm)
- **Diet:** Worms, crustaceans, insects
- **Water temperature:** 72 to 77°F (22 to 25°C)
- **Species tank**

This fairly short, high-backed cichlid has a rounded forehead and a laterally compressed body. The dorsal and anal fins of the male are elongated and have pointed tips. In old males the dorsal fin may extend back almost to the end of the caudal fin, and the ventral fins may reach the anal fin. The upper lobe of the caudal fin is slightly longer than the lower lobe. In general, the body is beige to pale brown and the flanks have 12 or 13 longitudinal rows of darker dots. A curved black band runs from the front end of the dorsal fin, across the eye, to the lower edge of the gill cover. The most characteristic feature, however, is a very dark blotch with a pale border that lies near the back and beneath the last spiny rays of the dorsal fin.

Keyhole Cichlid is a very peaceful fish, which can be kept in a tank with a few plants and rocks to provide shelter, and plenty of open water for swimming. The composition of the water is not critical but a portion—about one third—should be changed every three or four weeks. The eggs are laid on a previously cleaned rock and are guarded by both parents. They hatch in a few days, and the fry will feed on fine live food. They will continue to be guarded by the parents.

Right: **Aequidens maronii**
*This is a very undemanding cichlid, which has even bred in a community tank. The young may remain with the parent fishes for a period of six months.*

162

**A practical reminder**
A major contribution to keeping fishes in prime condition is a varied diet of high-quality food including living foods. Fishes will naturally become bored with any single type of food, however high the quality.

Family CICHLIDAE
# Aequidens pulcher
*Blue Acara*
- **Distribution:** Central and northern South America
- **Length:** Up to 6.3in (16cm)
- **Tank length:** 36in (90cm)
- **Diet:** Worms, crustaceans, insects
- **Water temperature:** 72 to 79°F (22 to 26°C)
- **Species tank**

This oval-shaped cichlid has a broad forehead. The rear part of the body is laterally compressed. The dorsal and anal fins of the male are very elongated with pointed tips—the dorsal fins may even extend over the caudal fin. The fins of the female are not as well-developed as those of the male. The back is olive, and the flanks are yellow-brown or grayish brown with a bluish iridescence. The underparts are much paler. The flanks have between five and eight broad transverse bars, which are sometimes indistinct. Each scale on the flanks has a large iridescent blue-green or pale blue spot. The gill cover and cheeks are marked with shiny blue-green dots and lines. The lips are pale

Above: **Aequidens pulcher**
*These fine cichlids are well named for the striking blue iridescent scales on their flanks.*

blue. The iris of the eye is golden-yellow with a red border. Except for the caudal fin, which is reddish, the fins are greenish or bluish. The dorsal fin has a red border. At spawning time the flanks show six to eight rows of greenish dots. The female is similarly colored.

The peaceful Blue Acara can be kept in a tank with some plants as well as rocks and roots, and a sandy substrate. Both sexes clean a rock that will be the spawning site. The female lays her eggs on the rock. There they are fertilized by the male. Both sexes tend the eggs—which hatch in two to five days—and they continue to look after the fry for some weeks. Once the fry are free-swimming they will feed on rotifers and small nauplii.

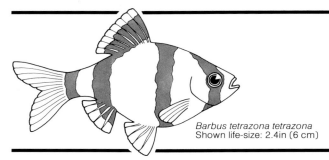

*Barbus tetrazona tetrazona*
Shown life-size: 2.4in (6 cm)

Family CICHLIDAE

## Apistogramma agassizi
*Agassiz's Dwarf Cichlid*
- **Distribution:** Brazil and Bolivia
- **Length:** Up to 3.2in (8cm) in males, to 2.4in (6cm) in females
- **Tank length:** 24in (60cm)
- **Diet:** Worms, crustaceans, insects, dried food
- **Water temperature:** 73 to 77°F (23 to 25°C)
- **Community tank**

Agassiz's Dwarf Cichlid is a moderately elongated small cichlid. It has a very long dorsal fin whose rear end draws out to a point—strikingly so in the male. The caudal fin of the male has central rays that are much longer than the outer ones. In the female this fin is rounded. The back of the male is greenish blue, and the

flanks are orange in front and iridescent greenish blue at the back. Both gill covers and cheeks are marked with brilliant blue dots and lines. A dark line extends from the mouth, across the eye, and back along the flanks to the root of the tail. The basal part of the dorsal fin is blackish, the front part blue-green, and the rear part smoky-gray with the edge and tip poppy-red. The inner part of the caudal fin is blue-green and the edges are gray-green. These two areas are separated by a smoky-gray section. The female is lemon-yellow with markings similar to those of the male.

This cichlid can be kept in a tank with rocks and plants. The water should be soft, slightly acid, and filtered through peat. The members of the genus *Apistogramma* spawn in small caves—not out in the open. In an aquarium provide the fishes with a small inverted flowerpot or half a

coconut shell for spawning. Either one can be propped up on one side to provide an entrance. The male guards a relatively large territory; within this area a number of females occupy smaller territories. The male courts and mates with each female. The eggs are laid on the roof of the cave and tended by the females. The eggs hatch in three or four days, and the fry are tended for a time by the female. When free-swimming they can be fed on rotifers and small nauplii.

Below: **Apistogramma agassizi** ♂
*One of the best dwarf cichlids, this species will not dig up the plants.*

Family CICHLIDAE

## Apistogramma borelli
*Yellow Dwarf Cichlid*
- **Distribution:** South America, in Rio Paraguay
- **Length:** Up to 2in (5cm)
- **Tank length:** 24in (60cm)
- **Diet:** Worms, crustaceans, insects, dried food
- **Water temperature:** 73 to 77°F (23 to 25°C)
- **Community tank**

*Apistogramma borelli* is a laterally compressed cichlid that is not as elongated as *Apistogramma agassizi*. The dorsal and anal fins of the Yellow Dwarf Cichlid are tall and pointed at the back. In the male the elongated tips of these fins reach the rear end of the caudal fin, but they are considerably shorter in the female. The caudal fin is fan-shaped. In the male the background coloration is grayish yellow, with a pale yellow belly. When in good condition, the flanks show bluish iridescence and the cheeks and gill cover are marked with numerous bright green spots. The dorsal fin is yellowish at the rear end and more greenish in front with a bluish iridescence. There are dark dots at the base. The caudal fin is yellowish. Several dark transverse or longitudinal markings may appear on the flanks. This usually occurs when the fish is excited. The female is darker, but becomes yellow at spawning time.

This cichlid requires soft, slightly acid water in a tank with rocks or other objects—artificial or otherwise—to supply shelter and caves for spawning. The male and female Yellow Dwarf Cichlids have the same territorial system as the Agassiz's Dwarf Cichlids. The female lays 30 to 60 red eggs, and she tends these and the fry. Her maternal instinct is very strong.

Left: **Apistogramma borelli**
*If her eggs fail to hatch, the female has been known to gather together a little shoal of* Daphnia *and guard them as her brood.*

**A practical reminder**
If you catch your pets' live food, try to collect it from fish-free waters. This will avoid the risk of introducing any fish diseases into the aquarium. Check all wild-caught food for dangerous aquatic larvae.

Family CICHLIDAE

# Astronotus ocellatus
*Oscar*

● **Distribution:** South America: Orinoco to Rio Paraguay
● **Length:** Up to 14in (35cm)
● **Tank length:** 48in (120cm)
● **Diet:** Worms, crustaceans, insects, chopped meat, dried food
● **Water temperature:** 72 to 79°F (22 to 26°C)
● **Species tank**

The Oscar is an oval cichlid with only moderate lateral compression of the body. The ventral fins are pointed, but the dorsal, caudal, anal, and pectoral fins are rounded. The general coloration varies greatly and depends, to some extent, on age. In sexually mature specimens the flanks may be dark brown, bluish black, or olive. They are marked with very irregular pale yellowish streaks and blotches. The caudal peduncle has a black spot encircled by a bright red ring—this is one of the Oscar's few constant characteristics. The fins are dark at the outside and paler at the base. The eyes are relatively small.

Ideally the tank should have a substrate of sand or gravel, a number of rocks and roots, and some floating plants. Rooted plants are not advised since Oscars are great diggers. Some aquarists use potted plants well anchored in the substrate. Both sexes carefully clean a suitable spawning site—often a flat rock. The eggs adhere to this site and are guarded by both parents. They hatch in three or four days, and the parents move the fry to a shallow pit in the sand where they remain for six or seven days. Once they are free-swimming they will take rotifers and small brine shrimp nauplii.

Above: **Astronotus ocellatus**
*In spite of its large size, this is quite a peaceful fish, but its digging activities make it unsuitable for a community tank.*

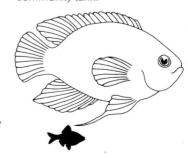

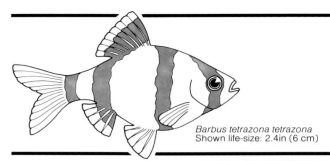

*Barbus tetrazona tetrazona*
Shown life-size: 2.4in (6 cm)

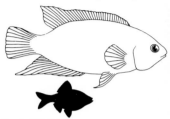

Family CICHLIDAE

# Cichlasoma biocellatum

*Jack Dempsey*

- **Distribution:** Southern Mexico to Honduras.
- **Length:** Up to 7in (18cm)
- **Tank length:** 48in (120cm)
- **Diet:** Worms, crustaceans, insects, fish, chopped meat, dried food
- **Water temperature:** 66 to 77°F (19 to 25°C)
- **Species tank**

The Jack Dempsey, named for the heavyweight boxing champion, is another laterally compressed cichlid. It is sometimes known as *C. octofasciatum*. The dorsal and anal fins of the male are pointed at the rear and reach to about the middle of the caudal fin; in the female these fins are shorter and more rounded. The caudal fin is fan-shaped with a convex rear edge. The background coloration is gray-brown, marked particularly in young specimens by seven or eight rather poorly defined dark transverse bars. A bright blue or blue-green dot appears on each scale. This helps to enliven the otherwise dull coloring. A dark longitudinal line extends from the gill cover to the central part of the flanks, where it ends as a black spot. The dorsal, caudal, and anal fins are dark with blue dots. The dorsal one has a red border.

This is an aggressive species that is best kept in a tank with a substrate of gravel and a few large rocks. Rooted plants are unwise because the fishes dig vigorously—particularly at spawning time. A few floating plants would, however, be quite suitable. Spawning takes place on the bottom and both sexes protect the brood very carefully. They drive away any intruders. Jack Dempseys are sensitive to old water, so about one quarter should be replaced every three or four weeks. The tank should have adequate aeration.

**A practical reminder**
Micro-, grindal and white worms can be cultured by any fishkeeper. These tiny worms are fed on cereal foods and the cultures should be changed periodically to avoid their turning sour.

Family CICHLIDAE
## Cichlasoma/ Mesonauta festivus
*Festive Cichlid*
● **Distribution:** Tropical South America
● **Length:** Up to 6in (15cm)
● **Tank length:** 36in (90cm)
● **Diet:** Worms, crustaceans, insects, plant matter, dried food
● **Water temperature:** 68 to 79°F (20 to 26°C)
● **Community tank:** Will eat smaller species, such as characins

Left: **Mesonauta festivus**
*Once established, a pair of these fishes will continue to breed. This species is peaceful enough to be kept with Angelfishes.*

When viewed from the side, the Festive Cichlid appears oval with pronounced lateral compression. The dorsal and anal fins are elongated at the rear, where they end in a point. In older specimens the tip of the dorsal fin may reach the rear end of the caudal fin. Coloration may vary somewhat, but the characteristic feature is the oblique black band that extends from the lower half of the eye to the rear half of the dorsal fin. The band continues onto the fin tip. Above the band the upperparts are usually brown, but below it the flanks are yellow with some iridescence. The gill cover is iridescent greenish or yellow, and the caudal peduncle has a well-defined black marking surrounded by a golden-yellow area. The iris is also golden-yellow with splotches of red above.

This shy, non-aggressive cichlid should be kept in a well-aerated tank with rocks and roots, and a few rooted plants. Spawning takes places on a rock or leaf and the parents guard the eggs and fry assiduously. The fry become free-swimming about two days after hatching, and can be fed at first on fine live food.

Family CICHLIDAE
## Cichlasoma cyanoguttatum
*Rio Grande Perch*
● **Distribution:** Northern Mexico and Texas
● **Length:** Up to 12in (30cm)
● **Tank length:** 36in (90cm)
● **Diet:** Worms, crustaceans, insects, chopped meat, plant matter
● **Water temperature:** 59 to 77°F (15 to 25°C)
● **Species tank**

Also known as *Herichthys cyanoguttatus*, this species is an elongated, laterally compressed cichlid with an arched back and a bulging forehead. The dorsal fin is pointed but not elongated, and the caudal fin is slightly concave. Adults are blue-gray or chestnut-brown with an irregular pattern of blue or green streaks and dots that extend onto the dorsal, caudal, and anal fins. The pectoral fins are colorless, and the rays of the anal fin are bright blue-green. Females are similarly—but less intensely—colored. Young individuals are clay-colored with a few dark markings on the flanks.

Above: **Cichlasoma cyanoguttatum**
*This is the only member of the family that is native to the United States. Also known as Texas Cichlid.*

Rio Grande Perch is an aggressive cichlid that uproots plants. The tank should contain only rocks and roots positioned to form separate compartments so that the fishes can establish territories. A few floating plants would be suitable. Good aeration is essential and a portion of the water must be replaced at regular intervals as this species is sensitive to old water. The 400 to 500 eggs are laid in the open in large spawning pits or sometimes on rocks cleaned by the fishes.

The eggs hatch in five to seven days. The parents do not always protect their brood.

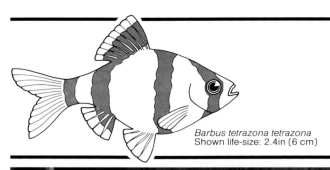

*Barbus tetrazona tetrazona*
Shown life-size: 2.4in (6 cm)

# Cichlasoma meeki
*Firemouth Cichlid*

- **Distribution:** Central America
- **Length:** Up to 6in (15cm)
- **Tank length:** 36in (90cm)
- **Diet:** Worms, crustaceans, insects, dried food
- **Water temperature:** 68 to 77°F (20 to 25°C)
- **Community tank**

*Cichlasoma meeki* is a fairly tall, laterally compressed cichlid with a large head. The forehead in front of the eyes is slightly concave. The dorsal fin starts far forward on this fish—roughly above the rear edge of the gill cover. In the male it ends behind in a pointed tip. The anal fin has a similar pointed tip. In the female the fin tips are noticeably shorter. In older inidividuals the rear edge of the caudal fin becomes slightly concave and the outer rays are elongated. The general coloration is blue-gray with violet iridescence. The belly is yellow-green to orange, but the throat and breast are characteristically bright red, hence the popular name. The flanks have from five to seven dark transverse bars, which are usually not very well defined. The scales have red edges. Apart from the pectoral fins, which are

Above: **Cichlasoma meeki** ♂
*This photograph shows a male guarding a large shoal of very young fry. With its brilliant red underparts, this is one of the most striking of the cichlids.*

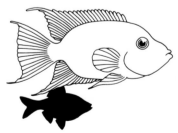

transparent, the other fins have brownish red rays, and the tissue between them is marked with blue-green dots. The edges of the caudal and anal fins are black. The edge of the dorsal fin is red.

This is a peaceful cichlid except towards smaller members of its own species. It requires a tank with a substrate of clean sand, rocks and roots, and a few robust plants. The plants will not be attacked except possibly during breeding. Spawning takes place on the bottom and then both sexes protect the eggs and, subsequently, the fry.

Firemouth Cichlids are also found in subterranean waters.

**A practical reminder**
Fishes needing vegetable matter may have their diet supplemented with lettuce leaves, spinach, or wheatgerm. Carnivores can be given scraps of raw, lean meat such as ox heart, and will enjoy chopped earthworms.

Family CICHLIDAE
# Cichlasoma nigrofasciatum
*Zebra Cichlid*
- **Distribution:** Central America: Guatemala (in Lakes Atitlan and Amatitlan)
- **Length:** Up to 4in (10cm), possibly more
- **Tank length:** 36in (90cm)
- **Diet:** Worms, crustaceans, insects, fish, chopped meat, plant matter, dried food
- **Water temperature:** 68 to 79°F (20 to 26°C)
- **Species tank**

The Zebra Cichlid is moderately elongated and laterally compressed. It has a small mouth and eight or nine dark transverse bars on the flanks. In the male, the dorsal fin, which starts above the gill slit, is elongated and pointed toward the end. The tip reaches back to the middle of the caudal fin or even beyond. There is a large black spot on the caudal peduncle and on the gill cover. The caudal, dorsal, and anal fins are iridescent green, the last two having red borders. The female is not as brightly colored as the male. At spawning time the transverse bars of the male are scarcely visible, but those of the female are black.

This is a quarrelsome fish that is suitable only for a tank with large rocks, a gravel substrate, and no rooted plants. The diet should contain a high proportion of plant matter, such as boiled lettuce or spinach and soaked oat flakes. (Boiling and soaking will soften the food.) Spawning takes place on the bottom in the open, not in a cave. The eggs are laid on a previously cleaned spawning site and are guarded assiduously by both parents, who chase away any intruders. The fry are still tended by the parents, and they become free-swimming about six to eight days after hatching. They can then be fed on tiny live food, such as brine shrimp nauplii and micro-worms. Brood protection continues for three or four weeks after hatching.

Right: **Cichlasoma nigrofasciatum**
*This is a boisterous fish that will quickly destroy any tank decor.*

Family CICHLIDAE
# Crenicichla lepidota
*Pike Cichlid*
- **Distribution:** Brazil to northern Argentina.
- **Length:** Up to 8in (20cm)
- **Tank length:** 36in (90cm)
- **Diet:** Worms, insects, fish
- **Water temperature:** 68 to 79°F (20 to 26°C)
- **Species tank**

Pike Cichlid is another elongated cichlid. It has moderate lateral compression, a pointed snout, and a deeply cleft mouth. The body looks somewhat like that of a pike. The upperparts are olive-green or gray-green and the underparts are whitish, pale brown, or yellowish. The flanks are green and sometimes tinged with yellow. A dark longitudinal band, sometimes broken, runs

Left: **Crenicichla lepidota**
*This predatory cichlid needs an abundant supply of live food.*

back from the mouth to a point just behind the insertion of the pectoral fins. The area behind the gill cover has a large black marking, which may be encircled with silvery or golden spots. The rear part of the caudal peduncle has a similar marking. In general, the coloration of this cichlid varies greatly, which is not surprising in view of its extensive geographical range.

This voracious cichlid should be kept in a covered tank with a sandy substrate, rocks and roots arranged to provide shelter, and a few robust rooted plants. The composition of the water is not critical. Spawning takes place in shallow pits in the substrate. The female lays a number of very small, whitish eggs. In this species the protection of the brood is carried out primarily by the male, who should be given a varied and abundant diet of large insects and small fishes during this period. Once they are free-swimming the fry can be fed on tiny live food.

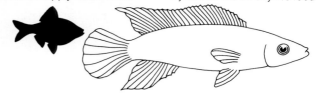

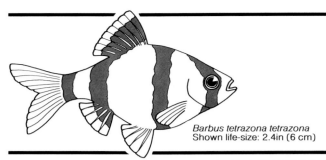

*Barbus tetrazona tetrazona*
Shown life-size: 2.4in (6 cm)

Right: **Etroplus maculatus**
*One of the few Asiatic cichlids, this modestly sized species is highly suitable for an aquarium.*

Family CICHLIDAE

# Etroplus maculatus
*Orange Chromide*

- **Distribution:** India and Sri Lanka
- **Length:** Up to 3.2in (8cm)
- **Tank length:** 24in (60cm)
- **Diet:** Worms, crustaceans, insects, fish, plant matter, dried food
- **Water temperature:** 72 to 83°F (22 to 28°C)
- **Community tank**

The slightly elongated Orange Chromide has strong lateral compression. When viewed from the side the body is ovate and less angular than the Green Chromide. The forehead is very slightly concave, the head is pointed, and the eyes are large. The fins are not very impressive compared with those of other cichlids. The anal and dorsal fins are low and quite long. At spawning time the back is grayish blue or dark brown. The yellow or pale orange flanks are marked with three broad transverse bars that do not usually extend to the back and underparts. Each scale on the flanks has a red dot. The dorsal fin is orange with dark red dots and a red border. The anal fin is yellow at the base but dark at the edge. The caudal fin is yellow, becoming reddish towards the edge. The eyes are large with golden or iridescent red irises.

This is a better fish for the small aquarium than the Green Chromide. It can be kept in a tank with rocks and a few plants, which will not normally be attacked. The water should be hard with added sea salt (about two teaspoonsful to every 2.5 gallons/10 liters of tank water). If kept in pure fresh water this species is susceptible to fungal disease. Spawning habits are identical to those of the Green Chromide; the eggs and fry are guarded by both parents. Before they become free-swimming the fry adhere to the parents' flanks.

**A practical reminder**
Brine shrimp (Artemia salina) eggs hatch in salt water (4oz of natural sea salt per gallon/30gm per liter) in 24 to 26 hours. They provide nutritious, disease-free, live food just the right size for the majority of fry.

Family CICHLIDAE
## Etroplus suratensis
*Green Chromide*
- **Distribution:** Sri Lanka
- **Length:** Up to 16in (40cm)
- **Tank length:** 36in (90cm)
- **Diet:** Worms, insects, chopped meat
- **Water temperature:** 73 to 83°F (23 to 28°C)
- **Species tank**

*Etroplus suratensis* is a short oval cichlid with a deep, laterally compressed body. The forehead is very slightly concave, and the caudal fin is convex with pointed corners. The dorsal and anal fins are low and very long. This is not a particularly colorful fish except at spawning time. The general coloration is grayish to gray-green and the flanks are marked with six to eight dark transverse bars, which are often very indistinct. Depending upon the angle of the light, the flanks show a certain amount of iridescence and the scales in this area have large bright blue or green spots. In general the fins are greenish or faintly blue, with the exception of the pectoral fins, which are pale yellow with a clearly defined dark marking at the base.

The Green Chromide should not be kept in fresh water for any length of time. In the wild it lives in shoals in brackish water, occasionally moving into the sea, where it suffers no harm. In fact, it has been observed that sea water enhances the colors of the fish. The tank can have some dense vegetation, and the water must be hard, with added sea salt (about two teaspoonsful to every 2.5 gallons/10 liters of fresh water). Spawning takes places on a previously cleaned rock or other object. The eggs are guarded by both parents, and they hatch in two to five days. When they are free-swimming, the fry will start to feed on brine shrimp nauplii and other very small live food.

Family CICHLIDAE
## Geophagus/ Satanoperca jurupari
*Earth-eater*
- **Distribution:** Tropical South America
- **Length:** Up to 10in (25cm)
- **Tank length:** 36in (90cm)
- **Diet:** Worms crustaceans, insects
- **Water temperature:** 72 to 83°F (22 to 28°C)
- **Community tank:** Size may intimidate smaller species

Earth-eater is a moderately elongated, laterally compressed cichlid with an arched back and forehead and a strikingly massive head. The dorsal fin is very long and its rear end is pointed. The anal fin, on the other hand, is quite short but it too is pointed. The sexes are similarly colored. In general, the flanks are iridescent greenish or yellowish and the back is somewhat darker. The belly is usually pale yellow, but it may be grayish. The fins are greenish with pale dots and streaks. The head and gill cover have many shiny dots and streaks.

In spite of its somewhat predatory appearance, this is a most peaceful fish and will not bother the other occupants of the tank. It feeds on the bottom, burrowing in the substrate for its food — hence the popular and generic names (*Geophagus* means 'earth-eater'). The tank should have rocks and roots to provide hiding-places, some robust plants, and a substrate of fine sand. The continuous digging makes the water cloudy, so the filtration system must be efficient. Spawning usually takes place on a rock, where the eggs remain for about 24 hours. During this period they are fanned by the fins of both parents. They are then taken up into the female's mouth, where they are incubated. Some aquarists say that the male also takes part in mouth-brooding. So the breeding behavior falls between that of the typical open spawners, such as *Cichlasoma*, and that of the mouth-brooders, such as *Labeotropheus*.

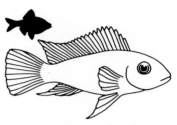

Below: **Satanoperca jurupari**
*Although it appears aggressive, this is a reasonably peaceful fish.*

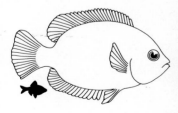

Left: **Etroplus suratensis**
*This cichlid is ideal for a home aquarium when young. A shoal of mature specimens makes a splendid exhibit in a public aquarium.*

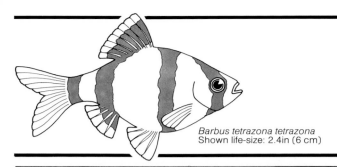

*Barbus tetrazona tetrazona*
Shown life-size: 2.4in (6 cm)

Family CICHLIDAE

# Hemichromis bimaculatus

*Jewel Cichlid*

- **Distribution:** Africa (Rivers Nile, Niger, Zaire)
- **Length:** Up to 6in (15cm)
- **Tank length:** 36in (90cm)
- **Diet:** Worms, crustaceans, insects, chopped meat
- **Water temperature:** 72 to 83°F (22 to 28°C)
- **Species tank**

This elongated, laterally compressed cichlid has a roundish caudal fin, but the dorsal and anal fins are pointed. The back is gray-brown or dark olive with greenish iridescence, and the belly is yellowish. The flanks are greenish yellow with a dark longitudinal band that expands on the gill cover, mid-flanks, and tail base to form large blotches. The fins are dark ocher to greenish. At spawning time the coloration becomes much more brilliant. The back and forehead are olive with red iridescence, and the markings on the gill cover and flanks become almost black. The dorsal fin is pale red in the middle,

Above:
**Hemichromis bimaculatus** ♂(t), ♀(b)
*Eggs can be seen just below the female of this spawning pair.*

becoming deep red at the base and edge. The rays of the ventral fins are blue-green. The iris is blood-red with a thin golden inner edge.

This is a quarrelsome fish and an inveterate digger—in a short time, a small group of Jewel Cichlids will uproot all the plants, dig pits in the substrate, and undermine the rocks. This should be taken into consideration when furnishing the tank. Typical open breeders, they usually spawn on a rock. Brood protection is particularly assiduous, and the young are tended until they are 0.4in (1cm) or more in length. The digging activities make the water cloudy, so there should be a good system of filtration.

**A practical reminder**
Well-fed fishes can be left without food over a two-week vacation period. If you can trust a neighbor not to overfeed them, you have found a 'fish-sitter' but always remember— overfeeding kills.

Left: **Hemihaplochromis multicolor**
*This excellent mouth-brooder has been a favorite since about 1905.*

## Hemihaplochromis multicolor
*Egyptian Mouth-brooder*
● **Distribution:** Eastern Africa, particularly the Nile area
● **Length:** Up to 3.2in (8cm)
● **Tank length:** 18in (45cm)
● **Diet:** Worms, crustaceans, insects, chopped meat, dried food
● **Water temperature:** 68 to 79°F (20 to 26°C)
● **Community tank**

Also known as *Pseudocrenilabrus multicolor,* the Egyptian Mouth-brooder is a moderately elongated cichlid with lateral compression, particularly in the rear of the body. The caudal fin is fan-shaped and the rear parts of the dorsal and anal fins are rounded. The general coloration is yellow to pale red, with greenish or golden iridescence; the back is iridescent blue. The dorsal fin of the male is usually red with a blue-green border and a black edge; the anal fin has the same coloration, but is bright red at the rear end. The caudal fin is yellow-green with three rows of dark dots. The iris is golden-yellow and the gill cover is green with a black spot ringed in gold. The female is not as brightly colored, and the anal fin lacks the red tip.

This is altogether a truly multicolored fish, and one that is highly suitable for a beginner. It can be kept in a tank with a sandy substrate, dense marginal vegetation, a few floating plants, and rocks and roots to provide hiding-places. The composition of the water is not critical. Spawning takes place in a small pit that has been previously dug by the male. There may be 30 to 60 eggs— sometimes more—and they are immediately taken up into the mouth of the female, where they are incubated until they hatch after about 10 days. The fry start to feed immediately on very fine live food, but they continue to use the female's mouth as a refuge when threatened, and also at night, for as long as six or seven days.

## Julidochromis ornatus
*Golden Julie*
● **Distribution:** East Africa, in Lake Tanganyika
● **Length:** Up to 2.8in (7cm)
● **Tank length:** 24in (60cm)
● **Diet:** Worms, crustaceans, insects, plant matter, dried food
● **Water temperature:** 72 to 77°F (22 to 25°C)
● **Species tank**

This elongated, spindle-shaped cichlid has a small mouth, a long snout, and a fan-shaped caudal fin. The flanks are marked by

Left: **Julidochromis ornatus**
*This cichlid needs plenty of swimming space in a species tank.*

three well-defined, broad, dark brown or almost black longitudinal bands. The uppermost of these bands runs along the back and extends onto the base of the dorsal fin; the central band runs from the forehead above the eye to the upper edge of the caudal peduncle; and the lower band extends from the upper lip, across the lower half of the eye, to the caudal peduncle and continues onto the caudal fin as a large, round spot. All the fins are yellow and the dorsal, caudal, and anal fins have dark edges.

This is a territorial cichlid best kept as a single species to avoid male rivalry. The tank should be furnished with rocks, arranged to provide small caves. The water must be hard and slightly alkaline. A typical cave spawner, the female lays eggs in a small cave or on the underside of an overhanging rock. The male, which is larger than the female, takes the major part in brood protection. After hatching, the fry remain at the spawning site for four to six days and are then free-swimming. At this stage they can be fed on nauplii and other tiny live food.

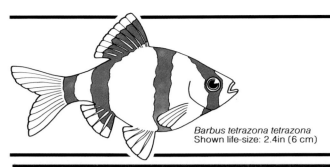

*Barbus tetrazona tetrazona*
Shown life-size: 2.4in (6 cm)

Above and left:
**Labeotropheus fuelleborni** ♂(t), ♀(l)
*This active cichlid needs plenty of swimming space and rocks.*

**Family CICHLIDAE**

# Labeotropheus fuelleborni
*Fuelleborn's Cichlid*

- **Distribution:** East Africa, in Lake Malawi
- **Length:** Up to 4.7in (12cm)
- **Tank length:** 36in (90cm)
- **Diet:** Worms, crustaceans, insects, plant matter, dried food
- **Water temperature:** 72 to 77°F (22 to 25°C)
- **Species tank**

A moderately elongated, relatively high-backed cichlid, *Labeotropheus fuelleborni* has pointed dorsal and anal fins. The upper lip is quite large and overhangs the lower lip, so the mouth of Fuelleborn's Cichlid is ventral. The teeth are chisel-shaped and well adapted for grazing on the thick algal mats that cover the inshore rocks of their native Lake Malawi. These algal mats also contain the larvae of midges and other small insects.

The males of this species are blue with darker transverse bars. The rear edge of the caudal fin is red. Some of the females are also blue and very similar to the males, but others are orange with dark spots and blotches, giving a marbled appearance.

This active cichlid needs a tank that includes groups of plants with tough leaves and an arrangement of rocks and roots to provide hiding-places. The water should be medium-hard. These cichlids—especially the males—tend to be quarrelsome, so they are best kept as a pair in a separate species tank. Spawning takes place on the bottom. After the eggs have been laid they are taken up into the female's mouth, where they are incubated for two to four weeks. A large female may lay up to 60 eggs. Once hatched the fry will be free-swimming and ready to feed on small live food after about three weeks.

**A practical reminder**
Regular maintenance chores include pruning plants, removing dead leaves and detritus, and cleaning front and cover glasses. Change the filter wool when you do partial water changes. Check pump filter pads.

Family CICHLIDAE
# Labeotropheus trewavasae
*Trewavas's Cichlid*
- **Distribution:** East Africa Lake Malawi
- **Length:** Up to 4in (10cm)
- **Tank length:** 36in (90cm)
- **Diet:** Worms, crustaceans, insects, plant matter, dried food
- **Water temperature:** 72 to 77°F (22 to 25°C)
- **Species tank**

Another elongated, robustly built cichlid from Lake Malawi, Trewavas's Cichlid is similar in shape to Fuelleborn's Cichlid. The males are pale blue with darker transverse bars and a reddish brown dorsal fin. Some of the females are colored like the males, but many of them are yellowish brown or orange with a pattern of red and black marbling. Young males are mostly violet-blue. The upper lip is overhanging and the teeth are shaped for scraping algae off the rocks.

This is an active, rather quarrelsome cichlid, which establishes and defends a territory. The tank should be furnished with a few rooted plants with tough leaves, and some rocks and roots arranged to provide hiding-places The water should be medium-hard. Spawning takes place on the bottom, and the eggs are taken up into the mouth of the female, where they are incubated for three or four weeks. Normally a female does not lay a large number of eggs—usually about a dozen—but because of the mouth-brooding behaviour these eggs have a greater chance of survival than those spawned at random by so many other tropical fishes, such as characins and barbs.

Lake Malawi, one of the East African Rift Valley lakes, has over 200 cichlids that can be found nowhere else—these are known as endemic species.

Left and below:
**Labeotropheus trewavasae** ♀(l),♂(b)
*As this fish scrapes algae off rocks in the wild it also takes in small crustaceans and worms.*

Family CICHLIDAE
# Nannacara anomala
*Golden-eyed Dwarf Cichlid*
- **Distribution:** Guyana
- **Length:** Up to 3.2in (8cm)
- **Tank length:** 24in (60cm)
- **Diet:** Worms, crustaceans, insects
- **Water temperature:** 72 to 83°F (22 to 28°C)
- **Community tank**

An elongated and laterally compressed cichlid, Golden-eyed Dwarf Cichlid has an oval profile when seen from the side. The caudal peduncle is very short, but the dorsal fin is long, with a pointed tip at the rear that reaches to the middle of the caudal fin. The anal fin is similarly elongated and pointed, but the caudal fin has a rounded edge. The coloration and pattern vary considerably, but in the male the upperparts are olive to chestnut-brown and the flanks iridescent olive-green or almost golden. Each scale is marked with a dark brown spot. When the fish is excited the flanks may show two dark longitudinal bands and some transverse markings. The outer edge of the iris is brown and the center is reddish with an orange border. The gill covers and cheeks are iridescent green, characteristically marked with black spots and streaks. The female is more soberly colored, but retains some trace of the flank markings.

This peaceful cichlid swims mainly in the middle and lower water layers. It can be kept in a tank with patches of dense vegetation and a few rocks. It does not burrow in the substrate or attack the plants. The water must be soft, slightly acid, and preferably filtered through peat. The eggs are laid on a clean object and guarded only by the smaller female—she chases away the male when spawning has finished. Remove the male.

Left: **Nannacara anomala** ♂
*This specimen has an exceptionally well developed dorsal fin.*

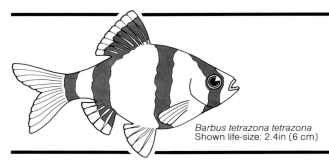

*Barbus tetrazona tetrazona*
Shown life-size: 2.4in (6 cm)

## Family CICHLIDAE
## Nanochromis parilus

- **Distribution:** Central Africa, in the Zaire River
- **Length:** Males up to 2,8in (7cm), females 2in (5cm)
- **Tank length:** 24in (60cm)
- **Diet:** Worms, crustaceans, insects, dried food
- **Water temperature:** 72 to 83°F (22 to 28°C)
- **Species tank**

Another elongated and somewhat dorso-ventrally compressed cichlid with a cylindrical body form, *Nanochromis parilus* has a fairly blunt head and a steep forehead. The dorsal fin is particularly long and low, and the caudal fin is rounded, and pale in the lower half, the upper half being attractively striped in claret and yellow with hints of blue. The caudal and dorsal fins are edged with a white inner and black outer stripe. The body is yellowish with an overlying iridescent blue sheen. There are no distinct external sex differences in this species.

This is a very attractive small cichlid. The males may quarrel among themselves, but they do not bother the females. They swim in the lower water layers and spend much time in small caves. The tank, therefore, should have dense vegetation around the edges and some rocks, which should be arranged to form caves. The water must be soft, slightly acid and filtered through peat; or some peat can be incorporated in the substrate. For breeding, it is advisable to keep only a single male with two or three females. The eggs are laid in groups on the roof of a small cave, and are guarded by the female; there may be 80 to 100 eggs in a brood. They hatch in about three days and are free-swimming three days later. The fry can be fed initially on very small live food.

Below: **Nanochromis parilus**
*A coconut or flowerpot will serve as a spawning site for this species.*

## Family CICHLIDAE
## Melanochromis auratus

*Malawi Golden Cichlid*

- **Distribution:** East Africa, in Lake Malawi
- **Length:** Males up to 4.3in (11cm), females to 3.5in (9cm), larger specimens not unusual
- **Tank length:** 36in (90cm)
- **Diet:** Worms, crustaceans, insects, plant matter, dried food
- **Water temperature:** 72 to 77°F (22 to 25°C)
- **Species tank**

This cichlid is elongated and only slightly laterally compressed. The rear end of the caudal fin is slightly concave and the dorsal and anal fins are rounded, not elongated, at the rear. Coloration of the sexes is very different. The male is dark brown with a paler band running along the flanks from the forehead to the caudal peduncle. The back is yellow. The bases of the caudal and anal fins are dark; the outer parts are pale yellow. The dorsal fin is turquoise-blue. The female is golden-yellow with three blackish brown bands, one along the middle of the flanks, the second near to the midline of the back, and the third on the dorsal fin. The fins are yellowish. The upper part of the caudal fin shows dark markings and the tips of the dorsal fin rays are reddish to orange.

The Malawi Golden Cichlid is rather aggressive. It should be kept in a tank with gravel substrate, a few tough plants, and rocks and roots arranged to divide up the area. This fish will graze algae from the rocks and aquarium glass. The water should be medium-hard. For breeding the temperature should be raised to 79°F (26°C). The eggs are laid in the open and immediately taken up into the female's mouth. They remain there for about three weeks before hatching. Only about 30 eggs are laid, but they are quite large. The newly hatched fry start to feed immediately on tiny crustaceans and other small live food.

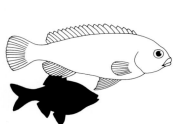

Left:
**Melanochromis auratus** ♂(t),♀(b)
*In the wild this very active cichlid lives in the rocky areas of Lake Malawi. The juveniles' coloration is similar to that of the adult female. This species is suitable only for the experienced aquarist.*

**A practical reminder**
Prevent disease by quarantining all new fishes and by disinfecting new plants. Watch each fish for the first sign of any spots, folded fins, or abnormal behavior. Isolate any doubtful fishes at once.

Family CICHLIDAE
# Pelvicachromis pulcher
*Kribensis*
- **Distribution:** West Africa, in southern Nigeria
- **Length:** Up to 4in (10cm)
- **Tank length:** 24in (60cm)
- **Diet:** Worms, crustaceans, insects, dried food
- **Water temperature:** 75 to 83°F (24 to 28°C)
- **Community tank**

The Kribensis is an elongated, moderately compressed cichlid with a short but tall caudal peduncle and a rounded forehead. The long dorsal fin starts very far forward and the caudal fin has a convex rear edge. The tips of the dorsal and anal fins are elongated and pointed in the male, but rounded in the female. The coloration varies greatly. In general, however, the upperparts are brownish with bluish or violet iridescence, and the underparts are white with a bluish tinge. On either side of the belly there is a brilliant red blotch with poorly defined edges. The rear end of the gill cover has a dark brown marking, bordered above by a red area and below by a steel-blue area. The upper part of the male's caudal fin usually has from one to five dark spots, each with a pale yellow border. In the adult female the dorsal fin has a dark marking. On the whole the females are more brightly colored than the males, which is a rare occurence for fishes.

This cichlid was formerly called *Pelmatochromis kribensis,* hence the popular name. There is still a certain amount of confusion about the naming of this and related fishes.

The tank should have rocks and roots for shelter together with some areas of dense vegetation. The water should have added sea salt (about 5 teaspoonfuls per 2.5 gallons/10 liters of water) because this species comes from brackish waters. Spawning takes place in small caves and the red-brown

Above:
**Pelvicachromis pulcher** ♀(t),♂(b)
*The photograph shows a breeding pair; the free-swimming fry are clearly visible.*

eggs are guarded by both parents, though some aquarists say only by the female. They hatch in two or three days, and the fry are free-swimming about four days later. They can then be fed on tiny live food.

177

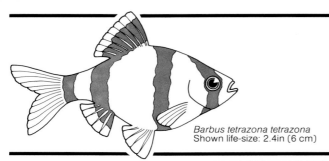

*Barbus tetrazona tetrazona*
Shown life-size: 2.4in (6 cm)

Right: **Pseudotropheus zebra** ♂
*The pale spots on the anal fin are
egg dummies; the female may bite
at these marks to stimulate the
male to release the fertilizing milt.*

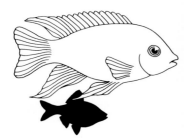

Family CICHLIDAE

# Pseudotropheus zebra

*Malawi Blue Cichlid*

- **Distribution:** East Africa, in Lake Malawi
- **Length:** Up to 6in (15cm)
- **Tank length:** 36in (90cm)
- **Diet:** Worms, crustaceans, insects, plant matter, dried food
- **Water temperature:** 72 to 77°F (22 to 25°C)
- **Species tank**

Another fish from Lake Malawi, this squat, high-backed cichlid has thick lips, a bulging forehead, and a caudal peduncle that is short but relatively tall. The rear parts of the dorsal and anal fins are elongated and pointed. In this species there are several different color phases. The commonest has a pale blue background coloration and seven or eight blue-black transverse bars. The dorsal, caudal, and ventral fins are blue. In another color phase the body is blue, but without dark transverse bars. An alternative phase is almost white; and in another—which occurs only in females—the body is bluish white with irregular orange, brown, and black markings. There may well be other color phases.

Like *M. auratus,* the Malawi Blue Cichlid is an aggressive species, which can be kept in a shoal in a tank with a number of rocks and roots arranged to form hiding-places. A few robust plants would probably not be attacked, although this species is a keen grazer of algae. The water must be medium-hard. Spawning takes place on or near the bottom, where the female collects up the relatively few but rather large eggs and incubates them in her mouth for 22 to 24 days. After hatching, the fry start to feed on small nauplii and other live food of similar size.

**A practical reminder**
Calculate medication doses accurately. Remove carbon from filters but leave the filters running. Increase aeration to keep the oxygen level high. Change the water gradually to normal following treatments.

Family CICHLIDAE
## Pterophyllum scalare
*Angelfish*
● **Distribution:** South America: Amazon and some tributaries
● **Length:** Up to 6in (15cm)
● **Tank length:** 24in (60cm)
● **Diet:** Worms, crustaceans, insects, plant matter, dried food
● **Water temperature:** 72 to 86°F (22 to 30°C)
● **Community tank**

One of the most popular of all tropical aquarium fishes, the Angelfish was introduced to the aquarium in the early part of the 20th century. It is a laterally compressed, disk-shaped cichlid

Left: **Pterophyllum scalare**
*This elegant favorite is now available in many different forms.*

with very large fins. Excluding the fins, the body is only one third longer than the height. Including the fins, the total height is about 10in (25cm), although this size cannot be achieved in a home aquarium. The flanks of the common Angelfish are silvery with a brownish tinge and with four prominent black transverse bars. The first bar runs in a curve from the nape across the eye to the insertion of the ventral fins; the second from the front part of the dorsal fin to the anus; the third and broadest from the tip of the dorsal to the tip of the anal fin; and the fourth across the caudal peduncle. The extended rays of the ventral fins are bluish white and the rays of the dorsal fin are yellow-brown to blackish. The sexes are very difficult to distinguish.

This undemanding, peace-loving cichlid should be kept in a shoal in a deep tank with marginal vegetation and plenty of space for swimming. In accordance with its origins in the Amazon region, the water should be soft, but it will tolerate medium-hard water. Spawning takes place on leaves and plant stems that have been previously cleaned. Both parents take part in guarding and fanning fresh water over the eggs, which hatch in 24 to 36 hours. The fry hang from the plants for four or five days and are then taken by the parents to a shallow pit in the substrate. They start to look for food and, at this stage, should be fed on rotifers and small nauplii.

Family CICHLIDAE
## Sarotherodon mossambicus
*Mozambique Mouth-brooder*
● **Distribution:** Eastern Africa
● **Length:** Up to 14in (35cm)
● **Tank length:** 39in (100cm)
● **Diet:** Worms, crustaceans, insects, chopped meat, plant matter, dried food
● **Water temperature:** 70 to 77°F (21 to 25°C)
● **Species tank**

Also known as *Tilapia mossambica,* the Mozambique Mouth-brooder is a particularly hardy cichlid that has been introduced into many parts of the tropics, particularly Southeast Asia, as a food fish. The body is thick-set with some lateral compression, a large head, and thick fleshy lips. In the home aquarium this fish usually attains a total body length of 8in (20cm). Outside the breeding period both sexes are gray or green with a silvery sheen and a dark green marking on the gill cover. At spawning time, the female

Above: **Sarotherodon mossambicus**
*This very adaptable freshwater fish has been bred in sea water.*

remains the same, but the male becomes an intense blue, the back an even darker blue. The gill cover is iridescent blue-green with a black marking. The ventral fins—and usually also the anal fin—become almost black. The dorsal and caudal fins acquire a bright red border.

This very active cichlid should be kept in a small shoal. It grows very quickly. The tank should have a well-washed gravel substrate, and rocks and roots to provide hiding-places. It should not contain rooted plants, as this is an inveterate digger, particularly at spawning time. A few floating plants, however, would be very suitable. The composition of the water is not important; the species is often found in brackish waters. After spawning, the female takes the eggs up into her mouth for incubation. They hatch in about 10 to 12 days and the fry continue to be protected by the female for a while longer.

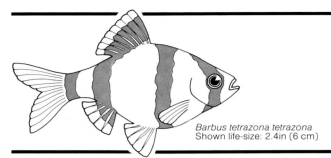

*Barbus tetrazona tetrazona*
Shown life-size: 2.4in (6 cm)

Family CICHLIDAE

# Symphysodon aequifasciata axelrodi

*Brown Discus*

- **Distribution:** South America: Amazon (near Belém)
- **Length:** Up to 4.7in (12cm)
- **Tank length:** 39in (100cm)
- **Diet:** Worms, crustaceans, insects, plant matter
- **Water temperature:** 77 to 86°F (25 to 30°C)
- **Species tank:** Usually fare better in groups of six or more

The body shape of the Brown Discus is exactly the same as that of the Blue Discus. The general coloration is yellow-brown to chestnut-brown with nine narrow transverse bars. These may be well developed, but are sometimes completely absent except for the bar that runs across the eye. The brown coloration extends onto the basal parts of the dorsal and anal fins. The outer parts of these fins are almost colorless—except for a few rust-red dots—and they are separated from the basal parts by a broad dark brown longitudinal band. The caudal fin is yellowish to greenish. The head has a masklike pattern of iridescent pale spots and lines.

This subspecies of the genus *Symphysodon* requires exactly the same aquarium conditions as the Blue Discus, and its breeding behavior is the same.

The third subspecies, *Symphysodon aequifasciata aequifasciata,* known as the Green Discus, comes from Santarém and Tefé on the Amazon. It is dark brownish green with the same pattern of transverse bars. The caudal fin is translucent with pale dots. The dorsal and anal fins are blackish at the base and olive-green with pale spots towards the edge. There are horizontal dark streaks on the back and the dorsal and anal fins, but these features may be lacking in the middle of the body. The iris is reddish-brown in color.

Below:
**Symphysodon a. axelrodi**
*Like other discus fishes this one needs soft, bacteria-free water.*

Family CICHLIDAE

# Symphysodon aequifasciata haraldi

*Blue Discus*

- **Distribution:** South America: Amazon (Letitia and Benjamin Constant area)
- **Length:** Up to 4.7in (12cm) often larger
- **Tank length:** 39in (100cm)
- **Diet:** Worms, crustaceans, insects, plant matter
- **Water temperature:** 77 to 86°F (25 to 30°C)
- **Species tank:** Usually fare better in groups of six or more

The Blue Discus is a disk-shaped, almost circular cichlid with strong lateral compression, a small mouth, and a very steep forehead. The dorsal and anal fins have a long insertion. In this form the general coloration is brownish, becoming pale blue with age. The head is somewhat darker with a purple sheen. The flanks are marked with nine dark transverse bars—the first crossing the eye, the last at the root of the tail. The dorsal and anal fins are dark, almost black, with reddish iridescence. The iris is red. This subspecies is characterized by having several horizontal iridescent pale blue lines on the flanks that extend onto parts of the dorsal and anal fins.

This rather delicate cichlid is best left to the advanced aquarium hobbyist. It requires a deep tank with rocks and roots, a dark substrate, some marginal vegetation, and a few isolated plants with large leaves. The composition of the water is extremely important. It must be soft, slightly acid, and filtered through peat (or the substrate can contain peat). Spawning takes place on a previously cleaned leaf or rock, and the eggs hatch in about two days. The fry at first hang from leaves for two or three days and then become free-swimming. At this stage they move to the flanks of the parents where they start to feed on a mucus secretion produced by the parents' skin. The fry soon take small live food as well and gradually become independent of the parent fishes.

Below:
**Symphysodon aequifasciata haraldi**
*Coloration varies in this species, tending toward pale blue with age.*

**A practical reminder**
Breeding any species requires a true pair of fishes. Learn to sex your fishes accurately. Some species will spawn collectively in a shoal. Condition the sexes separately for two or three weeks before breeding.

Family CICHLIDAE
# Symphysodon discus
*Discus*

● **Distribution:** South America: Amazon at Manaus and Tefé, also in the Rio Negro
● **Length:** Up to 8in (20cm)
● **Tank length:** 39in (100cm)
● **Diet:** Worms, crustaceans, insects, plant matter
● **Water temperature:** 77 to 86°F (25 to 30°C)
● **Species tank**

The shape of the body and fins of *S. discus* is the same as that of the Blue, Brown, and Green Discus. The general coloration is chestnut-brown with pale blue iridescence, which is particularly striking on the flanks. The fifth bar in the middle of the body is broader and darker than the remainder of the bars. The flanks are patterned with wavy iridescent pale blue lines that extend onto parts of the otherwise sky-blue dorsal and anal fins. There is also a pattern of lines on the head.

The aquarium conditions for this species should be the same as those described for the Blue Discus. Spawning and parental care are also similar, although successful rearing may be even more difficult.

The classification of the various members of the genus *Symphysodon* is rather confused. Some authorities maintain that they are all merely color variants of a single species, *Symphysodon discus,* and do not accord them the status of subspecies. It is quite likely that this view will be upheld in the years to come.

Other known forms are the Red Discus, in which the body and the bases of the dorsal and anal fins are deep red, and the so-called Royal Blue Discus, in which the transverse bars are very prominent and the horizontal stripes are brilliant blue.

Above: **Symphysodon discus**
*This is the largest and perhaps the most beautiful discus fish, but it is often very difficult to breed.*

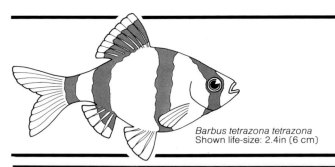

*Barbus tetrazona tetrazona*
Shown life-size: 2.4in (6 cm)

Family CICHLIDAE

# Uaru amphiacanthoides

*Waroo*

● **Distribution:** South America: Guyana and Amazon.
● **Length:** Up to 10.4in (26cm)
● **Tank length:** 36in (90cm)
● **Diet:** Worms, crustaceans, insects
● **Water temperature:** 81 to 86°F (27 to 30°C)
● **Species tank**

The Waroo is a high-backed, very laterally compressed cichlid with a rather small mouth and, in older specimens, a bulging forehead. The rear parts of the dorsal and anal fins are rounded in the young but pointed in old individuals, and the fins stretch halfway along the caudal fin. In small specimens (about 1.2 to 2in/3 to 5cm long), the body and the pectoral and ventral fins are dark. The other fins are colorless. Half-grown individuals (about 4in/10cm) are yellowish to yellow-brown with some pale or greenish spots. The adults are yellowish to brown with blue-green iridescence. The lower half of the body has a large black, almost triangular marking that is broadest at the front end. There are smaller dark markings just behind the eye and on the upper part of the caudal peduncle. The fins are yellowish or blue-green and the iris is pale red. The sexes cannot be distinguished by color.

This cichlid comes from the same waters as the Discus and Angelfish, and it should be kept in a tank with a few large plants and rocks to provide shelter. The water must be soft, slightly acid, and filtered through peat. Spawning takes place in a dark corner — under a rock or in a broken flowerpot — and both parents guard the eggs, which

Above: **Uaru amphiacanthoides**
*This cichlid is usually peaceful but males may fight when spawning.*

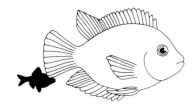

hatch in 30 to 36 hours. After they have become free-swimming the fry should be given rotifers and small nauplii, but they are not easy fishes to rear successfully.

182

**A practical reminder**
Live-bearers of the same species will interbreed regardless of color variety. To maintain pure strains, keep color varieties separate. Give gravid females a well-planted nursery tank rather than a breeding trap.

Family CICHLIDAE
## Tropheus moorei
*Brabant Cichlid*
- **Distribution:** East AFrica, in Lake Tanganyika
- **Length:** Up to 4.7in (12cm)
- **Tank length:** 24in (60cm)
- **Diet:** Worms, crustaceans, insects, plant matter, dried food
- **Water temperature:** 77 to 83°F (25 to 28°C)
- **Species tank**

This relatively high-backed, laterally compressed cichlid has a broad ventral mouth, spatulate teeth, and a steep forehead. The edge of the caudal fin is truncated or slightly concave. The general coloration is dark olive to velvety-black and the middle of the body is marked with a red or yellow band that broadens out on the back and belly. The part of the dorsal fin that lies immediately above the band is an intense red. In general, the females may be more deeply colored than the males.

The Brabant Cichlid is a rather quarrelsome fish in the confines of an aquarium. It is best kept in a shoal in a tank with rocks but no rooted plants; floating plants will help to subdue the light. The water must be hard. Spawning takes place after a courtship that involves vigorous shaking of the fishes' bodies. The female lays only a few eggs (eight to 16), but they are very large—with a diameter of 0.28in (7mm). The female collects the eggs up into her mouth before they have sunk to the bottom and then moves to the genital area of the male. There the sperm are shed and taken into the female's mouth, where they fertilize the eggs. After about four weeks' incubation the eggs hatch, and the fry leave the female's mouth, fully formed and free-swimming. They are then up to 0.6in (15mm) long and ready to feed on a variety of food, such as small crustaceans, chopped white worms, and grindal worms.

Below: **Tropheus moorei**
*This hard water cichlid is best kept in a shoal in a species tank.*

Left: **Brachygobius xanthozona**
*The newly-hatched fry of this fish at first swim in open water and later move down to the bottom.*

Family GOBIIDAE
These small fishes come from shallow coastal waters in Europe and particularly in tropical Asia. Some species have the ventral fins fused into a suction organ that allows the fish to adhere to rocks.

Family GOBIIDAE
## Brachygobius xanthozona
*Bumblebee Fish*
- **Distribution:** Borneo, Sumatra, Java
- **Length:** Up to 1.8in (4.5cm)
- **Tank length:** 18in (4.5cm)
- **Diet:** Worms, crustaceans, insects, dried food
- **Water temperature:** 75 to 86°F (24 to 30°C)
- **Species tank**

A very squat, thick-set fish with the body cylindrical in front, laterally compressed at the rear. There are two dorsal fins, clearly separated, the second one lying directly above the anal fin. The caudal fin has a rounded rear edge. As in other members of the family Gobiidae, the ventral fins are fused to form a suction disk.

The sexes can be distinguished at spawning time, the female being stouter than the male. The ground coloration is yellow marked with a very variable pattern of bands and spots. In most individuals there are four blackish bands, the first passing over the head in the region of the eye, the second and third over the body and extending onto the fins, and the fourth across the caudal peduncle. The areas between these bands may have wedge-shaped markings. In general, the dark areas become reduced in size with increasing age.

The tank for this unusual, rather shy fish should have some plants and a few rocks and roots to provide hiding-places; in a community tank this species would remain timid owing to disturbance by the other inmates and would probably die quite soon. The water should contain some added salt (approximately two teaspoonsful to every 2.5 gallons/10 liters).

For breeding, the tank can have a few small plants of the genus *Cryptocoryne*, which tolerates the salt, and some rocks. Spawning takes place after a period of courtship, and the 200 to 300 eggs are laid in groups on rocks. The female should then be removed and the eggs will be guarded by the male. They hatch over a period of several days and the fry are free-swimming about 48 hours after hatching. They can be fed at first on very small *Cyclops* nauplii and after five days on brine shrimp nauplii.

# THE LABYRINTH FISHES

Above: *Colisa fasciata,* one of the attractive
labyrinth fishes from Southeast Asia.
Right: A quiet, slow-flowing stream in Thailand,
the typical home of labyrinth fishes.

*T*his group of small to medium-sized freshwater fishes is
native to Africa and Southeast Asia, the Philippines, and
Indonesia. Some inhabit estuaries. All members of the suborder
have an accessory respiratory organ, the labyrinth organ, which lies
in the gill cavity and enables the fish to take in atmospheric air
at the surface and extract its contained oxygen. The labyrinth
consists of a number of many-folded lamellae (thin sheets of
tissue) with a rich blood supply. This ability to use atmospheric air
for respiration is highly advantageous in the poorly oxygenated
waters of so many tropical areas. In fact, most anabantoids rely so
heavily on this method of respiration that they will die if denied
access to the air, even if the water is rich in oxygen. In damp,
humid conditions the Climbing Perch of Africa is able to leave
the water and move overland for long distances, thus enabling it to
colonize new waters.

In most of the species the male builds a floating nest at the
surface of the water. This consists of numerous bubbles of air
coated with saliva and it often incorporates a certain amount of
plant matter. Courtship takes place beneath the nest with the male
coiling around the female and turning her upside down. The eggs
are lighter than water and when they are shed they float upwards
and land in the bubble nest. There they are guarded by the male;
even after hatching he still tends the fry, spitting back into the
nest any that stray. In some species the eggs are laid on the
substrate and taken into the mouth (usually of the male) where
they are incubated.

The suborder has four families: the Anabantidae with the
genera Anabas *and* Ctenopoma; *the* Belontiidae *with* Belontia,
Betta, Colisa, Macropodus, Sphaerichthys, *and* Trichogaster;
*the* Helostomatidae *with* Helostoma; *and the* Osphromenidae *with*
Osphronemus.

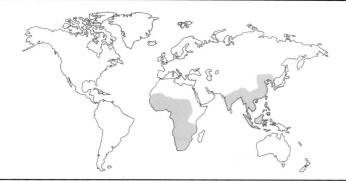

Left: The map shows the distribution of the labyrinth fishes, which are restricted to parts of Africa and southern Asia. They are not as fastidious in their water requirements as the characins. This is due largely to the possession of an accessory respiratory organ that makes them independent of water quality. Only the Gourami of Southeast Asia is economically important as a food fish for human use.

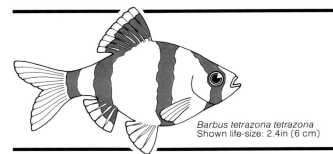

*Barbus tetrazona tetrazona*
Shown life-size: 2.4in (6 cm)

Family ANABANTIDAE
## Anabas testudineus
*Climbing Perch*
- **Distribution:** India, Sri Lanka, Southeast Asia to southern China
- **Length:** Up to 10in (25cm)
- **Tank length:** 36in (90cm)
- **Diet:** Worms, crustaceans, insects, plant matter, dried food
- **Water temperature:** 75 to 86°F (24 to 30°C)
- **Species tank**

The Climbing Perch is not a true perch and is the only species in its genus. This is an elongated, perchlike fish with large scales and a large mouth with tooth-bearing jaws. The edge of the gill cover is spiny and the pectoral fins are particularly well developed. The general coloration is grayish brown to silvery gray, the edges of the scales being paler. The fins are yellowish or pale brown. The only constant markings are a dark spot on the gill cover and another spot on the root of the tail.

This is a rather shy but quarrelsome fish. During wet weather and usually at night they climb out of the water and move across damp land, propelling themselves with the tail and using the pectoral fins and gill covers primarily as props. In this way they can move from one body of water to another. During such journeys they use the labyrinth organ for respiration. They have also been seen climbing along the trunks of fallen trees. Climbing Perch live mainly in weedy streams, rice fields, muddy ponds, and also brackish water. When the dry season is imminent, they dig down into the mud and remain more or less dormant. They can be kept in a spacious tank with a good lid—to stop them from climbing out—and some dense vegetation. The composition of the water is not critical. Spawning takes place at random among the plants and the eggs hatch in 24 to 36 hours. The fry are neither protected by the parent fishes nor molested by them.

This is an interesting labyrinth fish that is suitable for the home aquarium only when relatively small. It commonly lives for more than five years. It is used as a food fish in some parts of India.

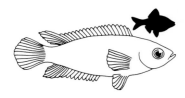

Right: **Anabas testudineus**
*This fish needs a secure tank to prevent it crawling or jumping out.*

Family BELONTIIDAE
## Belontia signata
*Combtail*
- **Distribution:** Sri Lanka
- **Length:** Up to 5in (13cm)
- **Tank length:** 18in (45cm)
- **Diet:** Worms, crustaceans, insects, dried food
- **Water temperature:** 75 to 83°F (24 to 28°C)
- **Community tank:** Best to keep only young specimens as older fish tend to be quarrelsome

The Combtail is a moderately elongated, laterally compressed fish with an ovate caudal fin. Some of the central rays of the caudal fin extend beyond the edge

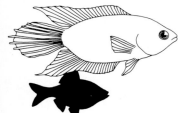

Left: **Belontia signata** ♀(t),♂(b)
*Spawnings of this fish may produce about 200 young. The eggs are laid in a bubble-nest or under floating leaves. The male then guards them.*

186

**A practical reminder**
Cichlid fishes choose their own partners and should be allowed to do so. Raise a few of each species from juveniles and any pairs that 'self-select' are likely to remain together for life and make good parents.

Family ANABANTIDAE

# Ctenopoma nanum
*Dwarf Climbing Perch*
● **Distribution:** Africa: southern Cameroon, Congo
● **Length:** Up to 3in (7.5cm)
● **Tank length:** 18in (45cm)
● **Diet:** Worms, crustaceans, insects, fish, dried food
● **Water temperature:** 79 to 84°F (26 to 29°C)
● **Species tank**

Dwarf Climbing Perch is another labyrinth fish. It is elongated and moderately compressed, and its dorsal and ventral profiles are equally convex. The very long dorsal fin starts just behind the head and almost reaches the caudal fin. The anal fin is shorter, starting at about the middle of the belly. Both fins are pointed at the rear in the males and, in general, are more fully developed than in the females. The caudal fin is rounded and the ventral fins are saberlike, not filamentous as in the genus *Colisa*. Coloration varies greatly and may be green, olive-brown, or red-brown. The head and flanks are marked with six to nine dark transverse bars, which extend onto the bases of the dorsal and anal fins. The fins are pale greenish to pale yellowish. Young individuals have a conspicuous round spot on the base of the tail.

This peaceful fish may sometimes be rather shy, so the tank should have several areas of dense vegetation to provide shelter. It should also have some roots. The water should be soft, slightly acid, and filtered through peat. This species has been bred on several occasions. The male builds a bubble-nest at the surface, but it is not always very well constructed. The male and female court beneath the nest. The female produces several hundred eggs in batches of about 20. The male guards the eggs and, subsequently, the fry, which require very fine live food when free-swimming. Members of the related *Ctenopoma oxyrhynchus* do not build a bubble-nest and after spawning the eggs merely float to the surface because of their high oil content.

Below: **Ctenopoma nanum**
*This warmth-loving labyrinth fish is highly suitable for an aquarium, but too shy for a community tank.*

of the fin in older males. The first rays of the ventral fins are prolonged to form filaments. The dorsal and anal fins of the males are prolonged at the rear and are pointed. The flanks are gray-green to olive-green, the back being somewhat darker. In older individuals the general coloration becomes reddish with greenish and violet shading when seen in reflected light. The dorsal, caudal, and anal fins are reddish, increasing in intensity towards the edge. There is a distinct dark marking at the base of the rear part of the dorsal fin. The other fins are green. In females the coloration is duller and the fins are not so prolonged.

The tank should have patches of dense vegetation and rocks and roots arranged to provide hiding-places. The composition of the water is not critical. For breeding the male builds a nest of air bubbles coated with mucus. The eggs cling to the nest and are guarded by the male. They hatch in about 24 hours and the fry can be fed at first on small nauplii. Evidently this species may occasionally spawn without a bubble-nest. In this instance, the eggs are laid under floating leaves at the surface.

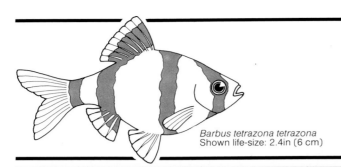

*Barbus tetrazona tetrazona*
Shown life-size: 2.4in (6 cm)

## Family BELONTIIDAE
## Betta splendens
*Siamese Fighting Fish*
- **Distribution:** Southeast Asia
- **Length:** Up to 2in (5cm) in the wild
- **Tank length:** 24in (60cm)
- **Diet:** Worms, crustaceans, insects, dried food
- **Water temperature:** 77 to 83°F (25 to 28°C)
- **Species tank**

The Siamese Fighting Fish is an elongated, laterally compressed fish with a very long anal fin and an almost circular caudal fin. The ventral fins are saber-shaped and the dorsal fin starts behind the middle of the back. By planned breeding and the careful selection of offspring, it has been possible over the course of many years to

Left: **Betta splendens** ♂
*Several color forms are available of this highly ornamental fish.*

produce forms with enlarged dorsal and anal fins. Such specimens may be up to 2.6in (6.5cm) long. In the wild, the general coloration is red-brown with blue-green iridescence and numerous red, green, or blue dots—usually arranged in rows. The caudal and anal fins have red or brown rays separated by areas of blue-green. The dorsal fin is red-brown, usually with greenish stripes. The female is brownish with faint transverse bars. Males of selected forms bred for aquarium use are available in a wide color range, including green, blue, red or violet.

The males are particularly aggressive and should never be kept together. A single male and one or two females could be kept in a community tank with shallow water and areas of dense vegetation, but the colors show better when a pair is kept in a species tank. The composition of the water is not important. The male builds a bubble-nest near the surface and guards the 400 to 500 eggs laid by the female. The fry can be fed at first on a supply of infusorians and rotifers.

There is a related Fighting Fish, *Betta brederi*, in Java and Sumatra. The male of this species incubates the eggs in his mouth.

## Family BELONTIIDAE
## Colisa chuna
*Honey Gourami*
- **Distribution:** Northeastern India, Bangladesh
- **Length:** Up to 2.8in (7cm)
- **Tank length:** 12in (30cm)
- **Diet:** Worms, crustaceans, insects, dried food
- **Water temperature:** 75 to 79°F (24 to 26°C)
- **Species or community tank**

A somewhat stocky, laterally compressed fish, the Honey Gourami has an ovate profile when seen from the side. The dorsal and anal fins have a long insertion, but they are not tall. The rear ends of these fins are not prolonged. The ventral fins are filamentous and considerably longer than the height of the body. The rear end of the caudal fin is slightly concave. The general coloration is pale yellow, with silvery iridescence that becomes more pronounced towards the underparts. The iris is reddish. There is a dark brown longitudinal stripe running from the eye to the root of the caudal fin. The female and the young males are brownish and much duller with a distinct longitudinal stripe. When excited, such as at spawning time, the flanks, caudal fin, and the rear parts of the dorsal and anal fins of

the males become golden-yellow. At the same time, the head, nape, underparts, and the front part of the anal fin become almost black with greenish iridescence. The ventral fins turn orange.

Although this species can be kept in a community tank it is better in a species tank. This gives the males a chance to establish their own territories and to develop their full colors. The composition of the water is not critical. The male builds a small bubble-nest, which is fairly compact. The eggs hatch in about 24 hours and the fry remain in the nest for three to five days, while consuming the contents of the

Above: **Colisa chuna** ♂(l), ♀(r)
*This species thrives in a peaceful tank; disturbance causes shyness.*

yolk-sac. The male guards the fry until they leave the nest. They should be fed at first on infusorians and rotifers, later on brine shrimp nauplii.

## Family BELONTIIDAE
## Colisa lalia
*Dwarf Gourami*
- **Distribution:** Northeastern India, Assam, Bangladesh
- **Length:** Up to 2in (5cm)
- **Tank length:** 12in (30cm)
- **Diet:** Worms, crustaceans, insects, dried food
- **Water temperature:** 68 to 79°F (20 to 26°C)
- **Community tank**

The Dwarf Gourami is stocky and laterally compressed with a longish-ovate profile when seen from the side. The dorsal and anal fins begin in the front part of the body, unlike *Betta,* and are only separated from the fan-shaped caudal fin by a short distance. The ventral fins are filamentous and fairly long—about the same as the body height. The dorsal and anal fins are more fully developed in the male than in the female. The male is scarlet with narrow oblique double rows of blue or green dots that give it a striped appearance. The throat and breast are deep blue-green, and the ventral fins are orange. The female is much duller, usually brownish with oblique gray-blue stripes on the flanks, and even these are visible only in the central part of the body. The front of the underparts is silvery-gray. The

**A practical reminder**
Egg-scattering fishes are notorious egg-eaters. Use nets, marbles, or thick bunches of plants to trap the eggs. Remove the adults after spawning, and shade the tank, but watch closely for first signs of the young

dorsal and anal fins are rounded at the rear.

This small, peaceful gourami is very suitable for the beginner. It should be kept in a tank with feathery-leaved rooted plants and a few floating plants. Roots and rocks arranged on the bottom will provide shelter, and there must be sufficient open water for swimming. The tank should receive some sunshine. Algal growth on the glass is desirable because these fishes like to graze on it. The composition of the water is not critical. The male builds a relatively deep bubble-nest, often incorporating parts of the neighboring floating plants.

Above: **Colisa lalia** ♂
*An extremely popular dwarf species.*

After spawning the female should be removed from the tank, and the male then guards the brood. The eggs hatch in about 24 hours, and the fry remain in the nest for three to five days longer. When they leave the nest, they will, at first, require a plentiful supply of infusorians and rotifers.

Family BELONTIIDAE
# Colisa fasciata
*Banded Gourami*
● **Distribution:** India to Malaya
● **Length:** Up to 4.7in (12cm)
● **Tank length:** 24in (60cm)
● **Diet:** Worms, crustaceans, insects, dried food
● **Water temperature:** 72 to 79°F (22 to 26°C)
● **Community tank**

The body of this gourami is longish-ovate with marked lateral compression. The dorsal and anal fins are very long with the rear ends drawn out to a point in the male. Unlike *Colisa chuna*, these fins are rounded posteriorly in the female and young males. The ventral fins are filamentous and, when laid back, reach approximately to the end of the anal fin. Coloration varies. In males the back is brownish and the flanks greenish brown with blue iridescence. A number of oblique, reddish stripes mark the flanks. The gill cover has a bright blue-green pattern. The dorsal fin is bluish; the tips of the spiny rays are white, and the rear part of the fin has red spots and streaks. The ventral fins are mainly orange, the bases whitish. The anal fin is bluish-in front, becoming green to red at the rear. The caudal fin is greenish or reddish yellow with

Above: **Colisa fasciata** ♂
*This is a highly prolific fish; broods of 1000 eggs are possible.*

red dots. In general, the females are more soberly colored.

This is a hardy gourami with a number of local varieties, which is not surprising in view of its extensive geographical range. It can be kept in a tank with rooted plants and a few floating plants at the surface. Provide roots and rocks for hiding-places. The composition of the water is not critical. The male builds a large bubble-nest, sometimes up to 4in (10cm) across, and guards it assiduously. As soon as spawning has finished and the eggs are in the nest, the female should be removed from the tank. The male adds more air bubbles at the bottom of the nest, so that the eggs are well protected. They hatch in about 24 hours and remain in the nest for four to five days while consuming the yolk-sac contents. The fry then swim free at the surface and require large amounts of infusorians and rotifers; then brine shrimp nauplii.

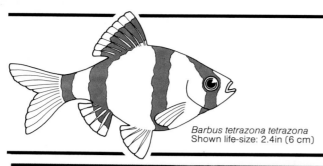
*Barbus tetrazona tetrazona*
Shown life-size: 2.4in (6 cm)

Family BELONTIIDAE

## Macropodus cupanus dayi
*Brown Spike-tailed Paradisefish*
- **Distribution:** Malabar Coast, Burma, southern Vietnam
- **Length:** Up to 3in (7.5cm)
- **Tank length:** 24in (60cm)
- **Diet:** Worms, crustaceans, insects, dried food
- **Water temperature:** 64 to 79°F (18 to 26°C)
- **Community tank:** Sometimes aggressive; should be watched with smaller species

An elongated, laterally compressed labyrinth fish, the Brown Spike-tailed Paradisefish has a small head and a slightly upturned mouth. The caudal fin is elongated and ends in a spike, hence the popular name. The dorsal and anal fins are also elongated and pointed at the rear. The upperparts are dark brown and the underparts red-brown or red. The flanks are usually chestnut-brown and marked with two dark brown longitudinal bands. One of these bands starts at the upper edge of the gill cover, the other at the mouth. Both extend back to the root of the tail. The caudal fin is reddish at the base and becomes bright red in the center; the elongated rays are bluish. The dorsal fin is marked with small brown dots. The other fins are reddish with green edges. The female is similarly colored,

Above:
**Macropodus cupanus dayi ♂**
*The coloration of both sexes intensifies at spawning time.*

but with the dorsal and anal fins more rounded in shape.

This warmth-loving labyrinth fish can be kept in a tank with areas of dense vegetation and a few floating plants, leaving sufficient open water for swimming. The composition of the water is not critical. For breeding the water temperature can be allowed to rise to 86°F (30°C). The male builds a bubble-nest at the surface and guards the eggs while they develop. At this point the female should be removed from the tank. The eggs hatch in about 24 hours and the fry remain in the nest for four to five days longer while they consume the contents of the yolk-sac. They will then feed on infusorians.

The related subspecies *Macropodus cupanus cupanus* comes from India, Sri Lanka, and Malaya. It is usually pale brown with greenish iridescence and dark underparts. The fins are pale gray, although the coloration varies.

Family BELONTIIDAE

## Sphaerichthys osphromenoides
*Chocolate Gourami*
- **Distribution:** Sumatra, Malaysia
- **Length:** Up to 2.4in (6cm)
- **Tank length:** 18in (45cm)
- **Diet:** Crustaceans, insects
- **Water temperature:** 79 to 86°F (26 to 30°C)
- **Species tank**

This is a tall, relatively short labyrinth fish with a laterally compressed body and a ventral profile that is more convex than the dorsal. The head is pointed and the mouth is small. The dorsal and anal fins start in the front half of the body and are slightly pointed at the rear. The ventral fins have well-developed spiny rays and the first soft ray is elongated and filamentous. The sexes are very similar and scarcely distinguishable except that the female is stouter when ready to spawn. Also she usually has a more rounded dorsal fin. The general coloration is chocolate-brown, sometimes red-brown, with dark-edged scales. The flanks have irregularly arranged pale yellow or whitish transverse bars. The first very thin bar extends from iris to iris across the forehead; the second, broader bar usually runs across the gill cover to the insertion of the ventral fins. The other bars are in the rear part of the body. The fins are brown,

Above:
**Sphaerichthys osphromenoides**
*Breeding, which rarely occurs, may produce 20 to 50 young.*

except for the rays of the ventral fins, which are yellowish.

This is the most delicate of the labyrinth fishes. It should be kept in a tank with areas of dense vegetation, a dark substrate, and sufficient open water for swimming. The lighting should be subdued, possibly by having some floating plants, and the water must be soft, slightly acid, and filtered through peat. This is a fish for the advanced aquarist only. It was formerly thought to be live-bearing but is now known to be a mouth-brooder. After spawning the eggs are taken up into the male's mouth, where they are incubated for about two weeks. Some say the female also broods eggs. Other reports say that a bubble-nest is built, into which the female spits the eggs that she has held in her mouth. In any case, the fry must be fed at first on infusorians.

**A practical reminder**
Male bubble-nest-building fishes can be tough on the female if she is not ready for spawning. And after spawning the female should be removed from the tank for her own safety. The male will guard the nest.

Family BELONTIIDAE
# Macropodus opercularis
*Paradisefish*
- **Distribution:** Korea, China, Vietnam, Taiwan
- **Length:** Up to 3.5in (9cm)
- **Tank length:** 24in (60cm)
- **Diet:** Worms, crustaceans, insects, plant matter, dried food
- **Water temperature:** 59 to 75°F (15 to 24°C)
- **Species tank**

This is a moderately elongated labyrinth fish with lateral compression, particularly in the rear half of the body. The caudal fin has upper and lower lobes very elongated. The rear parts of the dorsal and anal fins are also elongated, particularly in the males. The coloration varies greatly. In the males the head and nape are olive with brownish marbling; the flanks are marked with alternate blue-green and red transverse bars. The gill cover has a conspicuous blackish longitudinal marking that shows greenish iridescence and has an orange or red border. The caudal fin is red with dark dots and streaks in the center. The dorsal and anal fins also have dark markings that become increasingly red towards the tips. The ventral fins are red with white tips. In the females the coloration is duller and only the flanks have red transverse bars.

This interesting fish was introduced into the aquarium in Europe in 1869. It can be very aggressive, particularly at spawning time, so it is best kept without other species. The tank should have patches of dense vegetation, including a small number of floating plants, and sufficient open water for swimming. Algal growth on the glass as well as the troublesome planarians which so often infest aquarium tanks will be consumed by the fish. Neither the composition of the water nor the temperature is critical—even 68 to 75°F (20 to 24°C) is sufficient for breeding. The male builds a bubble-nest at the surface and, after spawning, spits the eggs into the nest from below. He then guards them assiduously. They hatch in about 24 hours and after three to five days in the nest the fry become free-swimming and can be fed initially on infusorians.

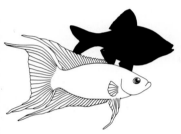

Left and below:
**Macropodus opercularis**
*Two males of this colorful species.*

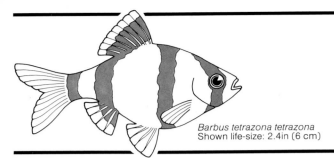

Barbus tetrazona tetrazona
Shown life-size: 2.4in (6 cm)

Family BELONTIIDAE
## Trichogaster leeri
*Pearl Gourami*
- **Distribution:** Thailand, Malaysia, Sumatra, Borneo
- **Length:** Up to 4.3in (11cm)
- **Tank length:** 24in (60cm)
- **Diet:** Worms, crustaceans, insects, dried food
- **Water temperature:** 75 to 86°F (24 to 30°C)
- **Community tank**

The Pearl Gourami is a moderately elongated, laterally compressed labyrinth fish. The ventral fins are very long and threadlike. The dorsal fin has a short base and is positioned in the middle of the back, unlike the genus *Colisa*. The anal fin has a very long base and it starts in the front part of the belly. The caudal fin is deeply cleft. The dorsal and anal fins are more fully developed in the male than in the female. The general coloration of the male is reddish brown, but this is overlaid by a pearly, dense pattern of iridescent bluish violet dots. The

underparts are orange or red. A somewhat interrupted dark brown longitudinal band extends from the snout across the eye and ends in an enlarged spot on the root of the tail. The pearly pattern extends onto the bases of the dorsal and anal fins. The female is more brownish with silvery-white underparts.

This very attractive labyrinth fish can be kept in a tank with areas of dense vegetation—particularly plants with feathery leaves—and a few floating plants. The composition of the water is not critical. Sexual maturity is reached relatively late. The male builds a large bubble-nest at the water surface. Courtship is particularly stormy and mostly takes place beneath the nest. The female lays a large number of eggs and should then be removed from the tank along with any other fishes—except the male, who will guard the nest. The eggs hatch in about 24 hours. The fry remain in the nest for four or five days and then feed on very small live food.

Family BELONTIIDAE
## Trichogaster trichopterus
*Three-spot Gourami*
- **Distribution:** Thailand, Malaysia, Java, Sumatra, Borneo
- **Length:** Up to 6in (15cm)
- **Tank length:** 24in (60cm)
- **Diet:** Worms, crustaceans, insects, dried food
- **Water temperature:** 75 to 84°F (24 to 29°C)
- **Community tank:** May harass smaller species

The body of *T. trichopterus* is somewhat stockier than that of the Pearl Gourami, but in other ways is very similar. Both sexes of the Three-spot Gourami have

threadlike ventral fins that, when laid back, reach approximately to the middle of the caudal fin. The dorsal fin in the male is taller and more pointed than in the female. The edge of the caudal fin is concave. The general coloration is silvery-olive, becoming darker on the back and paler on the belly. The flanks often have rather indistinct transverse bars. There are two characteristic black spots—one in the middle of the flank, the other on the caudal peduncle. These two spots, together with the eye, account for the popular name. The dorsal, caudal, and anal fins are grayish or green with white or pale orange dots and they show bluish iridescence in reflected light. The

subspecies *T. trichopterus sumatranus* (known as the Blue Gourami) is blue with more distinct transverse bars, particularly at spawning time, and iridescent pearly dots on the fins. Another variety, called the Cosby, is blue with dark marbling on the flanks.

This is a peaceful gourami that can be kept in a tank with clumps of rooted plants, a few floating plants, and some roots to provide hiding-places. The composition of the water is not critical, although it has been recommended that the Blue Gourami be kept in soft, slightly acid water. The male builds a bubble-nest at the surface. Spawning takes place below the nest after very vigorous driving by

Above: **Trichogaster trichopterus**
*This is a very prolific species. The fry must be sorted into size groups to prevent cannibalism.*

the male. The eggs, which have been guarded by the male, hatch in about 24 hours. The fry are free-swimming four or five days later and ready to be fed initially on infusorians.

**A practical reminder**
Killifish eggs may not hatch the first time
they are re-immersed in water. This is
nature's way of protecting them against
short rain showers. Dry out the eggs again,
and re-immersion usually does the trick.

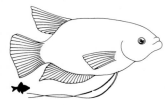

**Left: Osphronemus goramy**
*Young specimens of this fish are
suitable to mix with larger species.*

Family OSPHRONEMIDAE
## Osphronemus goramy
*Gourami*
- **Distribution:** Originally Borneo,
  Sumatra, Java
- **Length:** Up to 24in (60cm),
  possibly more
- **Tank length:** 36in (90cm)
- **Diet:** Worms, crustaceans,
  insects, plant matter, dried food
- **Water temperature:** 66 to 79°F
  (19 to 26°C)
- **Community tank**

This squat gourami has large
scales and a very laterally
compressed body. It looks ovate
when seen from the side. The
head is relatively small, with a
distinct projecting chin in old
individuals. The ventral fins are
elongated and threadlike. Young
specimens are not as tall-bodied
and they have a more pointed
head. The dorsal and anal fins of
the males are elongated and
pointed posteriorly. The edge of
the caudal fin is straight or slightly
concave. Adults are brownish or
reddish with pale iridescence; the
upperparts are a little darker in
color and the belly is either pale
yellow or silvery. There are several
dark spots scattered over the
body. Young individuals are
reddish brown with a number of
dark transverse bars. On the rear
part of the anal fin is a more or
less circular marking with a yellow
or silvery border. The ventral fins
are orange; all the other fins are
bluish.

This labyrinth fish is, of course,
suitable for the home aquarium
only when quite small. It has
been introduced to many other
parts of Southeast Asia and also
to Australia as a food fish. When
young (about 8in/20cm long) it
can be kept in a community tank
with floating plants and a large
area of open water for swimming.
The water composition is not
critical. The essential plant part of
the diet can include lettuce and
soaked oat flakes. The male builds
a bubble-nest which often
includes pieces of plant. The eggs,
which are guarded by the male,
hatch in 24 to 36 hours and the
fry are free-swimming a few days
later. They feed at first on
infusorians and rotifers.

Family HELOSTOMATIDAE
## Helostoma temmincki
*Kissing Gourami*
- **Distribution:** Southeast Asia:
  Thailand, Malaysia, Sumatra,
  Java, Borneo
- **Length:** Up to 12in (30cm)
- **Tank length:** 36in (90cm)
- **Diet:** Worms, crustaceans,
  insects, plant matter, dried food
- **Water temperature:** 75 to 83°F
  (24 to 28°C)
- **Community tank:** Often
  aggressive, particularly to
  smaller species.

Well known for its habit of
extending its thick fleshy lips and
'kissing,' this gourami is an ovate
labyrinth fish. When viewed from
the side, it shows strong lateral
compression. The flat broad lips
are well adapted for browsing on
algal mats. These lips also
protrude during kissing when the
fishes touch lip to lip. This kissing
behavior is probably a form of
sparring. The forehead is slightly
concave particularly in young
individuals. The dorsal and anal
fins start far forward and extend
back to the tail. The caudal fin is
slightly concave. The rear parts of
the dorsal and anal fins are taller
than the front spiny parts. The
upperparts are olive-green to
gray; the belly is paler. A few, often
indistinct, darkish longitudinal
stripes appear on the flanks and
two short dark transverse bars
mark the gill cover. The fins are
greenish to grayish yellow. The
coloration of old males is
somewhat more intense. The
sexes are very difficult to

distinguish. There is also a poorly
pigmented form of the Kissing
Gourami that is uniformly pink
and without markings.

This is a largely vegetarian fish,
which usually grows to a length of
about 4in (10cm) in the home
aquarium. It can be kept in a tank
with plenty of plants, preferably
those with tough leaves. The
composition of the water is not
important. The fish reaches sexual
maturity at three to four years of
age. Spawning takes place at
dusk or during the night, after a
period of stormy courtship. The
eggs are lighter than water and
they rise towards the surface,
many adhering to plants on the
way. They hatch in about 50
hours and the fry are free-

**Above: Helostoma temmincki**
*The fry of this very prolific fish —
up to 1000 eggs per brood — are
usually not molested by the parents.*

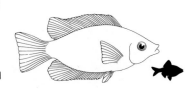

swimming after three to five days.
They must then be fed on
infusorians and also on pulverized
oatmeal scattered at the surface of
the water. At first they grow
rapidly, but later on more slowly.

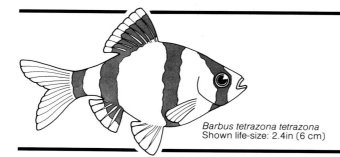

Barbus tetrazona tetrazona
Shown life-size: 2.4in (6 cm)

## Suborder ATHERINOIDEI

The suborder Atherinoidei contains a small number of families. Those found in the aquarium are the Atherinidae *Bedotia* and *Telmatherina*, and the Melanotaeniidae with the genus *Melanotaenia*. They live in shallow coastal areas of many parts of the world, including Europe.

Family MELANOTAENIIDAE

## Melanotaenia maccullochi
*Dwarf Rainbowfish*

- **Distribution:** Northern Australia
- **Length:** Up to 2.8in (7cm)
- **Tank length:** 24in (60cm)
- **Diet:** Worms, crustaceans, insects, dried food
- **Water temperature:** 68 to 77°F (20 to 25°F)
- **Community tank**

Also known as *Nematocentris maccullochi,* this is a moderately elongated and laterally compressed fish with almost symmetrical dorsal and ventral profiles. There are two separate dorsal fins. The anal fin starts in the middle of the body and has a relatively long base. The second dorsal fin and the anal fin are separated from the caudal fin by a gap. The first dorsal fin is pointed in the male, more rounded in the female. The small mouth faces slightly upward. The male is silvery-gray with bluish iridescence. The rows of scales on the flanks show pearly iridescence and between them run seven red-brown longitudinal stripes. The gill cover is iridescent blue-green with a bright red spot edged in golden-green. The throat and the edge of the belly are red and the back is brownish. The dorsal and anal fins are red with a greenish base. The female has more subdued coloration.

This is an active, hardy fish that lives mostly in the middle water layers. It can be kept in a shoal in a tank with a sandy substrate and groups of feathery-leaved rooted planted arranged to leave sufficient space for the small shoal to swim about. The water must not be too soft, and should preferably be medium-hard. Add about one teaspoonful of sea salt per gallon (4 liters) of water. Spawning takes place over a period of days, but most of the eggs are laid on the first day, often during the morning. The darkly pigmented eggs are attached by short filaments to feathery leaves. They hatch in seven to 10 days and the fry are free-swimming a few days later. They can be fed initially on *Paramecium*, rotifers and brine shrimp nauplii. At first they grow rather slowly but, after reaching a length of about 0.4in (1cm), the growth rate increases.

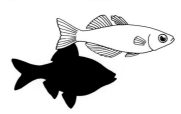

Right: **Melanotaenia maccullochi**
*This peaceful fish can be kept as a small shoal in a community tank.*

Family MELANOTAENIIDAE

## Melanotaenia nigrans
*Red-tailed Rainbowfish*

- **Distribution:** Eastern Australia, south to Sydney
- **Length:** Up to 4in (10cm)
- **Tank length:** 36in (90cm)
- **Diet:** Worms, crustaceans insects, dried food
- **Water temperature:** 64 to 79°F (18 to 26°C)
- **Community tank**

Also known as *Nematocentris fluviatilis,* this is an elongated torpedo-shaped fish with strong lateral compression. The anal fin, which has a long base, starts approximately below the first dorsal fin, and its pointed tip extends over the base of the caudal fin. The second dorsal fin has the same general shape, but with a shorter base. The caudal fin is forked. In the male the back is yellow to grayish yellow and the belly is whitish. The flanks are iridescent green or blue-green. The relatively large scales have a dark front edge and a red hind edge, forming a netlike pattern. There are several dark longitudinal stripes separated by iridescent zones. The caudal peduncle is green and the gill cover has a triangular blood-red marking with a red, green, and white border. The dorsal and anal fins are yellow with a black edge; the other fins are yellowish. In the female the flanks do not show iridescence on the scales, and the dorsal and anal fins do not have a black border.

This is an active but peaceful fish, which should be kept in a shoal in a tank with a sandy substrate and scattered clumps of feathery-leaved plants. The water must be medium-hard or hard, and neutral in pH, with about five percent added sea water. (This is equivalent to adding 5 teaspoons-ful per 2.5 gallons/10 liters of water). The species is often found in coastal brackish waters. For breeding the temperature should be 73 to 77°F (23 to 25°C). The eggs are attached by short filaments to leaves and they hatch in eight to 10 days. A few days after hatching the fry will be free-swimming and ready to feed on rotifers and brine shrimp nauplii. They are not difficult to rear.

Left: **Melanotaenia nigrans**
*In common with M. maccullochi, this species will not molest its brood.*

194

**A practical reminder**
Keep careful written records of all attempts
at breeding new fishes. If you get it right,
you may well forget that important factor
(such as an increase in temperature) that
brought success at last.

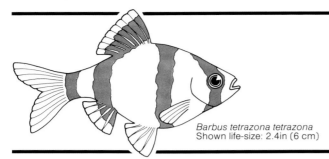

*Barbus tetrazona tetrazona*
Shown life-size: 2.4in (6 cm)

## Family ATHERINIDAE
# Bedotia geayi
*Madagascar Rainbowfish*
- **Distribution:** Madagascar
- **Length:** Up to 6in (15cm)
- **Tank length:** 24in (60cm)
- **Diet:** Worms, crustaceans, insects, plant matter, dried food
- **Water temperature:** 73 to 77°F (23 to 25°C)
- **Community tank**

The Madagascar Rainbowfish is an elongated, laterally compressed fish with symmetrical dorsal and ventral profiles. The head is pointed, the eyes are large, and the mouth faces slightly upward. The very short first dorsal fin is usually folded down. The second dorsal fin and the anal fin are low with long bases. The caudal fin is fan-shaped with a straight or slightly concave rear edge. The coloration of the male varies somewhat, but the back is usually yellowish brown and bordered on each side by a broad dark band. This band is decorated with a number of iridescent golden to grass-green scales and extends back to the root of the tail. There is another less conspicuous dark longitudinal band near the belly. The iris of the eye is golden above and green below. The second dorsal fin and the anal fin have pale yellow bases, but the fins themselves are orange with blackish borders. The main part of the caudal fin is bluish or colorless but the rear border has a semi-circular blue-gray band and a blood-red outer edge. The female is less brightly colored and lacks the dark borders to the fins.

This is an active fish of the upper and middle water layers, which should be kept in a small shoal in a tank with a few feathery-leaved plants and plenty of space for swimming. The water should be medium-hard and quite clear of any cloudiness caused by infusorians, since this species is very sensitive to them. The relatively large, pale yellowish eggs are laid among the plants and hang by short filaments. They are not molested by the parent fishes. The eggs hatch in six to seven days and the fry feed at first on rotifers and a little later on small brine shrimp nauplii.

Right: **Bedotia geayi** ♂
*This elegant midwater fish takes food from near the water surface.*

## Family ATHERINIDAE
# Telmatherina ladigesi
*Celebes Sailfish*
- **Distribution:** Southeast Asia, Celebes only
- **Length:** Up to 2.8in (7cm)
- **Tank length:** 24in (60cm)
- **Diet:** Worms, crustaceans, insects, dried food
- **Water temperature:** 68 to 77°F (20 to 25°C)
- **Community tank**

An elongated, laterally compressed fish, the Celebes Sailfish has symmetrical dorsal and ventral profiles. The first dorsal fin is very small and positioned roughly above the ventral fins. The second dorsal fin and the anal fin are much larger. In mature males the first rays of these fins grow filamentous extensions, producing a rather ragged appearance. In females and young males these fins are rounded. The mouth is small and faces slightly upward. In the male the back, the upperpart of the caudal peduncle, and the underparts are yellow. The flanks are yellowish with blue-green iridescence, and marked with a narrow shiny blue-green longitudinal band. The iris of the eye is yellowish green. The first dorsal fin is copper-colored. The second dorsal fin and the anal fins are yellow, becoming more orange-red at the bases; but the first rays of the fins are black. The caudal fin and the ventral fins are yellowish, the former with dark streaks at the upper and lower edge. The pectoral fins are colorless. The female is less brightly colored, and the first rays of the anal fin and the second dorsal fin are not black.

This is a peaceful fish, living mainly in the middle water layers. It can be kept in a shoal in a tank with scattered plants around the edges and a sufficient amount of space for swimming. The water should be medium-hard with about five per cent added sea water. (Equivalent to adding 5 teaspoonsful of sea salt per 2.5 gallons/10 liters of tank water.) Spawning usually takes place in the morning; the eggs are laid in batches over a period of several days. They hatch in 11 or 12 days, and can be fed immediately on very fine live food. They grow slowly and may not reach a length of 0.8in (2cm) until eight weeks.

Above:
**Telmatherina ladigesi** ♀(t),♂(b)
*After a slow start, this fish is sexually mature in seven months.*

**A practical reminder**
There is more to fishkeeping than just fishes. You make lots of friends and develop new skills. The aquarium that was only intended to light up a dark corner will brighten your whole life!

## Family TETRAODONTIDAE

The pufferfishes, so called because of their ability to inflate their bodies, occur in tropical seas and brackish waters, with a few species in fresh waters. They have a very powerful beaklike dentition that can crush even the shells of mollusks.

Family TETRAODONTIDAE

# Tetraodon fluviatilis
*Green Pufferfish*

- **Distribution:** Southeast Asia, Philippines, Malay Archipelago
- **Length:** Up to 6.7in (17cm)
- **Tank length:** 24in (60cm)
- **Diet:** Worms, crustaceans, insects, chopped meat, plant matter
- **Water temperature:** 72 to 79°F (22 to 26°C)
- **Species tank**

This is a stocky fish with a very broad forehead and slightly protruding eyes. The dorsal and anal fins are roundish and lie opposite one another. The caudal fin is fan-shaped and there are no ventral fins. The skin is leathery with numerous small spines. The colors vary according to age and locality. In adults the upperparts and head are marked with large brown or blackish blotches on a yellowish green background. The underparts are gray and often spotted, but in young individuals the belly is white. The fins are translucent and yellowish, and the caudal fin may be marked with black spots or have a black border. There are no reliable external sex differences.

In the wild this species lives in fresh and brackish waters. The popular name refers to the ability to inflate the body when disturbed or attacked. It can be kept in a tank with dense vegetation and an arrangement of rocks and roots to provide hiding-places. Young specimens are peaceful, but older ones are usually aggressive towards one another. They appear to do best in brackish water, so the tank water should have one teaspoonful of sea salt added per gallon (4 liters) of water. Spawning takes place after a period of courtship near the bottom. The pale, glassy eggs are laid close to one another on a rock. They are tended by the male and usually hatch in six or seven days. The fry, which resemble tiny tadpoles, are taken by the male to a small pit on the bottom where he continues to guard them. They are not easy to feed but should be offered brine shrimp nauplii and rotifers, or possibly micro-worms.

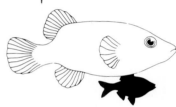

Below: **Tetraodon fluviatilis**
*Some specimens of this species have lived for nine years.*

197

# FURTHER READING

## Books

Axelrod, H. et al. *Breeding Aquarium Fishes,* Vols 1-6, T.F.H., 1967, 1971, 1973, 1976, 1978, 1981.

Axelrod, H. et al. *Exotic Tropical Fishes,* T.F.H., 1981.

Dal Vesco, et al. *Life in the Aquarium,* Octopus, 1975.

Duijn, C. van. *Diseases of Fishes,* 3rd edition, Butterworth Group, 1973.

Favre, H. *Dictionary of the Freshwater Aquarium,* Ward Lock, 1977.

Federation of British Aquatic Societies. *National Show Fish Sizes,* F.B.A.S., 1981. *National Show Guide to Cultivated Fishes,* F.B.A.S., 1981. *Dictionary of Common/Scientific Names of Freshwater Fishes,* F.B.A.S., 1982. *Scientific Names of Fishes and Their Meanings,* F.B.A.S., 1980.

Frank, Dr. S. *Illustrated Encyclopedia of Aquarium Fish,* Octopus, 1980.

Gilbert, J. ed. *Complete Aquarists Guide to Freshwater Tropical Fish,* revised edition, Peter Lowe, 1981.

Goldstein, R. *Cichlids of the World,* T.F.H., 1973.

Guery, Dr. *Characoid Fishes,* T.F.H., 1980.

Hervey, and Hems. *A Guide to Freshwater Aquarium Fishes,* Hamlyn, 1973.

Hoedeman, J.J. *Naturalists's Guide to Freshwater Aquarium Fishes,* Sterling Pub. Inc., 1974.

Hunman, Milne, and Stebbing. *The Living Aquarium,* Ward Lock, 1981.

Jacobsen, N. *Aquarium Plants,* Blandford Press, 1979.

Mayland, H.J. *The Complete Home Aquarium,* Ward Lock, 1975.

Mills, D. *Know the Game: Aquaria,* EP Publishing, 1978. *Aquarium Fishes,* Kingfisher Books, 1980. Canada: John Wiley, 1980. *Illustrated Guide to Aquarium Fishes.* Kingfisher Books/Ward Lock, 1981.

Ramshorst, Dr. J.D. van. *Complete Aquarium Encyclopedia of Tropical Freshwater Fishes,* Elsevier Phaidon, 1978.

Rataj, and Horeman. *Aquarium Plants,* T.F.H., 1977.

Schiotz, and Dahlström. *Collins Guide to Aquarium Fishes & Plants,* Collins, 1972.

Singleton, V. and Mills, D. *How About Keeping Fish,* EP Publishing, 1979.

Spotte, S. *Fish & Invertebrate Culture,* Wiley Interscience, 1970, 1979.

Sterba, G. *Freshwater Fishes of the World,* Studio Vista, 1966. *Aquarium Care,* Studio Vista, 1967. *Dr Sterba's Aquarium Handbook,* Pet Library, 1973.

Thabrew, Dr. V. de. *Popular Tropical Aquarium Plants,* Thornhill Press, 1981.

Vevers, G. *Pocket Guide to Aquarium Fishes,* Mitchell Beazley, 1980.

Whitehead, P. *How Fishes Live,* Elsevier Phaidon, 1975.

## Periodicals

*The Aquarist and Pondkeeper.* Dog World, 9 Tufton Street, Ashford, Kent TN23 1QN, England.

*Practical Fishkeeping,* E.M.A.P. National Publications, Bretton Court, Bretton, Peterborough, Cambs., England.

*Tropical Fish Hobbyist,* T.F.H. Publications Inc., 211 West Sylvania Avenue, P.O. Box 27, Neptune City, New Jersey 07753, U.S.A.

*Freshwater and Marine Aquarium,* 120 West Sierra Madre Boulevard, Sierra Madre, California 91024, U.S.A.

Roloffia occidentalis ♂

# GLOSSARY

Words in *italics* refer to separate entries within the glossary and, in some cases, to scientific names.

**Adipose fin** Small, non-rayed *fin* carried by some species between the *dorsal fin* and *caudal fin.*

**Aeration** The introduction of compressed air into the aquarium via an *airstone* to produce water movement and turbulence. This has the effect of allowing carbon dioxide to be released and oxygen to be taken up at the air-water interface.

**Aerobic** Oxygen-loving, oxygen-dependent. Often applied to bacteria.

**Airline** Neoprene tubing used to carry compressed air from the air pump to the equipment within the aquarium.

**Airstone** Block of porous material which, when supplied with air, produces a stream of bubbles.

**All-glass** Term used to describe tanks made from five panes of bonded glass.

**Anabantids** Fishes equipped with auxiliary breathing organ in the head. See *Labyrinth fishes.*

**Anal fin** Single *fin* projecting vertically downward beneath the body.

**Annual fishes** Fishes with a natural lifespan of one year; those fishes that inhabit waters which completely dry out each summer. See *Killifishes.*

**'Apple' snail** Species of water snail (*Ampullaria*) often used in *fry*-raising tanks, as it produces quantities of *infusorians* from its droppings.

**Artemia salina** Brine shrimp.

**Barbels** Whisker-like growths, often equipped with taste cells, around the mouths of some species, especially catfishes.

**Biological filter** Method of filtration using bacterial activity instead of a trapping *filter medium*. Usually known as an undergravel filter.

**Brine shrimp** *Artemia salina*. The eggs can be hatched (in *salt* water) to provide an excellent live food for *fry*.

**Cably tidy** A junction box for electrical connections to aquarium apparatus (via switches for non-continuously operated equipment).

**Caudal fin** Single, vertically set *fin* at rear end of fish; the tail.

**Caudal peduncle** Part of fish's body that connects immediately with the *caudal fin*.

**Compost** Term often applied to any aquarium base-covering medium.

**Conditioning** The bringing of fishes into peak physical condition (by isolation and increased feeding of quality foods) for breeding or showing purposes.

**Cover glass** A sheet of glass placed between the water surface and the tank hood. It reduces evaporation and damage to the lamps from water spray, and prevents dust getting in and fishes jumping out.

**Crown** The junction between root and stem of aquatic plants; should not be buried in the gravel.

**Daphnia** *Daphnia pulex*, the water flea; a freshwater crustacean collected and sold commercially as live food for aquarium fishes.

**Detritus** Layer of material found on the floor of the aquarium, usually dead plant leaves, uneaten food, fish droppings, etc. Also known as mulm.

**Dorsal fin** Single *fin* projecting vertically from the top of the fish's body; some species may have two dorsal fins.

**Driving** The pursuit of the female fish by the male, which stimulates the release of eggs when the female eventually succumbs to a spawning embrace, usually in clumps of plants or artificial spawning mops.

**Egg-layers** Term applied to fishes whose eggs are laid and fertilized outside the female's body. Although the *mouth-brooding* species' fertilized eggs are incubated in the female's mouth, these genera are still classed as egg-layers within the hobby.

**Emerse** Mode of plant growth in which the roots are anchored in the substrate under water and the leafy shoots and flowers develop above the surface.

**Fancy goldfish** Any of the cultivated forms of *Carassius auratus*, the Goldfish.

**Filter** Device for cleaning the aquarium water. Various types are available.

**Filter medium** Usually a man-made fiber used as a trapping device held within the body of the *filter*.

**Fins** Propelling and stabilizing external appendage of a fish. Usually seven in number: *dorsal, anal, caudal, pelvic* or *ventral* (2), and *pectoral* (2). An extra fin may be present, either as an additional *dorsal* or as an *adipose fin*.

**Fry** The young of a fish.

**Gallon** Measurement of liquid volume.
1 U.S. gallon=3.78 liters.
1 Imperial gallon=4.55 liters.

**Gills** Fish's organs by means of which dissolved oxygen is extracted from the water during respiration.

**Gonopodium** The male *live-bearer's anal fin*, modified into a reproductive organ for internal fertilization of the female.

**Gravid** Pregnant.

**Hardness** Measurement of the amount of dissolved mineral salts in water.

**Heater** Heating device, usually a submersible glass- or aluminium-encased electric element controlled by a *thermostat*.

**Hood** (Reflector) Tank cover housing the aquarium lights, usually with a hinged lid to facilitate feeding.

**Infusorians** Minute, water-living organisms that include *rotifers* and protozoans. Often used as a first food for young fishes. May be cultured by the aquarist. See *'Apple' snail*.

**Killifishes** Members of the family Cyprinodontidae. A large number of species of this group are *annual fishes*.

**Labyrinth fishes** Members of the family Anabantidae (Gouramies, Siamese Fighting Fishes). See *Anabantids*.

**Lateral line** A vibration-detecting nervous system, whose sensors appear as a row of pierced *scales* along the flanks of the fish.

**Length (of fish)** Standard length is measured from tip of snout to end of *caudal peduncle; caudal fin* is excluded from this measurement.
Total length is measured from tip of snout to extreme rear end of *caudal fin* (or projections).

**Liter** Measurement of liquid volume.
1 liter=0.26 U.S. gallon.
1 liter=0.22 Imperial gallon.

**Live-bearer** Fish whose eggs are fertilized and develop inside the female.

**Milt** Fertilizing fluid containing spermatozoa released during spawning by the male fish.

**Mops** Bunches of nylon wool, acting as plant substitutes, in which fishes can deposit fertilized eggs. Mostly used by *Killifish* breeders.

**Mouth-brooders (-breeders)** Fishes whose females incubate the fertilized eggs in the mouth and buccal cavity.

**Mulm** See *detritus*.

**Nauplii** Microscopic, free-swimming larval stages of some crustaceans. Frequently used as first food for very young fishes.

**Operculum** External bony covering to the *gills*.

**Ovipositor** Egg-depositing tube extended from the body of some female fishes at breeding time. May also be used to describe milt-depositing tube of the male fish of the same species.

**Pectoral fins** Paired *fins* immediately behind the *operculum*.

**Pelvic fins** Paired *fins* on fish's ventral surface ahead of *anal fin*. Often referred to as ventral fins. May be lacking in some marine species.

**pH** Unit measurement of water's acidity or alkalinity. Neutral is pH7.

**Photosynthesis** Process by which plants under illumination absorb carbon dioxide and give off oxygen as they build up simple carbohydrates.

**Power filter** Common name given to any design of *filter* that uses small electrically driven impeller to move water through the filter, as opposed to those operated by compressed air.

**Quarantine** Period of isolation of new fishes designed to prevent disease introduction into the aquarium.

**Rays** Spines supporting *fin* tissues.

**Rotifers** Microscopic, mostly free-swimming animals so called because they have an arrangement of tiny hairs resembling a rotating wheel. Used as live food for *fry*.

**Runners** Young plants sent out from an established, adult plant.

**Salt** Sodium chloride (NaC1). Used as a prophylactic bath. Only natural sea salt should be used in aquarium applications.

**Scales** Thin, overlapping plates covering the fish's body.

**Scutes** Large, overlapping armored plates replacing scales in some species, particularly catfishes.

**Sealant** Silicone-rubber adhesive used in bonding glass.

**Shoal** A large number of one species of fish. Also called a 'school'.

**Siphon (tube)** Method of transferring water from a higher to a lower level. Can be used to drain tanks or during partial water changes, when it can also be useful in clearing *detritus* from the aquarium floor.

**Spawning** Act of reproduction in fishes; in aquarium terms may be applied to the whole procedures of courtship, mating, and raising of the young.

**Swim-bladder** Hydrostatic organ giving neutral density (neither floating up nor sinking down) within the fish's body.

**Tail** See *caudal fin*.

**Thermometer** Device for measuring water temperature.

**Thermostat** Electromechanical device for controlling the supply of electric current to the aquarium heater, thus controlling the water temperature.

**Tubifex** Small red worms, often found in sewage-infested river mud, used as live food.

**Undergravel filter** See *biological filter*.

**Variety** Fishes of same species whose coloration or finnage has been developed into fixed recognizable patterns by selective breeding programs.

**Ventral fin** See *Pelvic fin*.

**Water Flea** See *Daphnia*.

**Worms** Excellent foods for fishes. Sizes may range from cultures of micro-, grindal or white worms up to earthworm proportions.

Aequidens maronii ♂

# GENERAL INDEX

Page numbers in **bold** type indicate major references; those in *italics* refer to illustrations.

## A

Acriflavine 43
Aeration **15**
*Aeshna* (Dragonfly) 38
African Rift Valley Lakes
   hard water fish species 22, *25*
Air flow valves *27, 30,31*
Air pumps 15, *28*
Airstone *15, 26, 28, 41*
Algae 11, 13, 23
   as fish food *37, 39*
   tank cleaning *39*
Anchor worm *40*
Anus *35*
Aquarist magazines 48
Aquarist societies 48, 49
Aquarium
   cleaning *39*
   cover glass 13, 30, *31*
   filling *9, 28*
   filtration systems **13**, *26, 28*
   fish selection *36*
   furnishing **22**
   health criteria 41
   heaters *12, 28, 30* (table)
   hood 13, 30, *31*
   hygiene 40, 41
   lighting *13, 23, 31*
   maintenance routine 39
   planting method 30
   plants **16**, *28*
   rockwork *28*
   setting up **26-33**
   siting *10,* **11**, *48*
   size 10
   stands 11
   stock calculations *10,* 36
   tank types **10**
   thermostats *12*
   water changes *25, 41*
   water surface area 10
   *see also* Marine aquarium and
      Tanks
Aquarium Terrarium Inter-
     national 48
*Artemia salina* (Brine shrimp)
   *38, 39*
A.T.I. (Aquarium Terrarium
     International) 48
Axelrod, Dr. Herbert 67

## B

Bacteria
   *Nitrobacter* 15
   *Nitrosomonas* 15
Barbels *34, 35, 92,* 120
Barbs 51, 92
   natural habitat *93*
B.B.A.T. (Belgique Bond
     Aquaria Terraria) 48
Belgique Bond Aquaria Terraria 48
Bloodworms 38
Breeding 24, **44**
   culling 47
   selection 44
   spawning records 47
   tanks 44, *46*
   trap *46*
Breeding patterns
   Anabantoidei (Labyrinth
     fishes) 184
   Characidae 54
   Cichlidae (Cichlids) 160

Cyprinidae 92
Cyprinodontidae (Egg-laying
   Toothcarps) 132
Poeciliidae (Live-bearing
   Toothcarps) 144
Brine shrimp eggs *38, 39*
Bubble-nest 44, *45, 47*
'Bunch' plants 20

## C

C.A.A.C. (Canadian Association
     of Aquarium Clubs) 48
Canadian Association of
     Aquarium Clubs 48
Carp 51, 92
Catfishes 51
   natural habitat *121*
Characins 51
   natural habitat *55*
Charbonnier, M. 128
*Chilodonella* 43
Chromatophores 23, 35
Cichlids 51
   geographical distribution *55
     160, 161, 175*
   natural habitat *161*
Clark Scale *25*
Clubs 48, 49
Cold water aquarium planting 30
Color in fishes 23, 35
Community aquarium 36
Competitions 48, 49
   classes 48
   color-fed fish 35
   judging *49*
Coral 22
Cork bark *23*
*Costia* (Slimy skin disease) *43*
Cover glass 13, 30, *31*

## D

*Dactylogyrus* (Gill flukes) 42, *43*
Dansk Akvarie 48
*Daphnia pulex* (Water flea) 38
°dH 24, *25*
Diseases
   diagnosis and treatment 40, 41
     *43*
   'dropsy' 42
   eye infections, *43*
   'finrot' *42*
   fungus *42*
   gill flukes 42, *43*
   'hole-in-the-head' *40*
   hospital tank regimen *41*
   *lymphocystis* 42
   mouth fungus *43*
   pox *42*
   'shimmying' *42*
   skin flukes 42, *43*
   slimy skin 41, *43*
   stress component 36, 40
   symptoms *37*
   tapeworms 43
   threadworms 43
   treatments
     individual bath 41, *43*
     'long-term' bath 41, *43*
     'out of water' 41, *43*
   tuberculosis *37, 43,* 69
   velvet disease *43*
   white spot 42, *43*

D.K.A. (Dansk Akvarie) 48
Dragonfly larvae 38
'Dropsy' 42, *43*
   *Dytiscus marginalis* (Great diving
     beetle) 38

## E

Earthworms 38
Eggs 44
Electric 'cable tidy' *28, 29, 31*
Electric power supply 11, 12, 30
Esophagus *35*
Eye *35*
   infections *43*

## F

F.A.A.S. (Federation of American
     Aquarium Societies) 48
F.B.A.S. (Federation of British
     Aquatic Societies) 48
Fédération Français des
     Associations Aquaphile et
     Terrariophile 48
Federation Luxembourg Aquario-
     phile et Terrariophile 48
Federation of American
     Aquarium Societies 48
Federation of British Aquatic
     Societies 48
Federation of New Zealand
     Aquatic Societies 48
Feeding
   breeding fishes 45, *46*
   frequency 38, 39
   mouth adaptation 34, 35
   F.F.A.A.T. (Fédération Français
     Associations Aquaphile et
     Terrariophile) 48
Filter media 14, *15, 26*
Filters **13**
   air operated 14, *26*
     internal box type *14, 26*
     external box type 14, *26*
     sponge type *14, 15, 26*
   biological *14, 26, 27*
   breeding tank requirements 15
   chemical 14
   hospital aquarium *41*
   mechanical 'power' *14, 15, 26,
     28*
'Finrot' *42*
Fins 34
   adipose 34, *35*
   anal 34, *35,* 44, *45*
   caudal 34, *35*
   diseases *42*
   dorsal *34*
   pectoral 34, *35*
   pelvic 34, *35*
   ventral 34, *35*
Fish
   anatomy *34, 35*
   bubble-nest builders 44, *45*
   camouflage 35
   egg-buriers 44
   egg-depositors 44, *45*
   egg-scatterers *19,* 44
   introduction to aquarium *32,* 37
   lateral line system 35
   live-bearing 44, *46*
     gestation period 44

mouth-brooders 44, *45*
nocturnal coloration 35
nutrition *38*
pigmentation 23, 35
   cells 35
selection criteria 36
senses 34, 53
sexing *37*
transporting 37
Fishkeeping 9, 24
F.L.A.T. (Federation
     Luxembourg Aquariophile et
     Terrariophile) 48
*Flexibacter columnaris* 43
Food
   'color' foods 35
   dried
     floating pellets *38*
     flour-fine fry food *38,* 47
     freeze-dried shrimp *38*
     freeze-dried *Tubifex*
       cubes *38*
     granulated high protein *38,* 57
     green (vegetable formula)
       flake *38*
     multiflavoured flake *38*
     'stick-on' tablet *38*
   infusorians 47
   liquid for fry, tubed *38,* 47
   live
     bloodworms *38*
     brine shrimp *38,* 47
     *Cyclops* nauplii 183
     *Daphnia* larvae *38,* 47
     grindal worms *39,* 47
     micro-worms 39, 47
     mosquito larvae *38*
     *Paramecium* 83, 194
     rotifers 56
     white worms 39, 47
     wild-caught 38
   *see also* Feeding
Food fishes 89, *193,* 92, *185, 186*
Formalin 43
Freshwater coldwater species
     tank population guide *10*
Freshwater tropical species
     tank population guide *10*
Fry 44, *46, 47*
Fungus 42
Furnishings
   cork bark *23*
   for egg-scatterers 44, *46*
   gravel 14, 22, *27*
   hospital aquarium *40*
   imitation plants 23
   peat 14, *17,* 44
   rock 22, 23, *27, 28*
   wood *23*

## G

Geographical distribution 51
   Anabantoidei (Labyrinth fishes)
     184, *185*
   Anostomidae 54
   Characidae 54
   Cichlidae (Cichlids) 160, *161*
   Citharinidae 54
   Curimatidae 54
   Cyprinidae *93*
   Cyprinodontidae *134*
   Gasteropelecidae (Hatchet-
     fishes) 54
   Lebiasinidae 54

Poeciliidae (Live-bearing Tooth-
    carps) 144, *145*
Serrasalmidae (Piranhas) 54
Siluriformes (Catfishes) 120,
    *121*
Gill cover *34*
Gill flukes 42, *43*
Gills *35*
    diseases 42, *43*
Gnat larvae 38
Gravel 14, 16, 22
    color 22
    particle size 16, 22
    planting depth 23, *26, 27*
Great diving beetle larvae 38
Guanin 35
Guppy, Robert John Lechmere 149
*Gyrinus* (Whirligig beetle) 38
*Gyrodactylus* 42, *43*

**H**

Hatchetfishes
    geographical distribution 54
Heart *35*
Heaters **12**
    capacity (Watts) calculation 12
        30 (table)
    combined heater/ thermostat
        units 12, *27, 28*
    hospital aquarium *40*
Hood 13, 30, *31*
*Hydra* 38
Hygiene 40, 41

**I**

*Ichthyobodo 43*
*Ichthyophthiriasis* (White
    spot disease) 42, *43*
Imitation plants *23*
Innes, W.T. 73
Intestine *35*

**K**

Kidney *35*

**L**

Labyrinth fishes 51, **184**
Lateral line system *35*
*Lernaea* (Anchor worm) *40*
*Libellula* (Dragonfly) 38
Lighting *12, 13*
    color-enhancing lamps *35*
    direction *13*
    duration/brightness 13, 32
    fluorescent 13
    high-intensity 13
    hood installations *12, 13, 31*
    hospital aquarium *40*
Live-bearers 44, *46*, 144, 149
    natural habitat *145*
Liver *35*
*Lymphocystis 42*

**M**

Marine aquarium 10
    all-glass construction 10

calcareous rocks 22
    evaporation loss replacement 25
Marine shark
    absence of swim-bladder 35
Marine tropical species
    tank population guide *10*
Medication and treatment 41
Methylene blue 43
Metriphonate 43
Mosquito larvae *38, 146*
Mouth *35*
    adaption for feeding in an
        environment *34, 35*
    diseases *43*

**N**

N.A.F. (Norsk Akvarieforbund)
    48
Nauplii *39*
N.B.A.T. (Nederlands Bond
    Aquaria et Terraria) 48
Nederlands Bond Aquaria et
    Terraria 48
Nets
    isolation and disinfection 40
Norsk Akvarieforbund 48
Nostril *35*
*Notonecta* (Water boatman) 38

**O**

*Oodinium* (Velvet disease) *43*
Operculum (Gill cover) *34*
Ovary *35*

**P**

Parasites
    anchor worm *(Lernaea sp.) 40*
    *Costia 43*
    *Dactylogyrus* 42, *43*
    *Gyrodactylus* 42, *43*
    *Ichthyophthiriasis* 42, *43*
    *Lernaea 40*
Peat 14, 17, *44, 47*
pH scale *25*
Photography 49
    camera/tank set up *49*
Physical characteristics
    Anabantoidei (Labyrinth
        fishes) 184
    Characidae (Characins) 54
    Cichlidae (Cichlids) 160
    Cyprinidae (Carps and Barbs)
        92
    Cyprinodontidae (Egg-laying
        Toothcarps) 132
    Siluriformes (Catfishes) 120
    Poeciliidae (Live-bearing
        Toothcarps) 144
Planting out *9, 28, 30*
    medium requirements 16, 17
Plant stick *17*
Plants 16
    aquarium layout *16, 17, 28-9, 30*
    as food 16
    as shelter 16
    as spawning sites 16, 18,
        19, 44
    cuttings or 'bunch' **20**, 21
    floating 13, **20**, *21*

potassium permanganate
        wash 40
    pots 17, 18
    preparations for aquarium 40
    propagation *21*
    rhizome species *(Aponogeton)*
        *17, 18*
    rooted 16
    *see also* separate Aquatic Plants
        Index
Polski Zwiazeke Akwarystow 48
Potassium permanganate 40, 41
Pox *42*
Ppm 25
Predators
    great diving beetle larvae 38
P.Z.A. (Polski Zwiazeke
    Akwarystow) 48

**Q**

Quarantine 40, 41

**R**

Rock 22, *23, 27, 28*
    calcareous 22
Rocky aquarium 37

**S**

*Saprolegnia 42*
S.A.R.F. (Sveriges Akvariet-
    föreningars Riksförbund) 48
Scales 34, *35*
    dropsical condition 34, *35*
Senses 34
    Mormyridae electric sense
        organ 53
'Shimmying' *42*
Showing *see* Competitions
Skin Flukes *43*
Slimy skin disease 41, *43*
Snails 21, 40
Societies 48, 49
Spawning *44, 46*
Species aquariums 37
Spray bar 14, *26, 28*
Stomach *35*
Stress component in disease 36, 40
Sveriges Akvarietföreningars
    Riksförbund 48
Swim-bladder *35*
*Sympetrum* (Dragonfly) 38

**T**

'Tailrot' *42*
Tanks
    all-glass, adhesive bonded *10*
    angled-iron framed 10
    breeding 10, *44, 46*
    filtration 15
    cover glass 13, 30
    hood 13, 30
    hospital 10, *41*
    installations **11**
    insulation 11, 12
    leaks 11
    nursery 10, *46*
    plastic molded *10*

quarantine 10, 40
sealant *11*
water capacities and weights
    (table) 30
water surface area *10*
*see also Aquarium*
Tapeworms 43
Thermometers *13, 30*
Thermostats 12, *27, 31*
    combined heater/thermostat
        units 12, 28
Threadworms 43
Tools 27
    planting stick *17*
    tank 'vacuum cleaner' *39*
Toothcarps 51
    natural habitat *132, 145*
*Tubifex* worms 38, *38*

**U**

Urinogenital opening *35*

**V**

V.D.A. (Verband Deutscher
    vor Aquarien) 48
Velvet disease *43*
Vent *35*
Verband Deutscher vor Aquarien
    48

**W**

Water **24**
    carbon dioxide 10, 16
    chemical effect on rocks 22,
        *23, 24*
    conditioners 31
    contamination 40
    filling the tank *28*
    filtration *13*
    hardness 24, 25
        °Clark (UK) 25
        °dH (Germany) 25
        °fH (France) 25
        general (GH) 25
        °hardness (USA) 25
        ppm (parts per million
            $CaCO_3$) 25
        temporary (KH) 25
    oxygen content 10
    pH scale 25
    pH test kits *24*
    quality 24
    soft (acidic) *24*
    temperature 12, *32*, 37
    transfer between tanks 40
Water boatman larvae 38
Water fleas 38
    larvae *38*
Whirligig beetle larvae 38
White spot disease 42, *43*
    infection cycle *42*
Wood 23
Worm cataract *43*
Worms
    grindal 39
    micro- 39
    *Tubifex* 38, *38*
    white 39

# INDEX OF PLANTS

Page numbers in *italics* refer to illustrations.

## A

*Acorus gramineus* var.
    *pusilus* (Dwarf Japanese Rush)
    *16, 18*
Amazon Sword Plant 18, 85
*Aponogeton* 18
    *crispus 17*
    *madagascariensis* (Madagascar
        Laceplant) *17,* 18
Arrowhead *18*
*Azolla* 20
    *caroliniana* (Fairy Moss) *19*

## C

*Cabomba* 20, 25, *30*
    *caroliniana 18*
*Ceratophyllum* 20
    *demersum* (Hornwort) *19*
*Ceratopteris* 18
    *thalictroides* (Indian Fern) 21
*Cryptocoryne* 18, 124, 183
    *balansae* 20
    *wendtii 21*
    *willisii* 20
Crystalwort *16*

## D

Dwarf Amazon Sword Plant 18, *19*
Dwarf Japanese Rush *16,* 18

## E

*Echinodorus* 25, 86
    *bleheri 18*
    *brevipedicellatus* (Amazon
        Sword Plant) 18, 85
    *magdalensis* (Dwarf
        Amazon Sword Plant)
        18, *19*
Eelgrass *16*
*Egeria densa* 20
*Eleocharis*
    *acicularis* (Hairgrass) 18

## F

Fairy Moss *19*
*Fontinalis* (Willow Moss) 19

## H

Hairgrass 18
Hornwort *19*
*Hygrophila* 18, 20, *30,* 84
    *difformis* (Water Wisteria) *18*
    *polysperma 17*

## I

India Fern 21

## J

Java Fern *16*
Java Moss 19, *21,* 83

## L

*Lemna* 20, 21
*Limnophila* 20
*Ludwigia* 18, 84
    *repens 19*

## M

Madagascar Laceplant *17,* 18
*Microsorium* 19
    *pteropus* (Java Fern) *16*
Milfoil 20, 66, 76, 97, 107, 108,
    115
*Myriophyllum* (Milfoil) 20, 66, 76,
    97, 107, 108, 115

## N

*Najas* 20
    *guadelupensis (N. microdon)*
    *16*
Needlegrass (Hairgrass) 18
*Nomaphilia stricta 17*

## P

*Pistia* 20
    *stratiotes* (Water Lettuce) *18*

## R

*Riccia* 20
    *fluitans* (Crystalwort) *16*

## S

*Sagittaria* 18, *30*
    *subulata* (Arrowhead) *18*
*Salvinia* 20
    *natans 17*
*Synnema triflorum* (Water
    Wisteria) *18*

## V

*Vallisneria* 18, 25, *30*
    *natans* (Eelgrass) *16*
*Vesicularia*
    *dubyana* (Java Moss) 19, *21,* 83

## W

Water Lettuce *18*
Water Wisteria *18*
Willow Moss 19

A beautifully planted freshwater tank

A pair of Poecilia latipinna

# INDEX OF FISHES

Page numbers in **bold** type indicate the major references for each fish, including accompanying illustrations. Page numbers in *italics* refer to other illustrations.

## A

*Abramites hypselonotus* (Headstander) **86**
*microcephalus* (Headstander) **86**
*Acanthophthalmus kuhli* (Coolie Loach) **34**
Acara
  Blue **163**
  Port **162**
*Aequidens maronii* (Keyhole Cichlid) **162**, *200*
*portalegrensis* (Port Acara) **162**
*pulcher* (Blue Acara) **163**
African Glass Catfish **122**
African Knifefish **52**
African Redfin **91**
Agassiz's Dwarf Cichlid **164**
*Alestes chaperi* (Chaper's Characin) **56**
*longipinnis* (Long-finned Characin) **56**
American Flagfish *47*, **140**
Anabantidae **34**, **47**, **184**, **186**
Anabantoidei **184**, **186**
*Anabas testudineus* (Climbing Perch) **184**, **186**
Anablepidae **143**
*Anableps anableps* (Four-eyes) **143**
Angelfish **18**, *34*, *36*, *51*, **105**, *179*
*Anoptichthys jordani* (Blind Cave Characin) **35**, **59**
Anostomidae **54**, **86**
*Anostomus anostomus* (Striped Anostomus) **86**
*trimaculatus* (Three-spot Anostomus) **86**
*Aphyocharax anisitsi* (Bloodfin) **56**
*Aphyosemion australe* (Lyretail) *37*, *132*, **134**, **135**
*filamentosum* (Plumed Lyretail) **135**
Hjerresen's **134**
*Apistogramma agassizi* (Agassiz's Dwarf Cichlid) **164**
*borelli* (Yellow Dwarf Cichlid) **164**
*Aplocheilichthys macrophthalmus* (Lamp-eye Panchax) **137**, **140**
*Aplocheilus blocki* (Green Panchax, Dwarf Panchax) **134**
*Aplocheilus dayi* (Ceylon Killifish) **136**
*panchax* (Blue Panchax) **136**
Archerfish **157**
Argentine Pearlfish *44*, **138**
Argusfish **156**
Armored Catfish **34**, *39*, **124**, **127**
*Arnoldichthys spilopterus* (Red-eyed Characin) **57**
Arulius Barb **94**
*Astronotus ocellatus* (Oscar) *37*, **165**
*Astyanax bimaculatus* **58**
*mexicanus* **35**, **59**
Atherinidae **196**
Atherinoidei **194**

## B

*Badis badis* (Badis) **158**
Banded Barb **105**
Banded Gourami *184*, **189**

Banded Knifefish **119**
Banded Leporinus **87**
Banded Loach **116**
Barbs **92**
  Arulius **94**
  Banded **105**
  Checker **101**
  Cherry **107**
  China **103**
  Clown **97**
  Cuming's **97**
  Dwarf **101**
  Everett's **97**
  Flying Fox **108**
  Golden **103**
  Golden Dwarf **98**
  Green **103**, **105**
  Half-banded **103**
  Island **101**
  Lined **98**
  Orange **95**
  Purple-headed *36*, **100**
  Pygmy **101**
  Red *46*, **96**
  Rosy *46*, **96**, **103**
  Schubert's **103**
  Schwanenfeld's **102**
  Spanner **99**
  Stoliczka's **104**
  Striped **98**
  Sumatran **105**
  Swamp **95**
  Tiger **35**, *46*, **105**
  Tinfoil **102**
*Barbus arulius* (Arulius Barb) **94**
*barilioides* (Orange Barb) **95**
*chola* (Swamp Barb) **95**
*conchonius* (Rosy Barb) *46*, **96**, **103**
*cumingi* (Cuming's Barb) **97**
*everetti* (Clown Barb, Everett's Barb) **97**
*fasciatus* (Striped barb) **98**
*gelius* (Golden Dwarf Barb) **98**
*lateristriga* (Spanner Barb) **99**
*lineatus* (Lined Barb) **98**
*nigrofasciatus* see (Black Ruby, Purple-headed Barb) *36*, **92**, **100**, **101**
*oligolepis* (Island Barb, Checker Barb) **101**
*phutunio* (Dwarf Barb, Pygmy Barb) **101**
*'schuberti'* (Golden Barb, Schubert's Barb) **103**
*schwanenfeldi* (Schwanenfeld's Barb, Tinfoil Barb) **102**
*semifasciolatus* (Green Barb, China Barb, Half-banded Barb) **103**, **105**
*stoliczkanus* (Stoliczka's Barb) **104**
*tetrazona partipentazona* (Banded Barb) **105**
*tetrazona tetrazona* (Sumatran Barb, Tiger Barb) **35**, *46*, **105**
*ticto stoliczkae* (Stoliczka's Barb) **104**
*titteya* (Cherry Barb) **107**
Beacon fish *36*, **62**
*Bedotia geayi* (Madagascar Rainbowfish) **196**
*Belontia signata* (Combtail) **186**

Belontiidae **184**, **186**
Bengal Danio **108**
*Betta brederi* (Mouth-brooder Betta) **188**
*splendens* (Siamese fighting fish) *35*, *45*, *47*, **188**
Black-bellied Limia **149**
Black-line Tetra **68**
Black Molly **42**, **147**
Black Neon **67**, **68**
Black Phantom Tetra **69**, **70**
Black Ruby *36*, *92*, **100**, **101**
Black-spotted Corydoras **126**
Black Tetra **60**
Black-winged Hatchetfish **78**
Bleeding Heart Tetra **65**
Blind Cave Characin **35**, **59**
Blood Characin **64**
Bloodfin **56**
Blue Acara **163**
Blue Discus *37*, **180**
Blue Gourami **192**
Blue Panchax **136**
Boehlke's Penguin Fish **76**
*Botia hymenophysa* (Banded Loach) **116**
*macracantha* (Clown Loach) *37*, **116**
*modesta* (Orange-finned Loach) **118**
*morleti* **117**
*sidthimunki* (Dwarf Loach, Chained Loach) **119**
Brabant Cichlid **183**
*Brachydanio albolineatus* (Pearl Danio) **106**
*rerio* (Zebra Danio) *36*, *44*, *46*, **107**
*Brachygobius xanthozona* (Bumblebee Fish) **183**
Brilliant Rasbora **111**
Bronze Corydoras *36*, *120*, **124**
Brown Discus **180**
Brown Spike-tailed Paradisefish **190**
Buenos Aires Tetra **61**, **62**, **63**
Bumblebee Fish **183**
Butterflyfish **53**

## C

*Calamoichthys calabaricus* (Reedfish) **52**
Callichthyidae **34**, **120**, **124**
*Callichthys callichthys* (Armored Catfish) *39*, **124**, **127**
Cardinal Tetra **59**, **73**
*Carnegiella marthae* (Black-winged Hatchetfish) **78**
*strigata* (Marbled Hatchetfish) **79**
Catfishes **120**
  African Glass **122**
  Armored **34**, **124**
  Bronze Corydoras *36*, *120*, **124**
  Electric **35**
  Glass **122**
  Golden Otocinclus *36*, **130**
  Suckermouth **131**
  Upside-down **123**
Celebes Sailfish **196**
Centrarchidae **154**
Centropomidae **155**
Ceylon Killifish **136**
Chained Loach **119**
Chalceidae **58**
*Chalceus macrolepidotus* (Pink-

tailed Characin) **58**
*Chanda ranga* (Indian Glassfish) **155**
Chaper's Characin **56**
Characidae **54**, **56**, **85**
Characins **54**
  Blind Cave **35**, **59**
  Blood **64**
  Chaper's **56**
  Long-finned **56**
  One-striped African **90**
  Pike **91**
  Pink-tailed **58**
  Red-eyed **57**
  Spraying *44*, **88**
Characoidei **34**, **54**, **56**
Checker Barb **101**
*Cheirodon axelrodi* (Cardinal Tetra) **59**, **73**
Cherry Barb **107**
*Chilodus punctatus* (Spotted Headstander) **88**
China Barb **103**
Chocolate Gourami **190**
Chromide
  Green **170**, **171**
  Orange **170**
*Cichlasoma* **171**
*biocellatum* (Jack Dempsey) **166**
*cyanoguttatum* (Rio Grande Perch) **167**
*festivus* (Festive Cichlid) **167**
*meeki* (Firemouth Cichlid) **168**
*nigrofasciatum* (Zebra Cichlid) **169**
*octofasciatum* **166**
*portalegrensis* **162**
Cichlids **160**
  Agassiz's Dwarf **164**
  Blue Acara **163**
  Brabant **183**
  Earth-Eater **171**
  Festive **167**
  Firemouth **168**
  Fuelleborn's **174**
  Golden-eyed Dwarf **175**
  Golden Julie *37*, **173**
  Jack Dempsey **166**
  Jewel *45*, **172**
  Keyhole **162**
  Kribensis ('Kribs') *45*, **177**
  Malawi Blue *23*, *37*, **178**
  Malawi Golden *37*, **176**, **178**
  Oscar *37*, **165**
  Pike **169**
  Port Acara **162**
  Rio Grande Perch **167**
  Trewavas's *37*, **175**
  Waroo **182**
  Yellow Dwarf **164**
  Zebra **169**
Cichlidae **15**, *35*, *46*, *47*, **160**
Citharinidae **89**
Clariidae **120**
Climbing Perch **184**, **186**
Clown Barb **97**
Clown Loach *37*, **116**
Cobitidae **116**
*Colisa* **20**, **187**
*chuna* (Honey Gourami) **188**, **189**
*fasciata* (Banded Gourami) *184*, **189**
*lalia* (Dwarf Gourami) **15**, **188**
Combtail **186**
Common Carp **92**

Common Hatchetfish 76
Common Pencilfish 82
Congo Tetra 70
Coolie Loach *34*
*Copeina* 85
  *arnoldi* 81
  *guttata* (Red-spotted Copeina) 80
*Copella* 85
  *arnoldi* (Spraying Characin) *44*, 81
*Corydoras* 34, 35
  *aeneus* (Bronze Corydoras) *36*, *120*, 124
  *julii* (Leopard Corydoras) 126
  *leopardus* 126
  *melanistius* (Black-spotted Corydoras) 126
  *myersi* (Myers' Corydoras) 127
  *paleatus* (Peppered Corydoras) 128
  *reticulatus* (Reticulated Corydoras) 128
*Crenicichla*
  *lepidota* (Pike Cichlid) 169
Crescenty Black Molly 147
*Ctenobrycon*
  *spiluris* (Silver Tetra) 60
*Ctenopoma*
  *nanum* (Dwarf Climbing Perch) 187
  *oxyrhynchus* 187
Cuban Limia 149, 150
Cuming's Barb 97
Curimatidae 54, 88
*Cynolebias* 47
  *bellotti* (Argentine Pearlfish) *44*, 138
  *nigripinnis* (Dwarf Argentine Pearlfish) 138
Cyprinidae 92, 94
Cyprinodontidae 46, *132*, 134
*Cyprinus carpio* (Common Carp) 92


**D**

*Danio*
  *aequipinnatus* (Giant Danio) 108
  Bengal 108
  *devario* (Bengal Danio) 108
  giant 108
  pearl 106
  *regina* 108
  *zebra* *36*, *44*, *46*, *107*, 108
*Dermogenys*
  *pusillus* (Halfbeak) 154
Diamond Tetra 71, 72
Discus *24*, *160*, 181
  Blue *37*, 180
  Brown 180
  Green 180
  Red 181
  Royal Blue 181
Disk Tetra *54*, 60, 74
*Distichodus sexfasciatus* (Six-banded Distichodus) 89
Dwarf Argentine Pearlfish 138
Dwarf Barb 101
Dwarf Climbing Perch 187
Dwarf Gourami 15, 188
Dwarf Loach 119
Dwarf Panchax 134
Dwarf Rainbowfish 194


**E**

Earth-eater 171
Egyptian Mouth-brooder, *45*, 173
*Elassoma evergladei* (Everglades Pygmy Sunfish) 154
Electric Catfish 35
Electric Eel 53
Elephant Nose 53
Emperor Tetra 73
*Epalzeorhynchus kallopterus* (Flying Fox) 108
*Ephippicharax orbicularis* 74
*Epiplatys sexfasciatus* (Six-barred Epiplatys) 139
*Erpetoichthys calabaricus* (Reedfish) 52
*Etroplus maculatus* (Orange Chromide) 170
  *suratensis* (Green Chromide) 170, 171
*Eutropiellus debauwi* (African Glass Catfish) 122
Everett's Barb 97
Everglades Pygmy Sunfish 154
Exocoetidae 154
Eye-spot Rasbora 112


**F**

False Rummy-nose 74
Featherfin Panchax 142
Festive Cichlid 167
Fingerfish 156
Firemouth Cichlid 168
Fire Rasbora 115
Flag Tetra 67, 68
Flame Tetra 65, 66
Flying Fish 34
Flying Fox 108
Four-eyes 143
Fuelleborn's Cichlid 174


**G**

*Gambusia*
  *affinis* (Mosquito Fish) 146
  *affinis affinis* 146
  *affinis holbrooki* 146
Gasteropelecidae 54, 76
*Gasteropelecus levis* (Silver Hatchetfish) 78
  *sternicla* (Common Hatchetfish) 76
*Geophagus jurupari* (Earth-eater) 171
Giant Danio 108
Glass Catfish 122
Glass Tetra 71, 72
Glassfish
  Indian 155
Glowlight Tetra 62
*Gnathonemus petersi* (Elephant Nose) 53
Gobiidae 183
Gold Platy 152
Golden Barb 103
Golden Dwarf Barb 98
Golden-eyed Dwarf Cichlid 175
Golden Julie *37*, 173
Golden Otocinclus *36*, 130
Golden Pencilfish 81
Gourami 34, 47, 193
  Banded 189
  Blue 192


Chocolate 190
  Dwarf 15, 188
  Honey 188, 189
  Kissing 193
  Pearl *36*, 192
  Three-spot 192
Graceful Pimelodella 124
Green Barb 103
Green Chromide 170, 171
Green Discus 180
Green Panchax 134
Green Pufferfish 197
Griem's Tetra 65, 66
Guppy *36*, 149
Gurnard 34
*Gymnocorymbus ternetzi* (Black Tetra) 60
*Gymnotidae* 119
*Gymnotus carapo* (Banded Knife-fish) 119


**H**

Half-banded Barb 103
Half-banded Pyrrhulina 84
Halfbeak 154
Harlequin Fish 18, *36*, 113
Hatchetfish 34, 54, 76
  Black-winged 78
  Marbled 79
  Silver 78
Headstander 86
  Spotted 88
*Helostoma temmincki* (Kissing Gourami) 193
Helostomatidae 184, 193
*Hemichromis bimaculatus* (Jewel Cichlid) *45*, 172
*Hemigrammus caudovittatus* (Buenos Aires Tetra) 61, 62, 63
  *erythrophthalmus* 68
  *erythrozonus* (Glowlight Tetra) 62
  *ocellifer* (Beacon Fish) *36*, 62
  *ocellifer falsus* 62
  *ocellifer ocellifer* 62, *62*
  *pulcher* (Pretty Tetra) 63
  *rhodostomus* (Red-nosed Tetra) 74
*Herichthys cyanoguttatum* 167
*Heterandria formosa* (Least Killifish) 146
Hjerresen's Aphyosemion 134
Honey Gourami 188, 189
*Hyphessobrycon callistus* (Blood Characin) 64
  *erythrostigma* (Bleeding Heart Tetra) 65
  *flammeus* (Flame Tetra) 65, 66
  *georgettae* (Strawberry Tetra) 66
  *griemi* (Griem's Tetra) 65, 66
  *herbertaxelrodi* (Black Neon) 67, 68
  *heterorhabdus* (Flag Tetra) 67, 68
  *innesi* 73
  *metae* 68
  *'minor'* 64
  *pulchripinnis* (Lemon Tetra) 68
  *rubrostigmata* (Bleeding Heart Tetra) 65
  *scholzei* (Black-line Tetra) 68
  *serpae* 64
*Hypostomus punctatus* 131


**I**

Indian Glassfish 155
Island Barb 101


**J**

Jack Dempsey 166
Jewel Cichlid *45*, 172
*Jordanella floridae* (American Flagfish) *47*, 140
*Julidochromis* 22
  *ornatus* (Golden Julie) *37*, 173


**K**

Keyhole Cichlid 162
Killifish *47*
  Ceylon 136
  Least 146
Kissing Gourami 193
Knifefish
  Banded 119
Kribensis ('Kribs') *45*, 177
*Kryptopterus*
  *bicirrhis* (Glass Catfish) 122


**L**

*Labeo bicolor* (Red-tailed Labeo) 110
*Labeotropheus* 22, 171
  *fuelleborni* (Fuelleborn's Cichlid) 174
  *trewavasae* (Trewava's Cichlid) *25*, *37*, 175
Labyrinth Fishes 184
Lamp-eye Panchax 137, 140
Leaf-fish
  Schomburgk's 159
  South American 158
Least Killifish 146
Lebiasinidae 54, 80
Lemon Tetra 68
Leopard Corydoras 126
*Lepomis gibbosus* (Pumpkinseed) 154
*Leporinus fasciatus* (Banded Leporinus) 87
  *striatus* (Striped Leporinus) 88
*Lebistes reticulatus* (Guppy) 149
Limia
  Black-bellied 149
  Cuban 149, 150
*Limia vittata* 149, 150
Lined Barb 98
Loach
  Banded 116
  Clown *37*, 116
  Dwarf 119
  Orange-finned 118
Long-finned Characin 56
*Loricaria filamentosa* (Whiptail) 129
Loricariidae 120, 129
Lyretail *37*, *132*, *134*, 135
  Plumed 135


**M**

*Macropodus cupanus cupanus* 190
  *cupanus dayi* (Brown Spike-tailed Paradisefish) 190

*opercularis* (Paradisefish)
47, 191
Madagascar Rainbowfish 196
*Malapterurus electricus* (Electric
Catfish) 35
Malawi Blue Cichlid 23, 37,
160, 178
Malawi Golden Cichlid 37, 176
178
Marbled Hatchetfish 79
*Megalamphodus megalopterus*
(Black Phantom Tetra) 69, 70
*sweglesi* (Red Phantom Tetra)
70
*Melanochromis auratus* (Malawi
Golden Cichlid) 37, 176, 178
*Melanotaenia*
*maccullochi* (Dwarf Rain-
bowfish) 194
*nigrans* (Red-tailed
Rainbowfish) 194
Melanotaeniidae 194
*Mesonauta festivus* 167
Mexican Sailfin molly 34, 37, 151
*Micralestes interruptus* (Congo
Tetra) 70
*Microgeophagus ramirezi* end-
papers, copyright page
Mochokidae 34, 120, 123
*Moenkhausia oligolepis* (Glass
Tetra) 71, 72
*pittieri* (Diamond Tetra) 71, 72
*sanctaefilomenae* (Red-eye
Tetra) 72
*Mollienisia velifera* 147
Molly
Black 42, 147
Crescenty Black 147
Mexican Sailfin 37, 151
Pointed-mouth 147, 150
Sailfin 34, 147, 148, 151
*Monocirrhus polyacanthus* (South
American Leaf-fish) 158
Monodactylidae 156
*Monodactylus argenteus*
(Fingerfish) 156
*sebae* (Striped Fingerfish) 156
Mormyridae 53
Mosquito fish 146
Mountain Minnow 115
Mouth-brooder
Betta 188
Egyptian 45, 173
Mozambique 160, 179
Mozambique Mouth-brooder 160,
179
Myers' Corydoras 127

### N

Nandidae 158
*Nannacara anomala* (Golden-eyed
Dwarf Cichlid) 175
*Nannaethiops unitaeniatus* (One-
striped African Characin) 90
*Nannostomus* 35, 85
*beckfordi* (Golden Pencilfish)
81
*beckfordi anomalus* 81
*beckfordi aripirangensis* 81
*eques* (Tube-mouthed
Pencilfish) 82
*espei* (Common Pencilfish) 82

*trifasciatus* (Three-banded
Pencilfish) 35, 83
*unifasciatus* (One-lined
Pencilfish) 84
*unifasciatus ocellatus* 84
*Nanochromis parilus* 176
*Nematobrycon palmeri* (Emperor
Tetra) 73
*Nematocentris fluviatilis* (Red-
tailed Rainbowfish) 194
*maccullochi* (Dwarf
Rainbowfish) 194
*Neolebias ansorgii* (African
Redfin) 91
Neon Tetra 43, 51, 62, 73
Notopteridae 52
*Notopterus afer* 52

### O

One-lined Pencilfish 84
One-striped African Characin 90
Orange Barb 95
Orange Chromide 170
Orange-finned Loach 118
*Oryzias melastigma* 140
Oscar 37, 165
Osphronemidae 184, 193
*Osphronemus goramy* (Gourami)
34, 47, 193
*Otocinclus affinis* (Golden
Otocinclus) 36, 130

### P

*Pachypanchax playfairi* (Playfair's
Panchax) 141
Panchax
Blue 136
Dwarf 134
Featherfin 142
Green 134
Lamp-eye 137, 140
Playfair's 141
*Pantodon buchholzi* (Butterflyfish)
53
Pantodontidae 53
*Paracheirodon axelrodi* (Cardinal
Tetra) 59
*meinkeni* 59
*innesi* (Neon Tetra)
43, 51, 62, 73
Paradisefish 47, 191
Brown spike-tailed 190
Pearl Danio 106
Pearl Gourami 36, 192
Pearly Rasbora 115
*Pelmatochromis kribensis* 177
*Pelvicachromis pulcher* (Kribensis,
'Kribs') 45, 177
Pencilfish 35, 82
Golden 81
One-lined 84
Three-banded 35, 83
Tube-mouthed 82
Peppered Corydoras 128
*Petitella georgiae* (False
Rummy-nose) 74
*Phago loricatus* 91
*maculatus* (Pike Characin) 91
*Phenacogrammus interruptus* 70

Pike Characin 91
Pike Cichlid 169
*Pimelodella gracilis* (Graceful
Pimelodella) 124
Pimelodidae 34, 120, 124
Pink-tailed Characin 58
Piranha 35, 36, 54, 77
Platy 152
Gold 152
Red 152
Red Variatus 153
Tuxedo 152
Variatus 153
*Platypoecilus maculatus* 152
Playfair's Panchax 141
*Plecostomus commersoni* 131
*puntactus* (Suckermouth
Catfish) 131
Plumed Lyretail 135
*Poecilia hybrid* (Black Molly) 42,
147
*latipinna* (Sailfin Molly) 34, 147
148, 151, 204
*melanogaster* (Black-bellied
Limia) 149
*reticulata* (Guppy) 36, 149
*sphenops* (Pointed-mouth
Molly) 147, 150
*velifera* (Mexican Sailfin
Molly) 34, 37, 151
*vittata* (Cuban Limia) 149, 150
Poeciliidae 144, 146
*Poecilobrycon* 85
*eques* (Tube-mouthed
Pencilfish) 82
*unifasciatus* (One-lined
Pencilfish) 84
Pointed-mouth Molly 147, 150
*Polycentrus schomburgki*
(Schomburgk's Leaf-fish) 159
Polypteridae 52
*Polypterus* 52
*Poptella orbicularis* (Disk Tetra)
54, 60, 74
Port Acara 162
Pretty Tetra 63
*Pristella maxillaris* (X-ray Fish,
Water Goldfinch) 75
*Pseudocrenilabrus multicolor*
Egyptian Mouth-brooder) 45,
173
*Pseudotropheus* 22
*zebra* (Malawi Blue Cichlid)
23, 37, 160, 178
*Pterolebias longipinnis*
(Featherfin Panchax) 142
*Pterophyllum* 18, 34
*scalare* (Angelfish) 18, 34, 36,
51, 105, 179
Pufferfish
Green 197
Pumpkinseed 154
Purple-headed Barb 36, 92, 100
Pygmy Barb 101
*Pyrrhulina laeta* (Half-banded
Pyrrhulina) 84
*metae* (Rio Meta Pyrrhulina) 85
vittata (Striped Vittata) 84

### R

Rainbowfish
Dwarf 194
Madagascar 196
Red-tailed 194

*Rasbora borapetensis* (Red-tailed
Rasbora) 110
*dorsiocellata* (Eye-spot Rasbora)
112
*dorsiocellata macrophthalma*
112
*einthoveni* (Brilliant Rasbora)
111
*heteromorpha* (Harlequin Fish)
18, 36, 113
*maculata* (Spotted Rasbora) 113
*trilineata* (Scissor-tail) 114
*vaterifloris* (Pearly Rasbora, Fire
Rasbora) 115
Red Aphyosemion 142
Red Barb 46, 96
Red Discus 181
Red-eye Tetra 72
Red-eyed Characin 57
Red-nosed Tetra 74
Red Phantom Tetra 70
Red Piranha 77
Red Platy 152
Red-spotted Copeina 80
Red-tailed Labeo 110
Red-tailed Rainbowfish 194
Red-tailed Rasbora 110
Red-tailed Shark 110
Red Tetra 65
Red Variatus Platy 153
Reedfish 52
Reticulated Corydoras 128
Rio Grande Perch 167
Rio Meta Pyrrhulina 85
*Roloffia occidentalis* (Red
Aphyosemion) 142, 198
*Rooseveltiella nattereri* 77
Rosy Barb 46, 96, 103
Royal Blue Discus 181

### S

Sailfin Molly 34, 147, 148, 151
Sailfish, Celebes 196
*Sarotherodon mossambicus*
(Mozambique Mouth-brooder)
160, 179
*Satanoperca jurupari* 171
Scatophagidae 156
*Scatophagus argus* (Argusfish) 156
*rubrifrons* 156
Schilbeidae 120, 122
Schomburgk's Leaf-fish 159
Schubert's Barb 103
Schwanenfeld's Barb 102
Scissors-tail 114
Serrasalmidae 54, 77
*Serrasalmus nattereri*
(Red Piranha) 77
Siamese Fighting Fish 35, 45, 47
188
Siluridae 120, 122
Siluriformes 120
Silver Hatchetfish 78
Silver Tetra 60
Six-banded Distichodus 89
Six-barred Epiplatys 139
South American Leaf-fish 158
Spanner Barb 99
*Sphaerichthys osphromenoides*
(Chocolate Gourami) 190
Spotted Headstander 88
Spotted Rasbora 113
Spraying Characin 44, 81
Stoliczka's Barb 104

Strawberry Tetra 66
Striped Anostomus 86
Striped Barb 98
Striped Fingerfish 156
Striped Leporinus 88
Striped Vittata 84
Suckermouth Catfish 131
Sumatran Barb 105
Sunfish
    Everglades Pygmy 154
Swamp Barb 95
Swordtail *34, 36,* 152
*Symphysodon aequifasciata
    aequifasciata*
        (Green Discus) 180
    *aequifasciata axelrodi*
        (Brown Discus) 180
    *aequifasciata haraldi*
        (Blue Discus) *37,* 180
    *discus* (Discus) *24,* 160, **181**
*Synodontis
    nigriventris* (Upside-down
        Catfish) **123**

*T*

*Tanichthys albonubes*
    (White Cloud Mountain
    Minnow) **115**
*Telmatherina ladigesi*
    (Celebes Sailfish) **196**

Tetra
    Black 60
    Black-line 68
    Black Neon 67
    Black Phantom 69
    Bleeding Heart 65
    Buenos Aires 61, 62, 63
    Cardinal 59, 73
    Congo 70
    Diamond 71, 72
    Disk *54,* 60
    Emperor 73
    Flag 67, 68
    Flame 65, 66
    Glass 71, 72
    Glowlight 62
    Griem's 65, 66
    Lemon 68
    Neon *43,* 62, 73
    Pretty 63
    Red 65
    Red-eye 72
    Red-Nosed 74
    Red Phantom 70
    Silver 60
    Strawberry 66
*Tetraodon fluviatilis*
    (Green Pufferfish) **197**
Tetraodontidae 197
*Thayeria boehlkei* (Boehlke's
    Penguin Fish) **76**
    *obliqua* 76

Three-banded Pencilfish *35,* 83
Three-spot Anostomus 86
Three-spot Gourami 192
Tiger Barb 35, *46,* 105
*Tilapia mossambica*
        (Mozambique Mouth-
        brooder) 160, 179
Tinfoil Barb 102
Toothcarps 46, **132,** 134, 136, 138,
        139, 142, **144**
*Toxotes jaculator*
        (Archerfish) **157**
    *jaculatrix* (Archerfish) **157**
Toxotidae 157
Trewavas's Cichlid *25, 37,* 175
*Trichogaster leeri* (Pearl Gourami)
    *36,* **192**
    *trichopterus* (Three-spot
        Gourami) **192**
    *trichopterus sumatranus*
        (Blue Gourami) **192**
*Tropheus duboisi* (Brabant
        Cichlid) **183**
    *moorii* (Brabant Cichlid) **183**
Tube-mouthed Pencilfish **82**
Tuxedo Platy 152

*U*

*Uaru
    amphiacanthoides* (Waroo) **182**
Upside-down Catfish **123**

*V*

Variatus Platy *144,* **153**

*W*

Waroo **182**
Water Goldfish 75
Whiptail **129**
White Cloud Mountain Minnow
    115
Wrestling Halfbeak **154**

*X*

X-ray Fish 75
*Xenomystus
    nigri* (African Knifefish) **52**
*Xiphophorus
    helleri* (Swordtail) *34, 36,* **152**
    *maculatus* (Platy) **152**
    *variatus* (Variatus Platy) *144,* **153**

*Y*

Yellow Dwarf Cichlid **164**

*Z*

Zebra Cichlid **169**
Zebra Danio *36, 44, 46,* **107,** 108

# CREDITS

**Artists**
Copyright of the artwork illustrations on the pages following the artists' names is the property of Salamander Books Ltd.

**Color artwork**
David Nockels: 34, 35, 36, 37, 42-3(B), 44, 45

Colin Newman (Linden Artists): 16-7(B), 18-9, 20-1, 23, 29, 42(T)

Tony Payne (Tudor Art Studios Ltd.): 46, 47, 49

Brian Watson (Linden Artists): 10, 11, 12-3, 14-5, 24, 41

**Line artwork**
Alan Hollingbery: 17(TR), Maps: 55, 93, 121, 133, 145, 161, 185

Sarah-Gay Wolfendale: 52-197

**Photographs**
The Publishers wish to thank the following photographers and agencies who have supplied photographs for this book. The photographs have been credited by page number and position on the page: (B) Bottom, (T) Top, (C) Center, (BL) Bottom left etc.

David Allison: 40(TL), 61(BR), 70, 76-7(T), 99, 109(BR), 163(B)

Heather Angel/Biofotos: 21, 22, 25(T, Murray Watson), 34, 98(B), 101(T), 124, 125(B), 152, 174(T), 195

Bruce Coleman Ltd: 50 (Jane Burton), 55 (Luiz Claudio Marigo), 65 (Hans Reinhard), 78-9 (T, Burton), 80-1 (T, Hans Reinhard), 90-1 (T, Hans Reinhard), 92 (Hans Reinhard), 100 (Jane Burton), 108-9 (T, Hans Reinhard), 113 (T, Hans Reinhard), 121 (Sandro Prato), 133 (Fritz Wollmar), 145 (M.S.L. Fogden), 154 (T, Jane Burton), 155 (T, Hans Reinhard), 161 (Peter Davey), 185 (Fritz Wollmar), 193 (T, Hans Reinhard)

Eric Crichton ©Salamander Books Ltd: 8, 12, 22, 23, 26, 27, 28, 29, 30, 31, 32, 33, 38, 39

Michael Dyer Associates ©Salamander Books Ltd: 15

Andreas Hartl: 87(BR), 110-11(B)

Ideas into Print: 38(TL)

Jan-Eric Larsson: 25(B), 47(R), 53(B), 56, 58(BL), 59(B), 60(BL), 62, 67, 68, 69(T), 73(B), 86(BL), 98(T), 105(T), 107, 113(T), 117(T), 120, 123, 126, 146-7(T), 160, 163(T), 172-3(B), 174(BL), 174-5(B), 175(CR), 178(B), 180(R), 183(T), 189(B), 197(B)

Arend van den Nieuwenhuizen: Half-title page, title page, copyright page, contents page, 16, 19, 24(TL), 35, 37, 44, 45, 46, 47(L), 52, 53(T), 54, 57, 58-9(T), 60-1(T), 63, 64, 66, 69(B), 71, 72, 73(T), 74-5, 75, 76(BL), 77(BR), 78(BL), 79(B), 80(BL), 81(BR), 82, 83, 84, 85, 88(B), 89(B), 90(B), 91(BR), 94, 95, 96, 97, 98(B), 101(B), 102, 103, 104(T), 106(B), 110(T), 111(T), 112, 113(B), 114, 115, 116, 117(B), 118, 119, 125(T), 127, 128, 129, 132, 134, 135, 136, 137, 138, 139, 140, 141, 142, 143, 144, 146-7(B), 148, 149, 150, 151, 153(TL, BL),

154(B), 155(B), 156-7(T), 157, 159, 162, 166(T), 167, 168(T), 169(T), 170, 171, 172(T), 173(T), 175(T), 176(C, B), 177, 178(T), 179, 181, 182, 183(B), 184, 186(B), 187(B), 188, 189(T), 190, 191(B), 192, 193(B), 196(B), 198, 200, 203, 204

Barry Pengilley: 86-7(T), 88-9(T), 130(T), 131(T), 156(BL), 165, 166(B), 180(L), 186-7(T), 194, 196-7(T), endpapers

Seaphot: 108(L)

Mike Sandford: 104-5(B), 122, 158

Ian Sellick: 176(T)

Touchstone ©Salamander Books Ltd: 27(BL)

W. A. Tomey: 10, 11, 17, 24(C), 36, 43, 48, 74(T), 93, 106(T), 130(B), 153(TR), 164, 168-9(B), 191(T)

**Acknowledgments**
The Publishers would like to thank the following individuals and organizations for their help in the preparation of this book: J. Reddick, Aquatic and Pet Supplies Ltd; J.N. Carrington, Interpet Ltd; Dr. C. Andrews; John Allan Aquariums Ltd; Mr. Dutta, Fish Tanks Ltd; Freshwater and Marine Aquarium magazine, Practical Fish-keeping magazine; Ian Sellick, British Cichlid Association; Federation of British Aquatic Societies (F.B.A.S.); Roger Paine, F.B.A.S. judge; South-East London Aquarist Society; East Dulwich Aquarist Society; Janet Parr (for typing the manuscript of part one): Carol Warren (for design assistance); Maureen Cartwright (for copy-editing); Stuart Craik (for preparing the index).